EXISTING LEGAL LIMITS TO SECURITY COUNCIL VETO POWER IN THE FACE OF ATROCITY CRIMES

In this book, the author outlines three independent bases for the existence of legal limits to the veto by UN Security Council permanent members while atrocity crimes are occurring. First, the Council must not act inconsistently with *jus cogens* (peremptory norms of international law). Second, the veto power (created by the UN Charter) must be exercised in accordance with the UN's "Purposes and Principles." Third, there are also positive obligations imposed by the Geneva and Genocide Conventions – conventions to which all permanent members are parties. The author demonstrates how vetoes and veto threats have blocked the Security Council from pursuing measures that could have prevented or alleviated atrocity crimes (genocide, crimes against humanity, and/or war crimes) in places such as Myanmar, Darfur, Syria, and elsewhere. As the practice continues despite regular condemnation by other UN Member States and the existence of voluntary veto restraint initiatives, the book explores how the legality of such vetoes could be challenged.

Jennifer Trahan is Clinical Professor at New York University's Center for Global Affairs, School of Professional Studies. She is a prolific scholar in the field of international justice, having written scores of law review articles, book chapters, and comprehensive digests on the case law of the Yugoslav and Rwanda Tribunals.

Existing Legal Limits to Security Council Veto Power in the Face of Atrocity Crimes

JENNIFER TRAHAN
New York University

CAMBRIDGE
UNIVERSITY PRESS

University Printing House, Cambridge CB2 8BS, United Kingdom

One Liberty Plaza, 20th Floor, New York, NY 10006, USA

477 Williamstown Road, Port Melbourne, VIC 3207, Australia

314–321, 3rd Floor, Plot 3, Splendor Forum, Jasola District Centre, New Delhi – 110025, India

79 Anson Road, #06–04/06, Singapore 079906

Cambridge University Press is part of the University of Cambridge.

It furthers the University's mission by disseminating knowledge in the pursuit of education, learning, and research at the highest international levels of excellence.

www.cambridge.org
Information on this title: www.cambridge.org/9781108487016
DOI: 10.1017/9781108765251

© Jennifer Trahan 2020

This publication is in copyright. Subject to statutory exception and to the provisions of relevant collective licensing agreements, no reproduction of any part may take place without the written permission of Cambridge University Press.

First published 2020

A catalogue record for this publication is available from the British Library.

Library of Congress Cataloging-in-Publication Data
NAMES: Trahan, Jennifer, author.
TITLE: Existing legal limits to Security Council veto power in the face of atrocity / Jennifer Trahan, New York University.
DESCRIPTION: Cambridge, United Kingdom ; New York, NY, USA Cambridge University Press, 2020. | Includes index. | Includes bibliographical references.
IDENTIFIERS: LCCN 2019058610 (print) | LCCN 2019058611 (ebook) | ISBN 9781108487016 (hardback) | ISBN 9781108765251 (ebook)
SUBJECTS: LCSH: United Nations. Security Council – Voting. | International criminal law. | Atrocities – Law and legislation.
CLASSIFICATION: LCC KZ6025 .T73 2020 (print) | LCC KZ6025 (ebook) | DDC 341.23/23–dc23
LC record available at https://lccn.loc.gov/2019058610
LC ebook record available at https://lccn.loc.gov/2019058611

ISBN 978-1-108-48701-6 Hardback

Cambridge University Press has no responsibility for the persistence or accuracy of URLs for external or third-party internet websites referred to in this publication and does not guarantee that any content on such websites is, or will remain, accurate or appropriate.

Contents

Foreword		*page* xiii
Richard J. Goldstone		
Acknowledgments		xvi
Introduction		1
1	**The Origins and History of the Veto and Its Use**	9
	Introduction	9
	1.1 The UN Charter Negotiations	10
	1.1.1 Positions on the Veto Leading into the San Francisco Conference	10
	1.1.2 Positions on the Veto at the San Francisco Conference	16
	1.2 Early General Assembly Attempts to Avoid Security Council Paralysis during the Cold War	21
	1.2.1 General Assembly Resolutions Calling for Veto Restraint	21
	1.2.2 The "Uniting for Peace" Resolution	22
	1.2.3 Use of the "Uniting for Peace" Resolution and Other Methods to Shift Debate to the General Assembly	26
	1.3 Overview of Veto Use Including during the Commission of Atrocity Crimes	30
	1.3.1 Overview of Veto Use	30
	1.3.2 Veto Use and Veto Threats during the Commission of Atrocity Crimes	33
	1.4 Security Council Reform Proposals	47
	1.4.1 Proposed Reforms to the Composition of the Security Council	48

		1.4.2	Recent Attempts to Curb Veto Use	50
	1.5	\multicolumn{2}{l	}{The Rationale for Reconsidering How the Veto Is Used in the Face of Atrocity Crimes}	51

2 Acting in the Face of Atrocity Crimes – Humanitarian Intervention and the Responsibility to Protect 53

Introduction 53
2.1 The Doctrine of "Humanitarian Intervention" 54
    2.1.1 Limited Historical Precedent 54
    2.1.2 The 1999 NATO Intervention in Kosovo 58
    2.1.3 Lingering Wariness about "Humanitarian Intervention" 63
2.2 The Development of the "Responsibility to Protect" 65
    2.2.1 Difficulties for R2P: Libya and Syria 70
        2.2.1.1 Libya as R2P 70
        2.2.1.2 Syria as an R2P Failure 72
    2.2.2 The Need to Revitalize R2P: Emphasizing the "Hard Law" Obligations Underlying It 75
2.3 Revisiting the Legal Status of "Humanitarian Intervention" Post-R2P 86
    2.3.1 Proposed Military Strikes in 2013 in Response to Chemical Weapons Attacks 86
    2.3.2 Military Strikes in Syria in 2017 and 2018 in Response to Chemical Weapons Attacks 90
    2.3.3 The Extent to Which "Humanitarian Intervention" Continues as a Viable Doctrine 95
    2.3.4 The Relationship between "Humanitarian Intervention" and the International Criminal Court's Crime of Aggression 97
2.4 Conclusion 99

3 Initiatives to Voluntarily Restrain Veto Use as to the Face of Atrocity Crimes 102

Introduction 102
3.1 The Different Approaches to Voluntary Veto Restraint as to the Face of Atrocity Crimes 103
    3.1.1 The Responsibility Not to Veto within R2P 104
    3.1.2 The "S5 Initiative" 107
    3.1.3 The French/Mexican Initiative 110
    3.1.4 The ACT Code of Conduct 114

		3.1.5	The Proposal of "The Elders"	117
		3.1.6	A US Proposal for Veto Restraint under the Obama Administration	118
	3.2	Evaluation of the Different Approaches to Voluntary Veto Restraint		119
		3.2.1	The Weight of the "Responsibility Not to Veto" as Articulated in These Initiatives	120
		3.2.2	Variations as to the Different Approaches	122
			3.2.2.1 Which Crimes to Include	123
			3.2.2.2 Whether to Call for the Vetoing Permanent Member to Articulate Its Reasoning	126
			3.2.2.3 Whether to Permit a Veto in the Face of "Vital National Interests" or "Vital State Interests"	127
			3.2.2.4 Whether the Crimes Need to Be Occurring or the Threat of Their Occurrences Also Triggers the Obligation Not to Veto	130
			3.2.2.5 Who Determines Whether Genocide, Crimes against Humanity, or War Crimes Are Occurring, or Are at Serious Risk of Occurring?	131
			3.2.2.6 Whether to Include the Threat of Veto Use by a Permanent Member	134
			3.2.2.7 Whether *All* Vetoes in the Face of Atrocity Crimes Should Be Encompassed	135
	3.3	Conclusion		138
4	Questioning the Legality of Veto Use in the Face of Genocide, Crimes against Humanity, and/or War Crimes			142
	Introduction			142
	The Need for an Approach Guided by Existing Hard Law Obligations			144
	Summary of Legal Arguments			148
	4.1	Consideration of the Relationship between Use of the Veto and *Jus Cogens*		150
		4.1.1	*Jus Cogens*/Peremptory Norms	150
		4.1.2	The Prohibitions of Genocide, Crimes against Humanity, and, at Least Certain, War Crimes Are Peremptory Norms Protected as *Jus Cogens*	153
		4.1.3	The Content of the Peremptory Norms as to Genocide, Crimes against Humanity, and War Crimes	155

	4.1.4		The Obligations of the UN and Its Organs, Including the Security Council, to Respect *Jus Cogens* Norms	158
		4.1.4.1	The Security Council Is Not Above the Law	158
		4.1.4.2	The Security Council Is Bound to Respect *Jus Cogens* Norms	161
	4.1.5		Legal Consequences of *Jus Cogens* Norms Being Binding on the Security Council	165
		4.1.5.1	The Security Council Cannot Explicitly Authorize Violations of *Jus Cogens*	165
		4.1.5.2	The Security Council May Not Violate *Jus Cogens* in Its Resolutions/a Resolution That Conflicts with a *Jus Cogens* Norm Will Be Void	165
	4.1.6		The Relationship between the Veto and *Jus Cogens*	168
		4.1.6.1	The Veto Should Not Be Used in Circumstances Where It Has the Effect of Facilitating the Commission of *Jus Cogens* Violations	169
		4.1.6.2	The Veto Should Not Be Used in a Way That Undermines the Duty of Other Security Council Members to Cooperate and Make an Appropriate Response to a Serious Breach of a *Jus Cogens* Norm	172
		4.1.6.3	The Veto Should Be Used in a Way That Is Consistent with *Jus Cogens*	175
		4.1.6.4	Individual Permanent Members Are Bound to Respect *Jus Cogens*	177
4.2			Limitations Imposed on the Security Council by the "Purposes and Principles" of the United Nations	179
	4.2.1		The Obligation of the Security Council to Act in Accordance with the "Purposes and Principles" of the United Nations	179
	4.2.2		Whether a Veto in the Face of Genocide, Crimes against Humanity, and/or War Crimes Accords with the Obligation to Act in Accordance with the "Purposes" of the United Nations	185
		4.2.2.1	The "Purposes" of the United Nations	185
		4.2.2.2	Veto Use Must Be in Accordance with the "Purposes" of the United Nations	191

		4.2.3	Whether a Veto in the Face of Genocide, Crimes against Humanity, and/or War Crimes Accords with the Obligation to Act in Accordance with the "Principles" of the United Nations and the General Obligation of "Good Faith"	194
		4.2.4	Whether the Vetoes Related to the Situation in Syria Are in Accordance with the "Purposes and Principles" of the United Nations	198
			4.2.4.1 Resolutions Vetoed Related to the Situation in Syria	199
			4.2.4.2 The Objections of States to Veto Use Related to the Situation in Syria and More Generally in the Face of Atrocity Crimes	201
			4.2.4.3 Other Resolutions Did Not Obviate the Need for the Resolutions That Were Vetoed Related to the Situation in Syria	206
4.3	Consideration of the Treaty Obligations of Individual Permanent Member States			209
	4.3.1	Legal Obligations under the Genocide Convention		210
	4.3.2	Legal Obligations under the 1949 Geneva Conventions		215
	4.3.3	Whether Legal Obligations Created under These Foundational Treaties Apply to States while Serving on the Security Council		220
	4.3.4	Treaty Obligations Potentially Relevant to Veto Use		224
	4.3.5	Treaty Obligations Potentially Relevant to Drafting, Negotiating, and Voting on Resolutions		228
	4.3.6	Application of Foundational Treaty Obligations to Veto Use		230
		4.3.6.1 The Situation in Myanmar		230
		4.3.6.2 Veto Threats		235
		4.3.6.3 The Situation in Syria		237
4.4	Seeking an Advisory Opinion from the International Court of Justice and the Issue of Judicial Review			242
	4.4.1	The ICJ May Review Security Council Actions for Compliance with the UN Charter and/or Other Bodies of International Law		243
	4.4.2	Security Council Actions Do Not Constitute Non-justiciable "Political" Question, at Least Where There Are Legal Standards against Which to Review Them		251

		4.4.3	Why the ICJ Should Exercise Its Discretion to Render an Advisory Opinion	254
		4.4.4	Advisability of Seeking Judicial Review by the ICJ and Possible Alternatives	256
	4.5	Conclusion		257
5	**Case Studies – Veto Use Related to the Situation in Syria and Veto Threats Related to the Situation in Darfur**			**260**
	Introduction			260
	5.1	Analysis of Veto Use Related to the Situation in Syria		262
		5.1.1	A Brief Background	263
		5.1.2	The First Vetoes Related to the Situation in Syria: Blocking Condemnation of Crimes	269
			5.1.2.1 Vetoing a Call to End Violence and Hold Perpetrators Accountable	269
			5.1.2.2 Vetoing Condemnation of Arbitrary Detention, Enforced Disappearances, and Other Crimes	271
			5.1.2.3 Vetoing Condemnation of Bombing and Shelling of Population Centers and Detention of Thousands in Government-Run Facilities	272
		5.1.3	Vetoing Referral of the Situation in Syria to the ICC	274
			5.1.3.1 Acceleration of Crimes	274
			5.1.3.2 The Sarin Gas Attack on Al-Ghouta	276
			5.1.3.3 The Dire Consequences of Siege Warfare	277
			5.1.3.4 Vetoing ICC Referral	278
			5.1.3.5 ISIL Crimes against the Yazidis	280
		5.1.4	Vetoes Related to the Siege of Aleppo	283
			5.1.4.1 The Siege of Aleppo	283
			5.1.4.2 Vetoing Expressions of Outrage at the Alarming Number of Civilian Casualties, Including Those Caused by Indiscriminate Aerial Bombing, in Aleppo	285
			5.1.4.3 Vetoing a Seven-Day Ceasefire in Aleppo That Would Have Allowed Humanitarian Assistance	287
		5.1.5	Vetoes Related to Chemical Weapons Use	288
			5.1.5.1 Attempts at Destroying Syria's Chemical Weapons Stockpile	289

		5.1.5.2	Continued Chemical Weapons Use	291
		5.1.5.3	Vetoing Condemnation of Chemical Weapons Use	292
		5.1.5.4	Further Vetoing Condemnation of Chemical Weapons Use, and Requests for Documentation Such as Flight Plans and Access to Air Bases from Which Chemical Weapons Were Believed to Have Been Launched	293
		5.1.5.5	Vetoing Renewal of the Mandate for Investigations That Would Have Attributed Responsibility to the Side Using Chemical Weapons	295
		5.1.5.6	Further Vetoing Condemnation of Chemical Weapons Use, and Furthering Vetoing Renewal of the Mandate for Inspections That Would Have Attributed Responsibility	295
	5.1.6	Overall Impact of the Vetoes Related to the Situation in Syria		298
5.2	Analysis of Veto Threats Related to the Situation in Darfur			302
	5.2.1	A Brief Background		303
	5.2.2	How Veto Threats Hampered the Security Council's Ability to Pass Resolutions Related to the Situation in Darfur		309
	5.2.3	How Veto Threats Weakened Sanctions		312
		5.2.3.1	The First Implicit Threat to Veto Sanctions	312
		5.2.3.2	A Second Threat to Veto Sanctions	320
		5.2.3.3	The Third Threat to Veto Sanctions	322
		5.2.3.4	The Fourth Threat to Veto Sanctions	324
		5.2.3.5	The Fifth Threat to Veto Sanctions	329
	5.2.4	How Veto Threats Weakened Peacekeeping		330
		5.2.4.1	The First Veto Threat Related to Peacekeeping	331
		5.2.4.2	The Second Veto Threat Related to Peacekeeping	333
		5.2.4.3	The Lingering Impact of Veto Threats Weakening Peacekeeping	336
	5.2.5	Threats Blocking Follow-Up on the ICC Referral		337

		5.2.6 Overall Impact of the Veto Threats Regarding the Situation in Darfur	340
	5.3	Conclusion	342

Index 343

Foreword

Richard J. Goldstone

In 1945, the then global community paid a very high price for enticing the five most powerful powers to join the United Nations and subscribe to its Charter. That price was the recognition in Article 23 of the Charter of their permanent membership in the Security Council and the accompanying veto power over apparently all but procedural resolutions of the Council conferred on each of them by Article 27. There is no question that without permanent membership and the veto power, China, the Soviet Union, the UK, and the US would not have joined the newly forming organization. Those powers were extended also to France. The reality is that, at the present time, there is very little prospect of the Charter being amended, as it would require the agreement of all five permanent members. Those privileges must therefore be accepted as permanent features in the architecture of the United Nations.

In the face of this reality, Member States of the United Nations have sought through a number of ways to temper the use of the permanent members' veto power in the most critical situations. In 1950, the General Assembly passed the Uniting for Peace resolution pursuant to which, when the Security Council is unable to act to secure international peace and security because of lack of unanimity on the part of the permanent members, the General Assembly may consider the situation and issue its own recommendations for the restoration of international peace and security. While such a resolution, under the Charter, has no binding consequences, it is a prominent demonstration by the Member States of the United Nations of their frustration with veto use. This mechanism under the Uniting for Peace resolution has been used on approximately eleven occasions since 1950.

A feature of the veto that is all too often overlooked is the frequency with which the mere threat of its exercise by a permanent member effectively blocks resolutions from being formally presented to the Security Council. For the most part, threatened vetoes manifest themselves during informal meetings of the Security Council and a paper trail is usually difficult to find. It is in a comparatively small number of cases that the resolutions are put formally to the Security Council only to be defeated by the use of the veto power. As appears in Chapter 5, this has occurred no less than fourteen times with regard to the devastating war that has been raging since 2011 in Syria.

In this book, Professor Jennifer Trahan describes in impressive and depressing detail how permanent members of the Security Council have used their veto powers to block measures from being adopted by the Council that have been aimed at preventing or punishing atrocity crimes (genocide, crimes against humanity, and/or war crimes). That is the context in which she presents her major thesis, in Chapter 4, that the use or threat of use of the veto in a way that contravenes fundamental norms of international law or the "Purposes and Principles" of the United Nations is unlawful and therefore falls outside the proper exercise of power of the Security Council and each of its members. She demonstrates with faultless logic that the powers of the Security Council and its members, including the use of the veto, are subordinate to:

(1) the norms of *jus cogens*;
(2) the provisions of Article 24(2) of the Charter which require that in discharging its duties the Security Council shall act in accordance with the "Purposes and Principles" of the United Nations; and
(3) the provisions of specific treaties such as the Genocide Convention and the Geneva Conventions which impose certain legal obligations on states that are parties to them.

In the final chapter of the book, Professor Trahan provides as examples and describes in equally impressive detail the manner in which the veto or threat of the exercise of the veto has been used to thwart action by the Security Council in the situations in Darfur and Syria – in both of which it was clear that atrocity crimes were taking place.

The author recognizes that the permanent members of the Security Council will not likely acknowledge any limits to their veto power. She offers some new ideas on options for challenging unlimited veto use. One proposal is that the General Assembly could decide to approach the International Court of Justice for an advisory opinion declaring that the veto powers of the permanent members of the Security Council are limited by existing international law. She also suggests that in addition to the many examples of individual UN Member States' statements over the years, the General Assembly could, by resolution, also recognize these legal limits and call on the permanent members to exercise a consequential restraint in the use of the veto or its threatened use relating to genocide, crimes against humanity, and/or war crimes.

For the past few years Professor Trahan, with notable success, has launched a project with the aim of seeking support for her thesis and objectives from members of the United Nations, international criminal law experts, and civil society organizations. She has spoken on the issue at many conferences, meetings, and side-events including at the United Nations in New York and at the annual meetings of the Assembly of States Parties of the International Criminal Court.

It has been my privilege to work with and encourage the author in furtherance of her project. Like this book, her endeavors reflect impressive scholarship, imagination, and countless hours of hard work. I am optimistic that this initiative will continue to gather support and discourage some of the permanent members of the Security Council from persisting in their folly of thwarting the Council from functioning when so many lives threatened by mass atrocity crimes are on the line. The veto, while a power granted under the UN Charter, is not paramount to the Charter or other norms of international law. It is one provision under that Charter and subject to the rules and norms of international law.

Acknowledgments

Many people helped me in the process of writing this book, and I am deeply appreciative of their assistance. To start, I must thank Hans Corell, who heard me in a speech question the legality of how the veto is used even during the commission of atrocity crimes and said "you *must* work on this"; he has continued to provide encouragement along the way. I have also received much advice and wisdom from Richard Goldstone and Andras Vamos-Goldman, and for this I am extremely grateful. I am deeply appreciative of those who have read and commented on chapters of the book: Belinda Cooper, Susan Hulton, Andras Vamos-Goldman, Mohammad Al Abdallah, and Eric Reeves. I have been heartened by NGO representatives who encouraged my work on the topic, including Gareth Sweeney of Crisis Action, David Donat-Cattin of Parliamentarians for Global Action, Fernando Travesi and Anna Myriam Roccatello of the International Center for Transitional Justice, and James Goldstone of the Open Society Justice Initiative. I have been encouraged by the positive responses I have received from the legal advisers of numerous states, and am particularly appreciative of those who workshopped the legal arguments with me, courtesy of the law firm of Foley Hoag LLP and the Global Justice Center, especially Akila Radhakrishnan. Thanks also go to Taylor Ackerman, Alejandro Garcia, Isabelle Glimcher, Erin Lovall, Kara McDonald, and Samantha Wynne for their research assistance. Thank you to my "anonymous peer reviewers" who showed enthusiasm about the manuscript proposal and to the excellent publications team at Cambridge University Press. Thank you also to my many, many supportive friends, and my colleagues at NYU Center for Global Affairs.

I deeply appreciate my children, Teddy Trahan Rashkover and Nicole Paige Rashkover. I write in memory of my father, Donald H. Trahan, and my mother, Elizabeth Welt Trahan, who survived the atrocities of World War

II and without whose guiding example I would probably not be working in this field.

Above all, I write on behalf of victims of atrocity crimes that the international community potentially could have prevented, yet failed to prevent. I am convinced of the linkage (sometimes direct, sometimes distant) between vetoes recklessly or self-interestedly cast in the Security Council and continuing death tolls on the ground, when measures that could have attempted to alleviate suffering or advanced accountability were blocked. We must not only acknowledge this linkage exists but also do our utmost to ensure that the UN Charter's voting provisions are *never* used in a way that directly or indirectly facilitates or enables the ongoing perpetration of genocide, crimes against humanity, or war crimes.

Introduction

This book examines veto use by the permanent members of the UN Security Council while atrocity crimes are being committed – genocide, crimes against humanity, and/or war crimes. The veto power, conferred by UN Charter Article 27(3), allows any one of the five permanent members – the US, the UK, Russia, China, or France – to block a substantive resolution within the Council by casting a negative vote. Both today, and in the past, permanent members use, or have used, their veto power to block resolutions, including those designed to curtail or alleviate the commission of atrocity crimes,[1] with dire consequences sometimes resulting on the ground. For example, when chemical weapons inspections that would have attributed responsibility to the side using the weapons in Syria are blocked by the veto and chemical weapons attacks continue, veto use appears to be costing lives. (This appears particularly true because the chemical weapons attacks had decreased or stopped when the inspections commenced.) When measures are never proposed and the Security Council is simply unresponsive to unfolding atrocities, such as those in Myanmar, it is harder to detect, but the unresponsiveness can be traced to the existence of the veto power. Many states have voiced alarm at this state of affairs as seen by the fact that close to two-thirds of UN Member States call for "voluntary veto restraint" – that the permanent members should voluntarily refrain from using their veto while genocide, crimes against humanity, and/or war crimes are occurring. Yet, when three permanent members refuse to endorse that approach (which is the situation), there *is no veto restraint*. The book makes a case for another, complementary, approach: to revisit – based on existing legal obligations – whether veto use

---

[1] This book uses the phrase "atrocity crimes" to mean genocide, crimes against humanity, and/or war crimes.

while there is ongoing genocide, crimes against humanity, and/or war crimes is in accordance with international law.

The book's chapters examine, first, the origins of the veto, tracing negotiations of the UN Charter in San Francisco, and then providing an overview of veto use, or veto threats, while ongoing atrocity crimes are being committed. The situations examined include South Africa (during apartheid), Rwanda, Darfur, Israel, Sri Lanka, Yemen, Syria, and Myanmar.

Second, the book examines the doctrines of humanitarian intervention, intermittently invoked when the Security Council is paralyzed by the veto or anticipated veto. The chapter concludes that states will still be tempted to invoke this doctrine – utilizing force without Security Council authorization in the face of atrocity crimes – until this vexing problem of veto use in the face of atrocity crimes is solved. The book additionally examines the related doctrine of the responsibility to protect (R2P) and calls for its revitalization, recognizing that there are hard law legal obligations underlying it so that it should not simply be considered "soft law."

Third, the book examines the various "voluntary veto restraint" initiatives that have developed over the past nearly twenty years, the most recent of which are the ACT (Accountability, Coherence and Transparency) Group's "Code of Conduct" and the "French/Mexican initiative." Along with their predecessor initiatives, these initiatives have been significantly helpful in galvanizing momentum towards a shared recognition that something must be done about unrestrained veto use while genocide, crimes against humanity, and/or war crimes are occurring; the initiatives have also succeeded in increasing the "political cost" of such veto use. Yet, in light of three permanent members not endorsing the initiatives, the initiatives are not currently reining in veto use in the face of atrocity crimes.

Fourth, the book explores a complementary approach: to examine the legality of veto use while genocide, crimes against humanity, and/or war crimes are occurring, measured against three types of legal obligations, those provided by: (a) *jus cogens*, (b) the UN Charter, and (c) foundational treaties. This chapter suggest options available to the international community, such as for states to raise these legal arguments any time a permanent member invokes the veto during the commission of atrocity crimes. It also suggests the General Assembly consider seeking an Advisory Opinion from the International Court of Justice (ICJ) on a question such as: Does existing international law contain limitations on the use of the veto power by permanent members of the UN Security Council in situations where there is ongoing genocide, crimes against humanity, and/or war crimes?

Finally, by way of more detailed case studies, the fifth chapter examines one situation where the veto was used and one situation where the veto was threatened during ongoing atrocity crimes. It examines the fourteen vetoes cast related to the situation in Syria while mass atrocities were occurring there, and the numerous veto threats made related to the situation in Darfur while mass atrocities were occurring there. The selection of these two case studies is intended as illustrative, as the book aims its arguments at all veto use while there are ongoing atrocity crimes.

DETAILED SYNOPSIS OF CHAPTERS

Chapter 1. The Origins and History of the Veto and Its Use

This chapter traces the origins of the veto power of the permanent members of the UN Security Council from the negotiations leading into the San Francisco Conference to the finalization of the UN Charter. It then examines an early response to Security Council paralysis – resolutions in the late 1940s by the General Assembly calling for veto restraint, as well as the "Uniting for Peace" resolution in 1950, which provides a mechanism for the General Assembly to make recommendations related to international peace and security when the Security Council's work is blocked. Even though expectations for the Security Council have probably gone beyond the intention of the drafters of the UN Charter, especially since the end of the Cold War it is clear that when there is sufficient political will, this body has the legal ability to prevent and/or stop many situations of catastrophic consequences to communities, countries, and regions around the world. Concomitantly, when the Council does not take on such a role, there is widespread disenchantment with its performance. Despite numerous efforts, attempts to reform the composition of the Council have, to date, largely failed to reach fruition. The lack of responsiveness to the commission of mass atrocity crimes (genocide, crimes against humanity, and/or war crimes), which have occurred virtually unimpeded (just taking the last few decades) in places such as Rwanda, Darfur, Syria, Sri Lanka, Myanmar, and Yemen, has come at a staggering toll in terms of lives lost. Much of the time, inaction by the Council can be specifically traced to use of the veto, or the threat of the veto, by one or more of the permanent members. Recent, broadly endorsed, encouraging initiatives aimed at curtailing veto use in the face of atrocity crimes provide strong evidence that the international community wants the Security Council to be more effective in these situations. Yet, because of the voluntary natures of these initiatives (waiting for all permanent members to join them), this chapter makes the case that it is time to reconsider existing hard law legal obligations, and recognize that these in fact impose limitations on the use of the veto in the face of atrocity crimes.

Chapter 2. Acting in the Face of Atrocity Crimes

This chapter explores two doctrines that developed in response to Security Council paralysis or inaction in the face of atrocity crimes. The first is the doctrine of humanitarian intervention, most famously invoked in 1999 to justify the intervention of the North Atlantic Treaty Organization (NATO) in Kosovo, although largely dismissed by most states as impermissible, at least under a strict reading of the UN Charter. The second doctrine is the "responsibility to protect" (R2P), which was first formulated in 2001 but has since undergone significant modifications. Because the later formulations of R2P require Security Council authorization for any forceful intervention, R2P ultimately fails to address the problem of Security Council paralysis in the face of atrocity crimes (although the "responsibility not to veto" contained within formulations of R2P attempts to do so). Furthermore, because R2P was invoked as part of the 2015 intervention in Libya, which left a destabilized state, and appears to have been largely ignored with respect to atrocities in Syria, enthusiasm for R2P may be waning and could use revitalization; some ideas for revitalization are explored in the chapter. The chapter makes the case that until the international community solves the problem of veto use in the face of atrocity crimes, some states still *will* be tempted to invoke, or engage in, humanitarian intervention because there are currently no satisfactory alternatives to addressing Security Council paralysis blocking forceful intervention; yet, there remain significant dangers to such an approach. Ultimately, the chapter concludes that by addressing the problem of use, and threatened use, of the veto in the face of atrocity crimes, one could both strengthen R2P and lessen any need to invoke humanitarian intervention.

Chapter 3. Initiatives to Voluntarily Restrain Veto Use in the Face of Atrocity Crimes

This chapter explores initiatives that have sought voluntarily to restrain use of the veto in the face of atrocity crimes. They include: the "responsibility not to veto" found in the "responsibility to protect," the "S5 initiative," the French/Mexican initiative not to veto in the face of atrocity crimes, the ACT Code of Conduct, and a proposal by a group known as "The Elders." In addition to explaining the initiatives and providing background on them, this chapter evaluates the merits of each of the different approaches. Because all the initiatives call for *voluntary* veto restraint, until the recalcitrant permanent members of the Security Council (China, Russia, and the US) join these initiatives – which appears unlikely – the initiatives will not fully solve the problem of veto use, or the threat of veto use, in the face of atrocity crimes.

Chapter 4. Questioning the Legality of Veto Use in the Face of Genocide, Crimes against Humanity, and/or War Crimes

This chapter makes the case that it is appropriate, and justified, to revisit – based on existing international legal obligations – the problem of veto use in the face of genocide, crimes against humanity, and/or war crimes. This chapter will show a clear tension between existing legal obligations and the use of the veto when such crimes are occurring, or when they are at serious risk of occurring; consequently, use of the veto in such circumstances is arguably outside the proper exercise of Security Council power. The chapter presents three main legal arguments that indicate there are legal limits (or constraints) on the use of the veto in the face of genocide, crimes against humanity, and/or war crimes. First, the chapter argues that the veto power, which is conferred by the UN Charter, is subordinate to the highest level *jus cogens* norms; as a consequence, the veto should not be used (i) where it has the effect of facilitating ongoing *jus cogens* violations, (ii) where it undermines the duty of other Security Council members to cooperate to make an appropriate response to a serious breach of a *jus cogens* norm, or (iii) where its use is inconsistent with *jus cogens* protections. Second, the chapter argues that the veto power sits within the context of the UN Charter, which states that the Security Council must act pursuant to the UN's "[p]urposes and [p]rinciples"; a veto in the face of genocide, crimes against humanity, and/or war crimes does not accord with the UN's "[p]urposes and [p]rinciples." Third, the chapter argues that there are also treaty obligations that bind individual permanent member states, such as those under the Genocide Convention[2] and 1949 Geneva Conventions,[3] and veto use should not be contrary to

---

[2] Convention on the Prevention and Punishment of the Crime of Genocide, Dec. 9, 1948, 78 UNTS 277.
[3] Geneva Convention I for the Amelioration of the Condition of the Wounded and Sick in Armed Forces in the Field, Aug. 12, 1949, 75 UNTS 31; Geneva Convention II for the Amelioration of the Condition of Wounded, Sick and Shipwrecked Members of Armed Forces at Sea, Aug. 12, 1949, 75 UNTS 85; Geneva Convention III Relative to the Treatment of Prisoners of War, Aug. 12, 1949, 75 UNTS 135; Geneva Convention IV Relative to the Protection of Civilian Persons in Time of War, Aug. 12, 1949, 75 UNTS 287.

obligations created under these treaties. Furthermore, these treaty obligations are not overridden by UN Charter Article 103 because the norms protected by these treaties are also protected by *jus cogens* and/or the UN's "[p]urposes and [p]rinciples"; alternatively, the veto power should be read in a way that is consistent with the legal obligations created under these foundational treaties.

In light of the issues raised, the chapter considers the scope of judicial review by the ICJ, concluding that the above legal questions are ones on which the ICJ could, and should, opine. Ultimately, the chapter suggests that the General Assembly consider requesting an advisory opinion from the ICJ on a question such as: Does existing international law contain limitations on the use of the veto power by permanent members of the UN Security Council in situations where there is ongoing genocide, crimes against humanity, and/or war crimes? The chapter proposes that it is time to stop reading the veto as a *carte blanche*, above all other sources of law. The General Assembly could ask the ICJ to opine on this significant question given the strong arguments that exist that the veto power is not superior to all sources of international law but must be used in a way that is consistent with, or limited by, them. The chapter also suggests the alternative possibility of the General Assembly, in a resolution, confirming its understanding of such hard law obligations regarding veto use while genocide, crimes against humanity, and/or war crimes are occurring, or are at serious risk of occurring. In the meanwhile, the chapter additionally suggests that states at the UN should continue to build a consistent precedent by invoking legal arguments, such as those outlined above and detailed in this chapter, whenever a permanent member exercises its veto while there are ongoing atrocity crimes or they are at serious risk of occurring.

Chapter 5. Case Studies

This final chapter presents two case studies, one where the veto was utilized while atrocity crimes were being committed, and one where the veto was threatened (expressly or implicitly) while atrocity crimes were being committed. The first case study traces climbing death tolls and growing recognition that mass atrocity crimes were occurring in Syria, while Russia, sometimes joined by China, invoked the veto on fourteen separate occasions. The vetoes blocked recognition of crimes, investigation of crimes, prosecution of crimes, as well as other measures. While sometimes somewhat comparable resolutions later passed, in other situations the veto resulted in permanent blockage. It is not claimed that passage of any single one of the vetoed resolutions would have halted all the crimes. On the other hand, that a significant number of resolutions that would have condemned regime and/or opposition crimes failed to pass or were significantly delayed could not have failed to send a metaphorical "green light" to the perpetrators; thus, the vetoes are partly responsible for the still unfolding human tragedy.

The second case study traces climbing death tolls in the early 2000s while the Sudanese military and Janjaweed militia committed mass atrocity crimes against the Fur, Masalit, Zaghawa, and other ethnic groups in the Darfur region of Sudan. These crimes likely constituted genocide, and, at minimum, war crimes and crimes against humanity. During the key years when the crimes were occurring, China blocked by threat of the veto: Initially, any imposition of sanctions on the Government of Sudan, and, permanently, any oil embargo, as well as peacekeeping that was not consensually negotiated with the Government of Sudan. Eventually, a hybrid peacekeeping mission was agreed to and deployed, but only after the height of the killing had occurred and with a weakened mandate. While there were no express vetoes cast related to the situation in Darfur, the Security Council's delays and tepid approach to sanctions and peacekeeping, which significantly increased the death toll, are at least partly attributable to Chinese threats (both express and implied) to use the veto. One might also view the two situations discussed in this chapter through the lens of Russia having strategic and military ties to the regime of Syrian President Bashar al-Assad (and, in fact, militarily involved in the war in Syria), and China having economic and strategic ties to the regime of then-Sudanese President Omar Hassan Ahmad al-Bashir, including as a major importer of Sudanese petroleum. China was also a weapons supplier to the Sudanese military.[4]

CONCLUSION

The book ultimately makes the case that the General Assembly, and states more generally, should continue to challenge the current state of affairs, where any single permanent member may cause complete Security Council paralysis, at massive cost to lives lost on the ground through the commission of genocide, crimes against humanity, and/or war crimes. Can this really be a correct, and legally defensible reading of the UN Charter's voting provisions – that the UN system's highest organ can countenance the commission

---

[4] As mentioned above, while this chapter presents these two case studies, all veto use or threats of veto use in the face of ongoing genocide, crimes against humanity, and/or war crimes (or the serious risk of these crimes occurring) is repugnant, regardless of which permanent member is utilizing the veto or threat of veto. The selection of these two case studies is by no means intended to suggest they are the only problematic situations.

of such crimes through politicized use of the veto? The author hopes her arguments, or similar ones, can spur states to continue to create a consistent precedent by raising legal questions such as those presented in this book any time a permanent member blocks or threatens to block the Security Council in the face of ongoing atrocity crimes. Furthermore, states should seriously consider requesting an Advisory Opinion from the ICJ questioning the legality of veto use while there is ongoing genocide, crimes against humanity, and/or war crimes. For too long has the veto power been treated as if it is above all sources of international law, when it is not.

1

The Origins and History of the Veto and Its Use

[U]nless the Security Council can unite around the aim of confronting massive human rights violations and crimes against humanity ... then we will betray the very ideals that inspired the founding of the United Nations.[1]

INTRODUCTION

This chapter traces the origins of the veto power of the permanent members of the UN Security Council from the negotiations leading into the San Francisco Conference to the finalization of the UN Charter. It then examines an early response to Security Council paralysis – resolutions in the late 1940s by the General Assembly calling for veto restraint, as well as the "Uniting for Peace" resolution in 1950, which provides a mechanism for the General Assembly to make recommendations related to international peace and security when the Security Council's work is blocked. Even though expectations for the Security Council have probably gone beyond the intentions of the drafters of the UN Charter, especially since the end of the Cold War it is clear that when there is sufficient political will, this body has the legal ability to prevent and/or stop many situations of catastrophic consequences to communities, countries, and regions around the world. Concomitantly, when the Council does not take on such a role, there is widespread disenchantment with its performance. Despite numerous efforts, attempts to reform the composition of the Council have, to date, largely failed to reach fruition. The lack of responsiveness to the commission of mass atrocity crimes (genocide, crimes against humanity, and/or war crimes), which have occurred virtually unimpeded (just taking the last few

---

[1] Kofi Annan, Uniting the Security Council in Defence of Human Rights, Address to the Centennial of the First International Peace Conference, The Hague, May 18, 1999, *in* THE QUESTION OF INTERVENTION: STATEMENT BY THE SECRETARY-GENERAL, at 33 (1999).

decades) in places such as Rwanda, Darfur, Syria, Sri Lanka, Myanmar, and Yemen, has come at a staggering toll in terms of lives lost. Much of the time, inaction by the Council can be specifically traced to use of the veto, or the threat of the veto, by one or more of the permanent members. Recent, broadly endorsed, encouraging initiatives aimed at curtailing veto use in the face of atrocity crimes provide strong evidence that the international community wants the Security Council to be more effective in these situations. Yet, because of the voluntary nature of these initiatives (waiting for all permanent members to join them), this chapter makes the case that it is time to reconsider existing hard law legal obligations, and recognize that these in fact impose limitations on the use of the veto in the face of atrocity crimes.

1.1 THE UN CHARTER NEGOTIATIONS

1.1.1 *Positions on the Veto Leading into the San Francisco Conference*

By December 1943, US President Franklin Delano Roosevelt had a vision of the "great powers" as the "Policemen" who would maintain international peace and security in the future: "Britain, Russia, China and the United States and their allies represent more than three-quarters of the total population of the earth. As long as these four nations with great military power stick together in determination to keep the peace there will be no possibility of an aggressor Nation arising to start another world war."[2] His vision translated into what became, with the addition of France, the permanent members of the United Nations Security Council. As permanent members, pursuant to the UN Charter, these states would have veto power over substantive votes, which both ensured, in 1945, their participation in the newly forming organization, but also over the years has generated a vast amount of controversy and discontent as to the Security Council's performance, particularly, as to the use of the veto power.

In the early negotiations of what would become the UN Charter, the US, UK, USSR, and China agreed they would have veto in the Security Council on substantive votes.[3] What emerged as a principle point of contention in their

---

[2] The American Presidency Project, Franklin Delano Roosevelt, Fireside Chat (Dec. 24, 1943), *at* www.presidency.ucsb.edu/ws/index.php?pid=16356.

[3] Although France was accepted as a permanent member of the Security Council, France was not present during negotiations at the Dumbarton Oaks Conference or the Yalta Conference. *See infra* notes 15–17 and accompanying text. China was also not at Yalta (and appears to have played a much lesser role in the negotiations than the US, UK, and USSR), and was only at a resumed session of the Dumbarton Oaks Conference. EDWARD C. LUCK, UN SECURITY COUNCIL: PRACTICE AND PROMISE 12 (2006) ("Because Moscow refused to meet with a Chinese delegation representing the Chiang Kai-Shek regime, the Dumbarton Oaks

negotiations – primarily conducted by the US, USSR, and the UK[4] – was whether this should extend to voting (and hence veto use) as to situations to which they themselves were a party.[5]

The Soviet Union refused to agree to any plan in which they might not have veto power even as to matters involving themselves. However, the US and the UK initially had qualms about such an approach. Ultimately, as detailed below, the US and the UK acquiesced to the Soviet Union's position during negotiations at the Yalta Conference, held February 4–11, 1945.[6] The USSR's position was based on the "principle of unanimity," which it viewed as requiring consensus in all instances. The USSR argued that without unanimity or consensus among the "great powers," there would be discord that could undermine international peace and security. Of course, the veto would also permit the permanent members to maintain power on perhaps the most crucial matters that would face the newly forming organization. Ultimately, other states later argued against including the veto, and, alternatively, against including the veto as to matters under Chapter VI of the Charter (pacific settlement of disputes),[7] and when a permanent member was a party to the dispute including under Chapter VII, but did not prevail.

In 1943, the US had put forth a proposal regarding how Security Council voting might work in its "US Plan for the Establishment of an International Organization for the Maintenance of International Peace and Security."[8] The US plan included the possibility of requiring a three-quarters majority (suggesting the US did not originally insist on veto power), or "unanimity of all members with indeterminate tenure" for voting, and exclusion from voting of a state involved in the conflict at issue. The UK appeared supportive of the veto but with constraints: "Sir Alexander Cadogan [UK Permanent Under-Secretary

meetings had to proceed in two tripartite phases, the first including the Soviet Union and the second, the briefer, China.").

[4] "China's role in the whole process was merely symbolic while France had no say." JAMES A. PAUL, OF FOXES AND CHICKENS: OLIGARCHY AND GLOBAL POWER IN THE UN SECURITY COUNCIL 23 (2017).

[5] There have been two shifts in the composition of the permanent members, with the Russian Federation in 1991 assuming the seat previously held by the USSR, and the People's Republic of China assuming in 1971 the seat previously held by the Republic of China (Taiwan). Id. at 27–28. The Charter still states that the Republic of China and the USSR are the permanent members. UN Charter, Art. 23.1.

[6] The conference took place at the Black Sea resort of Yalta, in Crimea, with the US represented by President Franklin D. Roosevelt, the UK represented by Prime Minister Winston Churchill, and the USSR represented by Premier Joseph Stalin.

[7] LUCK, *supra* note 3, at 13–14. *See* Charter of the United Nations (1945), 892 UNTS 119 (1945) (hereinafter UN Charter), Chapter VI. There is an exclusion from voting under Chapter VI for a party to a dispute. *See* note 62 *infra*.

[8] Memorandum by the Secretary of State to President Roosevelt, December 29, 1943, FRUS, 1944, General Vol. 1, *at* https://history.state.gov/historicaldocuments/frus1944v01/d376.

for Foreign Affairs] stated that he had been instructed to propose that voting in the Council be on the basis of a two-thirds vote in all cases [including the unanimous votes of all permanent members] and further that states which are parties to disputes should not vote."[9] China accepted such an approach.[10]

The Soviet Union argued against such voting procedures. For instance, in the Informal Minutes of Meeting No. 14 of the Joint Steering Committee held September 13, 1944, at the Dumbarton Oaks Conference in Washington, DC, Soviet Ambassador Andrei Gromyko maintained that "in the Soviet opinion the American and British proposal as to voting in the Council would violate the principle of unanimity."[11] Instead, the Soviet Union demanded the requirement of consensus among permanent members, even where a permanent member was a party to the dispute. Initially, the US and the UK refused to concede to the Soviet proposal.

Summarizing the disagreement, in a memorandum to President Roosevelt and US Secretary of State Cordell Hull on September 21, 1944, Under-Secretary of State Edward R. Stettinius wrote:

> The problem with which we are most concerned is whether a permanent member of the Council should vote on matters relating to a dispute to which it is a party and, in consequence of the unanimity rule, have the power of veto. The Soviets insist they should have this right and that permanent members should have the power of veto on all questions, except procedural matters, including the question of whether a dispute may be considered in the Security Council. The British maintain that no state party to a dispute should be entitled to vote.[12]

The US archives of the Dumbarton Oaks conversations reveal that both sides were unwilling to compromise on their positions at the Conference.[13]

---

[9] Memorandum by the Under Secretary of State (Stettinius) to the Secretary of State, August 22, 1944, FRUS, 1944, General Vol. 1, *at* https://history.state.gov/historicaldocuments/frus1944v01/d420.

[10] Tentative Chinese Proposals for a General International Organization, August 23, 1944, FRUS, 1944, *at* https://history.state.gov/historicaldocuments/frus1944v01/d422.

[11] Informal Minutes of Meeting No. 14 of the Joint Steering Committee Held at 10:30 a.m. at Dumbarton Oaks, September 13, 1944, FRUS, 1944 "Dumbarton Oaks Conversations," 798, *at* https://history.state.gov/historicaldocuments/frus1944v01/pg_798.

[12] Memorandum by the Under Secretary of State (Stettinius) to President Roosevelt and the Secretary of State, September 21, 1944, FRUS, 1944, Vol. 1, at 834–36, *at* https://history.state.gov/historicaldocuments/frus1944v01/pg_835.

[13] In a memorandum by Stettinius to Hull, entitled "Progress Report on Dumbarton Oaks Conversations – Twenty-first day," September 13, 1944, Stettinius assessed that there was "[n]o indication of any inclination on the part of the Soviet group to recede from the principle of unanimity of the great powers … ." Memorandum by the Under Secretary of State (Stettinius) to the Secretary of State: Progress Report on Dumbarton Oaks Conversations – Twenty-first day, September 13, 1944, FRUS, 1944, *at* https://history.state.gov/historicaldocuments/frus1944v01/d459.

1.1 The UN Charter Negotiations

The "principle of unanimity" was repeatedly pointed to by the Soviet Union. In a letter to President Roosevelt, Stalin wrote: "otherwise, we will be brought to naught the agreement at the Teheran Conference . . . , first of all the unanimity of agreement of four powers [the USSR, US, UK, and China] necessary for the struggle against aggression in the future."[14] (Although France did not participate at the Dumbarton Oaks Conference or Yalta, France was included as a permanent member by the time of the Yalta Conference[15] at the insistence of the UK.[16] Indeed, at the beginning of negotiations at Dumbarton Oaks, there was already general support to include France as a permanent member.)[17]

While voting at the Security Council was only one of the points of contention in the Charter negotiations,[18] disagreement over Security Council voting threatened to undermine talks to form the United Nations.[19] Both sides echoed the importance of the matter of Security Council voting procedures for the success of the UN and as a matter of importance for their states. The Soviet Union conceded on various points during negotiations,[20] but would not abandon their position on Security Council voting.

---

[14] The Chairman of the Council of People's Commissars of the Soviet Union (Stalin) to President Roosevelt, in Foreign Relations 1944, Vol. 1, *at* https://history.state.gov/historicaldocuments/frus1944v01/pg_806. The Teheran Conference occurred in Teheran, Iran, from November 28 to December 1, 1943, with negotiations between Stalin, Roosevelt, and Churchill. It followed the Cairo Conference, and preceded the Yalta and Potsdam Conferences.

[15] Office of the Historian, The Yalta Conference, 1945, *at* https://history.state.gov/milestones/1937-1945/yalta-conf.

[16] W. W. KULSKI, DE GAULLE AND THE WORLD: THE FOREIGN POLICY OF THE FIFTH FRENCH REPUBLIC 90 (1966).

[17] Franklin D. Roosevelt, Joint Statement with Churchill and Stalin on the Yalta Conference, *in* Presidential Speeches, February 11, 1945, *at* https://millercenter.org/the-presidency/presidential-speeches/february-11-1945-joint-statement-churchill-and-stalin-yalta; Memorandum by the Under Secretary of State (Stettinius) to President Roosevelt, in Foreign Relation 1944, Vol. 1, *at* https://history.state.gov/historicaldocuments/frus1944v01/d427.

[18] In a memorandum to President Roosevelt near the end of the Dumbarton Oaks conversations, Stettinius remarked that, in addition to the Security Council's voting procedure, agreement had not been reached on "determination of initial members," "treatment of matters within the domestic jurisdiction of member states," "human rights and fundamental freedoms," and "provision for the amendment of the Charter." Memorandum by the Under Secretary of State (Stettinius) to President Roosevelt and the Secretary of State, in Foreign Relations 1944, Vol. 1, September 21, 1944, *at* https://history.state.gov/historicaldocuments/frus1944v01/pg_835.

[19] Extract from the Personal Diary of the Under Secretary of State (Stettinius), in Foreign Relations 1944, Vol. 1, September 18, 1944, *at* https://history.state.gov/historicaldocuments/frus1944v01/pg_823; Extracts from the Personal Diary of the Under Secretary of State (Stettinius) in Foreign Relations 1944, Vol. 1, September 14, 1944, *at* https://history.state.gov/historicaldocuments/frus1944v01/d465.

[20] During a meeting between USSR Ambassador Gromyko, Under Secretary of State Stettinius, and President Roosevelt, Ambassador Gromyko offered to accept the Economic and Social Council, to concede on the proposal for an international air force, and to "yield on everything else," except the

At one point, the UK and US discussed an informal formula that would have postponed negotiations on the matter of voting to a future UN conference.[21] Yet, President Roosevelt and Prime Minister Churchill ultimately rejected it, as Churchill believed the Soviets would refuse to delay a decision on voting.[22]

The US delegation sent a proposal for voting to the USSR in the negotiation ahead of the Yalta Conference. While it included the veto, the US was still proposing that a party to a dispute should abstain from voting on the resolution in question, including permanent members, thereby removing the veto in those instances.[23] The Soviets, however, refused to accept the removal of the vote in cases where the permanent member was a party to the dispute, a refusal made clear in letters from Stalin, while the UK was amendable to the US proposal.[24] Stalin again emphasized that "there must be full agreement of powers which are permanent members."[25] Stalin argued that removal of the

---

issue of voting. Extracts from the Personal Diary of the Under Secretary of State (Stettinius), September 8, 1944, FRUS 1944, at https://history.state.gov/historicaldocuments/frus1944v01/d452.

[21] Extracts from the Personal Diary of the Under Secretary of State Stettinius, September 14, 1944, FRUS, 1944, at 810, at https://history.state.gov/historicaldocuments/frus1944v01/pg_810.

[22] President Roosevelt to Under Secretary of State (Stettinius), September 15, 1944, FRUS, 1944, at https://history.state.gov/historicaldocuments/frus1944v01/d469.

[23] The memorandum from the US delegation proposed the following text:

Proposal for section c of the chapter on the security council

C. Voting
1. Each member of the Security Council should have one vote.
2. Decisions of the Security Council on procedural matters should be made by an affirmative vote of seven members.
3. Decisions of the Security Council on all other matters should be made by an affirmative vote of seven members including the *concurring votes of the permanent members; provided that*, in decisions under Chapter VIII, Section A, and under paragraph 1 of Chapter VIII, Section C, *a party to a dispute should abstain from voting*.

Proposed Formula for Voting Procedure in the Security Council of the United Nations Organization and Analysis of the Effects of that Formula, February 6, 1945, *at* https://history.state.gov/historicaldocuments/frus1945Malta/d357 (emphasis added). The references to Chapter VIII became Chapter VII. The requirement of a vote by seven members existed when the Security Council was comprised of eleven members, as it was initially; it was only by amendment in 1965 that the Council expanded to the current fifteen members, with a voting requirement of nine affirmative votes. In 1965, Article 23 was amended to enlarge the Security Council from eleven to fifteen members, and Article 27 was amended to increase the required number of Security Council votes from seven to nine.

[24] The Acting Counsellor of the British Embassy (Wright) to the Special Assistant to the Secretary of State (Pasvolsky), January 14, 1945, FRUS, 1945, *at* https://history.state.gov/historicaldocuments/frus1945Malta/d89.

[25] Marshal Stalin to President Roosevelt, December 27, 1944, FRUS, 1945, *at* https://history.state.gov/historicaldocuments/frus1945Malta/d84. Stalin wrote to President Roosevelt: "the principle of unanimity of permanent members is necessary in all decisions of the Council in

veto for permanent members, even when they are parties to the dispute, could "put certain powers in opposition to other great powers,"[26] allowing aggression. He took the position that "small countries" would also benefit because "a split among great powers, united for tasks of maintenance of peace and security for all peace-loving countries is pregnant with the most dangerous consequences for all these nations."[27]

Following the letter from Stalin rejecting the US proposal, sentiment began to waver within the US administration about the issue of disqualifying a permanent member from voting on a matter to which it was a party. One memorandum recorded that President Roosevelt: "said that he was still worried as to what the situation would be if a controversy arose between, say, the United States and Mexico, and the matter was taken up by the Security Council without the United States having a vote in whatever decisions might be taken."[28] Yet, thereafter, the US apparently reverted back to the position that a permanent member should not vote, and thus have no veto, as to a dispute to which it was a party.[29]

At the Yalta Conference, Stalin once again made clear that he saw the Soviet Union as a "great power" entitled to exceptionalism. According to the Bohlen Minutes of the Yalta Conference: "Marshal Stalin said that he was prepared in concert with the United States and Great Britain to protect the rights of the small powers but that he would never agree to having any action of any of the Great Powers submitted to the judgment of the small powers."[30] Later in that same dinner, Churchill again began to waver.[31]

---

regard to determination of a threat to peace as well as in respect to measures of elimination of such a threat or for suppression of aggression or other violations of peace." *Id.*

[26] *Id.*

[27] *Id.* Similarly, in a conversation between Soviet Ambassador Gromyko and Special Assistant to the Secretary of State Leo Pasvolsky: "The Ambassador repeated the arguments which he has so often given us: that what the small countries are primarily interested in is peace; that peace is unobtainable unless unity prevails among the great powers; and that unity among great powers will inevitably be impaired if the unanimity rule is not maintained throughout in the voting procedures of the Security Council." Memorandum by the Special Assistant to the Secretary of State, January 11, 1945, Subject: Conversation with the Soviet Ambassador on the Dumbarton Oaks Document, FRUS, 1945, *at* https://history.state.gov/historicaldocuments/frus1945Malta/d87.

[28] Memorandum by the Special Assistant to the Secretary of State (Pasvolsky), January 8, 1945, FRUS 1945, *at* https://history.state.gov/historicaldocuments/frus1945Malta/d86.

[29] *Id.*

[30] Bohlen Minutes, February 4, 1945, FRUS, 1945, *at* https://history.state.gov/historicaldocuments/frus1945Malta/d331.

[31] *Id.*

The voting procedure was finally agreed on at Yalta, by the USSR, US, and UK,[32] with the veto available even when a permanent member was a party to a dispute.[33]

1.1.2 Positions on the Veto at the San Francisco Conference

The idea of the permanent members of the Security Council having veto power generated considerable backlash at the United Nations Conference on International Organization or San Francisco Conference, where fifty delegations from forty-eight countries[34] gathered from April 25 to June 26 at the War Memorial Opera House to finalize negotiations of the UN Charter. As might have been predicted, small and middle-sized states pushed back against the inequitable distribution of power that would be created by bestowing veto power on the permanent members of the Security Council,[35] and, indeed, the concept of having "permanent members" of the Security Council[36] – which

---

[32] See note 3 *supra*.
[33] Bohlen Minutes, February 7, 1945, FRUS, 1945, *at* https://history.state.gov/historicaldocuments/frus1945Malta/d373 (hereinafter Feb. 7, 1945, Bohlen Minutes); *see also* Buel W. Patch, *Veto Power in United Nations*, CQ Researcher (Sept. 18, 1946), *at* http://library.cqpress.com/cqresearcher/document.php?id=cqresrre1946091800#H2_1 (agreement at Yalta on the voting formula). *See* note 66 *supra* (procedural votes not subject to veto). The report given on February 6, 1945, by Under-Secretary of State Stettinius with the revised American proposal reflected that agreement had been reached:

> Mr. Molotov [Soviet Minister of Foreign Affairs] said that yesterday we have heard Mr. Stettinius give a full report and explanations of the President's proposals and that this report and explanation had been satisfactory and had made the issue clear to the Soviet Delegation. He said that they had always also followed closely Mr. Churchill's remarks on the subject. He added that after hearing Mr. Stettinius' report and Mr. Churchill's remarks, which had clarified the subject, the Soviet Government felt that these proposals fully guaranteed the unity of the Great Powers in the matter of preservation of peace. Since this had been the main Soviet purpose at Dumbarton Oaks and they felt that the new proposals fully safeguarded this principle, he could state that they were entirely acceptable and that they had no comments to offer. He felt that there was full agreement on this subject.

Feb. 7, 1945, Bohlen Minutes, at 712.
[34] S.D. Bailey & S. Daws, The United Nations: A Concise Political Guide 15 (3d ed. 1995). The number fifty is frequently used, although forty-eight appears more accurate. The difference depends on whether one counts Ukraine and Byelorussia, which sent delegations, but were not in fact independent states.
[35] United Nations, 1945: The San Francisco Conference, *at* www.un.org/en/sections/history-united-nations-charter/1945-san-francisco-conference/index.html.
[36] *See, e.g.*, Luck, *supra* note 3, at 112 ("[v]igorous challenges were voice in San Francisco to the size of the Council ... [and] to the notion of permanent seats set aside for the self-selected few ...").

was seen as a form of "victors' justice" and an infringement on the concept of sovereign equality of states.[37]

Thus, for example, during a June 20 meeting of Commission III (charged with drafting the part of the Charter pertaining to the Security Council),[38] the Australian Ambassador argued against the veto power on the grounds that "each one of the five powers can prevent a decision being reached . . . ."[39] Peru expressed concern that the veto would amount to the "right of certain interests, political or economic, to stop rule of reason and concession."[40] There was general concern that a single vote could make it impossible for the Security Council to adopt "any decision of importance, upon which the peace of the world may rest."[41] El Salvador expressed concern about a lack of procedures in place under the Charter if the permanent members could not all agree on an "emergency affecting the peace of the world."[42] Australia argued that if the UN failed to settle disputes, just as the League of Nations had failed, disputes would still need to be settled, and they would be settled outside the UN system, in a manner contrary to the principles of the United Nations.[43] Belgium voiced concern that the veto "gave any one of the five powers a right to invoke its provisions when wishing to obstruct the action of the Organization."[44] Cuba opined that the Security Council's failure to act could amount to an encouragement of war.[45]

---

[37] Jan Wouters & Tom Ruys, *Security Council Reform: A New Veto for a New Century?*, at 5 (Royal Institute for Int'l Relations, Egmont Paper 9, Aug. 2005).

[38] The drafting of the Charter was divided into four parts, each taken up by a "Commission." "Commission one dealt with the general purposes of the organization, its principles, membership, the secretariat and the subject of amendments to the Charter. Commission two considered the powers and responsibilities of the General Assembly, while Commission three took up the Security Council. Commission four worked on a draft for the Statute of the International Court of Justice." United Nations, 1945: The San Francisco Conference, *supra* note 35.

[39] Verbatim Minutes of the Fourth Meeting of Commission III, Opera House, June 20, 1945, Doc. 1149, at 20. Australia also presented an amendment which would have ruled out use of the veto regarding peaceful settlement of disputes, but it was rejected. Wouters & Ruys, *supra* note 37, at 6. Ironically, France had earlier suggested a similar restriction, prior to when it was awarded permanent membership. Id.

[40] Commission III: Security Council, Committee 1, Summary Report of Seventeenth Meeting of Committee III/I, June 11, 1945, Doc. 922, at 4.

[41] Continuation of the Report on the Activities of Committee III/I Concerning Sections A, B, C, and D of Chapter VI of the Dumbarton Oaks Proposals Submitted by the Rapporteur Hector David Castro, Restricted WD 359, June 16, 1945, at 6.

[42] Summary Report of Sixteenth Meeting of Committee III/1, June 9, 1945, Doc. 897, III/1/42, at 7.

[43] Verbatim Minutes of the Fourth Meeting of Commission III, *supra* note 39, at 25.

[44] Commission III: Security Council, Committee 1, Summary Report of Seventeenth Meeting of Committee III/I, *supra* note 40, at 2.

[45] Id. at 7.

Small and middle-sized states also criticized the permanent members' inability to articulate the reasoning behind having veto power, particularly their failure to answer with specific responses questions put to them in a questionnaire about concerns for the veto's implications.[46] Some states found the logic behind the veto to be a paradox. Cuba argued: "if unanimity really existed among the great powers [then] the veto was superfluous."[47] Belgium took the view that providing the veto to some states and not others "belied the principle of sovereign equality."[48] Other states objected to "a too rigid designation of permanent members in the Charter [which] might hamper the ability of the United Nations to adapt to the changing nature of power in the international system in the future."[49]

States also objected to the absence of a provision disqualifying a permanent member from voting on a matter when it was a party to the dispute. For instance, a report of proceedings reflected that: "[a] general consensus of all delegations seems to have existed at all times concerning the abstention from voting which is required of every member of the Security Council who is a party to a dispute submitted to the Council."[50]

The USSR then argued that the issue of whether a matter could even be discussed at the Council related to international peace and security should be subject to the veto, but did not prevail.[51]

In the end, the "great powers" made it clear their participation in the UN hinged on obtaining veto power on substantive votes, including Chapter VII matters to which they were a party.[52] Indeed, one of the US delegates famously threatened that without the veto power, other states could forget about having a UN, and dramatically tore up his draft of the Charter. Tom Connally, a Democrat from Texas, described the incident:

[46] Continuation of the Report on the Activities of Committee III/I Concerning Sections A, B, C, and D of Chapter VI of the Dumbarton Oaks Proposals, *supra* note 41, at 9, in Vol. XI, at 612. In response to the questionnaire, the four sponsoring nations (China, US, UK, and USSR) "handed over a public statement, the so-called 'San Francisco Declaration', with which France later concurred . . . ." Wouters & Ruys, *supra* note 37, at 6, citing source.
[47] Commission III: Security Council, Committee 1, Summary Report of Seventeenth Meeting of Committee III/I, *supra* note 40, at 7.
[48] *Id.* at 2.
[49] Security Council Report, The Veto, at 2 (2016, No. 3), *quoting* Luck, *supra* note 3, at 13–14.
[50] Commission III: Security Council, Committee 1, Continuation of the Report of the Activities of Committee III/1 concerning Sections A, B, C, and D of Chapter VI of the Dumbarton Oaks Proposals, Submitted by the Rapporteur, Hector David Castro, June 16, 1945, Document 922, at 7, in Vol. 11, at 610.
[51] *See* Patch, *supra* note 33. Some "branded the proposed curb on discussion a 'Russian gag rule.'" *Id.* Note, however, that a permanent member can veto that a matter is procedural, in order to use the veto once the matter is discussed on substance.
[52] *Id.* Chapter VII governs "Action with Respect to Threats to the Peace, Breaches of the Peace, and Acts of Aggression."

"You may go home from San Francisco – if you wish," I cautioned the delegates, "and report that you have defeated the veto. Yes," I went on, "you can say you defeated the veto . . . . But you can also say, 'We tore up the Charter!'" At that point I sweepingly ripped the Charter draft in my hands to shreds and flung the scraps with disgust on the table.[53]

Other states realized they needed to capitulate in order to have a United Nations and because they perceived they would need to rely on the military power of the permanent members to engage in enforcement measures.[54] Edward C. Luck describes the situation:

The dilemma for most delegations in San Francisco could not have been starker. On the one hand, they objected to the veto both because it was inequitable and because it could prevent Council action when most needed. On the other hand, they realized that the viability and effectiveness of the UN – like the League before it – would depend heavily on the continued collaboration of the great powers.[55]

The League of Nations had been "without enforcement capabilities," and this was seen as the key reason for its ineffectiveness, and how the "the United Nations" – originally, a term for a military alliance[56] – was designed to be different.[57]

The final vote on the "unanimity clause" (that is, veto provision) was thirty-three in favor, two against (Colombia and Cuba),[58] with fifteen abstentions.[59] As some recompense, Article 11(2) of the Charter allows the General Assembly to "discuss any question relating to the maintenance of international peace

---

[53] SENATOR TOM CONNALLY, MY NAME IS TOM CONNALLY 283 (1954) (emphasis in original), cited in Luck, supra note 3, at 14.
[54] Security Council Report, The Veto, supra note 49, at 3. Wouters & Ruys point out that in fact the permanent members are not major troop contributing countries to UN peacekeeping operations. Wouters & Ruys, supra note 37, at 28.
[55] Luck, supra note 3, at 14.
[56] The "United Nations" military alliance was established in a "Declaration by the United Nations," signed originally by President Roosevelt, Prime Minister Churchill, Maxim Litvinov of the USSR, and T.V. Soong of China, and twenty-two other states on January 1, 1942, in Washington, D.C. The declaration, later joined by twenty-one additional states, was a pledge by governments to engage their militaries against the Axis powers, and to "cooperate" with each other and refuse to make any separate peace agreements with the Axis powers. Declaration by United Nations, January 1, 1942, Washington, E.A.S. 236, at www.loc.gov/law/help/us-treaties/bevans/m-ust000003-0697.pdf.
[57] Thomas G. Weiss, Foreword, in Luck, supra note 3, at xiii.
[58] Verbatim Minutes of the Fifth Meeting of Commission III, June 20, 1945, at 3, Doc. 1150, in UNIO, DOCUMENTS OF THE UNITED NATIONS CONFERENCE OF INTERNATIONAL ORGANIZATION SAN FRANCISCO, 1945, VOL. XI, at 165.
[59] Jean Krasno and Mitushi Das, The Uniting for Peace Resolution and Other Ways of Circumventing the Authority of the Security Council, in THE UN SECURITY COUNCIL AND THE POLITICS OF INTERNATIONAL AUTHORITY 176 (Bruce Cronin & Ian Hurd eds., 2008).

and security brought before it,"[60] as long as the Council is not exercising its functions related to the matter.[61] Additionally, the provision excluding a Security Council member from voting on a matter to which it was a party would apply under Chapter VI.[62]

Thus, on June 26, 1945, the UN Charter was signed, with the permanent members of the Security Council having veto power on substantive matters (under both Chapters VI and VII), and without any provision in Chapter VII excluding a permanent member from voting on a matter to which it was a party. "The framers of the UN Charter foresaw that the Great Powers would accept the privilege of the veto with a concomitant obligation to shoulder a more substantial burden for the maintenance of international peace and security."[63] Thus, the Charter – which does not use the word "veto"[64] – states in Article 27(3) that decisions on all but procedural matters: "shall be made by an affirmative vote of

---

[60] Article 11(2) states: "The General Assembly may discuss any question relating to the maintenance of international peace and security brought before it by any Member of the United Nations, or by the Security Council, or by a state which is not a Member of the United Nations ... and ... may make recommendations with regard to any such questions to the state or states concerned or to the Security Council or both." UN Charter, Art. 11(2).

[61] Article 12(1) states: "While the Security Council is exercising in respect of any dispute or situation the functions assigned to it in the present Charter, the General Assembly shall not make any recommendation with regard to that dispute or situation unless the Security Council so requests." UN Charter, Art. 12(1). *See also* UN Charter, Art. 10 (allowing the General Assembly to discuss "any questions or any matters within the scope of the present Charter" and make recommendations, except as provided in Article 12). Practice, however, has allowed the two bodies to deal with a matter in parallel:

   [I]n its 2004 *Wall* Advisory Opinion, the ICJ recognized that four decades of practice had modified article 12(1) so as to permit the General Assembly to deal with a matter in parallel with the Security Council. The Court accepted that in practice "It is often the case that, while the Security Council has tended to focus on the aspects of such matters related to international peace and security, the General Assembly has taken a broader view, considering also their humanitarian, social and economic aspects."

   Andrew J. Carswell, *Unblocking the UN Security Council: The Uniting for Peace Resolution*, 18 J. CONFLICT & SEC. L. 453, 469 (2013), *quoting* Legal Consequences of the Construction of a Wall in the Occupied Palestinian Territory, Advisory Opinion, 2004 ICJ Rep. 136, 149–50 (July 9).

[62] *See* UN Charter, Art. 27(3) ("in decisions under Chapter VI, and under paragraph 3 of Article 52 [pacific settlement of disputes through regional arrangements], a party to a dispute shall abstain from voting"). This exclusion from voting applies to both elected and permanent members of the Council. Wouters & Ruys, *supra* note 37, at 12. Wouters and Ruys point out that the exclusion has been inconsistently applied. *Id.* at 13.

[63] Carswell, *supra* note 61, at 457; Luck, *supra* note 3, at 10 ("[T]he most powerful states were given special rights and responsibilities concerning the maintenance of international peace and security.").

[64] Krasno & Das, *supra* note 59, at 175.

seven [amended in 1965 to nine][65] members including the concurring votes [that is, absence of veto][66] of the permanent members."[67] This was, quite simply, the cost other countries would have to bear if they wanted the United Nations to exist at all. It was a "sine qua non for the establishment of the UN, ensuring the participation of the most powerful states in the world body."[68]

1.2 EARLY GENERAL ASSEMBLY ATTEMPTS TO AVOID SECURITY COUNCIL PARALYSIS DURING THE COLD WAR

Not long after the Charter's 1945 creation, states began to see the ramifications of this extraordinary power they had granted, or been forced to grant, the permanent members of the Security Council. Exacerbated by the polarized climate of the Cold War, use of the veto soon began to create deadlock within the Council. By August 1, 1950, "the Soviet Union had all but [paralyzed] the Security Council by vetoing forty-five draft resolutions since the creation of the UN."[69] The fear was that the UN could lapse into the dysfunctionality that had stymied the League of Nations.[70] If the Security Council could not utilize its Chapter VII enforcement powers due to veto use, it was feared the UN could suffer the same fate as the League of Nations, unable to prevent world war.

1.2.1 *General Assembly Resolutions Calling for Veto Restraint*

Already by 1946 – only one year after the Charter's creation – one sees an early General Assembly resolution that demonstrates frustration with veto use. The General Assembly "earnestly request[ed]" the permanent members to "make

---

[65] See note 23 *supra* (amendment).
[66] While the Charter states that it requires "the concurring votes of the permanent members," in practice, this has been read also to permit a permanent member to abstain from voting. Thus, nine affirmative votes are required for procedural matters; nine affirmative votes, including either concurrence or abstention by the permanent members, are required for substantive matters. S.C. Rep., The Veto, at 2 (2016, No. 3); Wouters & Ruys, *supra* note 37, at 8.
[67] UN Charter, Art. 27(3).
[68] Security Council Report, The Veto, *supra* note 49, at 2 (quoting a point made during a September 20, 2015 ministerial-level meeting in New York on veto restraint co-hosted by France and Mexico).
[69] Dominik Zaum, *The Security Council, The General Assembly, and War: The Uniting for Peace Resolution, in* THE UNITED NATIONS SECURITY COUNCIL AND WAR: THE EVOLUTION OF THOUGHT AND PRACTICE SINCE 1945, at 156 (Vaughan Lowe, et al. eds., 2008).
[70] "The failures of the League of Nations were still fresh in the minds of diplomats who did not want the newly created UN to be paralysed in the same way as the League had been." Krasno & Das, *supra* note 59, at 177. *See* Wouters & Ruys, *supra* note 37, at 5 ("under the League of Nations ... unanimity among all members was required").

every effort ... to ensure that the use of the [veto] does not impede the Security Council in reaching its decision."[71] In 1947, the General Assembly likewise called for Security Council members to "consult with one another on the problem of voting in the Security Council.[72] By 1949, the General Assembly again voiced frustration with veto use:

> **290 (IV). Essentials of Peace**
> *The General Assembly ...*
> *Calls upon the five permanent members of the Security Council, ...*
> 10. *To broaden* progressively their cooperation and to exercise restraint in the use of the veto in order to make the Security Council a more effective instrument for maintaining peace.[73]

Similar sentiments were reflected in a 1949 General Assembly resolution, which recommended the veto be used "only when [the permanent members] consider the question of vital importance ... and to state upon what ground they consider this condition to be present."[74]

1.2.2 The "Uniting for Peace" Resolution

Momentum to combat veto use then manifested in what came to be known as the "Uniting for Peace" resolution,[75] originally also known as the "Acheson Plan"[76] for US Secretary of State Dean Acheson. It passed the General Assembly in 1950 by fifty votes, five abstentions (the Soviet bloc), and two opposed (Argentina and India).[77] It states in relevant part:

> **377(V). Uniting for Peace**
> ...
> *Reaffirming* the importance of the exercise by the Security Council of its primary responsibility for the maintenance of international peace and security, and the duty of the permanent members to seek unanimity and to exercise restraint in the use of the veto, ...
> *Conscious* that failure of the Security Council to discharge its responsibilities on behalf of all the Member States ... does not relieve Member States of

---

[71] UN GA Res. 40(I), para. 3 (Dec. 13, 1946).
[72] UN GA Res. 117(II), para. 3 (Nov. 21, 1947).
[73] UN GA Res. 290 (IV) (Dec. 1, 1949).
[74] UN GA Res. 267 (III), para. 3.c (Apr. 14, 1949). This resolution is discussed more extensively in Chapter 3.
[75] For discussion of the history of Resolution 290 and the Uniting for Peace resolution, see Krasno & Das, *supra* note 59.
[76] Keith S. Petersen, *The Uses of the Uniting for Peace Resolution since 1950*, 13 INT'L ORG. 219, 219 (1959).
[77] Krasno & Das, *supra* note 59, at 181.

their obligations or the United Nations of its responsibility under the Charter to maintain international peace and security,

Resolves that if the Security Council, because of lack of unanimity of the permanent members, fails to exercise its primary responsibility for the maintenance of international peace and security in any case where there appears to be a threat to the peace, breach of the peace, or act of aggression, the General Assembly shall consider the matter immediately with a view to making appropriate recommendations to Members for collective measures, including in the case of a breach of the peace or act of aggression the use of armed force when necessary, to maintain or restore international peace and security.[78]

The Uniting for Peace resolution thus builds on Article 24 of the Charter, which states that the Council has "primary responsibility" in the maintenance of international peace and security.[79] This implies the Security Council does not have *exclusive* responsibility in the maintenance of international peace and security, suggesting "the existence of a secondary or subsidiary responsibility ... laid upon the General Assembly."[80] The Uniting for Peace resolution specifies that in instances of Security Council deadlock, matters may be taken up by the General Assembly, at least in the form of recommendations – which power the General Assembly expressly has under the UN Charter.[81] The ability of the General Assembly to address matters in situations of Security Council paralysis was later recognized by the International Court of Justice (ICJ), in 1962, in the *Certain Expenses* case, which recognized that the Security Council has "primary" but not "exclusive" authority and that "whilst the taking of enforcement action was the exclusive prerogative of the Security Council under Chapter VII this did not prevent the Assembly from making recommendations under Articles 10 and 14."[82]

According to one scholar, there are four preconditions to using the Uniting for Peace resolution: (1) the Security Council must have failed "to exercise its primary responsibility for the maintenance of international peace and security"; (2) "[t]he Security Council's failure to exercise its primary responsibility

---

[78] General Assembly A/RES/377 A, 5 U.N. GAOR, Supp. (No. 20) 10–12, U.N. Doc. A/1775 (1950). For additional background on negotiations of the Uniting for Peace Resolution, see, e.g., Harry Reicher, *The Uniting for Peace Resolution on the Thirtieth Anniversary of Its Passage*, 20 COLUM. J. TRANSNAT'L L. 1 (1981).

[79] UN Charter, Article 24 states: "In order to ensure prompt and effective action by the United Nations, its Members confer on the Security Council primary responsibility for the maintenance of international peace and security . . . ." UN Charter, Art. 24.

[80] Juraj Andrassy, *Uniting for Peace*, 50 AM. J. INT'L L. 563 (1956).

[81] *See, e.g.*, UN Charter, Arts. 10, 11(2).

[82] Certain Expenses of the United Nations, Advisory Opinion, 1962 ICJ Rep. 151 (July 20). *See* UN Charter, Arts. 10, 14.

must have been occasioned by ... the lack of unanimity of its permanent members"; (3) there must appear to be "a threat to the peace, breach of the peace or act of aggression"; and (4) the matter must have "at the very least been discussed in the Council."[83] (Note, however, that even if these preconditions are not met, the General Assembly also has residual powers directly under the UN Charter to discuss matters and make recommendations.)[84] The Uniting for Peace resolution also authorized creation of a Peace Observation Commission, a panel of military experts, and a Collective Measures Committee.[85]

Somewhat ironically – given changed political dynamics today – it was the US that spearheaded[86] passage of the Uniting for Peace resolution, so matters related to the Korean War (June 25, 1950–July 27, 1953) could be taken up by the General Assembly because the USSR's presumptive veto would have blocked passage at the Council. "The purpose initially was to wrestle the use of the veto away from the Soviet Union at the time when the United States and the West wanted the United Nations to legitimize action taken to defend South Korea from encroachment from the north."[87] Three resolutions on Korea did pass the Council – including a recommendation for the use of force[88] – but only because the USSR was absent for the vote:

> In 1950, the Soviet Union had boycotted the Security Council on grounds that the UN had failed to grant the People's Republic of China (Communist China), which had achieved control of the mainland after 1949, the seat of China in the UN and on the Council. Instead the UN continued to recognize the Chiang Kai-shek regime in Taiwan as the legitimate member.[89]

---

[83] Reicher, *supra* note 78, at 9–16. That author raises question as to exactly what the Security Council must have done to be said to have failed to exercise its responsibilities, *id.* at 10, and who exactly determines whether there is a "threat to the peace, breach of the peace, or act of aggression," suggesting it is the Council, but noting this could become problematic if that determination is subject to the veto. *Id.* at 12–13.

[84] UN Charter, Arts. 10, 11, 14. *See also* Reicher, *supra* note 78, at 37 ("These various references [in the UN Charter] support the residual power argument by collectively creating an image of [the General Assembly as] an organ with a general supervisory function ready to assume, at the very least, the role of peacekeeping 'backstop' should the need arise."). *See also* note 61 *supra* (allowing the two bodies to deal with a matter in parallel despite the language of Article 12(1)).

[85] UN GA Res. 377(V). None of these mechanisms were significantly used. *See* Petersen, *supra* note 76, at 220–21.

[86] Krasno & Das, *supra* note 59, at 179.

[87] *Id.* at 173.

[88] UN SC Res. 84 (July 7, 1950) (recommending "that Members of the United Nations furnish such assistance to the Republic of Korea as may be necessary to repel the armed attack and to restore international peace and security in the area").

[89] Krasno & Das, *supra* note 59, at 178.

1.2 General Assembly Attempts to Avoid SC Paralysis in Cold War

US delegate to the UN John Foster Dulles explained the need for the Uniting for Peace resolution:

> We must organize dependably the collective will to resist. If the Security Council does not do so, then this Assembly must do what it can by invoking its residual power of recommendation.[90] As the world moves in the path that this resolution defines, it will move nearer and nearer to the Charter ideal.[91]

The UK[92] and France[93] also supported the resolution, which was opposed by the USSR.[94] While cleverly captioned the "Uniting for Peace" resolution, Dean Acheson made clear the resolution was designed to avoid the Soviet veto: "We have been confronted with many and complex problems, but the main obstacle to peace is easy to identify, and there should be no mistake in anyone's mind about it. That obstacle has been created by the policies of the Soviet Union."[95] The resolution was thus designed to allow the UN to respond, at least through discussion and some preliminary measures, in the face of aggressive use of force.[96]

Commentators' views on the Uniting for Peace resolution vary considerably, with some emphasizing that "the Uniting for Peace Resolution 'did not confer upon the General Assembly a competence which it did not have under the

---

[90] United Nations General Assembly Session 5, Process Verbal 299, A/PV.299, at 4, John Foster Dulles (Nov. 1, 1950).

[91] *Id.* at 5.

[92] United Nations General Assembly Session 5, Process Verbal 300, A/PV.300, at 1, Kenneth Gilmour Younger (Nov. 2, 1950) ("The Soviet Union ... has attributed to the Council a power which it has never had under the Charter, namely, the power to insist that, because the Council has itself been reduced to impotence in the face of aggression by disagreement among its permanent members, the entire world Organisation shall wash its hands of the whole matter and let aggression take its course. The Council has never possessed any such right. Indeed, it is impossible to conceive that the authors of the Charter at San Francisco would have lent themselves to a proposition so far out of tune with the hopes and wishes of the peoples of the world.").

[93] United Nations General Assembly Session 5, Process Verbal 299, A/PV.299, at 10, Jean Chauvel (Nov. 1, 1950).

[94] "The Soviet argument was that the UN could not be strengthened by weakening the Security Council which would be the result if the proposals were adopted. The Soviet ambassador referred to the 'primary responsibility' give to the Security Council for the maintenance of international peace and security as an 'exclusive right.'" Krasno & Das, *supra* note 59, at 180. For further drafting history of the Uniting for Peace resolution, see *id.* at. 180 *et seq.*

[95] Statement of Mr. Acheson (Sept. 20, 1950), 5 U.N. GAOR, 279th plen. mtg., at 23, para. 28, U.N. Doc. A/PV. 279 (1950).

[96] US Delegate to the UN, John Foster Dulles noted the UN's response in the Korean situation, "which had proved that the Organization could be an effective instrument for suppressing aggression." Statement of Mr. Dulles, 5 U.N. GAOR, C.1, 354th mtg., at 63, para. 1, U.N. Doc. A/C.1/354 (1950).

Charter.'"[97] Yet, the resolution is also described as "one of the most important attempts by the US and its allies to change the institutional balance of power between the Security Council and the General Assembly at a time when the Council was deadlocked because of regular Soviet vetoes . . . ."[98] It appears to have been both – drawing upon existing General Assembly powers under the Charter, but designed to shift discussion of matters of international peace and security from the Security Council to the General Assembly. At the time, the General Assembly was seen as a reliable ally to the US as it "could command a safe pro-Western majority."[99] The composition of the General Assembly has, of course, significantly shifted with its greatly increased membership, from 51 states in 1945[100] to 193 today, in large part due to the process of decolonization.[101]

1.2.3 *Use of the "Uniting for Peace" Resolution and Other Methods to Shift Debate to the General Assembly*

The first use of the concept behind the Uniting for Peace resolution occurred already prior to the resolution's adoption, when the General Assembly in 1947 took up the issue (after it was vetoed by the USSR at the Security Council) of

---

[97] Reicher, *supra* note 78, at 34, quoting Remarks of Mr. Spender (Australia), 5 U.N. GAOR, C.1, 364th mtg., at 134, para. 63, U.N. Doc. A/C.1/SR. 364 (1950). *See also* Reicher, *supra* note 78, at 48 ("The Uniting for Peace Resolution was a constitutional landmark in the history of the Charter – not in the sense of creating *new* powers, but in the sense of revealing a latent potential in the Charter itself, and setting it on a firm foundation."). "It 're-legitimized' what was already there." *Id. See also* Andrassy, *supra* note 80, at 572 ("The Resolution grants the Assembly no greater powers than those it has under Article 10 and 11, paragraph 2."); Carswell, *supra* note 61, at 476 ("[T]he resolution serves to reveal the latent potential of the Assembly already residing within the UN Charter, and constructs a procedural framework for its exercise."). *But see* Luck, *supra* note 3, at 50 (calling the resolution "constitutionally dubious"); Christian Tomuschat, *Uniting for Peace* 2 (UN Audiovisual Library of International Law, 2008) ("originally resolution 377 A (V) [the Uniting for Peace resolution] was hardly reconcilable with the Charter").

[98] Zaum, *supra* note 69, at 155; Tomuschat, *supra* note 97, at 4 ("Resolution 377 A (V) has a potential that could subvert the well-equilibrated balance of power within the United Nations.").

[99] Zaum, *supra* note 69, at 155.

[100] The Charter was signed by representatives of fifty states, with Poland, which was not present at the Conference, joining as a member thereafter. United Nations, History of the United Nations, at www.un.org/en/sections/history/history-united-nations/. *But see* note 34 *supra* (divergence between counting as forty-eight or fifty states).

[101] *See* Zaum, *supra* note 69, at 165 ("decolonization and the resulting increase of the General Assembly's membership has made it an increasingly unpredictable body, less likely to follow the lead of the great powers in the Security Council"); *id.* at 156 ("the growing number of developing and non-aligned countries in the General Assembly as a consequence of decolonization in the 1950s and 1960s, contributed to the marginalization of the General Assembly, in particular by the US and Western states, who could no longer rely on the support of the majority of states in the Assembly").

1.2 General Assembly Attempts to Avoid SC Paralysis in Cold War

sending a UN Special Commission on the Balkans as a fact-finding mission, which the General Assembly authorized.[102] Subsequently, the Uniting for Peace resolution has been utilized a number of times, including in relation to: the Suez Crisis (1956), Hungary (1956), Lebanon (1958), Congo (1960), the Middle East (1967), East Pakistan/Bangladesh (1971), Afghanistan (1980), Grenada (1983), Panama (1989), the Middle East (1997), and Israel (2003).[103]

The Uniting for Peace resolution has been used for a variety of divergent purposes:

> It has been employed to request the creation of a peacekeeping mission (Suez), and to confirm or strengthen the mandate of UN missions (Korea, Congo). It has been used to condemn armed interventions (Suez, Hungary, Lebanon and Jordan, Afghanistan, and the Golan Heights), and to call for ceasefires (Suez and India-Pakistan). It has been used, by both the Security Council and the General Assembly, to condemn some of Israel's policies in the occupied territories, and finally, has been invoked to promote decolonization in Namibia.[104]

Thus, use of the Uniting for Peace resolution has morphed beyond its original design (responding to North Korean aggression), to various purposes, and the motivations for using it have also shifted (from avoiding the Soviet veto), to providing General Assembly members a voice in the face of a veto or presumptive veto by any permanent member or Security Council inaction more generally. As a result, "the General Assembly has increasingly come to use the tool of Uniting for Peace resolutions and emergency special sessions to raise ... issues ... to have their voices heard"[105] and "to take a stand against the increasing dominance of the UN by the Security Council."[106] (An "emergency special session" was a process created under the Uniting for Peace resolution whereby the General Assembly may meet, triggered by request of the Security Council or General Assembly, in an emergency special session within twenty-four hours if not in session at the time.)[107]

By 2001, a report by the International Commission on Intervention and State Sovereignty (ICISS) – the commission that famously first formulated the

---

[102] Krasno & Das, *supra* note 59, at 177.
[103] For details, see *id.* at 183–86, 189.
[104] Zaum, *supra* note 69, at 163. Zaum also notes that "the initiative for using the Uniting for Peace resolution has increasingly moved from the Security Council to the General Assembly[.]" *Id.*
[105] *Id.* at 166.
[106] *Id.* at 174.
[107] Uniting for Peace Resolution, *supra* note 78, at para. A.1. "[T]he transfer of an issue from the Council to the General Assembly is considered a procedural issue, and therefore not subject to a veto by a Permanent Member." Zaum, *supra* note 69, at 159.

concept of the "responsibility to protect"[108] – identified the Uniting for Peace resolution as "one possible important instrument if the Council fails to act to address major human rights violations or humanitarian emergencies."[109]

The General Assembly, of course, can also raise issues without convening an emergency special session (which was a more important tool when the General Assembly was in session less frequently during the year). Today, the emergency special session can still prove useful to convey a sense of urgency and bypass some of the timelines for General Assembly action. When an emergency special session is called, voting must be by two-thirds. When the General Assembly takes up issues related to "international peace and security" as well as certain other specific areas without an emergency special sessions, this also requires a two-thirds vote, whereas other matters require a simple majority.[110]

The Uniting for Peace resolution, as well as the General Assembly simply taking up a topic when the Council is deadlocked – such as with the recent creation of the International, Impartial and Independent Mechanism (IIIM) to investigate crimes in Syria[111] – have thus developed as methods to attempt to circumnavigate Security Council paralysis particularly in the face of veto use. Indeed, when the IIIM was recently created – after Russia and China vetoed referral of the situation in Syria to the International Criminal Court (ICC)[112] – then-Secretary General Ban Ki-moon announced: "[t]he General Assembly today demonstrated that it can take the reins on questions of justice in the face of Security Council deadlock."[113]

[108] For further discussion of the "responsibility to protect" generally, see Chapter 2; for discussion of the "responsibility not to veto" contained within the "responsibility to protect," see Chapter 3.

[109] Zaum, *supra* note 69, at 173, citing International Commission on Intervention and State Sovereignty, *The Responsibility to Protect*, INTERNATIONAL DEVELOPMENT RESEARCH CENTRE, at 53 (Ottawa, 2001).

[110] Other "important questions" on which a two-thirds vote is required are: "the election of the non-permanent members of the Security Council, the election of the members of the Economic and Social Council, the election of members of the Trusteeship Council . . ., the admission of new Members to the United Nations, the suspension of the rights and privileges of membership, the expulsion of Members, questions relating to the operation of the trusteeship system, and budgetary questions." UN Charter, Art. 18.2.

[111] The full name is "The International, Impartial and Independent Mechanism to Assist in the Investigation and Prosecution of Those Responsible for the Most Serious Crimes under International Law Committed in the Syrian Arab Republic Since March 2011." UN GA Res. A/71/L.48 (Dec. 19, 2016), *at* www.un.org/ga/search/view_doc.asp?symbol=A/71/L.48. The IIIM is tasked to "collect, consolidate, preserve and analyse evidence" and "prepare files in order to facilitate and expedite fair and independent criminal proceedings." *Id*., para. 4.

[112] Draft Res. S/2014/348 (vetoed by Russia and China).

[113] Human Rights Watch, *UN General Assembly Adopts Resolution on War Crimes Investigations* (Dec. 21, 2017), *at* www.hrw.org/news/2016/12/21/syria-un-general-assembly-adopts-resolution-war-crimes-investigations.

1.2 General Assembly Attempts to Avoid SC Paralysis in Cold War

Yet, such approaches are far from a complete answer to Security Council deadlock due to veto use.[114] Because the General Assembly is generally only empowered to make recommendations (except in areas such as UN management and budget),[115] it is unclear how far the General Assembly can go in its actions.[116] Avoiding the Council may not always be possible. For instance, if some form of military force is required (for instance, even the creation of a "no fly zone" unless consent of the host country is obtained, is a form of military force), this should receive Security Council authorization.[117] It is clear the General Assembly cannot approve enforcement action.[118] Furthermore, a two-thirds vote in the General Assembly (under the Uniting for Peace procedure) is a fairly high threshold that is not always achievable. While the General Assembly was successful in creating the IIIM,[119] an investigative mechanism

---

[114] Zaum, *supra* note 69, at 156 ("While the Uniting for Peace Procedure provided an opening for the General Assembly to get involved more actively in addressing threats to international peace and security, the record shows that it failed to do so effectively. The resolution has thus contributed little to strengthening the UN's capacity for collective security."); Carswell, *supra* note 61, at 476 ("When one considers that well over 200 vetoes have been cast in the Security Council since the Uniting for Peace resolution was passed, the [now eleven] emergency special sessions called represent but a small fraction of the Assembly's potential.").

[115] See, e.g., UN Charter, Art. 17.1 ("The General Assembly shall consider and approve the budget of the organization"); see Andrassy, *supra* note 80, at 571, n. 27 (citing areas where the General Assembly can make binding decisions as: "[a]dmission, exclusion, suspension of Members, approval of trusteeship agreements and of agreements entered into with specialized agencies, approval of budgets, [and] apportionment of expenses among Members"). The General Assembly may also establish "such subsidiary organs as it deems necessary for the performance of its functions." UN Charter, Art. 22.

[116] For example, a member of the US team who worked on the resolution suggested the General Assembly could even "take certain preparatory measures" in "setting up a system of contribution of forces by Members States and providing for their suitable military organization." Krasno & Das, *supra* note 59, at 181, interview of Leonard Meeker (1990). Reicher notes that the Uniting for Peace Resolution allows the General Assembly to make recommendations as to use of force. Reicher, *supra* note 78, at 17. However, the view that the General Assembly can authorize humanitarian intervention is a minority view. See Michael Ramsden, *"Uniting for Peace" and Humanitarian Intervention: The Authorising Function of the U.N. General Assembly*, 25 WASH. INT'L L.J. 267 (2016).

[117] A strict reading of the UN Charter *requires* such authorization under Chapter VII; however, Chapter 2 makes an argument for a narrowly construed doctrine of bona fide humanitarian intervention as consistent with the Charter's Purposes and Principles. If one were to solve the problem of veto use in the face of atrocity crimes (as this author urges in Chapter 4), then one would no longer need to try to utilize the doctrine of humanitarian intervention because the Charter would be working as designed.

[118] "It is only the Security Council which can require enforcement by coercive action against an aggressor." *Certain Expenses*, *supra* note 82, at 163; Luck, *supra* note 3, at 50.

[119] The IIIM is not the only investigative mechanism that has been created. The Security Council also created the United Nations Investigative Team to Promote Accountability for Crimes Committed by Da'esh/ISIL (UNITAD) – charged with investigating ISIL

has no prosecutorial capacity and is never an adequate alternative to measures aimed at preventing the crimes in the first place. As overviewed below in Section 1.3.2 and detailed in Chapter 5, veto use and veto threats in the face of atrocity crimes[120] can still block the Security Council, while staggering death tolls mount.[121]

1.3 OVERVIEW OF VETO USE INCLUDING DURING THE COMMISSION OF ATROCITY CRIMES

1.3.1 *Overview of Veto Use*

There is fairly widespread sentiment that the veto and threat of veto continue to "play considerable parts in the growing disappointment with how the Council is managed."[122] "From the Cold War until the present day, the fact that the UN system has failed to live up to the lofty expectations of its framers can be attributed in significant part to the threat and exercise of the veto by individual Permanent Five (P5) members of the Council."[123] There is a broad "perception among many member states that the veto or threat of the veto is at times abused to the detriment of international peace and security"[124] and that it is used to defend the permanent members' "perceived national interests, or to uphold a tenet of their foreign policy."[125] There is no requirement in the Charter or in the Provisional Rules of Procedure of the

---

crimes committed in Iraq – and the Human Rights Council created the United Nations Independent Investigative Mechanism for Myanmar (IIMM). *See* S/RES/2379 (Sept. 21, 2017) (creating UNITAD); Hum. Rts. Council, Res. 39/2 (Sept. 28, 2018) (creating the IIMM).

[120] This book uses the term "atrocity crimes" to mean genocide, crimes against humanity, and/or war crimes. The term "ethnic cleansing" is also sometimes utilized in this context but does not have a specific definition for purposes of international criminal law, and is often used when it is unclear whether or not crimes constitute genocide.

[121] *See* Chapter 5 (detailed analysis of veto use regarding Syria and veto threats regarding Darfur).

[122] Security Council Report, The Veto, *supra* note 49, at 2.

[123] Carswell, *supra* note 61, at 453.

[124] Security Council Report, The Veto, *supra* note 49, at 2.

[125] *Id.* at 3. *See also* Richard Butler, *Reform of the United Nations Security Council*, 1 Penn. St. J. L. & Int'l Aff. 23 (2012) ("The Permanent Five have behaved and continue to behave in ways that suggest that they see the power that they hold as rightful and free, to be exercised by them in whatever manner they choose."); Ramsden, *supra* note 116, at 300 ("[P]ermanent members have vetoed resolutions for extraneous purposes. The United States vetoed the extension of peacekeeping mandates in Bosnia and Herzegovina because it had not received a concession in the drafting of the [resolution regarding a carve-out from ICC jurisdiction].") (footnotes omitted).

1.3 Overview of Veto Use 31

Security Council[126] that permanent members even explain a reason for their use of the veto.[127]

There are actually a number of vetoes built into the UN Charter. In addition to the veto on substantive matters, the permanent members have veto over the selection of the next UN Secretary-General, veto on matters of admission of new states to the UN, and veto over any amendment to the Charter.[128] One expert describes these vetoes (in addition to the substantive veto) as "four vetoes, not one."[129] There is also a veto over whether a matter on the Security Council's agenda is procedural or substantive, so that a "double veto" can be employed – vetoing that a matter is procedural, in order to use the veto once the matter is discussed on substance.[130] A veto may be made by a permanent member on its own behalf to serve its own agenda, or "delivered on behalf of a non-permanent member."[131] Thus, "permanent members sometimes use the privilege to shield friendly States with whom they maintain close economic and diplomatic relations from condemnation or the imposition of economic sanctions."[132] "This sends out the manifestly wrong signal that States that stand close to one of the [permanent members] can get away with recurrent human rights violations and/or unlawful military incursions into neighbouring States."[133]

---

[126] Provisional Rules of Procedure of the Security Council, S/96/Rev. 7 (1982), *at* www.un.org/en/sc/inc/pages/pdf/rules.pdf. The Provisional Rules basically say nothing about Security Council voting other than it is governed by the UN Charter. *See id.*, Rule 40 ("Voting in the Security Council shall be in accordance with the relevant Articles of the Charter and of the Statute of the International Court of Justice.").

[127] "States often fail to provide clarification of their exact motives for casting a vote. Even when States do give a public explanation, this will not necessarily correspond to the real reason." Wouters & Ruys, *supra* note 37, at 9, *citing* S.D. BAILEY & S. DAWS, THE PROCEDURE OF THE UN SECURITY COUNCIL, at 228 (3d ed. 1998). As discussed in Chapter 3, not all permanent members should be grouped together in this respect. Both the UK and France have called for curtailing veto use in the face of atrocity crimes, joining voluntary veto restraint initiatives that the US, China, and Russia fail to join. *See* Chapter 3.

[128] Butler, *supra* note 125, at 29.

[129] *Id.*

[130] *Id.* at 30; *see also* Patch, *supra* note 33, at 6 ("[T]he Big Five made it plain at San Francisco that they reserved the right to control decisions on what questions were procedural or substantive. This gave them a sort of double veto power. It has been the position of the small nations, and originally also of the United States and Britain, that determination of such questions should be governed by a procedural vote"). According to Wouters and Ruys the double veto has not been used since 1959. Wouters & Ruys, *supra* note 37, at 8.

[131] Butler, *supra* note 125, at 31. During the Cold War, "vetoes cast by [the USSR] and the United States were cast largely ... in defense of their client states." *Id.* at 30.

[132] Wouters & Ruys, *supra* note 37, at 14.

[133] *Id.* Wouters and Ruys point out fifty-six vetoes regarding South Africa (cast by the US, the UK, and France) and nearly half of the US's vetoes exercised regarding the Israeli/Palestinian

Overall, the veto has been used a total of 201 times during or before the Cold War and, as of early 2020, a total of 54 times thereafter, with uses by the Soviet Union/Russia (115 times), the US (81 times), the UK (29 times), France (16 times), and China (14 times).[134] While there was hope that with the end of the Cold War extensive veto use could become a relic of the past – which may have been true during the 1990s[135] – recent voting patterns suggest this is no longer the case. Indeed, there is a sense that geopolitics are no longer fully "out" of the Cold War, but hearkening back to it, or that the international system is in a new "post, post–Cold War."[136]

While this book primarily emphasizes the problems of veto *use*, the threat of the veto can be equally pernicious because it can block measures just as effectively as an actual veto, only it is often harder to detect. As explained in Chapter 5, a "threat" is not necessarily a statement made by a permanent member in threatening language, but simply a permanent member stating or even implying it will not support certain measures or certain language in a resolution.[137] According to former Australian Ambassador to the UN Richard Butler: "It would simply be impossible to calculate how many times the decision making process of the Security Council, in an informal, private session, has been shaped by the threat of a veto to be cast in a formal session by one of the Permanent Members."[138] This problem is further exacerbated because a "great proportion of what takes place in the Council is not seen publicly."[139] Sometimes a threat of a veto is referred to as a "hidden veto" or "silent veto."[140]

A parallel problem exists where, due to a permanent member's political alignment, it is simply understood the permanent member would veto, so no resolution is ever drafted, and nothing is ever put to a vote. This is even harder to detect. Yet, it can operate just as effectively as an actual veto or a veto threat, because certain measures or language is presumptively "off the table." In

---

situation. *Id.* at 15. For a recent book discussing the veto power and its uses, see Paul, *supra* note 4.

[134] *Security Council Veto List* (Jan. 21, 2020), *at* http://research.un.org/en/docs/sc/quick.

[135] "After the Cold War, beginning about 1990, the Council enjoyed an unprecedented burst of activity." Paul, *supra* note 4, at 14.

[136] *See, e.g.,* Ramsden, *supra* note 116, at 269 ("[R]ecent tensions among the permanent members over Russia's intervention in Crimea have provoked references to a 'new Cold War.'"); James Stavridis, *Are We Entering a New Cold War?*, For. Pol'y (Feb. 17, 2016); Daniel L. Dreisbach, *UN Head Sees the Return of Cold War*, Wisc. St. J. (Apr. 23, 2018), *at* www.wisc24.com/international/un-head-sees-the-return-of-cold-war-232302.html.

[137] *See* Chapter 5 (interview with Andras Vamos-Goldman).

[138] Butler, *supra* note 125, at 30. Ambassador Butler also served as chief weapons inspector in Iraq during the 1990s with the United Nations Special Commission to Disarm Iraq (UNSCOM).

[139] *Id.*

[140] Paul, *supra* note 4, at 35 (also referring to the "closet veto").

1.3.2 Veto Use and Veto Threats during the Commission of Atrocity Crimes

effect, the would-be-proponent(s) of the resolution and the Security Council member state charged with drafting, "the penholder," self-censor themselves – not drafting a resolution known to have no chance of passing, and/or not wishing to antagonize a particular permanent member.[141]

As detailed above, negotiations among the major powers leading to the creation of the UN Charter made clear that the veto was implemented primarily to require unanimity for military action in order to maintain international peace and security.[142] It was also undoubtedly implemented "so that the permanent members could protect their security and sovereignty,"[143] as well as vital national interests. What was never granted in San Francisco was the power to use the veto in a way that contravened basic tenets of international law or the UN's "[p]urposes and [p]rinciples" (like enabling genocide, crimes against humanity, or war crimes to happen or to continue). Yet, veto use has morphed into such contexts, including, as will be detailed, blocking measures in the face of ongoing atrocity crimes (that is, genocide, crimes against humanity, and/or war crimes). For example, vetoes have blocked recognition of atrocity crimes, blocked calls to stop their commission, blocked criminal investigations, and blocked criminal prosecutions or referrals for prosecution.[144] Such uses of the veto are far from the originally stated rationale for creation of the veto power, which, as illustrated above, was never designed to be used in such circumstances.[145] In 1945, of course,

---

[141] See Chapter 5 (interview with Andras Vamos-Goldman).
[142] See section 1.1 supra ("The UN Charter negotiations"). Edward C. Luck observes that the

> Council's track record in maintaining international peace and security ... has been spotty at best. Surely nothing close to the dependable system of collective security sought by the UN's far-sighted founders has been achieved. Clearly the Council has been more willing and able to grapple with some kinds of conflicts and with some regions than others. And the degree of consensus among its more influential members has ebbed and flowed ....

Luck, supra note 3, at 3.
[143] Stop Illegitimate Vetoes, *Legitimate Concerns: The Use of the UN Security Council Veto and How to Improve without Reform*, at http://stopillegitimatevetoes.org/wp-content/uploads/2018/03/Legitimate-Concerns-Revision-14.pdf.
[144] See, e.g., Chapter 5 (detailing such vetoes regarding the situation in Syria).
[145] See Chapter 1.1 supra ("The UN Charter negotiations"). See also Wouters & Ruys, supra note 37, at 25 ("the raison d'être underlying the veto privilege ... is based on the need to guarantee peaceful relations among the world's main powers and to assure the new body of their support in order to make it sufficiently credible and vigorous").

the field of international justice was only nascent and much of the law we now have was underdeveloped; ergo, in 1945, there was no debate about the interaction of the veto power and atrocity crimes.

For example, threat of the veto to avoid action in the face of atrocity crimes occurred in 1994, when France, the US, and, by some accounts, the UK, used the implied veto threat[146] to delay sending a more robust intervention force to Rwanda, and avoid formal acknowledgment of the crimes as genocide.[147] In the face of Security Council paralysis and the existence of only a minimal UN troop presence in Kigali (UNAMIR),[148]

---

[146] See JOHN HEIECK, A DUTY TO PREVENT GENOCIDE: DUE DILIGENCE OBLIGATIONS AMONG THE P5, at 66 (2018), citing Ariela Blätter & Paul D. Williams, The Responsibility Not to Veto, GLOB. RESP. PROTECT 301, 311 (2011) ("An example of implied vetoes occurred during the Rwanda genocide, when the 'Western P3' – France, the UK, and the US – repeatedly pressured other Council members not to propose draft resolution on the floor of the Security Council."); see also note 177 infra (express and implied threats).

[147] Wouters & Ruys, supra note 37, at 16 ("When the Security Council considered the possibility of intervening to halt the massacres, two permanent members, France and the United States (the latter partially motivated by the loss of eighteen soldiers in Somalia in 1993) blocked the establishment of a robust intervention force. The two countries moreover used their hidden veto to weaken the definition of the crisis under international law, carefully avoiding the term 'genocide.'"), citing Céline Nahory, The Hidden Veto, GLOB. POL'Y (May 2004), at www.globalpolicy.org/security-council/42656-the-hidden-veto.html ("Hidden vetoes can have terrible consequences. The Security Council failed to act during the Rwandan genocide in 1994 due to the hidden vetoes of France and the US. Paris and Washington not only blocked UN action, but also used their hidden veto to weaken the definition of the crisis under international law . . . ."). This situation is explained as follows:

> One source attributes the political pressure to three permanent members – France, the US, and the UK: Although Rwanda's 1994 genocide is not a case where a P5 member threatened a veto in order to stop a proposed military intervention, it is relevant because it demonstrates the potential power that P5 members can exert over the Security Council's decision-making process in response to mass atrocities. The central point of controversy that is relevant here is the way in which several P5 members, notably France, the UK and the US, used their influence during the Council's private deliberations to (1) prevent the development of a reinforced peacekeeping operation in the first few weeks after the genocide began in April 1994; and (2) prevent the use of the label genocide to describe the violence in Rwanda thereby closing down any serious discussion of possibly humanitarian military intervention.

Blätter & Williams, supra note 146, at 311 (footnotes omitted); see also Heieck, supra note 146, at 66 (similar). France of course had long supported the Hutu regime in power at the time of the genocide, including by providing arms in the lead-up to the genocide. See Daniel H. Levine, Some Concerns About the Responsibility Not to Veto, 3 GLOB. RESP. PROTECT 323, 327 (2011) ("The French have been involved with the Rwandan government long before the genocide.").

[148] The UN Assistance Mission for Rwanda (UNAMIR) was led by Canadian Lieutenant-General Roméo Dallaire and sent originally with a mandate to implement the Arusha Peace Accords. When UNAMIR troops found themselves in the midst of a genocide (after the April 6, 1994 downing of the airplane carrying the Presidents of Rwanda and Burundi),

with outside efforts focused only on rescuing foreign nationals,[149] approximately 800,000 to one million predominantly Tutsi perished over approximately 100 days.[150] The Security Council did eventually authorize sending nearly 5,500 troops (UNAMIR II), but they arrived only when much of the killing was over.[151] Meanwhile, the French-led operation, "Opération Turquoise," prior to UNAMIR II's arrival, inter alia, had the effect of facilitating the escape of Hutu perpetrators into Zaire.[152] The almost inconceivable mass slaughter was subsequently held by the International Criminal Tribunal for Rwanda (ICTR) to constitute genocide.[153] Of course, the implied veto threat was used because there

> Dallaire did his utmost to obtain peacekeeping reinforcements, a change of mandate, and to rescue those UNAMIR could, given the limited resources at its disposal, particularly after Belgium withdrew its troop contingent. See generally ROMÉO DALLAIRE, SHAKE HANDS WITH THE DEVIL: THE FAILURE OF HUMANITY IN RWANDA (2004).

[149] In early April 1994, France launched Opération Amaryllis to evacuate foreign nationals. "Five years after the events, the Report of the UN Independent Inquiry on Rwanda concluded that 'a force numbering 2,500 should have been able to stop or at least limit' the massacres which took place following the shooting of the Rwandan President's airplane." Wouters & Ruys, supra note 37, at 16, citing Report of the Independent Inquiry into the Actions of the United Nations During the 1994 Genocide in Rwanda, at 30, S/1999/1257 (Dec. 16, 1999).

[150] For background, see ALISON DES FORGES, LEAVE NONE TO TELL THE STORY: GENOCIDE IN RWANDA (HUMAN RIGHTS WATCH, 1999).

[151] UNAMIR II troops did not start arriving until June 1994. LINDA MELVERN, CONSPIRACY TO MURDER: THE RWANDAN GENOCIDE at 411 (2004).

[152] According to former Rwandan ambassador to France and co-founder of the RPF Jacque Bihozagara, "Opération Turquoise was aimed only at protecting genocide perpetrators, because the genocide continued even within the Turquoise zone." France Accused on Rwanda Killings, BBC NEWS (Oct. 24, 2006). Daniel H. Levin writes:

> [E]ven if Opération Turquoise did some good, it was motivated in significant part by cynical French geopolitics – a combination of (former) alliance with the genocidal regime and desire to halt the advance of the RPF, who were perceived as allied with the anglophone (and, hence, US-aligned) Ugandans. And even if its main intent was not to protect the genocidaires, it served to cover the retreat of genocidal elements out of Rwanda, notably into the Democratic Republic of Congo (DRC, then Zaire). Philip Gourevitch puts it bluntly: "the signal achievement of the Opération Turquoise was to permit the slaughter of Tutsis to continue for an extra month, and to secure safe passage for the genocidal command to cross, with a lot of its weaponry, into Zaire."

Levine, supra note 147, at 328, quoting PHILIP GOUREVITCH, WE WISH TO INFORM YOU THAT TOMORROW WE WILL BE KILLED WITH OUR FAMILIES: STORIES FROM RWANDA 160–61 (1998).

[153] The first case to establish the killing as genocide was the ICTR's Akayesu case that not only recognized the crimes as genocide but held that rape could constitute an underlying crime of genocide. Prosecutor v. Jean-Paul Akayesu, Case No. ICTR-96-4-T, Trial Chamber Judgment (Sept. 2, 1998); Prosecutor v. Jean-Paul Akayesu, Case No. ICTR-96-4-A, Appeals Chamber Judgment (June 1, 2001). For a digest of the case law of the ICTR, see JENNIFER TRAHAN, GENOCIDE, WAR CRIMES AND CRIMES AGAINST HUMANITY: A DIGEST OF THE CASE

was basically no will to act.[154] That is, permanent members were hesitant to utilize the word "genocide" for fear it would be seen to trigger a responsibility to respond,[155] which no state appeared willing to do in the circumstances.[156] In such a situation, the veto power is being used as a tool to avoid responding to the unfolding tragedy.

In 1998 and 1999, when ethnic cleansing by Serb forces was commencing in Kosovo, Russia and China made clear they would veto any forceful intervention designed to curtail the atrocities.[157] When Serbian President Slobodan Milošević dismissed all attempts to peacefully settle the conflict, and after discovery of a massacre in Rajac,[158] the North Atlantic Treaty Organization (NATO) launched a military intervention absent Security Council authorization. (NATO's operations, termed by some "humanitarian intervention," are discussed in Chapter 2.) NATO's actions show that the threat or anticipation of a veto in the face of atrocities can, rather than always resulting in inaction, alternatively, in some instances, cause other states to be tempted to slip from a strict reading of the use of force framework of the UN Charter – something that appears to have been

---

LAW OF THE INTERNATIONAL CRIMINAL TRIBUNAL FOR RWANDA (Human Rights Watch, 2010). The tribunal was able to be created by the Security Council, along with its sister tribunal, the International Criminal Tribunal for the former Yugoslavia (ICTY), because in the 1990s there was a more conducive political climate.

[154] "The decision by the Security Council on 21 April to reduce UNAMIR [from 2,500] to a minimal force [of 270] in the face of the killing which were by then known to all, rather than to make every effort to muster the political will to try and stop the killing has led to widespread bitterness in Rwanda. It is a decision which the Inquiry finds difficult to justify. The Security Council bears a responsibility for its lack of political will to do more to stop the killing." Report of the Independent Inquiry into the Action of the United Nations During the 1994 Genocide in Rwanda ("Carlsson Report"), at 32, U.N. Doc. S/1999/1257 (Dec. 16, 1999).

While the veto, or recognition that the veto would be invoked, is often to blame, the lack of will to become involved can also prove a massive impediment. See, e.g., Michael Byers & Simon Chesterman, Changing the Rules about Rules? Unilateral Humanitarian Intervention and the Future of International Law, in J. L. HOLZGREFE AND R. KEOHANE, HUMANITARIAN INTERVENTION: ETHICAL, LEGAL, AND POLITICAL DILEMMAS 202 (2003) ("States are not champing at the bit to intervene in support of human rights around the globe, prevented only by an intransigent Security Council and the absence of clear criteria to intervene without its authority. The problem, instead, is the absence of the will to act at all.").

[155] See Heieck, supra note 146, at 103 (recounting governments' statements that the killing in Rwanda should not be labeled "genocide" because that might obligate them to "do something" about it).

[156] With what happened in Mogadishu fresh in everyone's minds the question that states that had the capacity to respond quickly were struggling with was how intervention could be done without casualties like in Mogadishu. Thus, the paralysis was likely also due to a lack of a viable solution to this dilemma.

[157] Wouters & Ruys, supra note 37, at 17, citing R. Watson, UN Left on Sidelines, BBC NEWS (Apr. 3, 1999).

[158] Wouters & Ruys, supra note 37, at 17.

1.3 Overview of Veto Use

repeated with US missile strikes in spring 2017,[159] and US, French, and UK missile strikes in spring 2018 in response to chemical weapons attacks in Syria.[160] (These missile strikes are also further discussed in Chapter 2.) Both NATO's intervention and the 2017–18 missile strikes demonstrate that inappropriate veto threats and knowledge that the veto would be used can, and do, lead to both the undermining of international law when its rules are ignored (as will be detailed in Chapter 4), and challenges for the law, when states are forced to go beyond a strict reading of the Charter's use of force norms.

Vetoes have also been used in the face of a variety of human rights abuses and crimes, including, for example, in Gaza and Zimbabwe:

- On 13 July and 11 November 2006, the US cast vetoes on draft resolutions calling on Israel to halt military operations in Gaza;
- Following the violent elections in Zimbabwe in June 2008, China and Russia cast vetoes on an 11 July 2008 draft resolution that would have condemned the government for a campaign of violence against civilians and the political opposition, while imposing an arms embargo on Zimbabwe and designating individuals participating in the violence for a travel ban and assets freeze.[161]

The US consistently vetoes Security Council resolutions related to Israel,[162] despite allegations of war crimes and crimes against humanity. An example would include violations allegedly committed by both Israeli forces and Palestinian

---

[159] Michael R. Gordon, Helene Cooper & Michael D. Shear, *Dozens of U.S. Missiles Hit Air Base in Syria*, N.Y. Times (Apr. 6, 2017), *at* www.nytimes.com/2017/04/06/world/middleeast/us-said-to-weigh-military-responses-to-syrian-chemical-attack.html.

[160] Zachary Cohen & Kevin Liptak, *US, UK and France Launch Syria Strikes Targeting Assad's Chemical Weapons*, CNN (Apr. 14, 2018), *at* www.cnn.com/2018/04/13/politics/trump-us-syria/index.html.

[161] Security Council Report, The Veto, *supra* note 49, at 3.

[162] "The United States . . . has routinely used its veto power to shield Israel from Security Council measures demanding it show greater restraint in its dealings with the Palestinians." Colum Lynch, *Rise of the Lilliputians*, For. Pol'y (May 10, 2012), *at* http://foreignpolicy.com/2012/05/10/rise-of-the-lilliputians/. *Compare* Citizens for Global Solutions, *The Responsibility Not to Veto: A Way Forward*, at 4 (suggesting not all US vetoes have been in the face of atrocity crimes, and suggesting some vetoes may have been warranted due to "language [that] can be interpreted as unbalanced and aggressive"). For one analysis of US vetoes related to Israel, see UN Security Council: US Vetoes of Resolutions Critical to Israel (1972–present), *at* www.jewishvirtuallibrary.org/u-s-vetoes-of-un-security-council-resolutions-critical-to-israel. *See also* Blessing Nneka Iyase & Sheriff Folami Folarin, *A Critique of Veto Power System in the United Nations Security Council*, 11(2) Acta Universitatis Danubius 104, 107 (2018); Serdar Yurtsever & Fatih Mohamad Hmaidan, *From League of Nations to the United Nations: What Is Next?*, 12(62) J. Int'l Soc. Res. 449 (2019) (stating that from 1946 to 2016 the US used the veto seventy-nine times regarding Israel/Palestine); Wouters & Ruys, *supra* note 37, at 15 (listing various US vetoes related to Israel).

armed groups related to the 2008–09 incursion into Gaza ("Operation Cast Lead") as well as the 2014 incursion ("Operation Protective Edge").[163] The US of course has well-known military, financial, and diplomatic ties to the State of Israel.[164]

Other examples of veto use include, historically, US, UK, and French vetoes over decades, protecting the apartheid regime in South Africa.[165] Wouters and Ruys write:

> With regard to South Africa, no less than 56 vetoes were cast (26 by the United Kingdom, 20 by the United States and 10 by France). In 1986 for example the UK and the US blocked draft resolutions that condemned South African attacks against Angola, Zambia, Botswana and Zimbabwe. In 1987 and 1988, the same permanent members moreover vetoed the imposition of economic sanctions against the apartheid regime . . . .[166]

Apartheid was acknowledged in 1973 to constitute a crime against humanity that violates "the principles of international law, in particular the purposes and principles of the Charter of the United Nations."[167]

As detailed more extensively in Chapter 5, in the early 2000s, China used the threat of the veto on multiple occasions to block any meaningful response to the crimes, including war crimes, crimes against humanity, and, most likely, genocide,[168] unfolding in Darfur, Sudan, at the hands of the Janjaweed and

---

[163] The ICC has an open Preliminary Examination covering the latter Gaza incursion. *See* International Criminal Court, Office of the Prosecutor, *Report on Preliminary Examination Activities 2017*, paras. 51–78 (Dec. 4, 2017), *at* www.icc-cpi.int/itemsDocuments/2017-PE-rep/2017-otp-rep-PE_ENG.pdf. The latter incursion occurred after Palestine deposited an instrument of accession to the ICC's Rome Statute. *See* Rome Statute of the International Criminal Court, Arts. 6-8, July 17 July 1998, U.N. Doc. A/CONF.183/9; ICC Press Release, *The State of Palestine Accedes to the Rome Statute*, ICC-ASP-20150107-PR1082 (Jan. 7, 2015), *at* www.icc-cpi.int/Pages/item.aspx?name=pr1082_2.

[164] *See, e.g.*, Stephen Zunes, *Why the U.S. Supports Israel*, INST. POL'Y STUD. (May 1, 2002), *at* https://ips-dc.org/why_the_us_supports_israel/); Charles D. 'Chuck' Freilich, *Can Israel Survive without America?*, 59(4) SURVIVAL 135 (2017).

[165] Wouters & Ruys, *supra* note 37, at 15.

[166] *Id.* (citations omitted). *See, e.g.*, Draft Resolution S/12312/Rev.1 (the question of South Africa (Apartheid)) (vetoed by the US, UK, and France); Draft Resolution S/12311/Rev.1 (the question of South Africa (Apartheid, the South African Border War, and South Africa's Nuclear Weapons program)) (vetoed by the US, UK, and France); Draft Resolution S/12310/Rev.1 (the question of South Africa (Apartheid and the South African Border War)) (vetoed by the US, UK, and France).

[167] International Convention on the Suppression and Punishment of the Crime of Apartheid, 1015 UNTS 243, Art. 1.1 (1973, *entry into force* 18 July 1976). The US, UK, and France had known economic ties to South Africa.

[168] *See, e.g.*, Jennifer Trahan, *Why the Killing in Darfur Is Genocide*, 31 FORDHAM INT'L L.J. 990 (2008). The charges levelled against then Sudanese President Bashir by the ICC include genocide. Prosecutor v. Omar Hassan Ahmad Al Bashir, Case No. ICC-02/05-01/09, First

1.3 Overview of Veto Use

Sudanese military.[169] The death toll is estimated at approximately 400,000,[170] predominantly members of the Fur, Masalit, Zaghawa, as well as other ethnic groups, with over two million displaced.[171] There, the threat of a veto was basically as effective as the veto in blocking and weakening sanctions, and weakening and delaying UN peacekeeping.[172] For example, veto threats ensured there were no effective sanctions, such as an oil embargo, on the Government of Sudan, whose military was heavily implicated in atrocity crimes along with the Janjaweed militia, which the Government was arming and supplying.[173] The lack of oil sanctions also "protected" Sudanese oil exports to China, the permanent member that made the veto threats.[174] Weakening the arms embargo also "protected" Chinese arms sales to Sudan.[175]

China has also used its veto power to downplay atrocities committed in Sri Lanka's 1983–2009 civil war by both Government forces and the Liberation Tigers of Tamil Eelam (LTTE).[176] It is difficult to determine the exact number of veto threats (express or implied)[177] by China related to Sri Lanka, as it appears that China's support for the Government has translated into a consistent understanding that China would not support

---

Warrant of Arrest (Mar. 4, 2008), Second Warrant of Arrest (July 12, 2010). Even if the crimes in Darfur are characterized as crimes against humanity and war crimes, these are still atrocity crimes, which the Security Council could have done far more to halt, were it not for multiple veto threats. *See* Chapter 5.

[169] *See* Chapter 5.
[170] While fatality estimates are often in the 200,000–300,000 range, a more accurate figure is probably 400,000. Phillip Manyok, *Oil and Darfur's Blood: China's Thirst for Sudan's Oil*, 4 J. POL. SCI. & PUB. AFF. (2016), *at* www.omicsonline.org/open-access/oil-and-darfurs-blood-chinas-thirst-for-sudans-oil-2332-0761-1000189.php?aid=69390 ("The UN Office for the Coordination of Humanitarian Affairs (OCHA) estimated that 396,563 people have died as a result of war in Darfur alone."); *see also* Eric Reeves, *Quantifying Genocide: Darfur Mortality Update, August 6, 2010 (updated November 2016)*, SUDAN: RESEARCH, ANALYSIS, AND ADVOCACY (Jan. 5, 2017), *at* http://sudanreeves.org/2017/01/05/quantifying-darfur-mortality-update-august-6-2010/.
[171] The UN often uses the figure of 2.7 million displaced. *See* Chapter 5.
[172] "Liechtenstein stated that while 'the use of the veto is ... the most extreme expression of [the Council's] lack of unity, [this is] closely followed by the threat of the veto.'" Security Council Report, The Veto, *supra* note 49, at 7. Details of the veto threats regarding Darfur are in Chapter 5.
[173] *See* Chapter 5.
[174] *Id.*
[175] *Id.*
[176] Human Rights Watch, *We Cannot Ignore Sri Lanka* (Apr. 27, 2009), *at* www.hrw.org/news/2009/04/27/we-cannot-ignore-sri-lanka.
[177] Sometimes blockage can be "express" in that a permanent member states that it will not accept certain measures or certain language in a resolution; sometimes the blockage is more "implied" – that due to a permanent member's political alignment, measures are never even drafted, debated, or brought to a vote.

Security Council action related to Sri Lanka.[178] Russia and China have also at least once used leverage to avoid having a meeting on Sri Lanka put on the Council's agenda.[179] Meanwhile, there were an estimated 80,000–100,000 fatalities during the civil war,[180] with an estimated 40,000 fatalities alone during a particularly brutal phase towards the end of the war.[181] The Report of the Secretary-General's Panel of Experts on Accountability in Sri Lanka found reason to believe crimes against humanity and war crimes were committed by both Government forces and the LTTE.[182] China has financial ties to the Government of Sri Lanka.[183]

---

[178] Security Council Report, Update No. 5: Sri Lanka, (Apr. 21, 2009), at www.securitycouncilreport.org/update-report/lookup-c-glKWLeMTIsG-b-5113231.php; *Blame Russia and China for Sri Lanka Failure, Not UN's Ban*, CHANNEL 4 NEWS (Apr. 26, 2011), at www.channel4.com/news/blame-russia-and-china-for-sri-lanka-failure-not-uns-ban; Security Council Report, Update No. 1: Sri Lanka (June 4, 2009), at www.securitycouncilreport.org/update-report/lookup-c-glKWLeMTIsG-b-5214273.php; Patrick Hein, *Riding with the Devils: China's Role in the Cambodian and Sri Lankan Conflict*, 73 INDIA Q. (2017). *China Pledge to Support Sri Lanka at UNHRC and UN Security Council*, NEWS. LK, OFF. GOV'T NEWS PORTAL OF SRI LANKA (Apr. 25, 2017), at www.news.lk/news/business/item/440-china-pledge-to-support-sri-lanka-at-unhrc-and-un-security-council; *UN Split on Sri Lankan Issue*, SUNDAY TIMES (Mar. 22, 2009), at www.sundaytimes.lk/090322/News/sundaytimesnews_01.html.

[179] See *UN Split on Lankan Issue: US Backing Move for Security Council Briefing; China, Russia Against*, SUNDAY TIMES (Mar. 22, 2009), at www.sundaytimes.lk/090322/News/sundaytimesnews_01.html ("China is 'vehemently' opposing any discussion in the Security Council on the issue of civilians trapped in the fighting between government Security Forces and the LTTE arguing that it is 'purely an internal matter.'"); Evelyn Leopold, *Sri Lanka: UN Security Council Makes Its First Move*, HUFFPOST (May 25, 2011), at www.huffpost.com/entry/sri-lanka-un-security-cou_b_203259 ("Russia, China, Libya and Vietnam had opposed putting the issue [of Sri Lanka] on the agenda of the Security Council, the U.N.'s most powerful body, considering the war an internal matter rather than a threat to international peace and security. But they relented in issuing a statement . . . .").

[180] Human Rights Watch, *Sri Lanka: Country Summary* (Jan. 2010), at www.hrw.org/sites/default/files/related_material/srilanka_0.pdf. Compare *Sri Lanka Marks 10 Years since Civil War's End*, VOA NEWS, AGENCE FRANCE-PRESSE (May 18, 2019), at www.voanews.com/south-central-asia/sri-lanka-marks-10-years-civil-wars-end (estimating over 100,000 fatalities and 20,000 missing); International Crisis Group, *Picturing Sri Lanka's Undead War* (May 17, 2019), at www.crisisgroup.org/asia/south-asia/sri-lanka/picturing-sri-lankas-undead-war (estimating over 150,000 fatalities).

[181] Report of the Secretary-General's Panel of Experts on Accountability in Sri Lanka, para. 137 (Mar. 31, 2011), at www.refworld.org/docid/4db7b23e2.html.

[182] Id.

[183] *See, e.g.*, Bharath Gopalaswamy, *Sri Lanka's Political Shake-Up Is a Win for China*, FOR. POL'Y (Oct. 29, 2018), at https://foreignpolicy.com/2018/10/29/sri-lankas-political-shake-up-is-a-win-for-china (discussing China's economic ties to Sri Lanka, including loans and large infrastructure projects).

China, joined by Russia, additionally in 2007 vetoed a resolution that would have condemned crimes in Myanmar against the Rohingya.[184] This pattern continues today, as China blocks (expressly or implicitly)[185] Security Council resolutions related to crimes against the (Muslim) Rohingya by the (Buddhist) Burmese military, despite acknowledgment that the crimes being committed "very likely" amount to war crimes, crimes against humanity, and genocide.[186] Fatalities from the Burmese military's so-called "clearance operations" stand at over 10,000,[187] with approximately 740,000 since 2017 having fled the violence,[188] which includes mass rape, burning of villages, and burning of persons to death inside their homes.[189] As with Sri Lanka, it is difficult to determine the exact number of threats of veto used by China

---

[184] Draft Security Council Res. S/2007/14 (Jan. 12, 2007) (vetoed by China and Russia), at www.un.org/en/ga/search/view_doc.asp?symbol=S/2007/14 (sponsored by the UK and US, the resolution would have called on "the Government of Myanmar to cease military attacks against civilians in ethnic minority regions and in particular to put an end to the associated human rights and humanitarian law violations against persons belonging to ethnic nationalities, including widespread rape and other forms of sexual violence carried out by members of the armed forces").

[185] See note 177 *supra*.

[186] The Independent International Fact-Finding Mission on Myanmar established by the UN Human Rights Council concluded that credible evidence exists that war crimes, crimes against humanity, and genocide have been committed against members of the Rohingya minority group. Report of the Detailed Findings of the Independent International Fact-Finding Mission on Myanmar, U.N. Doc. A/HRC/39/CRP.2 (Sept. 17, 2018) (concluding that named senior generals of the Myanmar military should be investigated and prosecuted in an international criminal tribunal for genocide, crimes against humanity, and war crimes). *See also* Report of the Independent International Fact-Finding Mission on Myanmar, U.N. Doc. A/HRC/42/50 (Aug. 8, 2019), *at* https://documents-dds-ny.un.org/doc/UNDOC/GEN/G19/236/74/PDF/G19 23674.pdf?OpenElement; Doug Bock Clark, *Inside the Rohingya Refugee Camps, Traumatised Exiles Ask Why the World Won't Call the Humanitarian Crisis "Genocide*," POST MAG. (Jan. 16, 2018), *at* www.scmp.com/magazines/post-magazine/long-reads/article/2128432/inside-rohingya-refugee-camps-traumatised-exiles (discussing a Burmese document titled "Rohingya Extermination Plan"); Justin Lynch, *Western Officials Ignored Myanmar's Warning Signs of Genocide*, FOR. POL'Y (Aug. 20, 2018), *at* https://foreignpolicy.com/2018/08/30/western-officials-ignored-myanmars-warning-signs-of-genocide/.

[187] James Bennett, *Rohingya Death Toll Likely Above 10,000, MSF Says Amid Exodus*, ABC NEWS (Dec. 14, 2017), *at* www.abc.net.au/news/2017-12-14/rohingya-death-toll-in-the-thousands-says-msf /9260552. Compare Laignee Barron, *More Than 43,000 Rohingya Parents May Be Missing. Experts Fear They Are Dead*, TIME (Mar. 8, 2018), *at* https://time.com/5187292/rohingya-crisis-missing-parents-refugees-bangladesh (a report by ASEAN Parliamentarians for Human Rights estimating that over 40,000 parents are missing, and presumably killed).

[188] UNHCR, Operational Portal Refugee Situations, Refugee Response in Bangladesh, *at* https://data2.unhcr.org/en/situations/myanmar_refugees (estimating 914,998 Rohingya refugees, of whom 744,400 arrived after August 2017).

[189] Then High Commissioner for Human Rights Zeid Ra'ad Al-Hussein cited a long list of atrocities committed against the Rohingya including "deliberately burning people to death inside their homes, murders of children and adults, indiscriminate shooting of fleeing

related to Myanmar, as it appears that China's support for Myanmar has translated into a consistent understanding that China would not support significant Security Council action related to Myanmar.[190] There are at least several reported incidents where China used its leverage to undermine any potential for Security Council resolutions.[191] For example, a resolution was blocked in 2017 by veto threat from China, resulting in the Security Council issuing only a non-binding Presidential Statement,[192] with Security Council press statements having also been blocked.[193] China has known political and financial ties to the Government of Myanmar.[194]

While relevant to accountability – but not made during the commission of atrocity crimes – in 2015, Russia vetoed a resolution that would have commemorated the twentieth anniversary of the Srebrenica massacre as genocide.[195] The

civilians, widespread rapes of women and girls, and the burning and destruction of houses, schools, markets and mosques." James Bennett, *Myanmar's Persecution of Rohingya May Be Genocide, UN Human Rights Watchdog Says*, ABC News (Dec. 5, 2017), *at* www.abc.net.au/news/2017-12-06/myanmars-persecution-of-rohingya-may-be-genocide-un-says/9230366.

[190] Security Council Report, Briefing on the Situation in Myanmar, WHAT'S IN BLUE (Mar. 16, 2017), *at* www.whatsinblue.org/2017/03/briefing-on-the-situation-in-myanmar.php; Security Council Report, February 2009 Monthly Forecast (Jan. 29, 2009), *at* www.securitycouncilreport.org/monthly-forecast/2009-02/lookup_c_glKWLeMTIsG_b_4916577.php.

[191] Security Council Report, Update Report No. 1: Myanmar (June 1, 2006), *at* www.securitycouncilreport.org/update-report/lookup_c_glkwlemtisg_b_1722297.php; Security Council Report, Update Report No. 4: Myanmar (Sept. 27, 2006), *at* www.securitycouncilreport.org/update-report/update-report-no-4-myanmar.php.

[192] HUMAN RIGHTS WATCH, WORLD REPORT 2018, MYANMAR, *at* www.hrw.org/world-report/2018/country-chapters/burma ("In response to the Rohingya crisis, in September [2017] the UN Security Council held its first open discussion of the situation in Burma in eight years. A draft Security Council resolution was blocked by a veto threat from China. Instead, in November it adopted a Presidential Statement expressing grave concern over reports of human rights violations in Rakhine State by Burma's security forces and calling on Burma to cooperate with UN investigative bodies.").

[193] *See, e.g.*, *China, Russia Block U.N. Council Concern About Myanmar Violence*, REUTERS (Mar. 17, 2017), *at* www.reuters.com/article/us-myanmar-rohingya-un/china-russia-block-u-n-council-concern-about-myanmar-violence-idUSKBN16O2J6 ("China, backed by Russia, blocked a short U.N. Security Council statement on Myanmar on Friday, diplomats said, after the 15-member body met to discuss the situation in Rakhine state, where the country's military is conducting a [so-called] security operation.").

[194] *See, e.g.*, Subir Bhaumik, *Why Do China, India Back Myanmar Over the Rohingya Crisis?*, S. CHINA MORNING POST (Oct. 18, 2017), *at* www.scmp.com/week-asia/geopolitics/article/2115839/why-do-china-india-back-myanmar-over-rohingya-crisis ("Heavy investments in Rakhine state have seen the two countries take a markedly different approach to the Western powers." "Burmese politicians are reluctant to openly criticise China because the country depends on its northern neighbour for support in the UN to counter resolutions critical of its human rights record in Rakhine.").

[195] Draft Res. S/2015/508 (July 8, 2015), *at* www.un.org/en/ga/search/view_doc.asp?symbol=S/2015/508 (sponsored by Jordan, Lithuania, Malaysia, New Zealand, the UK, and the US).

1.3 Overview of Veto Use

veto came despite the ICTY (which was created by the Security Council)[196] having pronounced in numerous decisions that the killing in and around Srebrenica constituted genocide.[197] Russia then vetoed a resolution that would have established an international criminal tribunal to prosecute the downing of Malaysia Airlines Flight MH17, shot down over Ukraine with 298 commercial airlines passengers and crew aboard.[198] The missile that downed the plane was Russian-made and launched from pro-Russian separatist-controlled territory in Ukraine.[199]

As explored in more depth in Chapter 5, Russia (sometimes in conjunction with China), as of January 2020, used the veto fourteen times related to the situation in Syria.[200] For example, it has vetoed resolutions to:

- condemn the continued widespread and gross violations of human rights and fundamental freedoms in Syria;[201]
- condemn the bombing and shelling of population centers and condemn the detention of thousands in government-run facilities;[202]
- refer the situation in Syria to the ICC;[203]
- express outrage at the alarming number of civilian casualties, including those caused by indiscriminate aerial bombings in Aleppo;[204]

---

[196] See S/RES/827 (May 25, 1993) (creating the ICTY).

[197] The first ICTY case to do so was the *Krstić* case. See Prosecutor v. Krstić, Case No. IT-98-33, Trial Chamber Judgment (Aug. 2, 2001); Prosecutor v. Krstić, Case No. IT-98-33-A, Appeals Chamber Judgment (Apr. 19, 2004).

[198] Security Council Report, The Veto, *supra* note 49, at 1. See also *MH17: Julie Bishop Says Russian Veto of Proposed UN-Backed Tribunal to Prosecute Suspects "Compounds Atrocity,"* ABC News (July 30, 2015), at www.abc.net.au/news/2015-07-30/russia-vetoes-proposal-for-un-backed-tribunal-over-mh17/6658620.

[199] Nick Miller, *Malaysia Airlines Flight MH17 Was Shot Down from Pro-Russian Rebel Controlled Territory, Investigation Finds* (Sept. 29, 2016), at www.smh.com.au/world/malaysia-airlines-flight-mh17-was-shot-down-from-prorussian-rebel-controlled-territory-investigation-finds-20160928-grqter.html (The "head of the central crime investigation department of the national police of the Netherlands, said MH17 was shot down by a missile 'launched from a Buk trailer that was brought in from the territory of the Russian federation and after launch was returned to Russian Federation territory.'"); *id.* ("The plane had been hit by a Russian-made surface to air missile."). The Netherlands is now pursuing domestic prosecutions, in absentia, related to the downing of MH17, as the majority of those on board were Dutch. *Dutch Prosecutor Names Four to Be Tried for Murder in Downing of MH17*, RadioFreeEurope/RadioLiberty (June 19, 2019), at www.rferl.org/a/jit-name-suspects-charges-mh17-ukraine-malaysia-russia-shootdown/30007817.html.

[200] For a compilation of statements by other Security Council members condemning Russian and Chinese vetoes related to Syria, see Carswell, *supra* note 61, at 454.

[201] Draft Res. S/2011/612 (vetoed by Russia and China).

[202] Draft Res. S/2012/538 (vetoed by Russia and China).

[203] Draft Res. S/2014/348 (vetoed by Russia and China).

[204] Draft Res. S/2016/846 (vetoed by Russia).

- decide on a seven-day ceasefire in Aleppo and demand that humanitarian assistance be allowed;[205]
- condemn the use of toxic chemicals as weapons and demanded compliance with the Organisation for the Prohibition of Chemical Weapons (OPCW);[206]
- renew the mandate of the Joint Investigative Mechanism (JIM) conducting chemical weapons inspections that would have attributed responsibility to the side using them;[207]
- condemn "any use of any toxic chemical, including chlorine, as a weapon in the Syrian Arab Republic and express ... its outrage that civilians continue to be killed and injured by chemical weapons and toxic chemicals as weapons in the Syrian Arab Republic";[208] and
- implement a ceasefire for Syria's war-torn Idlib province, call for a halt to an aerial bombing campaign there, and demand humanitarian access and safe passage for medical personnel.[209]

Meanwhile, the Independent International Commission of Inquiry on the Syrian Arab Republic[210] has documented the commission of large-scale war crimes and crimes against humanity including by regime forces,[211] as well as genocide against the Yazidis.[212] Regime crimes include mass use of torture in

---

[205] Draft Res. S/2016/1026 (vetoed by Russia and China).
[206] Draft Res. S/2017/172 (vetoed by Russia and China).
[207] Draft Res. S/2017/884 (vetoed by Russia).
[208] Draft Res. S/2018/321 (vetoed by Russia). Sometimes comparable resolutions did pass, but in most instances of veto use related to Syria, the measures under debate were simply blocked. *See* Chapter 5.1 for details.
[209] Draft Res. S/2019/756 (vetoed by the Russian Federation and China). "The Syrian Observatory for Human Rights says the offensive [in Idlib] has killed close to 1,000 civilians." French Press Agency – AFP, *Russia's 13 UN Security Council Vetoes on Syria*, DAILY SABAH MIDEAST (Sept. 20, 2019), at www.dailysabah.com/mideast/2019/09/20/russias-13-unsecurity-council-vetoes-on-syria.
[210] *See* Resolution Adopted by the Human Rights Council at its Seventeenth Special Sess., S-17/1, Situation of Human Rights in the Syrian Arab Republic, *at* www.ohchr.org/Documents/HRBodies/HRCouncil/CoISyria/ResS17_1.pdf (mandating the Commission to investigate alleged violations of international human rights law since March 2011 in the Syrian Arab Republic).
[211] *See* reports of the Independent Commission of Inquiry on the Syrian Arab Republic, *at* www.ohchr.org/EN/HRBodies/HRC/IICISyria/Pages/Documentation.aspx.
[212] Report of the Independent International Commission of Inquiry on the Syrian Arab Republic, "They Came to Destroy": ISIS Crimes against the Yazidis, para. 165, U.N. Doc. A/HRC/32/CRP.2 (June 15, 2016) ("The Commission has determined that ISIS has committed, and is committing, the prohibited acts with the intent to destroy, in whole or in part, the Yazidis of Sinjar, and has, therefore, committed the crime of genocide."). *See also* Joshua

1.3 Overview of Veto Use

detention facilities[213] – documented in the now infamous "Caesar photos"[214] – as well as use of chemical weapons.[215] As of December 2019, over half a million Syrians had been killed,[216] over 5.6 million Syrians had fled the country,[217] and an estimated 6.6 million had been internally displaced.[218] Russia strongly supports the Syrian Government of Bashar al-Assad, including through both military assistance and direct military involvement.[219]

Most recently, the veto has also been used related to the conflict in Yemen, where some reports place the death toll at 100,000,[220] with 3.65 million

> Berlinger, *Who Are the Religious and Ethnic Groups Under Threat from ISIS?* CNN (Aug. 8, 2014), at www.cnn.com/2014/08/08/world/meast/iraq-ethnic-groups-under-threat-isis/index.html (Da'esh has threatened the Yazidi, Christian, and Shia Muslim minorities in northern Iraq and eastern Syria with genocide).

[213] See, e.g., Human Rights Watch, *If the Dead Could Speak: Mass Deaths and Torture in Syria's Detention Facilities* (Dec. 16, 2015), at www.hrw.org/report/2015/12/16/if-dead-could-speak/mass-deaths-and-torture-syrias-detention-facilities.

[214] Human Rights Watch reports:

> [I]n January 2014, news emerged that a defector had left Syria with tens of thousands of images, many showing the bodies of detainees who died in Syria's detention centers. A team of international lawyers, as well as Syrian activists, interviewed the defector, code-named "Caesar," who stated that, as an official forensic photographer for the Military Police, he had personally photographed bodies of dead detainees and helped to archive thousands more similar photographs. These photographs were taken apparently as part of a bureaucratic effort by the Syrian security apparatus to maintain a photographic record of the thousands who have died in detention since 2011 as well as of members of security forces who died in attacks by armed opposition groups.

> *Id.* "The largest category of photographs, 28,707 images, are photographs of people Human Rights Watch understands to have died in government custody . . . ." *Id.*

[215] See, e.g., Report of the Independent International Commission of Inquiry on the Syrian Arab Republic, U.N. Doc. A/HRC/36/55 (Aug. 8, 2017) (concluding Syrian forces used weaponized chlorine). *See also* Chapter 5 (detailing chemical weapons attacks).

[216] HUMAN RIGHTS WATCH, WORLD REPORT 2019, SYRIA: EVENTS OF 2018, at www.hrw.org/world-report/2019/country-chapters/syria (citing Syrian Observatory for Human Rights reporting a death toll of 511,000 as of March 2018).

[217] UNHCR, Operational Portal Refugee Situations, Syria Regional Refugee Response, at https://data2.unhcr.org/en/situations/syria#_ga=2.182664928.793357314.1564411227-1268904042.1516508364 (refugee count as of July 4, 2019 at 5,625,871).

[218] UNHCR, Syria Emergency, at www.unhcr.org/en-us/syria-emergency.html (estimating IDPs as of April 19, 2018 at 6.6 million).

[219] See, e.g., *Russia Establishing Permanent Presence at Its Syrian Bases*, REUTERS (Dec. 26, 2017), at www.reuters.com/article/us-mideast-crisis-syria-russia-bases/russia-establishing-permanent-presence-at-its-syrian-bases-ria-idUSKBN1EK0HD. Many other countries are also involved in the conflict, including Iran, the US, and Turkey. *See* Chapter 5 (chronology of hostilities).

[220] Rod Austin, *Human Cost of Yemen War Laid Bare as the Death Toll Nears* 100,000, GUARDIAN (June 20, 2019), at www.theguardian.com/global-development/2019/jun/20/human-cost-of-yemen-war-laid-bare-as-civilian-death-toll-put-at-100000.

displaced.[221] Yemen's civil war began in 2014, when Houthi rebels (later supported by Iran) took control of the capital.[222] Beginning in March 2015, a coalition of Gulf States led by Saudi Arabia and the UAE started to launch air strikes against the Houthi, with US logistical and intelligence support.[223] Fighting has continued ever since, with large-scale accusations of war crimes.[224] As to veto use, draft Resolution S/2018/156, regarding sanctions, was vetoed by Russia due to a reference to a Yemen Panel of Experts' finding that Iran was in non-compliance with the arms embargo that had been imposed.[225] There are also reports of a veto threat by the US, stalling a UK-drafted resolution until it dropped language on the need for accountability for war crimes and guaranteeing humanitarian deliveries.[226] Another source mentions US, UK, and French veto threats to quash attempts at restraining the Saudi-led coalition or implicating its members in war crimes.[227]

---

[221] UNHCR Operational Update, Yemen (Aug. 9, 2019), at http://reporting.unhcr.org/sites/def ault/files/UNHCR%20Yemen%20Operational%20Update%20-%209AUG19.pdf.
[222] Council on Foreign Relations, Global Conflict Tracker, *War in Yemen*, at www.cfr.org/inte ractive/global-conflict-tracker/conflict/war-yemen.
[223] *Id.*
[224] *See, e.g.*, Amnesty International, *Yemen: The Forgotten War*, at www.amnesty.org/en/latest/ news/2015/09/yemen-the-forgotten-war.
[225] Sec. Council Rep., Chronology of Events, Yemen (Feb. 2018), at www.securitycouncilreport .org/chronology/yemen.php. The same day a similar resolution passed without that language, S/RES/2402. *Id.*; *see also* Rick Gladstone, *Russia Vetoes U.N. Resolution to Pressure Iran over Yemen Missiles*, N.Y. Times (Feb. 26, 2018), at www.nytimes.com/2018/02/26/world/mid dleeast/iran-yemen-security-council.html ("Russia blocked a resolution at the United Nations Security Council on Monday that would have pressured Iran over the illegal use of Iranian-made missiles by Houthi insurgents in Yemen.").
[226] The resolution later passed as S/RES/2451 (2018), without language on an independent investigation for breaches of international humanitarian law, and with more limited language regarding humanitarian deliveries. Julian Borger, *UN Agrees Yemen Ceasefire Resolution After Fraught Talks and US Veto Threat*, Guardian (Dec. 21, 2018), at www.theguardian.com/world/2018/dec/21/un-yemen-ceasefire-stockholm-resolution-us; *see also* Patrick Wintour, *Saudi and US Resistance Delays UN Resolution on Yemen Ceasefire*, Guardian (Dec. 20, 2018), at www.theguardian.com/world/2018/dec/20/saudi-and-us-resistance-delays-un-resolution-on-yemen ("Saudi Arabia is meanwhile insisting the draft contains no reference to an independent investigation into breaches of international humanitarian law during the three-year civil war, so protecting its pilots from UN investigations into the deliberate targeting of civilians." "A previous British attempt to pass a UN resolution on Yemen in November had to be shelved following US and Saudi objections over the wording.").
[227] *See* Sana'a Center for Strategic Studies, Category: Yemen at the UN, at http://sanaacenter.org /category/publications/yemen-at-the-un ("The United States (US), United Kingdom (UK) and France – all veto-wielding permanent UNSC members, as well as the Saudi-led military coalition's primary arms suppliers – have also quashed attempts at the UNSC to restrain the coalition or to implicate its members in war crimes. Representatives from other UNSC

Some of the permanent members employing these vetoes and veto threats seemingly fail to perceive, or do not care to perceive, that when they block Security Council measures in the face of atrocity crimes, the Council's credibility and efficacy is undermined. (Alternatively, perhaps the "protection" of economic or strategic allies in particular situations simply outweighs any such concerns.) When the Council appears incapable of responding to these highly publicized instances of mass atrocities, not only do the victims bear the most direct costs, but the inaction engenders widespread doubts about the efficacy of the UN system. These glaring failings then strengthen other states and NGOs in their calls for Security Council reform, for implementing voluntary veto restraint (endorsed by two permanent members),[228] and/or for bypassing the Council entirely, as occurred with the General Assembly's creation of the IIIM.[229]

1.4 SECURITY COUNCIL REFORM PROPOSALS

Widespread disenchantment with the performance and composition of the Security Council has led to a host of reform proposals related to the Council's composition and changes to its "decision-making methodology"[230] (that is, voting methods). Yet, a formal Charter amendment would be required to change the composition or formal voting of the Council, and this would require the vote and ratification by two-thirds of all UN Member States, including – most significantly – *the permanent members of the Council*.[231]

---

member states told the Sana'a Center in 2017 that the council had thus exhausted all plausible options for action regarding Yemen and had essentially been reduced to an observer of the crisis."). "Throughout 2017 three permanent members, namely the United States (US), UK, and France, continued to back the [Saudi-led military] coalition through arms sales worth billions of US dollars. The US also continued to provide technical, intelligence, and air refuel support to the Saudi-led military coalition." *Id.* If this account is accurate, it is perplexing to see particularly the reference to French and UK veto threats, as both countries have pledged to support veto restraint in the face of atrocity crimes. *See* Chapter 3. While the threat of veto is admittedly not covered by their pledges (which pertain to veto *use*), it appears, at minimum, inconsistent to threaten to do what one has pledged not to do.

[228] Both France and the UK have pledged themselves to support voluntary veto restraint in the face of atrocity crimes. See Chapter 3.

[229] *See* note 111 *supra* and accompanying text. Human rights groups, for instance, also called for the Security Council to be bypassed (after Russia's veto use) to create a mechanism to attribute responsibility for chemical weapons attacks in Syria. *See UN Secretary-General Should Activate Independent Mechanism to Attribute Responsibility for Chemical Attacks in Syria*, RELIEF WEB (Apr. 13, 2018), *at* https://reliefweb.int/report/syrian-arab-republic/un-secretary-general-should-activate-independent-mechanism-attribute.

[230] Butler, *supra* note 125, at 32.

[231] Charter amendments require vote and ratification by two-thirds of UN Member States "including all the permanent members of the Security Council." UN Charter, Art. 108.

"Any of the five would have the option, in other words, of vetoing any attempts to constrain or limit their veto power."[232] Accordingly, most such current proposals[233] appear doomed to failure *ab initio*, as it appears obvious that the permanent members are fairly unlikely to dilute their own veto power.[234]

1.4.1 Proposed Reforms to the Composition of the Security Council

Because many countries are discontent with the composition of the Security Council – and, particularly, the permanent positions five countries hold and their veto power – as an anachronistic reflection of the dominant powers of 1945,[235] there have been repeated calls for Security Council reform to increase representation and reform working methods.[236]

For instance, in 1992, Security Council reform was added to the agenda of the General Assembly's 48th session, spearheaded by India and twenty-five other members of the Non-Aligned Movement (NAM), later joined by Japan.[237] In 1993, the Secretary-General's report with Member States' proposals for reform was distributed,[238] resulting in the

---

[232] Luck, *supra* note 3, at 15.

[233] As noted above, there was a successful UN Charter amendment in 1965 changing the composition of the Council by increasing its number of members. See note 23 *supra*.

[234] See Wouters & Ruys, *supra* note 37, at 22 ("reform proposals stand little chance of being incorporated into the Charter, as the permanent members, most notably the United States and Russia, have repeated time and again that they will not accept any limitations to the veto"), citing statements by the US and Russia. However, there appears some willingness to add Japan and Germany to the ranks of permanent members, with the idea of possibly adding additional states at a later date.

[235] "[M]uch of the membership perceives the Council to be too small and too elitist, with an over-representation of rich and powerful states, and an under-representation of developing ones." Luck, *supra* note 3, at 56; *see also* Carswell, *supra* note 61, at 477 ("the [P5] are no longer fully representative of the global balance of power"); Wouters & Ruys, *supra* note 37, at 26 ("the current allocation of the veto is a product of the Allied victory in the Second World War and no longer reflects the modern-day distribution of economic and military power"). Luck, however, notes that while there is a perception the permanent members "no longer represent current power realities," in fact "they remain five of the world's six largest defense spenders (with Japan topping the United Kingdom for fifth place)." *Id.* at 57, citing INTERNATIONAL INSTITUTE FOR STRATEGIC STUDIES, MILITARY BALANCE, VOL. 103, at 335–40, Table 33 (2003).

[236] *See generally* Center for UN Reform Education, *Timeline UN Security Council Reform* (Nov. 2015), *at* www.centerforunreform.org/sites/default/files/Timeline%20November%202015%20final.pdf. For an overview of UN reform attempts since 1950, see J. MULLER, REFORMING THE UNITED NATIONS: THE STRUGGLE FOR LEGITIMACY (2006).

[237] UN GA Res. 47/62 (Dec. 11, 1992) ("Question of Equitable Representation on and Increase in the Membership of Security Council").

[238] UN GA Res. 48/264 (July 29, 1994) ("Revitalization of the Work of the General Assembly").

1.4 Security Council Reform Proposals 49

establishment of the Open-Ended Working Group (OEWG).[239] The resolution added to the provisional agenda the "question of equitable representation on and increase in the membership of the Security Council."[240] In 1997, there was a paper by the PGA/Chairman of the OEWG calling for adding five permanent and four non-permanent seats; this proposal, however, was rejected.[241] The 2000 Millennium Summit document called, inter alia, for "intensifying efforts to achieve comprehensive reform of the Council."[242] On December 2, 2004, then Secretary-General Kofi Annan distributed a report calling for (model A) six new permanent seats with no veto and three new two-year non-permanent seats, or (model B) no new permanent seats but a new category of eight four-year renewable-term seats and one new two-year non-permanent (and non-renewable) seat.[243] The 2005 World Summit Outcome Document "support[ed] early reform of the Security Council" and "recommend[ed] that the Security Council continue to adapt its working methods."[244] In September 2007, recommendations in an OEWG report called for "equitable representation on and increase in the membership of the Security Council," to be achieved "through intergovernmental negotiations."[245] In September 2008, a decision was adopted by consensus on the "question of equitable representation on and increase in the membership of the Security Council and related matters."[246] It called for work on five key issues: "categories of membership; the question of the veto; regional representation; size of an enlarged Security Council and working methods of the Council; and the relationship between the Council and the General Assembly."[247] This is only a sampling of the various proposals. There have been other campaigns lobbying for France to give its seat to the European

---

[239] UN GA Res. 48/26 (Dec. 3, 1993) ("Question of Equitable Representation on and Increase in the Membership of Security Council").
[240] Id.
[241] UN GA Res. 53/30 (Dec. 1, 1998) ("Question of Equitable Representation on and Increase in the Membership of Security Council").
[242] UN GA Res 55/2, United Nations Millennium Declaration, para. 30 (Sept. 8, 2000).
[243] Report of the Secretary-General's High-Level Panel on Threats, Challenges and Change: A More Secure World: Our Shared Responsibility, paras. 252–53, A/59/565 (Dec. 2, 2004).
[244] UN GA Res. 60/1, World Summit Outcome, paras. 153–54 (Oct. 24, 2005).
[245] Rep. of the Open-Ended Working Group on the Question of Equitable Representation on and Increase in the Membership of the Security Council and Other Matters Related to the Security Council, U.N. Doc. A/61/47 (Sept. 14, 2007).
[246] UN GA Dec. 62/557, U.N. Doc. A/63/49 (Vol. III) (Sept. 15, 2008).
[247] Id.

Union, for a permanent African seat, for a seat for India, Japan, Germany, Brazil, Mexico, and/or the Islamic and Arab States.[248]

Because many of these proposals would necessitate a Charter amendment, which requires the agreement of all permanent members, it is almost[249] a foregone conclusion that the permanent members will not agree.

1.4.2 Recent Attempts to Curb Veto Use

Potentially of more pragmatic utility are initiatives aimed at changing voting or veto practices – particularly in the face of genocide, crimes against humanity, and/or war crimes – which do not require a Charter amendment. Yet, herein lies the catch: if there is no Charter amendment, these initiatives cannot be made mandatory for permanent members. If it is voluntary to join such initiatives and not all permanent members agree, this ultimately limits what these initiatives can achieve.

Interesting recent initiatives specifically designed to tackle the problem of veto use in the face of such crimes are explored in Chapter 3. They include the "responsibility not to veto" found within the "responsibility to protect," the "S5 initiative" (by Costa Rica, Jordan, Liechtenstein, Singapore, and Switzerland), the French/Mexican initiative not to veto in the face of atrocity crimes (endorsed as of early 2020 by 105 states), and the ACT (Accountability, Coherence and Transparency) Group's Code of Conduct (endorsed as of early 2020 by 122 states).[250]

---

[248] See Global Policy Forum, *Background on Security Council Reform, Membership Including Expansion and Representation*, at www.globalpolicy.org/security-council/security-council-reform/membership-including-expansion-and-representation.html.

[249] Some bids to expand the number of permanent members apparently have received support from individual permanent members. See Wouters & Ruys, *supra* note 37, at 20 (citing France, UK, and Russia supporting adding permanent seats for Germany, Japan, India, and Brazil; China supporting India's bid; and the US supporting Japan's bid). See also note 234 *supra* (general support for adding Germany and Japan). *But see* Vijay Sharma, *Wikileaks Exposes US' Double-Game on UN Security Council Expansion*, GLOB. POL'Y FORUM (July 25, 2011), *at* www.globalpolicy.org/security-council/security-council-reform/50519-wikileaks-exposes-us-double-game-on-un-security-council-expansion.html?itemid=id#913 ("The G4 (India, Brazil, Germany, Japan) and the African Union have led talks about the expansion of the Security Council from 5 to 10 or 11 seats for at least two decades. The US has publicly supported these initiatives and has recently backed India's bid for a permanent seat. However, diplomatic cables revealed by Wikileaks show that US backdoor diplomacy has done everything to prevent a Security Council expansion. Indeed, the US fears losing its influence in the executive body of the UN and its privileges, such as the veto right. China and Russia share similar views.").

[250] See Chapter 3.

1.5 Reconsidering Veto Use in the Face of Atrocity Crimes

The existence of these initiatives suggests a collective shifting of conscience that many states recognize the UN *must not keep failing in its response to atrocity crimes,* and that use of the veto is a key impediment. The number of states that have joined the French/Mexican initiative and Code of Conduct demonstrates widespread support for these initiatives, including, importantly, from two permanent members of the Security Council.[251] Yet, as explored further in Chapter 3, it is problematic that the other three permanent members fail to join any of these initiatives.

1.5 THE RATIONALE FOR RECONSIDERING HOW THE VETO IS USED IN THE FACE OF ATROCITY CRIMES

The penultimate chapter, Chapter 4, makes the case for recognizing that there are legal limits to the use of the veto imposed by existing international law. That chapter presents three main arguments. First, it argues that the UN Charter must be read in a way that is consistent with, and certainly not violative of, the highest-level norms in the international legal system, *jus cogens*, a higher source of legal authority than the UN Charter (which created the veto power). Second, the chapter argues that use of the veto power needs to be consistent with the UN's "Purposes and Principles," with which the Security Council, under Article 24(2) of the Charter, is bound to act in accordance.[252] A third source of authority that arguably informs the permanent member's obligations regarding veto use can be found in certain foundational treaties such as the Genocide Convention,[253] and four 1949 Geneva Conventions,[254] to which all permanent members are parties.[255] After also

---

[251] As mentioned above, the UK and France are signatories to the Code of Conduct and France sponsored the French/Mexican initiative.
[252] *See* UN Charter, Art. 24(2).
[253] Convention on the Prevention and Punishment of the Crime of Genocide, Dec. 9, 1948, 78 U.N.T.S. 277.
[254] Geneva Convention I for the Amelioration of the Condition of the Wounded and Sick in Armed Forces in the Field, Aug. 12, 1949, 75 U.N.T.S. 31; Geneva Convention II for the Amelioration of the Condition of Wounded, Sick and Shipwrecked Members of Armed Forces at Sea, Aug. 12, 1949, 75 U.N.T.S. 85; Geneva Convention III Relative to the Treatment of Prisoners of War, Aug. 12, 1949, 75 U.N.T.S. 135; Geneva Convention IV Relative to the Protection of Civilian Persons in Time of War, Aug. 12, 1949, 75 U.N.T.S. 287.
[255] United Nations, Treaty Collection, *at* https://treaties.un.org/Pages/ViewDetails.aspx?src=I ND&mtdsg_no=IV-1&chapter=4&clang=_en; International Committee of the Red Cross, Treaties, State Parties, and Commentaries, *at* https://ihl-databases.icrc.org/applic/ihl/ihl.nsf /States.xsp?xp_treatySelected=380&xp_viewStates=XPages_NORMStatesParties. *See also* Chapter 4.3.3 for discussion of the interaction between these foundational treaties and the provisions of Article 103 of the Charter.

considering the question of judicial review,[256] the chapter concludes that the General Assembly should consider requesting the ICJ to render an advisory opinion on a question such as: does existing international law contain limitations on the use of the veto power by permanent members of the UN Security Council in situations where there is ongoing genocide, crimes against humanity, and/or war crimes? The General Assembly could alternatively confirm in a resolution its understanding of the legal limits to veto use in the face of genocide, crimes against humanity, and/or war crimes imposed by existing international law.

Only such a "top-down" approach – recognizing there are legal limits to veto use in the face of atrocity crimes *imposed by existing law* – can solve this pressing conundrum. Waiting for the recalcitrant members of the Council to join the Code of Conduct or French/Mexican initiative will, quite simply, come at the cost of too many victims' lives. In the meanwhile, states at the UN should continue to create a consistent precedent by invoking legal arguments, such as those suggested above and detailed in Chapter 4, whenever a permanent member exercises its veto or threatens to veto while there are ongoing atrocity crimes. As will be demonstrated in Chapter 4, far from accepting unlimited veto use in the face of genocide, crimes against humanity, and/or war crimes, states have vociferously objected to such veto use,[257] such that there certainly has been no acquiescence to a practice of veto use in the face of such crimes.

The veto, at times, is being used in a way that was not envisioned when the UN Charter was created – with vetoes having the consequence of shielding the commission of genocide, crimes against humanity, and war crimes. Reform proposals that would necessitate a Charter amendment have hit a roadblock because the permanent members will not limit their own veto power; initiatives that call for voluntary veto restraint hit a roadblock when three permanent members fail to join them. Thus, it is time to revisit existing hard law legal obligation and recognize, once and for all, that the veto power is *not above all sources of international law*, but there are legal limits to its use.

---

[256] *See, e.g.*, Dapo Akande, *The International Court of Justice and the Security Council: Is There Room for Judicial Control of Decisions of the Political Organs of the United Nations*, 46 INT'L & COMP. L. Q. 309, 310 (1997) ("It will be contended that there are legal limits to the powers of the Security Council, even when it is acting to maintain or restore the peace, and that the International Court of Justice is, in proper cases, able to determine whether or not the Security Council has crossed those limits.").

[257] *See* Chapter 4.2.4.2 ("The objections of states to veto use related to the situation in Syria and more generally in the face of atrocity crimes.").

2

Acting in the Face of Atrocity Crimes

Humanitarian Intervention and the Responsibility to Protect

All that is necessary for the triumph of evil is that good men [and women] do nothing.[1]

INTRODUCTION

This chapter explores two doctrines that developed in response to Security Council paralysis or inaction in the face of atrocity crimes. The first is the doctrine of humanitarian intervention, most famously invoked in 1999 to justify the intervention of the North Atlantic Treaty Organization (NATO) in Kosovo, although largely dismissed by most states as impermissible, at least under a strict reading of the UN Charter. The second doctrine is the "responsibility to protect" (R2P), which was first formulated in 2001 but has since undergone significant modifications. Because the later formulations of R2P require Security Council authorization for any forceful intervention, R2P ultimately fails to address the problem of Security Council paralysis in the face of atrocity crimes (although the "responsibility not to veto" contained within many formulations of R2P attempts to do so). Furthermore, because R2P was invoked as part of the 2015 intervention in Libya, which left a destabilized state, and appears to have been largely ignored with respect to atrocities in the Syrian Arab Republic (Syria), enthusiasm for R2P may be waning and could use revitalization; some ideas for revitalization are explored below. The chapter makes the case that until the international community solves the problem of veto use in the face of atrocity crimes, some states still *will* be tempted to invoke, or engage in,

---

[1] Attributed to Edmund Burke. *But see* Quote Investigator, *at* https://quoteinvestigator.com/2010/12/04/good-men-do (casting doubt on the attribution). Another source attributes the quote to John Stuart Mill. *See* Independent, *The Top 10 Misattributed Quote Applications*, *at* www.independent.co.uk/voices/the-top-10-misattributed-quotations-a7910361.html.

humanitarian intervention because there are currently no satisfactory alternatives to addressing Security Council paralysis blocking forceful intervention; yet, there remain significant dangers to such an approach. Ultimately, the chapter concludes that by addressing the problem of use, and threatened use, of the veto in the face of atrocity crimes, one could both strengthen R2P and lessen any need to invoke humanitarian intervention.

2.1 THE DOCTRINE OF "HUMANITARIAN INTERVENTION"

2.1.1 *Limited Historical Precedent*

Historically, only a few instances can be pointed to in the practice of states as "humanitarian intervention" – that is, intervention by one or more states for humanitarian purposes (to halt or alleviate the commission of mass atrocity crimes)[2] that receives neither Security Council authorization nor the consent of the state in question.[3] Frequently cited are: Vietnam's 1978 invasion of Cambodia, ending the Khmer Rouge regime; India's invasion of East Pakistan (which became Bangladesh) in 1971, ending killings by the West Pakistani army; and Tanzania's 1979 invasion of Uganda, ending the regime of Idi Amin.[4] Scholars varyingly invoke these as examples of humanitarian intervention,[5] or dismiss them as not having been termed "humanitarian

---

[2] Unless specifically otherwise defined, "atrocity crimes" in this chapter means genocide, crimes against humanity, and/or war crimes.

[3] *See also* Jane Stromseth, *Interventions and International Law: Legality and Legitimacy*, in CAN MIGHT MAKE RIGHTS? BUILDING THE RULE OF LAW AFTER MILITARY INTERVENTIONS, at 34 (Jane Stromseth, Rosa Brooks & David Wippman eds., 2006) ("[H]umanitarian intervention" may be defined as "the use of force by a state or group of states to protect individuals in another state from severe human rights abuses without the consent of that state's government."); Arman Sarvarian, *Humanitarian Intervention After Syria*, 36(1) LEGAL STUD. 20, 22 (2016) ("[H]umanitarian intervention is defined as the 'use of force to protect people in another State from gross and systematic human rights violations committed against them, or more generally to avert a humanitarian catastrophe, when the target State is unwilling or unable to act.' It entails the right of states to use force, individually or collectively, without authorization by the Security Council ... ."), *quoting* V. Lowe & A. Tzanakopoulos, *Humanitarian Intervention*, in MAX PLANCK ENCYCLOPAEDIA OF PUBLIC INTERNATIONAL LAW, at para. 3 (2011).

[4] JEFFREY L. DUNOFF, STEVEN R. RATNER & DAVID WIPPMAN, INTERNATIONAL LAW NORMS, ACTORS, PROCESS: A PROBLEM-ORIENTED APPROACH 771 (4th ed. 2015); Claus Kreβ, *Major Post-Westphalian Shifts and Some Important Neo-Westphalian Hesitation in the State Practice on the International Law on the Use of Force*, 1 J. USE FORCE & INT'L L. 11, 19 (2014) (invoking the same examples); Michael Wood, *International Law and the Use of Force: What Happens in Practice?*, 53 INDIAN J. INT'L. L. 345, 362 (2013) (invoking the same examples); Christopher Greenwood, *Humanitarian Intervention: The Case of Kosovo*, 2002 FINNISH Y.B. INT'L L. 141, 163 (2002) (invoking the same examples).

[5] *Id.*

intervention" at the time or having been subsequently contested by other states.[6] Sometimes the French 1979 intervention in the Central African Empire supporting the coup against Emperor Jean-Bedel Bokassa is also included.[7] In prior eras, one also finds certain interventions attempting to prevent massacres of religious minorities, such as intervention by Great Britain, France, and Russia in Greece in the 1820s following massacres of Greek Christians, and French intervention in Syria in 1860 following massacres of Christians there.[8] These again are either invoked as early examples of humanitarian intervention,[9] dismissed as largely motivated by other interests,[10] or dismissed as occurring before the Charter era and thus irrelevant to the Charter's *jus ad bellum* regime.[11]

---

[6] See Gareth Evans, After Syria: The Future of the Responsibility to Protect, Speech delivered at Princeton, March 12, 2014 ("Vietnam's invasion of Cambodia in 1978, which stopped the Khmer Rouge in its tracks, was universally attacked as a violation of state sovereignty, not applauded. And Tanzania had to justify its overthrow of Uganda's Idi Amin in 1979 by invoking 'self-defense', not any larger human rights justification. The same had been true of India's intervention in East Pakistan in 1971."); Claus Kreβ, *The State Conduct Element, in* THE CRIME OF AGGRESSION: A COMMENTARY 492 (Claus Kreβ & Stefan Barriga eds., 2017) (The three examples "did not, however, set powerful precedents for such a right [of humanitarian intervention], for the following two reasons. First, each of the intervening states attempted to justify its use of force on grounds other than humanitarian intervention. Second the international reaction was not such that it could have been interpreted as even implicitly embracing the idea of a new unwritten exception to the prohibition of the use of force when force is used to avert an impending humanitarian catastrophe.") (footnotes omitted).

[7] See Nigel S. Rodley, *Humanitarian Intervention, in* THE OXFORD HANDBOOK OF THE USE OF FORCE IN INTERNATIONAL LAW, at 783 (Marc Weller ed., 2015) (also considering the Soviet invasion of Afghanistan and the French 1979 intervention in the Central African Empire); Louise Arbour, *The Responsibility to Protect as a Duty of Care in International Law and Practice*, 34(3) REV. INT'L STUD. 445, 446 (2008) (also considering the Central African Empire); L. HENKIN, HOW NATIONS BEHAVE 129, at 151–52 (1968) (same).

[8] DUNOFF, RATNER & WIPPMAN, *supra* note 4, at 771; Rodley, *supra* note 7, at 775 ("The doctrine [of humanitarian intervention has] origins in 19th century European interventions in situations of perceived persecution of Christians in territories under Ottoman Turkish rule . . . ."); *see also* Michael N. Schmitt & Christopher M. Ford, *Assessing U.S. Justifications for Using Force in Response to Syria's Chemical Attacks: An International Law Perspective*, 9 J. NAT'L SECURITY L. & POL'Y 283, 294 (2017) (citing various interventions in the 1800s). *See also* Jean-Pierre Fonteyne, *The Customary International Law Doctrine of Humanitarian Intervention: Its Current Validity Under the UN Charter*, 4 CAL. W. INT'L L.J. 203, 214 (1974) (tracing humanitarian intervention theory to St. Thomas Aquinas and Hugo Grotius and analyzing views of early scholars).

[9] *Id.*

[10] See SEAN D. MURPHY, HUMANITARIAN INTERVENTION: THE UNITED NATIONS IN AN EVOLVING WORLD ORDER 51 (1996) (concluding such interventions resulted when "the increasingly dominant, industrializing, and economically robust European powers sought to extend their influence worldwide, including to areas under Ottoman rule").

[11] See Peter Hilpold, *Humanitarian Intervention: Is There a Need for a Legal Reappraisal?*, 12(3) EUR. J. INT'L L. 437, 443–44 (2001) (pre-Charter interventions are "beside the point," because at that time "recourse to war was not legally regulated"); Christian J. Tams, *Prospects for Humanitarian Uses of*

More recently, those who support humanitarian intervention point to interventions by the Economic Community of West African States (ECOWAS) in Liberia in 1990[12] and Sierra Leone in 1998,[13] both of which received approval from ECOWAS (a regional actor), but only after-the-fact Security Council approval.[14] Technically, it is *prior* Security Council approval that is required under the UN Charter.[15]

Additionally, in 1991, in the wake of the first Gulf War ("Operation Desert Storm"), the US, the UK, and France implemented, without Security Council authorization, a no-fly zone[16] over Kurdish areas of Northern Iraq in order to protect the Kurdish population. The Kurds had previously faced mass slaughter, including through the use of chemical weapons, under the regime of then-Iraqi President Saddam Hussein.[17] After Iraq's expulsion from Kuwait, both the Kurdish and Shi'ite populations revolted and faced massive retaliation by Iraqi forces, with more than

---

Force, in REALIZING UTOPIA: THE FUTURE OF INTERNATIONAL LAW 368 (A. Cassese ed., 2012) ("one cannot draw support from pre-Charter practice").

[12] "On 7 August 1990, the [ECOWAS] Standing Mediation Committee established a Military Observer Group (ECOMOG), to help resolve an armed internal conflict which had broken out in Liberia the previous year." *ECOWAS and the Subregional Peacekeeping in Liberia*, J. HUMANITARIAN ASSISTANCE (Sept. 25, 1995), *at* https://sites.tufts.edu/jha/archives/66.

[13] "ECOWAS sent an ECOMOG force into [Sierra Leone] led by Nigeria. It engaged the [Armed Forces Revolutionary Council] and [Revolutionary United Front] fighters in battle and was able to reinstate [President] Kabbah to power by March 1998." *Economic Community of West African States on the Ground: Comparing Peacekeeping in Liberia, Sierra Leone, Guinea Bissau, and Côte D'Ivoire*, 2:2–3 AFRICAN SECURITY 119 (Dec. 15, 2009), *at* www.tandfonline.com/doi/pdf/10.1080/19362200903361945.

[14] *See* Stromseth, *supra* note 3, at 33, 34 ("The ECOWAS interventions in Liberia and Sierra Leone revealed the Security Council's own willingness to accept regional action first with Council endorsement after the fact"); Schmitt & Ford, *supra* note 8, at 296 ("The U.N. Security Council has sometimes approved humanitarian interventions after their launch. Such approval would logically be inconsistent with the unlawfulness of the operations *ab initio*."); THOMAS M. FRANCK, RECOURSE TO FORCE: STATE ACTION AGAINST THREATS AND ARMED ATTACKS, at 155–62 (2002) (analyzing ECOWAS interventions in Liberia and Sierra Leone); *compare* Kreβ, *supra* note 4 [Major Post-Westphalian], at 22, 23 (discussing ECOWAS's intervention in Liberia as humanitarian intervention, but distinguishing ECOWAS's Sierra Leone intervention as consensual); Rodley, *supra* note 7, at 784–85 (discussing ECOWAS's intervention in Liberia); Wood, *supra* note 4, at 362 (same).

[15] Charter of the United Nations, 892 UNTS 119 (1945) [hereinafter, UN Charter], at Art. 53.1.

[16] *See* Schmitt & Ford, *supra* note 8, at 298 (noting also the deployment of military personnel from Australia, Belgium, Canada, France, Germany, Italy, Luxembourg, the Netherlands, Portugal, Spain, Turkey, and the UK).

[17] These crimes are the subject of the second case tried by the Iraqi High Tribunal, the *Anfal* case, which examined the chemical and conventional weapons bombardment of the Kurds in 1988 during the so-called "Anfal" campaign. *See* Jennifer Trahan, *A Critical Guide to the Iraqi High Tribunal's Anfal Judgment: Genocide against the Kurds*, 30 MICH. J. INT'L L. 305 (2009).

2.1 The Doctrine of "Humanitarian Intervention" 57

a million Kurds attempting to flee.[18] A similar no-fly zone was imposed in the South of Iraq to protect the Shi'ites, who also had been victims of mass repression under Saddam Hussein's government.[19] While UN Security Council Resolution 688[20] is often cited in support of the implementation of such no-fly zones, the resolution contains no express authorization.[21]

Clearly, such interventions (at least those in the modern era) would have been appropriate as a matter of international law had they received prior UN Security Council authorization under Chapter VII of the UN Charter,[22] yet none did.

---

[18] See, e.g., Franck, *supra* note 14, at 152–53.

[19] See Chris Mooney, *Did the United Nations Authorize "No-Fly" Zones Over Iraq?*, SLATE (Nov. 19, 2002), *at* www.slate.com/articles/news_and_politics/explainer/2002/11/did_the_united_nations_authorize_nofly_zones_over_iraq.html ("Following the Gulf War, no-fly zones were set up north of the 36th parallel to protect Iraq's Kurdish minority and, later, south of the 32nd parallel to protect the country's Shiite Muslims.").

[20] See S/RES/688 (Apr. 5, 1991). "[T]he United States, in particular, made an attempt to justify 'Operation Provide Comfort' by reference to Security Council Resolution 688." Kreβ [The State Conduct Element], *supra* note 6, at 494. The UK Foreign Secretary, by contrast, claimed the right to unilateral humanitarian intervention "in case of extreme humanitarian need." *Id.*, citing CHRISTOPHER GREENWOOD, ESSAYS ON WAR IN INTERNATIONAL LAW, at 154–57 (2006); *see also* Ved P. Nanda, *Tragedies in Northern Iraq, Liberia, Yugoslavia, and Haiti – Revisiting the Validity of Humanitarian Intervention Under International Law – Part I*, 20 DENVER J. INT'L L. & POL'Y 305, 333 (1992) (analyzing the Kurdish intervention as humanitarian intervention); Rodley, *supra* note 7, at 785–86 (considering the Kurdish no-fly zone as a possible instance of humanitarian intervention).

[21] See, e.g., Rodley, *supra* note 7, at 786 (concluding resolution 688 did not authorize enforcement action); Schmitt & Ford, *supra* note 8, at 298 (same).

[22] See UN Charter, Ch. VII. Some controversy could have arisen as to whether atrocities solely internal to a country are properly subject to Chapter VII; however, this proposition is generally now fairly well-accepted. See, e.g., Frank, *supra* note 14, at 136 ("Although the Charter text does not specifically authorize the Council to apply Chapter VII's system of collective measures to prevent gross violations of humanitarian law and human rights [to a situation internal to a country], in practice it has done so occasionally; for example by authorizing members to use coercive measures to counter apartheid in South Africa and revoke Rhodesia's racially motived Unilateral Declaration of Independence (UDI), as well as to help end egregious ethnic conflicts in Yugoslavia, Somalia, and Kosovo and to reverse a Haitian military coup that sought to undo a UN-supervised democratic election."); Marc Weller, *Introduction: International Law and the Problem of War*, in THE OXFORD HANDBOOK OF THE USE OF FORCE IN INTERNATIONAL LAW, at 30 (Marc Weller ed., 2015) ("It is clear that the U.N. Security Council can act under Chapter VII to authorize the use of force on behalf of populations threatened by extermination, starvation, or forcible expulsion at the hands of their own government, or other groups exercising effective control over them. While the Council has had to emphasize the unique nature of virtually every situation it has addressed in this way, a pattern of practice has emerged which puts the authority of the Council to address essentially internal matters of this kind beyond question.").

2.1.2 *The 1999 NATO Intervention in Kosovo*

The classic example frequently invoked to support a doctrine of humanitarian intervention is that of NATO in 1999 in the Federal Republic of Yugoslavia (FRY) in response to atrocity crimes being committed in Kosovo against Kosovar Albanians.[23] These events followed on the heels of mass atrocity crimes in the wars in the 1990s in the former Yugoslavia, including the Srebrenica massacre, with UN peacekeeping forces stationed nearby. Against this backdrop of prior ethnic slaughter (with UN intervention in Bosnia having been roundly criticized as late and insufficient); the commencement of massacres in Kosovo by the army of the FRY and Serbian police;[24] failed attempts at peace talks in Rambouillet, France to resolve the situation in Kosovo;[25] and a near certain Russian (and perhaps Chinese) veto of any resolution that would have authorized military intervention,[26] NATO, on March 24, 1999, based on mutual agreement of its nineteen member states,[27] commenced an eleven-week air campaign ("Operation Allied Force").[28] "NATO's intervention was, in the end, effective in stopping the mass expulsions and persecution of Kosovo Albanians."[29]

That a regional organization, NATO, had authorized the intervention certainly improved its legitimacy over, for instance, a unilateral intervention or multilateral intervention not authorized by a regional actor. Yet, under a strict reading of UN Charter Article 53.1, intervention by a regional actor still requires UN Security Council prior approval.[30]

---

[23] For background on the crisis, see, e.g., Hilpold, *supra* note 11, at 438–41.

[24] See Greenwood [Kosovo], *supra* note 4, at 146 *et seq.* (chronicling the various massacres and massive refugee flows).

[25] See *id.* at 146 *et seq.* (detailing the diligent attempts by the "Contact Group" (US, UK, France, Germany, Italy, and Russia) to reach a negotiated settlement).

[26] Indeed, Russia sponsored a resolution condemning the intervention. See U.N. Doc. S/PV.3989 (1999).

[27] Schmitt & Ford, *supra* note 8, at 299.

[28] See Press Statement of NATO Secretary-General Javier Solana, NATO Press Release 040 (1999) (authorizing the Supreme Commander Europe to initiate air operations in the Federal Republic of Yugoslavia).

[29] Greenwood [Kosovo], *supra* note 4, at 143–44. See also Hilpold, *supra* note 11, at 448 ("intervention by NATO forces helped finally to stop the carnage and induced Serb forces to retreat from Kosovo").

[30] UN Charter Article 53.1 states "no enforcement action shall be taken under regional arrangements or by regional agencies without the authorization of the Security Council." UN Charter, Art. 53.1. The African Union Constitutive Act identifies one of the Union's operative principles as "the right of the Union to intervene in a Member State pursuant to a decision of the Assembly in respect of grave circumstances, namely: war crimes, genocide and crimes against humanity." African Union Constitutive Act of 2000, Art. 4(h), *at* www.achpr.org/files/instruments/au-constitutive-act/au_act_2000_eng.pdf. However, that would not constitute authorization at the Charter level.

In advance of the NATO intervention, in October 1998, the UK circulated a note to NATO allies explicitly advancing a legal basis for military action based on a narrowly tailored concept of humanitarian intervention.[31] As to the participation of other NATO members, it has been claimed that:

> [a]lthough only few of the other NATO States that participated in the Kosovo military action in 1999 came out publicly to explain the legal basis of their action, there can be little doubt that most, if not all, considered that action to be lawful. And, absent any other legal basis for that action, it is evident that the legal basis relied upon by NATO and its participating States – even if not expressed publicly – was that of humanitarian intervention.[32]

In statements at the Security Council, the UK defended its actions as "humanitarian intervention,"[33] with the US, Canada, and the Netherlands taking the position that intervention was necessary to prevent "humanitarian catastrophe" and for "humanitarian considerations."[34]

After NATO's intervention, the Security Council arguably endorsed the result, in Resolution 1244 (adopted by fourteen votes at the Security Council), imposing terms similar to those that had been sought at Rambouillet and authorizing an international security presence in Kosovo.[35] A Russian-sponsored resolution that would have condemned the intervention failed to pass, with only three votes in favor and twelve votes against.[36]

Thereafter, the FRY sued ten NATO member states at the International Court of Justice (ICJ) challenging the legality of the intervention.[37] Belgium

---

[31] Sir Daniel Bethlehem, *Stepping Back a Moment — The Legal Basis in Favour of a Principle of Humanitarian Intervention*, EJIL: TALK! (Sept. 12, 2013), at www.ejiltalk.org/stepping-back-a-moment-the-legal-basis-in-favour-of-a-principle-of-humanitarian-intervention. *See also* Greenwood [Kosovo], *supra* note 4, at 157 (discussing the UK's note).

[32] Bethlehem, *supra* note 31.

[33] Greenwood [Kosovo], *supra* note 4, at 158 (quoting the March 24, 1999, statement by the UK Permanent Representative to the UN).

[34] *Id.* at 159–60 (quoting statements by the Representatives of the US, Canada, and the Netherlands). Then President Bill Clinton also "vaguely referred to NATO as having helped 'to vindicate the principles and purposes of the Organization's Charter . . . .'" Henkin [How Nations Behave], *supra* note 7, at 170, *quoting* Press Release GA/9599 (Sept. 21, 1999).

[35] *See* S/RES/1244 (1999). *See also* Louis Henkin, *Kosovo and the "Law of Humanitarian Intervention,"* 93 AM. J. INT'L L. 824, 826 (1999) (the resolution "effectively ratified the NATO action and gave it the Council's support"); *but see* Rodley, *supra* note 7, at 787 ("It is disputed whether the Security Council [in Resolution 1244] was thereby ratifying the intervention."); Hilpold, *supra* note 11, at 441 ("the fact that the Security Council [in Resolution 1244] does not refer to the NATO military action can hardly be seen as evidence for an acquiescence to the intervention").

[36] Henkin [Kosovo], *supra* note 35, at 825.

[37] Legality of Use of Force (Serb. & Montenegro v. Belg.), Application of the Federal Republic of Yugoslavia (Int'l Ct. Just. Apr. 29, 1999).

defended on the merits the concept of "humanitarian intervention,"[38] while other states limited their arguments to the issue of jurisdiction. Because the ICJ ultimately dismissed the case for lack of jurisdiction,[39] it did not reach the issue of the legality of the intervention.[40]

Those writing on the legality of the Kosovo intervention generally concluded it was "legitimate" if not "fully legal," or similar formulations[41] – that there is a moral imperative to act to try to prevent mass atrocity crimes, but that the intervention was not perhaps fully legal, at least under a strict reading of the UN Charter. A strict reading of the UN Charter clearly does not reach a satisfying result, as it suggests, absent Security Council authorization, one simply permits a people in peril to be massacred. The dilemma is eloquently stated in the report of the Independent International Commission in Kosovo ("Kosovo Commission Report")[42] commissioned by Sweden: "[T]he Commission feels strongly that the moral imperative of protecting vulnerable people in an increasingly globalized world should not be lightly cast aside by adopting a legalistic view of international responses to humanitarian catastrophes. The effectiveness of rescue initiatives would seem to take precedence over formal niceties."[43] Others have written: "If it is morally right to use force to prevent a humanitarian emergency, then it should be legally permissible as well."[44] "While law and morality will, of course, sometimes be out of step with

---

[38] Stromseth, *supra* note 3, at 36, n. 50 (Belgium argued before the ICJ that NATO's action was a "lawful armed humanitarian intervention"), *citing* Argument of Belgium before the ICJ, at 7 (May 10, 1999); *see also* Legality of Use of Force (Serb. & Montenegro v. Belg.), Oral Proceedings, CR/99/15 (Int'l Ct. Just. May 10, 1999).

[39] Legality of Use of Force (Serb. & Montenegro v. Belg.), Provisional Measures, Order, 1999 ICJ Rep. 124 (June 2); Legality of Use of Force (Serb. & Montenegro v. Belg.), Preliminary Objections, Judgment, 2004 ICJ Rep. 279 (Dec. 15) (dismissal on the merits).

[40] While the conduct of NATO's intervention additionally faced criticisms such as the use of high-altitude bombing, use of depleted uranium, and as to target selection, these are issues of *jus in bello*, and raise separate issues than the legality of the intervention, *jus ad bellum*.

[41] Richard Falk wrote: "It is jurisprudentially problematic *both* to regard 'ethnic cleansing' as intolerable to the international community and to condemn the form and substance of the NATO interventionary response designed to prevent it. And yet just such doctrinal tensions seem to follow from the perspectives of international law and world order." Richard A. Falk, *Kosovo, World Order, and the Future of International Law*, 93 Am. J. Int'l L. 847, 852 (1999). *See also* Wood, *supra* note 4, at 350 (referring to the Kosovo intervention as "unlawful but justified"); Greenwood [Kosovo], *supra* note 4, at 144 (noting others calling it "morally right but unlawful").

[42] The Commission was chaired by eminent South African jurist Richard Goldstone, former Chief Prosecutor of the International Criminal Tribunal for the former Yugoslavia (ICTY) and the International Criminal Tribunal for Rwanda (ICTR).

[43] The Independent International Commission on Kosovo, The Kosovo Report: Conflict, International Response, Lessons Learned 176 (2000).

[44] Greenwood [Kosovo], *supra* note 4, at 144.

one another, a dichotomy between what is 'lawful' and what is 'legitimate' is undesirable in any society and particularly undesirable in international law.... "[45]

While the UN Charter, in its express language, of course, contains no mention of "humanitarian intervention," there are potentially creative readings of the Charter that have been invoked to suggest its permissibility. For instance, one can argue that the "Purposes" of the UN, as reflected in Article 1(3), mandate respect for human rights, and the Charter's preamble affirms "the dignity and worth of the human person," both of which should inform how one reads the Charter.[46] One could argue that humanitarian intervention is not aimed at the "territorial integrity" or "political independence" of the intervened-in state and thus does not violate Article 2(4)[47] – which prohibits use of force against "the territorial integrity or political independence of any state, or in any other manner inconsistent with the Purposes of the United Nations."[48] One could argue that the Charter should be read in an updated way[49] that does not sanction mass atrocities, and perhaps revives some

---

[45] *Id.* at 145.
[46] UN Charter, Art. 1(3), pmbl.
[47] *See, e.g.*, Larry May, *Aggression, Humanitarian Intervention, and Terrorism*, 41 CASE W. RES. J. INT'L L. 321, 331–32 (2009) (Michael Reisman argues: "Since a humanitarian intervention seeks neither a territorial change nor a challenge to the political independence of the State involved and is not only not inconsistent with the purposes of the United Nations but is rather in conformity with the most fundamental peremptory norms of the [Charter], it is a distortion to argue that it is precluded by Article 2(4)."), *citing* W. Michael Reisman & Myres McDougal, *Humanitarian Intervention to Protect the Ibos*, in HUMANITARIAN INTERVENTION AND THE UNITED NATIONS 177 (Richard Lillich ed., 1973); Rodley, *supra* note 7, at 778 (noting the same argument); Christian Henderson, *The UK Government's Legal Opinion On Forcible Measures in Response to the Use of Chemical Weapons by the Syrian Government*, 64 INT'L & COMP. L. Q. 179, 186, n. 49 (2015) (noting that Belgium argued that it "never questioned the political independence and the territorial integrity of the Federal Republic of Yugoslavia," and thus NATO's intervention was "compatible with Article 2, paragraph 4, of the Charter, which covers only intervention against the territorial integrity or political independence of a State"). *Compare* Kreβ [The State Conduct Element], *supra* note 6, at 489–90 ("Article 2(4) of the UN Charter opens a small window of textual ambiguity. But this window is immediately closed in the light of the fact that the *travaux préparatoires* unambiguously confirm that, apart from a use of force in self-defense, the prohibition contained in article 2(4) was intended not to leave room for exceptions in cases of a use of force pursuing a benign purpose...."); Henderson, *supra* note 47, at 186 (noting, although not endorsing, the argument "that force which does not deprive another State of all or a part of its territory, or that does not remove a government or deprive it of any meaningful independence, is excluded from the purview of Article 2(4)").
[48] UN Charter, Art. 2(4).
[49] *See, e.g.*, RONALD C. SLYE & BETH VAN SCHAACK, ESSENTIALS: INTERNATIONAL CRIMINAL LAW 92 (2009) ("It is generally accepted at the international level that treaties are to be treated as living documents. In other words, they are to be interpreted in the context

preexisting customary notion of humanitarian intervention.[50] Or, one could argue that a sovereign massively abusing the population should forfeit some of the protections normally associated with "sovereignty."[51] Yet, admittedly, none of these arguments "quite carr[y] the day."[52]

The Kosovo Commission Report ultimately concluded that NATO's intervention was "illegal" but "justified." Specifically, the report stated: "It was illegal because it did not receive prior approval from the United Nations Security Council. However, the Commission considers that the intervention was justified because all diplomatic avenues had been exhausted and because the intervention had the effect of liberating the majority population of Kosovo from a long period of oppression under Serbian rule."[53] The Commission ultimately wrote that "the intervention was not compatible with Charter norms but still 'legitimate,'"[54] falling into a legal "gray zone of ambiguity."[55]

---

of the time in which they are being applied, and not as they would have been interpreted at the time of their drafting.").

[50] See, e.g., Simon Chesterman, *Just War or Just Peace? Humanitarian Intervention and International Law* 235 (2002) ("There were long-standing arguments that a right of unilateral intervention pre-existed th[e] [UN] Charter.").

[51] Greenwood [Kosovo], *supra* note 4, at 162 ("[I]nternational law does not require that respect for the sovereignty and integrity of a State must in all cases be given priority over the protection of human rights and human life, no matter how serious the violations of those rights perpetrated by that State."); *id.* at 174 ("An oppressive government can no longer violate the most basic tenets of human rights and international humanitarian law, inflict loss of life and misery on a huge scale upon part of its population and expect to hide behind the concept of State sovereignty . . . ."); Statement of the Netherlands at the UNSC, U.N. Doc. S/PV.4001 (June 10, 1999), at 12 ("Today, we regard it as a generally accepted rule of international law that no sovereign State has the right to terrorize its own citizens."); LASSA OPPENHEIM, INTERNATIONAL LAW: A TREATISE 280 (Hersch Lauterpacht ed., 6th ed. 1947) ("When a State renders itself guilty of cruelties against and persecution of its nationals, in such a way as to deny their fundamental human rights and so shocks the conscience of mankind, intervention in the interests of humanity is legally permissible."); Weller [Introduction], *supra* note 22, at 311 ("Action undertaken on behalf of a population to save it from manifest abuses of its rights ... would, according to this view, not amount to intervention. After all, such action would be undertaken to vindicate the rights, or presumed will, of the population under threat. That population, of course, is the true sovereign of the state, rather than the government or effective authority.").

[52] Ruth Wedgewood, *NATO's Campaign in Yugoslavia*, 93 AM. J. INT'L L. 828–33, 828 (1999) (Wedgewood's full quote is that "no single argument quite carries the day, even while the ensemble seems sufficient.").

[53] Kosovo Commission Report, *supra* note 43, at 4.

[54] Tom J. Farer, *Agora: Future Implication of the Iraq Conflict: The Prospect for International Law and Order in the Wake of Iraq*, 97 AM. J. INT'L L. 621, at n. 13 (2003) (citing the Kosovo Commission Report).

[55] The Report stated that it "puts forward an interpretation of the emerging doctrine of humanitarian intervention. This interpretation is situated in a gray zone of ambiguity between an extension of international law and a proposal for an international moral consensus. In essence,

2.1.3 Lingering Wariness about "Humanitarian Intervention"

The reason states are wary of endorsing a doctrine of "humanitarian intervention" is fairly obvious. First, there is the challenge of defining it to ensure any intervention is truly "humanitarian" and not geopolitical or pretextual.[56] Absent such a definition of when the doctrine might be appropriately invoked, it is clearly susceptible to abusive invocations.[57] Furthermore, even appropriately defined, would the intervening state (or states) be the sole arbiters of the propriety of the intervention? That also presents dangers.[58] Second, presumably some limitations (limiting criteria) would need to be placed upon the conduct of the intervenor. Absent such criteria, the scope of the intervention could become a proverbial "Pandora's box." One might, for instance, limit the intervention in time and scope to alleviating the humanitarian crisis (and for no other purpose), require any intervention to adhere to the principles of distinction and proportionality, and require any intervention to last no longer than required to accomplish its purpose.[59] Yet, again, would the intervening state (or states) be the only arbiters of whether such criteria are being correctly applied? That poses risks. Third, even if there were an accepted definition and accepted criteria, one might still have concerns about a permissive reading of the UN Charter, especially one that arguably loosens the protection provided by Article 2(4) – the core UN Charter norm prohibiting aggressive use of

---

this gray zone goes beyond strict ideas of legality to incorporate more flexible views of legitimacy." Kosovo Commission Report, *supra* note 43, at 164.

[56] *See, e.g.*, Nanda, *supra* note 20, at 309 ("The doctrine of humanitarian intervention is subject to a major criticism: only powerful states are able to exercise the alleged right, and hence they are likely to abuse it, especially since international law has traditionally lacked effective safeguards against such abuse.").

[57] *See id.* at 311 ("An observer must nevertheless acknowledge the absence of a genuine consensus on the definition of humanitarian intervention, the set of criteria to judge its permissibility or impermissibility under international law, and the safeguards necessary to prevent its abuse."); *see, e.g.*, Mark Kersten, *Does Russia Have a Responsibility to Protect Ukraine? Don't Buy It*, GLOBE & MAIL (Apr. 3, 2014), *at* www.theglobeandmail.com/opinion/does-russia-have-a-responsibility-to-protect-ukraine-dont-buy-it/article17271450 (noting Russian Foreign Minister Sergey Lavrov evoking R2P language as a justification for military intervention in Crimea). *Compare* ROSELYN HIGGINS, PROBLEMS AND PROCESS: INTERNATIONAL LAW AND HOW WE USE IT 247 (1994) ("We delude ourselves if we think that the role of norms is to remove the possibility of abusive claims ever being made.").

[58] *See also* Carsten Stahn, *Between Law-Breaking and Law-Making: Syria, Humanitarian Intervention and "What the Law Ought to Be"* (Oct. 22, 2013), *at* https://ssrn.com/abstract=2343582 or http://dx.doi.org/10.2139/ssrn.2343582 (concerned about a "system where nations become the arbiters over the legality of their claims to intervene").

[59] These criteria are based on the UK's criteria for humanitarian intervention. *See* note 198 *infra*. *See, e.g.*, Fonteyne, *supra* note 8, at 249 (suggesting that states fearing that humanitarian intervention will be abusively invoked should work to develop precise criteria for its permissible use).

force.⁶⁰ Fourth, even if one overcomes such concerns, how does one justify the intervention as a matter of international law – that is, where, precisely, in the UN Charter does one ground such a reading of the permissibility of humanitarian intervention? For example, if one argues that humanitarian intervention does not violate Article 2(4), what provision actually *allows* one to read in the authorization for humanitarian intervention?⁶¹

These are the types of questions that cause most states,⁶² as well as legal scholars,⁶³ to reject the doctrine of "humanitarian intervention" as too susceptible to abusive invocations and not grounded in a strict reading of the text of the UN Charter. Put differently, on the world stage, numerically, there are more small and middle-sized states that see themselves as potential unwilling recipients of such an intervention and thus remain wary of the concept; there are numerically far fewer states that see themselves as would-be intervenors, and some of these intervenors have long histories of intervention, the record of which is checkered by colonial and neo-imperialist legacies.⁶⁴ Gareth Evans,

---

⁶⁰ See Rodley, *supra* note 7, at 794 ("The primacy of the norm prohibiting the use of force was at the heart of the UN at its birth"). According to former UN Secretary-General Kofi Annan: "No principle of the Charter is more important than the principle of the non-use of force as embodied in Article 2, paragraph 4.... Secretaries-General confront many challenges in the course of their tenures but the challenge that tests them and defines them inevitably involve the use of force." R. ZACKLIN, THE UNITED NATIONS SECRETARIAT AND THE USE OF FORCE IN A UNIPOLAR WORLD: POWER V. PRINCIPLE, at xii–xiii (2010) (quoting the Secretary-General). Louis Henkin calls Article 2(4) the "principal norm of contemporary international law." Henkin [How Nations Behave], *supra* note 7, at 129.

⁶¹ See Franck, *supra* note 14, at 138 ("A state using military force without Council authorization against another in 'humanitarian intervention' is thus engaging in an action for which the Charter text provides no apparent legal authority."); *compare* note 244 *infra* (Sir Daniel Bethlehem suggesting how one might read a customary international law doctrine of humanitarian intervention and the Charter together).

⁶² See, e.g., Group of 77 South Summit, Declaration of the South Summit, Havana, Cuba, April 10–14, 2000, para. 54 (rejecting "the so-called 'right' of humanitarian intervention, which has no basis in the United Nations Charter or in the general principles of international law") (emphasis added); *see also* GA Res. 68/38, para. 6 (Dec. 10, 2013) (requesting "the States parties to the relevant instruments on weapons of mass destruction to consult and cooperate among themselves in resolving their concerns with regard to cases of non-compliance as well as on implementation, in accordance with the procedures defined in those instruments, *and to refrain from resorting or threatening to resort to unilateral actions* . . . .") (emphasis added).

⁶³ See Rodley, *supra* note 7, at 775–76 (noting that the majority of scholars reject the lawfulness of unilateral humanitarian intervention); *see, e.g.*, Hilpold, *supra* note 11 (concluding that NATO's 1999 intervention was not a "watershed" moment changing the law).

⁶⁴ See Stahn [Between Law-Breaking and Law-Making], *supra* note 58, at 35 ("Members of the Global South perceive calls for greater legalization of 'humanitarian intervention' as the claim of a few to reshape the law in a way that is seen as a tool for domination by others."); Michael Byers & Simon Chesterman, *Changing the Rules about Rules? Unilateral Humanitarian Intervention and the Future of International Law*, in HUMANITARIAN INTERVENTION: ETHICAL, LEGAL,

who served as Chair of the International Commission on Intervention and States Sovereignty (ICISS), explains the dynamic as follows:

> It was very much a North-South debate [on humanitarian intervention], with the many new states born out of decolonization being very proud of their new won sovereignty, very conscious of their fragility, and all too conscious of the way in which they had been on the receiving end in the past of not very benign interventions from the imperial and colonial powers, and not very keen to acknowledge their right to do so again, whatever the circumstances.[65]

At the same time, it is deeply unsatisfying to accept that if Security Council authorization to intervene is not forthcoming, the international community is expected simply to allow the slaughter of a population in peril. In 1999, UN Secretary-General Kofi Annan posed the conundrum to the General Assembly, asking:

> [i]f, in those dark days and hours leading up to the [Rwandan] genocide, a coalition of States had been prepared to act in defence of the Tutsi population, but did not receive prompt Council authorization, should such a collation have stood aside and allowed the horror to unfold?[66]

To this author, the international community has not yet satisfactorily answered Kofi Annan's question.

2.2 THE DEVELOPMENT OF THE "RESPONSIBILITY TO PROTECT"

Responding to questions such as the one posed by Kofi Annan, in the aftermath of NATO's Kosovo intervention and the UN's glaring failures to prevent mass atrocities in both Rwanda and Bosnia,[67] the international community began reexamining its approach to situations of mass atrocities. This reexamination developed into the doctrine of the "responsibility to protect" (R2P) – the concept

---

AND POLITICAL DILEMMAS, at 190 (J. L. Holzgrefe & R. Keohane 2003) ("The novel conception of international law that is being constructed and reinforced [on humanitarian intervention] by a limited group of Anglo-American international lawyers is possible only by ignoring the wider circle of states and international lawyers around the world.").

[65] Evans, *supra* note 6.
[66] Secretary-General's Address to the General Assembly, Press Release SG/SM/7136, U.N. Doc. A/9596 (1999).
[67] See Report of the Independent Inquiry into the Actions of the United Nations During the 1994 Genocide in Rwanda, S/1999/1257 (Dec. 16, 1999); Report of the Secretary-General Pursuant to General Assembly, Res. 53/55, U.N. Doc. 1/54/549 (1999) (on Srebrenica).

that the international community *does* indeed have a responsibility to protect a population when it faces, or is at risk of, mass atrocity crimes.

The most aggressive formulation of R2P was, ironically, its first formulation, in 2001. (Unfortunately, one cannot say that this first formulation is where R2P stands today.) The first formulation was promulgated by the twelve-member ICISS, convened by Canada.[68] The Commissioners formulated the concept that there is indeed an obligation owed by the international community to protect a people in peril: "[S]overeign states have a responsibility to protect their own citizens from avoidable catastrophe – from mass murder and rape, from starvation – but that when they are unwilling or unable to do so, that responsibility must be borne by the broader community of states."[69] The ICISS Report also suggests criteria for intervention, namely: an ongoing or imminent "serious and irreparable harm" involving "large scale loss of life" or "large scale 'ethnic cleansing,'" the use of force as a last resort, and the use of "proportional means," meaning that "[t]he scale, duration and intensity of the planned military intervention should be the minimum necessary to secure the defined human protection objective."[70] (The ICISS Report, in this respect, was foreshadowed by the Kosovo Commission Report, which also contained criteria for judging the validity of "humanitarian intervention.")[71] As to who should implement this responsibility to protect, the ICISS Report states that

---

[68] International Commission on Intervention and State Sovereignty (ICISS), *The Responsibility to Protect, Report of the International Commission on Intervention and State Sovereignty* (International Development Research Centre, Ottawa, December 2001) [hereinafter, ICISS Report]. Louise Arbour traces Francis Deng and Roberta Cohen as developing already in 1996 the first tentative formulations of what became R2P. *See* Arbour, *supra* note 7, at 447, citing Roberta Cohen & Francis M. Deng, *Normative Framework of Sovereignty, in* Francis M. Deng, et al., SOVEREIGNTY AS RESPONSIBILITY: CONFLICT MANAGEMENT IN AFRICA (1996).

[69] ICISS Report, *supra* note 68, at VIII, para. 1.

[70] *Id.* at 37, para. 4.39.

[71] The Kosovo Commission Report suggested guidelines for judging the validity of humanitarian intervention:

1. There are two valid triggers of humanitarian intervention. The first is severe violations of international human rights or humanitarian law on a sustained basis. The second is the subjection of a civilian society to great suffering and risk due to the "failure" of their state, which entails the breakdown of governance at the level of the territorial sovereign state.
2. The overriding aim of all phases of the intervention involving the threat and the use of force must be the direct protection of the victimized population.
3. The method of intervention must be reasonably calculated to end the humanitarian catastrophe as rapidly as possible, and must specifically take measures to protect all civilians, to avoid collateral damage to civilian society, and to preclude any secondary punitive or retaliatory action against the target government.

Kosovo Commission Report, *supra* note 43, at 193–94. The report additionally enumerated eight other "contextual principles" that it would require. *See id.* at 194.

while the decision to intervene *should* be made by the Security Council, if the Council "fails to discharge its responsibility to protect in conscience-shocking situations crying out for action, concerned states may not rule out other means to meet the gravity and urgency of that situation."[72] This formulation would thus leave an opening for "humanitarian intervention" when the Security Council is failing to act in the face of mass atrocities.

However, by 2004, in the *UN Secretary-General's High-Level Panel on Threats, Challenges and Change* ("2004 R2P Report"),[73] while more detailed criteria are provided for when intervention would be appropriate, the report also states that it is the Security Council that must authorize any form of forceful intervention. Specifically, the 2004 R2P Report "endorses the emerging norm that there is a collective international responsibility to protect... in the event of genocide and other large scale killing, ethnic cleansing or serious violations of international humanitarian law which sovereign Governments have proved powerless or unwilling to prevent."[74] The 2004 R2P Report also suggests the following criteria by which to judge the appropriateness of intervention:

(a) *Seriousness of threat.* Is the threatened harm to State or human security of a kind, and sufficiently clear and serious, to justify prima facie the use of military force? In the case of internal threats, does it involve genocide and other large-scale killing, ethnic cleansing or serious violations of international humanitarian law, actual or imminently apprehended?
(b) *Proper purpose.* Is it clear that the primary purpose of the proposed military action is to halt or avert the threat in question, whatever other purposes or motives may be involved?
(c) *Last resort.* Has every non-military option for meeting the threat in question been explored, with reasonable grounds for believing that other measures will not succeed?
(d) *Proportional means.* Are the scale, duration, and intensity of the proposed military action the minimum necessary to meet the threat in question?
(e) *Balance of consequences.* Is there a reasonable chance of the military action being successful in meeting the threat in question, with the consequences of action not likely to be worse than the consequences of inaction?[75]

---

[72] ICISS Report, *supra* note 68, at XIII, para. 3(F).
[73] Report of the Secretary-General's High-Level Panel on Threats, Challenges and Change, A More Secure World: Our Shared Responsibility, U.N. Doc. A/59/565 (Dec. 2, 2004) [hereinafter, 2004 R2P Report].
[74] *Id.*, para. 203.
[75] *Id.*, para. 207.

Yet, the 2004 R2P Report also makes clear that military intervention, which is to be exercised as a last resort, is only "exercisable by the Security Council."[76] The report suggests the applicability of its criteria as guidelines to the Security Council or "anyone else involved in these decisions."[77]

A similar approach was articulated in the 2005 World Summit Outcome Document adopted unanimously by the General Assembly.[78] As to the crimes covered, the General Assembly here shifted from the ICISS terminology "large scale loss of lives"[79] to recognizing that "[e]ach individual State has the responsibility to protect its populations from genocide, war crimes, ethnic cleansing and crimes against humanity."[80] Yet, the World Summit Outcome Document states that the Security Council must authorize any form of forceful intervention.[81] Criteria for intervention were also omitted, perhaps out of an attempt to avoid "automaticity" – that is, avoiding the assumption that if the criteria are met, a response by the international community should follow.[82] In Resolution 1674 (2006) on protecting civilians in armed conflict, the Security Council first endorsed R2P as articulated in the World Summit Outcome Document.[83]

By 2009, a more nuanced approach to R2P appeared in the *Report of the Secretary-General, "Implementing the Responsibility to Protect."*[84] There, the

---

[76] *Id.*, para. 203.
[77] *Id.*, synopsis. *See also id.*, para. 209 ("It would be valuable if individual Members States, whether or not they are members of the Security Council, subscribed to the [criteria].").
[78] United Nations General Assembly, 60th Sess., 2005 World Summit Outcome, GA Res. A/60/1 (Sept. 20, 2005) [hereinafter, World Summit Outcome Document].
[79] Vito Todeschini, *The Place of Aggression in the Responsibility to Protect Doctrine*, in BEYOND RESPONSIBILITY TO PROTECT: GENERATING CHANGE IN INTERNATIONAL LAW 306 (Richard Barnes & Vassilis Tzevelekos eds., 2016).
[80] World Summit Outcome Document, *supra* note 78, para. 138.
[81] *Id.*, para. 139. It states: "We are prepared to take collective action, in a timely and decisive manner, though the Security Council, in accordance with the UN Charter, including Chapter VII, on a case by case basis and in cooperation with relevant regional organizations as appropriate, should peaceful means be inadequate and national authorities are manifestly failing to protect their populations from genocide, war crimes, ethnic cleansing and crimes against humanity." *Id.*
[82] *See* Dorota Gierycz, *From Humanitarian Intervention (HI) to Responsibility to Protect (R2P)*, 29 CRIM. JUST. ETHICS 100, 116 ("By avoiding the identification of general 'threshold' criteria, [the World Summit Outcome Document] attempts to diminish fears that intervention will be 'automatically' triggered . . . .").
[83] Arbour, *supra* note 7, at 449, *citing* S/RES/1674 (2006) (on protection of civilians in armed conflict, which "[r]eaffirms the provisions of paragraphs 138 and 139 of the 2005 World Summit Outcome Document regarding the responsibility to protect populations from genocide, war crimes, ethnic cleansing and crimes against humanity").
[84] Report of the Secretary-General: Implementing the Responsibility to Protect, U.N. Doc. A/63/677 (Jan. 12, 2009), *at* www.un.org/ruleoflaw/files/SG_reportA_63_677_en.pdf [hereinafter, 2009 R2P Report].

responsibility to protect is formulated in terms of three "pillars" of responsibility. Pillar I emphasizes that states have the primary responsibility to protect their own populations "from genocide, war crimes, ethnic cleansing and crimes against humanity, and from their incitement."[85] Pillar II focuses on the "commitment of the international community to assist States in meeting those obligations."[86] Pillar III stresses "the responsibility of Member States to respond collectively in a timely and decisive manner when a State is manifestly failing to provide such protection."[87] R2P thus encompasses a broad "continuum of prevention, reaction and rebuilding, spanning from early warning to diplomatic pressure, and to coercive measures."[88] Yet, again, for any kind of forceful (Pillar III) intervention, Security Council approval is required.[89] While there are later years' R2P reports, the basic approach of requiring Security Council approval for any form of forceful intervention remains consistent.[90]

Thus, while R2P represented a remarkable achievement in recognizing the responsibility of the international community to act in the face of atrocity crimes, and in articulating the different ways by which such protection should be accomplished, it ultimately does not answer Kofi Annan's original question. In response to the question of what to do if the Security Council is not acting (aside from the original ICISS formulation),[91] R2P responds that states wait for the Security Council to act, at least for Pillar III intervention. As will be discussed in Chapter 3, R2P also includes the concept of a "responsibility not to veto" – that the permanent members of the UN Security Council should refrain from utilizing their veto in situations where mass atrocity crimes are occurring.[92] *If* that were being implemented (which, as discussed in Chapter 3, it is not, as only two permanent members endorse such an approach),[93] that would make R2P's contribution more viable. As it stands,

---

[85] *Id.*, para. 11(a).
[86] *Id.*, para. 11(b).
[87] *Id.*, para. 11(c).
[88] Tomoko Yamashita, *Responsibility to Protect as a Basis for "Judicial Humanitarian Intervention,"* in Barnes & Tzevelekos, *supra* note 79, at 367. See also Arbour, *supra* note 7, at 448 ("The protection duty [of R2P] encompasses a continuum of prevention, reaction, and commitment to rebuild, spanning from early warning, to diplomatic pressure, to coercive measures, to accountability for perpetrators and international aid.").
[89] 2009 R2P Report, *supra* note 84, para. 11(c).
[90] See, e.g., UN Secretary-General Report, The Role of Regional and Sub-Regional Arrangements in Implementing the Responsibility to Protect, U.N. Doc. A/65/877-S/2011/393 (June 27, 2011); UN Secretary-General Report, Responsibility to Protect: Timely and Decisive Response, U.N. Doc. A/66/874-S/2012/578 (July 25, 2012).
[91] See note 72 *supra* and accompanying text.
[92] See Chapter 3.1.1.
[93] See Chapter 3.

without all permanent members endorsing the responsibility not to veto, waiting for the Security Council to act in the face of atrocity crimes still leaves populations in peril while crimes are committed where the geopolitics are such that one or more permanent members of the Security Council chooses to block the Council's work.

2.2.1 Difficulties for R2P: Libya and Syria

To compound difficulties in this area, the fortunes of R2P may be waning (or, at least, are far from robust) given that the 2011 Libya intervention was widely described as an exercise of R2P[94] yet turned out fairly unsuccessfully. Furthermore, the massive crimes that have been perpetrated in Syria[95] should long ago have triggered more of a response from the international community, if there really were solid support for implementing R2P.

2.2.1.1 Libya as R2P

The 2011 intervention in Libya was lauded at the time as a successful example of R2P. Gareth Evans writes: "Libya especially, at least at the outset, seemed a textbook example of exactly how R2P is supposed to work in practice, at the reaction stage, in the face of a rapidly unfolding mass atrocity situation."[96] Thus, in February 2011, when forces of then-Libyan President Muammar al-Qaddafi started massacring anti-government protesters in the context of the "Arab Spring," with incendiary government rhetoric promising further killings,[97] the Security Council authorized intervention in Resolution 1973.[98] In both Resolution 1970 (referring the situation in Libya to the International Criminal Court (ICC)) and Resolution 1973 (the force authorization), the Council expressly mentioned R2P – namely, the Libyan authorities' "responsibility to protect" its population.[99] "The Libya intervention

---

[94] Evans, *supra* note 6; Ruben Reike, *Libya and The Responsibility to Protect: Lessons for the Prevention of Mass Atrocities*, 8 ST. ANTONY'S INT'L REV. 122, 122 (2012) ("Actors of the 'international community' repeatedly invoked the R2P in relation to the [Libya] crisis.").

[95] The armed conflict in Syria is often dated as having started March 15, 2011. *Syria's Civil War Explained from the Beginning: On March 15, the War Entered Its Eighth Year*, AL JAZEERA (Apr. 14, 2018), *at* www.aljazeera.com/news/2016/05/syria-civil-war-explained-160505084119966.html. See Chapter 5.1 regarding the crimes committed.

[96] Evans, *supra* note 6.

[97] Saif al-Islam threatened "rivers of blood," and Muammar Gaddafi said protestors would be "cleansed" "house by house." Reike, *supra* note 94, at 127.

[98] S/RES/1973 (2011).

[99] S/RES/1970 (2011); S/RES/1973 (2011).

marked the first time that the Security Council invoked [R2P] to approve the use of force by U.N. member states."[100]

Yet, the intervention, by a multilateral coalition led by NATO forces ("Operation Unified Protector"), was later criticized both for arguably exceeding the terms of the Security Council's force authorization and leaving Libya a destabilized state, with numerous armed militias and a weak central government unable to exert authority over the country.[101] These results have in turn created cynicism, or at least disappointment, about the doctrine of R2P.[102]

In terms of the scope of the intervention, the resolution authorized "all necessary measures" to "protect civilians and civilian populated areas under threat," and implementation of a "no fly zone."[103] What was accomplished was arguably "regime change."[104] While it does appear that the force authorization was exceeded, there are also contrary arguments – for instance, that "[i]f civilians were to be protected house-to-house in areas like Tripoli under Gaddafi's direct control, ... that could only be by overturning his whole regime."[105]

As to the success of the intervention, we will never know what crimes might have been averted, so the cost of nonintervention could have been considerable. An interesting additional question is whether the intervention, rather than serving as an example of R2P improperly invoked, simply terminated prematurely, with NATO countries failing to remain engaged long enough to ensure

---

[100] Catherine Powell, *Libya: A Multilateral Constitutional Moment?*, 106 AM J. INT'L L. 298, 315 (2012).

[101] Tom Esslemont, *As Syrian Deaths Mount, World's "Responsibility to Protect" Takes a Hit: Experts*, REUTERS (Oct. 24, 2016), *at* www.reuters.com/article/us-mideast-crisis-syria-law/as-syrian-deaths-mount-worlds-responsibility-to-protect-takes-a-hit-experts-idUSKCN12O2S3 ("After the Libyan leader's overthrow and death, the country became mired in a slow-burn civil war between two rival governments, one in Tripoli and one in the east.").

[102] *See, e.g.*, Sophie Rondeau, *The Responsibility to Protect Doctrine, and the Duty of the International Community to Reinforce International Humanitarian Law and Its Protective Value for Civilian Populations*, *in* Barnes & Tzevelekos, *supra* note 79, at 266 ("It is safe to say that R2P is not currently flourishing."), *citing*, inter alia, M. Hall Findlay, *Can RtoP Survive Libya and Syria* (Strategic Studies Working Group Papers, Nov. 2011); Camila Pupparo, *The Responsibility to Protect: Emerging Norm or Failed Doctrine?*, 9 GLOB. TIDES 12 (2015) ("Unfortunately, the doctrine [of R2P] lost much of its hard-earned credibility from the international community and suffered adversely when the principle was used to justify NATO['s Libya] deployment.").

[103] S/RES/1973 (2011).

[104] *See* Kreβ [Major Post-Wesphalian], *supra* note 4, at 32 ("Brazil, the Russian Federation, India, China and South Africa (the so-called 'BRICS states') took the view that the NATO states had overstepped their Security Council mandate and that they had abused that mandate to bring about an inadmissible regime change.").

[105] Evans, *supra* note 6 (noting the argument); Reike, *supra* note 94, at 136 ("Some observers argue that the protection of civilians in Libya ultimately required regime change. To some, regime change was seen as the only tool to permanently prevent mass atrocities in Libya, to deal with the root cause of the threat.").

a sufficiently stable state post-intervention. Put differently, this may not have been a failure of "the responsibility to protect," but, rather, a situation where not enough focus was placed on the "responsibility to rebuild" aspect of R2P.[106]

Reflecting on the difficulties of international intervention, one author writes:

> It is not easy for an outside intervenor to stop massive human rights violations .... It is even more difficult for outsiders, by way of military intervention, to change underlying causes of such violations and to guarantee that violations do not recur immediately after the withdrawal of intervening forces .... Therefore, [intervention] in order to be morally and legally justifiable, also has to be successful.[107]

2.2.1.2 Syria as an R2P Failure

In recent years, the near paralysis of the international community, including, in particular, the UN Security Council, with respect to the situation in Syria is most certainly not only a tragedy for the Syrian people, but, doctrinally, a further low point for R2P.[108] One might legitimately wonder, given the scope of atrocities occurring there (and in Myanmar, Sri Lanka, and Darfur) whether there really is endorsement of the concept of R2P and/or the "will" to operationalize it.

As detailed in Chapter 5, there have now been years of atrocity crimes committed in Syria, predominantly at the hands of the regime of President Bashar al-Assad and the forces of the so-called "Islamic State of Iraq and the Levant" (ISIL),[109] as well as other groups.[110] These crimes have been well-documented by the Independent International Commission of Inquiry on the Syrian Arab Republic (Commission of Inquiry),[111] which has issued numerous

---

[106] ICISS Report, *supra* note 68, at ch. 5, 39–45 ("The Responsibility to Rebuild"). *See, e.g.*, Evans, *supra* note 6 ("post-crisis rebuilding" is part of R2P); Yamashita, *supra* note 88, at 367 (R2P encompasses a broad continuum of measures that includes "rebuilding"); Todeschini, *supra* note 79, at 310 ("the R2P doctrine presents three dimensions: prevention ... reaction ... and rebuilding ...").

[107] Rein Muellerson, *Book Review: Sean D. Murphy, Humanitarian Intervention: The United Nations in an Evolving World Order*, 92 AM J. INT'L L. 583, 586 (1998).

[108] *See, e.g.*, Evans, *supra* note 6 (asking "how serious a setback to the consolidation and evolution of the new norm Syria has been").

[109] ISIL is also known as the Islamic State of Iraq and Syria (ISIS), the Islamic State (IS), or Da'esh.

[110] *See* Chapter 5.1.

[111] The Human Rights Council first created a Fact-Finding Mission on Syria in 2011, which was soon upgraded to a Commission of Inquiry. BETH VAN SCHAACK, IMAGINING JUSTICE FOR SYRIA: WATER ALWAYS FINDS ITS WAY (forthcoming) (Oxford University Press 2020) (unpublished manuscript on file with the author).

reports detailing the crimes.[112] Some of these crimes were glaringly thrust into the public spotlight when the infamous "Caesar" photos were smuggled out of Syria and placed on display, revealing the horrific torture occurring in Syrian detention facilities run by the Assad regime.[113] While international focus has sometimes been placed on the use of chemical weapons by the Syrian regime (discussed in Chapter 5) – which is, indeed, horrendous – it is actually other crimes by regime forces that have triggered the highest death tolls in Syria, for instance through indiscriminate aerial bombardment and torture.[114]

The argument that there has not been more of a response by the Security Council to the unfolding tragedy in Syria because the Libya intervention exceeded the terms of its force authorization rings hollow. It is quite clear that Russia's fourteen vetoes as of January 2020 related to the situation in Syria stem, not from the Libya precedent, but from Russia's larger perceived geostrategic interests in protecting the government of Bashar al-Assad. Thus, "Russia's position on Syria was from the outset manifestly *realpolitik*-driven."[115] Beth Van Schaack writes: "[t]he Libya comparison perhaps enjoyed a hint of sincerity when first uttered in connection with Syria, but it sounded increasingly pre-textual as time wore on and it became clear that the West would not commit serious troops against the Assad regime."[116]

In the face of all these years of atrocities, the Security Council has issued a meager trickle of resolutions related to the situation in Syria,[117] mainly

---

[112] For the work of the Commission, see www.ohchr.org/en/ hrbodies/hrc/iicisyria/pages/indepen dentinternationalcommission.aspx. The Commission was established on August 22, 2011, by the Human Rights Council through Resolution S-17/1 with a mandate to investigate all alleged violations of international human rights law since March 2011 in the Syrian Arab Republic. *Id.*

[113] Human Rights Watch, *Syria: Stories Behind Photos of Killed Detainees: Caesar Photos' Victims Identified* (Dec. 16, 2015), *at* www.hrw.org/news/2015/12/16/syria-stories-behind-photos-killed-detainees.

[114] *See, e.g.*, Syrian Network for Human Rights, *Death Toll*, *at* http://sn4hr.org/blog/category/c asualties/victims-death-toll-victims (compiling death tolls); *60,000 People Have Died in Assad's Prisons During Syria's War, Monitoring Group Says*, REUTERS & VICE NEWS (May 22, 2016), *at* https://news.vice.com/article/60000-people-have-died-bashar-al-assad-regime-prisons-syria-war (citing a report by the Syrian Observatory for Human Rights). Former Legal Adviser of the Department of State during the Obama Administration Harold H. Koh writes: "implicit in the Trump Administration's actions was its willingness to allow Assad to keep exterminating Syrian innocents by conventional means, so long as he doesn't use chemical weapons." Harold Hongju Koh, *The Real "Red Line" Behind Trump's April 2018 Syria Strikes*, JUST SECURITY (Apr. 16, 2018), *at* www.justsecurity.org/54952/real-red-linebehind-trumps-april-2018-syria-strikes.

[115] Evans, *supra* note 6.

[116] Van Schaack [IMAGINING JUSTICE], *supra* note 111.

[117] "The Security Council has only issued about two dozen formal resolutions, and half as many Presidential Statements, dedicated to the situation in Syria—a conflict [then] entering its eighth year." *Id.*

watered-down and sometimes, as "a key concession to Russia," suggesting a "rhetorical equivalency" between the crimes of the regime and opposition forces.[118] For example, in Resolution 2139, the Council condemned the "widespread violations of human rights and international humanitarian law by the Syrian authorities, as well as human rights abuses and violations of international humanitarian law by armed groups," and demanded that "all parties" put an end to all forms of violence and "cease all attacks against civilians."[119] The Council has also rarely mentioned R2P in its resolutions related to Syria. Resolution 2165, addressing humanitarian access, is a rare example, as its preamble mentions "the primary responsibility of the Syrian authorities to protect the population in Syria."[120] As detailed in Chapter 5, numerous resolutions related to Syria have faced the Russian veto, and sometimes also Chinese veto (that is, a "double-veto").[121] This series of vetoes has provided "the regime a sense of untouchability and impunity, leading to further repressive behaviour ... ."[122] The Council, by contrast, "generally reserved its strongest accountability language for Al Qaida, [ISIL], and their affiliates."[123]

To put it bluntly, if there really is endorsement by the international community of R2P, one might well ask where this support has been related to the situation in Syria. Canadian politician Michael Ignatieff is not alone in his frustration when he states: "Syria is a case that's begging for 'responsibility to protect' and no one is showing any responsibility whatever."[124] Certainly no "responsibility to protect" has been "operationalized" as to the situation in Syria, which appears to be our newest example of the failure of the call "never again."

As explored further in Chapter 5, while no single force authorization or any other single Security Council resolution could have ended the civil war or curtailed the commission of all the crimes, there are many steps that could have been taken by the Security Council, including the imposition of UN sanctions,

---

[118] Id.
[119] S/RES/2139 (2014).
[120] S/RES/2165, pmbl. (2014).
[121] See Chapter 5.1.
[122] Evans, *supra* note 6.
[123] Van Schaack [IMAGINING JUSTICE], *supra* note 111. See, e.g., S/RES/2170 (2014) (condemning gross, widespread abuse of human rights by extremist groups in Iraq and Syria, and expressing the need for accountability for "ISIL, [al Nusra Front] and all other individuals, groups, undertakings and entities associated with Al-Qaida"); S/RES/2393 (Dec. 19, 2017) (condemning a long list of crimes, and, inter alia, expressing "grave concern" "at the movement of foreign terrorist fighters and other terrorists and terrorist groups into and out of Syria"); S/RES/2347 (2017) (condemning destruction and smuggling of cultural heritage by terrorist groups, including ISIL).
[124] Esslemont, *supra* note 101. Ignatieff adds: "So it's as relevant as ever, normatively, morally, in terms of our conscience, but it is a dead letter internationally." Id.

a UN arms embargo,[125] referral of the situation to the ICC,[126] continued chemical weapons inspections that would have attributed responsibility to the side using the weapons,[127] and much more full-scale condemnation of crimes by Syrian forces.[128] All of these measures could have conveyed that the international community *was* watching. The failure to take such steps and all the numerous vetoes related to the situation, meanwhile, conveyed exactly the opposite: that the international community was abdicating its responsibilities.

In light of the Libya intervention and inaction regarding Syria, Gareth Evans well asks: "has the whole R2P project been seriously, and perhaps irreversibly tarnished?"[129]

2.2.2 *The Need to Revitalize R2P: Emphasizing the "Hard Law" Obligations Underlying It*

It is safe to say that, currently, the doctrine of R2P could use revitalization. One idea – which is explored below and parallels this author's ideas on "legal limits" to the use of the veto explored in Chapter 4 – is to examine the legal foundations for R2P, and bring more recognition to the fact that some obligations underlying R2P are *not soft law*, but hard law, obligations. A second idea – explored in Chapter 4 – is to recognize that existing law imposes certain legal limits (or constraints) on the use of the veto in the face of atrocity crimes (genocide, crimes against humanity, and/or war crimes), as it is often the veto power, or threat of veto, that blocks implementation of R2P.

As to the legal authority of R2P, the international community should refrain from treating all of R2P – which is widely described as "soft law"[130] – as

---

[125] *See, e.g.*, Human Rights Watch, *Syria: Impose Arms Embargo Following Deadly Airstrikes: Repeated Strikes on Douma Kill At Least 112* (Aug. 20, 2015), *at* www.hrw.org/news/2015/08/20/syria-impose-arms-embargo-following-deadly-airstrikes (calling for a UN arms embargo to be imposed after indiscriminate bombings in Douma).

[126] As discussed in Chapter 5, referral to the ICC was blocked by the veto. Draft Resolution S/2014/348 (vetoed by Russia and China).

[127] As discussed in Chapter 5, renewal of the mandate for such chemical weapons inspections was vetoed three times. Draft Resolution S/2017/884 (vetoed by Russia); Draft Resolution S/2017/962 (vetoed by Russia); Draft Resolution S/2017/970 (vetoed by Russia).

[128] *See* Evans, *supra* note 6 (suggesting sanctions, an arms embargo, threat of International Criminal Court prosecutions, and condemnation). As discussed in Chapter 5.1, condemnation of crimes, particularly by Government forces in the early years of the conflict, was also blocked by the veto.

[129] *Id.* Evans provides an optimistic response to that question. *Compare* Esslemont, *supra* note 101 ("R2P is a merely a 'high moral aspiration' that has 'floundered' on the complex realities of warfare today, according to Paddy Ashdown.").

[130] *See, e.g.*, Jennifer M. Welsh & Maria Banda, *International Law and the Responsibility to Protect: Clarifying or Expanding States' Responsibilities?*, 2 GLOB. RESPONSIBILITY TO PROTECT 3, 213 (2010) (arguing that R2P is soft law); William W. Burke-White, *Adoption of*

something "aspirational" or only embodying a "moral commitment." While the 2004 R2P Report referred to R2P as an "emerging norm" (that is, an emerging *legal* norm),[131] it does not appear to be treated that way.[132]

In fact, "R2P is grounded in existing international law."[133] One such hard law source underlying R2P[134] is the Convention on the Prevention and

> *the Responsibility to Protect, in* THE RESPONSIBILITY TO PROTECT 34 (Jared Genser & Irwin Cotler eds., 2012) (arguing that R2P is "best understood as a norm of international conduct" and that "[t]he trajectory of the Responsibility to Protect over the past decade is strongly suggestive of its development toward a rule of international law, but further political development and legal process will be required"); Todeschini, *supra* note 79, at 314 ("R2P has not yet been consolidated into a legal norm"); Hitoshi Nasu, *The UN Security Council's Responsibility and the "Responsibility to Protect," in* MAX PLANCK YEARBOOK OF UNITED NATIONS LAW, Vol. 15, at 377–418 (2011) ("The responsibility to protect has been widely considered a policy agenda, and not a legally binding commitment by UN Member States."); Pupparo, *supra* note 102, at 3, 5, 9 ("As established by the ICISS, the [R2P] doctrine was not a legal principle but 'merely a policy option.'" Arguing that R2P has "shifted toward becoming a norm," but is "having trouble achieving full [norm] compliance since multiple aspects of it remain unclear and leave room for susceptibility to manipulation and abuse.").

[131] 2004 R2P Report, *supra* note 73, paras. 201–02 (referring to an "emerging norm of a collective international responsibility to protect").

[132] *See* Carsten Stahn, *Responsibility to Protect: Political Rhetoric or Emerging Legal Norm?*, 101 AM. J. INT'L L. 99, 101 (2007) (examining whether R2P is really a "legal norm" and concluding that, although parts rest on existing hard law, much of it does not and there is "considerable doubt concerning whether and to what extent states intended to create a legal norm"). *See also* note 130 *supra*. Stahn also notes that the US in particular took the position that the World Summit Outcome Document was not a source of legal obligations, but that R2P was a form of "moral responsibility." *Id.* at 108, *citing* Letter by Ambassador John Bolton. Stahn also examines the "hard law" underlying R2P, although focuses on different aspects than this author.

[133] *See, e.g.*, Australian Red Cross, *International Humanitarian Law and the Responsibility to Protect: A Handbook*, at www.redcross.org.au/getmedia/d0338aa5-27c9-4de9-92ce-45e4c8f4d825/IHL-R2P-responsibility-to-protect.pdf.aspx; Arbour, *supra* note 7, at 447–48 (the responsibility to protect norm is "anchored in existing law"); JOHN HEIECK, A DUTY TO PREVENT GENOCIDE: DUE DILIGENCE OBLIGATIONS AMONG THE P5 3 (2018) (R2P encapsulates four binding legal norms). "Many proponents of a legal obligation argue that R2P . . . is rooted in pre-existing treaty obligations, notably in common article 1 of the 1949 Geneva Conventions, article 1 of the 1948 Genocide Convention, and in the Human Rights Covenants . . . ." Anne Peters, *The Security Council's Responsibility to Protect*, 8 INT'L ORG L. REV. 15, 22 (2011) (citing authorities and states that have made statements at the General Assembly that R2P derives from existing treaty law). Canada called R2P a "sophisticated normative framework based on international law." Irmgard Marboe, *R2P and the Abusive Veto – The Legal Nature of R2P and Its Consequences for the Security Council and Its Members*, 16 AUSTRIAN REV. INT'L & EUR. L. 115, 117 (2011), *citing* U.N. Doc. A/63/Pv.97-100 (23, 24, and 28 July 2019).

[134] Arbour writes: "At the very least, under the Genocide Convention and its norms, which have been incorporated into international customary law, States have a duty to prevent genocide." Arbour, *supra* note 7, at 339–40. *See also* Australian Red Cross [Handbook], *supra* note 133 (noting existing legal obligations relevant to R2P include those found in the Genocide Convention).

Punishment of the Crime of Genocide (Genocide Convention).[135] Thus, former High Commissioner for Human Rights and former Chief Prosecutor of the ICTY and ICTR Louise Arbour writes: "the heart of the responsibility to protect doctrine already rests upon an undisputed obligation of international law: the prevention and punishment of genocide."[136] The Genocide Convention imposes on all its 152 state parties[137] in Article 1 an obligation to "prevent and to punish" genocide.[138] The ICJ elaborated on the obligation to "prevent" genocide in the *Bosnia v. Serbia* Case,[139] in which the Court determined that Serbia had breached its duty to prevent genocide committed by Bosnian Serb forces in and around Srebrenica.[140]

In its ruling, the ICJ articulated a standard of due diligence, which Arbour explains:

> The Court elaborated that "the obligation of States is rather to employ all means reasonably available to them, so as to prevent genocide as far as possible" .... "If the State has available to it means likely to have a deterrent effect on those suspected of preparing genocide, or reasonably suspected of harboring specific intent, it is under a duty to make use of these means as the circumstances permit." In a nutshell, the Court posits that States must "do their best" to ensure that acts of genocide do not occur. The Court invokes here a notion of "due diligence," a concept well understood in international human rights law .....[141]

As also discussed in Chapter 4, the two most significant aspects of the Court's ruling for present purposes are: (1) its holding that a state's responsibility to prevent genocide varies based on the state's ability to influence the relevant actors;[142] and (2) that the ICJ did *not* limit a state's obligations under

---

[135] Convention on the Prevention and Punishment of the Crime of Genocide, Dec. 9, 1948, 78 UNTS 277 [hereinafter, Genocide Convention].

[136] *Id.* at 450; *see also* Nasu, *supra* note 130, at 386 (states "are required to prevent and punish genocide under the [Genocide Convention], which also requires states to exercise due diligence, within their power, in preventing genocide").

[137] United Nations Treaty Collection, as of Jan. 25, 2020, at https://treaties.un.org/Pages/View Details.aspx?src=IND&mtdsg_no=IV-1&chapter=4&clang=_en.

[138] Genocide Convention, *supra* note 135, Art. 1.

[139] Case Concerning Application of the Convention on the Prevention and Punishment of the Crime of Genocide (Bos. & Herz. v. Serb. & Montenegro), Judgment, 2007 ICJ Rep. 43 (Feb. 26) [hereinafter, *Bosnia v. Serbia* Case].

[140] *Id.*, para. 438.

[141] Arbour, *supra* note 7, at 451–52, *quoting Bosnia v. Serbia* Case, paras. 430–32.

[142] *Bosnia v. Serbia* Case, *supra* note 139, para. 430 ("Various parameters operate when assessing whether a State has duly discharged the obligation concerned. The first, which varies greatly from one State to another, is clearly the capacity to influence effectively the action of persons likely to commit, or already committing, genocide.").

the Genocide Convention to preventing genocide only within a state's own territory, but applied it vis-à-vis genocide being committed in another state. On the first point, the ICJ concluded that "responsibility is incurred if the State manifestly failed to take *all measures* to prevent genocide which were *within its power*, and which might have contributed to preventing genocide."[143] Thus, the Court held that the obligation to take action to prevent genocide is stronger for states with close geographical proximity, and based on the strength of their political and other ties.[144] On the second point, the extraterritorial implications of the ruling are clear as the Court was adjudicating the responsibility of Serbia (then part of the FRY)[145] to prevent genocide committed in July 1995 by Bosnian Serb forces in Bosnia-Herzegovina, an independent state as of 1992.[146]

There are also binding legal commitments contained in the four 1949 Geneva Conventions[147] that underlie R2P.[148] All UN Member States are

[143] *Id.* (emphasis added). The ICJ also recently reached such a ruling (at least at the provisional measures stage) in Gambia, et al.'s case against Myanmar alleging a breach of the Genocide Convention. *See* Application of the Convention on the Prevention and Punishment of the Crime of Genocide (The Gambia v. Myanmar), Order of 23 January 2020, para. 79 (Int'l Ct. of Just.) ("Bearing in mind Myanmar's duty to comply with its obligations under the Genocide Convention, the Court considers that ... Myanmar must, in accordance with its obligations under the Convention, in relation to the members of the Rohingya group in its territory, *take all measures within its power to prevent* the commission of all acts within the scope of Article II of the Convention . . . .") (emphasis added).

[144] *Id.* As to the issue of "proximity," Arbour writes: "While proximity may matter most in terms of promptness and effectiveness of response, it should not be used as a pretext for non-neighbours to avoid responsibility." Arbour, *supra* note 7, at 454.

[145] At that time, the FRY consisted of Serbia, Kosovo, and Montenegro.

[146] *See* Kreß [The State Conduct Element], *supra* note 6, at 491 ("In the *Genocide* case, the ICJ recognized the duty of states to prevent genocide even beyond their own borders."); Jan Wouters, *The Obligation to Prosecute International Law Crimes*, 32 COLLEGIUM at 8 (2005), *citing* Application of the Convention on the Prevention and Punishment of the Crime of Genocide (Bos. & Herz. v. Yugo.), Preliminary Objections, para. 31 (Int'l Ct. of Just. July 11, 1996) ("the obligation each State thus has to prevent and to punish the crime of genocide is not territorially limited by the Convention").

[147] Geneva Convention I for the Amelioration of the Condition of the Wounded and Sick in Armed Forces in the Field, Aug. 12, 1949, 75 UNTS 31 [hereinafter, Geneva Convention I]; Geneva Convention II for the Amelioration of the Condition of Wounded, Sick and Shipwrecked Members of Armed Forces at Sea, Aug. 12, 1949, 75 UNTS 85 [hereinafter, Geneva Convention II]; Geneva Convention III Relative to the Treatment of Prisoners of War, Aug. 12, 1949, 75 UNTS 135 [hereinafter, Geneva Convention III]; Geneva Convention IV Relative to the Protection of Civilian Persons in Time of War, Aug. 12, 1949, 75 UNTS 287 [hereinafter, Geneva Convention IV] [collectively, 1949 Geneva Conventions].

[148] *See, e.g.,* Rondeau, *supra* note 102; Australian Red Cross [Handbook], *supra* note 133, at 12 ("States obligations to 'respect and ensure respect for' international humanitarian law and their responsibilities under IHL are enumerated in the Geneva Conventions and Additional Protocols. These obligations are relevant to the war crimes responsibilities under R2P.").

2.2 The Development of R2P

parties to the 1949 Geneva Conventions.[149] These Conventions impose on States Parties an obligation to prosecute "grave breaches"[150] (a fairly broad subset of war crimes committed in international armed conflict).[151] The Conventions, in Common Article 3, also prohibit a set of war crimes committed in non-international armed conflict.[152] The Conventions additionally specify that "[e]ach High Contracting Party shall take measures necessary for the suppression of all acts contrary to the provisions of the present Convention[s] other than grave breaches . . . ."[153]

Additionally, Common Article 1 to the 1949 Geneva Conventions provides an obligation for States Parties to "undertake to respect and to ensure respect

---

[149] International Committee for the Red Cross (ICRC), *Treaties, States Parties, and Commentaries*, at https://ihl-databases.icrc.org/applic/ihl/ihl.nsf/States.xsp?xp_treatySelected=380&xp_viewStates=XPages_NORMStatesParties.

[150] Geneva Convention I, *supra* note 147, Art. 49 (obligation to prosecute grave breaches), Art. 50 (grave breaches); Geneva Convention II, *supra* note 147, Art. 50 (obligation to prosecute grave breaches), Art. 51 (grave breaches); Geneva Convention III, *supra* note 147, Art. 129 (obligation to prosecute grave breaches); Art. 130 (grave breaches); Geneva Convention IV, *supra* note 147, Art. 146 (obligation to prosecute grave breaches), Art. 147 (grave breaches).

[151] Grave breaches specified in the four 1949 Geneva Conventions, *supra* note 147 (Arts. 50, 51, 130, 147, respectively) are willful killing; torture or inhuman treatment; biological experiments; willfully causing great suffering or causing serious injury to body or health; and extensive destruction and appropriation of property, not justified by military necessity and carried out unlawfully and wantonly (except, this last provision is not included in Article 130, Geneva Convention III). Grave breaches specified in Geneva Conventions III and IV, *supra* note 147 (Arts. 130 and 147, respectively) additionally include compelling a prisoner of war or a protected civilian to serve in the armed forces of the hostile Power; and willfully depriving a prisoner of war or a protected person of the rights or fair and regular trial prescribed in the Conventions. Grave breaches specified in Geneva Convention IV, *supra* note 147 (Art. 147) additionally include: unlawful deportation or transfer; unlawful confinement of a protected person; and taking of hostages. International Committee for the Red Cross (ICRC), *Grave Breaches Specified in the 1949 Geneva Conventions and in Additional Protocol I of 1977*, at www.icrc.org/eng/resources/documents/misc/57jp2a.htm.

[152] Common Article 3 prohibits, in conflicts not of an international character:

(a) violence to life and person, in particular murder of all kinds, mutilation, cruel treatment and torture;
(b) taking of hostages;
(c) outrages upon personal dignity, in particular humiliating and degrading treatment;
(d) the passing of sentences and the carrying out of executions without previous judgment pronounced by a regularly constituted court, affording all the judicial guarantees which are recognized as indispensable by civilized peoples.

1949 Geneva Conventions, Common Article 3.

[153] Geneva Convention I, *supra* note 147, Art. 49, para. 3; Geneva Convention II, *supra* note 147, Art. 50, para. 3; Geneva Convention III, *supra* note 147, Art. 129, para. 3; Geneva Convention IV, *supra* note 147, Art. 146, para 3.

for the Geneva Conventions in all circumstances."[154] Identical language about the obligation to "respect and to ensure respect" is found in Article 1(1) of Protocol I and Article 1(1) of Protocol III.[155] The International Committee of the Red Cross (ICRC) explains Common Article 1 does not impose "an obligation to reach a specific result, but rather an 'obligation of means' to take *all possible appropriate measures* in an attempt to prevent or end violations of IHL."[156] Thus, the ICRC Commentaries to the Geneva Conventions state that that language "covers *everything* a state can do to prevent the commission, or the repetition, of acts contrary to the convention[s]."[157] ICRC experts Knut Dörmann and Jose Serralvo[158] explain

---

[154] 1949 Geneva Conventions, *supra* note 147, Common Art. 1. Common Article 1 appears to apply both to international armed conflict and non-international armed conflict. See Rondeau, *supra* note 147, at 266 (construing the phrase "in all circumstances" to mean Common Article 1 also applies in non-international armed conflict); Knut Dörmann & Jose Serralvo, *Common Article 1 to the Geneva Conventions and the Obligation to Prevent International Humanitarian Law Violations*, 96 INT'L REV. RED CROSS 707, 735 (2014) (same); Oona A. Hathaway, Emily Chertoff, Lara Dominguez, Zachary Manfredi & Peter Tzeng, *Ensuring Responsibility: Common Article 1 and State Responsibility for Non-State Actors*, 95 TEXAS L. REV. 539 (2017) ("It is also important to note that Common Article 1 places affirmative responsibilities on states in both a non-international armed conflict ... and an international armed conflict ...."), *citing* International Committee of the Red Cross, Commentary of 2016, Art. 1, para. 125 (2d ed. Mar. 22, 2016) ("The High Contracting Parties undertake to respect and to ensure respect for 'the present Convention' in all circumstances.... Thus, the High Contracting Parties must also ensure respect for the rules applicable in non-international armed conflict ...."). Of course, part of the 1949 Geneva Conventions applies to non-international armed conflict – Common Article 3 – so the obligation to "respect and to ensure respect for" the 1949 Geneva Conventions clearly at least applies to respecting and ensuring adherence to Common Article 3.

[155] Protocol Additional to the Geneva Conventions of 12 August 1949, and relating to the Protection of Victims of International Armed Conflicts (Protocol I), June 8, 1977 [hereinafter, Protocol I]; Protocol Additional to the Geneva Conventions of 12 August 1949, and relating to the Adoption of an Additional Distinctive Emblem (Protocol III), December 8, 2005 [hereinafter, Protocol III]. Article 89 of Protocol I also states: "In situations of serious violations of the Conventions or of this Protocol, the High Contracting Parties undertake to act, jointly or individually, in co-operation with the United Nations and in conformity with the United Nations Charter." Protocol I, Art. 89.

[156] Rondeau, *supra* note 147, at 263–64, *quoting* INCREASING RESPECT FOR INTERNATIONAL HUMANITARIAN LAW IN NON-INTERNATIONAL ARMED CONFLICT, at 10 (M. Mack ed., ICRC, Geneva, 2008) (emphasis added). *See also* Rondeau, *supra* note 147, at 264 ("The duty to 'use appropriate, humanitarian and other peaceful measures to help to protect populations from those crimes,' as stated in the 2005 World Summit [Outcome Document], is complementary to the obligation of High Contracting Parties to the 1949 Geneva Conventions to do everything to ensure that IHL is respected ....").

[157] Wouters, *supra* note 146, at 6, *citing* Commentary to the 1949 Geneva Conventions, *supra* note 147 (emphasis added).

[158] At the time of their publication, Dörmann served as Head of the Legal Division of the ICRC and Serralvo as legal adviser in the Legal Division.

that Common Article 1 creates both an "internal component" (ensuring respect for the Conventions on a state's own territory, for example, by its military, police, and civilians), and an "external component."[159] The latter mandates that "third States – that is States not taking part in an armed conflict have an international legal obligation to actively prevent IHL violations" "even in conflicts to which they are not a party."[160] ICRC Commentaries also explain that Common Article 1 imposes an obligation to ensure respect by other states, which "should do everything in their power to ensure that the humanitarian principles underlying the Conventions are universally applied."[161] The ICJ similarly recognized an obligation of third states in both the *Nicaragua* Case (where the US was admonished to ensure respect for the Conventions and humanitarian law more broadly),[162] and the *Wall*

---

[159] Dörmann & Serralvo, *supra* note 154, at 708.

[160] *Id.* at 709. This reading is also embraced by Oona Hathaway and Zachary Manfredi who explain:

> In the new [ICRC] commentary [2016] on Common Article 1, the ICRC explains that duties "to respect" are distinguishable from duties "to ensure respect." The former applies directly to states and their organs, and require[s] that they not directly violate the laws of armed conflict. The duty "to ensure respect," however, creates independent obligation on states to ensure *other* states and non-state actors do not violate their own duties under international law.

Oona Hathaway & Zachary Manfredi, *The State Department Adviser Signals a Middle Road on Common Article 1*, JUST SECURITY (Apr. 12, 2016), *at* www.justsecurity.org/ 30560/state-department- adviser-signals-middle-road- common-article-1/. For a more extensive discussion of what Common Article 1 requires, see also Hathaway, Chertoff, Dominguez, Manfredi & Tzeng, *supra* note 154. But see Nasu, *supra* note 130, at 387, n. 37 ("The crucial question is whether common article 1 extends to include an obligation to take action to prevent violations or to protect civilians outside one's own control.").

[161] Dörmann & Serralvo, *supra* note 154, at 715 (*citing* COMMENTARY: IV GENEVA CONVENTION RELATIVE TO THE PROTECTION OF CIVILIAN PERSONS IN TIME OF WAR 16 (ICRC, Jean Pictet ed., 1958)). For an article questioning what is required under Common Article 1 and concluding that "[C]ommon Article 1 is no more than a reminder of all obligations ... to 'respect' the Geneva Conventions" and a recommendation for states "to adopt lawful measures to induce other contracting states to comply with the Conventions," see Carlo Focarelli, *Common Article 1 of the 1949 Geneva Conventions: A Soap Bubble?*, 21 EUR. J. INT'L L. 125 (2010); *id.* at 128 ("It is unclear whether [C]ommon Article 1 proves for an obligation or rather a discretionary power [or recommendation].... It is also unclear ... what specific measures contracting states are bound (or authorized) [or recommended] to adopt."); *see also* Nasu, *supra* note 130 (considering what is required of the Security Council in terms of implementing R2P).

[162] Dörmann & Serralvo, *supra* note 154, at 717 (*citing* Military and Paramilitary Activities in and against Nicaragua (Nicar. v. U.S.), Judgment, Merits, 1986 ICJ Rep. 14, para. 220 (June 27) ("The Court considers that there is an obligation on the United States Government, in the terms of Article 1 of the Geneva Conventions, to 'respect' the Conventions and even 'to ensure respect' for them 'in all circumstances,' since such an obligation does not derive only from the

Case (where every state party was reminded of its obligation to ensure that Israel comply with the requirements of the Fourth Geneva Convention).[163] Similarly, in a report submitted to the Security Council by the Secretary-General, it was emphasized that the obligation to ensure compliance with the Fourth Geneva Convention particularly applies to states "that have diplomatic relations with" the state in question who should "use all the means at their disposal to persuade" the government to abide by the applicable Convention.[164] "[A] State with close political, economic and/or military ties (for example, through equipping and training of armed forces or joint planning of operations) to one of the belligerents has a stronger obligation to ensure respect for IHL by its ally."[165] Obligations of due diligence would be "even more pronounced if third States provide support, directly, or indirectly, to a party to an ongoing armed conflict."[166] Additionally, of course, "third States are under the obligation not to knowingly aid or assist in the commission of IHL violations."[167]

Crimes against humanity do not yet have their own convention, although one has been drafted by the International Law Commission.[168] When it is hopefully finalized and adopted, it too could provide a similar source of legal

Conventions themselves, but from the general principles of humanitarian law to which the Conventions merely give specific expression.")).

[163] Dörmann & Serralvo, *supra* note 154, at 717 (*citing* Legal Consequences of the Construction of a Wall in the Occupied Palestinian Territory (Wall Case), Advisory Opinion, 2004 ICJ Rep. 136, para. 158 (July 9) ("The Court would also emphasize that Article 1 of the Fourth Geneva Convention, a provision common to the four Geneva Conventions, provides that '[t]he High Contracting Parties undertake to respect and to ensure respect for the present Convention in all circumstances.' It follows from that provision that every State party to that Convention, whether or not it is a party to a specific conflict, is under an obligation to ensure that the requirements of the instruments in question are complied with.")).

[164] Dörmann & Serralvo, *supra* note 154, at 718 (*citing* Report Submitted to the Security Council by the Secretary-General in Accordance with Resolution 605 (1987), paras. 24–27, U.N. Doc. S/19443, January 21, 1988).

[165] Dörmann & Serralvo, *supra* note 154, at 724 (*citing* Hans-Peter Gasser, *Ensuring Respect for the Geneva Conventions and Protocols: The Role of the Third States and the United Nations*, in EFFECTING COMPLIANCE, at 28 (British Institute of International and Comparative Law, Hazel Fox & Michael A. Meyer eds., 1993)).

[166] Dörmann & Serralvo, *supra* note 154, at 725.

[167] *Id.* at 727 (*citing* Draft Articles on Responsibility of States for Internationally Wrongful Acts, ch. IV.E.1, Art. 16, November 2001, Supplement No. 10 (A/56/10)).

[168] *See* International Law Commission, Draft Articles on Prevention and Punishment of Crimes against Humanity, Adopted by the International Law Commission at Its Seventy-First Session and Submitted to the General Assembly as Part of the Commission's Report Covering the Work of that Session, U.N. Doc. A/74/10, *at* https://legal.un.org/docs/?path=./ilc/texts/instruments/english/draft_articles/7_7_2019.pdf&lang=EF. For additional background, see Sévane Garibian & Claus Kreß (eds.), *Special Issue: Laying the Foundations for a Convention on Crimes against Humanity*, 16(4) J. INT'L CRIM. JUST. (2018).

obligation.[169] Even absent the Convention, "under international human rights law, states are under a general duty of due diligence to ensure respect for human rights within their territory or jurisdiction."[170] Given that crimes against humanity entail massive human rights violations, there necessarily is a similar duty of due diligence to prevent crimes against humanity.[171] Articles 40 and 41 of the ILC's Articles on State Responsibility similarly recognize "a positive duty to cooperate to bring to an end any serious breaches, by a state, of an obligation arising under a peremptory norm of international law."[172] War crimes, crimes against humanity, and genocide all constitute "peremptory norms of international law."[173] Thus, there exists an obligation of due diligence to ensure *all three crimes* are not committed, and, if they are, an obligation to cooperate to bring such crimes to an end.[174] As noted above, at

---

[169] See id. Art. 3(2) ("Each State undertakes *to prevent* and to punish crimes against humanity, which are crimes under international law, whether or not committed in time of armed conflict") (emphasis added).

[170] Nasu, *supra* note 130, at 386 (citing Louise Arbour, *The Responsibility to Protect as A Duty of Care in International Law and Practice*, REV. INT'L STUD. 34, 45 *et seq*. (2008)).

[171] See Marko Milanović, *State Responsibility for Genocide*, 17(3) EUR. J. INT'L L. 553, 571 (2006) ("States have a duty to prevent and punish genocide in exactly the same way as they have to prevent and punish crimes against humanity or other massive human rights violation.").

[172] International Law Commission, Articles on the Responsibility of States for International Wrongful Acts, reproduced in A/RES/56/83, December 12, 2001, Arts. 40–41. If the underlying crimes involve torture or slavery, there are relevant conventions and these give rise to certain legal obligations as well — but they would be for the crimes of "torture" and "slavery" and not "crimes against humanity" per se. *See* Convention against Torture and Other Cruel, Inhuman or Degrading Treatment or Punishment, Dec. 10, 1984, GA Res. 39/46, Annex, U.N. Doc. A/39/51 (1984); 1465 UNTS 85; Convention to Suppress the Slave Trade and Slavery, Sept. 25, 1926, 60 UNTS 253; Supplementary Convention on the Abolition of Slavery, the Slave Trade, and Institutions and Practices Similar to Slavery, *entered into force* Apr. 30, 1957, 226 UNTS 3.

[173] *See* International Law Commission, Commentary on Article 40, Draft Articles on the Responsibility of States for Internationally Wrongful Acts, 283–84 (2001), at http://legal.un.org/ilc/texts/instruments/english/commentaries/9_6_2001.pdf ("In the light of the description by the ICJ of the basic rules of international humanitarian law applicable in armed conflict as 'intransgressible' in character, it would ... seem justified to treat these as peremptory."); International Law Commission, Commentary to Article 26 (including crimes against humanity and genocide as "clearly accepted and recognized" peremptory norms). *See also* Chapter 4.1.2 ("The Prohibitions of Genocide, Crimes against Humanity, and, at Least Certain, War Crimes Are Peremptory Norms Protected as *Jus Cogens*").

[174] There are also obligations to prosecute or extradite. For example, as to the crime of torture (which can, depending on the context, constitute a war crime, crime against humanity, or crime underlying genocide), such obligations are contained in the Torture Convention. *See* Convention against Torture, *supra* note 172. As noted above, the obligation to "punish" genocide is found in the Genocide Convention, and the obligations to prosecute at least "grave breaches" is found in the 1949 Geneva Conventions. These obligations would apply not only to crimes committed on a state's territory "but also those crimes committed on another State's territory," pursuant to applicable principles of jurisdiction. Wouters, *supra*

least vis-à-vis the crime of genocide, the ICJ in the *Bosnia v. Serbia* Case clarifies that the duty to prevent genocide includes genocide occurring in *another* state; Common Article 1 also suggests extraterritorial obligations vis-à-vis the 1949 Geneva Conventions and Protocols I and III thereto.[175] As to additional war crimes (beyond those enumerated in the 1949 Geneva Conventions and Protocols I and III) and as to crimes against humanity, the ILC's formulation of an obligation "to cooperate to bring to an end *any serious breaches*," in no way suggests a territorial limitation.

Thus, *the R2P-related obligations of states are actually not entirely "soft law*," but, where genocide, war crimes, or crimes against humanity are occurring, there are certain hard law legal obligations. Applying the ICJ's logic in the *Bosnia v. Serbia* Case, and those writing on the obligation to "ensure respect for" the Geneva Conventions, these obligations apply all the more to states holding stronger positions of influence. In this respect, an argument can be made that countries intervening in a situation, particularly those with ties to the regime, and countries serving on the UN Security Council (particularly the permanent members), would bear the strongest obligations of due diligence, as they hold the most influential positions.[176] As will be explored further in Chapter 4, it appears fairly clear that a state that is intervening, closely tied to the regime, and *not* exerting influence to end the commission of genocide, crimes against humanity, and/or war crimes, and/or a permanent member of the Security Council that has utilized its veto power, for example, to *prevent* investigation of chemical weapons use[177] (which can be both a war crime and crime against humanity),[178] and *prevent*

---

note 146, at 1. For further discussion by the ILC of the requirement to extradite or prosecute, see "The Obligation to Extradite or Prosecute (aut Dedere aut Judicare)," *Final Report of the International Law Commission* (2014), II(2) Y.B. INT'L L. COMM'N (2014). *See also* M. Cherif Bassiouni, *International Crimes*: Jus Cogens *and Obligation* Erga Omnes, 59 L. & CONTEMP. PROB. 63, 65 (for a peremptory norm there is a duty to extradite or prosecute created by virtue of the *erga omnes* nature of the obligations).

[175] *See* notes 145–46, 159–63 and accompanying text.
[176] *See also* Arbour, *supra* note 7, at 453 ("Because of the power they wield and due to their global reach, the members of the Security Council, particularly the Permanent Five Members (P5) hold an even heavier responsibility than other States to ensure the protection of civilians everywhere.").
[177] Draft Resolution S/2017/884 (would have renewed the mandate of the OPCW-UN Joint Investigative Mechanism "JIM" for a year) (vetoed by Russia); Draft Resolution S/2017/962 (would have renewed the mandate of the JIM for a year) (vetoed by Russia); Draft Resolution S/2017/970 (would have renewed the mandate of the JIM for 30 days) (vetoed by Russia).
[178] Use of chemical weapons constitutes both a war crime and crime against humanity, depending on the circumstances. Stahn [Between Law-Breaking and Law-Making], *supra* note 58. Chemical weapons use can also constitute a component of genocide. *See* Trahan [A Critical Guide], *supra* note 17 (discussing, inter alia, chemical weapons use by the Iraqi regime

referral to the ICC[179] (a measure that could have helped "prevent" all three crimes)[180] is breaching these due diligence obligations.[181]

Thus, while Syria is clearly an R2P failure, moving forward, it could strengthen the doctrine of R2P to more explicitly emphasize the hard law legal obligations underlying it, and perhaps even demand a remedy when breaches of such legal obligations occur.[182] It could assist the fortunes of R2P even further, if, as suggested in Chapter 4, one recognizes that under existing international law there are limits to veto use in the face of genocide, crimes against humanity, and/or war crimes.[183] As detailed in Chapters 1 and 5, measures that could have alleviated the commission of atrocity crimes are all too often blocked by veto use or threat of the veto.[184]

against the Iraqi Kurds during the 1988 "Anfal campaign," adjudicated to constitute genocide).

[179] Draft Resolution S/2014/348 (would have referred the situation in Syria to the ICC) (vetoed by Russia and China).

[180] The Commission of Inquiry documented extensive crimes against humanity and war crimes committed in Syria, as well as genocide committed against the Yazidis. For the work of the Commission, see note 112 *supra*.

[181] Arbour writes: "If their responsibility were to be measured in accordance with the International Court of Justice's analysis, it would seem logical to assume that a failure to act could carry legal consequences and even more so when the exercise or threat of a veto would block action that is deemed necessary by other members to avert genocide, or crimes against humanity." Arbour, *supra* note 7, at 453.

The Security Council is an organ of the UN, and, admittedly, none of the above-discussed treaty obligations apply directly to it; yet, the individual Member States that sit on the Security Council do have such treaty obligations, and these states are not divested of their treaty obligations by virtue of sitting on the Council. As will be explored more extensively in Chapter 4, the Security Council also has the obligation to "act in accordance with" the Charter's "Purposes and Principles," under UN Charter Article 24(2). Surely, adhering to obligations under treaties as fundamental as the Genocide Convention and 1949 Geneva Conventions must be part of acting in accordance with such Purposes and Principles. For further discussion of how Article 103 of the Charter interacts with the treaty obligations of individual Security Council Member States, see Chapter 4.3.3. While the author is here focusing on Syria, these arguments can be made as to a number of situations, most contemporaneously, the situation in Myanmar.

[182] The breach of hard law obligations should create a corresponding right to a remedy. Interesting questions exist as to what the ramifications of such breaches should be, how there could be remedies, and how they might be enforced. *See, e.g.*, Nasu, *supra* note 130, at 389; *id.* at 415 ("It remains unresolved whether the Security Council's failure to fulfill its responsibility to protect may entail legal consequences and, if it does, what those legal consequences might be."); Stahn [Political Rhetoric or Emerging Legal Norm?], *supra* note 132, at 117 (posing similar questions).

[183] See Chapter 4. *See also* Pupparo, *supra* note 102, at 15 ("RtoP's last and possibly most notable weakness is that it is subject to Security Council authorization. The Security Council can 'expressly reject a proposal for intervention where humanitarian or human rights issues are significantly at stake.'").

[184] *See* Chapter 1 (discussing South Africa under apartheid, Rwanda, Darfur, Israel, Sri Lanka, Syria, Myanmar, and Yemen); *see* Chapter 5 (detailed case studies of veto use regarding Syria and veto threats regarding Darfur).

2.3 REVISITING THE LEGAL STATUS OF "HUMANITARIAN INTERVENTION" POST-R2P

Regardless of whether the doctrine of R2P can be revitalized, another question arises: whether, subsequent to the development of R2P, there still exists any doctrine of "humanitarian intervention" (to the extent one maintains it previously existed), or whether it was replaced by R2P. This question has arisen in regard to the situation in Syria, particularly in light of the regime's use of chemical weapons, the contemplated use of force to respond in 2013, and actual uses of force to respond in 2017 and 2018.

Most states would probably answer the author's question in the negative – that, to the extent there was any doctrine of "humanitarian intervention," it is now replaced by R2P, which makes clear that (in all formulations other than the original ICISS formulation),[185] Security Council approval is required for any form of forceful (Pillar III) intervention.[186] (The term "forceful intervention," while encompassing large-scale uses of force, could also encompass lesser uses of force where there is no consent of the host country. These, for instance, might include creating a humanitarian aid corridor, authorizing a "no-fly zone" to prevent aerial bombardments, or protecting civilians in Internally Displaced Persons (IDP) camps. Presumably, lesser uses of force always would be attempted or explored as options before any larger-scale intervention,[187] so that any use of force, which always carries risks, is the minimum necessary. "Humanitarian intervention" thus should not be seen as synonymous with large-scale intervention or "regime change." There are also many other non-forceful tools that can be employed by the Security Council, by regional actors, or on a bilateral basis, and presumably these also would be explored prior to recourse to force.)

2.3.1 *Proposed Military Strikes in 2013 in Response to Chemical Weapons Attacks*

Despite the apparent demise of the doctrine of "humanitarian intervention" in the eyes of most states, questions about the propriety and legality of

---

[185] See note 72 *supra* and accompanying text (ICISS suggesting the possibility of intervention without Security Council authorization).

[186] See notes 73–89 *supra* and accompanying text (discussing the 2004 R2P Report, World Summit Outcome Document, and 2009 R2P Report).

[187] This "ratcheting up" of means is found in Chapter VII of the Charter, which suggests the propriety of a force authorization (Art. 42) only "[s]hould the Security Council consider that measures provided for in Article 41 [non-forceful measures] would be inadequate or have proved to be inadequate." UN Charter, Art. 42. *See also* Kofi Annan, Press Release, SG/SM/7136, Sept. 20, 1999 ("It is important to define intervention as broadly as possible, to include actions along a wide continuum from the most pacific to the most coercive.").

humanitarian intervention resurfaced in August 2013, when forces of the Assad regime launched a large-scale chemical weapons attack in the suburbs of Damascus,[188] killing hundreds and leaving an estimated 3,000 suffering from "neurotoxic symptoms."[189] The use of chemical weapons was later confirmed by a UN Investigative Commission.[190]

Previously, US President Barack Obama had stated that chemical weapons use would cross a "red line,"[191] and, after the 2013 attack, indicated he would seek Congressional authorization for a limited military strike into Syria in order to deter further use of chemical weapons.[192] In his 2009 Nobel Lecture, President Obama had earlier articulated the view "that force can be justified on humanitarian grounds, as it was in the Balkans . . . ."[193] However, in making a proposal to Congress in a draft resolution sent to the Senate Foreign Relations Committee, the US used a "mix of justifications" for the proposed use of force in Syria,[194] never clearly articulating the words "humanitarian intervention."[195] Then State

---

[188] See Arms Control Association, *Timeline of Syrian Chemical Weapons Activity, 2012–2018*, at www.armscontrol.org/factsheets/Timeline-of-Syrian-Chemical-Weapons-Activity. Those launching the attack had access to the Syrian military chemical weapons stockpile and expertise and equipment to manipulate large amounts of chemical agents, leading to the conclusion that the attack was launched by Government forces.

[189] Médecins Sans Frontières, *Syria: Thousands Suffering Neurotoxic Symptoms Treated in Hospitals Supported by MSF* (Aug. 24, 2013), at www.msf.org/syria-thousands-suffering-neurotoxic-symptoms-treated-hospitals-supported-msf.

[190] United Nations Mission to Investigate Allegations of the Use of Chemical Weapons in the Syrian Arab Republic, Report on the Alleged Use of Chemical Weapons in the Ghouta Area of Damascus on 21 August 2013, September 13, 2013, at www.un.org/zh/focus/northafrica/cw investigation.pdf (finding "clear and convincing evidence that surface-to-surface rockets containing the nerve agent Sarin were used").

[191] Glenn Kessler, *President Obama and the "Red Line" on Syria's Chemical Weapons*, WASH. POST (Sept. 6, 2013), at www.washingtonpost.com/news/fact-checker/wp/2013/09/06/president-obama-and-the-red-line-on-syrias-chemical-weapons/?noredirect=on&utm_term=.fdac9d3acdfa.

[192] Peter Baker & Jonathan Weisman, *Obama Seeks Approval by Congress for Strike in Syria*, N.Y. TIMES (Aug. 31, 2013), at www.nytimes.com/2013/09/01/world/middleeast/syria.html.

[193] Barack Hussein Obama, A Just and Lasting Peace, Nobel Lecture, December 10, 2009.

[194] Stahn [Between Law-Breaking and Law-Making], *supra* note 58, at 27. The closest the US comes to invoking humanitarian intervention is perhaps the cryptic statement of White House counsel Kathryn Ruemmler that while any forcible action against Syria without authorization by the Security Council would not fit "a traditionally recognized legal basis under international law," it would nonetheless be "justified and legitimate under international law." Charles Savage, *Obama Tests Limits of Power in Syria Conflict*, N.Y. TIMES (Sept. 8, 2013).

[195] The draft resolution sent to the Senate Foreign Relations Committee referenced three core objectives: "(i) respond to the use of weapons of mass destruction by the Syrian government in the conflict in Syria"; (ii) "deter Syria's use of such weapons in order to protect the national security interest of the United States and to protect our allies and partners against the use of such weapons"; and (iii) "degrade Syria's capacity to use such weapons in the future." In his Address to the Nation, President Obama combined arguments on deterrence, threats of

Department Legal Adviser Harold H. Koh was later critical of the US's failure to articulate a legal theory, arguing that "Syria is a law-making moment. It should be treated that way .... Continuing to threaten military action in Syria without stating a public legal rationale creates a dangerous precedent."[196] As discussed in Chapter 5, President Obama later postponed Congress' vote on the use of force while negotiations were pursued to implement a chemical weapons inspection and disarmament regime proposed by Russia.[197]

After that 2013 chemical weapons attack, the UK, by contrast, more clearly endorsed the doctrine of "humanitarian intervention," with the British Prime Minister's Office in August 2013 issuing a statement of the Government's legal position that "a legal basis [to use force was] ... available, under the doctrine of humanitarian intervention [subject to certain conditions] ... ."[198] The UK position paper also articulated criteria for the use of humanitarian intervention, requiring that:

> (i) there is convincing evidence, generally accepted by the international community as a whole, of extreme humanitarian distress on a large scale, requiring immediate and urgent relief;
>
> (ii) it must be objectively clear that there is no practicable alternative to the use of force if lives are to be saved; and
>
> (iii) the proposed use of force must be necessary and proportionate to the aim of relief of humanitarian need and must be strictly limited in time and scope to this aim (i.e. the minimum necessary to achieve that end and for no other purpose).[199]

The UK did not ultimately intervene either, due to lack of approval from Parliament.[200] In 2013, France also indicated a willingness to undertake

---

further attacks, collective self-defense, and enforcement of norms. *See* Remarks by the President in Address to the Nation on Syria, September 10, 2013, *at* https://obamawhitehouse.archives.gov/the-press-office/2013/09/10/remarks-president-address-nation-syria. *See also* Stahn [Between Law-Breaking and Law-Making], *supra* note 58 (discussing the US position).

[196] Sarvarian, *supra* note 3, at 30, *citing* Koh, *supra* note 114.
[197] Timeline of Syrian Chemical Weapons Activity, *supra* note 188; *see also* Chapter 5.1.
[198] UK Prime Minister's Office, Chemical Weapon Use by Syrian Regime: UK Government Legal Position, policy paper (Aug. 29, 2013), *at* www.gov.uk/government/publications/chemical-weapon-use-by-syrian-regime-uk-government-legal-position/chemical-weapon-use-by-syrian-regime-uk-government-legal-position-html-version [hereinafter, UK 2013 Legal Position].
[199] *Id.*
[200] *Syria Crisis: Cameron Loses Commons Vote on Syria Action*, BBC (Aug. 30, 2013), *at* www.bbc.com/news/uk-politics-23892783. *See also* Bethlehem, *supra* note 31 ("The debate in the UK Parliament, and the vote thereafter, cannot be taken as a rejection of a right of humanitarian intervention. References to the law in the debate were brief, passing and inconclusive.").

2.3 "Humanitarian Intervention" Post-R2P

military action in response to the chemical weapons attack, while also not expressly invoking the term "humanitarian intervention."[201]

The UK position paper thus not only defended the doctrine of "humanitarian intervention" post-R2P (as had President Obama), but, importantly provides criteria for its use. Such criteria are extremely important – if one defends "humanitarian intervention at all – in order to distinguish a bona fide humanitarian intervention (if one believes this concept exists) from one that is not. Denmark has issued a similar position paper.[202]

The UK Parliament, however, appears more cautious than the UK executive. A 2015 Briefing Paper by the House of Commons suggests the "UK is keen to develop international law on humanitarian intervention" (that is, suggesting that humanitarian intervention is not supported by existing law), and, while noting the criteria articulated by the UK in 2013, concludes "there is not yet enough consistent state practice and legal opinion to establish clear rules of customary international law on the criteria for humanitarian intervention."[203] Thus, there may not be full unanimity on this issue even within the branches of the UK government.[204]

After the massive August 2013 chemical weapons attack, there was no military response, as another approach appeared viable. As further explored in Chapter 5, pursuant to a US and Russian Framework Agreement,[205] Syria became a party to the Convention on the Prohibition of the Development, Production, Stockpiling and Use of Chemical Weapons and on their Destruction (CWC), with inspection and disarmament obligations

---

[201] *French Intelligence: Syria's Assad Behind Chemical Attack*, REUTERS (Sept. 2, 2013), at www.reuters.com/article/us-syria-crisis-france-chemical/french-intelligence-syrias-assad-behind-chemical-attack-idUSBRE9810GQ20130902 ("The dossier [suggesting Assad's fighters were behind the attack] is central to President François Hollande's calls for Assad to be punished with military action for the reported chemical attack on areas controlled by Syrian rebels …"); *see also* Sarvarian, *supra* note 3, at 34 (analyzing French Government statements in 2013, but noting the lack of express invocation of the term "humanitarian intervention").

[202] *General Principled Considerations on the Legal Basis for a Possible Military Operation in Syria*, UPN ALM. BILAG (Aug. 30, 2013), at www.ft.dk/samling/20121/almdel/upn/bilag/298/1276299/index.htm.

[203] House of Commons Library, Briefing Paper, No. 7404, Legal Basis for UK Military Action in Syria, at 21 (Dec. 1, 2015).

[204] The UK updated its legal position in 2018. See Policy Paper: Syria Action – UK Government Legal Position (Apr. 14, 2018), at www.gov.uk/government/publications/syria-action-uk-government-legal-position/syria-action-uk-government-legal-position. [hereinafter, April 14, 2018 UK Legal Position]

[205] Joint National Paper by the Russian Federation and the United States of America, Framework for Elimination of Syrian Chemical Weapons, EC-M-33/NAT.1 (Sept. 17, 2013), at www.opcw.org/fileadmin/OPCW/EC/M-33/ecm33nato1_e_.pdf.

memorialized in Security Council Resolution 2118,[206] and weapons-grade chemicals were shipped out of Syria.[207] In 2014, an OPCW Fact-Finding Mission (OPCW FFM) was created[208] and empowered to examine chemical weapons use in Syria,[209] and, in 2015, by Resolution 2235, the Security Council created an OPCW-UN Joint Investigative Mechanism (JIM) to identify those responsible for chemical weapons attacks.[210] As detailed more extensively in Chapter 5,[211] notwithstanding an initial dip in chemical weapons attacks after chemical weapons disarmament was pursued and after the creation of the investigative mechanisms,[212] chemical weapons attacks later continued.[213] The JIM's mandate expired in November 2017, after its renewal was vetoed three times by Russia.[214]

2.3.2 Military Strikes in Syria in 2017 and 2018 in Response to Chemical Weapons Attacks

The dilemma about humanitarian intervention again resurfaced in April 2017, when – despite various efforts to curtail Syria's ability to use chemical weapons[215] – the Assad regime on April 4, 2017, used sarin gas, a nerve agent, killing dozens of people in Syria's northern Idlib province.[216] In response, on

---

[206] See S/RES/2118 (2013) (requiring Syria to dispose of its chemical weapons stockpiles and cooperate with the Organisation for the Prohibition of Chemical Weapons).
[207] Van Schaack [IMAGINING JUSTICE], supra note 111.
[208] "In response to persistent allegations of chemical weapon attacks in Syria, the OPCW Fact Finding Mission (FFM) was set up in 2014 'to establish facts surrounding allegations of the use of toxic chemicals, reportedly chlorine, for hostile purposes in the Syrian Arab Republic.'" Organisation for the Prohibition of Chemical Weapons [hereinafter, OPCW], at www.opcw.org/special-sections/syria/the-fact-finding-mission.
[209] For reports of the OPCW-FFM, see id.
[210] See S/RES/2235 (2015). The JIM's mandate was extended twice. S/RES/2314 (2016); S/RES/2319 (2016). The OPCW-FFM's findings were the basis for the work of the JIM.
[211] Chapter 5 contains a chronological discussion of chemical weapons attacks in Syria and use of the veto. See Chapter 5.1.5.
[212] Creation of the two investigative mechanisms appears to have had a positive impact, in that after creation of the OPCW-FFM and through at least the early work of the JIM, there is a nearly two year gap in chemical weapons attacks documented by the Commission. See Chemical Weapons Attacks Documented by the Commission (Infographic), OHCHR, at www.ohchr.org/SiteCollectionImages/Bodies/HRCouncil/IICISyria/COISyria_ChemicalWeapons.jpg (listing no chemical weapons attacks between April 2014 and April 2016).
[213] Sarah Almukhtar, Most Chemical Attacks in Syria Get Little Attention. Here Are 34 Confirmed Cases, N.Y. TIMES (Apr. 13, 2018), at www.nytimes.com/interactive/2018/04/13/world/middleeast/syria-chemical-attacks-maps-history.html.
[214] See note 177 supra (three vetoes of the renewal of the JIM).
[215] As detailed in Chapter 5, efforts to curtail Syria's ability to use chemical weapons were undermined by a series of six vetoes related to chemical weapons. See Chapter 5.1.5.
[216] See Timeline of Syrian Chemical Weapons Activity, supra note 188.

April 6, 2017, the US (under the administration of President Trump) launched a missile strike targeting the air base from which the Assad regime is believed to have launched its attack.[217] No legal justification was provided by the US, leaving it somewhat unclear whether the US was invoking the theory of humanitarian intervention.[218] No other legal theory, however, appears to fit: (1) there was no Security Council authorization; (2) while the US has invoked self-defense as to ISIL and "al-Qaeda elements in Syria known as the Khorasan Group," it has not done so regarding the Assad regime;[219] and (3) while the Assad regime may have implicitly consented to (or at least to some extent tolerated) foreign military intervention in Syria against ISIL, it certainly has not consented to use of force against itself.

The same dilemma then resurfaced in April 2018 when the Assad regime again used chemical weapons, this time in Douma, a suburb outside Damascus, killing at least several dozen civilians, after smaller chlorine gas attacks in Douma on March 7 and 11.[220] This time, on April 13, 2018, a joint military strike by the US, UK, and France ensued, targeting three chemical weapons facilities. The UK justified the strike on the basis of "humanitarian intervention," stating in a summary of legal advice that the strike was "permitted under international law, on an exceptional basis, to take measures to alleviate overwhelming humanitarian suffering."[221] The US and France did not articulate separate legal theories, leaving the rationales for their uses of force somewhat unclear, although their silence perhaps suggested they were joining the UK's legal theory. In a televised address, President Trump stated: "The purpose of our actions tonight is to establish a strong deterrent against the production, spread and use of chemical

---

[217] See id.
[218] See also Koh [The Real "Red Line"], supra note 114 (noting '[t]he glaring absence of an official U.S. legal justification for humanitarian intervention …"); Schmitt & Ford, supra note 8, at 303 ("If … this commendable norm of [humanitarian intervention] is ever to fully crystallize, States must have the moral courage to set forth their legal basis for use of force in the form of explicit expressions of opinio juris.").
[219] Letter Pursuant to UN Charter Article 51, dated 23 September 2014, from the Permanent Representative of the Unites States of America to the United Nations Addressed to the Secretary-General, S/2014/695, at http://dag.un.org/bitstream/handle/11176/89298/S_2014_695-EN.pdf?sequence=21&isAllowed=y.
[220] Id.
[221] April 14, 2018 UK Legal Position, supra note 204. See also the 8233rd Meeting of the Security Council on April 14, 2018 (S/PV.8233).

weapons,"[222] which would be consistent with a theory of humanitarian intervention.[223]

Could these missile strikes into Syria have met the UK's test as permissible humanitarian intervention? Probably (although the intervening states should bear the burden of demonstrating this).[224] Certainly, in 2013 the criteria of "extreme humanitarian distress on a large scale, requiring immediate and urgent relief" would appear to have been met by the hundreds of fatalities and thousands of injuries caused by the August 2013 chemical weapons attack. The attacks in spring 2017 and spring 2018 resulted in far fewer fatalities, but by then the Assad regime had been implicated in many such attacks, so, possibly, the figures should be viewed on a cumulative basis.[225] Human Rights Watch, for example, has documented a total of eighty-five chemical weapons attacks in Syria since 2013.[226]

As to there being "no practicable alternative to the use of force," in 2013 there arguably did appear to be an alternative – the Russian plan for chemical weapons inspection and disarmament, which was then pursued. Many chemical weapons attacks later and in light of Russia's eventual veto (three times) of the renewal of the mandate of the JIM,[227] the inspections and disarmament regime appears to have failed in significant part. Thus, by 2017 and 2018, one can more credibly claim there was no practicable alternative.

Finally, the use of force in 2017 and 2018 was certainly limited, so likely meets the criterion of proportionality. Was it necessary? It certainly conveyed

---

[222] *President Trump on Syria Strikes: Full Transcript and Video*, N.Y. TIMES (Apr. 13, 2018), at www.nytimes.com/2018/04/13/world/middleeast/trump-syria-airstrikes-full-transcript.html.

[223] President Trump somewhat inconsistently then went on to say: "Establishing this deterrent is a vital national security interest of the United States," which sounds more like an invocation of self-defense. *Id.*

[224] The UK did argue that all three conditions were met in 2013. *See* UK 2013 Legal Position, *supra* note 198. Their memorandum predated Russia's proposal for a chemical weapons inspection regime, which then appeared to provide an alternative. It was only later that this "alternative" proved insufficient to halt further attacks – so, it was not in fact a viable alternative. The UK also issued a position paper in 2018 arguing that all three conditions were also met in 2018. April 14, 2018, UK Legal Position, *supra* note 204.

[225] *But see* Schmitt & Ford, *supra* note 8, at 302 (the 2017 strikes did not meet the quantum of harm required for humanitarian intervention).

[226] Sarah Almukhtar, *Most Chemical Attacks in Syria Get Little Attention. Here Are 34 Confirmed Cases*, N.Y. TIMES (Apr. 13, 2018), *at* www.nytimes.com/interactive/2018/04/13/world/middleeast/syria-chemical-attacks-maps-history.html (attributing most attacks discussed in that report to regime forces and some as "unknown" in source).

[227] *See supra* note 177 (three vetoes of the renewal of the JIM).

a message to the regime as to the complete impermissibility of chemical weapons use that does not appear to have been successfully conveyed previously. In terms of whether it was the "minimum necessary to achieve" its end, the strikes were indeed limited in scope. Thus, yes, the UK criteria arguably could have been met.[228]

Note, however, that these are only the UK's criteria. Whether they are the correct criteria for judging the bona fides of humanitarian intervention (for those who accept that concept) probably warrants additional legal scrutiny. That said, this author sees no obvious flaws in the UK's criteria.[229] Necessity and proportionality, for instance, are basic criteria required for any use of force.[230] Some have additionally suggested the criterion of the "disinterestedness of the intervening States and/or organizations,"[231] sometimes phrased as "political neutrality," although it is also suggested that complete disinterestedness or neutrality is unrealistic, since a completely disinterested or neutral state is unlikely to intervene.[232] Also suggested as criteria are "the inability or unwillingness

---

[228] See also Chatham House, *Syria and International Law: Use of Force and State Responsibility*, at 4 (International Law Discussion Group Summary, Elizabeth Wilmshurst, chair, Sept. 20, 2013) ("the conditions [for humanitarian intervention] were met in the case of Syria following the chemical weapons attack in eastern Damascus on 21 August 2013"); Ilan Fuchs & Harry Borowski, *The New World Order: Humanitarian Interventions from Kosovo to Liberia and Perhaps Syria?*, 65 SYRACUSE L. REV. 304, 342 (2015) (as to Syria "there is ample reason to intervene on humanitarian grounds without the approval of the Security Council").

[229] Concepts such as "just cause, right intention, last resort, and proportionality of means" "hark[en] back to ... just war doctrine." Stahn [Political Rhetoric or Emerging Legal Norm?], *supra* note 132, at 114.

[230] See, e.g., Henderson, *supra* note 47, at 181 ("necessity" and "proportionality" are "customary international law principles"); Rodley, *supra* note 7, at 790–91 (agreeing that necessity and proportionality are relevant criteria); Fuchs & Borowski, *supra* note 228, at 328 ("the principles of necessity, proportionality, and immediacy" are to be respected "if any intervention is to be deemed legal"); Nanda, *supra* note 20, at 311 ("any use of force is subject to the limitations of 'necessity' and 'proportionality'").

[231] Sarvarian, *supra* note 3, at 22, *quoting* Lowe & Tzanakopoulos, *supra* note 3, at para. 39.

[232] Rodley, *supra* note 7, at 789 ("It would be too much to demand immaculate selflessness, but that any external political advantage should be outweighed by the humanitarian motive. A fair test could be whether the intervention would not have happened *but for* the humanitarian exigency."). See also Murphy, *supra* note 10, at 323 ("To assert that states must be wholly 'disinterested' in participating in humanitarian intervention ignores rudimentary aspects of geo-political behavior and may discourage any interventions from occurring at all."); Hilpold, *supra* note 11, at 464 ("It is neither possible nor necessary to ascertain whether an act of humanitarian intervention has been carried out mainly or exclusively for purely humanitarian reasons. What really matters is whether the act of intervention has brought relief to the endangered population and to what extent the pursuit of self-interests ... constitutes a real threat to the peace ... .").

of the territorial state to address the situation" (which certainly would be met in the situation of Syria) and "multilateral action only (i.e. no unilateral action)" (which would be met by the 2018 strike, but not the 2017 unilateral strike).[233] Given that R2P is triggered by the commission of genocide, crimes against humanity, and/or war crimes[234] – as are the "responsibility not to veto" found in the ACT "Code of Conduct" and French/Mexican initiative (detailed in Chapter 3)[235] – the trigger for "humanitarian intervention" (to the extent it exists) should probably also be the occurrence of these crimes. They at least have precise definitions under the ICC's Rome Statute,[236] as opposed to the imprecise formulation "extreme humanitarian distress on a large scale."[237] (Either formulation would appear to have been met as to the situation in Syria, where war crimes and crimes against humanity have been well-documented in numerous reports of the Commission of Inquiry.)[238]

Initial reactions from the scholarly community to the 2017 and 2018 missile strikes have generally been negative, with most taking the view that the strikes

---

[233] Sarvarian, *supra* note 3, at 31, *citing* Lowe & Tzanakopoulos [Humanitarian Intervention], *supra* note 3. The International Law Association in 1974 suggested twelve criteria for judging the *bona fides* of humanitarian intervention. See Hilpold, *supra* note 11, at 455–56, *citing* Third Interim Report of the Subcommittee on the International Protection of Human Rights by General International Law, ILA Report of the Fifty-Sixth Conference, at 217 (1974). See also Fonteyne, *supra* note 8, at 258–68 (suggesting and analyzing possible criteria); Nanda, *supra* note 20, at 330 (suggesting criteria); Adam Roberts, *The So-Called Right of Humanitarian Intervention*, 3 Y.B. INT'L HUMANITARIAN L. 3, 33–44 (2000) (suggesting and evaluating criteria); Harold H. Koh, *Symposium on Unauthorized Military Interventions for the Public Good: Humanitarian Intervention: Time for Better Law*, 111 Unbound 287, 289 (suggesting criteria).

[234] See, e.g., Chapter 2.2 (2004 R2P Report, World Summit Outcome Document, 2009 R2P Report). Inclusion of "ethnic cleansing" in formulations of R2P is probably unnecessary as it is not a crime recognized under international criminal law. See Arbour, *supra* note 7, at 450 ("ethnic cleansing" "is not, as such, a legal term of art").

[235] See Chapter 3.1.3–4.

[236] Rome Statute of the International Criminal Court, Arts. 6–8, July 17, 1998, U.N. Doc. A/CONF.183/9 [hereinafter, Rome Statute].

[237] See Rodley, *supra* note 7, at 777 ("Earlier discussion had to cope with the problem of what types or levels of human rights violations or abuse could justify 'humanitarian intervention' if it were permitted at all. While problems of scope and intensity remain, the notions of genocide, ethnic cleansing, war crimes and crimes against humanity offer sufficient criteria of seriousness . . . .").

[238] See note 112 *supra* (COI reports). The Commission of Inquiry also found grounds to believe genocide was committed by ISIL. Report of the Independent International Commission of Inquiry on the Syrian Arab Republic: They Came to Destroy: ISIS Crimes against the Yazidis, U.N. Doc. A/HRC/32/CRP.2 (June 15, 2016), *at* www.ohchr.org/Documents/HRBodies/HR Council/CoISyria/A_HRC_32_CRP.2_en.pdf.

were breaches of the Charter system;[239] contrary views have also been articulated.[240] The reaction by states appears to have been far more positive.[241]

2.3.3 The Extent to Which "Humanitarian Intervention" Continues as a Viable Doctrine

Thus, at present, the doctrine of humanitarian intervention is quite contested. There appear to be only four states that endorse it recently, of which only two have done so expressly. That the US and France appear to selectively utilize "humanitarian intervention" without being willing to publicly articulate support for the doctrine is troubling. While three of the four states have significant military capabilities, even the practice of these states most likely does not constitute sufficient state "practice," and their legal positions (such as they are) likely do not constitute *opinio juris* for the international community as a whole – especially when so many other states deny the existence of a doctrine of "humanitarian

---

[239] See, e.g., Anders Henriksen, *The Legality of Using Force to Deter Chemical Warfare*, JUST SECURITY (Apr. 17, 2018) ("Most commentators agree that last week's missile strikes on Syria by the United States, the United Kingdom and France violated international law ... ."); Dapo Akande, *The Doctrine of "Humanitarian Intervention" and the Legality of the UK's Air Strikes against the Assad Government in Syria*, GLOB. RESEARCH (Apr. 26, 2018), at www.globalresearch.ca/the-doctrine-of-humanitarian-intervention-and-the-legality-of-the-uks-air-strikes-against-the-assad-government-in-syria/5637943 ("The military action taken was not in accordance with the United Nations Charter and international law."); Julian Ku, *Trump's Syria Strike Clearly Broke International Law – and No One Seems to Care*" (Apr. 19, 2017), at https://scholarlycommons.law.hofstra.edu/cgi/viewcontent.cgi?article=2159&context=faculty_scholarship; Schmitt & Ford, *supra* note 8, at 302 (the 2017 strikes "do not appear to qualify as lawful humanitarian intervention"); Marko Milanović, *The Clearly Illegal US Missile Strike in Syria*, EJIL: TALK! (Apr. 7, 2017), at www.ejiltalk.org/the-clearly-illegal-us-missile-strike-in-syria.
[240] See, e.g., Jennifer Trahan, *The Narrow Case for the Legality of Strikes in Syria and Russia's Illegitimate Veto*, OPINIO JURIS (Apr. 23, 2018), at http://opiniojuris.org/2018/04/23/the-narrow-case-for-the-legality-of-strikes-in-syria-and-russias-illegitimate-veto; Andrew Bell, *Syria, Chemical Weapons, and a Qualitative Threshold for Humanitarian Intervention*, JUST SECURITY (Apr. 10, 2018), at www.justsecurity.org/54665/syria-chemical-weapons-international-law-developing-qualitative-threshold-humanitarian-intervention (calling for an "improved legal framework using a qualitative threshold – legitimizing humanitarian intervention against regimes that use chemical and biological weapons (CBW) on civilians"); Koh, *supra* note 233 (analyzing the 2017 strikes as not per se illegal).
[241] Henriksen notes "international reactions to the missile strikes have been surprisingly positive." Henriksen, *supra* note 239. See also Schmitt & Ford, *supra* note 8, at 303 (citing public support for the 2017 strikes from the US, UK, Australia, Canada, Israel, Japan, Spain, Italy, Saudi Arabia, Jordan, and Turkey, with France and Germany issuing a joint statement implicitly support the US action, and positive statements by EU and NATO officials).

intervention."[242] Thus, "humanitarian intervention" probably is not "customary international law,"[243] and, even if it were, one has to also fit it into the UN Charter, and explain not only why "humanitarian intervention" is permissible under the Charter, but where it in fact is authorized or fits into the Charter.[244]

Scholarly views on humanitarian intervention remain similarly divided, with many opining on its illegality,[245] some opining on its

---

[242] The four states are also not a geographically representative sampling. See Byers & Chesterman, *supra* note 64, at 191, 193 ("The views [on humanitarian intervention] from African and other developing states are frequently overlooked by Anglo-American authors," also lamenting that "powerful states have always had a disproportionate influence on customary law-making.").

[243] See, e.g., *id.* at 187 (state practice is insufficient, based on the Kosovo intervention, to support a new rule of customary international law supporting humanitarian intervention); Wood, *supra* note 4, at 362 ("It is difficult to demonstrate that State practice and *opinio juris* since the safe havens in northern Iraq in 1991, or the Kosovo intervention in 1999, have moved in the direction of those claiming the existence in customary international law of such a right.").

[244] See, e.g., Sarvarian, *supra* note 3, at 24 ("Even if humanitarian intervention were to qualify [as] a norm of customary international law, it is contended that the comprehensive prohibition on the use of force in Art 2(4) of the Charter remains a superior norm."). Addressing how customary law on humanitarian intervention might interlay with the Charter, former UK Legal Adviser to the Foreign Office Sir Daniel Bethlehem writes:

> As regards the relationship of such a principle with the UN Charter, three possible constitutional theories are apparent: (a) the customary international law principle could sit alongside the UN Charter (following the reasoning of the International Court of Justice in the *Nicaragua* case); (b) the customary international law principle could operate at an interpretative level, by reference to the interpretative canon reflected in Article 31(3)(c) of the Vienna Convention on the Law of Treaties, as regards the interpretation of the scope of Article 2(4) and other provisions of the UN Charter; and/or (c) the principle could be regarded as a supervening, later in time, principle of customary international law for purposes of filling in the gaps in, or even prevailing over elements of, the UN Charter.

Bethlehem, *supra* note 31. Note that the Charter has been modified by custom in at least one respect – permitting a permanent member to abstain from voting which still allows a resolution to pass (despite the wording of UN Charter Article 27(3) requiring "concurring votes"). However, use of force issues are more complex, since the prohibition on aggressive force outside the Charter's framework is said to have *jus cogens* status. International Law Commission, Articles on the Responsibility of States for Internationally Wrongful Acts, Art. 26 ("Those peremptory norms that are clearly accepted and recognized include the prohibition[] of aggression ... .").

[245] See, e.g., Rodley, *supra* note 7, at 775–76 (the majority of scholars reject the lawfulness of unilateral humanitarian intervention); Kreß [The State Conduct Element], *supra* note 6, at 499 ("A majority of scholars are of the view that state practice since 1945 ... is insufficient to support the conclusion that a use of force that is carried out ... to avert a humanitarian catastrophe ... is lawful."); *see, e.g.*, Tams, *supra* note 11, at 367 ("the available evidence makes it extremely difficult to argue that contemporary international law recognizes a right of humanitarian intervention"); Chesterman, *supra* note 50, at 235 ("There is ... minimal state

legality,[246] and some (including this author) arguing it is legitimate if not fully legal and thus at least falls into a "grey area" in terms of legality.[247]

2.3.4 The Relationship between "Humanitarian Intervention" and the International Criminal Court's Crime of Aggression

A final related question arises whether "humanitarian intervention," if it is not fully legal, could fall within the ambit of the ICC's fourth crime, the crime of aggression, as to which jurisdiction activated on July 17, 2018.[248]

The author (and quite a few others) have argued that there is enough endorsement of the legitimacy of humanitarian intervention and/or ambiguity as to its legal status, that it can be said to at least fall within a "grey area" in terms of legality, so that its use, if bona fide (for example, meeting criteria of legitimacy) would not constitute the crime of aggression.[249] Specifically, the

practice and virtually no *opinio juris* that supports a general right of humanitarian intervention.").

[246] See, e.g., Greenwood [Essays on War], *supra* note 20, at 625; FERNANDO R. TESÓN, HUMANITARIAN INTERVENTION: AN INQUIRY INTO LAW AND MORALITY 313–17 (2d ed. 1997); Nanda, *supra* note 20, at 310–11, 334; Fonteyne, *supra* note 8, at 269; Richard B. Lillich, *Humanitarian Intervention: A Reply to Ian Brownlie and a Plea for Constructive Alternatives*, in LAW AND CIVIL WAR IN THE MODERN WORLD 229 (John N. Moore ed., 1974); Weller [Introduction], *supra* note 22, at 3, 31 (at least leaning in the same direction).

[247] See, e.g., Roberts, *supra* note 233; ROBERT KOLB, IUS CONTRA BELLUM: LE DROIT INTERNATIONAL RELATIF AU MAINTIEN DE LA PAIX 315 (2d ed. 2009); Franck, *supra* note 14, at 172; Tams, *supra* note 11, at 367 ("it is at best a case of 'dark grey'"); Jennifer Trahan, *Defining the "Grey Area" Where Humanitarian Intervention May Not Be Fully Legal, But Is Not the Crime of Aggression*, 2 J. USE FORCE & INT'L L. 42 (2015); Kreβ [The State Conduct Element], *supra* note 6, at 500 ("A third, and perhaps more rarely recorded, group of scholars, rather than expressing a view on the question of lawfulness, emphasise that a use of force to avert a humanitarian catastrophe will, if stringent conditions are met, fall in a legal grey area." "Perhaps this last formulation best captures the complex picture that results from the above-summarised practice of state."); *see also* Kosovo Commission Report, *supra* note 43, at 164 (discussing "a gray zone of ambiguity").

[248] ICC-ASP/16/Res.5 (Dec. 14, 2017) (activating resolution with ICC crime of aggression jurisdiction commencing July 17, 2018).

[249] See Trahan [Defining the "Grey Area"], *supra* note 247, at 58; Kreβ [The State Conduct Element], *supra* note 6, at 502 ("It follows that the use of force to avert a humanitarian catastrophe falls within the grey area of the current international law on the use of force."); Beth Van Schaack, *The Crime of Aggression and Humanitarian Intervention on Behalf of Women*, 11 INT'L CRIM. L. REV. 477, 479 (2011); CARRIE MCDOUGALL, THE CRIME OF AGGRESSION UNDER THE ROME STATUTE OF THE INTERNATIONAL CRIMINAL COURT 125 (2013); Roger S. Clark, *Amendments to the Rome Statute of the International Criminal Court Considered at the First Review Conference on the Court, Kampala, 31 May–11 June 2010*, 2 GÖTTINGEN J. INT'L L. 689, 698 (2010); Matthew Gillett, *The Anatomy of an International Crime: Aggression at the International Criminal Court?*, 13 INT'L CRIM. L. REV. 829, 853 (2013); Noah Weisbord, *Judging Aggression*, 50 COLUM. J. TRANSNAT'L L. 82, 167 (2011);

ICC crime of aggression only criminalizes individual conduct in relationship to a state act of aggression that constitutes a "manifest" violation of the UN Charter by its "character, gravity, and scale."[250] This requirement means that only clear cases should be prosecuted, which excludes anything in a legal "grey area."[251] Even if such a case were to proceed, there would be numerous potentially applicable affirmative defenses and mitigating factors that could extinguish or minimize responsibility, although it should be unnecessary to reach those as there would not have been a state act of aggression.[252]

Because the US is not a party to the ICC's Rome Statute (and excluded from the ICC's jurisdiction over the crime of aggression),[253] and the UK and France are not parties to the crime of aggression amendment to the Rome Statute (so there arguably is no jurisdiction related to UK and French uses of force),[254]

Joshua L. Root, *"First, Do No Harm": Interpreting the Crime of Aggression to Exclude Humanitarian Intervention*, 2 U. BALTIMORE J. INT'L L. 63, 88, 97 (2013–14); Keith A. Petty, *Criminalizing Force: Resolving the Threshold Question for the Crime of Aggression in the Context of Modern Conflict*, 33 SEATTLE U. L. REV. 105, 123 (2009); Tom Ruys, *The Meaning of "Force" and the Boundaries of the* Jus ad Bellum: *Are "Minimal" Uses of Force Excluded from UN Charter Article 2(4)?*, 108 AM. J. INT'L L. 159, 165 (2014).

[250] Rome Statute, *supra* note 236, Art. 8*bis*, para 1; *see, e.g.*, Kreβ [The State Conduct Element], *supra* note 6, at 508 (explaining the reasons for the "manifest" requirement or threshold).

[251] These arguments are explored in far greater detail in Trahan [Defining the "Grey Area"], *supra* note 247. *See also, e.g.*, I. Hurd, *Is Humanitarian Intervention Legal? The Rule of Law in an Incoherent World*, 25 ETHICS & INT'L AFF. (2011), 293, 311 ("Contemporary international law can be read as either allowing or forbidding international humanitarian intervention, and the legal uncertainty around humanitarian intervention is fundamental and irresolvable."); *see also* note 43 *supra* (Kosovo Commission Report describing humanitarian intervention as falling in a legal grey zone).

[252] *See* Trahan [Defining the "Grey Area"], *supra* note 247, at 62–65 (examining affirmative defenses and mitigating factors that would apply). The argument that Byers and Chesterman invoke, that humanitarian intervention is illegal, but should be done in exceptional circumstances ("exceptional illegality") does not mesh well with the activation of the jurisdiction of the ICC's crime of aggression. *See* Byers & Chesterman, *supra* note 64, at 200–01.

[253] Under the ICC crime of aggression, non ICC States Parties are completely excluded from ICC jurisdiction over the crime of aggression. *See* Rome Statute, *supra* note 236, Art. 15*bis*, para. 5.

[254] The activating resolution adopted at the December 2017 meeting of the ICC's Assembly of States Parties appears to have limited dramatically the ICC's jurisdiction over the crime of aggression for purposes of article 15*bis* (State Party referral and *proprio motu*). *See* ICC-ASP/16/Res.5 (Dec. 14, 2017). This author has raised questions as to whether that limitation is a valid construction of the Kampala crime of aggression amendment's jurisdictional regime, or has *changed* the jurisdictional regime, which change arguably should have been accomplished by another Rome Statute amendment, and not an activating resolution. *See* Jennifer Trahan, *From Kampala to New York—The Final Negotiations to Activate the Jurisdiction of the International Criminal Court over the Crime of Aggression*, 18 INT'L CRIM. LAW REV. 197 (2018). Thus, under the text of the activating resolution, there is no Article 15*bis* jurisdiction over a Rome Statute State Party that commits an act of aggression but has not

and ICC jurisdiction over the crime only commenced on July 17, 2018 and is not retroactive, these arguments are, at present, hypothetical.[255]

2.4 CONCLUSION

Because the problem of veto use, or threat of veto use, in the face of atrocity crimes has not been solved, and there are times that intervention will be blocked at the Security Council despite ongoing atrocity crimes, certain states probably still *will* be tempted to invoke and utilize "humanitarian intervention." This happened with NATO's intervention in Kosovo. More recently, the UK and Denmark still expressly support the doctrine; the US and France have implicitly relied on it; and the US (in 2017) and the US, UK, and France (in 2018) appear to have utilized the doctrine as a basis for justifying airstrikes into Syria in response to the regime's use of chemical weapons.

At the same time, "humanitarian intervention" is generally *not* endorsed by most states, and its implementation carries clear risks – both to the legal order, and on the ground (that is, whether it achieves any good). Even if one accepts "humanitarian intervention" in theory, it is unclear whether it has been adequately defined and/or whether the UK's criteria should be generally accepted criteria for evaluating its bona fides; it also is troubling to leave it to the intervening state or states to determine whether it is being properly invoked and/or the criteria are met.

While the doctrine of the "responsibility to protect" has provided critical momentum toward solidifying the norm that the international community does have a responsibility to act in the face of atrocity crimes, R2P ultimately provides a disappointing response when Security Council action is blocked.

---

ratified the crime of aggression amendment (and the UK and France have not ratified the crime of aggression amendment). If, however, the activating resolution is not valid in limiting jurisdiction, then there could be such jurisdiction. This interpretative question regarding jurisdiction could be clarified by the ICC in the event that a Rome Statute State Party that has not ratified the crime of aggression amendment commits an act of aggression against a Rome Statute State Party that has ratified the crime of aggression amendment.

[255] Bringing an ICC case based on anything that resembles "humanitarian intervention" (that is, not something only pretextually dubbed as humanitarian intervention) would create extremely poor optics and high potential for an unsuccessful prosecution. Humanitarian intervention is presumably initiated with the goal of trying to prevent the very same atrocity crimes (genocide, crimes against humanity, and war crimes) that the ICC prosecutes; thus, prosecuting individuals responsible for attempting to prevent or curtail the commission of such crimes (unless other ICC crimes are committed in the process) would appear antithetical to the ICC's mandate of prosecuting the gravest crimes of concern to the international community. *See* Trahan [Defining the "Grey Area"], *supra* note 247 (trying to differentiate between a bona fide humanitarian intervention and one that is not).

R2P does call for voluntary veto restraint (a "responsibility not to veto") discussed in Chapter 3, and, if that were working, it would make R2P a much more potent tool; however, at least three permanent members of the Council refuse to endorse such voluntary veto restraint.[256] Thus, R2P's answer that the UN Security Council needs to authorize any form of forceful intervention means that intervention (and lesser uses of force and non-forceful measures as well) can still remain blocked due to use, or threat of the use, of the veto, even in the face of atrocity crimes.

The fortunes of R2P also appear on the decline given its disappointing performance regarding the situation in Libya, and its having been largely ignored with respect to the situation in Syria. In order to revitalize R2P, it could help to more strongly emphasize the actual hard law legal obligations underlying it, reinforcing the proposition that implementing at least those aspects is legally required. In fact, ideally, consequences also should flow from the breach of such hard law legal obligations.

If states are troubled by the risks associated with the doctrine of humanitarian intervention, and/or concerned about the lack of operationalization of R2P, one might reflect that it is in fact *the veto power that has been the true culprit*. For example, NATO states presumably did not go to the Security Council to seek authorization for use of force in Kosovo despite atrocity crimes commencing, knowing such a request would face a near-certain Russian veto. Similarly, had Security Council referral of the situation in Syria to the ICC not been blocked by the veto, and had renewal of the mandate for chemical weapons inspections that had been attributing responsibility to the side using the weapons not been blocked by the veto, there might long ago have been reason for regime actors in Syria to be deterred. Had there been such deterrence, at least regarding chemical weapons attacks, we might never have reached the point where the US, UK, and France perceived the need to launch retaliatory strikes. (Other uses of the veto or threat of the veto, discussed in Chapters 1 and 5, are equally problematic, but have not resulted in anything resembling "humanitarian intervention" and thus are not discussed in this Chapter.)[257]

Any discomfort states have with the doctrine of "humanitarian intervention" – and there appears to be great discomfort for most states who fear its

---

[256] *See* Chapter 3.

[257] For example, the crimes in Myanmar, Sri Lanka, and Darfur have simply been allowed to proceed virtually unimpeded, with many, and, in some instances, all Security Council measures blocked by the veto, or threat of veto (express or implied) of China. *See* Chapter 1 (overview of all three situations); Chapter 5 (detailed chronology of veto threats as to Darfur).

2.4 Conclusion

abusive invocation – or concern states have with the failure to implement R2P, should provide states incentive to work toward solving the problem of veto use in the face of atrocity crimes.[258] Until this pressing dilemma is solved, it may be difficult to fully operationalize R2P, particularly its "Pillar III," and certain states will be tempted to engage in humanitarian intervention. While this author has some sympathy toward the UK position on humanitarian intervention, it admittedly carries risks. Thus, the preferable course of action would be, as explored in Chapter 4, to tackle the problem of veto use in the face of atrocity crimes – recognizing that there are in fact legal limits to its use in the face of genocide, crimes against humanity, and/or war crimes imposed by existing obligations under international law. The recognition of such limits could potentially both strengthen the ability to implement R2P and lessen the need to invoke or utilize humanitarian intervention.

---

[258] *See also* Stahn [Between Law-Breaking and Law-Making], *supra* note 58, at 37 ("A better way forward [than humanitarian intervention] might be to work towards a more responsible use of veto powers in the future (i.e. understandings on the non-use of the veto in specific situations) . . . .").

3

Initiatives to Voluntarily Restrain Veto Use as to the Face of Atrocity Crimes

The core challenge to the Security Council and to the United Nations as a whole in the next century... is to forge unity behind the principle that massive and systematic violations of human rights—wherever they may take place—should not be allowed to stand. – Kofi Annan[1]

INTRODUCTION

This chapter explores initiatives that have sought voluntarily to restrain use of the veto in the face of atrocity crimes. They include: the "responsibility not to veto" found in the "responsibility to protect," the "S5 initiative," the French/Mexican initiative not to veto in the face of atrocity crimes, the ACT (Accountability, Coherence and Transparency) group of states' Code of Conduct, and a proposal by a group known as "The Elders." In addition to explaining the initiatives and providing background on them, this chapter evaluates the merits of each of the different approaches. Because all the initiatives call for *voluntary* veto restraint, until the recalcitrant permanent members of the Security Council (China, Russia, and the US) join these initiatives – which appears unlikely – the initiatives will not fully solve the problem of veto use, or the threat of veto use, in the face of atrocity crimes.

As discussed in Chapter 1, there have been periodic calls for reform of the Security Council in terms of both the Council's working methods and composition. Related to these have been initiatives designed to limit the use of the veto in situations where mass atrocity crimes are occurring. Two of the earlier initiatives, the "responsibility not to veto," found in

---

[1] *Secretary-General Presents His Annual Report to the General Assembly*, UN Press Release SG/SM/7136, GA/9596 (Sept. 20, 1999), *at* www.un.org/press/en/1999/19990920.sgsm7136.html.

formulations of the responsibility to protect (R2P) and the so-called "S5" initiative, met with limited success. Yet, these early forays contributed to the formation of the two subsequent initiatives, the "French/Mexican initiative," and the ACT "Code of Conduct," both of which have attracted fairly widespread support among UN Member States, including from two permanent members of the Security Council – France and the UK. Ultimately, however, both documents probably are seen as "soft law" – that is, articulating moral and/or political commitments. A similar commitment to veto restraint was sought by a group of elder-statespersons known as "The Elders,"[2] and there has even been momentum towards veto restraint by an earlier US-based task force, although this did not manifest in any formal commitment by the US. The initiatives have contributed to making significant progress towards veto restraint in the face of genocide, crimes against humanity, or war crimes, but have not, ultimately, reined in the use, or threat of the use, of the veto in such circumstances. Furthermore, as long as three permanent members refuse to join the initiatives, the problem of veto use in the face of atrocity crimes remains. Chapter 4, therefore, will suggest a different, but complementary, approach: reexamining existing hard law legal obligations that demonstrate that there are in fact legal limits (or constraints) to the use of the veto in the face of genocide, crimes against humanity, and/or war crimes imposed by such obligations.

3.1 THE DIFFERENT APPROACHES TO VOLUNTARY VETO RESTRAINT AS TO THE FACE OF ATROCITY CRIMES

The concept of calling for veto restraint, as explained in Chapter 1, originated during the Cold War, when the Security Council was facing voting paralysis. This manifested in early calls by the General Assembly in 1946,[3] 1947,[4] and 1949[5] General Assembly resolutions, for the Security Council to use every effort not to use the veto. For example, by 1949, the General Assembly recommended the veto be used "only when [the permanent members]

---

[2] See section 3.1.5 for discussion of "the Elders."
[3] UN G.A. Res. 40(1), para. 3 (Dec. 13, 1946) ("earnestly requesting" the permanent members to "make every effort ... to ensure that the use of the [veto] does not impede the Security Council in reaching its decisions").
[4] UN G.A. Res. 117(II), para. 3 (Nov. 21, 1947) (calling for the Security Council members to "consult with one another on the problem of voting in the Security Council").
[5] UN G.A. Res. 290 (IV) (Dec. 1, 1949) (calling for the permanent members "*[t]o broaden progressively their cooperation and to exercise restraint in the use of the veto*").

consider the question of vital importance ... and to state upon what ground they consider this condition to be present."[6] Because the veto was utilized extensively during the Cold War, most frequently by the US and USSR,[7] these early calls for veto restraint do not appear to have had significant impact at the time.[8]

3.1.1 The Responsibility Not to Veto within R2P

A reinvigoration of earlier calls for veto restraint resurfaced in the aftermath of the Kosovo intervention by the North Atlantic Treaty Organization (NATO). As discussed in Chapter 2, the Security Council would have faced deadlock had a request been put to it to authorize NATO's intervention, despite the ongoing commission of atrocity crimes in Kosovo.[9] In the 2000 report of the Independent International Commission on Kosovo, the Commissioners voiced the sentiment that "the current system allowing any Permanent [Security Council] member to paralyze UN action through the use of the veto must be adjusted in a judicious manner to deal effectively with cases of extreme humanitarian crisis."[10]

The first modern veto restraint initiative then surfaced in reports on the "responsibility to protect" (R2P).[11] By 2001, as part of the report of the International Commission on Intervention and State Sovereignty (ICISS), which first formulated the "responsibility to protect," the Commissioners declared that "it is unconscionable that one veto can override the rest of humanity on matters of grave humanitarian concerns."[12] The report concluded: "[t]he Permanent Five members of the Security Council should agree not to apply their veto power in matters where their vital state interests are not involved, to obstruct the passage of resolutions

---

[6] UN G.A. Res. 267(III), para. 3.c (Apr. 14, 1949).
[7] See Chapter 1.2 for discussion of veto use during the Cold War.
[8] For discussion of the "Uniting for Peace" resolution as a method around Security Council paralysis, see Chapter 1.2.2.
[9] Justin Morris & Nicholas Wheeler, *The Responsibility Not to Veto: A Responsibility Too Far?*, in THE OXFORD HANDBOOK OF THE RESPONSIBILITY TO PROTECT, at 227 (Alex J. Bellamy & Tim Dunne eds., 2016). During the Kosovo crisis, the Security Council faced a "near-certain veto" by Russia and the "likelihood of the same by China"; thus, NATO engaged in military action without first seeking Security Council authorization. *Id.* at 231–32.
[10] *See* The Independent International Commission on Kosovo, Kosovo Report, at 198 (2000).
[11] For additional discussion of R2P, see Chapter 2.2.
[12] International Commission on Intervention and State Sovereignty (ICISS), *The Responsibility to Protect, Report of the International Commission on Intervention and State Sovereignty*, at 51 (International Development Research Centre, Ottawa, December 2001) [hereinafter, ICISS report].

authorizing military intervention for human protection purposes for which there is otherwise majority support."[13] The obligation not to veto would apply if the resolution had obtained nine votes required for it to pass.[14]

A call for veto restraint was rearticulated in 2004 in the UN Secretary-General's High-Level Panel on Threats, Challenges and Change (2004 R2P report),[15] which called for voluntary restraint as to use of the veto in cases of "genocide and large-scale human rights abuses."[16] The report stated:

> [A]s a whole the institution of the veto has an anachronistic character that is unsuitable for the institution in an increasingly democratic age and we would urge that its use be limited to matters where vital interests are genuinely at stake. We also ask the permanent members, in their individual capacities, to pledge themselves to refrain from the use of the veto in cases of genocide and large-scale human rights abuses.[17]

The report also recommended "that processes to improve transparency and accountability be incorporated and formalized in the Council's rules of procedure."[18]

When it came to the 2005 World Summit Outcome document, however, the General Assembly did not include the "responsibility not to veto."[19] Simon Adams, Executive Director of the Global Centre for the Responsibility to Protect, has optimistically written that, notwithstanding the omission, "[t]he Responsibility to Protect, adopted at the 2005 World Summit ... means that the five Permanent Members of the Security Council have a responsibility not to veto in a mass atrocity situation."[20] This author does not necessarily read the omission that way. Others have written that the "responsibility not to veto" was "jettison[ed]" from the World Summit Outcome Document upon concerted lobbying by then

---

[13]   Id. at xiii.
[14]   Morris & Wheeler, *supra* note 9, at 232.
[15]   Report of the Secretary-General's High-Level Panel on Threats, Challenges and Change: A More Secure World: Our Shared Responsibility, U.N. Doc. A/59/565 (Dec. 2, 2004) [hereinafter, 2004 R2P report].
[16]   Id., para. 256.
[17]   Id.
[18]   Id., para. 258.
[19]   UN G.A. Res. 60/1, paras. 138–39 (Oct. 24, 2005) [hereinafter, World Summit Outcome Document].
[20]   Global Centre for the Responsibility to Protect, The Responsibility Not to Veto, speech delivered by Dr. Simon Adams, January 21, 2015, *at* www.globalr2p.org/media/files/2015-january-adams-veto-restraint-remarks.pdf.

US Ambassador to the UN John Bolton who ensured the responsibility not to veto was "expunged from the final text."[21] Another account points to lobbying by the US, China, and Russia.[22] This suggests the omission was quite intentional.

The "responsibility not to veto" then resurfaced in 2009 in the Report of the Secretary-General, "Implementing the Responsibility to Protect."[23] Then Secretary-General Ban Ki-moon described the permanent members' veto power as a privilege, and "urge[d] them to refrain from employing or threatening to employ the veto in situations of manifest failure to meet obligations relating to the responsibility to protect, as defined in paragraph 139 of the Summit Outcome [Document], and to reach a mutual understanding to that effect."[24] A "responsibility not to veto" was also referenced in the 2015 R2P report of the Secretary-General.[25] There, the Secretary-General stated:

> I ... encourage permanent members to exercise restraint in their use of the veto in situations that include the commission of atrocity crimes and welcome any effort designed to enhance the Council's ability to discharge its responsibilities. If States employ the veto in such situations, they should explain publicly what alternative strategy they propose to protect populations at risk. All members of the Security Council should continue to make even greater efforts to agree on an effective course of action.[26]

The Secretary-General, in his February 2016 report for the World Humanitarian Summit, additionally called for "the permanent members to withhold their veto power on measures addressing mass atrocity."[27]

---

[21] Morris & Wheeler, *supra* note 9, at 228, 232, citing Ariela Blätter & Paul D. Williams, *The Responsibility Not to Veto*, in GLOBAL RESPONSIBILITY TO PROTECT, at 315–16 (2011). See also Citizens for Global Solutions, *A Responsibility Not to Veto: A Way Forward*, at 9–10 (2014) (finding it "telling" that "all references to the [responsibility not to veto] were removed from the final version of the 2005 World Summit Outcome Document despite being present in earlier drafts of the text").

[22] See Jean-Baptise Jeangène Vilmer, *The Responsibility Not to Veto: A Genealogy*, 24(3) GLOB. GOVERNANCE, at 4 (2018) ("ultimately [the responsibility not to veto] was not included in the final paragraphs on R2P due to objections by the United States, Russia and China").

[23] Report of the Secretary-General: Implementing the Responsibility to Protect, para. 61, U.N. Doc. A/63/677 (Jan. 12, 2009), *at* www.un.org/ruleoflaw/files/SG_reportA_63_677_en.pdf.

[24] *Id.*

[25] UN Secretary-General (UNSG), A Vital and Enduring Commitment: Implementing the Responsibility to Protect: Report of the Secretary-General, para. 63, U.N. Doc. A/69/981-S/2015/500 (July 13, 2015), *at* www.refworld.org/docid/55cb3cd44.html [2005 R2P report].

[26] *Id.*

[27] Report of the Secretary-General for the World Humanitarian Summit, para. 67, U.N. Doc. A/70/709 (Feb. 2, 2016), *at* www.securitycouncilreport.org/atf/cf/%7B65BFCF9B-6D27-4E9C-8CD3-\CF6E4FF96FF9%7D/A_70_709.pdf.

Thus, a "responsibility not to veto" appears still to be part of the doctrine of R2P, although commitment to it has been inconsistent given its omission from the 2005 World Summit Outcome Document. One can well comprehend the necessity of having a "responsibility not to veto" as part of R2P; otherwise, as discussed more fully in Chapter 2, R2P measures, including "Pillar III" intervention (but also other measures) are subject to being blocked by the veto of one or more permanent members of the Security Council.[28]

3.1.2 The "S5 Initiative"

The second initiative calling for voluntary veto restraint was the "S5 initiative," introduced in 2005,[29] when five states (Costa Rica, Jordan, Liechtenstein, Singapore, and Switzerland), referred to as "the Small Five," formed a cross-regional initiative. In 2006, these states circulated a draft resolution in the General Assembly with the title "Follow up to the Millennium Summit," including suggestions for opportunities for the wider membership to participate in the Council's deliberations.[30] While the 2006 draft was not put to a vote, it appears to have influenced a July 2006 Note by the President of the Security Council.[31] In 2008, the S5, assisted additionally by Belgium, were able to hold an open debate in the Security Council on efforts to enhance the efficiency and transparency of the Council's work, and in 2011, Portugal held another open debate on the same topic.[32]

By May 2012, the S5 tabled a second draft resolution entitled "Enhancing the accountability, transparency and effectiveness of the Security Council."[33] The resolution included a broad variety of practical recommendations related

---

[28] For a more extensive discussion, see Chapter 2. For discussion of the three "pillars" of R2P, see Chapter 2.2.

[29] Letter dated November 3, 2005, from Costa Rica, Jordan, Liechtenstein, Singapore, and Switzerland, at www.globalpolicy.org/images/pdfs/Swiss_S5_Resolution_November_10_2005 .pdf (letter with suggested draft General Assembly resolution).

[30] DANIEL MARTIN NIEMETZ, REFORMING UN DECISION-MAKING PROCEDURES: PROMOTING A DELIBERATIVE SYSTEM FOR GLOBAL PEACE AND SECURITY 41 (2015).

[31] Note of the President of the Security Council, U.N. Doc. S/2010/507 (July 26, 2010), at www.un.org/en/sc/repertoire/Notes/S-2010-507.pdf.

[32] The debates were on the implementation of the 2006 Note of the President of the Security Council, "Note 507." Id. Japan used its chairmanship of the Council's Working Group on Documentation "to transform the collection of various Notes and Statements into a ... guide to the Council's working methods," known as "Note 507." Joanna Harrington, *The Working Methods of the United Nations Security Council: Maintaining the Implementation of Change*, 66 INT. & COMP. L. Q. 39, 61 (Jan. 2017). Presidential notes can "function as supplements to the Council's Rules of Procedure." Id. at 40.

[33] Draft Resolution, Enhancing the Accountability, Transparency and Effectiveness of the Security Council, sponsored by Costa Rica, Jordan, Liechtenstein, Singapore, and

to the Council's working methods, aimed at making its work more inclusive and transparent.[34] As to veto use, the 2012 draft resolution stated:

Use of the veto
The following measures are recommended for consideration by the permanent members of the Security Council:
   19. Explaining the reasons for resorting to a veto or declaring its intention to do so, in particular with regard to its consistency with the purposes and principles of the Charter of the United Nations and applicable international law. A copy of the explanation should be circulated as a separate Security Council document to all members of the Organization.
   20. Refraining from using a veto to block Council action aimed at preventing or ending genocide, war crimes and crimes against humanity.[35]

The resolution also initially contained a proposal that the permanent members be able to utilize a "negative vote" on a resolution, which would express a permanent member's negative position, but would not constitute a veto; however, that language was omitted from the final resolution.[36]

While the 2012 draft resolution initially attracted considerable support, it was withdrawn from the General Assembly's consideration after, controversially, the Under-Secretary-General for Legal Affairs – apparently after pressure from permanent members of the Security Council[37] – took the position that the

---

Switzerland, U.N. Doc. A/66/L.42/Rev.2 (May 15, 2012), *at* www.securitycouncilreport.org/atf/cf/%7B65BFCF9B-6D27-4E9C-8CD3-CF6E4FF96FF9%7D/a%2066%20l.42%20rev2.pdf.

[34] It included encouraging the Security Council to: (1) seek the views of other states; (2) increase transparency; (3) evaluate effectiveness of the implementation of its decisions through a working group on lessons learned; (4) increase the transparency of the work of its subsidiary bodies and allow Member States more input as to them; (5) inform Member States more fully about relevant developments regarding the planning, preparation, conduct and termination of operations, special political missions mandated and on-site missions carried out by the Council; (6) ensure the consistent implementation of its agreed working methods including by adopting rules of procedure; and (7) implement certain measures related to the appointment of the Secretary-General. Draft Resolution, U.N. Doc. A/66/L.42/Rev.2, *supra* note 33, Annex. There was also agreement in the World Summit Outcome Document to improve the working methods of the Security Council in order to enhance its accountability and transparency. World Summit Outcome Document, *supra* note 19, para. 154 (mentioning the need "to increase the involvement of States not members of the Council in [the Council's] work, as appropriate, [and to] enhance its accountability to membership and increase the transparency of its work").

[35] Draft Resolution, U.N. Doc. A/66/L.42/Rev.2, *supra* note 33, paras. 19–20.

[36] Statement by H.E. Mr. Paul Seger, Permanent Representative, Permanent Mission of Switzerland to the UN, Follow-Up to the Outcome of the Millennium Summit, General Assembly 66th Sess. (May 16, 2012) (discussing removal of the "negative vote"). The concept of such a "negative vote" was proposed already in the 2004 High-Level Panel R2P report. 2004 R2P Report, *supra* note 15, para. 257.

[37] Volker Lehmann, *Reforming the Working Methods of the UN Security Council: The Next Act*, Friedrich Ebert Stiftung, at 3 (Aug. 2013); Morris & Wheeler, *supra* note 9, at 233.

resolution pertained to an "important question," and therefore under Article 18(2) of the UN Charter required a vote of two-thirds of UN Member States to pass, rather than a simple majority (present and voting).[38] Some suggest the S5 did not wish to risk establishing the precedent of a two-thirds voting requirement for such a resolution,[39] whereas they also may not have had enough votes to reach the two-thirds threshold after pressure had been exerted on countries.[40] "Behind closed doors, the P5 undertook concerted action to prevent member states from casting a positive vote on the proposal."[41] For example, the Russian Permanent Representative took the position: "The working methods themselves and any potential possible modification to them are the responsibility of the Council itself. That is a very sensitive issue in the context of the reform of the Council, and discussion on that topic should not be subjected to populism."[42] Switzerland's then-Permanent Representative, H.E. Mr. Paul Seger, in his speech withdrawing the resolution, made clear: "the P-5 have put considerable pressure upon us not to submit our draft for action," yet prophetically stated "[t]his is not the closing of a chapter, but the opening of a new one."[43] Indeed, the S5 initiative undeniably contributed momentum towards creating the Code of Conduct and the French/Mexican initiative.[44]

After defeat of the S5 initiative, the Singaporean Permanent Representative made clear his frustration with the hypocrisy of permanent members expressing outrage at inaction regarding Syria, and then uniting together to defeat the S5 initiative.[45]

[38] Legal Opinion of Patricia O'Brien Under-Secretary-General for Legal Affairs (May 14, 2012); Charter of the United Nations (1945), 892 UNTS 119 (1945) [hereinafter, UN Charter].
[39] Lehmann, *supra* note 37, at 4–5.
[40] *Id.* at 2 (the S5's work "crumbled in 2012 under the joint pressure exercised by the permanent five (P5) members of the UN Security Council"); *see also id.* at 3 ("The [Uniting for Consensus group of states] tactically reversed their previous support for the S-5, taking along enough member states to prevent a successful vote").
[41] *Id.* at 3. Morris and Wheeler write: "Russia reportedly viewed the S5 proposition as an 'affront' to the P5 and the UNSC whilst China used its influence with African states to sap their support for the initiative and the United States, having previously shown some appetite for the kind of practices encapsulated within the S5 scheme, came out in unequivocal opposition to them." Morris & Wheeler, *supra* note 9, at 233 (footnotes omitted).
[42] Niemetz, *supra* note 30, at 43 (quoting the Russian Permanent Representative).
[43] Statement by H.E. Mr. Paul Seger, *supra* note 36.
[44] The S5's 2006 draft resolution may also have helped spearhead Japan's production of a handbook on Security Council working methods. Harrington, *supra* note 32, at 45, *citing* Permanent Mission of Japan to the United Nations, *Handbook on the Working Methods of the Security Council* (Dec. 2006), *at* www.un.emb-japan.go.jp/jp/handbook.pdf. *See also supra* note 32.
[45] He noted: "Those permanent members that repeatedly express outrage at what is happening within the Council on issues like Syria are the same ones that blocked [the S5 proposal]." U.N. Doc. S/PV.6870, as quoted in Morris & Wheeler, *supra* note 9, at 234.

3.1.3 The French/Mexican Initiative

Interestingly, France early on broke ranks with the other permanent members of the Security Council and led the third initiative calling for veto restraint.[46] (Subsequently, the UK also joined the call for veto restraint, joining the ACT Code of Conduct, discussed below.)[47] The "French/Mexican" initiative not to veto in the face of atrocity crimes was initially proposed by France, then joined by Mexico, and is now endorsed by a large number of states.[48] "[It is] remarkable that a veto-wielding permanent member is willing to advance the idea."[49] One explanation is that the S5 initiative aimed at implementing veto limitations through a General Assembly resolution; the French/Mexican initiative calls for veto restraint to be implemented *by the permanent members* – so *they* would specify how it would operate. Additionally, the S5 initiative contained a variety of proposals related to Security Council working methods, not solely veto restraint in the face of atrocity crimes, so that the French/Mexican initiative is more limited in scope.

Veto restraint in atrocity situations was initially suggested in 2001 by French Foreign Minister Hubert Védrine at a roundtable sponsored by the ICISS in Paris.[50] He called for the permanent members to create a "code of conduct" for themselves and not to apply their veto to block humanitarian action where their own national interests were not involved.[51] In fact, it appears that France is also responsible for the concept of veto restraint when it first emerged in the

---

[46] See Morris & Wheeler, *supra* note 9, at 235 ("Given the hitherto united front of the P5 against any proposals for limiting the veto, it is notable that France ... has chosen to break ranks from the P5 and join the growing chorus of voices calling for veto restraint.").

[47] Thus, both the UK and France are in a different position on the issue of voluntary veto restraint than the other permanent members.

[48] As of early 2020, it was endorsed by 105 states. See note 63 *infra*. While the initiative was originally proposed by France, it became known as the "French/Mexican" initiative after France and Mexico jointly hosted Ministerial Side-Events at the UN on the initiative in 2014 and 2015. Merrow Golden, *Could a Code of Conduct Work? The Prospects for the French Proposal Limiting the Veto on the United Nations Security Council*, 55 COLUMBIA J. TRANSNAT'L L. 101, n. 5 (2017).

[49] David Bosco, *France's Plan to Fix the Veto*, FOR. POL'Y (Oct. 4, 2013), at http://foreignpolicy.com/2013/10/04/frances-plan-to-fix-the-veto.

[50] Corrie Hulse, *Will the Veto Ever be Restrained*, THE MANTLE (May 11, 2017), at www.mantlethought.org/international-affairs/will-veto-ever-be-restrained. For France's role in veto restraint, see generally Vilmer, *supra* note 22. There were also UK and Danish scholars early on calling for veto restraint. *Id.* at 3–4.

[51] The 2001 version was actually preceded by a newspaper article in *Le Monde*, where Védrine suggested "that the permanent members agree on situations where they would refrain from invoking [the veto] (severe oppression or confirmed massacres, failure or responsibility of the state concerned, emergency)." Vilmer, *supra* note 22, citing Hubert Védrine *La gestion de la crise du Kosovo est une exception*, LE MONDE, at 16 (Mar. 25, 2000).

3.1 Approaches to Voluntary Veto Restraint as to Atrocity Crimes 111

ICISS report, which states that the idea of a "responsibility not to veto" came from a "senior representative of one of the Permanent Five countries,"[52] that is, France.[53]

The French again became active in September 2012, when French Minister of Foreign Affairs Laurent Fabius expressed support for "a 'code of conduct' through which permanent members of the [Security Council] would commit not to exercise their right to veto in situations of serious humanitarian crises when their vital interest are not in play."[54] The following month, the French Ambassador to the UN repeated this position.[55] The European Parliament also on April 18, 2013, passed a resolution proposing that the High Representative of the Union for Foreign Affairs and Security Policy, Vice-President of the Commission, and the Council "propose to the five permanent members of the UN Security Council the adoption of a voluntary code of conduct which would limit the use of the right of veto in cases of genocide, war crimes, ethnic cleansing, or crimes against humanity."[56]

French President François Hollande provided further support to the initiative in his September 24, 2013, UN General Assembly address.[57] There, Hollande stated: "I am proposing that a code of good conduct be defined by the permanent members of the Security Council, and that in the event of a mass crime they can decide to collectively renounce their veto powers."[58]

---

[52] ICISS Report, *supra* note 12, para. 6.21. "France was also responsible, with the support of other Council members, notably Brazil and New Zealand, for initiating the first 'open debate' on working methods within the Council." Harrington, *supra* note 32, at 58–59. Before this Chapter sounds too congratulatory towards France, the author would like to note that France's voice on these issues was apparently found after French (and US and UK) inaction in 1994 in the face of the Rwandan genocide, and implicit threats to use the veto to block describing the crimes as "genocide" and block sending in robust peacekeeping forces, with UN reinforcements sent in only *after* the genocide was largely over. See Chapter 1.3.2.

[53] See Vilmer, *supra* note 22, at 2–3 (the French Policy Planning Staff recommended in 1999 that the French Minister of Foreign Affairs take the initiative on a "reform of the veto" in the face of humanitarian crises).

[54] *Id.*, at 5, *citing* Laurent Fabius, speech at Sciences Po, September 6, 2012, Diplomatic Archives.

[55] *Id.*, *citing* U.N. Doc. A/66/L. 42 (Mar. 28, 2012); U.N. Doc. A/66/L.42/Rev.2, *supra* note 33, para. 20.

[56] European Parliament Recommendation to the Council of 18 April 2013 on the UN Principle of the "Responsibility to Protect" (R2P), para. 2(f), EU, P7_TA (2013)0180 (Apr. 18, 2013), at www.europarl.europa.eu/sides/getDoc.do?pubRef=-//EP//TEXT+TA+P7-TA-2013-0180+0+ DOC+XML+Vo//EN&language=EN.

[57] Permanent Mission of France to the United Nations in New York, September 24, 2013, Opening of the 68th Sess. of the United Nations General Assembly, Statement by Mr. François Hollande, President of the Republic, *at* https://onu.delegfrance.org/24-September-2013-Opening-of-the.

[58] *Id.*

Hollande's statement was followed, on October 4, 2013, by an op-ed in the *New York Times* and *Le Monde* by French Foreign Minister Fabius. In the op-ed, "A Call for Self-Restraint at the U.N.," Fabius wrote:

> Our suggestion is that the five permanent members of the Security Council – China, France, Russia, Britain and the United States – themselves could voluntarily regulate their right to exercise their veto. The Charter would not be amended and the change would be implemented through a mutual commitment from the permanent members. In concrete terms, if the Security Council were required to make a decision with regard to a mass crime, the permanent members would agree to suspend their right to veto. The criteria for implementation would be simple: at the request of at least 50 member states, the United Nations secretary general would be called upon to determine the nature of the crime. Once he had delivered his opinion, the code of conduct would immediately apply. To be realistically applicable, this code would exclude cases where the vital national interests of a permanent member of the Council were at stake.[59]

In his 2015 address to the General Assembly, President Hollande additionally committed that "France will never use its right of veto where there have been mass atrocities."[60]

France then launched its "Political Declaration on Suspension of Veto Powers in Cases of Mass Atrocity."[61] It states:

> We consider that situations of mass atrocities, when crimes of genocide, crimes against humanity and war crimes on a large scale are committed, may constitute a threat to international peace and security and require action by the international community. In that regard, we recall that the Heads of State and government of the United Nations expressed their readiness to "take collective action, in a timely and decisive manner, through the Security Council, in accordance with the Charter" when national authorities fail to protect their populations from genocide, crimes against humanity or war crimes (World Summit Outcome Document of 2005).
>
> We therefore consider that the Security Council should not be prevented by the use of veto from taking action with the aim of preventing or bringing an end to situations involving the commission of mass atrocities. We underscore

---

[59] Laurent Fabius, *A Call for Self-Restraint at the U.N.*, N.Y. TIMES (Oct. 4, 2013), at www.nytimes.com/2013/10/04/opinion/a-call-for-self-restraint-at-the-un.html.

[60] Golden, *supra* note 48, at 103.

[61] 70th General Assembly of the United Nations, Political Declaration on the Suspension of Veto Powers in Cases of Mass Atrocities, Presented by France and Mexico, open to signature to the members of the United Nations, at www.globalr2p.org/media/files/2015-07-31-veto-political-declaration-final-eng.pdf.

that the veto is not a privilege, but an international responsibility. In that respect, we welcome and support the initiative by France, jointly presented with Mexico, to propose a collective and voluntary agreement among the permanent members of the Security Council to the effect that the permanent members would refrain from using the veto in case of mass atrocities. We express our strong resolve to continue our efforts to prevent and end the commission of mass atrocities.[62]

As of early 2020, the French/Mexican initiative was supported by 105 Member States.[63] (Signatures to the French/Mexican initiative were apparently boosted by an agreement to "signature trade," in that the twenty-five initial signatories to the ACT Code of Conduct – discussed below in Chapter 3.1.4 – agreed to sign the French/Mexican initiative, and, in turn, France agreed to sign the Code of Conduct.)[64] France is the only permanent member of the Security Council to have joined the French/Mexican initiative.[65]

Oddly, while the French/Mexican initiative sounds as if it is aimed at having all permanent members of the Security Council renounce the veto in the face of atrocity crimes, it has been suggested that the initiative does not truly aim to obtain such an agreement, but is more realistic, in that the goal is to make "improper use of the veto more politically costly" and "to counter narratives on the demise or obsolescence of the Council."[66] One might then cynically wonder if the whole French/Mexican initiative merely serves to enhance France's standing in the eyes of the international community, as a responsible member of the Council, while never actually intending to tackle the problem? Perhaps the French also acted in order to strengthen the Council's responsible use of the veto, thereby undercutting claims, periodically raised, about the need to abolish the veto.[67]

---

[62] Id.
[63] Trahan e-mail exchange with legal adviser of the Permanent Mission of Mexico to the UN.
[64] Vilmer, *supra* note 22, at 8.
[65] The UK agreed to sign the ACT Code of Conduct, but not the French/Mexican initiative. One source explains: "By supporting the ACT's Code, [the UK] hoped to have it both ways: to look good in front of civil society without going so far as to irritate the United States which had serious reservations about the French initiative." *Id.*, at 8.
[66] See id. at 3 ("the real objective of [the French/Mexican] proposal to restrict the veto is not so much to obtain an agreement in the P5 but rather to exert pressure, rendering the improper use of the veto more politically costly, and more deeply to counter narratives on the demise or obsolescence of the UNSC").
[67] As noted in Chapter 1, a UN Charter amendment would require agreement of all permanent members of the Security Council. UN Charter, Art. 108. Thus, the permanent members essentially have "veto power against possible amendments to the UN Charter." Golden, *supra* note 48, at 115. Ergo, abolishing the veto is virtually impossible.

3.1.4 The ACT Code of Conduct

The fourth significant[68] initiative to call for voluntary veto restraint – temporally evolving somewhat in parallel with the French/Mexican initiative – is the Accountability, Coherence and Transparency (ACT) Group of states' Code of Conduct. While it is the ACT Group that launched a "Code of Conduct," interestingly, it was France that, years before, had called for implementing a "code of conduct." The ACT Group was formed from the alliance of states that had launched the S5 initiative, minus Singapore, joined by a number of additional states from different geographical regions.[69] At the time of its launch in May 2013, the ACT Group had twenty-two members: Austria, Chile, Costa Rica, Estonia, Finland, Gabon, Hungary, Ireland, Jordan, Liechtenstein, Maldives, New Zealand, Norway, Papua New Guinea, Peru, Portugal, Saudi Arabia, Slovenia, Sweden, Switzerland, Tanzania (as observer), and Uruguay.[70]

The ACT Group was formed to work on a variety of Security Council related measures, not only veto restraint, but, as suggested by its title, more generally pressing to improve the working methods of the Security Council. The ACT Group explains its goals as follows:

> We believe that additional measures are needed to enable the Council – in its present composition – to carry out its mandate with maximum efficiency, effectiveness and legitimacy. ACT will therefore continue to offer concrete and pragmatic proposals to help improve the working methods of the Security Council, in dialogue with Council members as well as through building political momentum outside of the Council.[71]

When it reached twenty-five members, in July 2015, the ACT Group proposed a Code of Conduct regarding Security Council action against

---

[68] There have been other initiatives related to the veto – including to amend the UN Charter to require at least two vetoes for a Security Council resolution to be defeated; allowing a majority (for example, three-quarters of the Council) to overcome a veto; and a "bicameral arrangement" that would send an issue to the General Assembly where four-fifths of its members could override a veto. See Niemetz, *supra* note 30, at 78. Because those methods would require a Charter amendment, this author views the likelihood of their implementation as nearly nil. See Citizens for Global Solutions, *supra* note 21, at 11 ("there is almost no hope of amending the UN Charter").

[69] Niemetz, *supra* note 30, at 44; Harrington, *supra* note 32, at 46.

[70] Lehmann, *supra* note 37, at 2.

[71] Center for UN Reform, *FACT SHEET, The Accountability, Coherence and Transparency Group – Better Working Methods for Today's UN Security Council* (June 2015), *at* http://centerforunreform.org/sites/default/files/FACT%20SHEET%20ACT%20June%202015.pdf.

genocide, crimes against humanity, and war crimes.[72] The Code of Conduct was launched on October 23, 2015. The transmittal letter of the Code of Conduct from the Permanent Representative of Liechtenstein to the UN Secretary-General describes the Code as follows:

> At its heart, the code of conduct contains a general and positive pledge to support Security Council action against genocide, crimes against humanity and war crimes – to both prevent or put an end to those crimes. This is complemented by a more specific pledge to not vote against credible draft Security Council resolutions that are aimed at preventing or ending those crimes, which are all well defined in international law.
>
> The application of the code of conduct would be triggered by any situation involving those crimes – in other words, when the facts on the ground lead to Security Council action, following an assessment of relevant information by a State committed to the code of conduct. However, the Secretary-General would serve as an important authority to bring such situations to the attention of the Council, and her or his assessment of the situation would carry great weight.[73]

Specifically, the Code of Conduct calls on all UN Member States, inter alia, to:

> 1. *Pledge* to support timely and decisive action by the Security Council aimed at preventing or ending the commission of genocide, crimes against humanity or war crimes;
> 2. *Pledge* in particular to not vote against a credible draft resolution before the Security Council on timely and decisive action to end the commission of genocide, crimes against humanity or war crimes, or to prevent such crimes;
> 3. *Invite* the Secretary-General, making full use of the expertise and early warning capacities of the United Nations system, in particular the Office of the United Nations High Commissioner for Human Rights and the United Nations Office on Genocide Prevention and the Responsibility to Protect, to continue to bring to the attention of the Council situations that, in her or his assessment, involve or are likely to lead to genocide, crimes against humanity or war crimes[.][74]

---

[72] According to one account, the ACT Group could have proceeded earlier, but was waiting "for the French initiative to succeed, because it had the benefit of coming from within the P5 . . . ." Vilmer, *supra* note 22, at 7.

[73] Letter dated 14 December 2015 from the Permanent Representative of Liechtenstein to the United Nations addressed to the Secretary-General, U.N. Doc. A/70/621–S/2015/978 (Dec. 14, 2015), *at* www.globalr2p.org/media/files/n1543357.pdf.

[74] UN G.A. Res. A/70/621–S/2015/978, Annex I to the letter dated 14 December 2015 from the Permanent Representative of Liechtenstein to the United Nations addressed to the Secretary-

The Code specifies in a footnote: "The term 'war crimes' refers in particular to war crimes committed as part of a plan or policy or as part of a large-scale commission of such crimes."[75]

As of spring 2020, the Code of Conduct had been signed by 121 UN Member States, including France and the UK.[76] To date, the ACT Group has additionally worked on a variety of initiatives.[77] The Code of Conduct is also supported by a large number of non-governmental organizations (NGOs).[78]

The ACT Code of Conduct is thus somewhat different in focus than the French/Mexican initiative – which called for veto restraint to be agreed to *by* the permanent Security Council members; the Code of Conduct, by contrast, "was pitched to all States, as either current or future potential Council members."[79] Furthermore, the Code of Conduct is broader than veto restraint – calling for all states to support timely and decisive action by the Security Council aimed at preventing or ending the commission of genocide, crimes against humanity or war crimes, as well as other measures to make Security Council performance more accountable, coherent and transparent.[80]

General, Code of Conduct Regarding Security Council Action against Genocide, Crimes against Humanity or War Crimes (Dec. 14, 2015), at www.globalr2p.org/media/files/n1543357.pdf [hereinafter, Code of Conduct]. The Code was officially launched at the UN at an event organized by Liechtenstein Foreign Minister, H.E. Ms. Aurelia Frick. See Statement by H.E. Ms. Aurelia Frick, Launch of the Code of Conduct Regarding Security Council Action against Genocide, Crimes against Humanity or War Crimes, New York, October 23, 2015.

[75] *Id.* at n. 6.
[76] Trahan e-mail exchange with legal adviser of the Permanent Mission of Liechtenstein to the UN.
[77] These include:

> the preparation of submission to the Council and the dissemination of jointly agreed statements of position, particularly during the Council's annual open debate on working methods, as well as the close monitoring of the work of the Council's Informal Working Group on Documentation and Other Procedural Questions, with a view to influencing outputs and encouraging follow-up. ACT also hosts formal and informal discussions among States, and supports efforts to disseminate accurate information and informative analysis concerning the Council's working methods.

Harrington, *supra* note 32, at 48 (footnotes omitted). ACT also worked in 2015 towards making more open arrangements for selecting a new Secretary-General. *Id.*

[78] See untitled letter dated August 31, 2015, joined by thirty-four NGOs.
[79] Harrington, *supra* note 32, at 49.
[80] Explanatory Note on a Code of Conduct Regarding Security Council Action against Genocide, Crimes against Humanity or War Crimes, Sept. 1, 2015.

3.1.5 *The Proposal of "The Elders"*

Finally, on February 7, 2015, a group known as "The Elders," a "diverse and independent group of global leaders working to promote peace and human rights,"[81] launched four new proposals at the 2015 Munich Security Conference.[82] One proposal related to veto restraint called for the permanent members of the Security Council to pledge:

> not to use, or threaten to use, their veto [where populations are being subjected to, or threatened with, genocide or other atrocity crimes] without explaining, clearly and in public, what alternative course of action they propose, as a credible and efficient way to protect the populations in question. This explanation must refer to international peace and security, and not to the national interest of the state casting the veto, since any state casting a veto simply to protect its national interests is abusing the privilege of permanent membership.[83]

"What is interesting about the Elders' statement is that it focuses on requiring the [permanent members] to give an explanation for their use of the veto in situations of mass atrocities. It does not require a pledge to never use the veto, it only requires a pledge to explain why a veto is used,"[84] and what credible alternative course the permanent member proposes. This would, thus, "enhance transparency and accountability but is arguably weaker than the French[/Mexican] proposal and the ACT Code of Conduct, which both require the P5 not to use the veto power at all in specific circumstances."[85]

A related initiative, prior to the work of the Elders, had also been advanced by former Under-Secretary-General for Legal Affairs and Legal Counsel of the United Nations Hans Corell. While not formulated to address only use of the veto in the face of atrocity crimes, Corell's initiative called for the permanent members to agree not to use their veto unless their most serious direct national

---

[81] Security Council Report, The Veto (Nov. 3, 2016). Nelson Mandela launched "The Elders" on July 18, 2007. On their website, the following eminent persons are listed as "Elders": Nelson Mandela (founder), Mary Robinson, Ban Ki-moon, Graça Machel, Lakhdar Brahimi, Gro Harlem Brundtland, Zeid Raad Al Hussein, Hina Jilani, Ellen Johnson Sirleaf, Ricardo Lagos, Juan Manuel Santos, Ernesto Zedillo, Martti Ahtisaari (emeritus), Ela Bhatt (emeritus), Fernando H. Cardoso (emeritus), Jimmy Carter (emeritus), Desmond Tutu (emeritus), Kofi Annan (emeritus). The Elders, *Who are The Elders?*, at https://theelders.org/about.
[82] The Elders, *A UN Fit for Purpose*, at https://theelders.org/un-fit-purpose. The other proposals related to (1) a new category of member states for the Security Council, (2) providing civil society organizations more opportunities to brief the Security Council, and (3) selection of the Secretary-General. *Id.*
[83] The Elders, *Strengthening the United Nations, Statement by The Elders* (Feb. 7, 2015), at https://theelders.org/sites/default/files/2015-04-22elders-statement-strengthening-the-un.pdf.
[84] Golden, *supra* note 48, at 127.
[85] *Id.*

interests were affected and to explain, in case they did use the veto, the reasons for so doing.[86]

3.1.6 A US Proposal for Veto Restraint under the Obama Administration

While this did not morph into a veto restraint initiative at the UN (nor in the US joining either the ACT Code of Conduct or the French/Mexican initiative), it is worth noting the positive approach to veto restraint suggested by a high-level task force convened during the Obama Administration.

Specifically, the "Genocide Prevention Task Force," bipartisanly chaired by former US Secretary of State Madeleine Albright and US Senator William S. Cohen, endorsed voluntary veto restraint in an extensive report by the Task Force.[87] Recommendation 6-2 of that report stated: "The secretary of state should undertake robust diplomatic efforts toward negotiating an agreement among the permanent members of the United Nations Security Council on non-use of the veto in cases concerning genocide or mass atrocities."[88] The report further stated:

> The United States has a strong interest in improving the effectiveness of the UN Security Council in responding to mass atrocities. There is no substitute in the international system for a strong statement by the council; the United States must, therefore, invest diplomatic capital in negotiations within the council on specific cases, as well as in efforts to improve the functioning of the body itself. Too frequently, one of the five permanent members of the UN Security Council has made effective collective action virtually impossible by threatening veto, implicitly or explicitly. This has led to either watered-down, ineffectual resolutions, or no resolution at all. Uniquely empowered by the UN Charter, the five permanent members have unique responsibilities to fulfill the mission of the charter.
>
> The U.S. ambassador to the United Nations should initiate a dialogue among the five permanent members (P-5) of the Security Council on the special responsibility they have to prevent genocide and mass atrocities.

---

[86] See, e.g., Letter from Hans Corell to the Governments of the Members of the United Nations, Security Council Reform: Rule of Law More Important Than Additional Members, December 10, 2008, at www.havc.se/res/SelectedMaterial/20081210corelllettertounmembers.pdf.

[87] U.S. Genocide Prevention Task Force, Preventing Genocide: A Blueprint for U.S. Policymakers, Madeleine K. Albright and William S. Cohen Co-Chairs (Washington DC: The US Holocaust Memorial Museum, The American Academy of Diplomacy, and the US Institute of Peace 2008), at www.usip.org/sites/default/files/files/genocide_taskforce_report.pdf.

[88] Id. at 106.

A principal aim should be informal, voluntary mutual restraint in the use or threat of a veto in cases involving ongoing or imminent mass atrocities. The P-5 should agree that unless three permanent members were to agree to veto a given resolution, all five would abstain or support it. This should apply, in particular, to resolutions instituting sanctions and/or authorizing peace operations in situations when mass atrocities or genocide are imminent or underway. The P-5 should also agree that a resolution passed by two-thirds of the General Assembly finding that a crisis poses an imminent threat of mass atrocities should add further impetus to an expeditious Security Council response without threat of a veto. An agreement along these lines would make the Security Council a more effective vehicle in cases when a permanent member might otherwise prefer to block action.[89]

These views, articulated during the Obama Administration, do not represent current US Government views. Furthermore, as noted above, even under the Obama Administration the US joined neither the ACT Code of Conduct nor the French/Mexican initiative.[90] Moreover, based on the many vetoes the US has cast related to Israel (noted in Chapter 1),[91] it appears likely the US (while it may condemn certain uses of the veto, for instance by Russia or China),[92] will not endorse across-the-board veto restraint.

3.2 EVALUATION OF THE DIFFERENT APPROACHES TO VOLUNTARY VETO RESTRAINT

While the S5 initiative and "responsibility not to veto" represented early forays into voluntary veto restraint, they were important measures in revitalizing calls for veto restraint. Although, as discussed above, the concept of veto restraint originated with the General Assembly in the 1940s, it was aimed at alleviating

---

[89] Id. at 106–07.
[90] See also Vilmer, supra note 22, at 9 ("Even under the previous administration, the United States was reticent out of principle, not wanting to weaken the veto, which, until recently, it had used more than anyone else since the end of the Cold War, almost exclusively to protect Israel.").
[91] "The United States . . . has routinely used its veto power to shield Israel from Security Council measures demanding it show greater restraint in its dealings with the Palestinians." Colum Lynch, Rise of the Lilliputians, FOR. POL'Y (May 10, 2012), at http://foreignpolicy.com/2012/05/10/rise-of-the-lilliputians/. Compare Citizens for Global Solutions, supra note 21, at 4 (suggesting not all such US vetoes have been in the face of atrocity crimes, and suggesting some vetoes may have been warranted due to "language [that] can be interpreted as unbalanced and aggressive").
[92] See Morris & Wheeler, supra note 9, at 236 (noting a 2014 side-event to the General Assembly where the US and the UK criticized Russian and Chinese vetoes over Syria, but the US Ambassador did not widen the focus to broader concerns with the veto). See, e.g., U.N. Doc. S/PV.6870 (Nov. 26, 2012) (US statement).

Cold War voting paralysis at the Council, so occurred in a different context, not pertaining specifically to atrocity crimes. Thus, the idea of veto restraint very much needed to be resuscitated, and these two initiatives helped achieve this.

What the approaches discussed above share in common is, of course, a call for veto restraint in the face of atrocity crimes. Put together, these initiatives, pursued from 2001 to the present, represent almost two decades of development, galvanizing the view that there *is a significant problem* with veto use by permanent members of the Security Council in the face of atrocity crimes – a view now held by close to two-thirds of the Member States of the UN, if one considers the number of states that have joined the ACT Code of Conduct.[93]

3.2.1 *The Weight of the "Responsibility Not to Veto" as Articulated in These Initiatives*

On the other hand, in terms of the legal weight or authority of these initiatives, probably the most that can be said is that the "responsibility not to veto" in the face of atrocity crimes appears to be seen as a form of "soft law."[94] "Soft law" is of course in itself a perplexing concept, as "law" should not be "soft," and thus something "soft" should not constitute "law" – yet, this nomenclature is nonetheless employed.[95] A "code of conduct," for example, does not purport to constitute "hard law" but is a typical form of "soft law" obligation.[96] Furthermore, the French/Mexican initiative holds itself out as a "political declaration," thereby clearly not purporting to serve as a source of law.[97] Thus, while there are actual "hard law" obligations that are relevant regarding

---

[93] See note 76 *supra* (number of States that have joined the Code of Conduct).

[94] See, e.g., Theresa Reinold, *The "Responsibility Not to Veto," Secondary Rules, and the Rule of Law*, in GLOBAL RESPONSIBILITY TO PROTECT, VOL. 6, 269, 276 (2014) (referring to the "responsibility not to veto" as a "'soft' secondary rule" in the form of a "non-binding code of conduct").

[95] See, e.g., Andrew T. Guzman & Timothy L. Meyer, *International Soft Law*, 2 J. LEGAL ANALYSIS 172 (2010); Michèle Olivier, *The Relevance of "Soft Law" as a Source of International Human Rights*, 35 COMP. & INT'L L.J. S. AFRICA 289 (2002).

[96] See, e.g., Dinah L. Shelton, *Soft Law*, at 4 (The George Washington University Law School Public Law and Legal Theory Working Paper No. 322, Legal Studies Research Paper No. 322, 2008). "Soft law is a term used to describe a range of non-legally binding instruments used by States and international organizations in contemporary international relations, as opposed to hard law, which is always binding." André da Rocha Ferreira, Cristieli Carvalho, Fernanda Graeff Machry & Pedro Barreto Vianna Rigon, *Formation and Evidence of Customary International Law*, 2013 UFRGS MODEL UN J. 182, 194.

[97] See also Golden, *supra* note 48, at 117 ("The French Proposal is an example of soft law reform because it simply calls for voluntary commitments from the P5.").

3.2 Evaluation of Approaches to Voluntary Veto Restraint

genocide, crimes against humanity, and war crimes (discussed in Chapters 2 and 4), these initiatives, which call for "voluntary" veto restraint, do not – by their very terms – purport to create "binding" legal obligations. Similarly, the S5 initiative, even if it had been adopted as a General Assembly resolution, would not have created a binding obligation (and it was not adopted). Furthermore, even if the "responsibility not to veto" is considered part of R2P (despite its omission from the World Summit Outcome Document), R2P is unfortunately often seen as only "soft law."[98] (Chapter 2 argues that R2P could use "revitalization," and one idea would be to focus attention on the hard law legal obligations underlying it.)[99] Yet, even if R2P were considered to be customary international law, that would not necessarily impose binding legal obligations as to Security Council voting.[100]

An interesting additional question is, even if some of these obligations could be considered to be morphing into customary international law, whether General Assembly member states could form such obligations as to a practice solely utilized by the permanent members of the Security Council, or whether it is those permanent members that should be considered the "specially affected" states,[101] and therefore one should look particularly to their practice and statements as to whether something is becoming customary international law. Unfortunately, it is difficult to claim any such "morphing" is occurring; while calls for veto restraint are endorsed by a fair number of states (given the widespread support for the Code of Conduct and French/Mexican initiative), veto restraint is only endorsed by two of the five permanent

---

[98] See, e.g., Jennifer M. Welsh & Maria Banda, *International Law and the Responsibility to Protect: Clarifying or Expanding States' Responsibilities?*, in GLOBAL RESPONSIBILITY TO PROTECT, VOL. 2, 3, 213 (2010) (arguing that R2P is soft law); William W. Burke-White, *Adoption of the Responsibility to Protect*, in THE RESPONSIBILITY TO PROTECT 34 (Jared Genser & Irwin Cotler eds., 2012) (arguing that R2P is "best understood as a norm of international conduct" and that "[t]he trajectory of the Responsibility to Protect over the past decade is strongly suggestive of its development toward a rule of international law, but further political development and legal process will be required").

[99] See Chapter 2.2.2.

[100] Ferreira, Carvalho, Machry & Rigon, *supra* note 96, at 194–95. For ideas how customary international law could interact with the Charter, see Chapter 2, at 96, note 244 (discussing Sir Daniel Bethlehem's approach). Note that practice has already modified the Charter's voting provisions in one respect, in that "concurring votes of the permanent members" in UN Charter, Article 27(3) is read to permit abstention by a permanent member.

[101] "In the words of the International Court of Justice in the North Sea Continental Shelf cases, the practice must 'include that of States whose interests are specially affected.' ... If 'specially affected States' do not accept the practice, it cannot mature into a rule of customary international law... ." Jean-Marie Henchaerts, *Study on Customary International Humanitarian Law: A Contribution to the Understanding and Respect for the Rule of Law in Armed Conflict*, 87 INT'L REV. RED CROSS 175, 179 (2005).

members, and the vetoes being cast or threatened by at least three permanent members (discussed in Chapters 1 and 5) suggest there is not yet any practice of veto restraint. (Or, any practice that exists appears limited to the practice of two permanent members, who have not utilized the veto or threat of veto for the last couple of decades.)[102] Additionally, because calls for veto restraint are themselves formulated as soft law obligations (a voluntary code of conduct and a political declaration), and do not purport to state binding legal obligations, even if there were a "practice" of veto restraint, it would not stem from any "*opinio juris sive necessitatis*" (that is, a sense of legal obligation). Thus, neither component required to form customary international law – custom out of a sense of legal obligation[103] – appears present. (Chapter 4 presents a different way of viewing the veto in the face of atrocity crimes based on hard law legal obligations; the author here is simply stating that the "responsibility not to veto," as reflected in *these* various initiatives, is probably not yet viewed as customary international law.)

3.2.2 Variations as to the Different Approaches

There are also interesting variations in the approaches discussed above. (That variations exist may, in fact, make it somewhat difficult to say there is even a "soft law" obligation – precisely which formulation would embody the obligation?) Variations include: (1) which atrocity crimes are encompassed; (2) whether to call for the permanent members to articulate their reasoning either for invoking the veto, to explain how doing so would be consistent with international law and the "Purposes and Principles" of the UN, or to provide another explanation; (3) whether a veto should be permitted in the face of "vital national interests" of a permanent member; (4) whether the threat of atrocity crimes also should trigger the obligation not to veto or the crimes must be occurring; (5) whether a body or person outside the Security Council should be involved in making the determination that the crimes are occurring (that is, to serve as a "trigger mechanism"); (6) whether a threat of the veto by

---

[102] France and the UK last utilized the threat of veto, along with the US, during the 1994 genocide in Rwanda by blocking use of the word "genocide" and the sending of additional forces until the genocide was nearly over. *See* Chapter 1.3.2. All three states in 1989 also vetoed a draft resolution condemning the US invasion of Panama. UNSC Provisional Verbatim Record of the Two Thousand Nine Hundred and Second Meeting, at 18–20, U.N. Doc. S/PV.2902 (Dec. 23, 1989). There are additionally unconfirmed reports of veto threats by the UK and France (and US) regarding vetoes related to Yemen. *See* Chapter 1.3.2.

[103] *See* Restatement (Third) of the Foreign Relations Law, at §102(2) (1987) (the US describes customary international law as resulting "from a general and consistent practice of states followed by them from a sense of legal obligation").

a permanent member would be encompassed; and (7) whether the initiative would cover all vetoes in the face of atrocity crimes, or whether the obligation not to veto would arise only, for example, where there is a "credible draft resolution" before the Security Council, or where the resolution has attracted nine affirmative votes.

The existence of these variations could suggest massive divergences in approach; yet, the Code of Conduct and French/Mexican initiative – the two initiatives attracting the most support – are fairly consistent. Their major differences are that the French/Mexican initiative has a carve-out for the "vital national interests" of the vetoing permanent member, and the Code of Conduct has a carve-out whereby it applies only to the veto of a "credible draft resolution"; also, they differ in terms of whether a "trigger" mechanism is required to recognize that genocide, crimes against humanity, and/or war crimes are occurring. All the various divergences in approach are discussed below.

3.2.2.1 Which Crimes to Include

An obvious initial question is: precisely which crimes should trigger the responsibility not to veto? The ICISS report called on permanent members not to "obstruct the passage of resolutions authorizing military intervention for human protection purposes for which there is otherwise majority support,"[104] while elsewhere it discusses "conscience-shocking situation[s]," including: those covered under the Genocide Convention; the threat or occurrence of large-scale loss of life; different manifestations of "ethnic cleansing"; crimes against humanity and violations of the laws of war; situations of state collapse; and "overwhelming natural or environmental catastrophes."[105] The 2004 R2P report called for veto restraint "in cases of genocide and large-scale human rights abuses."[106] The S5 initiative encompassed "genocide, war crimes and crimes against humanity,"[107] as does the ACT Code of Conduct.[108] The French/Mexican initiative refers to "situations of mass atrocities, when crimes of genocide, crimes against humanity and war crimes on a large scale are committed . . . ."[109] The Elders' proposal covers "genocide or other atrocity

---

[104] ICISS Report, *supra* note 12, at xiii.
[105] *See id.* at 33, para. 4.20.
[106] 2004 R2P report, *supra* note 15, para. 255.
[107] Draft resolution, U.N. Doc. A/66/L.42/Rev.2, *supra* note 33, para. 20.
[108] Code of Conduct, *supra* note 74.
[109] Political Declaration on the Suspension of Veto Power in Cases of Mass Atrocities, *supra* note 61.

crimes."[110] Similarly, the US-based Task Force addressed "genocide and mass atrocities."[111]

A formulation such as "large-scale human rights abuses" is more inclusive, but is also more vague than, for instance, "genocide, crimes against humanity, and war crimes," which are defined crimes under, inter alia, the International Criminal Court's Rome Statute.[112] The term "atrocity crimes" is similarly unspecific unless the phrase "atrocity crimes" is defined to encompass "genocide, crimes against humanity, and/or war crimes."[113] While a broad formulation could be helpful from a human rights perspective and being inclusive in terms of the crimes covered, a narrower formulation achieves more precision as to when any obligation not to veto is triggered. There is now extensive case law on the parameters of genocide, crimes against humanity, and war crimes, and, whereas disputes can still exist, there is quite a lot of jurisprudential guidance upon which to base a determination whether or not such crimes are occurring.[114] Therefore, "genocide, crimes against humanity, and/or war crimes" appears to be the preferable formulation in terms of which crimes should be encompassed.

Sometimes the phrase "ethnic cleansing" is included in this context.[115] Yet, that term primarily appears to be used when it is unclear (or intentional ambiguity is sought) as to whether ethnically motivated crimes rise to the level of genocide. "Ethnic cleansing" does not have significant meaning in international criminal law, as it is genocide, crimes against humanity, and war crimes that are prosecuted before international and hybrid criminal tribunals.[116]

---

[110] The Elders, *Strengthening the United Nations, Statement by The Elders, supra* note 83.
[111] U.S. Genocide Prevention Task Force, *supra* note 87, at 106–07.
[112] Rome Statute of the International Criminal Court, Arts. 6–8, July 17, 1998, U.N. Doc. A/CONF.183/9.
[113] To the extent the author uses the phrase "atrocity crimes," it is intended to cover genocide, crimes against humanity, and/or war crimes.
[114] *See, e.g.,* JENNIFER TRAHAN, GENOCIDE, WAR CRIMES AND CRIMES AGAINST HUMANITY: A TOPICAL DIGEST OF THE CASE LAW OF THE INTERNATIONAL CRIMINAL TRIBUNAL FOR THE FORMER YUGOSLAVIA (Human Rights Watch 2006); JENNIFER TRAHAN, GENOCIDE, WAR CRIMES AND CRIMES AGAINST HUMANITY: A DIGEST OF THE CASE LAW OF THE INTERNATIONAL CRIMINAL TRIBUNAL FOR RWANDA (Human Rights Watch 2010). This author strenuously disagrees with the claim that "what constitutes a 'mass atrocity situation' is largely in the eyes of the beholder," Morris & Wheeler, *supra* note 9, at 238, *quoting* Bosco, *supra* note 49, if atrocity crimes are defined as genocide, crimes against humanity, and/or war crimes.
[115] *See* ICISS report, *supra* note 12, at 33, para. 4.20 (discussing different manifestations of "ethnic cleansing"); European Parliament Recommendation, *supra* note 56, para. 2(f).
[116] The crime of aggression may also now be prosecuted before the ICC. *See* ICC-ASP/16/Res.5. For additional discussion of the crime of aggression, see, e.g., Jennifer Trahan, *From Kampala to New York—The Final Negotiations to Activate the Jurisdiction of the International Criminal*

This was alluded to by Switzerland's then-Permanent Representative Paul Seger in explaining why the S5 initiative did not include the term "ethnic cleansing": "we limited ourselves to genocide, war crimes and crimes against humanity which are defined by the Rome Statute on the International Criminal Court, whereas the term 'ethnic cleansing' is not a legally defined crime under international criminal law."[117] Excluding "ethnic cleansing" from a call for veto restraint probably does not mean that atrocities would escape coverage, as, in such situations, genocide, crimes against humanity, or war crimes are likely also occurring.[118]

Another variation is whether there is reference to "large-scale" in terms of the crimes. For instance, the Code of Conduct specifies in a footnote: "The term 'war crimes' refers in particular to war crimes committed as part of a plan or policy or as part of a large-scale commission of such crimes."[119] The French/Mexican initiative refers to "situations of mass atrocities, when crimes of genocide, crimes against humanity and war crimes on a large scale are committed . . . ."[120] (The latter formulation is somewhat unclear whether it implies that genocide, crimes against humanity, and war crimes *are* large-scale, or there should be a separate large-scale requirement for the three crimes, or a large-scale requirement for war crimes.)

Specifying "large-scale" as to genocide and crimes against humanity appears unnecessary, as the contextual elements of those crimes almost necessarily require the crimes to occur on a large scale. Genocide occurs only where there is intent to destroy a national, ethnical, racial, or religious group as such;[121] crimes against humanity are committed "as part of a widespread or systematic attack directed against any civilian population" and "pursuant to or in furtherance of a State or organizational policy."[122] Yet, for war crimes, because a single murder or single rape could, for example, constitute a war crime if the crime occurs in the context of armed conflict (either international or non-

---

Court Over the Crime of Aggression, 18 INT'L CRIM. LAW REV. 197 (2018); Jennifer Trahan, *Negotiating the Amendment on the Crime of Aggression: Proceedings at the Kampala Review Conference on the International Criminal Court*, 11 INT'L CRIM. L. REV. 49 (2011). The Special Tribunal for Lebanon is an outlier, prosecuting the crime of terrorism.

[117] Statement by H.E. Mr. Paul Seger, *supra* note 36.
[118] *See* GARETH EVANS, THE FRENCH VETO RESTRAINT PROPOSAL: MAKING IT WORK 3 (2016), *at* www.globalr2p.org/media/files/vetorestraintparis21jan25i15rev.pdf ("'Ethnic cleansing' is not a separately recognized crime, but is rather a way [of] carrying out both 'genocide' and 'crimes against humanity' and need not be specifically spelt out.").
[119] Code of Conduct, *supra* note 74, at n. 6.
[120] Political Declaration on the Suspension of Veto Power in Cases of Mass Atrocities, *supra* note 61.
[121] Convention on the Prevention and Punishment of the Crime of Genocide, Dec. 9, 1948, 78 UNTS 277; Rome Statute, Art. 6.
[122] *See, e.g.*, Rome Statute, Arts. 7.1, 7.2(a).

international) and there is a nexus between the crime and the armed conflict, the Code of Conduct's footnote – which mirrors language in the Rome Statute[123] – appears to be a useful formulation (and one, presumably, acceptable to at least the 123 States Parties to the Rome Statute).[124]

3.2.2.2 Whether to Call for the Vetoing Permanent Member to Articulate Its Reasoning

Another variation in approach is whether to require the permanent member utilizing the veto to articulate either: (1) the reason(s) for the veto; (2) an explanation of how the veto is consistent with international law and the "Purposes and Principles" of the UN; (3) the reasons why the veto is in the state's vital, or serious direct, national interests; or (4) to explain a proposed alternative course of action.

Specifically, the S5 initiative called for explanation of "the reasons for resorting to a veto" and its "consistency with the purposes and principles of the Charter" and "applicable international law."[125] Former Under-Secretary-General Hans Corell called for the permanent members to agree not to use their veto unless their most serious direct national interests were affected and to explain, in case they did use the veto, the reasons for doing so.[126] Similarly, the 1949 General Assembly resolution called for an explanation of how the permanent member using the veto considered the question of vital importance.[127] The Elders called for the vetoing permanent members to explain "clearly and in public, what alternative course of action they propose, as a credible and efficient way to protect the populations in question."[128] Similarly, the 2015 R2P report calls for the state employing the veto to "explain publicly what alternative strategy they propose to protect populations at risk."[129] The requirement of an explanation was not adopted in either the Code of Conduct or French/Mexican initiative.

---

[123] Rome Statute Article 8 applies to war crimes "in particular when committed as a part of a plan or policy or as part of a large-scale commission of such crimes." Rome Statute, Art. 8.1.
[124] See International Criminal Court, The States Parties to the Rome Statute, at https://asp.icc-cpi.int/en_menus/asp/states%20parties/pages/the%20states%20parties%20to%20the%20rome%20statute.aspx. The Republic of Kiribati is the 123rd State Party.
[125] Draft Resolution, U.N. Doc. A/66/L.42/Rev.2, *supra* note 33, para. 19.
[126] *See, e.g.*, Letter from Hans Corell to the Governments of the Members of the United Nations, *supra* note 86.
[127] UN G.A. Res. 267(III), para. 3.c (Apr. 14, 1949).
[128] The Elders, *Strengthening the United Nations, Statement by The Elders*, *supra* note 83.
[129] 2015 R2P Report, *supra* note 25, para. 63.

Of course, if there really were veto restraint, then explanations would prove unnecessary. As veto restraint has not yet been achieved, a call for an explanation would appear helpful in trying to force a vetoing permanent member to articulate its basis for utilizing the veto, or to be in the awkward position of not having a defensible basis to articulate. Seeking an explanation of the veto's consistency with international law and/or the "Purposes and Principles" of the UN has the additional advantage of suggesting these *are* relevant criteria by which to examine the acceptability of the veto's use. The Elders' proposal – of requiring the vetoing permanent member to explain a credible and efficient alternative course of action – has some merit, except that if the alternative plan could not attract nine votes, then it is not a true alternative. H.E. Paul Seger defended the requirement of an explanation this way: "to explain the reasons for resorting to a veto is nothing fundamentally new since it is already practiced to some extent by the permanent members of the Security Council."[130] Others have defended this idea as follows: explaining a veto to the General Assembly as "an accountability mechanism is the minimal concession that permanent members should make if they wish to endow the Security Council with the legitimacy and support it requires."[131]

3.2.2.3 Whether to Permit a Veto in the Face of "Vital National Interests" or "Vital State Interests"

Another variation is whether there should be some sort of carve-out permitting veto use in the face of atrocity crimes where the permanent member's "vital national interests," or "vital state interests," are involved, or to permit the veto where the vetoing state's "most serious direct national interests [are] affected."[132]

For example, the ICISS report contained a carve-out for "vital state interests" – that "[t]he Permanent Five members of the Security Council should agree not to apply their veto power in matters *where their vital state interests are not involved*, to obstruct the passage of resolutions

---

[130] Niemetz, *supra* note 30, at 79, citing to Permanent Representative Seger.
[131] *Id.*, citing Jan Wouters & Tom Ruys, *Security Council Reform: A New Veto for a New Century?*, 44 MIL. L. & L. WAR REV. 139 (2005). *See also* Niemetz, *supra* note 30, at 79 ("Such an obligation to explain the reasons behind a veto would ... not only add transparency to the Council's deliberations, but also emphasize its accountability to the GA."). Liechtenstein also now has a new initiative that there should be mandatory discussion in a formal meeting of the General Assembly every time the veto is used in the Security Council. Trahan meeting at the Permanent Mission of Liechtenstein to the UN.
[132] *See, e.g.*, Letter from Hans Corell to the Governments of the Members of the United Nations, *supra* note 86.

authorizing military intervention for human protection purposes for which there is otherwise majority support."[133] The 2004 R2P report called for voluntary veto restraint in cases of mass atrocities, and urged the veto "be limited to matters where vital interests are genuinely at stake."[134] As to the French/Mexican initiative, the op-ed in the *New York Times* by French Foreign Minister Laurent Fabius stated: "To be realistically applicable, this code would exclude cases where the *vital national interests* of a permanent member of the Council were at stake."[135] Yet, when France launched its "Political Declaration on Suspension of Veto Powers in Cases of Mass Atrocity,"[136] it did not contain such a carve-out. Former Under-Secretary-General Hans Corell's initiative called for the permanent members to agree not to use their veto unless their "most serious direct national interests" were affected.[137] In complete juxtaposition, the Elders' proposal suggests that "national interests" of a state can *never* justify casting the veto, "since any state casting a veto simply to protect its national interests is abusing the privilege of permanent membership."[138]

Language about "vital national interests" or "vital state interests" was no doubt included to make veto restraint in the face of atrocity crimes more "palatable" to the permanent members,[139] who might otherwise view the initiatives as encroaching on their power, or too encroaching on their power under the Charter, because, admittedly, the initiatives *do* try somewhat to limit such power by chipping away at unrestrained veto use in the face of genocide, crimes against humanity, or war crimes.[140]

---

[133] ICISS Report, *supra* note 12, at xiii, 75 (emphasis added).
[134] 2004 R2P Report, *supra* note 15, para. 256.
[135] Fabius, *supra* note 59 (emphasis added).
[136] Political Declaration on the Suspension of Veto Power in Cases of Mass Atrocities, *supra* note 61.
[137] *See, e.g.*, Letter from Hans Corell to the Governments of the Members of the United Nations, *supra* note 86.
[138] The Elders, Strengthening the United Nations, Statement by The Elders, *supra* note 83.
[139] *See also* Golden, *supra* note 48, at 120 ("indeterminate proposals are more likely to attain political support at the international level because states can hide behind the vagueness in wording and interpret the proposals in a way that best serves their interests").
[140] Arguably, however, in 1945, the veto power that permanent members were granted under the Charter was already somewhat limited. For example, it had to be used in a way that was in accordance with the UN's "Purposes and Principles," and, even then, there were early writings on *jus cogens*, additional sources of international law, as well as the clear commitment to human rights contained in the Charter. *See* UN Charter, Art. 24(2) (obligation for the Security Council to "act in accordance with the Purposes and Principles of the United Nations"), Art. 1 (UN's "Purposes" including human rights), Art. 2 (UN's "Principles").

3.2 Evaluation of Approaches to Voluntary Veto Restraint

Yet, these phrases "vital national interests," "vital state interests," or "most serious direct national interests" appear inherently susceptible to abusive invocations[141] – as suggested by the Elders, who view such veto use as "abusing the privilege of permanent membership."[142] Thus, if "vital interests are defined too broadly, the [French/Mexican] proposal will lack any application at all."[143] Who is to determine if a permanent member's "vital national interests" or "vital state interests" are implicated? Could China claim it has unlimited veto power related to the situation in Myanmar despite atrocities occurring against the Rohingya because China has investment interests in Myanmar[144] and these are of "vital national interest"? Could Russia claim that it has unlimited veto power related to the situation in Syria, despite the regime being deeply implicated in atrocity crimes,[145] because Russia's vetoes are consistent with its foreign policy to support the regime of Bashar al-Assad in Syria which constitutes a "vital national interest"? And who would evaluate these claims, or would each permanent member simply be free to invoke them?

This leads to the conundrum: "any articulation of the responsibility [not to veto] which does not recognize an exception based on vital interests will be wholly unacceptable to the P5, but once recognized[,] the indefinable and illimitable nature of the exception has the potential to render the responsibility vacuous."[146] A strong argument can be made that it should *never* be considered to be in the "vital national interests" or "vital state interests" of a permanent member to use a veto that allows the continued perpetration of genocide, crimes against humanity, or war crimes. The author holds this view and would not support any such carve-out.[147] Neither the Code of Conduct nor the Elders' proposal contains such a carve-out. Put another way, "vital

---

[141] See, e.g., Morris & Wheeler, *supra* note 9, at 237 ("what counts as vital interests is open to wide contestation"); Citizens for Global Solutions, *supra* note 21, at 12 ("the exclusion where vital national interests are at stake is simply too broad of an exclusion. Repeated use of this exclusion for political purposes would weaken the integrity of any code").

[142] The Elders, *Strengthening the United Nations, Statement by The Elders*, *supra* note 83.

[143] Golden, *supra* note 48, at 132.

[144] Nathan Vadnjal, *The Changing Face of Chinese Investment in Myanmar*, FOR. BRIEF: GEOPOLITICAL RISK ANALYSIS (June 9, 2017), *at* www.foreignbrief.com/asia-pacific/south-east-asia/changing-face-chinese-investment-myanmar ("China is Myanmar's largest trading partner.").

[145] See Chapter 5 for a chronological discussion of Russia's (and sometimes China's) vetoes related to Syria.

[146] Morris & Wheeler, *supra* note 9, at 238.

[147] See also Speech delivered by Dr. Simon Adams, *supra* note 20 ("committing these crimes (or protecting a state or non-state actor that is committing them) can never be excused, exempted or misrepresented as being a matter of 'vital national interest'").

interests are usually the underlying reason why permanent members use the veto" so if this formulation is included, it "weaken[s] the idea of [veto] restraint."[148]

3.2.2.4 Whether the Crimes Need to Be Occurring or the Threat of Their Occurrences Also Triggers the Obligation Not to Veto

Another issue is whether genocide, crimes against humanity, and/or war crimes need to be *occurring* to trigger a responsibility not to veto, or whether the *threat*, or serious risk, of their occurrence should also trigger this obligation. In other words, when it is suspected that genocide is commencing, is there an obligation to wait and be certain that genocide (or crimes against humanity or war crimes) are occurring before there is an obligation not to veto, and, if so, how long does the Security Council wait? This question is related to the question of what level of atrocity crimes might justify intervention, an issue that emerged, for example, as to crimes in Libya and Kosovo, where crimes were commencing, but the interventions were prompt enough that the crimes may not have fully manifested.[149] In that context, the Security Council's powers under Chapter VII can be triggered by a "threat" to the peace, so it is not required to wait until that threat fully morphs into a "breach of peace" or "act of aggression" before it may utilize its Chapter VII powers.[150]

Most of the above initiatives appear to suggest the crimes need to be occurring, while the ICISS report also covered "conscience-shocking situation[s]," including "the *threat* or occurrence of large-scale loss of life."[151] The Elders' proposal also encompassed "where populations are being subjected to, *or threatened with*, genocide or other atrocity crimes."[152] The US Genocide Prevention Task Force additionally would have covered where "a crisis poses an *imminent threat* of mass atrocities."[153] The French/Mexican initiative and Code of Conduct (along with the S5 initiative) refer to resolutions aimed at "preventing or bringing an end to," or "preventing or ending," atrocity crimes (suggesting a focus on prevention), but then appear to

---

[148] Security Council Report, The Veto, *supra* note 81, at 5.
[149] These are very different examples, of course, because as to Libya, there was a force authorization (UNSC Res. 1973), whereas there was no Security Council force authorization for NATO's intervention in Kosovo. *See* Chapter 2 for further discussion of the Kosovo and Libya interventions.
[150] UN Charter, Art. 39.
[151] *See* ICISS Report, *supra* note 12, at 33, para. 4.20 (emphasis added).
[152] The Elders, *Strengthening the United Nations, Statement by The Elders*, *supra* note 83 (emphasis added).
[153] U.S. Genocide Prevention Task Force, *supra* note 87, at 106–07 (emphasis added).

apply only when the crimes are occurring, suggesting the threat of the crimes occurring is not encompassed in those initiatives.

Indeed, an argument could be made that it should be unnecessary to wait until the crimes have fully manifested before the responsibility not to veto is triggered. On the other hand, if the responsibility not to veto also applies where there is a "threat," or serious risk, of the crimes occurring, there may be a lack of clarity as to when that point has been reached. Thus, including a situation where the crimes are "threatened" or there is a serious risk of their occurring is the more protective of populations at risk, but a formulation that requires the crimes to be occurring has more specificity as to whether the obligation not to veto is triggered. As discussed in Chapters 2 and 4, the duty to prevent genocide, according to the International Court of Justice, is triggered by the "serious risk" of genocide occurring,[154] so legal responsibility attaches prior to the crime fully manifesting. Given this legal obligation, an argument can be made that voluntary veto restraint should follow an analogous approach.

3.2.2.5 Who Determines Whether Genocide, Crimes against Humanity, or War Crimes Are Occurring, or Are at Serious Risk of Occurring?

A separate question is: if the obligation not to veto is triggered by the occurrence of genocide, crimes against humanity, or war crimes, *who* determines whether the crimes are occurring? (Similarly, if the responsibility not to veto also includes the *threat* of the crimes occurring, or the serious risk of their occurrence, who makes those determinations?) Is the Security Council the only body that would make such a determination, or should some outside entity or person be involved in making that determination (that is, serve as a "trigger")? Or should the "facts on the ground" suffice to provide the "trigger"?[155]

---

[154] Case Concerning Application of the Convention on the Prevention and Punishment of the Crime of Genocide (Bosn. & Herz. v. Serb. and Montenegro), Judgment of 26 February 2007, para. 431. *See also* Application of the Convention on the Prevention and Punishment of the Crime of Genocide (The Gambia v. Myanmar), Order of 23 January 2020, paras. 72, 86 (observing that the Fact-Finding Mission on Myanmar "'conclude[d] on reasonable grounds that the Rohingya people remain at serious risk of genocide'" and granting provisional measures).

[155] The Code of Conduct provides for "no procedural trigger," as the "facts on the ground would be the trigger and lead to Security Council action." Explanatory Note on a Code of Conduct, *supra* note 74.

The concern is, of course, that if the obligation not to veto applies in the face of genocide, crimes against humanity, or war crimes (or their serious risk), will this then incentivize a permanent member opposed to Security Council action to deny the occurrence of the crimes (or their serious risk)? History is replete with examples of states avoiding the term "genocide," presumably out of concern if they admit genocide is occurring, then the state should be taking action under the Genocide Convention's obligation to "prevent" genocide.[156] In such situations, one sees obfuscation and essentially meaningless formulations, like "isolated acts of genocide might be occurring."[157] That is meaningless, as the *dolus specialis* – special mental state requirement[158] – of genocide is either present or not, and, if it is, and "underlying acts" of genocide are occurring,[159] then genocide *is* occurring; if either "underlying acts" or the *dolus specialis* is not satisfied, then genocide is *not* occurring – there is no middle ground.

In this respect, the Code of Conduct invites the Secretary-General "making full use of the expertise and early warning capacities of the United Nations system, in particular the Office of the United Nations High Commissioner for Human Rights and the United Nations Office on Genocide Prevention and the Responsibility to Protect, to continue to bring [situations] to the attention of the Council ...."[160] Thus, while this references other persons and offices being involved, their information would be presented to the Council. Yet, the Code of Conduct is also careful to state that the "events themselves" would provide the "trigger" – that is, there is no requirement of an outside determination.

---

[156] See Genocide Convention, Art. I (obligation "to prevent and to punish" genocide). The obligation to "prevent" genocide is discussed further in Chapters 2.2.2 and 4.3.1.

[157] The United States, related to Rwanda, "did not publicly use the word genocide until May 25 [1994] and even then diluted its impact by saying 'acts of genocide.'" *US Chose to Ignore Rwandan Genocide: Classified Papers Show Clinton Was Aware of "Final Solution" to Eliminate Tutsis*, THE GUARDIAN (Mar. 31, 2004), *at* www.theguardian.com/world/2004/m ar/31/usa.rwanda. *See also* Chapter 1.3.2 (discussing Rwanda).

[158] The mental state requirement necessitates proof of "intent to destroy, in whole or in part, a national, ethnical, racial or religious group, as such." Genocide Convention, Art. II.

[159] The "underlying acts" or "underlying crimes" are listed in subsections (a)–(e) of Article II of the Genocide Convention: "a. [k]illing members of the group; b. [c]ausing serious bodily or mental harm to members of the group; c. [d]eliberately inflicting on the group conditions of life calculated to bring about its physical destruction in whole or in part; d. [i]mposing measures intended to prevent births within the group; [and] e. [f]orcibly transferring children of the group to another group." Genocide Convention, Art. II (a)–(e). For an application of these provisions, see, e.g., Jennifer Trahan, *Why the Killing in Darfur is Genocide*, 31 FORDHAM INT'L L.J. 990 (2008).

[160] Code of Conduct, *supra* note 74, para. 3.

Another proposal is that "at the request of at least 50 member states, the United Nations secretary general would be called upon to determine the nature of the crime. Once he [or she] had delivered his [or her] opinion, the code of conduct would immediately apply."[161] This would have the Secretary-General (who certainly could be assisted by appropriate bodies) making the determination. One source, however, contends that fifty Member States would be "too low a number," as it would too easily allow the General Assembly to "make repeated and politically motivated requests," although that source maintains the Secretary-General "would make a good trigger" for determining whether the crimes are occurring.[162] Another source, by contrast, argues that "requiring the backing of fifty Member States will be too time-consuming in situations that would need quick response."[163]

Yet another approach, proposed by the US Genocide Prevention Task Force, would be if a resolution were passed by two-thirds of the General Assembly that a crisis poses an imminent threat of atrocity crimes, that "should add further impetus to an expeditious Security Council response without threat of a veto."[164] This approach suggests two-thirds of the General Assembly as the trigger without absolutely requiring it. Another suggestion is to utilize a "permanent Commission of Inquiry, consisting of eminent and independent experts" who would "pronounce on the nature and scope of ongoing crises,"[165] similar to the International Commission of Inquiry on Darfur, the Independent International Commission of Inquiry on the Syrian Arab Republic, or the International Fact-Finding Commission established under the 1977 Protocols to the Geneva Conventions.[166] Gareth Evans, who served as co-chair of the ICISS, has suggested a two-stage trigger of (1) a determination by the Office of the UN Secretary-General's Special Adviser on the Prevention of Genocide and R2P that a situation is one to which the "code of conduct" should apply, and (2) a signed statement from at least fifty members of the General Assembly, including at least five members of each regional group.[167]

An outside "trigger" mechanism could have an advantage of clarity, that once it is met, then the responsibility not to veto must apply. Yet, it would also

---

[161] Fabius, *supra* note 59.
[162] Citizens for Global Solutions, *supra* note 21, at 11–12.
[163] Golden, *supra* note 48, at 130.
[164] Genocide Prevention Task Force, *supra* note 87, at 106–07.
[165] Wouters & Ruys, *supra* note 131, at 163–64.
[166] Golden, *supra* note 48, at 130. See, e.g., website of the International Humanitarian Fact-Finding Commission, *at* www.ihffc.org/index.asp?page=aboutus_general.
[167] Evans, *supra* note 118, at 4–5.

add another layer of complexity, and maybe another layer at which the crimes could be denied. An outside trigger also could not be made "binding" on the Council unless all permanent members were to agree (which would appear unlikely). If the Council members do not agree to the outside trigger, then a layer of complexity has been added, without even ensuring that no veto will follow.

Perhaps the Code of Conduct takes the best approach of not having an additional trigger, but giving appropriate deference to outside actors such as the Secretary-General, relying on the Office of the United Nations High Commissioner for Human Rights, and the United Nations Office on Genocide Prevention and the Responsibility to Protect. Indeed, an argument could be made that initial determinations by such bodies or persons, or UN commissions of inquiry or commissions of experts, that they believe that genocide, crimes against humanity, and/or war crimes are occurring or are at serious risk (that is, there is a "prima facie" case), should suffice to trigger the responsibility not to veto.

3.2.2.6 Whether to Include the Threat of Veto Use by a Permanent Member

As illustrated in Chapters 1 and 5, the threat of the veto can be as pernicious as actual veto use,[168] and there is also the situation where, due to a permanent member's support for a government, it is understood that the permanent member would employ the veto, so that measures related to atrocity crimes are not even proposed or discussed in the Council. (As noted in Chapter 1, China's support for the Governments of Sudan, Sri Lanka, and Myanmar appears to have translated into a consistent understanding that China would veto most measures related to atrocity crimes committed in those countries, so that various measures related to those situations likely never reached the Council for deliberation or voting.)[169] None of the initiatives applies to the threat of veto, except for the Elders' proposal, which sought a pledge by the permanent member "not to use, *or threaten to use*, their veto" where populations are being subjected to, or threatened with, genocide or other atrocity crimes.[170]

---

[168] See also Golden, *supra* note 48, at 110–11 ("It is well document that the P5 use the threat of the veto as a bargaining chip in negotiations. Thus, the veto power is much more influential than initially appears"), citing Céline Nahory, *The Hidden Veto*, GLOB. POL'Y FORUM (May 2004).

[169] See Chapter 1.3.2. The use of China's veto threat related to crimes in Darfur is detailed in Chapter 5.2.

[170] The Elders, *Strengthening the United Nations, Statement by The Elders*, *supra* note 83 (emphasis added).

3.2 Evaluation of Approaches to Voluntary Veto Restraint

The failure of most initiatives to apply to situations other than actual veto use suggests the need for the permanent members who believe in veto restraint or the elected members of the Security Council to actually draft resolutions and try to ensure they are voted on, thereby triggering actual veto use, in order to make it transparent how the veto is being misused. If, in the face of momentum towards veto restraint, practice shifts to fewer measures being put to a vote, that would of course defeat the purpose of veto restraint, because Security Council action would remain stymied without the veto having to be invoked. On the other hand, if there really ever fully were veto restraint (for instance, because all permanent members have agreed to voluntary veto restraint, or veto use in certain circumstances is recognized as inconsistent with *jus cogens*, the "Purposes and Principles" of the UN, and/or foundational treaty obligations of the permanent members, as argued in Chapter 4), then it would diminish the potency of any threat (or implicit threat) of the veto as well.[171] Thus, if actual veto restraint were successful, then it could be unnecessary to include the threat of the veto, as a threat of veto in the face of atrocity crimes would become a hollow threat. Since this has not occurred, the Elders' inclusion of the "threat" of use of the veto has merit.

3.2.2.7 Whether *All* Vetoes in the Face of Atrocity Crimes Should Be Encompassed

A final difference in approach is whether to take the position that a veto in the face of atrocity crimes should *always* be considered problematic, or whether there might still be vetoes that, despite atrocity crimes occurring, might be permissible or warranted. Furthermore, if one accepts the proposition that some vetoes might still be appropriate, how would one define which ones to exempt from veto restraint?

In this respect, the ACT Code of Conduct – apparently at the insistence of the UK[172] – calls for states to pledge *"in particular* to not vote against a *credible draft resolution* before the Security Council on timely and decisive action to end the commission of genocide, crimes against humanity, or war crimes, or to

---

[171] Author's e-mail correspondence with Richard Goldstone, Spring 2018.
[172] Harrington, *supra* note 32, at 49 (noting that the Code of Conduct required a modification to its text to refer to a "credible" draft resolution); Vilmer, *supra* note 22, at 8 (similar); *see also* Statement by Ambassador Matthew Rycroft of the UK Mission to the UN at the ACT Group Event on the Code of Conduct, October 1, 2015, *at* www.gov.uk/government/speeches/im-proud-to-say-that-the-united-kingdom-is-signing-up-to-the-act-code-of-conduct ("I am proud to say today that we will never vote against *credible* Security Council action to stop mass atrocities and crimes against humanity.") (emphasis added).

prevent such crimes."[173] Thus, by calling for veto restraint to apply "in particular" where there is a "credible draft resolution," the Code of Conduct implicitly retains the veto in the case of a non-credible draft resolution. The Secretary-General in his *Report for the World Humanitarian Summit* in February 2016 echoed the Code of Conduct formulation.[174] Both documents, then, beg the question of what constitutes a "credible draft resolution."[175] Neither document attempts to define this.

One can imagine an argument that not every resolution drafted and put to a vote while there are ongoing atrocity crimes, or their serious risk, should necessarily pass. For example, there might be times that genocide, crimes against humanity, or war crimes are occurring and the proposed measures contained in a draft resolution purportedly aimed at curtailing or alleviating commission of the crimes are judged as likely to do more harm than good, or perhaps even pretextual excuses for full-scale intervention when lesser uses of force could be attempted (for example, no-fly zones, protection of persons in Internally Displaced People (IDP) camps, creating humanitarian aid corridors). For example, a force authorization by the Security Council would only be appropriate where there is no practical or viable alternative if lives are to be saved. The use of force must be necessary and proportionate to the aim of relief of humanitarian need, or alleviating or curtailing the commission of genocide, crimes against humanity, or war crimes, and must be strictly limited in time and scope to this aim (that is, the minimum necessary to achieve that end and for no other purpose). Vetoing a force authorization, if these criteria are not met, would be appropriate.[176]

At least one author appears to conflate support for a "responsibility not to veto" with support for military intervention in the face of atrocity crimes.[177] No

---

[173] Code of Conduct, *supra* note 74, para. 2.
[174] Report of the Secretary-General for the World Humanitarian Summit, at para. 67, U.N. Doc. A/70/709 (Feb. 2, 2016), *at* www.securitycouncilreport.org/atf/cf/%7B65BFCF9B-6D27-4E9C-8CD3-CF6E4FF96FF9%7D/A_70_709.pdf (calling for the permanent members "not to vote against credible resolutions aimed at preventing or ending [mass atrocities]").
[175] "Credibility being subjective – what is credible to a state that supports a resolution is not credible to a state that does not – the word provided some freedom for interpretation and was enough to reassure [the UK]." Vilmer, *supra* note 22, at 8. *See also* Golden, *supra* note 48, at 134 ("[t]he determination of what is or is not credible should not be left to the P5").
[176] These criteria are derived from a UK government policy paper. *See* Prime Minister's Office, Chemical Weapon Use by Syrian Regime: UK Government Legal Position, Policy Paper (Aug. 29, 2013) (UK), *at* www.gov.uk/government/publications/chemical-weapon-use-by-syrian-regime-uk-government-legal-position/chemical-weapon-use-by-syrian-regime-uk-government-legal-position-html-version.
[177] *See* Daniel H. Levine, *Some Concerns About "The Responsibility Not to Veto,"* in GLOBAL RESPONSIBILITY TO PROTECT 323 (2011) (criticizing supporters of the "responsibility not to

3.2 Evaluation of Approaches to Voluntary Veto Restraint

such automatic linkage should be presumed. Military intervention is one option in the face of atrocity crimes, but should be *the very last option considered*. For example, under Chapter VII, the Security Council reaches forceful measures, "[s]hould the Security Council consider that measures provided for in Article 41 [non-forceful measures] would be inadequate, or have proved to be inadequate."[178] Clearly, non-forceful measures should be attempted first (and/or Article 40 provisional measures, as appropriate). Moreover, even the term "forceful measure" can encompass a broad variety of measures such as those noted above (that is, no-fly zones, protection of persons in IDP camps, and creating humanitarian aid corridors). There are also many additional Security Council tools, such as targeted sanctions, weapons embargoes, travel restrictions, etc. That author is right to point out large-scale military interventions are not always successful and carry risks.[179] Yet, it is wrong to suggest those who support veto restraint necessarily support military intervention; there are many other measures the Security Council can implement (including authorization of chemical weapons inspection regimes, the creation of mechanism for atrocity crimes investigations, and/or referrals of situations for prosecution, as well as others measures listed above), and these also run the risk of veto.[180]

Thus, there should not be an automatic assumption that *any* Security Council resolution drafted while genocide, crimes against humanity, and/or war crimes are occurring should *necessarily* pass. One does not want to make "inappropriate interventions too easy to authorize."[181] Rather than using the Code of Conduct's formulation of a "credible draft resolution," a preferable position could be that veto restraint should apply to a resolution that has

---

veto" as favoring military intervention); *see, e.g., id.* at 324 (the "responsibility not to veto" "implicitly privileges *military* action over non-military action for human rights abuses").

[178] UN Charter, Art. 42.

[179] As discussed in Chapter 2, the Libya intervention received Security Council authorization, SC Res. 1973 (2015), yet, is not generally seen as a success. It may have halted Gaddafi regime atrocities (we will never know what would have happened absent the intervention), but certainly left a destabilized state in its wake. Yet, was this a result of a flawed decision to intervene, or the failure to invest sufficiently in post-intervention rebuilding? This author contends that much more attention should be focused on the concept of the "responsibility to rebuild." Intervention should come with responsibility for the post-intervention's aftermath. *See also* Chapter 2.2.1.1 (Libya as R2P).

[180] Some of the difficulty may come from the word "action," which can, but does not need to, be read to mean "military action." *See, e.g.,* Levine, *supra* note 177, at 325 (noting the "strong tendency to understand ... 'action' as military in nature").

[181] *See id.* at 324 (warning that circumventing "the veto passed on the seriousness of abuses rather than any characteristics of the proposed intervention" "risks making inappropriate interventions too easy to authorize").

attracted nine votes. That is, the veto is blocking a resolution that otherwise would pass; absent nine votes, there is no need to utilize the veto. Furthermore, presumably, there would not be nine affirmative votes by Security Council members unless the resolution is seen by at least those nine states as a credible response.

3.3 CONCLUSION

This chapter has explored initiatives having the goal of voluntary veto restraint in the face of atrocity crimes, including the "responsibility not to veto" found in R2P, the S5 initiative, the French/Mexican initiative, the ACT Code of Conduct, and a proposal by "The Elders." In analyzing the differences in the initiatives, an obvious tension appears. The broader the initiative is formulated in terms of the crimes it encompasses and the fewer carve-outs it contains, the more protective it potentially is of victims of the crimes; this may in turn incentivize states that are not permanent members of the Security Council to join the initiative. The narrower the formulation and more carve-outs that exist (for example, permitting veto use in certain circumstances), the more acceptable the initiative may be to permanent members, which increases the likelihood of their joining. The initiatives are clearly trying to achieve something of a balance – and have achieved enough balance that two permanent members support voluntary veto restraint.[182] The question is, does a restrained approach make it more likely the remaining permanent members might join such initiatives, or are they unlikely to join anyway, so moderation in approach is hardly an enticement, as they may adamantly reject any form of veto restraint, even voluntary?

Of the permanent members, the US would appear the more likely to endorse one of the initiatives, in that, at least during the Obama Administration, as explained above, a high-level US-based task force called for veto restraint. Yet, while the US periodically condemns certain veto use (for instance, by Russia or China),[183] the US appears unlikely to accept any across the board limitations on the veto (even voluntary), as it periodically invokes the veto, particularly regarding situations involving

---

[182] Another possibility is that the UK and France have joined these initiatives out of a sense that their seats as permanent members of the Security Council are more tenuous, as they are less militarily and economically powerful than other permanent members; therefore, perhaps the UK and France perceive more of a need – in light of years of discussion as to possible changes in the composition of the Security Council – to be seen as responsible in their Security Council voting.

[183] *See, e.g.*, Chapter 4.2.4.2 (statements by the US critiquing veto use related to Syria).

3.3 *Conclusion* 139

Israel.[184] The chances of Russia or China agreeing to veto restraint would appear even lower:

> Hostile to the initiative, [Russia and China] feel no pressure to grant it greater importance, and remain inflexible. Using a slippery slope argument, they pretend that any discussion on limiting the veto, even voluntarily, would eventually lead to calling it into question. China insists on the relative nature of the crimes in question, on the fact that each Security Council decision should be made on a case-by-case basis and not by pre-established rules, and on the need to win the P5's consensus, fully knowing this to be impossible. For a long time, Russia has equally shown its opposition.[185]

Furthermore, as shown in Chapters 1 and 5, Russia (sometimes accompanied by China) has freely invoked its veto repeatedly as to the situation in Syria, and China makes use of the leverage of having the veto, so that resolutions related to crimes occurring in Sudan, Myanmar, and Sri Lanka were frequently not even drafted or put to a vote.[186] (Detailed chronologies of veto use as to Syria and veto threats as to Darfur are contained in Chapter 5.)

The greatest impediment to the implementation of these initiatives lies not in their wording variations, but that they call for *voluntary* veto restraint, and thus, at most are seen as representing political or moral aspirations, and, accordingly, "soft law." (Admittedly, at the time the initiatives were created, likely only such "soft law" approaches would have been supported by states, as backing for the concept of "veto restraint" needed to be cultivated.) Thus, while all the initiatives have contributed to building crucial momentum towards veto restraint in the face of atrocity crimes – and they are *each* important in this respect – they do not purport to create binding legal obligations as to Security Council veto use. As to wording variations, while the author has evaluated a number of proposals, it is the Code of Conduct and French/Mexican initiative that have galvanized the most support among UN Member States, so it is on these two initiatives that focus should continue to be

---

[184] See Chapter 1.3.2. See also M. Byers & S. Chesterman, *Changing the Rules about Rules? Unilateral Humanitarian Intervention and the Future of International Law*, in J. L. Holzgrefe & R. Keohane, HUMANITARIAN INTERVENTION: ETHICAL, LEGAL, AND POLITICAL DILEMMAS, at 195 (2003) ("The United States has always been reluctant to subject its national interests to multilateral structures.").

[185] Vilmer, *supra* note 22, at 10. Vilmer then optimistically predicts China might, of the two, be more willing to join out of a goal to be perceived as a "norm entrepreneur." *Id*. This author does not share that optimism.

[186] See Chapters 1, 5.

placed. Both formulations, which are not significantly that different, have merit and warrant support.

The French/Mexican initiative and the ACT Code of Conduct *are* significantly helpful in increasing the "political cost" of veto use in the face of genocide, crimes against humanity, and/or war crimes. Not only do the initiatives focus the attention of states on such veto use, the countries that join the initiatives are then well-positioned to make statements at the UN about how a permanent member engaging in such vetoes is acting in disregard of its obligations to prevent atrocity crimes, in disregard of its obligations under the UN Charter,[187] and in disregard of the plight of the victims. The more states join these initiatives, the greater the costs become for the permanent members using (or abusing) the veto power in this way. Membership in these initiatives should thus be encouraged; in fact, one could even imagine membership in one of the initiatives being an important litmus test for a state's candidacy to serve as an elected member of the Security Council.[188] It would be ideal if all elected members of the Council would join at least one of the initiatives.

To truly change veto use in the face of genocide, crimes against humanity, and/or war crimes, there appear to be two possibilities (as most consider a UN Charter amendment not realistically possible).[189] The first is to convince the remaining permanent members to join either the Code of Conduct or French/Mexican initiative – so that voluntary veto restraint is agreed to by *all* permanent members. Second, in light of the possibility that the remaining permanent members will not join either initiative (or not all will do so), Chapter 4 suggests a complementary approach: revisiting existing hard law obligations that show there are legal limits (or constraints) on the use of the veto in the face of genocide, crimes against humanity, and/or war crimes based on existing international law. Chapter 4 will demonstrate that whereas the voluntary veto restraint initiatives (discussed in this chapter) are seen as "soft law," there are actually hard law legal obligations underlying them; thus, in fact, states should not be treating the matter of veto restraint in the face of atrocity crimes as such a "voluntary" matter.[190]

The voluntary restraint initiatives by themselves are very unlikely to achieve veto restraint in the face of atrocity crimes (because they are seen as voluntary,

---

[187] Obligations to prevent genocide, crimes against humanity, and war crimes, and obligations imposed by the UN Charter will be discussed in Chapter 4.
[188] Suggestions made by the Permanent Representative of Liechtenstein, Ambassador Christian Wenaweser, in statements at the UN.
[189] See *supra* note 67 (Charter amendments).
[190] A parallel argument is presented in Chapter 2, that these same hard law legal obligations underlie aspects of R2P, so not all of R2P should be treated as "soft law." *See* Chapter 2.2.2.

3.3 Conclusion

and will inevitably clash with the self-interest of at least certain permanent members). Where these initiatives make a significant difference – especially the French/Mexican initiative and the ACT Code of Conduct – is that they are supported by so many States (nearly two-thirds of UN Member States). They thereby demonstrate the longstanding and strengthening understanding of the international community, and especially of states, that there are supposed to be limits to permanent member veto use in the face of atrocity crimes, an understanding that can be derived from, and is actually mandated by the hard law legal obligations discussed in Chapter 4. This understanding,[191] and the repeated efforts of the international community to find ways to restrain unrestricted veto use, also clearly demonstrate that there has never been a practice of acquiescence by states to unlimited veto use in the face of atrocity crimes.

---

[191] *See* Chapter 4.2.4.2 (statements by states at the UN objecting to veto use in the face of atrocity crimes).

4

Questioning the Legality of Veto Use in the Face of Genocide, Crimes against Humanity, and/or War Crimes

Statement of the United Kingdom at the UN Security Council: "What has taken place in Syria to date is in itself a violation of the United Nations Charter. No purpose or principle of the Charter is upheld or served by the use of chemical weapons on innocent civilians. On the contrary: to stand by and ignore the requirements of justice, accountability and the preservation of the non-proliferation regime is to place all our security—not just that of the Syrian people—at the mercy of a Russian veto." S/PV.8231, April 13, 2018, at pp. 10–11.

Statement of the United States at the UN Security Council: "Russia's veto was the green light for the Al-Assad regime to use these most barbaric weapons against the Syrian people, in complete violation of international law . . . . We cannot stand by and let Russia trash every international norm that we stand for, and allow the use of chemical weapons to go unanswered." S/P.V.8233, April 14, 2018, at p. 5.

INTRODUCTION

This chapter makes the case that it is appropriate, and justified, to revisit – based on existing international legal obligations – the problem of veto use in the face of genocide, crimes against humanity, and/or war crimes. This chapter will show a clear tension between existing legal obligations and the use of the veto when such crimes are occurring, or when they are at serious risk of occurring; consequently, use of the veto in such circumstances is arguably outside the proper exercise of Security Council power. The chapter presents three main legal arguments that indicate there are legal limits (or constraints) on the use of the veto in the face of genocide, crimes against humanity, and/or war crimes. First, the chapter argues that the veto power, which is conferred by the UN Charter, is subordinate to the highest-level *jus cogens* norms; as a consequence, the veto should not be used (i) where it has the effect of facilitating ongoing *jus cogens* violations, (ii) where it undermines the duty of other Security Council members to cooperate to make an appropriate response to a serious breach of a *jus cogens* norm, or (iii) where its use is inconsistent with *jus cogens* protections. Second, the chapter argues that the veto power sits within the context of the UN Charter, which states that the Security Council must act pursuant to the UN's "[p]urposes and [p]rinciples"; a veto in the face of genocide, crimes against humanity, and/or war crimes does not accord with the UN's "[p]urposes and [p]rinciples." Third, the chapter argues that there are also treaty obligations that bind individual permanent Member States, such as those under the Genocide Convention[1] and 1949 Geneva Conventions,[2] and veto use should not be contrary to obligations created under these treaties. Furthermore, these treaty obligations are not overridden by UN Charter Article 103 because the norms protected by these treaties are also protected by *jus cogens* and/or the UN's "[p]urposes and [p]rinciples"; alternatively, the veto power should be read in a way that is consistent with the legal obligations created under these foundational treaties.

In light of the issues raised, the chapter considers the scope of judicial review by the International Court of Justice (ICJ), concluding that the above legal questions are ones on which the ICJ could, and should, opine. Ultimately, the chapter suggests that the General Assembly consider requesting an advisory opinion from the ICJ on a question such as: does existing international law contain limitations on the use of the veto power by permanent members of the UN Security Council in situations where there is ongoing genocide, crimes against humanity, and/or war crimes? The chapter proposes that it is time to stop reading the veto as a *carte blanche*, above all other sources of law. The General Assembly could ask the ICJ to opine on this significant question given the strong arguments that exist that the veto power is not superior to all sources of international law but must be used in a way that is consistent with, or limited by, them. The chapter also suggests the alternative possibility of the General Assembly, in a resolution, confirming its understanding of such hard law obligations regarding veto use while genocide, crimes against humanity, and/or war crimes are occurring, or are at serious

---

[1] Convention on the Prevention and Punishment of the Crime of Genocide, Dec. 9, 1948, 78 UNTS 277 [hereinafter, Genocide Convention].
[2] Geneva Convention I for the Amelioration of the Condition of the Wounded and Sick in Armed Forces in the Field, Aug. 12, 1949, 75 UNTS 31 [hereinafter, Geneva Convention I]; Geneva Convention II for the Amelioration of the Condition of Wounded, Sick and Shipwrecked Members of Armed Forces at Sea, Aug. 12, 1949, 75 UNTS 85 [hereinafter, Geneva Convention II]; Geneva Convention III Relative to the Treatment of Prisoners of War, Aug. 12, 1949, 75 UNTS 135 [hereinafter, Geneva Convention III]; Geneva Convention IV Relative to the Protection of Civilian Persons in Time of War, Aug. 12, 1949, 75 UNTS 287 [hereinafter, Geneva Convention IV] [collectively, 1949 Geneva Conventions].

risk of occurring. In the meanwhile, the chapter additionally suggests that states at the UN should continue to build consistent precedent by invoking legal arguments, such as those outlined above and detailed in this chapter, whenever a permanent member exercises its veto while there are ongoing atrocity crimes or they are at serious risk of occurring.

THE NEED FOR AN APPROACH GUIDED BY EXISTING HARD LAW OBLIGATIONS

There is a need for revisiting the use of the veto power in the face of genocide, crimes against humanity, and/or war crimes[3] – both for policy and legal reasons. On the policy side, while the growing call since 2001 for voluntary veto restraint has made an important contribution by increasing the "political" cost of using the veto in the face of such atrocity crimes, it has not prevented its use in such circumstances. Nearly twenty years after voluntary veto restraint first surfaced in the 2001 report of the International Commission on Intervention and State Sovereignty (ICISS),[4] the time is ripe for taking a fresh look at this issue. On the legal side, there is a pressing need to examine more closely how international law has developed since 1945 in prohibiting atrocity crimes and in specifying the legal obligations on states in the face of such crimes, and to consider how use of the veto power fits within this system of international law.

Let us turn first to the efforts to secure voluntary veto restraint and the limitations of such an approach. Other chapters discuss the actual use of the veto in the face of such atrocity crimes,[5] and the various efforts that have been and are being made – through, inter alia, the ACT Group of States' Code of Conduct and the French/Mexican Initiative – to ask the permanent members of the Security Council to voluntarily restrain veto use in such circumstances.[6] As also detailed, however, three permanent members do not endorse such voluntary veto restraint. At present, therefore, there is no veto restraint being practiced by those permanent members, even in the face of ongoing genocide,

---

[3] Some formulations of the crimes protected by the "responsibility to protect" (R2P) include "ethnic cleansing," but that term has no defined meaning under international criminal law, so is not used by the author. See, e.g., Rome Statute of the International Criminal Court, Arts. 6–8, UN Doc. A/CONF.183/9*, July 18, 1998 [hereinafter, the Rome Statute or ICC Statute] (defining genocide, crimes against humanity, and war crimes).
[4] International Commission on Intervention and State Sovereignty (ICISS), *The Responsibility to Protect, Report of the International Commission on Intervention and State Sovereignty* (International Development Research Centre, Ottawa, December 2001).
[5] See Chapter 1 (overview); Chapter 5 (detailed analysis regarding Syria and Darfur).
[6] See Chapter 3.

crimes against humanity, and/or war crimes. Moreover, there seems little likelihood those permanent members will endorse such an approach.

In Chapter 2, the author suggested that one might revitalize R2P by returning to the hard law legal obligations that underlie it, thereby moving away from considering all of R2P as "soft law," which generally appears the approach taken.[7] In this chapter, the author similarly turns to existing hard law legal obligations to examine those relevant to use of the veto in the face of genocide, crimes against humanity, and/or war crimes,[8] in order to question whether unrestrained veto use in the face of such crimes is consistent with all bodies of international law.

When the veto power was created in 1945 as part of the UN Charter,[9] there was less international law than presently exists.[10] Quite understandably, then, the question would not have arisen as to how the Genocide Convention (adopted in 1948)[11] or 1949 Geneva Conventions would interact with the veto power, as those treaties did not yet exist. For example, by 1945, "genocide" had been coined as a legal term[12] by Polish jurist Raphael Lemkin to put a name to mass killing of members of a protected group – motivated by Nazi attempted extermination of the Jewish populations of Europe, among others.[13]

---

[7] See Chapter 2.2.2.
[8] The crime of aggression, which recently had its jurisdiction activated as the fourth crime of the International Criminal Court (ICC), is also one of the most serious crimes of concern to the international community but is not encompassed within the author's present arguments. See Activation of the Jurisdiction of the Court Over the Crime of Aggression, ICC-ASP/16/Res.5, December 14, 2017, at https://asp.icc-cpi.int/iccdocs/asp_docs/Resolutions/ASP16/ICC-ASP-16-Res5-ENG.pdf.
[9] For discussion of the drafting history of what became the veto power, see Chapter 1.
[10] Jan Wouters and Tom Ruys write:

> One must not forget the enormous progress that international human rights, humanitarian law and international criminal law have made since 1945 .... [T]he world has grown wiser in the past decades resisting impunity and raising the standard that heads of State and government officials should live up to, by adopting a great variety of treaties in the areas of human rights, international humanitarian law and international criminal law....

Jan Wouters & Tom Ruys, *Security Council Reform: A New Veto for a New Century?*, at 32 (Egmont Paper 9, Academic Press Royal Institute for Int'l Relations).
[11] The Genocide Convention was adopted by the General Assembly on December 9, 1948, and entered into force on January 12, 1951.
[12] "Genocide" is a word that combines the Greek word *génos* ("race, people") and the Latin suffix *–cide* ("act of killing"). Gregory H. Stanton, *What Is Genocide?*, GENOCIDE WATCH, at http://genocidewatch.net/genocide-2/what-is-genocide.
[13] For discussion of the decades-long work of Raphael Lemkin, see SAMANTHA POWER, "A PROBLEM FROM HELL": AMERICA AND THE AGE OF GENOCIDE, 47–60 (2013); PHILIPPE SANDS, EAST WEST STREET: ON THE ORIGINS OF GENOCIDE AND CRIMES AGAINST HUMANITY (2016).

The crime, however, was not prosecuted before the International Military Tribunal at Nuremberg,[14] as the definition was only adopted in the Genocide Convention after the Tribunal's main trial had been completed.[15] In 1945, of course, similarly none of the ad hoc or hybrid criminal tribunals yet existed, so there was much less law on the crimes of genocide, crimes against humanity, or war crimes.[16] For instance, what is required by the obligation to "prevent" genocide contained in the Genocide Convention was only fairly recently elucidated by the ICJ in the *Bosnia v. Serbia* Case.[17] Yet, when the veto power was conferred in 1945, there were already nascent developments in what we now called the field of international justice and early writings (based on natural law) that developed into *jus cogens*.[18]

The strength of these nascent developments can be seen in the now extensive body of international law, including international criminal law on the crimes of genocide, crimes against humanity, and war crimes.[19] Furthermore, the veto power – conferred in Article 27(3) of the UN Charter[20] – sits within this system of international law, including the work of

---

[14] The United States of America, The French Republic, The United Kingdom of Great Britain and Northern Ireland, and The Union of Soviet Socialist Republics v. Goering et al., Indictment, International Military Tribunal, Trial of War Criminals, at 23 (Dept. of State Publication 2420, Washington, 1945), at http://digitalcollections.smu.edu/cdm/ref/collection/hgp/id/654.

[15] The main trial of the Nuremberg Tribunal took place from November 20, 1945, to October 1, 1946.

[16] The Security Council created the International Criminal Tribunal for the former Yugoslavia (ICTY) in 1993, and the International Criminal Tribunal for Rwanda (ICTR) in 1994. UN Doc. S/RES/827 (1993); UN Doc. S/RES/955 (1994).

[17] Case Concerning Application of the Convention on the Prevention and Punishment of the Crime of Genocide (Bosn & Herz. v. Serb. and Montenegro), Judgment of 26 February 2007, 2007 ICJ Rep. 43 (Feb. 26) [hereinafter, *Bosnia v. Serbia* Case].

[18] See, e.g., Kamrul Hossain, *The Concept of* Jus Cogens *and the Obligation Under the UN Charter*, SANTA CLARA J. INT'L L. 72, 73 (2005) ("The doctrine of international *jus cogens* was developed under a strong influence of natural law concepts, which maintain that states cannot be absolutely free in establishing their contractual relations. States were obliged to respect certain fundamental principles deeply rooted in the international community.").

[19] *See, e.g.*, JENNIFER TRAHAN, A TOPICAL DIGEST OF THE CASE LAW OF THE INTERNATIONAL CRIMINAL TRIBUNAL FOR THE FORMER YUGOSLAVIA (Human Rights Watch 2006); JENNIFER TRAHAN, A DIGEST OF THE CASE LAW OF THE INTERNATIONAL CRIMINAL TRIBUNAL FOR RWANDA (Human Rights Watch 2010). *See also* Theresa Reinold, *The Responsibility Not to Veto, Secondary Rules, and the Rule of Law*, 6 GLOB. RESP. PROTECT 269, 283 (2014) ("While it is true that at the founding of the United Nations in 1945 the UN Security Council was envisioned as a political body, not a law-enforcement agency, the global normative climate has certainly changed over the past two decades, and a normative expectation has begun to emerge that not only the UN Security Council, but international organisations more generally, abide by the rule of law standards that they seek to promote in member-states.").

[20] Charter of the United Nations (1945), 892 UNTS 119 (1945) [hereinafter, UN Charter]. Article 27(3) states that "[d]ecisions of the Security Council on all [non-procedural] matters shall be

the International Law Commission (ILC) on state responsibility.[21] Legal questions then arise as to how the veto power interacts with these bodies of international law as they have developed – because the veto power is not necessarily limited by how the Charter was read in 1945.[22] Furthermore, as will be discussed more extensively below, even in 1945, the Security Council did not obtain unlimited power, but was required by Article 24(2) of the Charter to exercise its duties "in accordance with the [p]urposes and [p]rinciples of the United Nations."[23] In 1945, our conception of the "[p]urposes and [p]rinciples" of the UN may not have been informed by the much more defined detail of international law developed since, yet in drafting the Charter, written in the

> made by an affirmative vote of nine members including the concurring votes of the permanent members ... ." *Id.* Art. 27(3). While the word "veto" is not mentioned, by requiring "concurring votes of the permanent members," the veto is implicitly provided for in Article 27(3), because when the veto is used, concurring votes are lacking. Practice has developed also to permit one or more permanent member to abstain from voting, which still allows a resolution to pass. *See* Legal Consequences for States of the Continued Presence of South Africa in Namibia (South West Africa) Notwithstanding Security Council Resolution 276 (1970), Advisory Opinion, 1971 ICJ Rep. 22 (June 21) [hereinafter, *Namibia* Advisory Opinion] ("members of the Council, in particular its permanent members, have consistently and uniformly interpreted the practice of voluntary abstention by a permanent member as not constituting a bar to the adoption of a resolution").

[21] Int'l L. Comm'n, Draft Articles on the Responsibility of States for Internationally Wrongful Acts, with Commentaries (adopted), UN Doc. A/56/10 (2001) [hereinafter, Articles on State Responsibility].

[22] "[T]he meaning of even fundamental provisions [of the UN Charter does] not necessarily remain static." Christian Henderson, *The UK Government's Legal Opinion On Forcible Measures in Response to the Use of Chemical Weapons by the Syrian Government*, 64 INT'L & COMP. L. Q. 179, 185 (2015); *see also* Oscar Schachter, Book Review, 60 YALE L.J. 189, 193 (1951) (reviewing HANS KELSEN, THE LAW OF THE UNITED NATIONS (1966) (the Charter "is a constitutional instrument whose broad phrases were designed to meet changing circumstances for an undefined future."); Blaine Sloan, *The United Nations Charter as a Constitution*, 1 PACE Y.B. INT'L L. 61, 119 n. 268 (1989) ("President George Bush, when he was Ambassador to the United Nations, said in the General Assembly: 'We have demonstrated in many other actions here that the Charter is a flexible document. It was written by wise men to cope with the unforeseeable.'"), *citing* UN Doc. A/PV. 1976, corr. (1971); President François Hollande, *Allocution du président de la République à l'occasion de la Conférence des Ambassadeurs*, August 27, 2013 ("International law must evolve with the times. It cannot be a pretext for permitting the perpetration of mass massacres."), cited in Arman Sarvarian, *Humanitarian Intervention After Syria*, 36(1) LEGAL STUD. 20, 34 (2016); RONALD C. SLYE & BETH VAN SCHAACK, ESSENTIALS: INTERNATIONAL CRIMINAL LAW 92 (2009) ("It is generally accepted at the international level that treaties are to be treated as living documents. In other words, they are to be interpreted in the context of the time in which they are being applied, and not as they would have been interpreted at the time of their drafting."); Sarvarian, *supra* note 22, at 24–25, *citing* Christopher Greenwood, *International Law and the NATO Intervention in Kosovo*, 49(4) INT'L & COMP. L. Q. 926, 929 (2000) (international law "is not static but develops through a process of State practice of actions and the reactions to those actions").

[23] For further discussion of this obligation, see Chapter 4.2 *infra*.

wake of the horrors of World War II, it was never agreed that the veto could be used to allow the occurrence of mass atrocity crimes.

SUMMARY OF LEGAL ARGUMENTS

As will be explored in detail below, this chapter presents three main legal arguments that indicate there are legal limits (or constraints) on the use of the veto in the face of genocide, crimes against humanity, and/or war crimes *based on existing international law*.[24]

First, international law can be thought of in terms of a hierarchical structure, with *jus cogens* norms positioned at the apex of the hierarchy. *Jus cogens* protections thus sit above the veto power, which is conferred by the UN Charter. *Jus cogens* norms receive the highest level of protection in the international legal system in that no derogations may be permitted from them except through the creation of a new norm of comparable character. The prohibition of genocide, crimes against humanity, and, at least certain,[25] war crimes are all recognized as *jus cogens* norms. Because the UN is bound to respect *jus cogens*, its principal organ, the Security Council, is similarly constrained. All states are additionally constrained to respect *jus cogens*. It follows that the permanent members are thereby also constrained, both as states and as members of the Security Council. Therefore, the actions of the permanent members (including veto use): (a) must not be used in circumstances such that their effect is to facilitate *jus cogens* violations, (b) must not undermine the duty of other Security Council members to cooperate to make an appropriate response to a serious breach of a *jus cogens* norm, and (c) must be consistent with *jus cogens*.

A *second* source of constraint on the veto power is found in the UN Charter itself. The Charter limits Security Council power in that Article 24(2) states that the Security Council must act "in accordance with" the "[p]urposes and [p]rinciples" of the UN.[26] The Security Council, including its permanent members, have no power to act beyond the confines of the UN Charter – the legal instrument that created their power – so all of their actions, including veto use, necessarily must respect the Charter. The "[p]urposes and [p]rinciples" in Articles 1 and 2 of the Charter include respecting "principles of justice and international law,"

---

[24] The following arguments are based on existing law (*lex lata*); they are not based on the law as it should be (*de lege ferenda*). In fact, most of the legal authority examined in this chapter is relatively old in origin – the 1948 Genocide Convention, the 1949 Geneva Conventions, and how they interact with the veto power contained in the UN Charter (1945).
[25] See notes 68–78 *infra* and accompanying text. The focus on "certain" war crimes should not in any way be taken as minimizing the severity of all war crimes.
[26] UN Charter, Art. 24(2).

"promoting and encouraging respect for human rights," "co-operation in solving international problems of [a] ... humanitarian character," and "good faith."[27] Arguably, many of the vetoes that have been, and are being, cast in the face of genocide, crimes against humanity, and/or war crimes are not "in accordance" with the UN's "[p]urposes and [p]principles."[28] (They also fail to satisfy the separate obligation of "good faith" imposed generally under international law.) A veto that does not accord with the "[p]urposes and [p]rinciples" of the UN should be seen as *ultra vires* of the proper exercise of Security Council power.

A *third* source of legal obligation that arguably constrains use of the veto in the face of atrocity crimes is the treaty obligations of the individual permanent Member States, such as those under the Genocide Convention and 1949 Geneva Conventions, to which all permanent members of the Council are parties.[29] The permanent members do not cease to be bound by their treaty obligations by virtue of sitting on the Security Council. These treaties impose certain legal obligations, for example, "to prevent and to punish" genocide, to "prosecute" "grave breaches," and to "respect and ensure respect for" the 1949 Geneva Conventions. Any veto that allows the continuing perpetration of genocide or "grave breaches,"[30] or blocks the prosecution of these crimes, would arguably run afoul of the obligation to "prevent and to punish" genocide, and/or, as to international armed conflict, the obligation to "prosecute" "grave breaches" and "ensure respect for" the 1949 Geneva Conventions. Where there is non-international armed conflict, the veto should be measured, at minimum, as to whether its use is consistent with ensuring the war crimes prohibited by Common Article 3 to the 1949 Geneva Conventions are not committed.[31] It is possible to make similar arguments with respect to other war crimes and crimes against

---

[27] UN Charter Arts. 1(1), 1(3), 2(2).
[28] For example, see Chapter 4.2.4.1 *infra* (discussing veto use related to the situation in Syria).
[29] See International Committee for the Red Cross (ICRC), *Treaties, States Parties, and Commentaries, at* https://ihl-databases.icrc.org/applic/ihl/ihl.nsf/States.xsp?xp_treatySelected=380&xp_viewStates=XPages_NORMStatesParties (parties to the 1949 Geneva Conventions); United Nations Treaty Collection, *at* https://treaties.un.org/Pages/ViewDetails.aspx?src=IND&mtdsg_no=IV-1&chapter=4&clang=_en (parties to the Genocide Convention).
[30] See note 360 *infra* (enumerating "grave breaches").
[31] See note 361 *infra* (enumerating Common Article 3 war crimes). As detailed below, because States Parties to the Geneva Conventions owe an obligation in Common Article 1 to "ensure respect for" the Conventions as a whole, a veto that facilitates, or allows the continued commission of, Common Article 3 violations is legally problematic. *See* Chapter 4.3.2 and notes 402–06 *infra* and accompanying text. Similar arguments can be made – for those permanent members parties to them – as to violations of Protocols I and III to the Geneva Conventions. *See* notes 365–67, 407–14 *infra* and accompanying text. As to how to interpret the permanent members' obligations under these treaties in light of Article 103 of the Charter, see *infra* Chapter 4.3.3.

humanity, although the latter would rest on general obligations under international law, as there is not yet a finalized treaty on crimes against humanity.[32]

4.1 CONSIDERATION OF THE RELATIONSHIP BETWEEN USE OF THE VETO AND *JUS COGENS*

4.1.1 Jus Cogens/*Peremptory Norms*

The term *jus cogens* means, in Latin, "compelling law."[33] "*Jus cogens*" or "peremptory norms" are defined in the Vienna Convention on the Law of Treaties (Vienna Convention or VCLT) as norms of "general international law ... accepted and recognized by the international community of States as a whole ... from which no derogation is permitted and which can be modified only by a subsequent norm of general international law having the same character."[34] While the Vienna Convention was adopted in 1969, it is generally considered to have codified preexisting international law.[35]

As noted above, international law can be thought of as consisting of a hierarchy of norms.[36] The Statute of the ICJ,[37] finalized in 1945, lists in

---

[32] See notes 426–30, 497–502 *infra* and accompanying text.
[33] M. Cherif Bassiouni, *International Crimes*: Jus Cogens *and* Obligatio Erga Omnes, 59 L. & CONTEMP. PROB. 63, 67; Marjorie M. Whiteman, Jus Cogens *in International Law, with a Projected List*, GA. J. INT'L & COMP. L. 609, n. 1 (1977) (same, adding that "*jus*" means "law," and "*cogens*" is the present participle of *cogere*, meaning to compel).
[34] Vienna Convention on the Law of Treaties, Art. 53, May 23, 1969, 1155 UNTS 331, 8 ILM 679 [hereinafter, VCLT]. *See also* RESTATEMENT OF FOREIGN RELATIONS LAW OF THE UNITED STATES (THIRD), Section 102(k) (1987) ("Some rules of international law are recognized by the international community of states as peremptory, permitting no derogation. These rules prevail over and invalidate international agreements and other rules of international law in conflict with them. Such a peremptory norm is subject to modification only by a subsequent norm of international law having the same character ....").
[35] Article 53 of the Vienna Convention is declaratory of an already existing international law concerning *jus cogens*. Hossain, *supra* note 18, at 82, *citing* JAMES CRAWFORD, THE CREATION OF STATES IN INTERNATIONAL LAW 80 (1979).
[36] N.G. Onuf & Richard K. Birney, *Peremptory Norms of International Law: Their Source, Function and Future*, 4 J. INT'L & POL'Y 187, n. 7 (1994) ("H[ans] Kelsen has argued the logical necessity of a hierarchical arrangement of positive norms in the international legal order."), *citing* HANS KELSEN, PRINCIPLES OF INTERNATIONAL LAW 408–38 (1952); ALEXANDER ORAKHELASHVILI, PEREMPTORY NORMS IN INTERNATIONAL LAW 9, 423 (2006) ("The superior rules [i.e., *jus cogens*], determine the frame[work] within which the inferior rules [i.e., custom, treaties and 'the rights and obligations' flowing therefrom] can be valid, while the inferior rules must comply with the content of the superior rules" in order to be lawful.).
[37] Statute of the International Court of Justice (1945), 15 UNCIO 355 (1945) [hereinafter, ICJ Statute].

Article 38 the sources of international law to be applied by the Court as: (a) international conventions, (b) international custom, (c) "general principles of law recognized by civilized nations," and (d) "judicial decisions and the teachings of the most highly qualified publicists ... as subsidiary means for the determination of rules of law."[38] Yet, implicitly, at the apex of that list are *jus cogens* norms.[39] *Jus cogens* is implicitly contained in this list as the highest form of customary international law, in that, unlike ordinary customary international law, no derogations are permitted from *jus cogens*.[40] While the ILC wrote in 1966, "the emergence of rules having the character of *jus cogens* is comparatively recent,"[41] the term in fact has very old origins, deriving from natural law traditions.[42]

The hierarchical nature of international law, with *jus cogens* or peremptory norms at the apex, is explained as follows: "Peremptory norms of international law or norms of *jus cogens* have a superior hierarchy in relation to other rules.

---

[38] *Id.* Art. 38.1.a.–d.
[39] *See* Bassiouni, *supra* note 33, at 67 ("A *jus cogens* norm holds the highest hierarchical position among all other norms and principles."); André da Rocha Ferreira, Cristieli Carvalho, Fernanda Graeff Machry & Pedro Barreto Vianna Rigon, *Formation and Evidence of Customary International Law*, 2013 UFRGS MODEL UN J. 182, 194 ("Peremptory norms of international law or norms of *jus cogens* have a superior hierarchy in relation to other rules."); JOHN HEIECK, A DUTY TO PREVENT GENOCIDE: DUE DILIGENCE OBLIGATIONS AMONG THE P5, at 185 (2018), *citing* R. Nieto-Navia, *International Peremptory Norms* (Jus Cogens) *and International Humanitarian Law*, at 5 (2003) ("states have already consented to the notion of hierarchically superior norms when they codified *jus cogens* in Articles 53 and 54 of the VCLT"); Onuf & Birney, *supra* note 36, at 190 ("Peremptory norms are one category intended to be set apart from the bulk of norms making up the legal order."); Hossain, *supra* note 18, at 73 ("the position of the rules of *jus cogens* is hierarchically superior compared to other ordinary rules of international law").
[40] *See, e.g.*, ARNOLD MCNAIR, LAW OF TREATIES 213–15 (1961) ("There are, however, many rules of customary international law which stand in a higher category and which cannot be set aside or modified by contracting States.").
[41] Int'l L. Comm'n, Draft Articles on the Law of Treaties with Commentaries, Commentary on the Final Draft of Article 53, Y.B. Int'l L. Comm'n, 1966, Vol. II, at 248.
[42] "During the years of 1963 to 1966, several members [of the ILC] pointed out in the ILC commentary that the emergence of rules having the character of *jus cogens* was not the product of recent time, rather it has more long-standing character. They further stated that the concept of *jus cogens* had originated in regard to such universal crimes as piracy and the slave-trade as well as such principles as the freedom of high seas and other rules on the law of the sea." Hossain, *supra* note 18, at 74, n. 7, *citing* LAURI HANNIKAINEN, PEREMPTORY NORMS (Jus Cogens) IN INTERNATIONAL LAW 161–62 (1988). "The doctrine of international *jus cogens* was developed under a strong influence of natural law concepts, which maintain that states cannot be absolutely free in establishing their contractual relations. States were obliged to respect certain fundamental principles deeply rooted in the international community." Hossain, *supra* note 18, at 73.

This classification is reflected in the text of Article 53 of the Vienna Convention ... , according to which a treaty is void if it conflicts with a peremptory norm of international law."[43] "Peremptory norms are normative principles that are considered to be so important for the welfare and even survival of the global community that they cannot be violated or derogated from."[44]

Sir Gerald Fitzmaurice, the ILC's Special Rapporteur on the Law of Treaties, explains:

> There are certain forms of illegal action that can never be justified .... These are acts which are not merely illegal, but *malum in se*, [namely] rules in the nature of *jus cogens* – that is to say obligations of an absolute character, compliance with which is not dependent on corresponding compliance by others, but is requisite in all circumstances ... .[45]

Professor Alfred Verdross, a member of the ILC writing in 1966, articulated the concept as follows: "[I]n the field of general international law there are rules having the character of *jus cogens*. The criterion for these rules consists in the fact that they do not exist to satisfy the needs of the individual states but the higher interest of the whole international community. Hence these rules are absolute."[46]

Useful background explaining the concept of *jus cogens* is additionally provided by Gordon Christenson:

> A peremptory norm is like a public-order imperative in municipal systems. It is used to override other less powerful norms by an external public authority, and it may not be changed except by a norm having the same quality. A *jus cogens* norm must have great staying power ... . There are some prescriptions of international law, for example, that sovereign states may not change or agree with others to change by *jus dispositivum*: several states ought not to be able to enter a valid agreement among themselves to enslave a minority people, to use force against another state, to liquidate a race thought particularly noxious or to brutalize dissidents contrary to fundamental human rights.[47]

---

[43] Ferreira, Carvalho, Machry & Rigon, *supra* note 39, at 194; Hossain, *supra* note 18, at 74 ("Rules contrary to the notion of *jus cogens* could be regarded as void, since those rules oppose the fundamental norms of international public policy.").

[44] JEREMY MATAM FARRALL, UNITED NATIONS SANCTIONS AND THE RULE OF LAW 71 (2007).

[45] Sir Gerald Fitzmaurice, *The General Principles of International Law Considered from the Standpoint of the Rules of Law*, 92 RECUEIL DES COURS 120 (1957), as cited in Whiteman, *supra* note 33, at 610.

[46] Alfred Verdross, *Jus Dispositivum and Jus Cogens in International Law*, 60 AM. J. INT'L L. 55, 58 (1966), as cited in Whiteman, *supra* note 33, at 612.

[47] Gordon A. Christenson, *The World Court and Jus Cogens*, 81 AM. J. INT'L L. 93, 95–96 (1987) (footnotes omitted).

An explanation of why *jus cogens* norms enjoy hierarchical superiority appears in the thoughtful Separate Opinion of Judge ad hoc John Dugard in the *Armed Activities on the Territory of the Congo (DRC v. Rwanda)* case (2006) [hereinafter, *Armed Activities*]:[48]

> Norms of *jus cogens* are a blend of principle and policy. On the one hand, they affirm the high principles of international law, which recognize the most important rights of the international order – such as the right to be free from aggression, genocide, torture and slavery and the right to self-determination; while, on the other hand, they give legal form to the most fundamental policies or goals of the international community – the prohibitions on aggression, genocide, torture and slavery and the advancement of self-determination. This explains why they enjoy a hierarchical superiority to other norms in the international legal order. The fact that norms of *jus cogens* advance both principle and policy means that they must inevitably play a dominant role in the process of judicial choice.[49]

4.1.2 The Prohibitions of Genocide, Crimes against Humanity, and, at Least Certain, War Crimes Are Peremptory Norms Protected as Jus Cogens

The Vienna Convention on the Law of Treaties does not contain an enumerated list of *jus cogens* norms. However, the ILC, in its commentary on Articles 26 and 40 of the Articles on the Responsibility of States for Internationally Wrongful Acts (Articles on State Responsibility), noted that a number of peremptory norms have been recognized as such in accordance with the criteria set out in Article 53 of the Vienna Convention.[50] Based on national and international court decisions and general agreement among states, the ILC observed that "[t]hose peremptory norms that are clearly accepted and recognized" include the prohibitions on genocide and crimes against humanity.[51] As to war crimes, the ILC states that the "basic rules of international humanitarian law" constitute "peremptory" norms.[52]

---

[48] Armed Activities on the Territory of the Congo (New Application: 2002) (Dem. Rep. Congo v. Rwanda), Jurisdiction and Admissibility, Judgment, 2006 ICJ Rep. 6 (sep. op., Dugard, J.) [hereinafter, *Armed Activities*].
[49] *Id.*, para. 10.
[50] Int'l L. Comm'n, Articles on State Responsibility, *supra* note 21, Arts. 16, 40.
[51] *Id.* Art. 26 ("Those peremptory norms that are clearly accepted and recognized include the prohibitions of aggression, *genocide*, slavery, racial discrimination, *crimes against humanity* and torture, and the right to self-determination.") (emphasis added).
[52] Int'l L. Comm'n, Articles on State Responsibility, *supra* note 21, at Commentary to Art. 40.

The ICJ for the first time acknowledged the existence of peremptory norms (*jus cogens*) in the *Armed Activities* Case,[53] holding that "the prohibition of genocide" is "assuredly" a "peremptory norm[] of general international law (*jus cogens*)."[54] There, Judge ad hoc Dugard observed: "It is strange that the Court has taken so long to reach this point because it has shown no hesitation in recognizing the notion of obligations *erga omnes*, which together with *jus cogens* affirms the normative hierarchy of international law."[55] Judge Lauterpacht, writing in the *Application of Genocide Convention* Case, for example, has written that the prohibition of genocide has long been accepted as a matter of *jus cogens*.[56]

As to war crimes, the ILC writes: "In the light of the description by the ICJ of the *basic rules of international humanitarian law* applicable in armed conflict as 'intransgressible' in character, it would ... seem justified to treat these as peremptory."[57] Others, for example, renowned international law scholar

---

[53] *Armed Activities, supra* note 48, para. 64 ("The Court will begin by reaffirming that 'the principles underlying the [Genocide] Convention are principles which are recognized by civilized nations as binding on States, even without any conventional obligation' and that a consequence of that conception is 'the universal character both of the condemnation of genocide and of the cooperation required "in order to liberate mankind from such an odious scourge" (Preamble to the Convention).' It follows that 'the rights and obligations enshrined by the Convention are rights and obligations *erga omnes*'" (internal citations omitted).). The Separate Opinion of Judge ad hoc Dugard stated that "this is the first occasion on which the Court has expressly acknowledged the existence of peremptory norms (*jus cogens*)." *Armed Activities, supra* note 48, at para. 2 (sep. op., Dugard, J. ad hoc).

[54] *Armed Activities, supra* note 48, para. 64.

[55] *Id.*, para. 4 (sep. op., Dugard, J. ad hoc).

[56] *See* Application of the Convention on the Prevention and Punishment of the Crime of Genocide (Bosn. & Herz. v. Yugoslavia (Serb. and Montenegro), Further Request for the Indication of Provisional Measures, Order of 13 September 1993, 1993 ICJ Rep. 325, 440, 95 ILR 1 (sep. op., Lauterpacht, J. ad hoc) [hereinafter, *Application of Genocide Convention Case*] ("[T]he prohibition of genocide ... has generally been accepted as having the status not of an ordinary rule of international law but of *jus cogens*. Indeed, the prohibition of genocide has long been regarded as one of the few undoubted examples of *jus cogens*."). For a recent discussion of the prohibition of genocide as *jus cogens*, see Int'l L. Comm'n, Fourth Report on Peremptory Norms of General International Law (*Jus Cogens*), by Dire Tladi, Special Rapporteur, A/CN.4/727 (Jan. 31, 2019).

[57] Int'l L. Comm'n, Articles on State Responsibility, *supra* note 21, at Commentary to Art. 40 (emphasis added), *citing* Legality of the Threat or Use of Nuclear Weapons, Advisory Opinion, 1996 ICJ Rep. 226, 257, para. 79 (July 8) [hereinafter, *Nuclear Weapons* Advisory Opinion]. *See also* Martti Koskenniemi, Fragmentation of International Law: Difficulties Arising from the Diversification and Expansion of International Law, Report of the Study Group of the International Law Commission, at para. 374, n. 522, UN Doc. A/CN.4/L.682 (Apr. 13, 2006) (citing the prohibition of genocide, crimes against humanity, and "basic rules of international humanitarian law" as among the "most frequently cited candidates for the status of *jus cogens*"); *see also* International Law Commission, Fourth Report on Peremptory Norms, *supra* note 56, at para. 60 (listing peremptory norms as including the prohibition of genocide, the prohibition of crimes against humanity, and basic rules of international humanitarian law).

M. Cherif Bassiouni, have written that the prohibition of genocide, crimes against humanity, and war crimes all constitute peremptory norms of international law.[58] Sir Nigel Rodley similarly writes that "war crimes" enjoy *jus cogens* status.[59]

4.1.3 *The Content of the Peremptory Norms as to Genocide, Crimes against Humanity, and War Crimes*

As to what is contained within the peremptory norms (that is, what are the applicable definitions of genocide, crimes against humanity, and war crimes), the clearest answer concerns the crime of "genocide." The definition of the crime of genocide has been remarkably consistent at the international level since first formulated in the 1948 Genocide Convention[60] and has remained the same in all subsequent international criminal tribunal statutes.[61]

The definitions of crimes against humanity and war crimes have evolved over time, with early articulations, for example, found in the London Charter establishing the Nuremberg Tribunal,[62] and later ones found in the Statutes of the International Criminal Tribunal for the former Yugoslavia (ICTY)[63] and the International Criminal Tribunal for Rwanda (ICTR).[64] The most modern and comprehensive formulation of the definitions of crimes against humanity and war crimes is contained in the ICC's Rome Statute.[65] Therefore, as to

---

[58] *See* Bassiouni, *supra* note 33, at 68 ("[T]he legal literature discloses that the following international crimes are prohibited by *jus cogens*: aggression, genocide, crimes against humanity, war crimes, piracy, slavery and slave-related practices, and torture.").

[59] *See* Nigel S. Rodley, *Humanitarian Intervention*, *in* THE OXFORD HANDBOOK OF THE USE OF FORCE IN INTERNATIONAL LAW 794 (Marc Weller ed., 2015) ("The prohibitions of committing crimes against humanity and war crimes enjoy [*jus cogens*] status."). *See also ICRC Report of the Meeting of Experts*, compiled by Christina Pellandini, ICRC Legal Advisor (1997), in chapter by André Andries, Director of the International Society for Military Law's Documentation Centre, at 34, 38, 43 (citing "war crimes" as *jus cogens*).

[60] Genocide Convention, Art. II.

[61] *See* Genocide Convention, Art. II; Statute of the International Tribunal for the former Yugoslavia, Art. 4, UN SCOR, 48th Sess., 3217th Mtg., at 1, UN Doc. S/RES/827 (1993) [hereinafter, ICTY Statute]; Statute of the International Tribunal for Rwanda, Art. 2, UN SCOR, 49th Sess., 3453rd Mtg., at 1, UN Doc. S/RES/955 (1994) [hereinafter, ICTR Statute]; ICC Statute, Art. 6.

[62] *See* Agreement for the Prosecution and Punishment of Major War Criminals of the European Axis and Charter of the International Military Tribunal, Art. 6(b)–(c), Aug. 8, 1945, London Charter, 59 Stat. 1544, 82 UNTS 279.

[63] ICTY Statute, Art. 2 ("Grave breaches of the Geneva Conventions of 1949"); ICTY Statute, Art. 3 ("Violations of the laws or customs of war"); ICTY Statute, Art. 5 ("Crimes against humanity").

[64] ICTR Statute, Art. 3 ("Crimes against humanity"); ICTR Statute, Art. 4 ("Violations of Article 3 Common to the Geneva Conventions and of Additional Protocol II").

[65] *See* ICC Statute, Art. 7 (crimes against humanity), Art. 8 (war crimes). Two war crimes amendments to the Rome Statute have since been adopted by the ICC's Assembly of States

what these crimes encompass today, the Rome Statute provides the most contemporaneous source and is often cited as embodying customary international law.[66] It is unclear, however, whether all the "underlying crimes" of crimes against humanity as they are formulated in the Rome Statute are protected by *jus cogens*.[67]

Similarly, there does not appear to be clarity regarding exactly *which* war crimes have been recognized as *jus cogens*.[68] For example, the ICC's Rome Statute contains fairly extensive lists of war crimes committed in

Parties. *See* Resolution RC/Res.5, Annex 1 (June 10, 2010), at https://treaties.un.org/doc/sour ce/docs/RC-Res.5-ENG.pdf (war crimes amendment adopted at the Kampala Review Conference); Resolution on Amendments to Article 8 of the Rome Statute of the International Criminal Court, ICC-ASP/16/Res.4, at https://asp.icc-cpi.int/iccdocs/asp_docs/ Resolutions/ASP16/ICC-ASP-16-Res4-ENG.pdf (war crimes amendment adopted at the 2017 Assembly of States Parties). *See also* Int'l L. Comm'n, Draft Articles on Prevention and Punishment of Crimes against Humanity, Adopted by the International Law Commission at its Seventy-First Session and Submitted to the General Assembly as Part of the Commission's Report Covering the Work of that Session, UN Doc. A/74/10, at https://legal .un.org/docs/?path=./ilc/texts/instruments/english/draft_articles/7_7_2019.pdf&lang=EF.

[66] The Rome Statute definitions of the crimes are frequently cited as customary international law. *See* Philippe Kirsch, *Foreword*, *in* KNUT DÖRMANN, ELEMENTS OF WAR CRIMES UNDER THE ROME STATUTE OF THE INTERNATIONAL CRIMINAL COURT xiii (2003) ("The development of the Elements of Crimes has proven to be a very useful exercise. Because of the general agreement that the definitions of crimes in the ICC Statute were to reflect existing customary international law, and not to create new law, states relied heavily on accepted historical precedents in crafting the definitions in Articles 6 and 8 of the ICC Statute."); Darryl Robinson & Herman von Hebel, *War Crimes in Internal Conflicts: Art. 8 of the ICC Statute*, 2 Y.B. INT'L HUMANITARIAN L. 193, 194 (1999) ("Delegations agreed that definitions of these crimes must be articulated in the Statute and that those definitions must reflect existing customary law."); Claus Kreβ, *War Crimes Committed in Non-international Armed Conflict and the Emerging System of International Criminal Justice*, 30 ISR. Y.B. HUM. RTS. 103, 109 (2000) ("States have, in their overwhelming and steadily growing majority solemnly expressed the view that the war crimes list [in the Statute] is based on customary law."); Leila Sadat, *Custom, Codification and Some Thoughts about the Relationship between the Two: Article 10 of the ICC Statute*, 49 DE PAUL L. REV. 909, 912, 920 (2000) ("With respect to the definition of crimes and the jurisdiction of the Court, the Working Group assumed that the customary international law and treaties on the subject would be incorporated by reference into the ICC Statute, rather than codified therein.... Thus, ... even the inclusion of article 10 cannot foreclose arguments that customary international law now includes the Statute's definitions.").

[67] The "underlying crimes" are formulated differently in the ICTY Statute, ICTR Statute, and ICC Statute. *Compare* ICTY Statute, Art. 5; ICTR Statute, Art. 3; ICC Statute, Art. 7. For a recent discussion of the prohibition of crimes against humanity as *jus cogens*, see Fourth Report on Peremptory Norms, *supra* note 56, at paras. 84–90 (but not addressing *which* underlying crimes against humanity are *jus cogens*).

[68] Int'l L. Comm'n, Fourth Report on Peremptory Norms, *supra* note 56, at para. 121 ("There are obvious issues of uncertainty in relation to *jus cogens* and basic rules of international humanitarian law, most notably which rules of international humanitarian law qualify as the 'most basic' and thus meet the criteria of *jus cogens*.").

international armed conflict, and those committed in non-international armed conflict.[69] Yet, as mentioned above, the ILC wrote that it is *"the basic rules of international humanitarian law applicable in armed conflict"* that are "intransgressible" and thus "peremptory norms," citing to the *Nuclear Weapons* Advisory Opinion.[70] In that case, the ICJ referred to the principle of distinction between combatants and non-combatants as well as the prohibition on unnecessary suffering as "cardinal principles contained in the texts constituting the fabric of humanitarian law" and "intransgressible principles of international customary law."[71] The Court also referenced The Hague and Geneva Conventions more broadly because they "have enjoyed a broad accession. Further these fundamental rules are to be observed by all States whether or not they have ratified the conventions that contain them, because they constitute intransgressible principles of international customary law."[72] Dire Tladi, as Special Rapporteur writing for the ILC recently on this issue, notes that "the basic rules of international humanitarian law" are sometimes referred to as "grave breaches" and sometimes "war crimes,"[73] but he notes the lack of clarity on specifically *which* war crimes are encompassed.[74]

Therefore, to be conservative, this chapter focuses primarily on a universally accepted subset of very well-established war crimes, "grave breaches" of the 1949 Geneva Conventions, and the war crimes prohibited by Common Article 3 thereto.[75] Because the 1949 Geneva Conventions are universally ratified or acceded to,[76] there would seem little doubt that *at least* the war crimes contained in those Conventions would be prohibited by *jus cogens*. This conclusion is bolstered by the writings of Cherif Bassiouni, where he explains, in terms of identifying which crimes are covered by *jus*

---

[69] *See* Rome Statute, Art. 8(2)(a) ("grave breaches" in international armed conflict); Art. 8(2)(b) ("[o]ther serious violations of the laws and customs applicable in international armed conflict"); Art. 8(2)(c) (violations of Common Article 3 in non-international armed conflict); Art. 8(2)(e) ("[o]ther serious violations of the laws and customs applicable in armed conflicts not of an international character"). *See also* note 65 *supra* (two Rome Statute war crimes amendments).

[70] Int'l L. Comm'n, Articles on State Responsibility, *supra* note 21, at Commentary to Art. 40 (emphasis added), *citing Nuclear Weapons* Advisory Opinion, *supra* note 57.

[71] *Nuclear Weapons* Advisory Opinion, *supra* note 57, at 257, para. 78.

[72] *Id.* at 257, para. 79.

[73] Int'l L. Comm'n, Fourth Report on Peremptory Norms of General International Law (*Jus Cogens*), *supra* note 56, para. 116.

[74] *Id.*, para. 121.

[75] *See* note 360 *infra* (listing "grave breaches"); note 361 *infra* (listing war crimes in Common Article 3).

[76] *See* note 76 *supra* (states parties).

cogens, factors include: "the large number of states which have ratified treaties related to the[] crimes," "the [number of] legal instruments that exist to evidence the condemnation and prohibition of a particular crime," "the number of states that have incorporated the given proscription in their national laws," and "the number of international and national prosecutions for the given crime and how they have been characterized."[77] Under these criteria, it would appear warranted to include *at least* the war crimes contained in the 1949 Geneva Conventions as prohibited by *jus cogens*.[78]

4.1.4 *The Obligations of the UN and Its Organs, Including the Security Council, to Respect* Jus Cogens *Norms*

Legal authority demonstrates that, just as the UN is bound by international law, so too is its organ,[79] the Security Council, and this includes being bound by the highest level of international law – *jus cogens*.

4.1.4.1 The Security Council Is Not Above the Law

Judicial decisions and decisions by individual judges support the proposition that the Security Council is bound by law, including international law. For example, in the Advisory Opinion in *Conditions of Admission of a State to Membership in the United Nations (Article 4 of the Charter)*, the ICJ established that the Security Council is not above all law, because it is bound to observe the UN Charter.[80] There, the ICJ stated that: "[t]he political character of the Organs of the United Nations [including the Security Council and General Assembly] ... cannot

---

[77] Bassiouni, *supra* note 33, at 70.
[78] The 1949 Geneva Conventions are universally ratified or acceded to, and, as to the number of instruments covering the crimes, in addition to the 1949 Geneva Conventions, "grave breaches" and "Common Article 3" war crimes are also contained in the ICTY Statute, ICTR Statute (as to Common Article 3), and ICC Statute. Many states also incorporate "grave breaches" and "Common Article 3" violations into their domestic laws, and these crimes are most certainly prosecuted. *See* ICRC, National Implementation of IHL (database of national implementation of IHL treaties); TRAHAN, DIGESTS, *supra* note 19 (compiling ICTY and ICTR law on war crimes, including prosecution of "grave breaches" and "Common Article 3" violations). Other war crimes may also have risen to the level of *jus cogens*; this author is being deliberately conservative by focusing only on "grave breaches" and "Common Article 3," and does not mean to suggest that other war crimes have not risen to this level.
[79] Dapo Akande, *The International Court of Justice and the Security Council: Is There Room for Judicial Control of Decisions of the Political Organs of the United Nations*, 46 INT'L & COMP. L. Q. 309, 312 (1997) (the Security Council is an "organ" of the United Nations).
[80] Conditions of Admission of a State to Membership in the United Nations (Article 4 of the Charter), Advisory Opinion, 1948 ICJ Rep. 57, 64 (May 28) [hereinafter, *Conditions of Admission of a State to Membership in the United Nations*].

release them from observance of the treaty provisions by which they are governed [the UN Charter], when the provisions constitute limitations on their power...."[81]

It is also specifically established that because the UN is subject to international law, so too is its "organ," the Security Council. Thus, Judge Fitzmaurice (dissenting) in the *Namibia* Advisory Opinion concluded that "the Security Council is as much subject to [international law] ... as any of its individual member States are, [just as] the United Nations is itself a subject of international law...."[82] Judge de Castro, also in the *Namibia* Advisory Opinion, wrote in his Separate Opinion that: "[t]he Court, as a legal organ, cannot co-operate with a [Security Council or General Assembly] resolution which is clearly void, contrary to the rules of the Charter, or contrary to the principles of law"[83] – implying that Security Council resolutions cannot be contrary to the Charter or principles of law.

Similarly, in his Dissenting Opinion in the ICJ's *Lockerbie* Case, Judge ad hoc Jennings eloquently affirmed that the Security Council is constrained by law: "all discretionary powers of lawful decision-making are necessarily derived from the law, and are therefore governed and qualified by the law.... It is not logically possible to claim to represent the power and authority of the law and, at the same time, claim to be above it."[84] Judge Weeramantry, also writing in dissent in the *Lockerbie* Case, similarly concluded that: "The history of the United Nations Charter thus corroborates the view that a clear limitation on the plenitude of the Security Council's powers is that those powers must be exercised in accordance with the well-established principles of international law."[85] Judge Bedjaoui, also writing in dissent in *Lockerbie*, similarly wrote: "is not the essential point of concern to us here the fact that the Council is bound to respect the principles of international law?...."[86]

---

[81] *Id.* at 5. For additional authority that the Security Council is bound to adhere to the UN Charter, see Chapter 4.2 *infra*.

[82] *Namibia* Advisory Opinion, *supra* note 20, diss. op., Fitzmaurice, J. Sir, para. 115.

[83] *Namibia* Advisory Opinion, *supra* note 20, sep. op., de Castro, J, at 168.

[84] Case Concerning Questions of Interpretation and Application of the 1971 Montreal Convention Arising from the Aerial Incident at Lockerbie (Libyan Arab Jamahiriya v. U.K.), Preliminary Objections, Judgment, 1998 ICJ Rep. 9, 110 (diss. op., Jennings, J. ad hoc) [hereinafter, *Lockerbie (Libya v. UK)* Preliminary Objections Judgment].

[85] Case Concerning Questions of Interpretation and Application of the 1971 Montreal Convention Arising from the Aerial Incident at Lockerbie (Libyan Arab Jamahiriya v. United Kingdom), Order of 14 April 1992, Request for the Indication of Provisional Measures, 1992 ICJ Rep. 3, 65 (diss. op., Weeramantry, J.) [hereinafter *Lockerbie (Libya v. UK)* Provisional Measures]; Questions of Interpretation and Application of the 1971 Montreal Convention Arising from the Aerial Incident at Lockerbie (Libyan Arab Jamahiriya v. United States of America), Order of 14 April 1992, 1992 ICJ Rep. 114, 175 Request for the Indication of Provisional Measures (diss. op., Weeramantry, J.) [hereinafter, *Lockerbie (Libya v. US)* Provisional Measures].

[86] *Lockerbie (Libya v. UK)* Provisional Measures, *supra* note 85, at 46 (diss. op., Bedjaoui, J.).

Additionally, in the *Tadić* Case, the Appeals Chamber of the ICTY opined on the limits of the Security Council's power, finding that the Council's powers are subject to limitations and not "unbound by law":

> It is clear from this text [of Article 39 of the Charter] that the Security Council plays a pivotal role and exercises a very wide discretion under this Article. But this does not mean that its powers are unlimited. The Security Council is an organ of an international organization, established by a treaty which serves as a constitutional framework for that organization. The Security Council is thus subjected to certain constitutional limitations, however broad its powers under the constitution may be. Those powers cannot, in any case, go beyond the limits of the jurisdiction of the Organization at large, not to mention other specific limitations or those which may derive from the internal division of power within the Organization. In any case, neither the text nor the spirit of the Charter conceives of the Security Council as *legibus solutus* (unbound by law) .... The Charter thus speaks the language of specific powers, not of absolute fiat.[87]

A number of scholars have similarly concluded that the Security Council is not above the law but subject to it. For example, Aristotle Constantinides writes:

> The initial question is whether the Security Council is bound by the law or whether it is omnipotent and *legibus solutus*. The answer to this question is that the Council is not sovereign; it is not above the law. Despite its predominantly and *par excellence* political character and functions, it is still an organ of an international organization, deriving its very broad powers from a treaty concluded by States. It is very unlikely that an organization based on the principle of sovereign equality of its Member States would confer unlimited powers to any of its organs. This has been reaffirmed in the early jurisprudence of the ICJ and more recently by the ICTY Appeals Chamber in the *Tadić* case.[88]

Dapo Akande similarly opines that: "To the extent that the United Nations is a subject of international law it follows that its organs are thereby subjected to international law."[89] Anne Peters concurs, writing: "The Security Council, as the most powerful organ of the organization, cannot be less subjected to legal obligations than the organization itself ... ."[90] She continues: "the

---

[87] Prosecutor v. Dusko Tadić, Case No. IT-94-1-AR72, Decision on the Defense Motion for Interlocutory Appeal on Jurisdiction, para. 28 (Oct. 2, 1995), 35 I.L.M.32.

[88] Aristotle Constantinides, *An Overview of Legal Restraints on Security Council Chapter VII Action with a Focus on Post-Conflict Iraq*, at 2, presented at European Society of International Law, Inaugural Conference, Florence, 2004, *at* http://esil-sedi.eu/wp-content/uploads/2018/04/Constantinides_o.pdf, *citing Conditions of Admission of a State to Membership in the United Nations, supra* note 80, at 64; *Tadić, supra* note 87, para. 28.

[89] Akande, *supra* note 79, at 320.

[90] Anne Peters, *The Security Council's Responsibility to Protect*, 8 INT'L ORG L. REV. 15, 31 (2011).

[Security Council] is not a purely political organ acting in a law-free zone, but is subject to legal limits."[91] Karl Doehring and Alexander Orakhelashvili additionally agree that the Security Council cannot be above the law.[92]

4.1.4.2 The Security Council Is Bound to Respect *Jus Cogens* Norms

A *fortiori*, if the Security Council is subject to international law, it necessarily must be subject to *jus cogens* norms, as they are at the apex of the international legal system. Thus, James Crawford writes: "It seems intuitively right that the Security Council should be bound by peremptory norms. They are by definition norms that cannot be derogated from except by subsequent norms of the same kind."[93] Simon Chesterman concurs:

> It is generally acknowledged that the Security Council's powers are subject to the UN Charter and norms of *jus cogens* . . . . The Council does not operate free of legal constraint. In strict legal terms this means that the Council's powers are exercised subject to the Charter and norms of *jus cogens*. More importantly, however, the Council's authority derives from the rule of law – respect for its decisions depends on respect for the Charter and international law more generally.[94]

---

[91] *Id.* at 30; *see also id.* ("[I]n a constitutionalising international system, the traditional view of Security Council actions in a basically law-free realm is no longer tenable. The rule of law governs decisions of the Security Council.").

[92] *See* Karl Doehring, *Unlawful Resolutions of the Security Council and Their Legal Consequences*, 11 MAX PLANCK. Y.B. UN L. 91, 108 (1997) ("The Security Council is obliged to respect the rules of international law, i.e. the limits of its own competencies under the Charter of the United Nations and the rules of general international law as well."). Orakhelashvili writes:

> In performing its tasks under the Charter, the Security Council is perhaps empowered to take decisions affecting the legal rights and duties of state and non-state actors, though this general power is subject to limitations. (The exclusion of the power to effect a permanent settlement is an instance of these limitations.) But this is not the same as having the Security Council exempted from the operation of law. That could not be reconciled with the Charter framework or practice. The ICJ, in *Namibia*, while interpreting the Council's powers broadly, emphasized that the Council is subject to legal standards. The ICTY Appeals Chamber vigorously confirmed that the Council is not *legibus solutus* (unbound by law).

Alexander Orakhelashvili, *The Impact of Peremptory Norms on the Interpretation and Application of United Nations Security Council Resolutions*, 16(1) EUR. J. INT'L L. 59, 62 (2005).

[93] JAMES CRAWFORD, "CHANCE, ORDER, CHANGE: THE COURSE OF INTERNATIONAL LAW" GENERAL COURSE ON PUBLIC INTERNATIONAL LAW, at 421, para. 546 (2013).

[94] Simon Chesterman, *The UN Security Council and the Rule of Law: The Role of the Security Council in Strengthening a Rules-Based International System Final Report and Recommendations from the Austrian Initiative, 2004–2008*, New York University School of Law Public Law & Legal Theory Research Paper Series Working Paper No. 08–57, paras. 29, 49 (Dec. 2008). *See also*

The European Court of First Instance (now known as the General Court) also held that *jus cogens* constitute "a body of higher rules of public international law *binding on all subjects of international law, including the bodies of the United Nations.*"[95] If *jus cogens* is "binding on all subjects of international law, including the bodies of the United Nations," then *jus cogens* is necessarily binding on the Security Council.[96]

This conclusion – that the Security Council is bound by *jus cogens* – can also be derived from application of the principle *nemo plus iuris transferre potest quam ipse habet*, that an international creature cannot acquire more powers than its creators. Hannah Yiu explains:

> [A] further justification for *jus cogens* being a direct and autonomous legal limit on the [Security Council] comes from the fact that the [Security Council], despite its wide powers, has only those powers that have been conferred on it by the UN's Member States. The [Security Council] is a creation of the UN, created by the UN's Member States, all of whom are bound by *jus cogens* norms. It follows then that the [Security Council], as a creation of the UN, is also bound by *jus cogens* norms because an international creature cannot acquire more powers than its creators – *nemo plus iuris transferre potest quam ipse habet*.[97]

Farrall, *supra* note 44, at 71 ("As [peremptory] norms are so essential [that they cannot be violated or derogated from], it can be argued that the Security Council is legally bound to respect them.").

[95] Case T-315/01, Kadi v. Council of the European Union and Commission of the European Communities 2005 E.C.R. II-03649 (emphasis added) [hereinafter, *Kadi*]; Case T-306/01, Yusuf and Al Barakaat International Foundation v. Council of the European Union and Commission of the European Communities, 2005 E.C.R. II-03533 [hereinafter, *Al Barakaat*].

[96] See Orakhelashvili [The Impact], *supra* note 92 ("There is a hierarchy in international law with direct impact on the scope of the Council's powers. Not only are the Council's resolutions part of secondary law subjected to the Charter, but also part of a system which in its entirety is subordinated to *jus cogens*."). "Given their non-derogable character, *jus cogens* norms are ... superior to all sources and binding on all subjects of international law." Heieck, *supra* note 39, at 189, *citing* Orakhelashvili [Peremptory Norms], *supra* note 36, at 9, 423; Erica De Wet, Jus Cogens *and* Obligations Erga Omnes, *in* THE OXFORD HANDBOOK OF HUMAN RIGHTS LAW, at 6 (Dinah Shelton ed., 2013).

[97] Hannah Yiu, Jus Cogens, *the Veto and the Responsibility to Protect: A New Approach*, 7 N.Z. Y.B. INT'L L. 207, 246 (2009), *citing* August Reinisch, *Developing Human Rights and Humanitarian Law Accountability of the Security Council for the Imposition of Economic Sanctions*, 95 AM. J. INT'L L. 851, 858 (2001); Eike Duckwitz, The Doctrine of *Jus Cogens* as a Limit on the Power of the United Nations' Security Council, at 28–30 (Master's Thesis, University of Auckland, 2009); Orakhelashvili [The Impact], *supra* note 92, at 68, n. 53 ("States cannot delegate to an international organization more powers than they themselves can exercise."); *id.* at 79 (citing cases) ("The encroachment on *jus cogens* is clearly outside the Council's competence. It is established in national and international jurisprudence (although on a different matter than considered here) that conduct outlawed under *jus cogens* is outside the functions of states. Organizations established by states cannot be endowed with functions and powers which states themselves are not entitled to exercise.").

4.1 The Relationship between the Veto and Jus Cogens

Another way to reach the above conclusion is that peremptory norms limit the Security Council's powers (including Chapter VII powers) – because *no treaty* (not even the UN Charter) can derogate from *jus cogens* norms.[98] Under Article 53 of the Vienna Convention, any treaty that conflicts with a peremptory norm is void.[99] The UN Charter, while the "constitutive instrument" of the UN system, is nonetheless still a treaty.[100] Thus, it too is subject to *jus cogens*.[101]

---

[98] *See* Bardo Fassbender, Review Essay Quis Judicabit? *The Security Council, Its Powers and Its Legal Control*, 111(1) EUR. J. INT'L L. 219, 226 (2000) (quoting and translating Fraas: "The constitutive treaty of an international organization, he says, may not contradict *jus cogens* rules. 'From this it follows that the organs of the organization may not be empowered to violate rules of *jus cogens*.'") (MICHAEL FRASS, SICHERHEITSRAT DER VEREINTEN NATIONEN UND INTERNATIONALE GERICHTSHOF: DIE RECHTMÄβIGKEITSPRÜFUNG VON BESCHLÜSSEN DES SICHERHEITSRATS DER VEREINTEN NATIONEN IM RAHMEN DES VII. KAPITELS DER CHARTA DURCH DEN INTERNATIONALEN GERICHTSHOF, at 77 (1998)); Yiu, *supra* note 97, at 236, 246 ("The [Security Council's] acts are subject to *jus cogens* in the same way that acts of any other international actor would be."). *See also* Nico Krisch, *Action with Respect to Threats to the Peace, Breaches of the Peace, and Acts of Aggression, Introduction to Chapter VII: The General Framework*, in THE CHARTER OF THE UNITED NATIONS: A COMMENTARY, VOL. 2, 1259, para. 45 (Bruno Simma, Daniel-Erasmus Khan, Georg Nolte & Andreas Paulus eds., 3d ed. 2012) ("[P]eremptory norms of international law are often regarded as a stricter limit on the [Security Council]. Many commentators have argued that these norms pose limits to Chapter VII powers since no international treaty, including the UN Charter, can derogate from them, and [Articles] 53 and 64 of the [VCLT] may seem to indicate such a result. The ICTY has followed this line, and several domestic and regional courts have adopted it with a particular view to human rights protections.") (citations omitted) (but arguing the prohibition on aggression must be understood in light of the Security Council's Chapter VII powers).

[99] VCLT, *supra* note 34, Art. 53.

[100] *See* Sloan, *supra* note 22, at 61 ("The Charter of the United Nations is a multilateral convention to which all members of the Organization are parties. In other words, the Charter is a treaty and consequently one will look to the [Vienna Convention on the] Law of Treaties for guidance in its interpretation."); *Tadić, supra* note 87, para. 28 ("the Security Council is an organ of an international organization, established by a treaty which serves as a constitutional framework for that organization"). Sloan did note that, strictly speaking, the VCLT would not govern the Charter due to the VCLT's non-retroactivity provision (VCLT, *supra* note 34, Art. 4), but he then went on to use the VCLT as an authoritative guide to interpreting the Charter. *See* Sloan, *supra* note 22, at 116 ("the provisions of the Vienna Convention relating to interpretation are, if not a codification, at least a crystallization of custom and, hence, binding as general international law. We will, therefore, look to the Vienna Convention for guidance in the interpretation of the Charter."). *See also* Orakhelashvili [The Impact], *supra* note 92, at 67 ("The law of treaties codified in VCLT 1969, also embodying customary law, applies to constituent instruments of international organizations, such as the UN Charter."); Hossain, *supra* note 18, at 89 ("To the extent that these [*jus cogens*] norms were pre-existent and merely codified in the Charter, the Charter becomes subject to the operation of *jus cogens* even though it came into force before the promulgation of the Vienna Convention.").

[101] "The Charter, like all other multilateral treaties, is subservient to *jus cogens*." Heieck, *supra* note 39, at 202.

Yet another way of reaching the conclusion that the Security Council may not violate *jus cogens* can be deduced as follows. Under UN Charter Article 24(2) the Council is bound to "act in accordance with the [p]urpose and [p]rinciples" of the UN[102] – an argument further examined below as to the limitations this imposes on the Security Council.[103] For present purposes, note that one of the "[p]urposes" of the UN, in UN Charter Article 1(1), is:

> To maintain international peace and security, and to that end: to take effective collective measures for the prevention and removal of threats to the peace, and for the suppression of acts of aggression or other breaches of the peace, and to bring about by peaceful means, and *in conformity with the principles of justice and international law*, adjustment or settlement of international disputes or situations which might lead to a breach of the peace[.][104]

While it could be read that the requirement of acting "in conformity with the principles of justice and international law" only applies to the "adjustment or settlement of international disputes or situations which might lead to a breach of the peace," Dapo Akande persuasively argues that it also applies to the Security Council when acting to maintain international peace and security – that in that situation as well, the Council must act "in conformity with the principles of justice and international law."[105] Thus, if Article 1(1), combined with Article 24(2), mandate that the Council act in conformity with international law – and ICJ judges writing in the *Lockerbie* Case further confirm that the Security Council must act in conformity with international law[106] – then, relying on the UN Charter, one again reaches the conclusion that the Council certainly must act in conformity with *jus cogens*, the highest form of international law.[107]

---

[102] UN Charter, Art. 24(2).
[103] *See* Chapter 4.2 *infra*.
[104] UN Charter, Art. 1(1) (emphasis added).
[105] Akande, *supra* note 79, at 320 ("Though this debate [at San Francisco during the Charter negotiations] was not conclusive it demonstrates that when the question of limitation of the enforcement powers of the Security Council was raised it was assumed that they were similarly limited by the principles of international law."). *See also* notes 120, 214 *infra* (how to reconcile the Security Council's Chapter VII powers and the requirement of adherence to international law).
[106] *See* notes 84–86 *supra* and accompanying text (Judges Jennings, Weeramantry, and Bedjaoui). *See also* notes 120, 214 *infra* (how to reconcile the Security Council's Chapter VII powers and the requirement of adherence to international law).
[107] "[J]us cogens norms bind international actors, and the [Security Council] is no exception." Yiu, *supra* note 97, at 232.

4.1.5 Legal Consequences of Jus Cogens Norms Being Binding on the Security Council

Based on the conclusion that *jus cogens* is binding on the Security Council, one might then ask what consequences flow from this?

4.1.5.1 The Security Council Cannot Explicitly Authorize Violations of *Jus Cogens*

First, one must conclude that the Security Council cannot explicitly authorize violations of *jus cogens*. For example, a resolution that would appear to require participation in genocide would clearly be void.

4.1.5.2 The Security Council May Not Violate *Jus Cogens* in Its Resolutions/a Resolution That Conflicts with a *Jus Cogens* Norm Will Be Void

Second, it has been suggested – and the author shares this view – that a Security Council resolution will be void or invalid if it conflicts with a norm of *jus cogens*. This issue was explored in the *Application of Genocide Convention* Case.[108] At issue was whether the Security Council's arms embargo imposed on Yugoslavia was void as conflicting with *jus cogens* as it allegedly assisted the better-armed Serbian forces within Bosnia, was contrary to the right of self-defense enshrined in Article 51 of the Charter, and stopped the Bosnian government from preventing the commission of genocide as required by Article 1 of the Genocide Convention.[109] The Government of Bosnia-Herzegovina argued that because of the conflict with *jus cogens*, Security Council Resolution 713, which imposed the embargo, should be deemed *ultra vires* of the proper exercise of Security Council power and without effect. Judge ad hoc Eli Lauterpacht considered the issue in a separate opinion and found that Resolution 713 "can be seen as having in effect called on Members of the United Nations, albeit unknowingly and assuredly unwillingly, to become in some degree supporters of the genocidal activity of the Serbs and in this manner and to that extent to act contrary to a rule of *jus cogens*."[110] In addressing the legal consequences that flow from this analysis, Judge Lauterpacht considered one possibility to be that "when the operation of paragraph 6 of Security Council resolution 713 (1991) began to make Members of the United Nations accessories to genocide it ceased to be valid and binding in its operation against Bosnia-Herzegovina[,] and that Members of the United

---

[108] *Application of Genocide Convention* Case, *supra* note 56.
[109] *Id.* at 327–28.
[110] ICJ Rep. at 441, para. 102; 95 ILR 159 (sep. op., Lauterpacht, J.).

Nations then became free to disregard it."¹¹¹ The ICJ did not ultimately take a position on this issue as it found that part of Bosnia-Herzegovina's request to be outside the scope of its jurisdiction.¹¹² Thus, while Resolution 713 was not actually declared invalid, James Crawford writes: "in the absence of effective action under Council auspices States were increasingly disinclined to obey it. To some extent this is, in effect, what happened with, for example, the Organisation of Islamic Conference declaring that it would not comply with the arms embargo."¹¹³

While Judge Lauterpacht went on to describe another possible conclusion from his analysis, he ultimately opined: "It is not necessary for the Court to take a position in this regard at this time. *Instead, it would seem sufficient that the relevance here of* jus cogens *should be drawn to the attention of the Security Council ..., so that the Security Council may give due weight to it in future reconsideration of the embargo.*"¹¹⁴ He therefore clearly suggested that *jus cogens is relevant* to the Security Council in order for the Council to give it "due weight" in its resolutions.

Judge Dugard reached a similar conclusion in his Separate Opinion in the *Armed Activities* Case, when he concluded that "States must deny recognition to a situation created by a serious breach of a peremptory norm":

> It is today accepted that a treaty will be void if at the time of its conclusion, it conflicts with "a peremptory norm of general international law" (Art. 53 of the Vienna Convention on the Law of Treaties of 1969); and that *States must deny recognition to a situation created by the serious breach of a peremptory norm* (Arts. 40 and 41 of the Draft Articles on the Responsibility of States for Internationally Wrongful Acts ...).¹¹⁵

This would again imply that a Security Council resolution should not be creating or recognizing a serious breach of a peremptory norm (that is, the Security Council must respect *jus cogens*).¹¹⁶

The European Court of First Instance also expressed agreement with this approach in the *Barakaat* and *Kadi* cases, "affirming that *jus cogens* norms

---

[111] *Id.*, para. 103.
[112] See *Application of Genocide Convention* Case, *supra* note 56, para. 41.
[113] Crawford [Chance], *supra* note 93, para. 550, *citing* Akande, *supra* note 79, at 322 (reaching a similar conclusion).
[114] *Application of Genocide Convention* Case, *supra* note 56, para. 104 (sep. op., Lauterpacht, J.) (emphasis added).
[115] *Armed Activities*, *supra* note 48, para. 8 (sep. op., Dugard, J.) (emphasis added).
[116] Judge Dugard's discussion of *jus cogens* occurred in the context of the DRC having argued that a breach of *jus cogens* conferred jurisdiction on the ICJ. The DRC also argued that Rwanda could not raise a reservation to the Court's jurisdiction because *jus cogens* would defeat the reservation. Both arguments were rejected. *Id.*, para 3.

are unconditionally binding on the [Security Council], and a resolution violating *jus cogens* would not be binding":[117]

> International law ... permits the inference that there exists one limit to the principle that resolutions of the Security Council have binding effect: namely, that they must observe the fundamental peremptory provisions of *jus cogens*. If they fail to do so, ... they would bind neither the Member States of the United Nations nor, in consequence, the Community.[118]

The issue there arose in the context of asset freezes pursuant to a Security Council resolution, and how the EU gave effect to that resolution.[119]

Legal scholars similarly conclude that the Security Council is not able in its resolutions to violate *jus cogens*.[120] Alexander Orakhelashvili writes:

---

[117] Yiu, *supra* note 97, at 245.
[118] *Kadi*, *supra* note 95, at 230; *Al Barakaat*, *supra* note 95, at 281. In that case, the Court of First Instance found the implementation of the asset freeze did not infringe fundamental rights protected by *jus cogens*. *Al Barakaat*, *supra* note 95, at paras. 263–346; *Kadi*, *supra* note 95, at paras. 212–291. On appeal, the Court of Justice of the European Communities (now known as the Court of Justice of the European Union) saw it somewhat differently, that its review should focus on how Community members *implement* Security Council resolutions. Joined Cases C-402/05 P and C-415/05 P, Yassin Abdullah Kadi and Al Barakaat International Foundation v. Council and Commission, 47 ILM 923, para. 287 (Eur. Ct. Just Sept. 3, 2008).
[119] The resolution imposed an assets freeze on individuals and entities allegedly associated with Osama bin Laden, the Al-Qaeda network, and the Taliban, and was implemented through a Sanctions Committee. For discussion of the case, see, e.g., Miša Zgonec-Rozej, Kadi & Al Barakaat v. Council of the EU & EC Commission: *European Court of Justice Quashes a Council of the EU Regulation Implementing UN Security Council Resolutions*, 12(22) ASIL INSIGHTS (Oct. 28, 2008), at www.asil.org/insights/volume/12/issue/22/kadi-al-barakaat-v-council-eu-ec-commission-european-court-justice.
[120] Admittedly, this requirement of adherence to international law and *jus cogens* is a bit complex, as there are times when the Security Council *is* permitted to violate what would otherwise be required under international law. For example, its Chapter VII, Article 42, powers to implement forceful measures would otherwise violate the sovereignty of the country in question (and the prohibition against aggression), were they not expressly authorized under the Charter. Thus, the requirement of acting in conformity with the principles of "international law" and *jus cogens* probably needs to be read in this light – that the Security Council cannot violate general principles of international law (for example, pass a discriminatory resolution), but certainly the Council has the powers granted to it under the Charter. *See* Akande, *supra* note 79, at 317 (there is "a duty on the part of the Council not to violate general international law *unless the Charter specifically allows it to do so*") (emphasis added). Another way of thinking of this is that *jus cogens* prohibits use of force or aggression *outside* the UN Charter's framework. Note that even a Chapter VII force authorization would have limitations – for example, it could not violate the "intransgressible" rules of International Humanitarian Law such as the need to respect distinction and proportionality, just as it could not authorize the commission of genocide. Thus, even the operation of Chapter VII must have some limits, so that *jus cogens* is respected. *See* discussion notes 70–71 *supra* and

Since peremptory norms safeguard the community interest as opposed to individual state interests, they possess absolute validity; this is in contrast to the relative validity of ordinary or non-peremptory norms.... Their rationale consists in invalidating or *prevailing over incompatible acts and transactions* in order to ensure the paramount superiority of fundamental community values and interests .... [T]he Security Council must respect peremptory norms because the core values protected by *jus cogens* are not derogable or waivable in the sense of *jus dispositivum*. A Council resolution violating *jus cogens* would indeed be a derogation from *jus cogens*, as it would be an attempt to use the UN system for the establishment of a new legal regime through a resolution contrary to *jus cogens*.[121]

Based on Judge Lauterpacht's separate opinion, Dapo Akande reaches a similar conclusion: "*Jus cogens* norms are peremptory norms of international law and by definition they cannot be derogated from. They are overriding norms of the international legal order and they supersede all other norms. Any Security Council decision in conflict with a norm of *jus cogens* must necessarily be without effect."[122]

4.1.6 *The Relationship between the Veto and* Jus Cogens

The question then arises, if *jus cogens* violations are occurring (for example, genocide) and the Security Council has before it a draft resolution aimed at curtailing or alleviating the commission of the crimes, whether the veto may

---

accompanying text (*Nuclear Weapons* Advisory Opinion opining that "intransgressible" rules of IHL are peremptory norms). *See also* Jordan J. Paust, *U.N. Peace and Security Powers and Related Presidential Powers*, 26 GA. J. INT'L & COMP. L. 15, 16 (1996) ("*Jus cogens* prohibitions, such as the prohibitions of aggressive force and genocide, should condition and limit UN peace and security powers. In particular, Security Council actions under Chapter VII of the Charter generally must not serve to encourage aggression and genocide, as some actions apparently have with respect to Bosnia Herzegovina. To the extent that they do, Members should not be bound to participate.").

[121] Orakhelashvili [The Impact], *supra* note 92, at 62–63 (emphasis added). *See also id.* at 88 ("One should ... bear in mind the special role of peremptory norms in the contemporary international legal system, and consider that the continuance in force of a Council resolution which is in conflict with jus cogens is nothing but the maintenance of a situation that is morally and ethically repugnant in the eyes of the international community."). *See also* Stefano Congiu, Jus Cogens: *The History, Challenges and Hope of* "A Giant on Stilts," 7 PLYMOUTH L. & CRIM. JUST. REV. 47, 48 (2015) ("*Jus cogens* binds the Security Council, with Judge Lauterpacht considering it 'as a matter of simple hierarchy of norms', with *jus cogens* outranking a Security Council resolution.").

[122] Akande, *supra* note 79, at 322 (footnoted omitted). *See also* Doehring, *supra* note 92, at 108 ("Peremptory norms of international law cannot be set aside by resolutions of the Security Council; those resolutions cannot produce binding force upon the members of the United Nations.").

be freely used when the result would potentially help to enable the continued perpetration of the crimes.

4.1.6.1 The Veto Should Not Be Used in Circumstances Where It Has the Effect of Facilitating the Commission of *Jus Cogens* Violations

It is the author's contention, supported by legal and policy considerations, that the veto power should not be used in the face of ongoing *jus cogens* violations (or even the serious risk of them).[123] Here, the vetoing permanent member would be using its powers, granted by a treaty (the UN Charter), in circumstances where it essentially enables, or at least helps to enable (even if indirectly), a continuing *jus cogens* violation.

This conclusion – that the veto should not be used in such a way – is supported by the reasoning of Judge Lauterpacht, who observed that when the operation of a Security Council resolution effectively "make[s] members of the United Nations accessories to genocide it cease[s] to be valid and binding," one conclusion that could be reached is that Member States are "free to disregard it."[124] If a resolution should not make members of the UN accessories to genocide, then veto use also should not make them accessories by helping to enable (even if indirectly) the continued commission of genocide. Because the prohibition on committing crimes against humanity and war crimes (or at least certain of them)[125] are similarly peremptory norms protected by *jus cogens*,[126] the same should be true for them.[127]

---

[123] As explored below, in the ICJ's *Bosnia v. Serbia* decision, the ICJ held that the duty to "prevent" genocide is triggered by the "serious risk" of the crime occurring. *See* text accompanying notes 340–41 *infra*. Thus, arguably, a response is warranted (and no veto should be utilized) already when there is a "serious risk" of the crime occurring. While the ICJ decision only pertains to the crime of genocide, there is no reason not to have an analogous approach vis-à-vis crimes against humanity and war crimes.

[124] *Application of Genocide Convention* Case, *supra* note 56, at 441.

[125] See discussion at Chapter 4.1.3 as to which war crimes are *jus cogens*.

[126] *See* Chapter 4.1.2 *supra*.

[127] Yiu, *supra* note 97, at 232 ("Where there is a [core crime] situation involving the breach of a *jus cogens* norm, the veto cannot be used in a manner that *facilitates* this breach because such usage would be a violation of a non-derogable norm of international law.") (emphasis added). Assume the permanent member can be shown to be aware of the crimes being committed. Also assume, for arguments sake, that the veto has a "substantial effect" in allowing the crimes to continue. Note, however, that Judge Lauterpacht believes that a resolution that "unknowingly" and "unwillingly" makes Security Council members accessories to genocide would be void. *Application of Genocide Convention* Case, *supra* note 56, at 441, para. 103. Thus, for him, "awareness" by member states on the Council of the crimes being committed does not seem critical.

This conclusion is also warranted based on the ILC's Articles on State Responsibility (Article 41.2) and, *mutatis mutandis*, the ILC's Articles on the Responsibility of International Organizations for Internationally Wrongful Acts (Article 42.2). These make clear that no state or international organization shall "recognize as lawful a situation created by a serious breach [of a peremptory norm], *nor render aid or assistance in maintaining that situation.*"[128]

If a veto is employed during ongoing genocide, crimes against humanity, and/or war crimes, where there is a resolution designed to address the crimes – even just through condemnation – the veto is arguably helping to maintain the status quo, where a serious breach of a peremptory norm is occurring.[129] Yet, the ILC clearly states that "[n]o State" or "international organization" shall "render aid or assistance in maintaining" a situation where there is a serious breach of a peremptory norm.[130] Accordingly, a veto made where there is a serious breach of a peremptory norm should be seen as void or *ultra vires* of the proper exercise of Security Council power.[131] "Where *jus cogens* norms are in issue ... the matter should no longer be considered purely as one of international peace and security under the [Security Council's] sole jurisdiction, but one where the use of veto by the permanent [members] ... would be unlawful as a breach of *jus cogens*."[132]

---

[128] Articles on State Responsibility, *supra* note 21, Art. 41.2; Int'l L. Comm'n, Draft Articles on the Responsibility of International Organizations for Internationally Wrongful Acts, with Commentaries (adopted), UN Doc. A/66/10, para. 87 (2001) [hereinafter, Articles on the Responsibility of International Organizations], Art. 42.2 (emphasis added). For discussion of the "weight" accorded to the ILC's Articles, see notes 142–44 *infra* and accompanying text.

[129] As noted above, responsibility arguably should already be triggered by the "serious risk" of the crimes. See note 123 *supra*.

[130] Articles on State Responsibility, *supra* note 21, Art. 41.2; Articles on the Responsibility of International Organizations, *supra* note 128, Art. 42.2. For discussion of what constitutes a "serious" breach of a peremptory norm, see note 140 *infra*.

[131] See Heieck, *supra* note 39, at 188 ("While a treaty, such as the UN Charter, may be valid on its face, the *application* of certain treaty provisions, such as the exercise of the [permanent members'] discretionary rights ... to impose binding decisions through Security Council resolutions under Articles 41 and/or 42, and to vote for or veto such resolutions under Article 27(3), may be invalid if it conflicts with a *jus cogens* norm.") (emphasis added); Yiu, *supra* note 97, at 232 (similar); Orakhelashvili [The Impact], *supra* note 92, at 68 ("Acts contrary to *jus cogens* are beyond the powers of an institution (*ultra vires*).").

[132] Yiu, *supra* note 97, at 208. See also Orakhelashvili [The Impact], *supra* note 92, at 68 ("States violate *jus cogens* not only by inserting explicit clauses in treaties, but also – and predominantly – by the manner in which they exercise their rights and prerogatives under a treaty not explicitly conflicting with *jus cogens*."); *id.* at 71 (arguing that the Council should not be giving implicit support for the breach of a peremptory norm). Yiu focuses on the veto preventing "intervention"; however, many of the vetoes that have been employed are preventing far less – for example, preventing even condemnation of crimes. This author is in no way making a case for full-scale military intervention in the face of genocide, crimes against

4.1 The Relationship between the Veto and Jus Cogens

While some might argue that where a resolution only "condemns" *jus cogens* violations (for example, ongoing genocide, crimes against humanity, and/or war crimes), but does not impose measures designed to halt or alleviate the commission of the crimes (whether through forceful or non-forceful means),[133] the veto would not "aid" or "assist" the continued commission of crimes, as a condemning resolution would have no "substantial effect"[134] on whether the crimes are committed or continue. First, the ILC states that neither "states" nor any "international organization" shall "render aid or assistance" to maintaining a serious breach of a peremptory norm (without mentioning any "substantiality" requirement).[135] Second, even if there is a requirement of "substantial" assistance, condemnation is often the first step before the Council takes other measures – thus, it may be a crucial initial step as the Council may be unlikely to implement measures without having first condemned the crimes, so blocking this critical step could have a "substantial" effect. Third, some countries *would* care about even a single resolution of condemnation, so that the veto of *even one* condemning resolution *could* have a substantial effect. Fourth, in a situation where there are multiple vetoes that effectively "protect" a regime that perpetrates crimes such as genocide, crimes against humanity, and/or war crimes, the vetoes could be viewed cumulatively in terms of their impact; the series of vetoes most definitely could have a substantial effect in conveying to the regime in question that it has a "protector" (or two) on the Council, who will ensure it is essentially treated as above the law.[136] Moreover, whether a resolution or series of resolutions would have prevented the crimes is arguably beside the point. The ICJ – in discussing the obligation to "prevent" genocide found in Article 1

---

humanity, and/or war crimes unless non-forceful measures have been sufficiently attempted, and, thereafter, forceful measures short of large-scale intervention have also been attempted, and any full-scale intervention is narrowly tailored and satisfies legal requirements such as distinction and proportionality.

[133] There are many measures the Security Council may impose short of a force authorization, and, as to force authorizations, there are many measures that can be utilized short of a full force authorization.

[134] Under international criminal law, for aiding and abetting or individual responsibility more generally, it is generally required that there be a "substantial effect" on the perpetration of the crime. *See, e.g.,* Prosecutor v. Blaškiç, IT-95-14-A, Appeals Chamber Judgment, para. 48 (July 29, 2004); Prosecutor v. Nahimana, Barayagwiza and Ngeze, ICTR-99-52-A, Appeals Chamber Judgment, para. 492 (Nov. 28, 2007). The author does not claim there is individual criminal responsibility attached to veto use.

[135] Articles on State Responsibility, *supra* note 21, Art. 41.1; Articles on the Responsibility of International Organizations, *supra* note 128, Art. 42.1.

[136] *See, e.g.,* Chapter 5 for discussion of the series of fourteen vetoes made related to the situation in Syria; *see also* Chapter 4.2.4 *infra*.

of the Genocide Convention[137] – finds "it is irrelevant whether the State whose responsibility is in issue claims, or even proves, that even if it had employed all means reasonably at its disposal, they would not have sufficed to prevent the commission of [the crimes],"[138] as the obligation is one of due diligence to do all that is lawfully within a state's power;[139] it is thus an obligation of "means," not to ensure the result.

4.1.6.2 The Veto Should Not Be Used in a Way That Undermines the Duty of Other Security Council Members to Cooperate and Make an Appropriate Response to a Serious Breach of a *Jus Cogens* Norm

The conclusion that there are legal limits to veto use where peremptory norms are being violated is additionally warranted based on another obligation reflected in the ILC's Articles on States Responsibility (Article 41.1) and, *mutatis mutandis*, the ILC's Articles on the Responsibility of International Organizations (Article 42.1). There, the ILC recognized that there exists a duty of states and international organizations to "cooperate to bring to an end through lawful means any serious breach" "of an obligation arising under a peremptory norm of general international law."[140] (The importance of cooperation is additionally made clear by Article 1(3) of the Charter, which mandates "international co-operation in solving international problems of a[] ... humanitarian character" as one of the UN's "[p]urposes.")[141]

While the ILC's Articles on States Responsibility remain uncodified, states and non-state litigants have increasingly relied on these articles and commentaries, and international courts and tribunals have also treated them as source

---

[137] A more extensive discussion of the case is contained in Chapter 4.3.1 *infra*.
[138] Bosnia v. Serbia Case, *supra* note 17, para. 430.
[139] *Id*.
[140] Articles on State Responsibility, *supra* note 21, Arts. 41.1, 40.1; Articles on the Responsibility of International Organizations, *supra* note 128, Arts. 42.1, 41.1. As to when a "serious" breach of a peremptory norm occurs, while the author would contend that the occurrence of genocide, crimes against humanity, and/or war crimes are all per se "serious," the ILC takes the view that a "breach of such an obligation is serious if it involves a gross or systematic failure by the responsible [state or international organization] to fulfil the obligation." Articles on State Responsibility, *supra* note 21, Art. 40.2 (regarding states); Articles on the Responsibility of International Organizations, *supra* note 128, Art. 41.2 (regarding international organizations). Taking the most straightforward application, assume the Security Council does nothing in the face of a breach of a peremptory norm (e.g., passes no Security Council resolutions) that would arguably entail a "gross or systematic failure by the responsible international organization to fulfil" its obligations.
[141] *See* UN Charter, Art. 1(3).

of international law on questions of state responsibility.[142] For instance, the Articles on State Responsibility have been widely cited before and by the ICJ, including Article 41 which has been referred to at least twenty-three times in its judicial decisions.[143] In many cases, the Articles on State Responsibility have been viewed to reflect existing customary international law.[144]

The Commentary on Article 41.1 of the Articles on State Responsibility provides a powerful call for effective action in the face of serious breaches of peremptory norms. It states: "What is called for in the face of serious breaches is a joint and coordinated effort by all States to counteract the effects of these breaches."[145] "Article 41.1 thus seeks to strengthen existing mechanisms of cooperation, on the basis that all States are called upon to make an appropriate response to the serious breaches referred to in article 40."[146]

---

[142] James R. Crawford, *State Responsibility*, in MAX PLANCK ENCYCLOPEDIA OF PUBLIC INTERNATIONAL LAW, at para. 65 (2006), *at* https://opil.ouplaw.com/view/10.1093/law:epil/9780199231690/law-9780199231690-e1093. *See also* Report of the Secretary-General: Responsibility of States for Internationally Wrongful Acts, Compilation of Decisions of International Courts, Tribunals and Other Bodies, UN Doc. A/71/80/Add.1, June 20, 2017, *at* https://undocs.org/a/71/80/Add.1.

[143] Report of the Secretary-General, Responsibility of States for Internationally Wrongful Acts, Compilation of Decisions of International Courts, *supra* note 142, at 6.

[144] Crawford [Chance], *supra* note 93, para. 65 (noting, however, that some provisions are more controversial). *See also* Christiane Ahlborn & Bart Smit Duijzentkunst, *70 Years of the International Law Commission: Drawing a Balance for the Future*, OPINIO JURIS (May 3, 2018), *at* http://opiniojuris.org/2018/05/03/70-years-of-the-international-law-commission-drawing-a-balance-for-the-future (further discussion on the status of the Articles on State Responsibility); *see also* Kristina Daugirdas, *Reputation and the Responsibility of International Organizations*, 25(4) EUR. J. INT'L L. 991, 997 (2014), *at* www.ejil.org/pdfs/25/4/2543.pdf (noting that states that have opposed negotiating a treaty based on the Articles on State Responsibility were motivated by a desire to protect the ILC's work, as they feared that unsuccessful multilateral negations would undermine claims that the articles reflect existing customary international law). By comparison to the ILC Articles on State Responsibility, which were built on a large body of practice, the ILC's Articles on the Responsibility of International Organizations have been described as an exercise in the progressive development of international law. Daugirdas, *supra* note 144, at 997. The ILC has acknowledged as much. Articles on the Responsibility of International Organizations, *supra* note 128, at 2–3, paras. 1, 5. For a discussion of how customary international law can be read in conjunction with the Charter, see Chapter 2, note 244 (Sir Daniel Bethlehem).

[145] Int'l L. Comm'n, Articles on State Responsibility, *supra* note 21, at Commentary to Art. 41, para. 3.

[146] *Id.* According to the ILC in its commentary on Art. 41 of the Articles on State Responsibility:

> As to the elements of "aid or assistance", article 41 is to be read in connection with article 16. In particular, the concept of aid or assistance in article 16 presupposes that the State has "knowledge of the circumstances of the internationally wrongful act". There is no need to mention such a requirement in article 41, paragraph 2, as it is hardly conceivable that a State would not have notice of the commission of a serious breach by another State.

Thus, if other member states on the Council – or at least nine of them[147] – are cooperating to try to pass a resolution attempting to end or alleviate the violation of a peremptory norm (genocide, crimes against humanity, and/or war crimes),[148] their implementation of this duty should not be blocked by a permanent member. The permanent member would both be violating its own duty of cooperation and preventing other members of the Security Council from fulfilling their duties.

While some might argue that veto use can at times prove helpful – that is, that not every resolution drafted while ongoing genocide, crimes against humanity, and/or war crimes are occurring necessarily deserves to be adopted – the author's arguments only apply to the veto of a resolution that has attracted nine votes. If there are not nine affirmative votes, as mentioned, then there is no reason to invoke the veto. (Of course, here, based on the obligations recognized by the ILC, all members of the Security Council should also be working diligently to cooperate and agree on a resolution to address a serious breach of a peremptory norm, so that there are nine affirmative votes.) Note also that some reassurance can be derived from "strength in numbers," in that if a resolution were likely to be unhelpful, cause more harm than good, or is legally problematic for some reason,[149] it presumably would not attract nine affirmative votes from Security Council Member States. Put another way, if a resolution has attracted nine affirmative votes, at least nine members of the Security Council must see it as an "appropriate response" to the situation.[150]

Int'l L. Comm'n, Articles on State Responsibility, *supra* note 21, Commentary to Art. 41, para. 11.

[147] The UN Charter is read to require nine affirmative votes for a procedural matter, and nine affirmative votes and no veto for a substantive matter. See UN Charter, Art. 27(2)–(3); *see also* note 20 *supra* (discussing abstention).

[148] See Chapter 4.1.3 as to which war crimes are covered by *jus cogens*.

[149] A force authorization that does not respect distinction and proportionality would be one example.

[150] Alternatively, another possible formulation is that the veto should be considered of questionable legality where used in the face of genocide, crimes against humanity, and/or war crimes, when it vetoes a "credible draft" resolution designed to curtail or alleviate the commission of the crimes. This formulation – using the words "credible draft" resolution – is found in the ACT Group of States' Code of Conduct, which seeks voluntary veto restraint (and a positive commitment to vote for a resolution) in the face of genocide, crimes against humanity, and/or war crimes where there is such a "credible draft" resolution. See Chapter 3.1.4. Yet, as pointed out in Chapter 3, the Code of Conduct nowhere defines "credible draft" resolution, leaving this term open to multiple interpretations and thus susceptible to manipulation. It would seem unhelpful to hold a veto legally problematic in the face of ongoing genocide, crimes against humanity, and/or war crimes, *only* where there is a "credible draft" resolution designed to curtail or alleviate commission of the crimes – unless one defines "credible." See also Chapter 3.2.2.7. Accordingly, the author prefers the argument that a veto of a resolution responding to the commission of genocide, crimes against humanity, and/or war crimes, which has attracted the nine affirmative votes required for passage, should be seen

4.1.6.3 The Veto Should Be Used in a Way That Is Consistent with *Jus Cogens*

One could also envision an alternative formulation to support the argument that the veto should not be used while there are ongoing violations of peremptory norms or the serious risk of them.[151] One might argue that the veto power must be read to empower members of the Council only to act in a way that is *consistent with jus cogens*. If *jus cogens* norms are the highest level of law from which no derogations are permitted, which "cannot be violated,"[152] which must be respected "in all circumstances,"[153] which "rules are absolute"[154] and binding on the UN Security Council[155] (propositions all established above), then the power of the Security Council, including the veto power of its permanent members, needs to be read, and utilized, in a way that, at minimum, is *consistent with* these highest level norms.[156]

An emphasis on the need for "consistency" was recently articulated – admittedly in a different context – by the European Court of Human Rights and European Court of Justice when construing UN Security Council resolutions that appeared inconsistent with protections under the European Convention for the Protection of Human Rights and Fundamental Freedoms (European Convention).[157] This issue arose in both the *Kadi*[158] and *Al-Jedda*[159] cases. In *Kadi*, the "European Court of Justice held that guarantees of fundamental rights under EU law could not be displaced by

---

as questionable in terms of legality – without making reference to the resolution also having to be "credible."

[151] *See* note 123 *supra* (why the "serious risk" of the crimes should be covered).
[152] *See* note 44 *supra* (Farrall).
[153] *See* note 45 *supra* (Fitzmaurice).
[154] *See* note 46 *supra* (Verdross).
[155] *See* Chapter 4.1.4 *supra*.
[156] *See, e.g.*, Yiu, *supra* note 97, at 236 ("The [Security Council] itself is bound by *jus cogens* such that any use of the veto (or threatened use of the veto) *in a manner inconsistent* with *jus cogens* tenders that action or omission a breach of international law.") (emphasis added).
[157] European Convention for the Protection of Human Rights and Fundamental Freedoms, *entered into force* Sept. 3, 1953, ETS No. 005.
[158] Joined Cases Kadi and Al Barakaat, *supra* note 118.
[159] Case of Al-Jedda v. The United Kingdom, App. No. 27021/08, Judgment, para. 102 (Eur. Ct. H.R. July 7, 2011) (Grand Chambre), *at* www.law.umich.edu/facultyhome/drwcasebook/Documents/Documents/14.6_Al-Jedda%202011%20ECHR.pdf. The issue in *Al-Jedda* was whether preventive detention authority granted to UK forces in Iraq under Security Council Resolution 1546 displaced protections under Article 5 of the European Convention. The court concluded the Security Council had never authorized indefinite detention without charges, as the Council presumably meant to act in accordance with the European Convention. *Id.*, para. 109.

Security Council resolution."[160] In *Al-Jedda*, the European Court of Human Rights interpreted the Security Council resolution in question and the European Convention harmoniously, assuming no breach of the Convention was intended by the Security Council.[161] The "harmonious interpretation doctrine" was also followed by the European Court of Human Rights in *Al-Dulimi v. Switzerland*.[162]

Logically then, if courts strive to interpret Security Council resolutions in a way that is *consistent with* the European Convention,[163] arguably one should see similar consistency between the Council's actions and *jus cogens*.[164] In

---

[160] Marko Milanović, Al-Skeini *and* Al-Jedda *in Strasbourg*, 23 EUR. J. INT'L L. 121, 134 (2012), citing *Kadi, supra* note 95.

[161] Milanović, *supra* note 160, at 137, citing *Al-Jedda, supra* note 159, paras. 97–110. See also August Reinisch, *Should Judges Second-Guess the UN Security Council?*, 6 INT'L ORGS. L. REV. 257, 283 (2009) (commenting that in the *Al-Jedda* case before the UK Law Lords, "the House of Lords adopted a human right confirming interpretation of international law obligations in order to avoid a conflict between UN law and the demands under the ECHR").

[162] Case of Al-Dulimi and Montana Management Inc. v. Switzerland, App. No. 5809/08, Judgment, para. 140 (June 21, 2016) (Grand Chambre); see also id., para. 148 ("The Security Council is required to perform its tasks while fully respecting and promoting human rights.... [T]he Court takes the view that paragraph 23 of [Security Council] Resolution 1483 (2003) cannot be understood as precluding any judicial scrutiny of the measures taken to implement it."). See Secil Bilgic, *Harmonious Interpretation Meets the UN Charter: The Derogation Presumption*, HARV. HUM. RTS. J. (2016), *at* http://harvardhrj.com/harmonious-interpretation-meets-the-un-charter-the-derogation-presumption (comparing the "*Bosphorus* presumption" and the "harmonious interpretation" approaches taken by the European Court of Human Rights when faced with Security Council resolutions that appear to contradict the European Convention).

[163] The European Court of Human Rights in *Al-Jedda* held:

> [T]he Court considers that, in interpreting [Security Council] resolutions, there must be a presumption that the Security Council does not intend to impose any obligation on Member States to breach fundamental principles of human rights. In the event of any ambiguity in the terms of a Security Council resolution, the Court must therefore choose the interpretation which is most in harmony with the requirements of the Convention and which avoids any conflict of obligations. In the light of the United Nations' important role in promoting and encouraging respect for human rights, it is to be expected that clear and explicit language would be used were the Security Council to intend States to take particular measures which would conflict with their obligations under international human rights law.

Al-Jedda, supra note 159, para. 102. The argument would apply somewhat differently as to *jus cogens*; while it would seem appropriate to assume the Security Council does not intend to contradict *jus cogens*, if it did, its resolution would arguably be void, as it has no power to contravene *jus cogens*.

[164] See, e.g., Yiu, *supra* note 97, at 236. Orakhelashvili writes:

> The terms of a resolution, if vague, must be construed as requiring an outcome that is consistent with *jus cogens*. According to Gasser, "doubtful wording of the Council's resolutions must always be construed in such a way as to avoid conflict with fundamental international obligations." [Security Council] Resolution 242 called for "a just settlement of the refugee problem" in Palestine. "Just settlement" can only refer to

fact, this argument should apply even more so to *jus cogens* — which the Council has no power to violate[165] — than the European Convention, which, as a treaty, would reside lower on the hierarchy of norms.[166] "[T]he provisions of the UN Charter on the powers of the Security Council have to be interpreted *and executed* in a way that is *compatible with* jus cogens; they must be deemed to contain respective implicit limitations on that organ's powers."[167]

4.1.6.4 Individual Permanent Members Are Bound to Respect *Jus Cogens*

Finally, it almost goes without saying that, if the Security Council as a whole is bound to respect *jus cogens* (which, as demonstrated above, it is),[168] then the permanent members, who form a subset of the Council, similarly must be bound. This proposition can be derived a number of ways.

First, under the logic of the *Tadić* Case, discussed above, the ICTY held that the Security Council's "powers cannot ... go beyond the limits of the jurisdiction of the Organization at large [the United Nations]."[169] Just as the Security Council, as an organ of the UN, cannot have powers greater than its parent body, the same is true of individual permanent members. They cannot have powers greater than those of the Council. Thus, if the Council is bound to respect *jus cogens*,[170] so are individual permanent members.

Second, while the permanent members have an exceptional power granted to them under the UN Charter (the veto power), they are nonetheless still "states" and, as such, subject to respect *jus cogens*.[171] Because *jus*

> a settlement guaranteeing the return of displaced Palestinians, and other interpretations of this notion may be hazardous. The Council must be presumed not to have adopted decisions validating mass deportation or displacement. More so, as such expulsion or deportation is a crime against humanity or an exceptionally serious war crime ....

Orakhelashvili [The Impact], *supra* note 92, at 80.
[165] See Chapter 4.1.4.2 *supra* ("The Security Council is bound to respect jus cogens norms").
[166] Heieck, *supra* note 39, at 9 ("In the case of a conflict between a norm in question and a provision of the UN Charter, Article 103 controls the resolution of the conflict in favor of the latter *unless* the norm in question is a *jus cogens* norm.").
[167] Orakhelashvili [The Impact], *supra* note 92, at 68 (emphasis added).
[168] See Chapter 4.1.4.2 *supra* ("The Security Council Is Bound to Respect *Jus Cogens* Norms").
[169] *Tadić*, *supra* note 87, para. 28.
[170] See Orakhelashvili [The Impact], *supra* note 92, at 68 ("Acts contrary to *jus cogens* are beyond the powers of an institution (*ultra vires*).").
[171] "The most conspicuous consequence of this higher rank [of *jus cogens*] is that *the principle at issue cannot be derogated from by States* through international treaties." Prosecutor v. Furundžija, Case No. IT-95-17/1-T, Trial Chamber Judgment, para. 153 (Dec. 10, 1998) (emphasis added).

cogens is "binding on *all subjects* of international law,"[172] no exception is made, even for permanent members of the Security Council.[173] The Dissenting Opinion of Judge Fitzmaurice in the *Namibia* Case also supports this proposition. While Judge Fitzmaurice was writing on the topic of territorial sovereignty, he wrote: "This is a principle of international law that is well-established as any there can be, – and the Security Council is as much subject to it (for the United Nations is itself a subject of international law) *as any of its individual Member States are.*"[174]

Third, this conclusion can be reached under application of the principle *nemo plus iuris transferre potest quam ipse habet* – discussed above[175] – that an international creature cannot acquire more powers than its creators. If states cannot violation *jus cogens*, then the states that created the UN, and with it the existence of permanent members of the Security Council, cannot have granted to those members the power to violate *jus cogens*.

Fourth, this conclusion can be reached yet another way. Under UN Charter Article 24(1), UN Member States conferred on the Security Council "primary responsibility for the maintenance of international peace and security," and agreed that "in carrying out its duties under this responsibility the Security Council *acts on their behalf.*"[176] If the Security Council "acts on their behalf,"

---

[172] Heieck, *supra* note 39, at 189 (emphasis added) ("Given their non-derogable character, *jus cogens* norms are ... superior to all sources and binding on all subjects of international law."), citing Orakhelashvili, [Peremptory Norms], *supra* note 36, at 9, 423; De Wet, *supra* note 96, at 6. Salahuddin Mahmud & Shafiqur Rahman, *The Concept and Status of* Jus Cogens: *An Overview*, 3(6) INT'L J. L. 111 (2017) ("According to *Oxford Dictionary of Law, jus cogens* refers to a 'rule or principle in international law that is so fundamental that it binds *all states* and does not allow any exception.' Thus the concept of *jus cogens* in the context of international law indicates that it is a body of fundamental legal principle which is *binding upon all members of the international community in all circumstances.*") (emphasis added).

[173] See Orakhelashvili [The Impact], *supra* note 92, at 69 ("The direct and immediate effect of *jus cogens* means that the Council's acts are subject to it in the same way as the acts of any other actor."); Hossain, *supra* note 18, at 78–79 ("States regard these rules [of *jus cogens*] as being so important to the international society of states and to how that society defines itself, such that they cannot conceive of an exception.").

[174] See *Namibia* Advisory Opinion, diss. op., Fitzmaurice, J. Sir, *supra* note 20, at 294.

[175] See text accompanying note 97 *supra*.

[176] UN Charter, Art. 24(1) (emphasis added). See also Anne Peters, *The Security Council, Functions and Powers, Article 24, in* Simma et al., *supra* note 98, at vol. 1, 776, para. 45 ("The Security Council, being an organ of the United Nations, formally acts on behalf of that legal person and *not* on behalf of the members individually. The Charter's term 'on their behalf' can best be understood as highlighting the fact that, despite the restricted membership of the Council, that body is supposed to act in the interests of *all* members."); *id.*, para. 46 ("'[t]he powers vested in the Council under the Charter are in the nature of a trust and a delegation *from the entire membership of the UN.*' From that perspective, the members

and UN Member States cannot violate *jus cogens*, then in "acting on their behalf" neither should the Security Council nor its permanent members violate *jus cogens*.[177]

Thus, because individual permanent members are also bound to respect *jus cogens*, they too should not be acting in a way, through their resolutions or veto use, that: (i) in the circumstances has the effect of facilitating the commission of continuing *jus cogens* violations; (ii) undermines the duty of other Security Council members to cooperate to make an appropriate response to serious breaches of *jus cogens* norms; or (iii) is inconsistent with respect for *jus cogens* norms.

In conclusion, the section above demonstrates that not even the Security Council's permanent members should be able to derogate from the protections provided to *jus cogens* norms by permitting or facilitating (even if indirectly), through conduct on the Council (including veto use), the continued perpetration of genocide, crimes against humanity, and/or war crimes. The use of Security Council powers – both to pass resolutions and in the exercise of the veto by permanent members – must necessarily be constrained by, and consistent with, *jus cogens*, as neither the Security Council as a whole nor its individual permanent members, have the authority to violate *jus cogens*, or facilitate (even if indirectly) *jus cogens* violations.

4.2 LIMITATIONS IMPOSED ON THE SECURITY COUNCIL BY THE "PURPOSES AND PRINCIPLES" OF THE UNITED NATIONS

4.2.1 The Obligation of the Security Council to Act in Accordance with the "Purposes and Principles" of the United Nations

A second source of law by which to consider whether there are legal limits to the use of the veto power in the face of genocide, crimes against humanity, and/or war crimes is the UN Charter itself. While use of the veto is commonly treated in practice as a *carte blanche* subject to no limitations and above all

---

should be allowed to claim 'a right of supervision on how this responsibility is exercised on their behalf.'") (citations omitted).

[177] "As the International Law Commission (ILC) emphasized, states cannot escape the operation of *jus cogens*, particularly its invalidating power, through the establishment of an international organization." Orakhelashvili [The Impact], *supra* note 92, at 68; *see also id*. at 60 ("If a relevant norm is peremptory, then states cannot derogate from it, establishing an organization with the power to act in disregard of *jus cogens*. Therefore, *jus cogens* is an inherent limitation on any organization's powers.").

law,[178] examination of the text of the Charter reveals at least two express limitations on the Council's powers.

First, Article 27(3) states that "in decisions under Chapter VI [pacific settlement of disputes], and under paragraph 3 of Article 52 [pacific settlement of disputes through regional arrangements under Chapter VIII], a party to a dispute shall abstain from voting."[179] If a party to a dispute "shall abstain from voting," that includes a permanent member of the Security Council, which, in those circumstances, would not be able to exercise the veto.[180] ("[T]he veto [also] does not apply to resolutions on procedural matters, the election of judges for the ICJ, or for the appointment of members of conferences dealing with filling seats in the ICJ.")[181]

Second, and more importantly for current purposes, Article 24(2) provides that "the Security Council shall act in accordance with the Purposes and Principles of the United Nations."[182] If the Council's actions must accord with the "[p]urposes and [p]rinciples" of the UN, then, as further detailed below in Chapter 4.2.2.2, it follows also that veto use (an action taken by permanent members while serving on the Council)[183] also must accord with

---

[178] This "practice" has met with persistent objections from many states, so, as will be demonstrated below, there has been no acquiescence to such a practice. See Chapter 4.2.4.2 infra.
[179] UN Charter, Art. 27(3).
[180] See Stephen Eliot Smith, Reviving the Obligatory Abstention Rule in the UN Security Council: Reform from the Inside Out, 12 N.Z. Y.B. INT'L L. 15, 19 (2014) ("The obligatory abstention rule applies equally to permanent and non-permanent members of the Security Council, but its application is limited to decisions on non-coercive measures that may be taken under Chapter VI and art 52(3)."); Wouters & Ruys, supra note 10, at 12 (similar); Hans Kelsen, Organization and Procedure of the Security Council of the United Nations, 59 HARV. L. REV. 1087, 1099 (1946) ("Under paragraph 3 of Article 52, a party to the dispute shall abstain from voting. Since this rule applies to the permanent members, such decisions require only the concurring votes of the representatives of those permanent members not parties to the dispute.").
[181] Yiu, supra note 97, at 248, citing UN Charter, Art. 27(2); ICJ Statute, Art. 10(2).
[182] UN Charter, Art. 24(2). As to the drafting of Article 24(2), it seems to have been settled at the end of the Dumbarton Oaks conversations without much controversy. The Dumbarton Oaks Proposal, agreed upon at the culmination of the Dumbarton Oaks conversations, states "in discharging these duties, the Security Council should act in accordance with the purposes and principles of the Organization." Proposal for the Establishment of a General International Organization, reprinted in Y.B. UN 1946–1947, at 6. Of course, the eventual language in Article 24(2) states that the Council "shall act" in accordance with the Purposes and Principles of the UN. UN Charter Art. 24(2). The idea behind what became Article 24(2) appears to first surface with the UK's Tentative Proposal which included a provision that "the World Council should only be empowered to take action in accordance with the principles and objects of the Organization." See Tentative Proposals by the United Kingdom for a General International Organization.
[183] As explored more fully below, a veto is an *action* taken by a permanent member in that it needs to be invoked. It causes inaction by the Security Council as a whole on the resolution in question, but a veto is *not* inaction. See notes 250–51 and accompanying text.

the "[p]urposes and [p]rinciples" of the UN.[184] Thus, the plain language of the Charter provides for at least these limitations on Security Council power.[185]

That the Council's powers are limited by Article 24(2) to those in accordance with the UN's "[p]urposes and [p]rinciples" was recognized, for example, by the ICJ as a whole in the *Namibia* Advisory Opinion, by Judge Weeramantry in the *Lockerbie* Case, and by Judge Lauterpacht in the *Application of Genocide Convention* Case. In the *Namibia* Advisory Opinion, the ICJ wrote: "[T]he Members of the United Nations have conferred upon the Security Council powers commensurate with its responsibility for the maintenance of peace and security. *The only limitations are the fundamental principles and purposes* found in Chapter 1 of *the Charter*...."[186] In *Lockerbie*,[187] Judge Weeramantry wrote in his Dissenting Opinion:

> Article 24 itself offers us an immediate signpost to such a circumscribing boundary [on the powers of the Security Council] when it provides in Article 24(2) that the Security Council, in discharging its duties under Article 24(1) "*shall* act in accordance with the Purposes and Principles of the United Nations". The duty is imperative and the limits are categorically stated.[188]

Similarly, Judge ad hoc Lauterpacht wrote in his Separate Opinion in the *Application of Genocide Convention* Case: "Nor should one overlook the significance of the provision in Article 24(2) of the Charter that, in discharging its duties to maintain international peace and security, the Security Council shall act in accordance with the Purposes and Principles of the United Nations."[189]

---

[184] See, e.g., Andrew J. Carswell, *Unblocking the UN Security Council: The Uniting for Peace Resolution*, 18 J. CONFLICT & SEC. L. 453, 480 (the veto must be exercised "in a manner that conforms with the object and purpose of the UN Charter"). Orakhelashvili writes that the "actions" and "decisions" of international organizations must conform to their constitutive instruments:

> Some organizations are more powerful than others, but their powers, extensive as they are, nevertheless derive from a constitutive instrument consented to by the member states. Therefore, in accordance with the principle of constitutionality, organizations have a fundamental obligation to secure the lawfulness of their actions and decisions and, inevitably, reviews to determine whether their decisions are in conformity with their constituent instruments.

Orakhelashvili [The Impact], *supra* note 92, at 60.

[185] Additional limits to the veto power were sought during the San Francisco negotiations of the UN Charter, but were not obtained. *See* Chapter 1; *see also* Akande, *supra* note 79, at 315.

[186] *Namibia* Advisory Opinion, *supra* note 20, at 51–52 (emphasis added).

[187] *Lockerbie (Libya v. UK)* Provisional Measures, *supra* note 85; *Lockerbie (Libya v. U.S.)* Provisional Measures, *supra* note 85.

[188] *Lockerbie (Libya v. UK)* Provisional Measures, *supra* note 85, at 61 (diss. op., Weeramantry, J.) (emphasis in original); *Lockerbie (Libya v. U.S.)* Provisional Measures, *supra* note 85, at 171 (diss. op., Weeramantry, J.) (emphasis in original).

[189] 1993 ICJ Rep. 325, 440, para. 101; 95 ILR 1, 158.

The ICTY Appeals Chamber in *Tadić*, discussed above, also recognized that "[t]he Security Council is ... subjected to certain constitutional limitations, however broad its powers under the constitution [the UN Charter] may be,"[190] writing that "neither the text nor the spirit of the Charter conceives of the Security Council as *legibus solutus* (unbound by law).'"[191] Judge Bedjaoui has also written in a non-judicial capacity: "It appears less acceptable than ever that sovereign States should have created an international organization equipped with broad powers of control and sanction vis-à-vis themselves but [which is] *itself* exempted from the duty to respect both the Charter which gave birth to it and international law."[192]

Numerous scholars[193] as well as states, including in statements made in formal meetings of the Security Council, have noted this limitation provided in Article 24(2) on the powers of the Security Council.[194]

---

[190] *Tadić, supra* note 87, para. 28; text accompanying note 87 (discussing *Tadić*). See also Farrall, *supra* note 44, at 69 (citing the *Tadić* case "that the Security Council is subject to constitutional limitations, no matter how broad its powers may be."), citing *Tadić, supra* note 87, para. 28.

[191] *Id.*

[192] MOHAMMED BEDJAOUI, THE NEW WORLD ORDER AND THE SECURITY COUNCIL – TESTING THE LEGALITY OF ITS ACTS, 7 (1994) (emphasis in original).

[193] *See, e.g.,* Akande, *supra* note 79, at 316 ("The main limitation on the powers of the Security Council [is] understood to be the duty to act in accordance with the purposes and principles of the Charter. This obligation is expressly contained in Article 24(2) of the Charter and the purposes and principles are those stated in Article 1 and 2."); Carswell, *supra* note 184, at 470 ("Article 24(2) requires the Council to 'act in accordance with the Purposes and Principles of the United Nations.'"); Constantinides, *supra* note 88, at 3 ("It is article 24 of the Charter and the very purposes and principles of the UN to which it is referring, that can serve as workable limits on the [Security Council's] powers."); Thomas M. Franck, *The "Powers of Appreciation": Who Is the Ultimate Guardian of UN Legality?*, 86 AM. J. INT'L L. 519, 523 (1992) ("The legality of actions by any UN organ must be judged by reference to the Charter as a 'constitution' of *delegated* powers."); *id.* at 520 ("Being a treaty that delegates enumerated powers, the Charter, somewhat like the U.S. Constitution, implicitly also limits the powers of the political organs to which the delegation is made."); Orakhelashvili, [The Impact], *supra* note 92, at 61 ("The Council [is] not ... exempt from legal constraints under the Charter and general international law."); Constantinides, *supra* note 88, at 2 (the Security Council "[d]espite its predominantly and *par excellence* political character and functions, it is still an organ of an international organization, deriving its very broad powers from a treaty concluded by States."); Doehring, *supra* note 92, at 108 ("The Security Council is obliged to respect the rules of international law, i.e. the limits of its own competencies under the Charter of the United Nations and the rules of general international law as well.").

[194] For example, Dapo Akande quotes the representative of Egypt when the Council was, in 1951, addressing the question of passage of ships through the Suez Canal:

"Although we do not want to pretend that the functions and powers of the Security Council are limited to those specific powers mentioned in paragraph 2 of Article 24 of the Charter, yet we affirm that those powers and duties are limited and should be strictly regulated and governed by the fundamental principles and purposes laid down in Chapter I of the Charter. Paragraph 2 of Article 24, on the 'functions and powers' of the Security Council reminds us that 'In discharging these duties the Security Council shall act in accordance

The negotiating history of Article 24(2) further reinforces that the Security Council must act in accordance with the "[p]urposes and [p]rinciples" of the UN. In San Francisco, the US delegate, referring to the "[p]urposes and [p]rinciples" under the Charter, stated that these "constituted the highest rules of conduct."[195] He went on to state that "the Charter had to be considered in its entirety and *if the Security Council violated its principles and purposes it would be acting ultra vires.*"[196] Thus, he continued: "[w]here the [ICJ] is asked to choose between the application of a provision of the Charter and a Security Council resolution or decision, the Court is bound to choose the 'higher law' which in this case is the Charter."[197]

That the Security Council's powers are limited by the UN's "[p]urposes and [p]rinciples" is further reinforced by the fact that under UN Charter Article 25, UN Members States only agree "to accept and carry out" Security Council decisions that are *"in accordance with"* the Charter.[198] Thus, in the *Namibia* Advisory Opinion, the ICJ wrote that the Security Council resolutions under consideration were "adopted in conformity with the purposes and principles of the Charter and in accordance with its Articles 24 and 25," and "[t]he decisions [were] *consequently* binding on all States Member of the United Nations, which [were] thus under obligation to accept and carry them out."[199] Jeremy Farrall writes that Article 25 "can be interpreted as meaning that states are only obligated to carry out Council decisions that are taken in conformity with the

> with the Purposes and Principles of the United Nations.' Those Purposes and Principles of the United Nations are laid down in Chapter I of the Charter...."

> Akande, *supra* note 79, 316, *quoting* SC Official Records (1951), 553rd meeting, at 22–25, as quoted by Mr. Stavropoulos, representative of the UN Secretary General, at the oral hearings of the *Namibia* Advisory Opinion before the ICJ. *See* Pleadings, Oral Arguments, Documents – *The Namibia Advisory Opinion*, Vol. 2, at 48. Lebanon, in a debate in the Security Council on May 17, 2018, for example, stated: "Let us not forget that Article 24, paragraph 2, of the Charter requires the Security Council to abide by the purposes and principles of the United Nations. Only through faithful respect for those provisions will we avoid double standards and selective application of international law." Security Council Debate, "Upholding International Law within the Context of the Maintenance of International Peace and Security," May 17, 2018, Provisional Verbatim Record S/PV.8262, at 76. Similarly, the UK on April 13, 2018, stated at the Security Council: "What has taken place in Syria to date is in itself a violation of the United Nations Charter. No purpose or principle of the Charter is upheld or served by the use of chemical weapons on innocent civilians." Statement of the UK, S/PV.8231, at 10–11 (Apr. 13, 2018). *See also* Chapter 4.2.4.2 (additional views of states).

[195] Akande, *supra* note 79, at 319, *quoting* Doc. 555.III/1/27, 11 UNCIO Docs., at 378 (May 24, 1945).
[196] *Id.* (emphasis added).
[197] *Id.* at 332.
[198] *See* UN Charter, Art. 25 (emphasis added).
[199] *Namibia* Advisory Opinion, *supra* note 20, para. 115 (emphasis added).

Charter."[200] He concludes: "by pointing to the UN Purposes and Principles and the provisions of the Charter in general, Articles 24 and 25 provide a clear indication that the Security Council's powers are not supposed to be exercised without limits."[201] Aristotle Constantinides, relying on the *Namibia* Advisory Opinion, similarly explains that "under [this] interpretation of Article 25, States should accept and carry out only those decisions of the Council which are *intra vires* and consistent with the Charter."[202] Dapo Akande reaches a similar conclusion based on the *Namibia* Advisory Opinion,[203] as does Jordan Paust.[204]

The conclusion that the Security Council must act in accordance with the UN's "[p]urposes and [p]rinciples" can be derived yet an additional way. As noted above, under UN Charter Article 24(1), UN Member States conferred on the Security Council "primary responsibility for the maintenance of international peace and security," and agreed that "in carrying out its duties under this responsibility the Security Council *acts on their behalf.*"[205] If the Security Council "acts on their behalf," and UN Member States are bound by the UN's "[p]urposes and [p]rinciples" (as they are),[206] then in "acting on their behalf" the Security Council and its permanent members must similarly be bound.

---

[200] Farrall, *supra* note 44, at 68–69. *See also* Orakhelashvili [The Impact], *supra* note 92, at 67 ("Article 25 makes the binding force of the Council's acts conditional upon such compliance [with the Purposes and Principles of the UN] .... [T]he Council's decisions are binding only if they are in accordance with the Charter.").

[201] Farrall, *supra* note 44, at 69.

[202] Constantinides, *supra* note 88, at 2–3, *citing Namibia* Advisory Opinion, *supra* note 20, para. 115.

[203] *See* Akande, *supra* note 79, at 335 (in the *Namibia* Advisory Opinion "the Court indicated that the Security Council resolutions in question were adopted in conformity with the purposes and principles of the Charter and its Articles 24 and 25. It then stated: 'The decisions are *consequently* binding on all States Members of the United Nations, which are thus under obligation to accept and carry them out.'"), *citing Namibia* Advisory Opinion, *supra* note 20, at 53, para. 115. Akande concludes: "This implies that the binding effect of the decision flows from the face that they are in conformity with the restrictions imposed on the competence of the Security Council. Therefore, once it is found that certain decisions are not in conformity with those limitations the consequence is that those decisions are not binding on States." Akande, *supra* note 79, at 335.

[204] *See* Paust, *supra* note 120, at 16 (limitations on Security Council power "are implicit in Article 25, since Members agree merely to carry out 'decisions of the Security Council [made] in accordance with the ... Charter,' and, thus, decisions made in accordance with the Purposes and Principles of the United Nations as well as other Charter-based limits and duties.").

[205] UN Charter, Art. 24(1).

[206] *See* UN Charter, Art. 2 ("The Organization *and its Members* ... shall act in accordance with the following Principles ....") (emphasis added).

4.2.2 Whether a Veto in the Face of Genocide, Crimes against Humanity, and/or War Crimes Accords with the Obligation to Act in Accordance with the "Purposes" of the United Nations

The section below considers whether use of the veto in the face of ongoing[207] genocide, crimes against humanity, and/or war crimes accords with the Security Council's obligation to act in accordance with the "[p]urposes" of the UN. (The obligation to act in accordance with the "[p]rinciples" of the UN is examined in the following section.)

4.2.2.1 The "Purposes" of the United Nations

Article 1 of the Charter lists the "[p]urposes" of the United Nations to include:

> 1.To maintain international peace and security, and to that end: to take effective collective measures for the prevention and removal of threats to the peace, and for the suppression of acts of aggression or other breaches of the peace, and to bring about by peaceful means, *and in conformity with the principles of justice and international law*, adjustment or settlement of international disputes or situations which might lead to a breach of the peace; ... [and]
>
> 3.To *achieve international co-operation in solving international problems of an* economic, social, cultural, or *humanitarian character*, and *in promoting and encouraging respect for human rights and for fundamental freedoms for all without distinction as to race, sex, language, or religion* ....[208]

In addition to the text of Article 1(1), the importance of "justice" and "international law" is further reflected in the preamble of the Charter, which states that the "peoples of the United Nations" are determined, inter alia, "to establish conditions under which *justice and respect for* the obligations arising from treaties and other sources of *international law* can be maintained."[209] Rüdiger Wolfrum explains further:

> At the San Francisco Conference, the view was expressed that the United Nations should not function only as a political organization – decisions based upon international law being left to the International Court of Justice as

---

[207] *See also* note 123 *supra* (obligations are likely triggered already when there is a "serious risk" of the crimes occurring.)
[208] UN Charter, Art. 1 (emphasis added).
[209] *Id.*, pmbl. (emphasis added).

suggested by the Dumbarton Oaks Proposals – but that it should also be committed to international law. This led to the respective enrichment of the Preamble as well as Articles 1 and 2.[210]

As mentioned above, Article 1(1) could be read that the requirement of acting "in conformity with the principles of justice and international law" only applies to the "adjustment or settlement of international disputes or situations which might lead to a breach of the peace." Yet, Dapo Akande persuasively argues that it also applies to the Security Council when acting to maintain international peace and security – that in that situation as well, the Council must act "in conformity with the principles of justice and international law."[211] This reading is reinforced by Judge Weeramantry, who, in *Lockerbie*,[212] explained: "The history of the United Nations Charter ... corroborates the view that a clear limitation on the plenitude of the Security Council's powers is that those powers *must be exercised in accordance with the well-established principles of international law*."[213] This reading is further reinforced by the emphasis on "justice" and "international law" contained in the preamble, the above negotiating history, and the writings of additional legal scholars.[214]

---

[210] Rüdiger Wolfrum, *Preamble*, in Simma et al., *supra* note 98, at vol. 1, 104, para. 9.

[211] Akande, *supra* note 79, at 320 ("Though this debate [at San Francisco during the Charter negotiations] was not conclusive it demonstrates that when the question of limitation of the enforcement powers of the Security Council was raised it was assumed that they were similarly limited by the principles of international law.").

[212] *See Lockerbie (Libya v. UK)* Provisional Measures, *supra* note 85, at 65 (diss. op., Weeramantry, J.); *Lockerbie (Libya v. U.S.)* Provisional Measures, *supra* note 85, at 175 (diss. op., Weeramantry, J.).

[213] *Id.* (emphasis added).

[214] *See* Orakhelashvili [The Impact], *supra* note 92, at 60–61 ("In the process of adoption of Resolution 1483 (2003), which confirmed the status of the occupying powers in Iraq, the President of the Security Council emphasized that the Council's powers are not open-ended or unqualified. They should be exercised in ways that conform with 'the principles of justice and international law' mentioned in Article 1 of the Charter. . . ."); *id.* at 61 ("The Council [is] not ... exempt from legal constraints under the Charter and general international law."). As noted above, this requirement of adherence to international law is a bit complex, as there are times the Security Council *is* permitted to violate what would otherwise be required under international law – for instance, if expressly authorized to do so under the Charter. *See* Akande, *supra* note 79, at 317 (there is "a duty on the part of the Council not to violate general international law *unless the Charter specifically allows it to do so*") (emphasis added.) Akande gives the example that the Security Council "is empowered to use force in the maintenance of international peace but this does not relieve it of its duty in using such force to respect international humanitarian law." *Id.* at 320. *Compare* HANS KELSEN, THE LAW OF THE UNITED NATIONS: A CRITICAL ANALYSIS OF ITS FUNDAMENTAL PROBLEMS, 294 (1951) (arguing that the Council need not act in accordance with international law when acting to maintain or restore international peace and security). There are admittedly other authorities who take views similar to Kelsen. Referring to Article 1(1) of the Charter, Crawford notes that there is at least some indirect textual basis for the view expressed by some that "international law

Similarly, Article 1.1 of the Apartheid Convention[215] states that apartheid constitutes a crime against humanity that violates "the principles of international law, *in particular* the purposes and principles of the Charter of the United Nations."[216] The Convention's language thus makes clear that "principles of international law" are part of the "[p]urposes and [p]rinciples" of the UN.

In addition to the text of Article 1(3), the important role human rights plays in the Charter is further reflected in the preamble, which recognizes "the dignity and worth of the human person"; Article 55, which states that "the United Nations shall promote ... universal respect for, and observance of, human rights and fundamental freedoms of all without distinction as to race, sex, language, or religion"; and Article 56, which provides that "[a]ll [UN] Members pledge themselves to take joint and separate action in co-operation with the Organization for the achievement of the purposes set forth in Article 55."[217]

The first of the UN's "[p]urposes" relates to maintaining international peace and security, and the third of the UN's "[p]urposes" includes "promoting and encouraging respect for human rights."[218] The UN, of course, in this respect has a dual function, as maintaining "peace and security" includes protecting existing states, for example, from aggressive war, a stability function; yet, the UN also has a role in protecting human rights. These dual roles are not easily reconciled, and, in the early days of the UN, there were vigorous debates whether human rights violations solely internal to a country were even the concern of the UN.[219] Today, however, it is generally recognized that abuses internal to a state *are*

comes second as concerns recommendations under Chapter VI, but nowhere as concerns actions under Chapter VII." Crawford [Chance], *supra* note 93, 411–12, para. 538. However, Crawford himself goes on to respond to this argument. While he acknowledges that in some cases the Security Council may depart from international law and derogate from the rights of States under international law, he concludes: "But it is not accurate that the Security Council is not generally bound by international law. The Security Council may deviate from international law but only to the extent that it is empowered to do so under the UN Charter." *Id.* at 413, para. 540. This view that international law still must be adhered to even when the Security Council acts under Chapter VII is indeed far more persuasive. For example, as mentioned above, the Security Council certainly can authorize use of force, but in doing so, should not violate the principles of distinction and proportionality; similarly, it could not make a force authorization to eliminate members of a "protected group" under the Genocide Convention. Even within the context of Chapter VII, international law clearly has some applicability.

[215] International Convention on the Suppression and Punishment of the Crime of Apartheid, Art. 1, *entered into force* July 19, 1976, 1015 UNTS 243.
[216] *Id.* Art. 1.1 (emphasis added).
[217] UN Charter, pmbl., Arts. 55–56.
[218] *Id.* Arts. 1(1), 1(3).
[219] For example, the UN's early focus on apartheid was met with claims by South Africa that the UN lacked the competence to examine conduct internal to South Africa.

indeed a matter of concern to the international community, as sovereignty must not shield human rights abuses.[220] Thus, the Security Council has on numerous occasions addressed human rights abuses occurring solely within a country.[221] Accordingly, one would not say that the first purpose of the UN, in Article 1(1), can outweigh the third "[p]urpose" in Article 1(3) (or vice versa), as both "[p]urposes" are central to the UN.[222] And, as noted above, Article 1(1) does not only pertain to "international peace and security" but also the need to act "in conformity with the principles of justice and international law."[223]

Dapo Akande highlights two ICJ cases that recognize that human rights violations violate the "[p]urposes and [p]rinciples" of the UN.[224] In *United States Diplomatic and Consular Staff in Tehran*, the ICJ held that "[w]rongfully to deprive human beings of their freedom and to subject them to physical constraints in conditions of hardship is in itself manifestly incompatible with the principles of the Charter of the United

---

[220] Christopher Greenwood, *Humanitarian Intervention: The Case of Kosovo*, 2002 FINNISH Y.B. INT'L L. 141, 162 (2002) ("International law does not require that respect for the sovereignty and integrity of a State must in all cases be given priority over the protection of human rights and human life, no matter how serious the violations of those rights perpetrated by that State."); *id.* at 174 ("An oppressive government can no longer violate the most basic tenets of human rights and international humanitarian law, inflict loss of life and misery on a huge scale upon part of its population and expect to hide behind the concept of State sovereignty . . . .").

[221] *See, e.g.,* THOMAS M. FRANCK, RECOURSE TO FORCE: STATE ACTION AGAINST THREATS AND ARMED ATTACKS 136 (2002) ("Although the Charter text does not specifically authorize the Council to apply Chapter VII's system of collective measures to prevent gross violations of humanitarian law and human rights [to a situation internal to a country], in practice it has done so occasionally; for example by authorizing members to use coercive measures to counter apartheid in South Africa and revoke Rhodesia's racially motived Unilateral Declaration of Independence (UDI), as well as to help end egregious ethnic conflicts in Yugoslavia, Somalia, and Kosovo and to reverse a Haitian military coup that sought to undo a UN-supervised democratic election."); Marc Weller, *Introduction: International Law and the Problem of War*, *in* THE OXFORD HANDBOOK OF THE USE OF FORCE IN INTERNATIONAL LAW, *supra* note 59, at 30 ("It is clear that the U.N. Security Council can act under Chapter VII to authorize the use of force on behalf of populations threatened by extermination, starvation, or forcible expulsion at the hands of their own government, or other groups exercising effective control over them. While the Council has had to emphasize the unique nature of virtually every situation it has addressed in this way, a pattern of practice has emerged which puts the authority of the Council to address essentially internal matters of this kind beyond question.").

[222] Constantinides writes that as to the UN's "[p]urposes and [p]rinciples," "the Council has to act in accordance with (all of) them and thus, strike in all cases the concrete and proper balance between the primary goal of maintaining peace and security and the other UN purposes." Constantinides, *supra* note 88, at 3.

[223] UN Charter, Art. 1(1).

[224] Akande, *supra* note 79, at 324. *See also id.* at 323 ("It would be anachronistic if the Security Council, an organ of the United Nations, was itself empowered to violate human rights when the whole tenor of the Charter is to promote the protection of human rights by and in States.").

Nations, as well as with the fundamental principles enunciated in the Universal Declaration of Human Rights."[225] In the *Namibia* Advisory Opinion, the ICJ found the "denial [by South Africa] of fundamental human rights is a flagrant violation of the purposes and principles of the Charter."[226] Additional legal scholars similarly recognize that the "[p]urposes" of the UN mandate respect for human rights, and this requirement accordingly limits Security Council power.[227]

If human rights violations violate the "[p]urposes and [p]rinciples" of the UN (as they do), then the commission of genocide, crimes against humanity, and/or war crimes – which entail *massive* human rights violations – necessarily do.[228] Genocide, crimes against humanity, and war crimes, are human rights abuses *so extreme* they are no longer characterized under the human rights framework, but under the international criminal law framework. For example, the crime against humanity of "extermination" necessarily entails human rights violations, as extermination (that is, mass killing meeting certain contextual requirements) violates, for example, the right to life protected under the International Covenant on Civil and Political Rights.[229] The same is true of genocide – massive human rights abuses necessarily occur, including crimes toward members of a protected group, which would, under the human rights framework, constitute not only violations of the right to life,

---

[225] 1980 ICJ Rep. 3, 42.

[226] 1971 ICJ Rep. 6, 57.

[227] See, *e.g.*, Peters, *supra* note 90, at 31 ("The Security Council is bound at least by the 'Purposes and Principles' of the Charter (*cf.* article 24(2) of the UN Charter), which include customary human rights law . . . ."); Orakhelashvili [The Impact], *supra* note 92, at 64 ("The Security Council can never be entitled to infringe upon human rights embodied in universal human rights instruments."). Jordan Paust also writes:

> The first such limitation [on Security Council power] can be found in paragraph 2 of Article 24, which assures a constitutional limit on power when directing that the Council, in discharging its duties with respect to the maintenance of international peace and security, "shall act in accordance with the Purposes and Principles of the United Nations." As noted in Article 1 of the Charter, such Purposes and Principles include human rights . . . . Thus, the constituted authority of the Security Council is conditioned by the need to serve, among other goals, human rights . . . .

Paust, *supra* note 120, at 15–16.

[228] See Task Force on the EU Prevention of Mass Atrocities, *The EU and the Prevention of Mass Atrocities: An Assessment of Strengths and Weaknesses*, at 21 (2013), *at* http://massatrocitiestaskforce.eu/Report_files/The%20EU%20and%20the%20prevention%20of%20mass%20atrocities%20-%20an%20assessment%20of%20strenghts%20and%20weaknesses.pdf ("Mass atrocities are the gravest and most extreme violation of human rights.").

[229] See International Covenant on Civil and Political Rights, Art. 6.1, *entered into force* Mar. 23, 1976, 999 UNTS 171 ("Every human being has the inherent right to life. This right shall be protected by law. No one shall be arbitrarily deprived of his life.").

but also mass discrimination.[230] Indeed, genocide has been recognized by the ICJ, in its *Advisory Opinion Concerning Reservations to the Genocide Convention* to be "contrary to moral law and to the spirit and aims of the United Nations."[231] Similar language is found in the preamble to the Genocide Convention, which recognizes that "genocide is ... contrary to the spirit and aims of the United Nations."[232]

Combining Article 24(2) with Article 1(3), the Security Council's actions must be in accordance with "promoting and encouraging respect for human rights,"[233] and "achieving international co-operation in solving international problems of [a] ... humanitarian character." Additionally, combining Article 24(2) with Article 1(1), the Security Council's actions must additionally be in accordance with "principles of justice and international law."[234] A Security Council resolution that is not in accordance with these "[p]urposes," would then presumably be invalid or *ultra vires*, as failing to satisfy these requirements of Articles 1(1) and 1(3), adherence to which is required of the Security Council by Article 24(2).[235]

Dapo Akande, as an example, highlights two instances where the Council appears to have been mindful, while in the exercise of its Chapter VII powers, to adhere to human rights protections in its resolutions. First, he points to resolutions where the Security Council imposed economic and diplomatic sanctions under Article 41 but took care not to act "in such a way that the basic human rights of the peoples of the territories concerned will be violated,"[236] and he notes that "medical supplies and foodstuffs required for humanitarian purposes are always excluded from UN sanctions regimes."[237] Second, he points out that in creating the ICTY, the Security Council "was careful to ensure that the basic rights of accused persons are respected,"[238] and the

---

[230] *Id.* Arts. 2.1, 26 (guarantees against discrimination "of any kind, such as race, colour, sex, language, religion, political or other opinion, national, or social origin, property, birth or other status").

[231] In its *Advisory Opinion Concerning Reservations to the Genocide Convention,* the ICJ concluded that genocide "is contrary to moral law and to the spirit and aims of the United Nations." Whiteman, *supra* note 33, at 609, *quoting* Advisory Opinion of the International Court of Justice on Reservations to the Convention on the Prevention and the Punishment of the Crime of Genocide, 1951 ICJ 15, 23 (May 28).

[232] Genocide Convention, *supra* note 1, pmbl.

[233] See notes 224–27 *supra* and accompanying text (scholars and ICJ judges concluding this).

[234] See notes 209–14 *supra* and accompanying text (scholars and ICJ judges concluding this).

[235] Akande, *supra* note 79, at 319 (quoting US delegate at San Francisco: "the Charter had to be considered in its entirety and *if the Security Council violated its principles and purposes it would be acting ultra vires*") (emphasis added).

[236] *Id.* at 324.

[237] *Id.* at 324, n. 56.

[238] *Id.* at 324.

ICTY's Statute (adopted by Security Council resolution) contained extensive fair trial protections.[239] The ICTR (whose Statute was also adopted by the Security Council and contains similar fair trial protections),[240] additionally found in the *Kanyabashi* Case that "the protection of International Human Rights is the responsibility of all United Nations organs, the Security Council included, without any limitation, in conformity with the UN Charter."[241]

4.2.2.2 Veto Use Must Be in Accordance with the "Purposes" of the United Nations

If the Council must act in accordance with the UN's "[p]urposes and [p]rinciples" in its resolutions (as the discussion above demonstrates it must), then a related question is whether veto use by permanent members must also be in accordance with the UN's "[p]urposes and [p]rinciples."

While serving as Jordan's Ambassador to the UN, Prince Zeid (who later served as High Commissioner for Human Rights) took this view that veto use must be in accordance with the UN's "[p]urposes and [p]rinciples," including adherence to "principles of justice and international law":

> Jordan's UN ambassador, Prince Ra'ad Zeid Al-Hussein, [stated] that there is also a legal case to be made that *the U.N. Charter itself places limits on the rights of the council's permanent members to veto council action aimed at preventing mass killings*. He argued that while the council bears "primary responsibility" for the maintenance of peace and security it also requires decisions be made in "conformity with the principle of justice and international law." *Genocide and mass slaughter, he said, are certainly not in conformity with those principles* ....[242]

The UK, on April 13, 2018, expressed a similar view in a statement made at the Security Council after a veto was cast related to the situation in Syria, stating: "What has taken place in Syria to date is in itself a violation of the United Nations Charter. No purpose or principle of the Charter is upheld or served by the use of

---

[239] ICTY Statute, Art. 21(1), (4) ("equality of arms"); ICTY Statute, Art. 21(4)(d) (requirement of the accused's presence at trial); ICTY Statute, Art. 24(1) (penalties limited to life in prison, thereby excluding the death penalty); Art. 25 (right of appeal).

[240] *See* ICTR Statute, Art. 20 (rights of the accused).

[241] Prosecutor v. Kanyabashi, Case No. ICTR-96-15-T, Decision on the Defence Motion on Jurisdiction, para. 29 (June 18, 1997). *See also* Orakhelashvili [The Impact], *supra* note 92, at 80 (noting that "[c]ertain resolutions contain explicit clauses requiring respect for human rights and humanitarian law in terms of the fight against terrorism, such as Resolution 1456 (2003), or for respect of territorial integrity and sovereignty of a state, such as Resolution 1244 (1999) ....").

[242] Colum Lynch, *Rise of the Lilliputians*, FOR. POL'Y (May 10, 2012), *at* https://foreignpolicy.com/2012/05/10/rise-of-the-lilliputians (emphasis added) (quoting interview with Prince Ra'ad Zeid Al-Hussein).

chemical weapons on innocent civilians."[243] The UK thereby clearly implied that veto use needs to accord with the "[p]urposes and [p]rinciples" set forth in the UN Charter. Statements by Egypt and Norway, during a May 17, 2018, Security Council session entitled "Upholding International Law," suggest similar positions.[244]

The proposition that veto use must accord with the UN's "[p]urposes and [p]rinciples" can be derived in multiple ways. First, the requirement of adherence to the UN's "[p]urposes and [p]rinciples" is contained in Article 24 under the caption "Functions and Powers" of the Security Council. Veto use is one of the "powers" of the permanent members of the Council – as it is a power conferred by the voting provisions of Article 27(3) of the Charter. Thus, the requirements of Article 24 apply to veto use.

Second, Article 27(3) (conferring the veto power) and Article 24(2) appear to have the same weight within the Charter, so there is nothing that carves out the permanent members in their veto use (Article 27(3)) from having also to adhere to the UN's "[p]urposes and [p]rinciples" (Article 24(2)).

Third, if the Council's actions as a whole must be in accordance with the "[p]urposes and [p]rinciples" of the UN (as they must under Article 24(2)), then – as discussed above in Chapter 4.1.6.4 – the individual permanent members (who are a subset of the Council) can have no greater power.[245] This argument is supported by the logic in *Tadić*, where the ICTY Appeals Chamber recognized the Security Council's "powers cannot ... go beyond the limits of the jurisdiction of the Organization at large [the United Nations]."[246] Logically, if the Security Council's powers cannot go beyond the powers of the UN, then the powers of individual permanent members cannot exceed the powers of the Security Council, of which they are a part.

Fourth, the maxim *"nemo plus iuris transferre potest quam ipse habet"* (that an international creature cannot acquire more powers than its creator)[247] is also

---

[243] Statement of the UK, S/PV.8231, *supra* note 194, at 10–11.
[244] See notes 299, 301 *infra* and accompanying text (statements by Egypt and Norway).
[245] See Mónica Lourdes de la Serna Galván, *Interpretation of Article 39 of the UN Charter (Threat to the Peace) by the Security Council: Is the Security Council a Legislator for the Entire International Community?*, XI ANUARIO MEXICANO DE DERECHO INTERNACIONAL 147, 152 (2011) ("Since the Security Council while determining a threat to the peace is the only one who decides *when to exercise or not its veto power*, the permanent members have the duty to comply with its obligations, they have to exercise their office in good faith, commensurate with their responsibility as members of the Council and bearing in mind the principles and purposes of the Organization.") (emphasis added).
[246] *Tadić*, *supra* note 87, para. 28.
[247] See Yiu, *supra* note 97, at 246, *citing* Reinisch, *supra* note 97, at 858; Duckwitz, *supra* note 97, at 28–30.

relevant. The status of being a permanent member is created by the Charter; ergo, the permanent members cannot have power broader than UN Member States that created the Charter. If UN Member States are bound by the UN's "[p]urposes and [p]rinciples" (as they are),[248] then so are the permanent members. The permanent members were quite simply never granted powers to go beyond the Charter's limits.

Fifth, the permanent members are also bound to adhere to the UN's "[p]urposes and [p]rinciples," because they are UN Member States, and *states* are bound to those "[p]urposes and [p]rinciples."[249]

A critic might object to reliance upon Article 24(2), which requires the Security Council to "act" in accordance with the UN's purposes and principles, arguing that veto use is not an "action" but results in "inaction" by the Security Council as a whole. While it is true that veto use blocks the Security Council as a whole and thus results in inaction, at the same time, the veto is something that needs to be invoked. That is, a permanent member needs to cast a negative vote, which is an "act."[250] Thus, Article 24(2) is relevant as it governs "act[s]," and veto use is an "act" by a permanent member of the Council.[251]

Finally, a critic might argue that the specific (veto power in Article 27(3)) outweighs the general (the requirement in Article 24(2) of acting in accordance with the "[p]urposes and [p]rinciples" of the UN). First, Article 24(2) is no less specific than Article 27(3), so this argument is not even logical; yet, assuming it were, its substance must be rejected. As explained above, if the Security Council as a whole must comply with Article 24(2), then individual permanent members necessarily must. There is no authority that permanent members are free to violate the "[p]urposes and [p]rinciples" of the UN, nor would such a proposition be sound. The status of being a permanent member

---

[248] *See* UN Charter, Art. 2 ("The Organization *and its Members* . . . shall act in accordance with the following Principles . . . .") (emphasis added).

[249] *Id.* The third, fourth, and fifth arguments were also discussed earlier in support of the proposition that individual permanent members are bound by *jus cogens*. *See* Chapter 4.1 *supra*.

[250] *See, e.g.*, Statement of the UK, S/PV/7915, at 5 (Apr. 5, 2017) ("The world should be under no illusion. What Russia does in this Chamber [in casting vetoes related to the situation in Syria] does not cause inaction; defending the indefensible causes suffering. Each and every abuse of its veto has consequences. For the people of Khan Shaykhun [where a chemical weapons attack occurred], those consequences have been unspeakable.").

[251] Even if veto use were considered inaction (which seems implausible as it requires a positive act), there are duties to act, as will be explored below, under both the Genocide Convention (the obligation to "prevent" genocide), and the 1949 Geneva Conventions (the obligation to "ensure" Convention protections). *See* Chapter 4.3 *infra*. Inaction can give rise to responsibility where there are duties to act. *See, e.g.*, Peters, *supra* note 90, at 32 ("The possibility of legal responsibility for inaction, omissions, or passivity is well established in all criminal legal systems, and also in tort law.") (citations omitted).

was created by the UN Charter, so it would defy logic for the permanent members to be able to violate the "[p]urposes and [p]rinciples" of the UN, when it is the Charter that granted them their power. Inherently, they cannot have been granted power to violate the UN's "[p]urposes and [p]rinciples."

4.2.3 Whether a Veto in the Face of Genocide, Crimes against Humanity, and/or War Crimes Accords with the Obligation to Act in Accordance with the "Principles" of the United Nations and the General Obligation of "Good Faith"

The discussion below considers whether vetoes invoked during ongoing[252] genocide, crimes against humanity, and/or war crimes accord with the general obligation of "good faith" imposed both under international law,[253] and as one of the "[p]rinciples" of the UN under Article 2(2) of the Charter.

International law recognizes: a duty to perform a treaty (here, the UN Charter) in good faith,[254] a duty to interpret a treaty (here, the UN Charter) in good faith,[255] and a duty to negotiate (presumably, including Security Council resolutions) in good faith.[256] The obligation of "good faith" is also expressly required as one of the "[p]rinciples" of the UN, found in Article 2(2), which requires that "[a]ll Members, in order to ensure to all of them the rights and benefits resulting from membership, shall fulfil in good faith the obligations assumed by them in accordance with the present Charter."[257] While the

---

[252] See note 123 supra (obligations are likely triggered already when there is a "serious risk" of the crimes occurring).

[253] Good faith is a general principle of international law. See, e.g., Andreas R. Ziegler & Jorun Baumgartner, *Good Faith as a General Principle of (International) Law*, in ANDREW D. MITCHELL, M. SORNARAJAH & TANIA VOON, GOOD FAITH AND INTERNATIONAL ECONOMIC LAW (2015); Carswell, supra note 184, at 471, citing OPPENHEIM'S INTERNATIONAL LAW 346 (Hersch Lauterpacht ed., 1955) (the general requirement of states to act in good faith). Good faith is also mandated by the VCLT. See VCLT, supra note 34, Art. 26.

[254] VCLT, supra note 34, Art. 26 ("Every treaty in force is binding upon the parties to it and must be performed by them in good faith."); Ziegler & Baumgartner, supra note 253, at 11 ("having ratified the treaty, [there is a duty] to perform it in good faith and not to frustrate its object and purpose"). See also Gabčíkovo-Nagymaros Project (Hung.-Slovk.), Merits, 1997 ICJ Rep. 7, 78–79 ("The principles of good faith obliges the Parties to apply [the treaty] in a reasonable way and in such a manner that its purpose can be realized.").

[255] VCLT, supra note 34, Art. 31 ("A treaty shall be interpreted in good faith.").

[256] Ziegler & Baumgartner, supra note 253, at 19 ("The rule of [pacta sunt servanda], as the Permanent Court of International Justice (PCIJ) and the ICJ have often confirmed entails a duty to negotiate in good faith.") (citing cases).

[257] UN Charter, Art. 2(2). For further discussion, see Robert Kolb, *Purposes and Principles, Article 2(2)*, in Simma et al., supra note 98, at vol. 1, 173, para. 17 ("Good faith is not merely a general and abstract principle. Practice and legal writings have determined a series of concrete, partial legal contents of the principle, which have developed into operational rules

permanent members are allocated special powers under the Charter (the veto power), they are nonetheless still "UN Member States," and thus bound by the good faith requirement in Article 2(2) and international law more generally. The Security Council as a whole is also mandated to adhere to the "good faith" requirement in that Article 24(2) requires that the Council act in accordance with the UN's "[p]rinciples," which include the good faith requirement in Article 2(2).

Andrew Carswell, for example, takes the view that veto use by the permanent members must accord with the good faith requirement. He reasons: "Reading articles 2(2), 24 and 1(1) collectively, we may deduce that the [permanent members] are obliged to discharge in good faith their responsibility for maintaining international peace and security. *Employment of the veto in a manner that does not coincide with this responsibility arguably amounts to a breach of the good faith requirement*."[258] Carswell reaches this conclusion based in part on a statement made in 1945 in San Francisco by four of the permanent members (the US, UK, USSR, and China)[259] where they assured other states that the veto would not be used abusively. They took the position: "It is not to be assumed ... that the permanent Members, any more than the non-permanent Members, would use their 'veto' power wilfully to obstruct the operation of the Council."[260] Noting also the obligation generally to act in "good faith," Carswell concludes: "It was on this basis that the UN Charter was ultimately ratified."[261] Bruno Simma's Commentary on the Charter suggests the same view, stating: "This duty to act in good faith and without abuse of rights has been stressed in different contexts [including] the right of veto."[262] (The requirement of good faith is also similar to one of the UN's "[p]urposes," to achieve "international co-operation" including on issues of a "humanitarian character.")[263]

Anne Peters, based on the *Conditions of Admission of a State to Membership in the United Nations* Advisory Opinion, similarly concludes that the

---

of international law. These partial legal contents are concretizations of the general principle of good faith.").

[258] Carswell, *supra* note 184, at 470 (emphasis added).

[259] It was originally envisioned that there would be only four permanent members, as France was a later addition. See Chapter 1.1.1.

[260] Statement by the Delegations of the Four Sponsoring Governments on the Voting Procedure in the Security Council (June 7, 1945), UNCIO, Vol. XI, at 754, cited in Carswell, *supra* note 184, at 471, n. 72.

[261] Carswell, *supra* note 184, at 471.

[262] Kolb, *in* Simma, et al., *supra* note 257, at 174, para. 21.

[263] See UN Charter, Art. 1(3) (listing as one of the "[p]urposes" of the United Nations, "[t]o achieve international co-operation in solving international problems of [a] ... humanitarian character").

obligation of good faith carries over to voting at the UN, including on the Security Council:

> [J]udges of the ICJ reminded all UN members that when participating in a ... decision either in the Security Council or in the General Assembly the Member is "legally entitled to make its consent ... dependent on any political consideration which seem to it to be relevant. [However,] [i]n the exercise of this power the member is *legally bound* to have regard to the principle of good faith." UN members must exercise their voting power "in good faith, in accordance with the Purposes and Principles of the Organization and in such a manner as not to involve any breach of the Charter."[264]

International law also requires that treaties be observed under the principle of *pacta sunt servanda*,[265] and this would include UN Charter Article 24(2), requiring adherence to the UN's "[p]urposes and [p]rinciples," as well as the "good faith" requirement in Article 2(2).

Finally, as Simma's Commentary also alludes,[266] international law also requires rights – if one considers the veto a "right" conferred on the permanent members under the Charter – not to be abused (*abus de droit*).[267] Thus, under this doctrine, "where the right confers upon its owner a discretionary power, this must be exercised honestly, sincerely, reasonably, in conformity with the spirit of the law and with due regard to the interests of others."[268] Andrew Carswell thus opines that "taking even a conservative view of the doctrine of abuse of rights, it is arguable that an employment of the veto in a blatantly *mala fide* manner can be characterized as legally abusive."[269] He concludes:

> employment of the veto can arguably be viewed as "abusive" in certain circumstances, even if article 27(3) is not breached as such. If a permanent

---

[264] Peters, *supra* note 90, at 43–44, citing *Conditions of Admission of a State to Membership in the United Nations*, *supra* note 80, at paras. 21, 25; *see also id.*, para. 9 ("We do not claim that a political organ and those who contribute to the formation of its decisions are emancipated from all duty to respect the law.").

[265] VCLT, *supra* note 34, Art. 26 ("*Pacta Sunt Servanda*"); *see also* International Judicial Monitor, General Principles of International Law, *Pacta Sunt Servanda*, at www.judicialmonitor.org/archive_0908/generalprinciples.html; Hossain, *supra* note 18, at 73 ("There are rules, which are preconditions for effective international activity, such as *pacta sunt servanda*.").

[266] *See* Kolb, *in* Simma, et al., *supra* note 257, at 174, para. 21 ("This duty to act in good faith and *without abuse of rights* has been stressed in different contexts [including] the right of veto.") (emphasis added).

[267] Ziegler & Baumgartner, *supra* note 253, at 30–32 (discussing the "abuse of rights" doctrine, requiring that "rights must be exercised reasonably and in good faith").

[268] *Id.* at 32; *see also id.* at 33 (citing WTO Appellate Body decisions referring to the abuse of rights doctrine).

[269] *Id.*

member exercises its veto in a bad-faith manner, legally constituting an abuse of the right contained in article 27(3) – and consequently in violation of the responsibility conferred upon it by the international community on whose behalf it acts – it can be logically inferred that the Security Council is not "exercising [in the dispute or situation in question] the functions assigned to it in the present Charter."[270]

Anne Peters agrees: "it seems possible to qualify the exercise of the veto in a [core crimes] situation as an *abus de droit.*"[271] She writes:

Members of the Security Council act as delegates of *all other* UN members, and as trustees of the international community. Due to this *triplement fonctionnel, their voting behaviour is subject to legal limits.* Their position as trustees prohibits them handling their participation rights in the collective body in an arbitrary fashion. As a minimum, the fiduciary obligation of the members of the Security Council brings with it an obligation to balance all relevant aspects. This means that the rule of law not only prohibits arbitrary decisions of the Security Council as a whole, as stated above, but should also govern the Council members' votes approving or preventing arbitrary decisions.[272]

---

[270] *Id., citing* BARDO FASSBENDER, UN SECURITY COUNCIL REFORM AND THE RIGHT OF VETO: A CONSTITUTIONAL PERSPECTIVE 175 (1998) (concluding that use of the veto to prevent an amendment to the UN Charter for reasons of purely national interest would constitute an abuse of right).

[271] Peters, *supra* note 90, at 44. Peters, admittedly, hedges on her conclusion, as her article discusses the consequences of R2P being recognized as binding law, so it is a little unclear whether she stands by her arguments without that assumption. *See also* Irmgard Marboe, *R2P and the Abusive Veto – The Legal Nature of R2P and Its Consequences for the Security Council and Its Members*, 16 AUSTRIAN REV. INT'L & EUR. L. 115, 130 (2011) ("Although it may be the right of a [permanent member] to exercise the veto, its exercise in a concrete situation may be abusive."); Yiu, *supra* note 97, at 244 ("It is arguable that the use of the veto in a case of genocide in which intervention is clearly warranted and would otherwise have been authorized would be just such an *abuse of powers*, in contravention of the Charter's Purposes and Principles, and thus unenforceable against member states.") (emphasis added); Peters, *supra* note 90, at 42 ("An abuse of right is present when a state does not behave illegally as such, but exercises rights that are incumbent on it under international law in an arbitrary manner or in a way which impedes the enjoyment of other international legal subjects of their own rights.").

[272] Peters, *supra* note 90, at 39 (emphasis added) (internal footnotes omitted), *citing Conditions of Admission of a State to Membership in the United Nations, supra* note 80, para. 20 ("the members of the Security Council ... [act] on behalf of all the Members of the United Nations"); *see also* Georges A. J. Scelle, *Le phénomène juridique de dédoublement fonctionnel, in* RECHTSFRAGEN DER INTERNATIONALEN ORGANISATION. FESTSCHRIFT FÜR HANS WEHBERG ZU SEINEM 70. GEBURTSTAG (Walter Schätzel & Hans Jürgen Schlochauer eds., 1956). One also might wonder how the "clean hands" doctrine interrelates with a permanent member voting on a resolution where, for instance, the permanent member has close political or military ties to, and/or is supplying weapons to, the country in question

While the author has not conducted a comprehensive survey, at least the UK,[273] Mexico,[274] and the Ukraine[275] have recently taken the position in formal statements made at the UN that veto use can constitute an abuse of the veto power.

4.2.4 Whether the Vetoes Related to the Situation in Syria Are in Accordance with the "Purposes and Principles" of the United Nations

If one examines the vetoes related to the situation in Syria, as an example,[276] one might consider whether each veto satisfies the requirement in Article 1(1) of acting in accordance with "principles of justice and international law," the requirements in Article 1(3) of acting in accordance with "promoting and encouraging respect for human rights" and "achieving international cooperation in solving international problems of [a] ... humanitarian character," and, thereby, the requirement in Article 24(2) of acting in accordance with the "[p]urposes and [p]rinciples" of the UN. One might also consider whether the vetoes satisfy the "good faith" requirement imposed as one of the

---

that is alleged to have committed the crimes under deliberation. *See* Ziegler & Baumgartner, *supra* note 253, at 29–30 (discussing the "clean hands" doctrine). Probably, however, the general doctrine, *lex generalis* (clean hands) would be outweighed by the particular, *lex specialis* (UN Charter Article 27(3) on Security Council voting, where there is no exclusion from voting under Chapter VII even if the permanent member is a party to the situation). It was an unfortunate decision in the drafting of the Charter not to have excluded from voting, under Chapter VII, a party involved in the situation being voted upon – which was the US and UK proposal. *See* Chapter 1.

[273] The UK stated: "The Security Council has been unable to act solely because Russia has *abused the power of veto* to protect Syria from international scrutiny for the use of chemical weapons against the Syrian people." Statement of the UK, S/P.V.8228, at 5–6 (Apr. 10, 2018) (emphasis added). *See also* Statement of the UK, S/P.V.8164, at 5–6 (Jan. 23, 2018) ("When the Al-Assad regime deliberately ignored its obligation to stop using chemical weapons and continued to do so with careless regard for human life, Russia chose to *abuse its power of veto* to protect that regime.") (emphasis added).

[274] Mexico stated that "*the veto in situations where mass atrocities are committed is an abuse of the law* that can trigger international responsibility for the State committing them and an abuse that leaves the Organization under the sad shadow of paralysis and irrelevance." Security Council Debate, "Upholding International Law," *supra* note 194, at 47 (emphasis added).

[275] Ukraine stated that "Russia's revanchist policy of using military force against other States" has taken place "against a backdrop of Russia's systematic *abuse of the right of veto* and blatant disregard of its obligation to maintain peace and security." *Id.* at 61 (emphasis added).

[276] The list of vetoes below is illustrative of the problem; it is by no means intended to suggest that the only problematic use of the veto in the face of genocide, crimes against humanity, and/or war crimes relates to the situation in Syria. *See* Chapter 1 (discussing other situations); *see* Chapter 5.2 (also discussing Darfur in depth).

UN's "[p]rinciples" and by international law more generally, as well as the promise made in San Francisco that the veto would not be used abusively.

4.2.4.1 Resolutions Vetoed Related to the Situation in Syria

While a detailed analysis of veto use related to the situation in Syria is contained in Chapter 5, the following resolutions, described only briefly here, have been vetoed:

- On October 4, 2011, a resolution was vetoed that would have demanded an end to use of force by the Syrian authorities, and called for an end to the violence and human rights violations;[277]
- On February 4, 2012, a resolution was vetoed that would have condemned continued widespread and gross violations of human rights and fundamental freedoms including arbitrary executions, killing and persecution of protesters and members of the media, arbitrary detention, enforced disappearances, interference with access to medical treatment, torture, sexual violence and ill treatment, including against children;[278]
- On July 19, 2012, a resolution was vetoed that would have condemned bombing and shelling of population centers, and condemned detention of thousands in government run facilities;[279]
- On May 22, 2014, a resolution was vetoed that would have referred the situation in Syria to the ICC;[280]
- On October 8, 2016, a resolution was vetoed that would have expressed outrage at the alarming number of civilian casualties, including those caused by indiscriminate aerial bombing, in Aleppo;[281]
- On December 5, 2016, a resolution was vetoed that would have implemented a seven-day ceasefire in Aleppo that would have allowed humanitarian assistance;[282]
- On February 28, 2017, a resolution was vetoed that would have condemned the use of chemical weapons and demanded compliance with the Organisation for the Prohibition of Chemical Weapons (OPCW);[283]

---

[277] S/2011/612 (vetoed by the Russian Federation and China).
[278] S/2012/77 (vetoed by the Russian Federation and China).
[279] S/2012/538 (vetoed by the Russian Federation and China).
[280] S/2014/348 (vetoed by the Russian Federation and China).
[281] S/2016/846 (vetoed by the Russian Federation).
[282] S/2016/1026 (vetoed by the Russian Federation and China).
[283] S/2017/172 (vetoed by the Russian Federation and China).

- On April 12, 2017, a resolution was vetoed that would have condemned the use of chemical weapons and requested documentation such as flight plans and access to air bases from which chemical weapons were believed to have been launched;[284]
- On October 24, 2017, a resolution was vetoed that would have renewed the mandate of the UN Joint Investigative Mechanism (JIM), which would have attributed responsibility to those using chemical weapons;[285]
- On November 16, 2017, a resolution was vetoed that would have condemned the use of toxic chemicals as weapons, renewed the mandate of the JIM, and stated "no party in Syria shall use, develop produce otherwise acquire, stockpile or retain, or transfer chemical weapons";[286]
- On November 17, 2017, another resolution was vetoed that would have renewed the mandate of the JIM;[287]
- On April 10, 2018, a resolution was vetoed that would have condemned "any use of any toxic chemical including chlorine as a weapon in the Syrian Arab Republic," expressed "outrage that civilians continue to be killed and injured by chemical weapons and toxic chemicals as weapons in the Syrian Arab republic," demanded access for an OPCW Fact Finding Mission and medical/humanitarian personnel, and established a UN Independent Mechanism of Investigation.[288]
- On September 19, 2019, a resolution was vetoed that would have implemented a ceasefire for Syria's war-torn Idlib province, called for a halt to a campaign of indiscriminate aerial bombardment occurring there, and demanded humanitarian access and safe passage for medical personnel.[289]
- On December 20, 2019, a resolution was vetoed that would have called for improved humanitarian assistance, reiterated the obligation to comply with international humanitarian law and international human rights law, and called for "safe, unimpeded and sustained access" for humanitarian convoys.[290]

---

[284] S/2017/315 (vetoed by the Russian Federation).
[285] S/2017/884 (vetoed by the Russian Federation).
[286] S/2017/962 (vetoed by the Russian Federation).
[287] S/2017/970 (vetoed by the Russian Federation).
[288] S/2018/321 (vetoed by the Russian Federation).
[289] S/2019/756 (vetoed by the Russian Federation and China). "The Syrian Observatory for Human Rights says the offensive [in Idlib] has killed close to 1,000 civilians." French Press Agency – AFP, *Russia's 13 UN Security Council Vetoes on Syria*, DAILY SABAH MIDEAST (Sept. 20, 2019), at www.dailysabah.com/mideast/2019/09/20/russias-13-unsecurity-council-vetoes-on-syria.
[290] S/2019/961 (vetoed by the Russian Federation and China).

It should be obvious, on its face, that this series of vetoes does not in any way satisfy the requirement of acting in accordance with "principles of justice and international law," "promoting and encouraging respect for human rights," or achieving "international co-operation in solving international problems of [a] ... humanitarian character," and, thereby, the requirement of acting in accordance with the "[p]urposes" of the UN. The vetoes also fail to meet the requirement of "good faith," and thereby, the requirement of acting in accordance with the "[p]rinciples" of the UN, as well as international law generally.[291]

4.2.4.2 The Objections of States to Veto Use Related to the Situation in Syria and More Generally in the Face of Atrocity Crimes

Numerous states, both Security Council members and non-members, in formal statements at the UN, have in fact decried the way the veto is being used, both generally, and related to the situation in Syria, including taking the position, inter alia, that, as a result, the Security Council is not adhering to its obligations under the UN Charter. These statements additionally demonstrate that there has been no acquiescence by states to a practice of using the veto in the face of atrocity crimes; rather, states are persistently lodging objections to such veto use.

For example, three of the permanent members have consistently decried the Russian (and sometimes accompanying Chinese) vetoes in Syria as violating international law,[292] failing to accord with the "[p]urposes and [p]rinciples" of the Charter,[293] an abuse of the veto

---

[291] The vetoes also appear to fail to satisfy the abuse of rights doctrine. The series of vetoes appear particularly questionable for all the above enumerated reasons given that one of the vetoing permanent members has close political and military ties, and is furnishing military assistance, to the regime in question. See, e.g., Special Report: How a Secret Russian Airlift Helps Syria's Assad, REUTERS (Apr. 6, 2018), at www.reuters.com/article/us-russia-flights/special-report-how-a-secret-russian-airlift-helps-syrias-assad-idUSKCN1HD18Y (Russia claims its assistance is limited to "air strikes, training of Syrian forces and small numbers of special forces troops.").

[292] Statement of the US, S/P.V.8233, at 5 (Apr. 14, 2018) ("Russia's veto was the green light for the Al-Assad regime to use these most barbaric weapons against the Syrian people, in complete violation of international law. ... We cannot stand by and let Russia trash every international norm that we stand for, and allow the use of chemical weapons to go unanswered."); Statement of the UK, S/PV.8073, at 7 (Oct. 24, 2017) ("Russia alone has chosen to abuse its veto to support a regime that has no regard for international treaties, no regard for the most basic rules of war, no regard for its own people.").

[293] Statement of the UK, S/PV.8231, supra note 194, at 10–11 ("What has taken place in Syria to date is in itself a violation of the United Nations Charter. No purpose or principle of the Charter is upheld or served by the use of chemical weapons on innocent civilians.").

power,[294] undermining of global norms,[295] a failure to exercise the duties required of a permanent member of the Security Council,[296] and a violation of international obligations to take action against chemical weapons use.[297] Similar criticisms of veto use related to Syria also have been articulated by numerous other states while serving as members of the Security Council.[298]

[294] Statement of the UK, S/P.V.8228, *supra* note 273, at 5–6 ("The Security Council has been unable to act solely because Russia has abused the power of veto to protect Syria from international scrutiny for the use of chemical weapons against the Syrian people."); Statement of the UK, S/P.V.8164, *supra* note 273, at 5–6 ("when the Al-Assad regime deliberately ignored its obligation to stop using chemical weapons and continued to do so with careless regard for human life, Russia chose to abuse its power of veto to protect that regime.").

[295] Statement of the UK, S/P.V.8228, *supra* note 273, 5–6 ("Russia's credibility as a member of the Council is now in question. We will not stand idly by and watch Russia continue to undermine the global norms that have ensured the security of all of us, including Russia, for decades.").

[296] Statement of France, S/PV.8231, at 9 (Apr. 13, 2018) ("Those vetoes had no other objective than to protect the Syrian authorities – to guarantee a regime of impunity, in defiance of all international standards. To allow the indefensible, Russia has deliberately chosen to sacrifice the ability of the Council to act, the most important tool of our collective security."); Statement of the UK, S/PV.8105, at 7 (Nov. 16, 2017) ("Let us make no mistake – the JIM has succeeded. It is Russia that has failed. It has failed in its duties as a permanent member of the Security Council. It has failed as a State party to the Chemical Weapons Convention. It has failed as a supposed supporter of peace in Syria."); Statement of France, S/PV.7922, at 3–4 (Apr. 12, 2017) ("We have failed yet again to measure up to the responsibility that we have assigned ourselves and to the fundamental values that we are supposed to support and ensure respect for. Almost four years after the Ghouta massacre in August 2013, the Council has taken a terrible step backwards.").

[297] Statement of the UK, S/PV.7893, at 5 (Feb. 28, 2017) ("As permanent members of the Security Council and as parties to the Chemical Weapons Convention, Russia and China have a clear responsibility to take action against the use and proliferation of chemical weapons. By vetoing the draft resolution today they have undermined the credibility of the Security Council and of the international rules preventing the use of these barbaric weapons."); *see also* Statement of the US, S/PV.8231, at 6 (Apr. 13, 2018) (similar).

[298] *See* Statement of Kuwait, S/PV.8231, at 15 (Apr. 13, 2018) ("The continued violations of international humanitarian law, international human rights law and the relevant Security Council resolutions, including resolution 2118 (2013), by the warring parties in Syria further convince us that, in the case of grave violations of human rights or crimes that amount to war crimes or crimes against humanity, there should be a moratorium on the use of the veto as a procedural matter, so that such tragedies for innocent civilians are not repeated."); Statement of Poland, *id.* at 18 ("It is regrettable that the establishment of an independent, impartial investigative mechanism on the use of chemical weapons in Syria was vetoed on Tuesday . . . , thereby enabling those responsible for chemical attacks to remain unpunished. Accountability for such acts is a requirement under international law and is central to achieving durable peace in Syria."); Statement of Peru, *id.* at 19–20 ("Peru expresses its deep-rooted concern at the divisions that have emerged in the Council, in particular between its permanent members, and at the regrettable use of the veto, which limits our capacity to

States, in formal statements at the UN, have additionally taken the view – more generally and not necessarily related to the situation in Syria – that the veto is being used in a way that is not in line with the Charter, international law, and similar positions. For instance:

- **Egypt** stated that "[t]he use of the veto undermines the implementation of the provisions of the Charter and of international law."[299]
- **Mexico** maintained that "the veto in situations where mass atrocities are committed *is an abuse of the law* that can trigger international responsibility for the State committing them and an abuse that leaves the Organization under the sad shadow of paralysis and irrelevance."[300]
- **Norway** asserted that: "The use of the veto to protect narrow national interests in situations of mass atrocities *is not in line with the spirit of the Charter.*"[301]
- **Turkey** added that the Security Council's failure to carry out its primary responsibility for the maintenance of peace and security "pursuant to Article 24 of the Charter" is a *"serious blow to international law."*[302]

---

maintain international peace and security and to resolve the humanitarian conflicts and crises that form our agenda."); Statement of Poland, S/P.V.8228, at 7 (Apr. 10, 2018) ("Because of the use of the veto by the Russian Federation, the Security Council failed once again today to establish an accountability mechanism. By that act, Russia undermined the ability of the Council to fulfil its primary responsibility under the Charter of the United Nations: to maintain international peace and security."); Statement of the Netherlands, S/P.V.8225, at 9 (Apr. 9, 2018) ("The Kingdom of the Netherlands would also like to point out that the majority of the States Members of the United Nations count on the permanent members of the Council not to use their veto in cases of mass atrocities. The international community should be able to count on the Council to uphold international humanitarian law and the international prohibition on the use of chemical weapons, and to act when international law is trampled."); Statement of Ukraine, S/PV.8073, at 8–9 (Oct. 24, 2017) ("Today's voting has demonstrated a much more dangerous tendency—one in which fundamental international norms are cynically ignored and independent structures are held hostage. Today's voting has demonstrated once again the increasing abuse of the right to veto. Today, the Council has failed to do its job again."); Statement of Uruguay, S/PV.7919, at 8 (Apr. 7, 2017) ("We must also reflect on the situation in which the Council finds itself owing to the existence of the privilege of the veto in the adoption of its resolutions, and the aggravating factor of the use or threat of the use of the veto with respect to resolutions relating to crimes against humanity. Uruguay, as a signatory to the Accountability, Coherence and Transparency Group code of conduct, calls once again on the members of the Council to commit to not use the veto in situations of this kind.").

[299] Security Council Debate, "Upholding International Law," *supra* note 194, at 39 (emphasis added).
[300] *Id.* at 47 (emphasis added).
[301] *Id.* at 66 (emphasis added).
[302] *Id.* at 80 (emphasis added).

- **The Netherlands** stated that *the special privilege of the veto* ought to be used "with maximum restraint" and that the Council would "force itself into irrelevance" and the "rules-based international order would break down" if instead this privilege were "used as a licence to kill, as a means to obstruct justice, as a way to prevent the truth from being told, *as a means to hold hostage those who want to uphold the principles of the Charter.*"[303]
- **Australia** stated: "We have been dismayed by the use of the veto to block the Council's ability to act in the face of the horrors we have witnessed .... We urge the Security Council to once again lead by example in the fight against impunity and the *maintenance of the international rules-based order.*"[304]

States have additionally objected to the use of the veto to protect national interests in situations of mass atrocities.[305]

Numerous states have also objected to the use of the veto in mass atrocity situations and vocalized support for voluntary veto restraint in the face of atrocity crimes. For example, in the debate leading to Resolution 1674, Liechtenstein stated that the "responsibility [of Security Council members] leads almost inevitably to the conclusion that *collective action to prevent and respond to genocide, crimes against humanity and war crimes must not be made impossible by a non-concurring vote* of one of the permanent members of the Council."[306] Latvia, during a May 17, 2018, debate, took the position: "*The special privilege of veto power* of the permanent members of the Council is also a responsibility – it must be used in the interests of common peace and security, and *not when mass atrocity crimes are committed.*"[307]

---

[303] *Id.* at 15 (emphasis added). Netherlands was then serving on the Security Council.

[304] *Id.* at 59 (emphasis added).

[305] For example, Sweden (then serving on the Security Council) stated: "the use of the veto to protect narrow national interests in situations of serious violations of international law is totally unacceptable." *Id.* at 22. Georgia stated: "following the war [in Georgia], in blatant disregard of the need to advance the peace process and ensure an international presence on the ground, the Russian Federation used its veto power to dismantle the United Nations Observer Mission in Georgia in order to avoid any kind of international engagement on the ground." *Id.* at 37. Ukraine stated that "Russia's revanchist policy of using military force against other States" has taken place "against a backdrop of Russia's systematic abuse of the right of veto and blatant disregard of its obligation to maintain peace and security." *Id.* at 61 (emphasis added).

[306] Peters, *supra* note 90, at 40, *quoting* Statement of Liechtenstein in the debate on SC Res. 1674, at 15 (Dec. 9, 2005) (S/PV.5319 (Resumption 1)) (emphasis added).

[307] Security Council Debate, "Upholding International Law," *supra* note 194, at 34 (emphasis added). Many states have articulated similar views. For example, France stated: "In 2013, in

States have also called for the General Assembly to step in where the Security Council fails to act. For example, Ireland specifically linked Security Council paralysis to the Council being unable to fulfill its duties under the Charter, including the Charter's "[p]urposes and [p]rinciples": "Where the Security Council is unable to act, and therefore *unable to fulfil its primary responsibility to work towards the purposes and principles of the United Nations*, other organs – including the General Assembly – must act."[308]

[308] *Id.* at 46. Additionally, Liechtenstein stated: "the General Assembly should step in where the Council is paralysed and therefore unable to take on its responsibility to ensure accountability in line with its authority under the Charter." *Id.* at 43. Ukraine stated: "As to the Security Council, its failure to exercise its primary responsibility in dealing with threats to peace, breaches of peace, or acts of aggression should trigger a reaction by the General Assembly." *Id.* at 61. Liechtenstein also has launched a new initiative that there should be mandatory discussion in a formal meeting of the General Assembly of any use of the veto in the Security Council.

order to prevent blockages in cases where mass atrocities have been committed, as in Syria or Burma, France called for a unilateral suspension of the veto in the form of a voluntary political commitment by the five permanent members of the Security Council." *Id.* at 29. Kuwait (then serving on the Security Council) stated: "Kuwait supports the Mexican-French initiative and the Accountability, Coherence and Transparency group code of conduct, which call for refraining from use of the veto in cases of genocide, crimes against humanity and war crimes." *Id.* at 32. Lithuania stated: "Among other things, restraint in the use of the veto would make the Council's responses to ongoing crises more effective and reduce veto-induced paralysis. Lithuania therefore strongly supports the French-Mexican initiative on limiting its use in cases of mass atrocities, genocide, war crimes and crimes against humanity. Lithuania also actively endorses the relevant initiatives of Liechtenstein and the Accountability, Coherence and Transparency group." *Id.* at 33. Liechtenstein stated: "The collective commitment of the United Nations membership to fight mass atrocity crimes is also expressed in the Accountability, Coherence and Transparency group's code of conduct on mass atrocities. We echo the call by many speakers in the Chamber on all Member States to join that initiative, which is supported by 116 [121 as of early 2020] States." *Id.* at 43. Belgium stated: "Belgium supports the Franco-Mexican initiative to regulate the right of veto in the case of crimes of atrocity and why we signed the code of conduct of the Accountability, Coherence and Transparency group." *Id.* at 52. Italy stated: "Today the Council could promote accountability, for example, by referring to the ICC situations in which war crimes and crimes against humanity are perpetrated and by supporting the Court, by limiting the veto power in cases of mass atrocities." *Id.* at 53. Austria stated: "Austria urges the members of the Security Council to refrain from using the veto to curtail Council action where it could prevent or stop violence or conflict, in accordance with the purposes and principles of the Charter. Austria therefore supports the code of conduct of the Accountability, Coherence and Transparency group, as well as the initiative by Mexico and France in that regard." *Id.* at 72. Cyprus stated: "Cyprus reiterates its unequivocal support for the code of conduct regarding Security Council action against genocide, crimes against humanity and war crimes." *Id.* at 80. Portugal stated: "restraint on the part of the permanent members from the use of veto, at least when crimes of genocide, crimes against humanity and war crimes are committed, would be a very important step." *Id.* at 85. Slovenia stated: "we stress once again that members of the Security Council should not veto resolutions that seek to prevent or end genocide, crimes against humanity and war crimes." *Id.* at 90.

These kinds of statements as well as the development of the "voluntary veto restraint" initiatives discussed in Chapter 3 (especially the ACT Code of Conduct and the French/Mexican initiative) – which two permanent members join – attest that, far from states acquiescing in a practices of unlimited veto use in the face of atrocity crimes, they are vociferously objecting to such use. The statements also make clear the belief of states that it is appropriate to measure veto use in terms of whether it accords with the UN's "[p]urposes and [p]rinciples" and other obligations under international law.

4.2.4.3 Other Resolutions Did Not Obviate the Need for the Resolutions That Were Vetoed Related to the Situation in Syria

Turning back to the situation of Syria, while the Security Council was able to issue a number of other resolutions, as detailed in Chapter 5, those resolutions did not in any way obviate the need for the vetoed resolutions. A number of Security Council resolutions that passed pertained to crimes of the so-called Islamic State (ISIL)[309] or provided generic condemnation of crimes committed by "all parties."[310] By contrast, many of the resolutions that would have been critical of regime crimes, or implemented measures to alleviate the suffering of those harmed through regime crimes, were systematically vetoed.

For example, when the renewal of the mandate of the JIM was vetoed (three times),[311] it meant that *no mechanism* was empowered to conduct chemical weapons inspections that would have attributed responsibility to the side using chemical weapons. One might then ask whether blocking attribution of those using chemical weapons was "promoting and encouraging respect for human rights," "achieving international co-operation in solving international problems of [a] ... humanitarian character," or in accordance with "principles of justice and international law," and, thereby, in accordance with the UN's

---

[309] See, e.g., S/RES/2170 (2014) (condemning gross, widespread abuse of human rights by extremist groups in Iraq and Syria, and expressing the need for accountability for "ISIL, [al Nusra Front] and all other individuals, groups, undertakings and entities associated with Al-Qaida"); S/RES/2393 (Dec. 19, 2017) (condemning a long list of crimes, and, inter alia, expressing "grave concern" "at the movement of foreign terrorist fighters and other terrorists and terrorist groups into and out of Syria"); S/RES/2347 (2017) (condemning destruction, smuggling of cultural heritage by terrorist groups, including ISIL).

[310] See, e.g., S/RES/2139 (2014) (condemning the "widespread violations of human right and international humanitarian law by the Syrian authorities, as well as human rights abuses and violations of international humanitarian law by armed groups," and demanding that "all parties" put an end to all forms of violence and "cease all attacks against civilians").

[311] S/2017/884 (vetoed by the Russian Federation); S/2017/962 (vetoed by the Russian Federation); S/2017/970 (vetoed by the Russian Federation).

"[p]urposes and [p]rinciples"? One might also ask whether the veto was employed in good faith? In fact, the preamble to the Chemical Weapons Convention[312] *implicitly recognizes chemical weapons use as contrary to the UN's purposes and principles.*[313] If the veto of the renewal of the mandate of the JIM violated the UN's "[p]urposes and [p]rinciples," as it appears to have, the veto would be *ultra vires* of the proper exercise of Security Council power.[314] In fact, such veto use appears much closer to being an accessory to ongoing crimes – as chemical weapons use can constitute a war crime, crime against humanity,[315] or part of genocide[316] – which Judge ad hoc Lauterpacht expressly warned against in the *Application of Genocide Convention* Case.[317]

---

[312] Convention on the Prohibition of the Development, Production, Stockpiling and Use of Chemical Weapons and on their Destruction, Jan. 13, 1993, 1947 UNTS 45 (1993) [hereinafter, Chemical Weapons Convention].

[313] The preamble recites that the Convention "contributes to the realization of the purposes and principles of the Charter of the United Nations." *Id.*, pmbl.

[314] Akande, *supra* note 79, at 319 (quoting US delegate at San Francisco Charter negotiations: "if the Security Council violated its principles and purposes it would be acting ultra vires").

[315] Use of chemical weapons can be either a war crimes or crime against humanity, depending on the circumstances. Carsten Stahn, *Between Law-Breaking and Law-Making: Syria, Humanitarian Intervention and "What the Law Ought to Be"* (Oct. 22, 2013), at https://ssrn.com/abstract=2343582 or http://dx.doi.org/10.2139/ssrn.2343582; Prime Minister's Office, Chemical Weapon use by Syrian Regime: UK Government Legal Position, policy paper (Aug. 29, 2013), *at* www.gov.uk/government/publications/chemical-weapon-use-by-syrian-regime-uk-government-legal-position/chemical-weapon-use-by-syrian-regime-uk-government-legal-position-html-version.

[316] *See, e.g.*, Jennifer Trahan, *A Critical Guide to the Iraqi High Tribunal's Anfal Judgment: Genocide against the Kurds*, 30 MICH. J. INT'L L. 305 (2009) (discussing, inter alia, chemical weapons use by the Iraqi regime against the Iraqi Kurds during the 1988 "Anfal campaign," adjudicated by the Iraqi High Tribunal to constitute genocide).

[317] *See* notes 110–11 *supra* and accompanying text. An additional question is whether veto use could ever be considered "aiding and abetting," or complicity in, an ongoing crime. *See, e.g.*, Peters, *supra* note 90, at 47, 48 ("a member of the Security Council could in principle be held legally responsible for the exercise of its vote in the Council, especially for its veto." "A *lex specialis* is the prohibition of complicity in genocide under Article III(e) of the Genocide Convention.") (citations omitted). According to Article 16 of the ILC's Articles on State Responsibility:

> A State which aids or assists another State in the commission of an internationally wrongful act . . . is internationally responsible for doing so if:
>
> (a) that States does so with knowledge of the circumstances of the internationally wrongful act; and
> (b) the act would be internationally wrongful if committed by that State.

Int'l L. Comm'n, Articles on State Responsibility, *supra* note 21, Art. 16. The ILC's Commentary (3) on this article includes the following: "Article 16 limits the scope of responsibility for aid or assistance in three way. First, the relevant State organ or agency providing such aid or assistance must be aware of the circumstance making the conduct of the

Another example of a questionable veto is veto of the referral of the situation in Syria to the ICC.[318] One might ask whether that veto was "promoting and encouraging respect for human rights," aimed at achieving "international co-operation in solving international problems of [a] ... humanitarian character," "in conformity with the principles of justice and international law," and made in "good faith," which it would need to be to accord with the UN's "[p]urposes and [p]rinciples." That veto basically blocked any kind of comprehensive prosecution of crimes against humanity and war crimes committed by, inter alia, regime actors.[319] It is hard to see how blocking international prosecution of atrocity crimes is "promoting and encouraging respect for human rights," achieving "international co-operation in solving international problems of [a] ... humanitarian character," "in conformity with the principles of justice and international law," or an exercise of "good faith." If veto use does not meet these requirements, it fails to be in accordance with the UN's "[p]urposes and [p]rinciples" and again would be *ultra vires* of the proper exercise of Security Council power.[320] (This argument should not be read to imply that *any* veto of an ICC referral necessarily would violate the "[p]urposes and [p]rinciples" of the UN; important factors would be whether the domestic system appears "willing and/or able" to conduct trials, or whether another prosecutorial mechanism is being established or can be utilized. If there appear to be credible alternatives for prosecution, the lack of ICC referral (and veto

---

assisted State internationally wrongful; secondly, the aid or assistance must be given with a view to facilitating the commission of that act; and thirdly, the completed act must be such that it would have been wrongful had it been committed by the assisting State itself." *Id.* at 149. *See also Bosnia v. Serbia Case*, *supra* note 17, at para. 432 (differentiating the failure to "prevent" genocide from complicity; "complicity always requires that some *positive action* has been take to furnish aid or assistance to the perpetrators") (emphasis added). Veto use is a "positive action," see notes 250–51 *supra* and accompanying text, as is furnishing military aid and training.

[318] S/2014/348 (vetoed by the Russian Federation and China).

[319] Documentation of crimes in Syria is being coordinated by the International, Impartial and Independent Mechanism to Assist in the Investigation and Prosecutor of Persons Responsible for the Most Serious Crimes under International Law Committed in the Syrian Arab Republic since March 2011 (IIIM), but the IIIM has no prosecutorial capacity. Absent a Security Council referral, the ICC has very limited jurisdiction over crimes in Syria, having jurisdiction only over crimes committed by "foreign fighters" from Rome Statute States Parties. *See* Rome Statute, Art. 12(2)(b) (jurisdiction over nationals of States Parties). While some prosecutions will likely be possible in the domestic courts of third-states through the use of universal jurisdiction or other forms of jurisdiction, that will not result in anything close to comprehensive prosecutions. Thus, the veto of the ICC referral means any chance of prosecuting, inter alia, regime crimes in a systematic way has been blocked.

[320] *See* Akande, *supra* note 79, at 319 (quoting US delegate at San Francisco Charter negotiations: "if the Security Council violated its principles and purposes it would be acting ultra vires").

blocking referral) would appear less problematic.)[321] While the General Assembly was able to create an investigative mechanism to compile crime evidence related to Syria (the IIIM), that mechanism is unable to conduct prosecutions, so is hardly a substitute for ICC referral.[322]

In light of the foregoing, it is urged that members of the Security Council (both elected and permanent) employ additional self-oversight as to whether the Council's actions, including veto use, are in accordance with: (1) "promoting and encouraging respect for human rights," (2) "principles of justice and international law," (3) achieving "international co-operation in solving international problems of [a] ... humanitarian character," (4) "good faith," and (5) therefore, the "[p]urposes and [p]rinciples" of the UN. If the Security Council's actions do not satisfy these requirements imposed by the Charter and international law (as to good faith), then the actions (including veto use), are outside the proper exercise of Security Council power. A compelling argument can be made that some of the vetoes that have been cast are failing to adhere to the Charter's requirements, and thus, are *ultra vires* of the proper exercise of Security Council power.

4.3 CONSIDERATION OF THE TREATY OBLIGATIONS OF INDIVIDUAL PERMANENT MEMBER STATES

A third source of legal obligation by which one might examine veto use in the face of genocide, crimes against humanity, and/or war crimes is the treaty obligations of the individual permanent member states. These include treaty obligations under the Genocide Convention[323] and the 1949 Geneva Conventions,[324] to which all permanent members of the Security Council are parties.[325] To what extent these constrain the actions of states while serving on the Council is complicated by the fact that under Article 103 of the Charter, the obligations under the Charter appear to prevail over inconsistent treaty obligations;[326] yet, as explored below, that does not necessarily imply these treaties are irrelevant when considering veto use.

---

[321] Neither of these alternatives exists with respect to the situation in Syria, where the domestic system cannot be utilized to prosecute "regime" crimes while the regime is in power and there is no other prosecutorial mechanism being established, as the IIIM (as noted above) is only empowered to compile information and related tasks. See note 319 *supra*.
[322] See note 319 *supra*.
[323] Genocide Convention, *supra* note 1.
[324] 1949 Geneva Conventions, *supra* note 2.
[325] See note 29 *supra* (parties to the Genocide Convention and 1949 Geneva Conventions).
[326] See UN Charter, Art. 103.

4.3.1 Legal Obligations under the Genocide Convention

As also explored in Chapter 2,[327] the Genocide Convention imposes in Article 1 an obligation to "prevent and to punish" genocide.[328] The ICJ elaborated on the obligation to "prevent" genocide in the *Bosnia v. Serbia* Case.[329] There, the ICJ determined that Serbia had breached its duty to prevent genocide committed by Bosnian Serb forces (VRS) in and around Srebrenica.[330]

Bosnia initially requested provisional measures, prior to the Srebrenica genocide. The ICJ held that both Bosnia and Serbia were under a "clear obligation to do all in their power to prevent the commission of any such acts [of genocide] in the future," and ordered Serbia to "take all measures within its power to prevent commission of the crime of genocide" by all "organizations and persons which may be subject to its ... influence."[331] Thereafter, the Security Council, in Resolution 819, also "took note" of the ICJ's provisional measures order that "the Government of the Federal Republic of Yugoslavia (Serbia and Montenegro) should immediately ... take all measures within its power to prevent the commission of the crime of genocide" in accordance with Article 1 of the Genocide Convention.[332]

In response to a second request for provisional measures, the ICJ held it could not indicate further provisional measures, but the parties should immediately and

---

[327] That chapter examined the Genocide Convention and 1949 Geneva Conventions as sources of hard law underlying R2P. *See* Chapter 2.2.2. Thus, the law is examined there for a different purpose.

[328] Genocide Convention, *supra* note 1, Art. 1. The duty to "prevent" crimes exists in several other conventions, including the Convention against Torture and Other Cruel, Inhuman or Degrading Treatment or Punishment (1984), the Convention on the Prevention and Punishment of Crimes against Internationally Protected Persons, Including Diplomatic Agents (1973), the Convention on the Safety of United Nations and Associated Personnel (1994), and the International Convention for the Suppression of Terrorist Bombings (1998). Heieck, *supra* note 39, at 18–19 (citing conventions).

[329] *Bosnia v. Serbia* Case, *supra* note 17.

[330] *Id.*, para. 438.

[331] Case Concerning Application of the Convention on the Prevention and Punishment of the Crime of Genocide (Bosn. & Herz. v. Yugo. (Serb. and Montenegro)), Request for the Indication of Provisional Measures, Order of 8 April 1993, 1993 ICJ Rep. 3, paras. 45, 52 (April 8). A similar provisional measures order was recently granted in the Gambia et al.'s case against Myanmar. *See* Application of the Convention on the Prevention and Punishment of the Crime of Genocide (Gam. v. Myan.), Order of 23 January 2020 (Int'l Ct. Just.) [hereinafter, *Gambia v. Myanmar* Case]. There the ICJ ruled that "Myanmar must, in accordance with its obligations under the Convention, in relation to the members of the Rohingya group in its territory, take all measures within its power to prevent the commission of all acts within the scope of Article II of the Convention ... ." *Id.*, para. 79.

[332] SC Res. 819 (Apr. 16, 1993).

effectively implement the previous order.[333] Judge ad hoc Lauterpacht concurred in his Separate Opinion but argued that additional measures should have been indicated,[334] reaffirming (as discussed above) that the prohibition of genocide is a *jus cogens* norm.[335] In the ICJ's Preliminary Objections Decision, the ICJ also recognized that "the rights and obligations enshrined by the [Genocide] Convention ... are rights and obligations *erga omnes*."[336]

In its ruling on the merits (in 2007), the ICJ articulated a standard of "due diligence" that is required to comply with the obligation to "prevent" genocide in Article 1 of the Convention:

> [I]t is clear that the obligation in question is one of conduct and not one of result, in the sense that a State cannot be under an obligation to succeed, whatever the circumstances, in preventing the commission of genocide: the obligation of States parties is rather to *employ all means reasonably available to them*, so as to prevent genocide so far as possible. A State does not incur responsibility simply because the desired result is not achieved; *responsibility is however incurred if the State manifestly failed to take all measures to prevent genocide which were within its power, and which might have contributed to preventing the genocide*. In this area the notion of "due diligence", which calls for an assessment *in concreto*, is of critical importance. Various parameters operate when assessing whether a State has duly discharged the obligation concerned. The first, which varies greatly from one State to another, is clearly *the capacity to influence* effectively the action of persons likely to commit, or already committing, genocide. This capacity itself *depends, among other things, on the geographical distance of the State concerned from the scene of the events, and on the strength of the political links, as well as links of all other kinds*, between the authorities of that State and the main actors in the events. The State's capacity to influence must also be assessed by legal criteria, since it is clear that every State may only act within the limits permitted by international law; seen thus, a State's *capacity to influence may vary* depending on its particular legal position vis-à-vis the situations and persons facing the danger, or the reality, of genocide. On the other hand, it is irrelevant whether the State whose responsibility is in issue claims, or even proves, that even if it had employed all means reasonably at its disposal, they would not

---

[333] Case Concerning the Application of the Convention on the Prevention and Punishment of the Crime of Genocide (Bosn. & Herz. v. Yugo. (Serb. and Montenegro)), Further Request for the Indication of Provisional Measures, Order of 13 September 1993, 1993 ICJ Rep., para. 61 (Sept. 13).

[334] *Id.*, sep. op., Lauterpacht, J., at para. 123.

[335] *Id.*, para. 100.

[336] Case Concerning the Application of the Convention on the Prevention and Punishment of the Crime of Genocide (Bosn. & Herz. v. Yugo. (Serb. and Montenegro)), Preliminary Objections, Judgment of 11 July 1996, para. 31.

have sufficed to prevent the commission of genocide. As well as being generally difficult to prove, this is irrelevant to the breach of the obligation of conduct in question, the more so since the possibility remains that the combined efforts of several States, each complying with its obligation to prevent, might have achieved the result – averting the commission of genocide – which the efforts of only one State were insufficient to produce.[337]

Thus, briefly summarized, what is required to satisfy the obligation in Article 1 of the Genocide Convention is for states to "employ all means reasonably available" to prevent genocide based on their "capacity to influence," which is judged by factors including "the strength of the political links, as well as links of all other kinds, between the authorities of that State and the main actors in the events."[338]

The ICJ additionally held that

[e]ven if and when ... organs [of the UN] have been called upon, this does not mean that the States parties to the Convention are relieved of the obligation to take such action as they can to prevent genocide from occurring, while respecting the United Nations Charter and any decisions that may have been taken by its competent organs.[339]

As mentioned above, the ICJ held that the duty to act is triggered when "the State learns of, or should normally have learned of, the existence of a *serious risk* that genocide will be committed."[340] "From that moment onward, *if the State has available to it means likely to have a deterrent effect* on those suspected of preparing genocide, or reasonably suspected of harbouring specific intent (*dolus specialis*), it is under a duty to make such use of these means ...."[341]

Ultimately,

the ICJ held that this linkage requirement of the due diligence standard [existed and was not met] because Serbia had [and failed to utilize] the capacity to effectively influence the VRS [Army of Republika Srpska], ... due to not only Serbia's close proximity to the Srebrenica enclave, but also Belgrade's strong political, military, and financial links with the authorities and armed forces of the Republika Srpska.[342]

---

[337] *Bosnia v. Serbia Case, supra* note 17, at para. 430 (emphasis added).
[338] *Id.*
[339] *Id.*, para. 427.
[340] *Id.*, para. 431 (emphasis added).
[341] *Id.* (emphasis added).
[342] Heieck, *supra* note 39, at 39, *citing id.*, paras. 237–41, 388, 394, 434, 435. Given all the means of modern communication and surveillance, the Court's emphasis on physical proximity is

4.3 Treaty Obligations of Individual Permanent Member States 213

As explained in Chapter 2, the two most significant aspects of the Court's ruling for present purposes are: (1) its holding that a state's responsibility to prevent genocide varies based on the state's ability to influence the relevant actors;[343] and (2) that the ICJ did *not* limit a state's obligations under the Genocide Convention to preventing genocide only within a state's own territory, but applied it vis-à-vis genocide being committed in another state.

On the first point, "according to the Court, the due diligence standard provides that if a state has the capacity to effectively influence genocidal actors and the knowledge that there exists a serious risk that genocide might occur, the state has a positive legal duty to use its best efforts within the means available to it to prevent the genocide from occurring."[344] One could imagine that such a duty of due diligence would be particularly high for any country that is a permanent member of the Security Council due to its capacity to influence.[345] For example, the UN Secretary-General has stated "the five permanent members bear particular responsibility because of the privileges of tenure and the veto power they have been granted under the Charter."[346] John Heieck similarly writes that "the 'great powers' of the international order – China, France, Russia, the UK and the US – have a *heightened* duty to cooperate in order to satisfy the due diligence standard and to discharge their duty to prevent genocide."[347] He continues: "This heightened duty is the result of these

---

somewhat puzzling, as a state could keep fully informed about another state's military or paramilitary activities without close geographic proximity. *See* Louise Arbour, *The Responsibility to Protect as a Duty of Care in International Law and Practice*, 34(3) REV. INT'L STUD. 445, 454 (2008) ("while proximity may matter most in terms of promptness and effectiveness of responses, it should not be used as a pretext for non-neighbours to avoid responsibility").

[343] *Bosnia v. Serbia* Case, *supra* note 17, para. 430 ("Various parameters operate when assessing whether a State has duly discharged the obligation concerned. The first, which varies greatly from one State to another, is clearly the capacity to influence effectively the action of persons likely to commit, or already committing, genocide.").

[344] Heieck, *supra* note 39, at 28. The need for a state to take "all measures within its power to prevent the commission [of genocide]" was recently reaffirmed in the ICJ's *Gambia v. Myanmar* Case. *See* note 331 *supra*.

[345] The Genocide Convention also specifically envisions UN organs (which would include the Security Council) playing a role in preventing genocide. *See* Genocide Convention, *supra* note 1, Art. VIII ("Any Contracting Party may call upon the competent organs of the United Nations to take such action under the Charter of the United Nations as they consider appropriate for the prevention and suppression of acts of genocide . . . .").

[346] Report of the UN Secretary-General: Implementing the Responsibility to Protect, UN Doc. A/63/677 (Jan. 12, 2009), *at* www.un.org/ruleoflaw/files/SG_reportA_63_677_en.pdf.

[347] Heieck, *supra* note 39, at 51.

five states' more extensive means, capacity to effectively influence, and access to timely information, which, in turn, is the product of not only their individual power and resources, but also their *privileged legal position* within the Security Council as veto-wielding members . . . ."[348] Anne Peters additionally writes:

> The [permanent members'] privilege within the Security Council, the veto power, is only justifiable in a constitutionalised order with a view to those members' special military and economic capabilities. The veto power is thus intrinsically correlated with a special responsibility. It is therefore submitted that the hard legal obligation to protect populations threatened by [core] crimes especially falls on the permanent members of the Security Council.[349]

One could further imagine such a duty of due diligence would be at its very highest for a state that is both a permanent member, and has political, military, and/or financial ties to the country in question, because its actions (or lack thereof) could have the greatest impact on what is happening on the ground.[350]

On the second point, the extraterritorial implications of the ruling are clear as the ICJ was adjudicating the responsibility of Serbia (then part of the Federal Republic of Yugoslavia (FRY))[351] to prevent genocide

---

[348] *Id.*

[349] Peters, *supra* note 90, 40. She continues:

> The conclusion drawn by the delegate of Liechtenstein in the debate leading to [Security Council] Resolution 1674 on the protection of civilians was: "That responsibility leads almost inevitably to the conclusion that collective action to prevent and respond to genocide, crimes against humanity and war crimes *must not be made impossible by a non-concurring vote* of one of the permanent members of the Council."

Id. (citing Statement of Liechtenstein in the debate on SC Res. 1674, at 15 (Dec. 9, 2005) (S/PV.5319 (Resumption 1)) (emphasis added by Peters)).

[350] Marko Milanović notes the different levels of cooperation required of states depending on their relative power:

> A minor state could probably be considered to have only the obligation to cooperate with other states, most of all diplomatically, in attempting to put pressure on a genocidal actor. The obligation would be similar in scope to the ones proposed by the ILC in Article 41 of its Articles on States Responsibility, regulating the aggravated regime of state responsibility for serious breaches of peremptory norms of international law. A great power, on the other hand, would have to be much more active in order to discharge this obligation, while a state which is in one way or another directly involved in the events, for instance by proving assistance and support to the genocidal actors, as Serbia was in Bosnia, would have the greatest obligation yet.

Marko Milanović, *State Responsibility for Genocide: A Follow Up*, 18 Eur. J. Int'l L. 669, 686 (2007).

[351] At that time, the FRY consisted of Serbia, Kosovo, and Montenegro.

committed in July 1995 by the VRS in Bosnia-Herzegovina, an independent state as of 1992.[352] In the Preliminary Objections Decision, the ICJ also expressly stated that "the obligation each state ... has to prevent and to punish the crime of genocide is not territorially limited by the Convention."[353] Thus, for any state party to the Genocide Convention, the obligation to take measures to the best of its ability to prevent genocide encompasses genocide occurring in another state. Marko Milanović thus writes: "The ICJ has made it clear that every state in the world has an obligation to prevent ... genocide, albeit to a greater or to a lesser extent ...";[354] "the Court makes the obligation to prevent genocide a truly global duty of every state to do what it reasonably can."[355]

4.3.2 Legal Obligations under the 1949 Geneva Conventions

As explained in Chapter 2,[356] there are also similar legal obligations contained in the four 1949 Geneva Conventions,[357] which are binding on all UN Member States, as all UN Member States are parties to those Conventions.[358] These conventions expressly impose on states parties an obligation to prosecute "grave breaches"[359] (a fairly broad subset of war crimes committed in international armed conflict).[360] The Conventions,

---

[352] See Claus Kreß, *The State Conduct Element*, in THE CRIME OF AGGRESSION: A COMMENTARY 373, 491 (Claus Kreß & Stefan Barriga eds., 2017) ("In the *Genocide* case, the ICJ recognized the duty of states to prevent genocide even beyond their own borders."); Jan Wouters, *The Obligation to Prosecute International Law Crimes*, 32 COLLEGIUM, at 8 (2005) (similar), *citing* Preliminary Objections, *supra* note 336, at para. 31.
[353] Preliminary Objections, *supra* note 336, para. 31.
[354] Milanović [Follow Up], *supra* note 350, at 687.
[355] *Id.* at 691.
[356] Again, that chapter examined these sources as hard law obligations underlying R2P, and thus the law was examined for a different purpose. See Chapter 2.2.2.
[357] 1949 Geneva Conventions, *supra* note 2.
[358] *See supra* note 29 (states parties to the 1949 Geneva Conventions).
[359] Geneva Convention I, *supra* note 2, Art. 49 (obligation to prosecute grave breaches), Art. 50 (grave breaches); Geneva Convention II, *supra* note 2, Art. 50 (obligation to prosecute grave breaches), Art. 51 (grave breaches); Geneva Convention III, *supra* note 2, Art. 129 (obligation to prosecute grave breaches); Art. 130 (grave breaches); Geneva Convention IV, *supra* note 2, Art. 146 (obligation to prosecute grave breaches), Art. 147 (grave breaches).
[360] Grave breaches specified in the four 1949 Geneva Conventions, *supra* note 2, Arts. 50, 51, 130, 147, respectively) are willful killing; torture or inhuman treatment; biological experiments; willfully causing great suffering; causing serious injury to body or health; and extensive destruction and appropriation of property, not justified by military necessity and carried out unlawfully and wantonly (except, this last provision is not included in Article 130, Geneva Convention III). Grave breaches specified in Geneva Conventions III and IV, *supra* note 2,

in Common Article 3, also prohibit certain war crimes committed in non-international armed conflict.[361]

Common Article 1 to the 1949 Geneva Conventions additionally provides an obligation for states parties to "undertake to respect and *to ensure respect for* the Geneva Conventions in all circumstances."[362] The Conventions further specify that, in addition to the obligation to prosecute "grave breaches," "[e]ach High Contracting Party shall take measures necessary for the suppression of all acts contrary to the provisions of the present Convention[s] other than grave breaches ... ."[363] Thus, there exists both an obligation in Common Article 1 to "ensure" "grave breaches" and Common Article 3 war crimes are not committed,[364] as well as an obligation more generally to "suppress" acts

---

Arts. 130 and 147, respectively, additionally include compelling a prisoner of war or a protected civilian to serve in the armed forces of the hostile Power; and willfully depriving a prisoner of war or a protected person of the rights or fair and regular trial prescribed in the Conventions. Grave breaches specified in Geneva Convention IV, *supra* note 2, Art. 147, additionally include: unlawful deportation or transfer; unlawful confinement of a protected person; and taking of hostages. International Committee for the Red Cross (ICRC), Grave breaches specified in the 1949 Geneva Conventions and in additional Protocol I of 1977, *at* www.icrc.org/eng/resources/documents/misc/57jp2a.htm.

[361] Common Article 3 prohibits, in conflicts not of an international character:

(a) violence to life and person, in particular murder of all kinds, mutilation, cruel treatment and torture;
(b) taking of hostages;
(c) outrages upon personal dignity, in particular humiliating and degrading treatment;
(d) the passing of sentences and the carrying out of executions without previous judgment pronounced by a regularly constituted court, affording all the judicial guarantees which are recognized as indispensable by civilized peoples.

1949 Geneva Conventions, Common Art. 3.

[362] 1949 Geneva Conventions, *supra* note 2, Common Art. 1 (emphasis added).

[363] Geneva Convention I, *supra* note 2, Art. 49, para. 3; Geneva Convention II, *supra* note 2, Art. 50, para. 3; Geneva Convention III, *supra* note 2, Art. 129, para. 3; Geneva Convention IV, *supra* note 2, Art. 146, para 3.

[364] For authority that Common Article 1 applies to Common Article 3, see Sophie Rondeau, *The Responsibility to Protect Doctrine, and the Duty of the International Community to Reinforce International Humanitarian Law and Its Protective Value for Civilian Populations*, in BEYOND RESPONSIBILITY TO PROTECT: GENERATING CHANGE IN INTERNATIONAL LAW 306, 366 (Richard Barnes & Vassilis Tzevelekos eds., 2016) (construing the phrase "in all circumstances" to mean Common Article 1 also applies in non-international armed conflict); Knut Dörmann & Jose Serralvo, *Common Article 1 to the Geneva Conventions and the Obligation to Prevent International Humanitarian Law Violations*, 96 INT'L REV. RED CROSS 707, 735 (2014) (same); Reuven (Ruvi) Ziegler, *Non-refoulement between "Common Article 1" and "Common Article 3,"* in REFUGE FROM INHUMANITY?: WAR REFUGEES AND INTERNATIONAL HUMANITARIAN LAW 396 (David James Cantor & Jean-François Durieux eds., 2014) ("CA1 precedes CA2 and CA3, so there is no systematic or contextual ground for excluding CA3 from the scope of CA1 . . . . Moreover, there is no reason

4.3 Treaty Obligations of Individual Permanent Member States 217

contrary to the Conventions. Language identical to Common Article 1 of the 1949 Geneva Conventions is also found in Article 1(1) of the 1977 First Protocol[365] and Article 1(1) of the Third Protocol,[366] to which some of the permanent members are parties.[367]

The International Committee of the Red Cross (ICRC) explains Common Article 1 does not impose "an obligation to reach a specific result, but rather an 'obligation of means' to take *all possible appropriate measures* in an attempt to prevent or end violations of [international humanitarian law (IHL)]."[368] The ICRC Commentaries to the Geneva Conventions state that that language "covers *everything* a state can do to prevent the commission, or the repetition, of acts contrary to the convention[s]."[369] Explaining further what Common Article 1 requires, ICRC experts Knut Dörmann and Jose Serralvo[370] write:

> [Common Article] 1 epitomizes the commitment of States to avoid IHL violations taking place in the future. It does so by creating a framework whereby States not party to a particular armed conflict must *use every means at their disposal* to

---

to exclude CA3 from the scope of the obligation to ensure respect *'for the present Convention.'* After all, the provision does not proclaim that States should 'ensure respect for the provisions of the present Convention *that are applicable in international armed conflicts.'*") (emphasis in original); Yves Sandoz, *Rights, Powers, and Obligations of Neutral Powers Under the Convention, in* THE 1949 GENEVA CONVENTIONS, A COMMENTARY, ch. 5, n. 131 (Andrew Clapham, Paola Gaeta & Marco Sassòli eds., 2015) ("Keeping in mind that the obligation to 'ensure respect' for the [Geneva Conventions] specified in CA 1 also covers CA 3, which in turn includes [non-international armed conflicts]").

[365] Protocol Additional to the Geneva Conventions of 12 August 1949, and Relating to the Protection of Victims of International Armed Conflicts, June 8, 1977 [hereinafter, Protocol I]. Article 89 of Protocol I also states: "In situations of serious violations of the Conventions or of this Protocol, the High Contracting Parties undertake to act, jointly or individually, in co-operation with the United Nations and in conformity with the United Nations Charter." Protocol I, Art. 89.

[366] Protocol Additional to the Geneva Conventions of 12 August 1949, and Relating to the Adoption of an Additional Distinctive Emblem December 8, 2005 [hereinafter, Protocol III].

[367] Of the permanent members, the US has not ratified Protocol I and Russia has withdrawn its ratification; Russia and China have not ratified Protocol III. See International Committee of the Red Cross, *Treaties, States Parties and Commentaries*, at https://ihl-databases.icrc.org/applic/ihl/ihl.nsf/States.xsp?xp_viewStates=Xpages_NORMStatesParties&xp_treatySelected=470, and https://ihl-databases.icrc.org/applic/ihl/ihl.nsf/States.xsp?xp_viewStates=XPages_NORMStatesParties&xp_treatySelected=615.

[368] Rondeau, *supra* note 364, at 263–64, *quoting* INCREASING RESPECT FOR INTERNATIONAL HUMANITARIAN LAW IN NON-INTERNATIONAL ARMED CONFLICT 10 (M. Mack ed., ICRC, Geneva, 2008) (emphasis added).

[369] Dörmann & Serralvo, *supra* note 364, at 731 (emphasis added), *citing* Commentary: I Geneva Convention for the Amelioration of the Condition of the Wounded and Sick in Armed Forces in the Field 367 (Jean Pictet ed., 1952).

[370] Dörmann served as Head of the Legal Division of the ICRC and Serralvo as legal adviser in the Legal Division.

ensure that the belligerents comply with the Geneva Conventions and [Additional Protocol] 1, and probably the whole body of IHL.... [Common Article] 1 is not a mere entitlement to act. Instead, it imposes upon third States an international legal obligation to ensure respect in all circumstances. This obligation, which applies in international and non-international armed conflicts, is one of *due diligence*: to avoid breaching it, *States must make every lawful effort in their power, regardless of whether they attain the desired result or not*. For that purpose, they can choose among the different means at their disposal – with the exception of military intervention, which would only be lawful if undertaken in accordance with the UN Charter. That said, as in many other branches of international law, *the larger the means, the greater the responsibility*.[371]

Common Article 1 thus appears to create a due diligence obligation quite similar to what the obligation to "prevent" genocide requires under the Genocide Convention, in that, what is required by Common Article 1, also depends on a state's capacity to influence. Thus, because "the larger the means, the greater the responsibility," the capacity to influence of a permanent member of the Security Council, particularly one with ties to the country at issue, would be particularly significant.

Dörmann and Serralvo also explain that Common Article 1 creates both an "internal component" (ensuring respect for the Conventions on a state's own territory, for example, by its military, police, and civilian authorities), as well as an "external component."[372] The latter mandates that "third States – that is States not taking part in an armed conflict have an international legal obligation to actively prevent IHL violations" *"even in conflicts to which they are not a party."*[373] ICRC Commentaries similarly explain that Common Article 1

---

[371] Dörmann & Serralvo, *supra* note 364, at 735 (emphasis added).
[372] *Id.* at 708.
[373] *Id.* at 709 (emphasis added). This reading is also embraced by Oona Hathaway and Zachary Manfredi who explain:

> In the new [ICRC] commentary [2016] on Common Article 1, the ICRC explains that duties "to respect" are distinguishable from duties "to ensure respect." The former applies directly to states and their organs, and require[s] that they not directly violate the laws of armed conflict. The duty "to ensure respect," however, creates independent obligation on states to ensure *other* states and non-state actors do not violate their own duties under international law.

> Oona Hathaway & Zachary Manfredi, *The State Department Adviser Signals a Middle Road on Common Article 1*, JUST SECURITY (Apr. 12, 2016), *at* www.justsecurity.org/ 30560/state-department-adviser-signals-middle-road-common-article-1. For a more extensive discussion of Common Article 1, see also Oona A. Hathaway, Emily Chertoff, Lara Dominguez, Zachary Manfredi & Peter Tzeng, *Ensuring Responsibility: Common Article 1 and State Responsibility for Non-state Actors*, 95 TEX. L. REV. 539 (2017). *But see* Hitoshi Nasu, The UN

4.3 Treaty Obligations of Individual Permanent Member States 219

imposes an obligation to ensure respect by other states, which "should do everything in their power to ensure that the humanitarian principles underlying the Conventions are *universally applied*."[374] In this respect, Common Article 1 also operates similarly to the obligation to "prevent" genocide under the Genocide Convention, which also carries this external obligation.[375]

The ICJ has recognized this external obligation in both the *Nicaragua* Case (where the US was admonished to ensure respect for the 1949 Geneva Conventions and international humanitarian law more broadly),[376] and the *Wall* Case (where every state party was reminded of its obligation to ensure that Israel comply with the requirements of the Fourth Geneva Convention).[377] Similarly, the UN Secretary-General in a report submitted to the Security Council emphasized that the obligation to ensure compliance with the Fourth Geneva Convention particularly applies to states "that have

---

Security Council's Responsibility and the "Responsibility to Protect," in MAX PLANCK YEARBOOK OF UNITED NATIONS LAW, VOL. 15, 377, 387, n. 37 (2011) ("The crucial question is whether common article 1 extends to include an obligation to take action to prevent violations or to protect civilians outside one's own control.").

[374] Dörmann & Serralvo, *supra* note 364, at 715 (emphasis added) (*citing* COMMENTARY: IV GENEVA CONVENTION RELATIVE TO THE PROTECTION OF CIVILIAN PERSONS IN TIME OF WAR 16 (ICRC, Jean Pictet ed., 1958)). For an article questioning what is required under Common Article 1 and concluding that "common Article 1 is no more than a reminder of all obligations ... to 'respect' the Geneva Conventions" and a recommendation for states "to adopt lawful measures to induce other contracting states to comply with the Conventions," see Carlo Focarelli, *Common Article 1 of the 1949 Geneva Conventions: A Soap Bubble?*, 21 EUR. J. INT'L L. 125 (2010); *id.* at 128 ("It is unclear whether common Article 1 provides for an obligation or rather a discretionary power [or recommendation] .... It is also unclear ... what specific measures contracting states are bound (or authorized) [or recommended] to adopt."). Focarelli's reading appears out of line with the ICJ's admonition in the *Nicaragua* and *Wall* Cases that states must "ensure respect for" the Conventions – so the ICJ obviously maintains that there is content to this requirement. See notes 376–77 *infra*.

[375] See notes 351–55 *supra* and accompanying text (external obligation under the Genocide Convention).

[376] Military and Paramilitary Activities in and against Nicaragua (Nicar. v U.S.). Merits, Judgment. 1986 ICJ Rep. 14 (June 27) [hereinafter, *Nicaragua* Case], para. 220 ("The Court considers that there is an obligation on the United States Government, in the terms of Article 1 of the Geneva Conventions, to 'respect' the Conventions and even 'to ensure respect' for them 'in all circumstances,' since such an obligation does not derive only from the Conventions themselves, but from the general principles of humanitarian law to which the Conventions merely give specific expression.").

[377] Legal Consequences of the Construction of a Wall in the Occupied Palestinian Territory, Advisory Opinion, 2004 ICJ Rep. 136, para. 158 (July 9) [hereinafter, *Wall* Case] ("The Court would also emphasize that Article 1 of the Fourth Geneva Convention, a provision common to the four Geneva Conventions, provides that 'The High Contracting Parties undertake to respect and to ensure respect for the present Convention in all circumstances.' It follows from that provision that every State party to that Convention, whether or not it is a party to a specific conflict, is under an obligation to ensure that the requirements of the instruments in question are complied with.").

diplomatic relations with" the state in question who should "use all the means at their disposal to persuade" the government to abide by the applicable Convention.[378] Thus, "a State with close political, economic and/or military ties (for example, through equipping and training of armed forces or joint planning of operations) to one of the belligerents has a stronger obligation to ensure respect for IHL by its ally."[379] Obligations of due diligence would be "even more pronounced if third States provide support, directly, or indirectly, to a party to an ongoing armed conflict."[380] Furthermore, the ILC has made it clear in its Articles on State Responsibility that "third States are under the obligation not to knowingly aid or assist in the commission of IHL violations."[381]

4.3.3 Whether Legal Obligations Created under These Foundational Treaties Apply to States while Serving on the Security Council

The next issue becomes whether these obligations on parties to the Genocide Convention and the 1949 Geneva Conventions create obligations that extend to states *while they are serving* on the Security Council, particularly, the permanent members who are all parties to these conventions.

The most relevant provision of the Charter in this regard is Article 103, which states: "In the event of a conflict between the obligations of the Members of the United Nations under the present Charter and their obligations under any other international agreements, their obligations under the present Charter shall prevail."[382] While this appears to suggest that, hierarchically, obligations under the Charter take precedence over inconsistent treaty obligations,[383] it may not actually address the current question.

The issue of inconsistent obligations created under a treaty and obligations created under the Charter arose in the ICJ's *Lockerbie* Case,[384] where an issue arose as to requests by the US and the UK for surrender of two suspects for trial,

---

[378] Dörmann & Serralvo, *supra* note 364, at 718 (*citing* Report Submitted to the Security Council by the Secretary-General in Accordance with Resolution 605 (1987), paras. 24–27, UN Doc. S/19443 (Jan. 21, 1988)).

[379] Dörmann & Serralvo, *supra* note 364, at 724 (*citing* Hans-Peter Gasser, *Ensuring Respect for the Geneva Conventions and Protocols: The Role of Third States and the United Nations*, in EFFECTING COMPLIANCE, at 28 (British Institute of International and Comparative Law, Hazel Fox & Michael A. Meyer eds., 1993)).

[380] Dörmann & Serralvo, *supra* note 364, at 725.

[381] *Id.* at 727 (*citing* Articles on State Responsibility, *supra* note 21, Art. 16).

[382] UN Charter, Art. 103.

[383] *See* Constantinides, *supra* note 88, at 4 ("By virtue of Article 103 of the Charter binding Security Council decisions prevail ... over treaty law.").

[384] *Lockerbie (Libya v. UK) Provisional Measures*, *supra* note 85; *Lockerbie (Libya v. U.S.) Provisional Measures*, *supra* note 85.

and whether the requests were consistent with the Montreal Convention.[385] After Libya filed a request for provisional measures, the Security Council passed Resolution 748, imposing mandatory sanctions to secure compliance with the request for surrender.[386] The ICJ then dismissed the provisional measures request on the grounds that, under Article 103, the Montreal Convention obligations were outweighed by obligations created under the Security Council resolution.[387]

Thus, if there were obligations created under the 1949 Geneva Conventions and/or Genocide Convention and these *conflict* with obligations created under a Security Council resolution, Article 103 could suggest that the obligations created under the resolution would prevail; yet, the 1949 Geneva Conventions and Genocide Convention protect *jus cogens* norms, whose protections also accord with the UN's "[p]urposes and [p]rinciples," so it is *not so clear* the Security Council should be creating, or even *can* create, obligations inconsistent with these foundational treaties. For example, could the Security Council pass a resolution that parts of IHL contained in the 1949 Geneva Conventions do not apply in a particular conflict? Could the Security Council pass a resolution that the obligation to "prevent" genocide does not apply to a particular country? Such resolutions would appear problematic, as they would fail to conform to international law (one of the UN's "[p]urposes" under Article 1(1) of the Charter), and therefore fail to accord with the "[p]urposes and [p]rinciples" of the UN as required of the Security Council by Article 24(2).[388] Such resolutions would additionally appear to violate the treaty obligations of individual states on the Security Council who are parties to those treaties.

Thus, even if Article 103 *generally* permits the Security Council, while acting under Chapter VII, to implement resolutions (or use its veto) in

---

[385] Convention for the Suppression of Unlawful Acts against the Safety of Civil Aviation [hereinafter, Montreal Convention].
[386] For discussion of the case, see, e.g., Akande, *supra* note 79, at 311, n.8.
[387] *Id.*
[388] *See* discussion Chapter 4.2 *supra*. Orakhelashvili writes:

> The UN is bound by humanitarian law, which must be complied with in every circumstance by its forces engaged in hostilities. The relevant rules are embodied in the Geneva Conventions, such as the rules protecting civilians and their property, and those distinguishing between military and non-military objectives. The Chapter VII economic sanctions are subject to peremptory norms, particularly the fundamental humanitarian rules, such as the principles of proportionality and necessity. All this implies an obligation not to deprive civilians of access to the goods necessary for their survival, and respective duties of the occupying powers. Any sanctions regime is governed by humanitarian norms essential for the survival of the civilian population, to secure food, water, shelter, medicines and medical care.

Orakhelashvili [The Impact], *supra* note 92, at 66–67.

a way that is inconsistent with treaty obligations, that *should not be* the result related to foundational treaty obligations, such as those contained in the Genocide Convention or 1949 Geneva Conventions, because they protect *jus cogens* norms and accord with the "[p]urposes and [p]rinciples" of the UN.

As argued above (when considering the question of the Council's actions and the need to be consistent with *jus cogens*),[389] recent law from the European Court of Justice and the European Court of Human Rights suggests the need for "harmonizing" obligations created under Security Council resolutions with those created under the European Convention. In *Kadi*,[390] the "European Court of Justice held that guarantees of fundamental rights under EU law could not be displaced by Security Council resolution."[391] And, in *Al-Jedda*,[392] the European Court of Human Rights interpreted the Security Council resolution in question and the European Convention harmoniously, assuming no breach of the Convention was intended by the Security Council.[393] The "harmonious interpretation doctrine" was also followed in *Al-Dulimi v. Switzerland*,[394] where the European Court of Human Rights stated: "unless the Resolutions *explicitly* state otherwise, the [court] presumes that the Council '*does not intend to*' contradict [International Human Rights law]."[395]

---

[389] See Chapter 4.1.6.3 (consistency argument).
[390] Joined Cases Kadi and Al Barakaat, *supra* note 118.
[391] Milanović, [*Al-Skeini* and *Al-Jedda*], *supra* note 160, at 134, citing *Kadi*, *supra* note 95.
[392] *Al-Jedda*, *supra* note 159.
[393] Milanović, *supra* note 160, at 137, citing *Al-Jedda*, *supra* note 159. See also *Al-Jedda*, *supra* note 159, para. 109. The European Court of Human Rights in *Al-Jedda* held:

> [T]he Court considers that, in interpreting [Security Council] resolutions, there must be a presumption that the Security Council does not intend to impose any obligation on Member States to breach fundamental principles of human rights. In the event of any ambiguity in the terms of a Security Council resolution, the Court must therefore choose the interpretation which is most in harmony with the requirements of the Convention and which avoids any conflict of obligations. In the light of the United Nations' important role in promoting and encouraging respect for human rights, it is to be expected that clear and explicit language would be used were the Security Council to intend States to take particular measures which would conflict with their obligations under international human rights law.

Al-Jedda, *supra* note 159, para. 102. While the *Al-Jedda* case suggests the Security Council could displace international human rights law, the *Kadi* case, by contrast, suggests it cannot be displaced. See Milanović, *supra* note 160, at 134. Regardless, the author's argument is that treaties that protect *jus cogens* norms should not be displaced.

[394] *Al-Dulimi*, *supra* note 162.
[395] See Bilgic, *supra* note 162 (comparing the "*Bosphorus* presumption" and the "harmonious interpretation" approaches taken by the European Court of Human Rights when faced with Security Council resolutions that appear to contradict the European Convention).

If courts interpret the Security Council as unable to displace the European Convention, and/or try to harmonize obligations created under Security Council resolutions with obligations created under the European Convention, the Genocide Convention and 1949 Geneva Conventions should receive *no less protective treatment*. That is – regardless of whether the UN Security Council could *ordinarily* displace treaty obligations – it should not be free to violate the obligations created under these foundational treaties (in its resolutions or veto use by permanent members) and/or its powers and resolutions should be harmonious with, and certainly not violate, these foundational treaties. Thus, there may be some inherent limits to the operation of Article 103. Alexander Orakhelashvili concludes that "Article 103 cannot make a resolution which is unlawful under the Charter prevail over other legal norms."[396]

August Reinisch similarly rejects a strict reading of Article 103 when human rights are at issue, on the grounds that Security Council resolutions *and* human rights law *both* need to be respected:

> [O]ne may doubt whether the UN Charter's "formal" solution to solve potential conflicts between international human rights obligations and obligations under binding UN Security Council resolutions in favor of the latter is fully adequate in such situations. Certainly, unconditional preference to UN law would enhance the effectiveness of that legal order. However, where this leads to a conflict with fundamental human rights obligations, a substantive assessment may be required to come to an adequate solution.... Safeguarding human rights standards, in itself an internationalist agenda, is of utmost importance; so is compliance with binding UN Security Council resolutions aiming at maintaining world peace and security. Thus, *it would appear crucial to find a way to achieve both goals at the same time.*[397]

The same approach should apply to respecting the obligations under the Genocide Convention and 1949 Geneva Conventions. "[I]t is 'the dignity and worth of the human person' which is the principal concern of the UN Charter. This concern must guide any interpretation of the instrument."[398]

---

[396] Orakhelashvili [The Impact], *supra* note 92, at 69.

[397] Reinisch [Should Judges Second-Guess], *supra* note 161, at 287 (emphasis added); *id.* (urging the Security Council to "adopt sanctions resolutions in a way that conforms to basic human rights obligations"). *See also* José E. Alvarez, *Judging the Security Council*, 90(1) AM. J. INT'L L. 1, 29 (Jan. 1996) ("Judge Oda [in *Lockerbie*] seemed to be suggesting that the Council might have violated customary international law [in its resolution], and, significantly, he did not add that Article 103 of the Charter licenses the Council to do so with impunity.").

[398] Fassbender, *supra* note 98, at 224, discussing and translating Martin Lailach's reading of the Charter in DIE WAHRUNG DES WELTFRIEDENS UND DER INTERNATIONALEN SICHERHEIT ALS AUFGABE DES SICHERHEITSRATES DER VEREINTEN NATIONEN (1998). Of course, the UN's first stated concern, as set out in the preamble of the Charter

4.3.4 Treaty Obligations Potentially Relevant to Veto Use

If the permanent members,[399] in fact, still hold these treaty obligations while acting on the Council, then:

i) By virtue of being parties to the Genocide Convention:
- They should not veto a resolution with the goal of preventing the commission of genocide, given the Genocide Convention's obligation to "prevent" genocide; and
- They should not veto a resolution with the goal of investigating[400] or prosecuting genocide, given the Genocide Convention's obligation to "punish" genocide.[401]

---

is "to save succeeding generations from the scourge of war." UN Charter pmbl. Yet, the dignity and worth of the human person is as least *a* principal concern of the UN Charter.

[399] Actually, even elected members of the Security Council, where parties to the relevant treaties, also should not vote against resolutions in the situations enumerated:

> An obligation to vote positively is incumbent on all members of the Council. However, the permanent members are in a legally different position to the non-permanent ones, because each of them can actually hinder a decision by itself through the veto. A non-permanent member does not have the power to block a Council decision on its own. Its negative vote can only co-determine the outcome, and it may in any case have a chilling effect on Security Council policies. So it seems that the obligations falling on the non-permanent members should be somewhat less strict than for the [permanent members].

Peters, *supra* note 90, at 39. Yet, even the obligation to vote positively should have caveats that in trying to end or alleviate the commission of atrocity crimes, international law must also be respected. Thus, a resolution designed to end genocide must, for example, not violate the principles of distinction and proportionality if there is a force authorization. Thus, the obligation to vote positively does not necessarily apply to *every* draft resolution put to the Council while atrocity crimes are occurring. *See* note 150 *supra* (similar and discussing the concept of a "credible draft" resolution).

[400] One cannot "punish" genocide if there is no investigation. The ILC recognizes that the obligation to "prosecute" necessarily must contain, preliminarily, an obligation to "investigate." *See* Final Report of the Int'l L. Comm'n, The Obligation to Extradite or Prosecute (*aut dedere aut judicare*) (2014), Y.B. Int'l L. Comm'n, vol. II (Part Two), para. 20 (2014) (discussing the obligation to "investigate" as part of the obligation to "prosecute"), relying upon Questions Relating to the Obligation to Prosecute or Extradite (Belg. v. Sen.), Judgment, 2012 ICJ Rep. 422, 453–54 (July 20). If the obligation to "prosecute" necessarily contains an obligation to "investigate," then the obligation to "punish" must similarly contain an obligation to "investigate."

[401] Here, the primary obligation to "punish" is presumably that of the state on whose territory the perpetrator is located. *See id.* Yet, there is also a positive duty of all states "to cooperate to bring to an end through lawful means any serious breach" "by a State of an obligation arising under a peremptory norm of general international law." Int'l L. Comm'n, Articles on State Responsibility, *supra* note 21, Arts. 40.1, 41.1. If genocide is ongoing, cooperation could potentially include cooperation to ensure investigations and/or prosecutions. Additionally,

4.3 *Treaty Obligations of Individual Permanent Member States* 225

ii) By virtue of being parties to the 1949 Geneva Conventions:
- They should not veto a resolution attempting to ensure compliance with the 1949 Geneva Conventions, given the obligation to "ensure respect for" the 1949 Geneva Conventions in Common Article 1, and that "[e]ach High Contracting Party shall take measures necessary for the suppression of all acts contrary to the provisions of the present Convention[s] other than grave breaches ...";[402]
- They should not veto a resolution with the goal of investigating[403] or prosecuting "grave breaches" of the 1949 Geneva Conventions, given the obligation to prosecute "grave breaches" in the 1949 Geneva Conventions;[404] and
- They should not veto a resolution with the goal of ensuring that "Common Article 3" violations do not occur or with the goal of their investigation or prosecution, given the obligation to "respect and ensure respect for" the 1949 Geneva Conventions and that Common Article 3 is contained in the Conventions,[405] and that the Conventions

---

the ILC explains that, in terms of the obligation to "extradite or prosecute," each State Party, by virtue of obligations *erga omnes*, has "a 'common interest' in [ensuring] compliance with such obligations." Final Report of the Int'l L. Comm'n, The Obligation to Extradite or Prosecute, *supra* note 400, para. 46. Thus, while limited, there appear to be some obligations of third-states where treaties mandate extradition or prosecution, at least regarding peremptory norms.

[402] Geneva Convention I, *supra* note 2, Art. 49, para. 3; Geneva Convention II, *supra* note 2, Art. 50, para. 3; Geneva Convention III, *supra* note 2, Art. 129, para. 3; Geneva Convention IV, *supra* note 2, Art. 146, para 3.

[403] See note 400 *supra* (discussing the need for investigation in order to punish); *see also* Claus Kress, *Reflection on the* Judicare *Limb of the Grave Breaches Regime*, 7 J. INT'L CRIM. JUST. 789 (2009) ("What the *judicare* limb of the grave breaches regime actual entails is a duty to investigate and, where so warranted, to prosecute and convict.").

[404] Again, the primary obligation to prosecute (or extradite) is presumably on the state on whose territory the perpetrator is located. *See, e.g.*, Final Report of the Int'l L. Comm'n, The Obligation to Extradite or Prosecute, *supra* note 400, para. 9 ("The four Geneva Conventions of 1949 contain the same provision whereby each High Contracting Party is obligated to search for persons alleged to have committed, or to have ordered to be committed, grave breaches, and to bring such persons, regardless of their nationality, before its own courts. However, it may also, if it prefers, ... hand such persons over for trial to another High Contracting Party ... ."). Yet, because all States Parties to the 1949 Geneva Conventions owe, under Common Article 1, a duty to "ensure respect" for the Conventions, and prosecuting "grave breaches" is required under the Conventions, then third-states also presumably owe an obligation to *ensure* that grave breaches are prosecuted. See ICRC, *at* https://ihl-databases.icrc.org/customary-ihl/eng/docs/v1_rul_rule144 (in discussion of "ensuring respect" under Common Article 1, listing "investigating possible violations, creating *ad hoc* tribunals and courts, [and] creating the International Criminal Court" as ways to ensure respect if violations occur).

[405] See note 361 *supra* (listing Common Article 3 violations); *see* note 364 *supra* (Common Article 1 applies to Common Article 3).

mandate that "[e]ach High Contracting Party shall take measures necessary for the suppression of all acts contrary to the provisions of the present Convention[s] other than grave breaches . . . ."[406]

iii) By virtue of being parties to Protocol I, as to permanent members who are parties:
- They should not veto a resolution attempting to ensure compliance with Protocol I, given its Article 1 requires states parties to "ensure respect for" its provisions;[407] and
- They should not veto a resolution with the goal of investigating[408] or prosecuting grave breaches enumerated in Protocol I,[409] given the obligation to ensure respect for Protocol I in its Article 1.[410]

iv) By virtue of being parties to Protocol III, as to permanent members who are parties:
- They should not veto a resolution attempting to ensure compliance with Protocol III, given its Article 1 requires states parties to "ensure respect for" its provisions;[411] and
- They should not veto a resolution with the goal of investigating[412] or prosecuting the misuse of distinctive emblems covered in Protocol III,[413] given the obligation to ensure respect for Protocol III in its Article 1, and the obligation in that Protocol "to take measures necessary for the prevention and repression, at all times, of any misuse of the distinctive emblems."[414]

Additionally, it is relevant to consider briefly when the duty to act is triggered. As mentioned above, under the Genocide Convention, the obligations of a state to do its utmost to prevent genocide is triggered when "the State learns of, or should normally have learned of, the existence of a serious risk that genocide will be committed."[415] While this issue is not explicitly addressed in the 1949 Geneva Conventions (or Protocols

---

[406] Geneva Convention I, *supra* note 2, Art. 49, para. 3; Geneva Convention II, *supra* note 2, Art. 50, para. 3; Geneva Convention III, *supra* note 2, Art. 129, para. 3; Geneva Convention IV, *supra* note 2, Art. 146, para 3.
[407] Protocol I, supra note 365, Art. 1.
[408] See note 400 *supra* (discussing the need for investigation in order to punish).
[409] Protocol I, *supra* note 365, Arts. 11, 85(3) (grave breaches)
[410] Id. Art. 1; see also id., Art. 89 (co-operation).
[411] Protocol III, *supra* note 366, Art. 1.
[412] See note 400 *supra* (discussing the need for investigation in order to punish).
[413] See Protocol III, *supra* note 366, Arts. 1–2.
[414] Id. Art. 1, Art. 6(1).
[415] *Bosnia v. Serbia* Case, *supra* note 17, para. 431.

I or III), there is no reason to think a different standard would apply to Geneva Convention violations. That is, the obligation to "ensure respect for" the Conventions (while it should apply at all times), would particularly be triggered when there is knowledge of, or reason to know of, a serious risk that violations are occurring.[416]

Note that "grave breaches" are fairly broadly formulated in the 1949 Geneva Conventions, and one of the grave breaches is "willfully causing great suffering or causing serious injury to body or health."[417] Certainly using chemical weapons, among other violations,[418] could constitute "willfully causing great suffering or causing serious injury to body or health"; thus, chemical weapons use could, arguably, constitute a "grave breach" if utilized during international armed conflict.[419] Similarly, "grave breaches" under Protocol I include "making the civilian population or individual civilians the object of attack" and "launching an indiscriminate attack affecting the civilian population or civilian objects."[420] If chemical weapons are launched toward a civilian population, and given that chemical weapons are "indiscriminate," their use could also constitute a "grave breach" of Protocol I.[421]

---

[416] In this respect, briefings to the UN Security Council would be particularly relevant to triggering a country's "knowledge" or "reason to know" of violations.

[417] Geneva Convention I, *supra* note 2, Art. 50; Geneva Convention II, *supra* note 2, Art. 51; Geneva Convention III, *supra* note 2, Art. 130; Geneva Convention IV, *supra* note 2, Art. 147.

[418] Chemical weapons use is prohibited under various treaties; the author is here examining whether it violates the 1949 Geneva Conventions and Protocol I because of the obligation to "ensure" those conventions are respected.

[419] "The use of chemical weapons is [specifically] prohibited in international armed conflicts in a series of treaties, including the Hague Declaration concerning Asphyxiating Gases, the Geneva Gas Protocol, the Chemical Weapons Convention and the Statute of the International Criminal Court." ICRC, IHL Database, Customary IHL, Rule 74. Chemical Weapons, *at* https://ihl-databases.icrc.org/customary-ihl/eng/docs/v1_rul_rule74#Fn_F4806E2_00001.

[420] *See* Protocol I, *supra* note 365, Art. 85(3)(a)–(b).

[421] Even for the permanent members not parties to Protocol I (the US and Russia), attacking a civilian population and indiscriminate attacks would constitute war crimes. *See, e.g.,* Waldemar A. Solf, *Protection of Civilians against the Effects of Hostilities under Customary International Law and under Protocol I*, 1(1) AM U. INT'L L. REV. 117, 129 (1986) ("Protocol I reaffirms and supports the customary principles that prohibit the attack on civilians and civilian objects, and that requires that distinctions be made between the treatment of combatants and civilians."); L. Lynn Hogue, *Identifying Customary International Law of War in Protocol I: A Proposed Restatement*, 13 LOY. LA INT'L & COMP. L. REV. 279, 297, 299, 300 (1990) (similar); Alexander Schwarz, *War Crimes, in* MAX PLANCK ENCYCLOPEDIA OF PUBLIC INTERNATIONAL LAW, para. 59 (last updated September 2014), *at* http://opil.ouplaw.com/view/10.1093/law:epil/9780199231690/law-9780199231690-e431 ("Due to the high ratification rate of the [Chemical Weapons Convention] (190 States as of September 2014), the prohibition of the use of chemical weapons *inter alia* forms part of customary international law.").

Chemical weapons use is also a violation and war crime if committed in non-international armed conflict.[422]

4.3.5 Treaty Obligations Potentially Relevant to Drafting, Negotiating, and Voting on Resolutions

An argument can also be made that (prior to the issue of the veto arising), all permanent members – indeed, all states serving on the Security Council[423] – additionally have obligations to use their best efforts to cooperate in drafting, negotiating, and voting on, in good faith, Security Council resolutions aimed at preventing or ending the commission of genocide, crimes against humanity, and/or war crimes.

John Heieck makes this argument vis-à-vis the crime of genocide, based on the obligation to "prevent" genocide found in Article I of the Genocide Convention.[424] Yet, as explored above, there are parallel obligations of due diligence contained in the 1949 Geneva Conventions (as well as Protocols I and III for states parties to them) for a state to do its utmost based on its

---

[422] Chemical weapons use could fall within "violence to life and person, in particular murder of all kinds, mutilation, [and] cruel treatment" under Common Article 3. See 1949 Geneva Conventions, Common Article 3(a). See also ICRC, IHL Database, Customary IHL, Rule 74. Chemical Weapons ("The prohibition of the use of chemical weapons contained in the Chemical Weapons Convention applies in all circumstances, including in non-international armed conflicts.").

[423] See notes 431–34 infra and accompanying text (obligation of all states to vote for resolutions in the face of atrocity crimes).

[424] He argues the "due diligence" obligation requires states "not only to cooperate in good faith in negotiating and drafting a resolution under Chapter VII, but also to impose binding decisions, rather than non-binding recommendations ... ." Heieck, supra note 39, at 64. He further argues that states must:

> use their best efforts to impose the necessary and appropriate measures under Article 41 and 42 [of the UN Charter] in an attempt to prevent or suppress the genocide in question. These Articles 41 and 42 measures include, inter alia, the referral of such situations to the International Criminal Court; the imposition of economic sanction, arms embargoes, asset freezes and travel bans; the deployment of international monitors, fact-finding missions and peace-enforcement forces, the institution of safe havens, humanitarian corridors, and no-fly zones, and the authorization of the use of force to protection national, ethnic, racial or religious groups under threat of genocide.

Id. at 64–65. Heieck also concludes that the "due diligence" obligation also "constrains each state from vetoing, either expressly or impliedly, draft resolutions aimed at preventing genocide under Article 27(3)." Id. at 65. See also Andreas Zimmermann, Article 27, in Simma et al., supra note 98, vol. 1, at 887 ("Responsibility under international law is incurred if a State, as a member of the [Security Council], manifestly fails to support or even delay possible [Security Council] measures aimed at preventing genocide, ... which might have contributed to preventing such acts.").

position of influence to "ensure" there are no violations.[425] Furthermore, the ILC finds there is "a positive duty [of all states] to cooperate to bring to an end *any serious breaches*, by a state, of an obligation *arising under a peremptory norm* of international law"[426] – so that cooperation obligations should, in fact, apply to *all three crimes* (including crimes against humanity).[427] "[I]nternational co-operation in solving international problems of ... [a] humanitarian character" is also mandated by UN Charter Article 1(3) as one of the "[p]urposes" of the UN, and this also would apply to all three crimes.[428] Additionally, as discussed above, there are general duties to act and negotiate in good faith that also would apply to all three crimes,[429] and, as discussed above, good faith is also mandated by UN Charter Article 2(2) as one of the "[p]rinciples" of the UN.[430]

While this book focuses primarily on the role of the permanent members of the Security Council (and particularly their veto use), obligations to use due diligence to try to prevent,[431] and/or cooperate in good faith to try to end,[432] the crimes should actually apply to *all states* in their various international capacities: (a) whether they serve as elected members of the Security Council, (b) whether serving as members of the UN General Assembly or in other capacities at the UN; (c) as members of regional organizations, and (d) even in their bilateral relations. This last obligation

---

[425] See Chapter 4.3.2 *supra* (discussing due diligence obligations under the Geneva Conventions).

[426] Int'l L. Comm'n, Articles on State Responsibility, *supra* note 21, Arts. 40.1, 41.1 (emphasis added).

[427] The commission of genocide, crimes against humanity, and war crimes *are* all "serious" breaches of peremptory norms, particularly where the war crimes are large-scale and/or committed pursuant to a plan or policy. Genocide and crimes against humanity, due to their contextual elements, are necessarily "serious" as they are almost necessarily large in scale. *See* Rome Statute, *supra* note 3, pmbl. (covering "the most serious crimes of concern to the international community); Art. 8 (jurisdiction over war crimes "in particular when committed as a part of a plan or policy or as part of a large-scale commission of such crimes").

[428] *See* UN Charter, Art. 1(3).

[429] *See* Chapter 4.2.3 *supra* (good faith obligations).

[430] UN Charter, Art. 2(2).

[431] This would be the obligation vis-à-vis genocide for parties to the Genocide Convention (by virtue of the obligation to "prevent" genocide), and vis-à-vis at least "grave breaches" and "Common Article 3 violations" by virtue of the obligation to "ensure respect" for the Geneva Conventions, and, for parties to them, Protocols I and III.

[432] This would be the obligation vis-à-vis *all three crimes* – genocide, war crimes, and crimes against humanity – as recognized by the ILC and by virtue of general obligations of good faith. *See* Int'l L. Comm'n, Articles on State Responsibility, *supra* note 21, Arts. 40.1, 41.1 (there is a positive duty of all states "to cooperate to bring to an end through lawful means any serious breach" "by a State of an obligation arising under a peremptory norm of general international law."); *see also* Chapter 4.2.3 *supra* (good faith obligations).

would be particularly relevant where a state, by virtue of its political, military, and/or economic ties, is in a position of influence regarding a regime implicated in, or at risk of committing, the crimes. Such bilateral relationships would also be relevant to the permanent members of the Security Council in that – *in capacities other than that of permanent members of the Security Council* – they also should exert their best efforts, where, by virtue of political, military, and/or economic ties, they hold positions of influence regarding a regime implicated in, or at risk of committing, the crimes. It is far from clear that states outside the context of the Security Council, and aside from the question of veto use, are fulfilling these obligations to the extent that they are able. As discussed in Chapter 3, a majority of Member States, many serving regularly as elected members of the Council (as well as two permanent members) are parties to the ACT Code of Conduct. This commits them to take "timely and decisive action to end the commission of genocide, crimes against humanity or war crimes, or to prevent such crimes,"[433] and provides another source of obligation for states that have joined the Code of Conduct.[434]

4.3.6 Application of Foundational Treaty Obligations to Veto Use

It may be helpful to take a closer look at some recent Security Council practice to see how these foundational treaty obligations apply to use of the veto. The situations discussed in this section relate to Myanmar and Syria.[435]

4.3.6.1 The Situation in Myanmar

Turning to the situation in Myanmar, the Independent International Fact-Finding Mission on Myanmar established by the UN Human Rights Council concluded by September 2018 that credible evidence exists that genocide (as well as war crimes and crimes against humanity) have been committed in Myanmar particularly against members of the Rohingya ethnic group.[436]

---

[433] "Code of conduct regarding Security Council action against genocide, crimes against humanity or war crimes." Annex I to UN Doc. A/70/621–S/2015/978, Dec. 14, 2015, at www.globalr2p.org/media/files/n1543357.pdf. See Chapter 3.1.4 for discussion of the Code of Conduct. Among the permanent members, France and the UK are parties.

[434] As explored in Chapter 3, while the Code of Conduct is drafted as a "soft law" document, there are actually hard law obligations underlying parts of it. *See* Chapter 3.2.1.

[435] As discussed in Chapters 1 and 5, these are by no means the only problematic situations of veto use or veto threats, but are illustrative.

[436] Report of the Detailed Findings of the Independent International Fact-Finding Mission on Myanmar, UN Doc. A/HRC/39/CRP.2 (Sept. 17, 2018). *See also* Report of the Independent

Specifically, the Fact-Finding Mission concluded that named senior generals of the Myanmar military should be investigated and prosecuted in an international criminal tribunal for genocide, crimes against humanity, and war crimes.[437] China then attempted to stop a Security Council briefing on Myanmar by the Chair of the UN Fact-Finding Mission.[438] While the 2018 report is fairly recent, such crimes in Myanmar have reportedly been occurring for quite a few years, so awareness of the serious risk of genocide and other crimes likely existed far earlier.[439]

Here, the obligation to "prevent" genocide is relevant, meaning every state must do whatever is within its power, legally,[440] to "prevent" genocide, even (according to the *Bosnia v. Serbia* decision) genocide occurring in *another* state.[441] A permanent member, by virtue of its position of influence, should have a particularly weighty obligation to "prevent" genocide, as well as any country with political, military, and/or economic ties to the country. Should any state be both a permanent member and have political, military, and/or economic ties to the country in question, the obligation of due diligence to do the utmost to "prevent" genocide would seem to apply the most.[442] Thus, given these obligations of due diligence to do whatever is within a state's power to

---

International Fact-Finding Mission on Myanmar, UN Doc. A/HRC/42/50 (Aug. 8, 2019), *at* https://documents-dds-ny.un.org/doc/UNDOC/GEN/G19/236/74/PDF/G1923674.pdf?OpenElement. The ICJ acknowledged this finding as the basis for its grant of provisional measures. See *Gambia v. Myanmar* Case, *supra* note 331, paras. 72, 86 (observing that the Fact-Finding Mission on Myanmar "'conclude[d] on reasonable grounds that the Rohingya people remain at serious risk of genocide'" and granting provisional measures).

[437] UN Doc. A/HRC/39/CRP.2, at Summary.

[438] Michelle Nichols, *China Fails to Stop U.N. Security Council Myanmar Briefing*, REUTERS (Oct. 24, 2018), *at* www.reuters.com/article/us-myanmar-rohingya-un/china-fails-to-stop-un-security-council-myanmar-briefing-idUSKCN1MY2QU. This is a good illustration of the efforts by a permanent member (China, in this case) to try to ensure that a situation is not considered (and followed-up on) as a separate agenda item.

[439] See note 451 *infra* and accompanying text (discussing a Burmese 1988 military document entitled "Rohingya extermination plan").

[440] See *Bosnia v. Serbia* Case, *supra* note 17, para. 430 ("The State's capacity to influence must also be assessed by *legal criteria*, since it is clear that every State may only act within the limits permitted by international law."). While the argument for "humanitarian intervention" can sometimes be made and has been made by some states, *see* Chapter 2, the ICJ is fairly clearly not endorsing it under Article 1 of the Genocide Convention, at least not in the *Bosnia v. Serbia* Case.

[441] See notes 337–55 *supra* and accompanying text.

[442] By this same logic, even the elected ten members of the Council should not vote against a resolution designed to "prevent" or alleviate the commission of genocide, as they too would have the obligation to use their best efforts to "prevent" genocide, if parties to the Genocide Convention. See Chapter 4.3.5 *supra* ("Treaty Obligations Potentially Relevant to Drafting, Negotiating, and Voting on Resolutions").

prevent genocide, the veto of a resolution designed to prevent or alleviate genocide against the Rohingya and/or other ethnic groups within Myanmar would be inconsistent with the obligation to "prevent" genocide in the Genocide Convention.[443] As explained above, because the Council's powers should be interpreted under the Charter in a way that is consistent with such a foundational treaty as the Genocide Convention, and because that Convention protects a *jus cogens* norm with which the Council's work should be consistent,[444] a veto in the face of ongoing genocide (such as thought to be occurring in Myanmar)[445] should be considered *ultra vires* of the proper exercise of Security Council power.[446]

While, as of the time of writing, there have not been recent vetoes related to the situation in Myanmar, more than ten years earlier, in January 2007, two vetoes were cast against a resolution related to the situation in Myanmar, which certainly appear legally questionable, particularly in light of subsequent developments. The vetoed resolution would have called on the Government of Myanmar "to cease military attacks against civilians in ethnic minority regions and in particular to put an end to the associated human rights and *humanitarian law violations* against persons belonging to *ethnic nationalities*, including *widespread rape and other forms of sexual violence* carried out by members of the armed forces."[447] First, as to the IHL violations, under Common Article 1 of the Geneva Conventions, responsibility is incurred if a state fails to "use every means at their disposal,"[448] which "covers *everything* a state can do to prevent the commission, or the repetition, of acts contrary to the convention[s]."[449] The crimes enumerated in the draft resolution overlap with Common Article 3 war crimes: "violence to life and person, in particular murder of all kinds,

---

[443] See Heieck, *supra* note 39, at 65 (arguing that the "due diligence" obligation "constrains each state from vetoing, either expressly or impliedly, draft resolutions aimed at preventing genocide"); Arbour, *supra* note 342, at 454 ("One has to wonder why the exercise of a veto blocking an initiative designed to reduce the risk of, or put an end to, genocide would not constitute a violation of the vetoing States' obligations under the Genocide Convention.").

[444] See Chapter 4.3.3 *supra* (consistency argument in this section).

[445] Obviously, the crimes have not yet been adjudicated to constitute genocide, but the responsibility to "prevent" genocide is triggered by a "serious risk" of the crimes occurring, so requires no such adjudication. See note 436 *supra* (ICJ ruling regarding Myanmar).

[446] "[G]enocide is a clear example of an act which is prohibited by *jus cogens* ... and that the permanent five must abide by a restriction of their power of veto under Article 27(3) of the Charter where genocide is occurring or where there is a *prima facie* case for suspecting its occurrence." Yiu, *supra* note 97, at 208.

[447] S/2007/14 (vetoed by China and the Russian Federation) (emphasis added).

[448] Dörmann & Serralvo, *supra* note 364, at 735.

[449] *Id.* at 731 (emphasis added), *citing* Pictet Commentary, *supra* note 369, at 367.

4.3 Treaty Obligations of Individual Permanent Member States

mutilation, cruel treatment and torture," and "outrages upon personal dignity, in particular humiliating and degrading treatment."[450] Calling on a state to end IHL violations is certainly one means at the disposal of Security Council Member States; thus, already in 2007, vetoing permanent members appear to be doing the opposite of *ensuring* respect for the 1949 Geneva Conventions. Second, as to genocide, the draft states the violence was being committed against "ethnic nationalities" (and, apart from the draft, it was well-known that particularly members of the Rohingya ethnic group have been and are being targeted). In fact, there has been a Burmese military document entitled the "Rohingya extermination plan" since 1988.[451] Given the responsibility to prevent genocide is triggered by the "serious risk" of genocide,[452] and that a state must "take *all measures* to prevent genocide which were within its power and *which might have contributed* to preventing the genocide,"[453] the resolution (had it passed) *might have contributed* to preventing genocide. Thus, the vetoes (cast by China and Russia) seem additionally questionable on this ground, also given the Security Council's

---

[450] 1949 Geneva Conventions, Common Article 3 (a), (c). See also note 364 *supra* (Common Article 1 applies to Common Article 3 war crimes).

[451] Doug Bock Clark, *Inside the Rohingya Refugee Camps, Traumatised Exiles Ask Why the World Won't Call the Humanitarian Crisis "Genocide,"* POST MAG. (Jan. 16, 2018) (discussing an "11-point scheme detailed in a government report ... titled 'Rohingya Extermination Plan'"), at www.scmp.com/magazines/post-magazine/long-reads/article/2128432/inside-rohingya-refugee-camps-traumatised-exiles. *See also* Zimmerman, *supra* note 424, 887 ("Responsibility under international law is incurred if a State, as a member of the [Security Council], manifestly fails to support or *even delay* possible [Security Council] measures aimed at preventing genocide, ... which might have contributed to the commission of such acts.") (emphasis added).

[452] *Bosnia v. Serbia* Case, *supra* note 17, para. 431.

[453] *Id.*, para. 430 (emphasis added); *see also Gambia v. Myanmar* Case, *supra* note 331 (ordering that "Myanmar must, in accordance with its obligations under the Convention, in relation to the members of the Rohingya group in its territory, take all measures within its power to prevent the commission of all acts within the scope of Article II of the Convention ...."). Admittedly, passage of that resolution (one of condemnation) likely would not in itself have prevented the crimes, but its veto may have emboldened the Government of Myanmar by suggesting it would be "protected" by the veto power from Security Council condemnation or other measures, and this may have contributed to the commission of later crimes, including genocide. *See Bosnia v. Serbia* Case, *supra* note 17, at para. 430 ("It is irrelevant whether the State whose responsibility is in issue claims, or even proves, that even if it had employed all means reasonably at its disposal, they would not have sufficed to prevent the commission of genocide. As well as being generally difficult to prove, this is irrelevant to the breach of the obligation of conduct in question, the more so since the possibility remains that the combined efforts of several States, each complying with its obligation to prevent, might have achieved the result – averting the commission of genocide – which the efforts of only one State were insufficient to produce.").

capacity to influence, and, in particular, China's capacity to influence the government of Myanmar.[454]

Similarly, by virtue of the Genocide Convention obligations to "prevent" and "punish" genocide (and the ILC's recognition that "investigation" is necessary to prosecute crimes),[455] and the obligation in the 1949 Geneva Conventions to "ensure" against violations, which should cover Common Article 3 war crimes,[456] one can envision a number of vetoes that could be problematic. For example, if there were a resolution put to the Council to: (i) create an investigative mechanism for crimes committed in Myanmar,[457] (ii) refer the situation in Myanmar to the ICC,[458] or (iii) create a hybrid or ad hoc international criminal tribunal to prosecute crimes committed in Myanmar, it would appear incumbent on permanent members not to veto such a resolution, assuming it attracts the nine votes otherwise required to pass.[459] Presumably, the other elected ten members, at least if parties to the Genocide Convention,[460] also ought to vote

---

[454] See, e.g., U.S. Institute of Peace, *China's Role in Myanmar's Internal Conflicts* (Sept. 14, 2018), at www.usip.org/publications/2018/09/chinas-role-myanmars-internal-conflicts ("Driven by security concerns, economic interests, and a desire for political influence in a country with which it shares a 1,500-mile border, China is playing a key role in Myanmar's internal security and peace process.").

[455] See note 400 *supra* (discussing the need for investigation in order to "punish"). The linkage between having criminal penalties and the obligation to "prevent" genocide was also acknowledged by the ICJ. See *Bosnia v. Serbia* Case, *supra* note 17, para. 426 ("One of the most effective ways of preventing criminal acts, in general, is to provide penalties for persons committing such acts, and to impose those penalties effectively on those who commit the acts one is trying to prevent."). As mentioned above, if one must "investigate" in order to "prosecute" (as the ILC establishes), then one must similarly "investigate" in order to "punish."

[456] See note 364 *supra* (Common Article 1 applies to Common Article 3 war crimes).

[457] Now that the Human Rights Council voted to create the Independent Investigative Mechanism for Myanmar (IIMM) the question whether the Security Council should create such a mechanism is likely moot. See UNGA, Human Rights Council, Situation of Human Rights of Rohingya Muslims and Other Minorities in Myanmar, UN Doc. A/HRC/39/L.22 (Sept. 25, 2018).

[458] Even if a permanent member were to somehow prove that an ICC referral would not have sufficed to prevent further acts of genocide, this would not be sufficient to impede attribution of state responsibility; the possibility would remain that a combination with other efforts would have had the desired effect. See *Bosnia v. Serbia* Case, *supra* note 17, para. 430. The ICC has jurisdiction over deportation and other crimes against the Rohingya where at least one element of the crime occurred in Bangladesh (a State Party to the Rome Statute). See Decision on the 'Prosecution's Request for a Ruling on Jurisdiction under Article 19(3) of the Statute,' ICC-RoC46(3)-01/18 (Sept. 6, 2018). However, this does not obviate the need for jurisdiction over crimes committed solely within Myanmar.

[459] As noted above, there is no need to veto unless there are nine affirmative votes.

[460] This obligation probably would also apply to a country not party to the Genocide Convention, given that there is "a positive duty [of all states] to cooperate to bring to an end any serious breaches, by a state, of an obligation arising under a peremptory norm of international law." Int'l L. Comm'n, Articles on State Responsibility, *supra* note 21, Arts. 40.1, 41.1. A mechanism to investigate and/or prosecute is one way to attempt to bring violations to an end.

4.3 Treaty Obligations of Individual Permanent Member States 235

in favor of such a resolution. It would not appear to matter much whether a permanent member votes in favor of the resolution or abstains, as it could pass in either event, although, given the obligation is to "prevent" and "punish" genocide, a positive vote would appear appropriate. Note that where accountability is blocked at the Security Council, if there is no other reasonable prospect of investigation and/or prosecution for the bulk of the crimes (for example, crimes occurring solely within Myanmar),[461] veto use by a permanent member acts like a de facto amnesty. Yet, under international law, amnesty is prohibited for genocide, crimes against humanity, and war crimes.[462]

As already discussed, the above logic does not lead to the conclusion that *every time* genocide, "grave breaches," or "Common Article 3" violations are suspected of occurring members of the Security Council *must* vote in favor of, or abstain from voting on, creating a tribunal or referral to the ICC.[463] Certainly, if there were a reasonable likelihood that: (i) investigations and/or prosecutions could occur in the country where the crimes occurred, (ii) a significant number of the perpetrators could be prosecuted in countries with universal jurisdiction laws or other forms of jurisdiction, or (iii) perpetrators could be prosecuted before another tribunal with jurisdiction over the situation, then such measure might prove unnecessary. (Of course, if there were viable alternatives, the Council probably would not be voting on implementing mechanisms for investigation and/or prosecution.)

4.3.6.2 Veto Threats

Related to the situation in Myanmar (as well as other situations), a further relevant question is if *use* of the veto is problematic, whether the *threat* of the

---

[461] See note 458 *supra* (limited ICC jurisdiction exists to the extent an element of the crime occurred in Bangladesh).

[462] "[A]mnesties for serious violations of human rights and humanitarian law — war crimes, crimes against humanity and genocide – are generally considered illegal." Office of the UN High Commission for Human Rights, Rule-of-Law Tools for Post-Conflict States: Truth Commissions, at 12 (2006). For example, when the UN endorsed the Sierra Leone Peace Agreement it was quite specific about excluding core international crimes. See Orakhelashvili [The Impact], *supra* note 92, at 81 ("Resolution 1260 (1999) welcomed the signing of the Peace Agreement in Sierra Leone, and called upon all parties to implement it fully. At its signing, the UN Secretary-General stated that the amnesty provided for in the agreement would not extend to perpetrators of international crimes. Therefore, the Council cannot be presumed to have endorsed immunity for perpetrators of international crimes. Although the Secretary General cannot speak for the Council, it must be assumed that the latter was aware that the former committed the UN with that qualification.").

[463] See text accompanying note 321 *supra*.

use of the veto is similarly problematic.[464] Such an argument could be made. For instance, in the *Nuclear Weapons* Advisory Opinion, the ICJ opined that: "If the use of force itself in a given case is illegal – for whatever reason – the threat to use such force will likewise be illegal."[465] That threats are indeed problematic is reinforced by the prohibition in Article 2(4) of the UN Charter of the "threat or use of force against the territorial integrity or political independence of any state, or in any other manner inconsistent with the Purposes of the United Nations."[466] Also suggesting that "threats" can be a serious matter, the Vienna Convention on the Law of Treaties provides that a treaty will be void if procured by the "threat or use of force."[467] Under analogous logic, if the *use* of the veto is problematic in the face of genocide, crimes against humanity, and/or war crimes, the *threat* of the veto should likewise be problematic. This conclusion can also be reached given the due diligence obligations required under the Genocide Convention and 1949 Geneva Conventions (and Protocols I and III for states parties to them). A state would hardly be doing its utmost to try to "prevent" genocide, or "ensure respect for" the Geneva Conventions, if it threatens to employ its veto related to condemnation of, or measures designed to alleviate or prevent, genocide or IHL violations.[468] Clearly, a threat to veto a resolution during ongoing genocide[469] can block a resolution just as much as veto use, and

---

[464] See Chapter 1.3.2 for a discussion of threats and inaction related to Myanmar and other situations. See Chapter 5 for a discussion of veto threats related to Darfur.

[465] *Nuclear Weapons* Advisory Opinion, *supra* note 57, para. 47. *See also* Sarvarian, *supra* note 22, at 28 ("It is averred that the use of force against Syria would have been unlawful, which by extension renders the threat of force unlawful.") (*citing Nicaragua* Case, *supra* note 376, at 107–08, para. 205; *Nicaragua* Case, *supra* note 376, para. 191 ("Every State has the duty to refrain from the threat or use of force to violate the existing international boundaries of another State or as a means of solving international disputes, including territorial disputes and problems concerning frontiers of States."), and *citing* GA Res. 2625 (XXV), Friendly Relations and Co-operation among States in accordance with the Charter of the United Nations).

[466] UN Charter, Art. 2(4).

[467] VCLT, *supra* note 34, Art. 52 (Coercion of a State by the Threat or Use of Force).

[468] *See* Heieck, *supra* note 39, at 65 (arguing that the "due diligence" obligation "constrains each state from vetoing, either expressly *or impliedly*, draft resolutions aimed at preventing genocide") (emphasis added); Yiu, *supra* note 97, at 236 ("The [Security Council] itself is bound by *jus cogens* such that any use of the veto (*or threatened use of the veto*) in a manner inconsistent with *jus cogens* tenders that action or omission a breach of international law.") (emphasis added). A threat to veto a resolution regarding crimes against humanity should also be problematic given the obligation to cooperate in ending such violations. *See* Int'l L. Comm'n, Articles on State Responsibility, *supra* note 21, Arts. 40.1, 41.1 (there is a positive duty of all states "to cooperate to bring to an end through lawful means any serious breach" "by a State of an obligation arising under a peremptory norm of general international law.").

[469] For discussion of French, US, and, by some accounts, also UK threats or implicit threats to veto any Security Council resolution using the word "genocide" or to send in more robust

should be viewed as equally legally problematic. When the highest body of the UN blocks condemnation of, or measures designed to prevent or curtail the commission of, genocide or IHL violations (whether by veto use or threat of the veto), that can appear to the country at issue as if it were being given a "green light" – that is, the distinct danger of a lack of condemnation is that it could be seen as akin to permission to commit or continue to commit crimes, or not rein in perpetrators under the state's control.[470]

4.3.6.3 The Situation in Syria

As to the situation in Syria, many of the vetoes cast (enumerated above)[471] appear legally problematic, particularly in light of Geneva Convention obligations. This section considers only a few examples: (a) veto of renewal of chemical weapons inspections that were attributing responsibility to the side using the weapons,[472] (b) veto of referral of the situation in Syria to the ICC;[473] and (c) veto of a resolution that would have condemned indiscriminate aerial bombardment in Aleppo.[474]

If chemical weapons use is considered a grave breach,[475] then the three vetoes cast against the renewal of the mandate of the JIM (which blocked identifying potential perpetrators and thus blocked investigations) and veto of the referral of the situation in Syria to the ICC (a court with jurisdiction to prosecute "grave breaches")[476] appear at odds with the obligation to "prosecute" "grave breaches" of the 1949 Geneva Conventions and/or Protocol I.[477] As previously noted, according to the ILC, part of the obligation to "extradite

---

forces during the 1994 genocide in Rwanda, see Chapter 1.3.2. For a detailed discussion of veto threats related to Darfur, see Chapter 5.2.

[470] The same argument can be made regarding crimes against humanity, although it is not treaty-based. See Chapter 4.3.5 *supra* (obligations covering all three crimes).

[471] See Chapter 4.2.4.1 *supra*.

[472] S/2017/884 (vetoed by the Russian Federation); S/2017/962 (vetoed by the Russian Federation); S/2017/970 (vetoed by the Russian Federation).

[473] S/2014/348 (vetoed by the Russian Federation and China).

[474] S/2016/1846 (vetoed by the Russian Federation).

[475] See notes 417–19 *supra* and accompanying text.

[476] See Rome Statute, Art. 8(2)(a) ("grave breaches").

[477] These vetoes – of renewal of the mandate of the JIM (three times) and referral of the situation in Syria to the ICC are also examined above. See Chapter 4.2.4 *supra*. But, there, they are examined as to whether the vetoes accord with the UN's "[p]urposes and [p]rinciples"; here, they are examined in terms of compliance with treaty obligations of the individual permanent member states. The veto of the ICC referral blocked not only prosecution of chemical weapons use, but also prosecution of other war crimes as well as crimes against humanity and genocide (by ISIL members), so is problematic for additional reasons.

or prosecute" includes the obligation to "investigate."[478] While the primary obligation to extradite or prosecute (and "investigate" before one prosecutes) is on the state on whose territory the perpetrator is located, as explained above, other States Parties to the 1949 Geneva Conventions and Protocol I owe an obligation to "ensure respect" for the Conventions,[479] which should include "ensuring" grave breaches are prosecuted.[480] If third states must help "ensure" grave breaches are prosecuted (and, first, investigated), it appears out of line with these obligations to veto renewal of the mandate of the JIM. Furthermore, the ILC recognizes that one way to fulfill the obligation to "extradite or prosecute" is to surrender the accused to a "competent international criminal tribunal" to conduct the investigation or prosecution.[481] Where national court investigations and/or prosecutions of grave breaches are not occurring (for instance, in Syria), and prosecution of "foreign fighters" returning to countries with universal jurisdiction laws or other forms of jurisdiction would likely result in only a limited number of prosecutions, it also appears out of line with the obligation to "ensure" that "grave breaches" are prosecuted to veto referral to the ICC. The veto of the ICC referral is also legally questionable in light of the obligation to "prevent" and "punish" genocide, given that ISIL members are suspected of committing genocide against the Yazidis.[482]

Note that "a State with close political, economic, and/or military ties (for example, through equipping and training of armed forces or joint planning of operations) to one of the belligerents has a stronger obligation to ensure

---

[478] See note 400 *supra* (duty to investigate).

[479] 1949 Geneva Conventions, *supra* note 2, Common Article 1; Protocol I, *supra* note 365, Common Article 1.

[480] Common Article 1 appears to apply to the whole 1949 Geneva Conventions, and hence would apply to the obligation to prosecute "grave breaches." See ICRC, at https://ihl-databases.icrc.org/customary-ihl/eng/docs/v1_rul_rule144 (in discussion of "ensuring respect" under Common Article 1, listing "investigating possible violations, creating ad hoc tribunals and courts, [and] creating the International Criminal Court" as ways to ensure respect if violations occur).

[481] Final Report of the Int'l L. Comm'n, The Obligation to Extradite or Prosecute, *supra* note 400, para. 27 ("With the establishment of the International Criminal Court and various *ad hoc* international criminal tribunals, there is now the possibility that a State faced with an obligation to extradite or prosecute an accused person might have recourse to a third alternative – that of surrendering the suspect to a competent international criminal tribunal.").

[482] See Report of the Independent International Commission of Inquiry on the Syrian Arab Republic, "They Came to Destroy": ISIS Crimes against the Yazidis, para. 165, UN Doc. A/HRC/32/CRP.2 (June 15, 2016). While there is an Iraq investigative team collecting evidence of crimes committed by ISIL, it has no capacity to prosecute. See S/RES/2379 (Sept. 21, 2017) (creating the United Nations Investigative Team to Promote Accountability for Crimes Committed by Da'esh/ISIL (UNITAD)).

respect for IHL by its ally."[483] Obligations of due diligence would be "even more pronounced if third States provide support, directly, or indirectly, to a party to an ongoing armed conflict."[484]

A similar argument can be made as to violations of Common Article 3, given the Geneva Conventions also obligate states to "ensure" these war crimes are not committed,[485] and the Rome Statute also has jurisdiction to prosecute violations of Common Article 3.[486] Whether one relies on (a) the "grave breaches" provision in the 1949 Geneva Conventions or Protocol I, or (b) Common Article 3, is determined by whether the situation in Syria, or the aspect of the conflict being examined, is characterized as international or non-international armed conflict. The main conflict appears to be non-international, with certain aspects being simultaneously international armed conflict.[487]

Another example of a questionable veto occurred on October 8, 2016, with veto of a resolution that would have expressed outrage at the alarming number of civilian casualties, including those caused by indiscriminate aerial

---

[483] Dörmann & Serralvo, *supra* note 364, at 724 (*citing* Gasser, *supra* note 379, at 28).

[484] *Id.* at 725. Additionally, of course, "third States are under the obligation not to knowingly aid or assist in the commission of IHL violations." *Id.* at 727 (*citing* Articles on State Responsibility, *supra* note 21, Art. 16).

[485] *See* note 364 *supra* (Common Article 1 applies to Common Article 3 war crimes).

[486] *See* Rome Statute, Art. 8(2)(c) (Common Article 3 violations).

[487] *Compare* Report of the Independent International Commission of Inquiry on the Syrian Arab Republic, A/HRC/34/64, Annex I, at 23 (Feb. 2, 2017) (classifying the situation in Syria as a non-international armed conflict); Terry D. Gill, *Classifying the Conflict in Syria*, 92 INT'L L. STUD. 353, 375 (2016) ("This author takes the position that this separate conflict [with ISIL] is ... non-international, notwithstanding the lack of consent by the Syrian government. Coalition actions are directed almost exclusively against [ISIL], which is in firm control of a significant portion of Syrian territory, population and infrastructure, rather than Syrian government-held territory, population or infrastructure; also classifying the conflict between the Kurds in Syria and Turkey as non-international."); *with* David Wallace, Amy McCarthy & Shane R. Reeves, *Trying to Make Sense of the Senseless: Classifying the Syrian War Under the Law of Armed Conflict*, 25 MICH. ST. INT'L L. REV. 555, 593 (2017) ("The Syrian hostilities are primarily non-international armed conflicts, with the exception of the U.S. and Syria, which are now involved in an international armed conflict."); *Situation in Syria Constitutes International Armed Conflict – Red Cross*, REUTERS (Apr. 7, 2017), at www.reuters.com/article/us-mideast-crisis-syria-redcross-idUSKBN17924T (spokesperson for the ICRC told Reuters: "The situation in Syria now 'amounts to an international armed conflict' after U.S. missile strikes on a Syrian air base."); *and with* Geneva Academy, *Rule of Law in Armed Conflicts, Classification, International Armed Conflicts in Syria*, at www.rulac.org/browse/conflicts/international-armed-conflict-in-syria ("Due to the use of force by the U.S.-led coalition against the Islamic State group in Syria without the consent of the Syrian government, there is an international armed conflict. In addition, Turkey is using force against both the Islamic State group and Kurdish militia in Syria without the consent of the Syrian government.").

bombardment, in Aleppo.[488] It is difficult to see how that veto is in line with the obligation to "ensure respect for" the 1949 Geneva Conventions (including Common Article 3) and Protocol I, when "launching an indiscriminate attack" is a "grave breach" under Protocol I.[489] During non-international armed conflict, "launching an indiscriminate attack" arguably constitutes a Common Article 3 violation.[490] Common Article 1 requires states to "use every means at their disposal" to ensure against violations,[491] which "covers *everything* a state can do to prevent the commission, or the repetition, of acts contrary to the convention[s]."[492] Calling on a state to end IHL violations such as "indiscriminate aerial bombardment" is most certainly something Security

---

[488] S/2016/846 (vetoed by the Russian Federation). Similar arguments can be made as to the veto cast on September 19, 2019 of a resolution that would have created a ceasefire in Idlib province and condemned indiscriminate aerial bombardment. See S/2019/756 (vetoed by the Russian Federation and China).

[489] Protocol I, *supra* note 385, Art. 85(3)(b). While two permanent members are not parties to Protocol I, "indiscriminate attacks" also constitute a war crime under customary international law. See note 421 *supra*.

[490] While lacking specificity, Common Article 3 prohibits "violence to life and person." 1949 Geneva Conventions, *supra* note 2, Art. 3(a).

[491] Dörmann & Serralvo, *supra* note 364, at 735.

[492] *Id.* at 731 (emphasis added), *citing* Pictet Commentary, *supra* note 369, at 367. John Heieck analyzes the situation as follows:

> In applying the law to the facts of Syria, Russia and China had a positive duty to prevent war crimes because all three prongs of the due diligence standard were satisfied. First, as two of the most powerful states in the world, Russia and China had a duty to do everything within their considerable power that might have contributed to the prevention of war crimes. Second, Russia and China had the capacity to effectively influence the government forces due to their extensive political, military and economic ties with the Assad family. And while they lacked the same ties with the opposition forces, Russia and China nevertheless had the capacity to effectively influence even these forces due to their position as permanent members on the [Security Council]. As [permanent] members ... , Russia and China had the ability, and arguably the obligation ... to cooperate with the other [Security Council] members to impose mandatory demands and binding decisions on the opposition—and government—forces through [Security Council] resolutions. As a result, Russia and China had the capacity to effectively influence *all* parties to the conflict. Third, Russia and China were aware, or should have been aware, of the existence of a serious risk that war crimes would occur in Syria due to numerous reports from the ... commission of inquiry .... Therefore, as early as 23 November 2011, Russia and China had a positive duty to prevent war crimes in Syria.

John Heieck, *Emerging Voices: Illegal Vetoes in the Security Council—How Russia and China Breached Their Duty under* Jus Cogens *to Prevent War Crimes in Syria*, OPINIO JURIS (Aug. 14, 2013), *at* http://opiniojuris.org/2013/08/14/emerging-voices-illegal-vetoes-in-the-security-council-how-russia-and-china-breached-their-duty-under-jus-cogens-to-prevent-war-crimes-in-syria. While Heieck analyzes the duty to act regarding war crimes as *"jus cogens,"* to this author, his analysis fits better as to duties of due diligence created by the Geneva Conventions.

4.3 Treaty Obligations of Individual Permanent Member States 241

Council Member States could do to try to "ensure" the Geneva Conventions are not violated, and the veto of the resolution appears to be the opposite of "ensuring" Geneva Conventions protections. Such obligations would apply to any situation, not solely the situation in Syria, and, again, the elected ten members also should not vote against a resolution aimed at punishing "grave breaches," "Common Article 3" violations, or ensuring respect for the 1949 Geneva Conventions, or (for the elected members who are parties to them) Protocols I and/or III, or probably IHL more broadly.[493]

Again, while it is arguable that all these treaty-based obligations could be outweighed (if one employs a strict reading of Article 103 of the Charter), the stronger argument would be that the Security Council *should be operating in a way that is consistent with the obligations under these foundational treaties* which protect *jus cogens* norms and accord with the "[p]urposes and [p]rinciples" of the UN. In short, one should not read Article 103 to permit states serving on the Security Council to disregard obligations under the Genocide Convention and 1949 Geneva Conventions.[494] The obligation of states to cooperate to end the commission of genocide, crimes against humanity, and war crimes applies regardless,[495] as would the obligations to negotiate and act in good faith.[496] These obligations would apply to all three crimes – genocide, crimes against humanity, and war crimes.

By focusing primarily on "grave breaches," violations of Common Article 3, and obligations under the 1949 Geneva Conventions (and to some extent Protocols I and III), the author in no way means to minimize the severity of other war crimes or crimes against humanity. While one can make similar arguments about other war crimes, this chapter takes a more conservative approach because all UN Member States, including all permanent members, are parties to the 1949 Geneva Conventions. It is also possible to make similar arguments with respect to crimes against humanity,[497] only, they would not at

---

[493] See Dörmann & Serralvo, *supra* note 364, at 735 ("[Common Article] 1 epitomizes the commitment of States to avoid IHL violations taking place in the future. It does so by creating a framework whereby States not party to a particular armed conflict must use every means at their disposal to ensure that the belligerents comply with the Geneva Conventions and [Additional Protocol] 1, *and probably the whole body of IHL*.") (emphasis added).

[494] See Chapter 4.3.3 *supra* (consistency argument this section).

[495] See Int'l L. Comm'n, Articles on State Responsibility, *supra* note 21, Arts. 40.1, 41.1.

[496] See Chapter 4.2.3 *supra* (good faith obligations).

[497] The ILC, for example, recognizes that there is an obligation to prosecute crimes against humanity. *See* Int'l L. Comm'n, 1996 Draft Code against the Peace and Security of Mankind with Commentaries, at 27, Art. 8 ("Without prejudice to the jurisdiction of an international criminal court, the State Party in the territory of which an individual alleged to have committed a crime set out in article 17 [genocide], 18 [crimes against humanity] ... or 20 [war crimes] is found shall extradite or prosecute that individual.").

present be treaty-based as the crimes against humanity treaty is not finalized.[498] When finalized and in force, it could facilitate making such arguments.[499] Meanwhile, arguments about the need to prevent and/or punish crimes against humanity and/or additional war crimes (and the obligation not to utilize the veto as to resolutions aimed at curtailing or preventing such crimes) would rest on *erga omnes* obligations,[500] general obligations to cooperate,[501] and obligations of good faith.[502]

4.4 SEEKING AN ADVISORY OPINION FROM THE INTERNATIONAL COURT OF JUSTICE AND THE ISSUE OF JUDICIAL REVIEW

Given the legal issues articulated in this chapter concerning use of the veto in the face of genocide, crimes against humanity, and/or war crimes, and whether such veto use is consistent with (a) *jus cogens*, (b) the "[p]urposes and [p]rinciples" of the UN, and/or (c) foundational treaty obligations of the individual permanent members, the question of obtaining judicial review regarding these legal issues arises. The author is here suggesting the need for judicial review of the questions in the abstract by way of an advisory opinion requested by the General Assembly, although it might be possible to pursue such issues also in the context of a contentious case. The ICJ would be the appropriate court to render such review, as Article 96 of the UN Charter provides that "[t]he General Assembly or the Security Council may request the International Court of Justice to give an advisory opinion on any legal question."[503]

---

[498] *See* Int'l L. Comm'n, Draft Articles on Prevention and Punishment of Crimes against Humanity, *supra* note 65.

[499] *See id.*, pmbl. ("*Affirming* that crimes against humanity, which are among the most serious crimes of concern to the international community as a whole, must be prevented in conformity with international law"); *id.* Art. 3(2) ("Each State undertakes to prevent and to punish crimes against humanity, which are crimes under international law, whether or not committed in time of armed conflict"); *id.* Art. 4 ("Each State undertakes to prevent crimes against humanity, in conformity with international law, including through: . . . (b) cooperation with other States, relevant intergovernmental organizations, and, as appropriate, other organizations.").

[500] For discussion of what states must do to fulfill obligations *erga omnes*, see Bassiouni, *supra* note 33.

[501] Int'l L. Comm'n, Articles on State Responsibility, *supra* note 21, Arts. 40.1, 41.1. Marko Milanović, *State Responsibility for Genocide*, 17(3) EUR. J. INT'L L. 553, 571 (2006) ("States have a duty to prevent and punish genocide in exactly the same way as they have to prevent and punish crimes against humanity or other massive human rights violation."). *See also* UN Charter, Art. 1(3) (UN "[p]urpose" "[t]o achieve international co-operation in solving international problems of [a] . . . humanitarian character").

[502] *See* Chapter 4.2.3 *supra* (discussing good faith obligations).

[503] UN Charter, Art. 96(1).

4.4 Seeking an Advisory Opinion from the ICJ

While the Charter makes clear a request for an advisory opinion may pertain to "any legal question,"[504] the section below: (1) demonstrates that actions of the Security Council are indeed subject to judicial review by the ICJ as to the Council's compliance with the UN Charter and/or other bodies of international law; (2) shows that the issues involved are legal in nature, preemptively refuting the argument that they present "non-justiciable political questions"; (3) demonstrates why the ICJ should exercise its discretion and render such review; yet also (4) articulates several caveats about seeking such judicial review and explores possible alternatives.

4.4.1 The ICJ May Review Security Council Actions for Compliance with the UN Charter and/or Other Bodies of International Law

Two contentious ICJ cases suggest that the ICJ may engage in judicial review of Security Council actions for compliance with the UN Charter and/or treaty obligations – Lockerbie[505] and the Application of Genocide Convention Case.[506]

In Lockerbie, Libya had challenged the validity of Security Council Resolution 731, which urged Libya "to provide a full and effective response" to requests by the US and the UK for the surrender for trial of two Libyan nationals accused of carrying out the bombing of Pan Am Flight 103. Libya filed a request for provisional measures, arguing that the surrender request violated the terms of the Convention for the Suppression of Unlawful Acts against the Safety of Civil Aviation (Montreal Convention).[507] The Security Council then adopted Resolution 748 which imposed mandatory sanctions on Libya which were to apply until the Security Council decided that the Libyan Government had complied with the demand for surrender.[508] The ICJ dismissed Libya's request for provisional measures, there, avoiding to address the justiciability of the Council's Article 39 determination, finding it sufficient to rely on the validity of the resolution as it was not "at [that] stage called upon to

---

[504] Id.; Akande, supra note 79, at 328 ("The General Assembly could request the Court to give an advisory opinion on the legality of Security Council decisions .... This is well within the scope of Article 96 ...."). This final section of this Chapter relies extensively on the excellent analysis of Dapo Akande, who has already explored these same arguments as to ICJ review of the Security Council. See Akande, supra note 79.
[505] Lockerbie (Libya v. UK) Provisional Measures, supra note 85; Lockerbie (Libya v. U.S.) Provisional Measures, supra note 85.
[506] Application of Genocide Convention Case, supra note 56.
[507] Montreal Convention, supra note 385.
[508] SC Res. 748 (Mar. 31, 1992).

determine definitively the legal effect" of the resolution.[509] However, the ICJ did find that under Article 25 of the Charter, UN Member States are obliged to accept and carry out decisions of the Security Council.[510] The ICJ held that that obligation extended to Resolution 748 which, by virtue of Article 103 of the Charter, prevailed over inconsistent treaty obligations under the Montreal Convention.[511] Ultimately, the two *Lockerbie* cases (one filed against the US and one against the UK)[512] were discontinued by consent in September 2003, so the matter was never decided on the merits.[513] In dissent, Judge Bedjaoui suggested that "Resolution 748 … may have been 'manifestly incompatible with the Charter' if its object or effect was to prevent the Court from exercising its judicial function invested by the Charter or to place the Court in a state of subordination."[514] While, here, the ICJ did not reach a final decision on the merits, the point is that it engaged in at least some judicial review of the

---

[509] *Lockerbie (Libya v. UK)* Provisional Measures, *supra* note 85, at 15–16, para 43; *Lockerbie (Libya v. U.S.)* Provisional Measures, *supra* note 85, at 16, para 43. Similarly, at the preliminary objections phase, the Court held that the issue again did not need to be addressed as it did not possess "an exclusively preliminary character." See *Lockerbie (Libya v. UK)* Preliminary Objections Judgment, *supra* note 84, at 22, paras. 49–50. *Lockerbie (Libya v. U.S.)*, Preliminary Objections Judgment, 1998 ICJ Rep. 115 133, para. 49.

[510] *Lockerbie (Libya v. UK)* Provisional Measures, *supra* note 85, at 15, para. 39; *Lockerbie (Libya v U.S.)* Provisional Measures, *supra* note 85, at 16, para. 42.

[511] *Id.* That the ICJ suggested it would uphold obligations created under Security Council resolutions over treaty obligations does not imply the same result would attach to analysis of the Genocide Convention or 1949 Geneva Conventions, which, as argued above, protect *jus cogens* norms and accord with the "[p]urposes and [p]rinciples" of the UN, so the UN Security Council should be acting in accordance with, and arguably has no power to act contrary to, these foundational treaties. See Chapter 4.3.3 *supra*.

[512] Questions of Interpretation and Application of the 1971 Montreal Convention arising from the Aerial Incident at Lockerbie (Libyan Arab Jamahiriya v. United Kingdom) (Int'l Ct. Just.); Questions of Interpretation and Application of the 1971 Montreal Convention arising from the Aerial Incident at Lockerbie (Libyan Arab Jamahiriya v. United States of America).

[513] Questions of Interpretation and Application of the 1971 Montreal Convention arising from the Aerial Incident at Lockerbie (Libyan Arab Jamahiriya v. United States of America), Order on Discontinuance (Sept. 10, 2003); Questions of Interpretation and Application of the 1971 Montreal Convention arising from the Aerial Incident at Lockerbie (Libyan Arab Jamahiriya v. United Kingdom), Order on Discontinuance (Sept. 10, 2003).

[514] *Lockerbie (Libya v. UK)* Provisional Measures, *supra* note 85, at 46, n. 1 (diss. op., Bedjaoui, J.); *Lockerbie (Libya v. US)* Provisional Measures, supra note 85, at 156, n. 1 (diss. op., Bejaoui, J.). Summing up, José Alvarez writes:

> The dissenters, Judges Bedjaoui, Weeramantry, Ajibola and El-Koshen, would have given Libya some of its requested provisional relief and all of them criticized the Council, sometimes trenchantly. Judge Bedjaoui found that the Montreal Convention's right to extradite or prosecute is a right recognized by international law, suggested that the Council turned to chapter VII as a pretext, cast doubt on whether the failure to extradite nationals accused of committing a bombing three years earlier was "today" an "urgent" threat to the international peace, affirmed that *the Council must*

enforceability of the Security Council resolutions in light of the Charter and inconsistent treaty obligations. Eminent international law scholar Thomas M. Franck summed up the *Lockerbie* holdings: "the Court has carefully, and quietly, marked its role as the ultimate arbiter of institutional legitimacy."[515] José Alvarez similarly writes: "some of the individual opinions in the *Lockerbie* Orders constitute nearly plaintive pleas for the Council to exercise some normative restraint .... They are cueing the Council to internalize the limits suggested and impose restraints on itself that would prevent violations of the law."[516]

As previously discussed, the *Application of Genocide Convention* Case resulted from a challenge brought by Bosnia-Herzegovina to Security Council Resolution 713, which imposed an arms embargo during the conflict in the former Yugoslavia.[517] Bosnia challenged the legality of the Security Council's resolution in a request for provisional measures, arguing that the arms embargo against Bosnia was contrary to the right of self-defense enshrined in Article 51 of the Charter and would stop the Bosnian government from preventing the commission of genocide as required by Article 1 of the Genocide Convention.[518] The ICJ rejected on technical grounds various of the provisional measures requests, finding that they were not aimed at a declaration of what provisional measures the respondent ought to take, but were aimed at a declaration that would clarify the legal situation for the entire international community.[519] The ICJ did not, however, in any way reject the argument that a Security Council resolution would need to accord with treaty obligations and the UN Charter, or that it had power to review the legality of Security Council actions.

Both cases are relevant in that the ICJ clearly suggests it could evaluate the legality of Security Council resolutions in light of the UN Charter and other treaty obligations. Dapo Akande concludes as to these cases: "The *Lockerbie* and *Bosnia* cases demonstrate that the validity of Security Council resolutions may be called into question in contentious cases between two states."[520] José

---

respect the Charter and international law and that the Court has competence to tell it to do so ....

José Alvarez, *Collective Security Law*, in THE LIBRARY OF ESSAYS IN INTERNATIONAL LAW, at https://archive.org/stream/in.ernet.dli.2015.49746/2015.49746.Collective-Security-Law_djvu.txt (emphasis added).

[515] Franck [Powers of Appreciation], *supra* note 193, at 523.
[516] Alvarez [Judging the Security Council], *supra* note 397, at 30.
[517] *Application of Genocide Convention* Case, *supra* note 56, at 345.
[518] *Id.* at 327–28.
[519] *Id.* at 345.
[520] Akande, *supra* note 79, at 331. *See also* Reinisch [Should Judges Second-Guess], *supra* note 161, at 290 ("The World Court has repeatedly upheld its jurisdiction in cases where the legality of measures of the UN Security Council or other UN organs was in issue.").

Alvarez similarly writes: "The judges' individual opinions in the *Lockerbie* and *Bosnia* cases suggest a Court that is ready to engage in ... judicial review, even if in advance or defiance of the expectations of some UN members."[521] Michael Frass also concludes: "Judicial review of the legality of [Security Council] decisions is both possible under procedural law and permitted under constitutional law of the UN."[522] Akande also concludes: "[in] so far as the Court is called upon to apply or not to apply or even to consider the applicability or consequences of a Security Council resolution, it may have to check to see whether the resolution is valid in the first place and may have to ensure that the Council has not exceeded its powers in passing such resolution or deciding on a course of action."[523] However, "[t]he Security Council cannot be party to a contentious case and thus cannot be bound by a decision made under contentious jurisdiction," as it would only be binding on the parties.[524]

The matter of judicial review by the ICJ is further elucidated by Judge Skubiszewski writing in dissent in *East Timor (Portugal v. Australia)* where he explained:

> The Court is competent, and this is shown by several judgments and advisory opinions, to interpret and apply the resolutions of the Organization. The Court is competent to make findings on their lawfulness, in particular whether they were *intra vires*. This competence follows from its function as the principal judicial organ of the United Nations. The decisions of the Organization (in the broad sense which this notion has under the Charter provisions on voting) are subject to scrutiny by the Court with regard to their legality, validity and effect.[525]

---

[521] Alvarez [Judging the Security Council], *supra* note 397, at 30.
[522] Fassbender, *supra* note 98, at 223 (quoting and translating Frass, *supra* note 98, at 255).
[523] Akande, *supra* note 79, at 331 n. 90, 332, *quoting* Judge Petrén, *Namibia* Advisory Opinion, *supra* note 20, at 131 ("So long as the validity of the resolutions upon which Resolution 276 (1970) was based had not been established, it was clearly impossible for the Court to pronounce on [its] legal consequences."), *quoting* sep. op., de Castro, J, *Namibia* Advisory Opinion, *supra* note 20 ("the Court, as a legal organ, cannot cooperate with a resolution which is clearly void, contrary to the rules of the Charter, or contrary to the principles of law.").
[524] Farrall, *supra* note 44, at 74–75. "The most the Court would find [in a contentious jurisdiction case] is that a particular Council decision as applied to these parties in the circumstances at issue would be illegal." *Id.* at 75. *Compare* Akande, *supra* note 79, at 336 ("A decision of the Court to the effect that a certain Security Council resolution or decision is invalid or beyond its powers [even in a contentious case that is only between the parties] would undermine the legitimacy of that decision [more broadly] and weaken its claim to compliance.").
[525] East Timor (Port. v. Austl.), Judgment, para. 86 (Int'l Ct. Just. June 30, 1995) (diss. op., Skubiszewski, J.). Orakhelashvili explains:

> [T]he Court is obliged to support only such action of the Council as is compatible with the Charter and relevant general international law. Judge Lauterpacht in *Bosnia* considered

Yet, if the Court has competence to determine that decisions are *intra vires*, it must also have competence to determine that decisions are *ultra vires*, as a determination that a decision is *not intra vires* (that is, is *ultra vires*) necessarily would be one of the possible outcomes of such judicial review. Any review that is only able to conclude that the Security Council acts *intra vires* would not in fact constitute true judicial review.

Nor does it appear problematic that the ICJ and Security Council could be pronouncing on the same situation, as there is no "hierarchy between the Security Council and the Court and neither organ is in any way subordinate to the other."[526] For instance, in the *Nicaragua* Case,[527] the Court observed:

> While in Article 12 of the Charter there is provision for a clear demarcation of functions between General Assembly and the Security Council . . . there is no similar provision anywhere in the Charter with respect to the Security Council and the Court. The Council has functions of a political nature assigned to it, whereas the Court exercises purely judicial functions. Both organs can perform their separate but complementary functions with respect to the same event.[528]

That the ICJ may adjudicate legal issues related to matters also before the Council was similarly noted by Judge Weeramantry in the *Nuclear Weapons* Advisory Opinion.[529] There, Judge Weeramantry, in a Dissenting Opinion, wrote that "even if the Security Council had expressly endorsed the use of such weapons, *it is this Court which is the ultimate authority on questions of legality*, and . . . such an observation, even if made, would not prevent the Court from making its independent pronouncement on this matter."[530] Jeremy Farrall

> that the Court is entitled, and indeed bound, to ensure respect for the rule of law within the United Nations system, and therefore to insist, in cases properly brought before it, on compliance by UN principal organs with the rules governing their operation. Judge Skubiszewski noted in *East Timor* that the Court is entitled to examine the Security Council's resolutions and draw appropriate conclusions if they are *ultra vires*. The ICTY in *Tadić* affirmed its power to review the Chapter VII measures of the Security Council. The powers of the Security Council under Chapter VII are not unlimited, but are bound by legal norms to be determined finally by the International Court, either in contentious or advisory proceedings. The Council possesses autonomy in the relevant field, but the Court determines the legal and constitutional boundaries of that autonomy.

Orakhelashvili [The Impact], *supra* note 92, at 87–88.
[526] Akande, *supra* note 79, at 313 (citing Gowlland-Debbas, *The Relationship between the International Court of Justice and the Security Council in the Light of the* Lockerbie *Case*, 88 AM. J. INT'L L. 643, 655 (1994)).
[527] *Nicaragua* Case, *supra* note 376.
[528] *Id.* at 435.
[529] *Nuclear Weapons* Advisory Opinion, *supra* note 57.
[530] *Id.* at 911 (emphasis added).

similarly observes that *Lockerbie* demonstrates that "the Court may ... consider the legal dimensions of a dispute that is concurrently under consideration by the Security Council."[531]

The Court may also pronounce on the Council's powers "under its advisory jurisdiction and its pronouncements [while advisory] would carry considerable weight as authoritative findings of law ...."[532] Two cases where the ICJ reviewed Security Council actions in the course of rendering advisory opinions are *Certain Expenses*[533] and *Namibia*.[534] Dapo Akande explains:

> In the [*Certain*] *Expenses Opinion* the Court was asked to decide whether the member States of the United Nations were responsible for the expenses of the UN Operations in Congo (ONUC) and the United Nations Emergency Force in the Middle East (UNEF).... The Court held that the rejection of [a] French amendment ... (that would have expressly required it to review the resolutions) did not preclude it from considering whether the expenditures were "decided on in conformity with the provisions of the Charter, if the Court finds such consideration appropriate". The Court went on to say that it "must have full liberty to consider all relevant data available to it in forming an opinion on a question posed to it for an advisory opinion". The Court then went on to [determine] whether both the General Assembly and the Security Council had the power to set up peacekeeping operations.[535]

In the *Namibia* Advisory Opinion, the Court was asked to give an opinion on the legal consequences for States of the continued presence of South Africa in South West Africa (Namibia) despite the General Assembly and Security Council resolutions terminating its mandate and requiring the withdrawal of its administration. The Court noted that it "does not possess powers of judicial review or appeal in respect of the decisions taken by the United Nations organs concerned" and that "the question of the validity or conformity with the Charter of General Assembly resolution 2145 (XXI) and related Security Council decisions does not form the subject matter of the request for advisory opinion". "However", the Court went on to say, "*in the exercise of its judicial function and since objections have been advanced*[,] the Court, in the course of its reasoning, will consider these objections before determining any legal

---

[531] Farrall, *supra* note 44, at 74 (citing *Lockerbie*). He also notes that the ICTY's *Tadić* case, the ICTR's *Kanyabashi* case, and the *Kadi* case heard by the Court of First Instance of the European Communities all "consider[ed] legal questions touching upon the powers of the Security Council." *Id*.
[532] Akande, *supra* note 79, at 75.
[533] Certain Expenses of the United Nations, Advisory Opinion,1962 ICJ Rep. 151 (July 20).
[534] *Namibia* Advisory Opinion, *supra* note 20.
[535] Akande, *supra* note 79, at 330, *quoting Certain Expenses, supra* note 533, at 151, 156, 157, 163–68.

4.4 Seeking an Advisory Opinion from the ICJ 249

consequences arising from those resolutions". The Court then examined the Security Council actions from the point of view of both procedural validity and substantive legality.... Substantively, the Court held that the Council did have the power to issue a resolution requiring South Africa to withdraw its administration from Namibia.[536]

Particularly, in the Namibia Advisory Opinion, the ICJ "reached the conclusions that the decisions made by the Security Council in [Resolution 276 (1970), Resolution 264 (1969), and Resolution 269 (1969)] *were in conformity with the purposes and principles of the Charter and in accordance with its Articles 24 and 25.*"[537]

Thus, in both Certain Expenses and Namibia, "the Court has demonstrated that when faced with questions as to the validity of the actions of the political organs it will look to see whether those actions have been validly taken and it will look to see whether the actions were *ultra vires* the organ that has taken them."[538] Karl Doehring explains why ICJ judges should conduct such review: "Neutral judges may be in a better position to control the legality of political actions and to test whether they overstep legal boundaries. Of course, decisions of a Court may also violate the law, but they are, at least, more acceptable than those of political organs acting more or less under the pressure of political interests. The veto-power clearly demonstrates this situation."[539]

Another case involving judicial review of the legality of a Security Council resolution is the ICTY's *Tadić* Case,[540] discussed above.[541] In that case, the accused brought a challenge to the legality of the Security Council's establishment of the ICTY, arguing, inter alia, that it was beyond the scope of the Council's authority to create a criminal tribunal and thus the Council had acted *ultra vires*.[542] The ICTY's Appeals Chamber first examined whether it had competence to rule on the question (which involved ruling on the legality of Security Council actions), concluding that it inherently had competence to rule on its own competence (*compétence de la compétence*).[543] Then, examining the Security Council's powers granted under Chapter VII, as noted above, the Appeals Chamber held that "[t]he Security Council is ... subjected to certain

---

[536] Akande, *supra* note 79, at 330–31, *quoting* Namibia Advisory Opinion, *supra* note 20, at 45, 53.
[537] Akande, *supra* note 79, *quoting* Namibia Advisory Opinion, *supra* note 20, at 53, para. 115 (emphasis added by Akande).
[538] Akande, *supra* note 79, at 326.
[539] Doehring, *supra* note 92, at 100–01.
[540] *Tadić*, *supra* note 87.
[541] See *supra* note 87 and accompanying text.
[542] *Tadić*, *supra* note 87, at para. 8.
[543] *Id.*, para. 22.

constitutional limitations, however broad its powers under the constitution [the UN Charter] may be."[544] "[N]either the text nor the spirit of the Charter conceives of the Security Council as *legibus solutus* (unbound by law)."[545] The Court ultimately concluded that the Security Council had acted properly in creating the ICTY, as it was exercising powers granted under Article 41 of the Charter, and therefore the Security Council's actions were not *ultra vires*.[546]

The ICTR has also issued a parallel decision in response to a challenge to the Security Council's creation of that Tribunal.[547] As in *Tadić*, the accused argued that creating a tribunal did not fall within the Security Council's Chapter VII powers; the ICTR, however, found that it did fit within Chapter VII, Article 41, as a measure toward "restoration and maintenance of peace," noting that the "list of actions contained in Article 41 is clearly not exhaustive but indicates some examples of measures which the Security Council might eventually decide to impose upon States."[548] There also exists a similar decision of the Appeals Chamber of the Special Tribunal for Lebanon in response to a challenge to the Security Council's creation of that Tribunal, where the Appeals Chamber unanimously upheld the Trial Chamber's finding that the Security Council had properly established the Tribunal under Chapter VII of the Charter.[549]

While in these cases the ICJ and other tribunals upheld the validity of Security Council resolutions, the point is that there may be such judicial review.[550] As Orakhelashvili concludes: "An organ cannot be the final judge of

---

[544] *Id.*, para. 28.
[545] *Id.*
[546] *Id.*, paras. 34, 40.
[547] See *Prosecutor v. Kanyabashi*, Case No. ICTR-96-15-T, Decision on the Defence Motion on Jurisdiction (June 18, 1997).
[548] *Id.*, para. 27. The argument that the Security Council's creation of the Tribunal violated Rwanda's sovereignty was also rejected. *Id.*, para. 15.
[549] See *The Prosecutor v. Ayyash, Badreddine, Oneissi, and Sabra*, Case No. STL-11-01/PT/AC/AR90.1, Decision on the Defence Appeals against the Trial Chamber's Decision on the Defence Challenges to the Jurisdiction and Legality of the Tribunal, headnote, at 1 (Oct. 24, 2012).
[550] While there appears dicta of the ICJ in the *Namibia* Advisory Opinion that it should not exercise jurisdiction over decisions by UN organs, the ICJ essentially did exercise such review. See *Namibia* Advisory Opinion, *supra* note 20, at para. 89 ("Undoubtedly, the Court does not possess powers of judicial review or appeal in respect of decisions taken by the United Nations organs concerned."). Yet, the Court went on to state: "[T]he question of the validity or conformity with the Charter of General Assembly resolution 2145 (XXI) or of related Security Council resolutions does not form the subject of the request for advisory opinion. However, in the exercise of its judicial function and since objections have been advanced[,] the Court, in the course of its reasoning, will consider these objections before determining any legal consequences arising from those resolutions." *Id.*

the legality of its acts."⁵⁵¹ "Even if each principal organ [of the UN] remains prima facie a judge of its competence, the exercise of such competence undoubtedly involves legal questions on which the ICJ is empowered to adjudicate."⁵⁵² José Alvarez similarly concludes: "For ICJ judges as for most lawyers, unchecked power in the hands of any single organ is 'law' in name only."⁵⁵³

If the ICJ may engage in judicial review of the Council's actions in light of the provisions of the UN Charter and other bodies of international law, it follows that it could similarly engage in judicial review of the legality of one or more permanent members' use of the veto, at least where measured against legal standards, such as those contained in the UN Charter or other bodies of international law, such as *jus cogens* or treaty obligations of individual permanent member states. This conclusion is also clear based on the UN Charter, which states that the General Assembly or Security Council "may request" the ICJ to give an advisory opinion "on *any* legal question."⁵⁵⁴

4.4.2 *Security Council Actions Do Not Constitute Non-Justiciable "Political" Question, at Least Where There Are Legal Standards against Which to Review Them*

Another issue that could potentially arise relates to the argument that the Security Council's actions, or the actions of individual permanent member states while serving on the Council, are "political," not "legal," and thus present "non-justiciable political questions." This argument is refuted below.

Initially, one sees from the cases discussed above that it certainly is not always the case that the Security Council's actions are viewed as "political" and incapable of judicial review, because in the cases above there *was* judicial review. However, that there was review does not imply there *always* would be. For example, this author does not deny that there are instances where Security Council actions could constitute wholly political ones, incapable of judicial review – such as generally the determination whether or not to utilize coercive Chapter VII powers or which measures to employ.⁵⁵⁵ Some of the separate and

---

⁵⁵¹ Orakhelashvili [The Impact], *supra* note 92, at 85.
⁵⁵² *Id.* at 87.
⁵⁵³ Alvarez [Judging the Security Council], *supra* note 397, at 35.
⁵⁵⁴ UN Charter, Art. 96 (emphasis added).
⁵⁵⁵ Even here, however, a justiciable question could arise if there were a credible draft Security Council resolution invoking Chapter VII forceful measures that was designed to curtail or alleviate the commission of atrocity crimes (meaning, e.g., it is the minimum force calculated to be necessary and carefully drafted to satisfy requirements of distinction, proportionality and limits on duration, etc.), and it is vetoed by a permanent member, when there is no credible

dissenting opinions in the *Lockerbie* cases and most authors also suggest the decision whether or not Chapter VII has been triggered – that is whether there was a "threat to the peace, breach of the peace, or act of aggression" under Article 39 of the Charter – is generally a determination left to the Council.[556]

As to how to differentiate when judicial review can occur, Dapo Akande suggests that cases illustrate that judicial review occurs where there is a *legal standard* against which the Security Council's actions may be reviewed.[557] By contrast, judicial review has been found inappropriate where there are no "judicially discoverable and manageable standards."[558] The ICTY Trial Chamber in *Tadić* also made this distinction, suggesting the issue of whether the Security Council properly invoked Chapter VII was "only for it [the Council]," as it was "not a justiciable issue, but one involving considerations of high policy and of a political nature."[559] Thus, the Trial Chamber concluded that the Council's *invocation* of Chapter VII was not an issue for a "judicial body."[560]

    alternative proposal for addressing the crimes. For example, assume the use of force being proposed as a Chapter VII measure is a "no fly zone" (which, absent consent of the host country, constitutes a coercive measure), and it is needed to halt ongoing genocide being perpetrated by the host state by means of aerial bombardment. Assume at least nine members of the Council agree on the need for passing such a resolution, which is blocked by one permanent member that has military, political, and/or economic ties to the host state. Use of the veto in such circumstances *ought* to receive judicial scrutiny as contrary to the *jus cogens* protections accorded to the crime of genocide, contrary to the "[p]urposes and [p]rinciples" of the UN, contrary to the general international law obligation of good faith, and contrary to the vetoing county's obligation under the Genocide Convention to "prevent" genocide.

[556] *See, e.g.,* Farrall, *supra* note 44, at 71 ("The ICJ has not pronounced itself definitively on this question. However, in the *Lockerbie* case various judges expressed the view that the Council retained exclusive discretion concerning the state of affairs that brings Chapter VII into operation."), *citing Lockerbie (Libya v. U.S.) Provisional Measures, supra* note 85, at 176 (diss. op., Weeramantry, J.); *Lockerbie (Libya v. UK) Preliminary Objections, supra* note 84, at 110 (diss. op., Jennings, J. ad hoc). The author notes that now that the ICC's crime of aggression has a definition, Rome Statute, Art. 8*bis*, at least the "act of aggression" under Article 39 could in theory be measured against an identified legal standard; however, the ICC's definition is for ICC purposes and not directly applicable to the Council. *See* Rome Statute, Art. 8*bis*, para. 2 ("For the purpose of this Statute, 'act of aggression' means . . . .").

[557] Akande, *supra* note 79, at 314–15.

[558] *Id., citing* Baker v. Carr, 369 U.S. 186, 217 (1962).

[559] *Tadić*, Case No. IT-94-1, Decision on the Defence Motion on Jurisdiction, para. 23 (Aug. 10, 1995).

[560] *Id.* The Appeals Chamber did not quite endorse this approach, finding "the determination that there exists such a threat [to the peace] is not totally unfettered discretion, as it has to remain, at the very least, within the limits of the Purposes and Principles of the Charter." *Tadić, supra* note 87, para. 29. It did not examine the issue further, as the Appeals Chamber recognized there is "an armed conflict … taking place in the territory of the former Yugoslavia," and Appellant "no longer contests the Security Council's power to determine whether the situation in the former Yugoslavia constituted a threat to the peace, nor the determination itself." *Id.*, para. 30.

By contrast, the ICJ "can review decisions of the Council to see whether they overstep the *legal limits* imposed on the Council . . . ."[561] For example, in *Certain Expenses*, the ICJ ruled:

> [I]t has been argued that the question put to the Court is intertwined with political questions, and that for this reason the Court should refuse to give an opinion. It is true that most interpretations of the Charter of the United Nations will have political significance, great or small. In the nature of things it could not be otherwise. The Court, however, cannot attribute a political character to a request which invites it to undertake an essentially judicial task . . . .[562]

The Appeals Chamber in *Tadić* cited this ruling to support the conclusion that it *could* engage in judicial review of whether the Security Council properly established the ICTY, and dismissed the argument that the question was "political" or "non-justiciable."[563] The Appeals Chamber in *Tadić* further suggested that arguments about "non-justiciable" "political questions" were generally outdated, having "receded from the horizon of contemporary international law."[564]

A similar conclusion that the political character of an organ does not exempt it from judicial scrutiny was affirmed by Judge ad hoc Jennings in *Lockerbie* who, as also quoted above, wrote in a Dissenting Opinion that:

> all discretionary powers of lawful decision-making are necessarily derived from the law, and are therefore governed and qualified by the law. This must be so if only because the sole authority of such decisions flows itself from the law. It is not logically possible to claim to represent the power and authority of the law, and at the same time, claim to be above the law.[565]

Consequently, Judge ad hoc Jennings rejected the view that Security Council resolutions adopted under Chapter VII of the Charter are immune from review according to applicable legal principles.[566] Two ICJ advisory opinions relating to admission to the UN similarly recognize that interpreting the Charter is a judicial task despite the "political character" of the organ whose actions are under review.[567]

---

[561] Akande, *supra* note 79, at 340 (emphasis added).
[562] *Certain Expenses*, *supra* note 533, at 155.
[563] *Tadić*, *supra* note 87, para. 25.
[564] *Id.*, para. 24.
[565] *Lockerbie (Libya v. UK)* Preliminary Objections Judgment, *supra* note 84, at 110 (diss. op., Jennings, J. ad hoc).
[566] Orakhelashvili [The Impact], *supra* note 92, at 60.
[567] See *Conditions of Admission of a State to Membership in the United Nations*, *supra* note 80, at 64 ("The political character of an organ cannot release it from the observance of treaty provisions

Dapo Akande concludes: "[t]he Court can ... decide that even if the measure is necessary in the view of the Council, it is not one open to the Council to take as such a measure would be contrary to norms of *jus cogens*, well-established principles of international law or fundamental human rights, or would otherwise be beyond the powers of the Council."[568] Because veto use would be measured against these same sources of law (*jus cogens*, the "[p]urposes and [p]rinciples" of the UN, and/or foundational treaty obligations), it presents the same type of justiciable question.

The above analysis leads to the conclusion that "there are legal limits to the powers of the Security Council, even when it is acting to maintain or restore the peace, and that the International Court of Justice is, in proper cases, able to determine whether or not the Security Council has crossed those limits."[569] If the ICJ is able to conduct judicial review of the Council's resolutions, it is not a significantly far step to conclude that it similarly has power to review permanent members' use of the veto power (a power granted under the UN Charter), at least where it can be measured against identifiable legal standards. Thus, "[i]n so far as the questions before the [ICJ] are legal ... and in so far as the Court has jurisdiction, the Court has a duty to decide the matter even when it involves examining whether another principal organ such as the Security Council has exceeded its powers."[570]

4.4.3 Why the ICJ Should Exercise Its Discretion to Render an Advisory Opinion

That the Security Council or General Assembly requests an advisory opinion, does not, however, guarantee that the ICJ will render such review. The Court has interpreted its power "to mean that the Court [also] has a discretionary

---

established by the Charter, when they constitute limitations on its powers or criteria for its judgment. To ascertain whether an organ has freedom of choice for its decisions, reference must be made to the terms of its constitution [the UN Charter].") (emphasis added); Competence of the General Assembly for the Admission of a State to the United Nations, Advisory Opinion, 1950 ICJ Rep. 4, 6 (Mar. 3) ("So far as concerns its competence, the Court will simply recall that, in a previous Opinion which dealt with the interpretation of Article 4, paragraph 1 [of the Charter], it declared that, according to Article 96 of the Charter and Article 65 of the [ICJ] Statute, it may give an Opinion on any legal question and that there is no provision which prohibits it from exercising, in regard to Article 4 of the Charter, a multilateral treaty, an interpretative function falling within the normal exercise of its judicial powers.").

[568] Akande, *supra* note 79, at 340–41.
[569] *Id.* at 310.
[570] *Id.* at 343.

4.4 Seeking an Advisory Opinion from the ICJ

power to decline to give an advisory opinion even if the conditions of jurisdiction are met."[571]

At the same time, the ICJ is "mindful of the fact that its answer to a request for an advisory opinion 'represents its participation in the activities of the Organization, and, in principle, *should not be refused*.'"[572] "Thus, the consistent jurisprudence of the Court is that only 'compelling reasons' may lead the Court to refuse its opinion in response to a request falling within its jurisdiction."[573] Absent such "compelling reasons for it to decline to respond" to a request for an advisory opinion, the ICJ will exercise judicial review.

In the recent advisory opinion in the *Chagos Islands* Case,[574] the ICJ concluded that it should exercise review, in part because (1) "the matter [raised there] of decolonization is of particular concern to the United Nations,"[575] and (2) despite the fact that there existed divergent views expressed by Mauritius and the UK, the ICJ concluded that the situation did not represent a bilateral dispute.[576]

---

[571] *Wall* Advisory Opinion, *supra* note 377, at 156, para. 44; Accordance with International Law of the Unilateral Declaration of Independence in respect of Kosovo, Advisory Opinion, 2010 (II) ICJ Rep. 403, 415–16, para. 29 (July 22) [hereinafter, *Kosovo* Advisory Opinion].

[572] Legal Consequences of the Separation of the Chagos Archipelago from Mauritius in 1965, para. 65 (Int'l Ct. Just. Feb. 25, 2019), *at* www.icj-cij.org/files/case-related/169/169-20190225-01-00-EN.pdf (emphasis added), *citing* Interpretation of Peace Treaties with Bulgaria, Hungary and Romania, First Phase, Advisory Opinion, 1950 (I) ICJ Rep. 65, 71 (Mar. 30); Difference Relating to Immunity from Legal Process of a Special Rapporteur of the Commission on Human Rights, Advisory Opinion, 1999 (I) ICJ Rep. 62, 78–79, para. 29 (Apr. 29); *Wall* Advisory Opinion, *supra* note 377, at 156, para. 44.

[573] *Chagos*, *supra* note 572, para. 65, *citing Wall* Advisory Opinion, *supra* note 377, at 156, para. 44; *Kosovo* Advisory Opinion, note 571 *supra*, at 416, para. 30.

[574] *Chagos*, *supra* note 572.

[575] *Id.*, para. 88.

[576] *Id.*, para. 89. Judge Donoghue, by contrast, concluded in dissent that "the Advisory Opinion has the effect of circumventing the absence of United Kingdom consent to judicial settlement of the bilateral dispute between the United Kingdom and Mauritius regarding sovereignty over the Chagos Archipelago . . . ." *Chagos*, *supra* note 572, (diss. op., Donoghue, J.).

In the ICJ's 2010 Advisory Opinion on Kosovo, the ICJ made clear that the motives of individual states which sponsor a resolution requesting an advisory opinion are not relevant to the Court's exercise of its discretion. *Kosovo* Advisory Opinion, *supra* note 571, at 417, para. 33. And, in the ICJ's 2004 *Wall* Advisory Opinion, an argument was raised that the Court should decline to exercise its jurisdiction on the basis that an advisory opinion "could impede a political, negotiated solution to the Israeli-Palestinian conflict"; more particularly, it was argued that "such an opinion could undermine the scheme of the 'Roadmap,'" a negotiating framework which had been endorsed by the Security Council. The ICJ did not regard this factor as a "compelling reason" to decline to exercise its jurisdiction, as it was not clear what influence the Court's opinion might have on Israeli-Palestinian negotiations. *Wall* Advisory Opinion, *supra* note 377, at 160–61, paras. 51–53. The Court found that it had "sufficient information and evidence to enable it to give the advisory opinion" and that "the

Here, how the veto power is used when there are ongoing atrocities is most certainly an issue of concern to the United Nations (as numerous statements by states at the UN attest).[577] Furthermore, by seeking a ruling on a legal question in the abstract – such as whether existing international law contains limitations on the use of the veto power by permanent members of the UN Security Council in situations where there is ongoing genocide, crimes against humanity, and/or war crimes – the situation in no way involves a bilateral dispute.

Moreover, far from "compelling reasons" not to exercise judicial review, the following provide compelling reasons why the court *should* exercise judicial review: (a) the urgency of the issue – with the lives of victims of atrocity crimes on the line;[578] (b) the fact that so many states view the way the veto is being used as problematic for the effective functioning of the Security Council and thereby also the UN; as well as (c) the clearly legal nature of the issues presented that only the ICJ is in a position to conclusively answer.

4.4.4 Advisability of Seeking Judicial Review by the ICJ and Possible Alternatives

A final note of caution warrants articulating. The ICJ is known as a fairly conservative court that frequently appears to construe questions so narrowly that it does not reach the real issue presented,[579] or provides a somewhat favorable and somewhat unfavorable ruling.[580] Accordingly, there is no guarantee that if the questions raised in this chapter were presented to the ICJ, that the Court would provide an answer. For example, while the author finds it unlikely the ICJ would hold that the veto is above all sources of international law, the Court probably could find a way to avoid opining on the question, or provide an answer that is so theoretical it gives no practical guidance for application in concrete situations. The Court could also provide an answer that does not significantly clarify or advance the state of the law.

As noted above, an alternative or additional possibility for states to consider is whether to draft some of the above-articulated legal conclusions directly into a General Assembly resolution. Perhaps, also, raising the issues presented in

---

circumstance that others may evaluate and interpret these facts in a subjective or political manner can be no argument for a court of law to abdicate its judicial task." *Id.* at 162, para. 58.

[577] For a compilation of statements, see Chapter 4.2.4.2 *supra*.

[578] For a compilation of death tolls in Rwanda, Darfur, Sri Lanka, Myanmar, Syria, see Chapter 1.3.2. *See also* Chapter 5 (death tolls in Syria and Darfur detailed chronologically).

[579] *See, e.g., Kosovo* Advisory Opinion, *supra* note 571.

[580] *See, e.g., Nuclear Weapons* Advisory Opinion, *supra* note 57.

this book, including hopefully increasingly by states at the UN,[581] and through additional legal scholarship,[582] will generate greater discussion of the issues, and further advance acceptance of some of the concepts articulated in this chapter, such that it could be more appropriate to seek ICJ review at a later date. In the interval, states could intensify what many have already been doing, which is speaking out critically at the UN each time the veto is used in violation of these existing legal norms. States could additionally further explore both options – having the General Assembly issue a resolution, and/or request an advisory opinion (or perhaps pursue some other way of highlighting the issues presented in this chapter) – depending on the political support for these measures.

4.5 CONCLUSION

The consequences of the use of the veto by permanent members of the Security Council in the face of genocide, crimes against humanity, and/or war crimes, is not just a breach of existing norms of international law – it costs lives. Precisely which lives are lost due to which vetoes in the face of such crimes is impossible to calculate. Lives are similarly lost due to the threat of the veto, or anticipation of veto use – when measures that could halt or alleviate the commission of genocide, crimes against humanity, and/or war crimes that a sufficient number of other Security Council members would have supported are not even presented or debated due to a permanent member's political alignment with the country in question. Yet, when a regime implicated in such crimes has a sense that it has a "protector" as a permanent member of the UN Security Council – whether in Syria, Darfur (Sudan), Myanmar, Sri Lanka, Israel, or elsewhere – that regime has little reason to restrain its conduct, and is likely emboldened to continue committing crimes (or not rein in perpetrators under its control), having been given essentially a "green light" by one or more permanent member.

Yet, as statements made during Security Council debates as well as thematic debates attest, UN Member States have been challenging the use of the veto in such circumstances, as being contrary, for example, to the "[p]urpose and [p]rinciples" of the UN and other obligations under

---

[581] As mentioned, states are already making legal arguments against unlimited veto use in the face of atrocity crimes. For a compilation of statements, see Chapter 4.2.4.2 *supra*.

[582] The author presents her arguments with some humility that they are not necessarily the only way these arguments could be approached. The author does not mean to suggest that a brief to the ICJ necessarily should present the arguments precisely as articulated herein.

international law.[583] Such pronouncements are highly relevant to support the argument that the time has come to reexamine veto practice in light of such legal obligations. Such statements additionally demonstrate that, far from acquiescing to a practice of unlimited veto use in the face of atrocity crimes, states have been vociferously objecting to such practices.

The legal challenge will not be brought by the groups perishing in the countries concerned, as they have little ability to harness the mechanisms of international law designed for their protection. Yet, as the ICJ has shown in the *Bosnia v. Serbia* decision, the obligation to "prevent" genocide, actually carries stringent legal obligations. There is no reason to believe the obligation to "ensure" respect for the 1949 Geneva Conventions – invoked by the ICJ in the *Nicaragua* and *Wall* cases[584] – does not carry similarly serious obligations. The veto power, conferred by the Charter, also should be used in a way that is consistent with *jus cogens*, does not undermine the duty of other Security Council members to cooperate to make an appropriate response to a serious breach of a *jus cogens* norm, and certainly should not be used in circumstances such that it has the effect of facilitating ongoing *jus cogens* violations. Veto use also must be in accordance with the UN's "[p]urposes and [p]rinciples." Current veto use in the face of genocide, crimes against humanity, and/or war crimes meets none of these legal obligations.

Not only the permanent members, but *all* UN Member States additionally must ensure that they are carrying out their treaty and other obligations to do what is in their power, legally, to ensure that genocide, crimes against humanity, and war crimes are not committed.[585] For example, the ICJ's *Bosnia v. Serbia* decision clarifies that states parties must "employ all means reasonably available" to prevent genocide,[586] and the ICJ just reaffirmed this in its provisional measures order in the *Gambia v. Myanmar* Case.[587] Common Article 1 to the 1949 Geneva Conventions requires states parties to use "every means at their disposal" to prevent

---

[583] For a compilation of statements, see Chapter 4.2.4.2 *supra*.
[584] See notes 376–77 *supra* and accompanying text.
[585] As to all three crimes, as previously mentioned, there is a positive duty "to cooperate to bring to an end through lawful means any serious breach." Int'l L. Comm'n, Articles on State Responsibility, *supra* note 21, Arts. 40.1, 41.1. As also previously discussed, parties to the Genocide Convention have the obligation to "prevent" genocide, and parties to the 1949 Geneva Conventions (and Protocols I and III) have the obligation to "ensure" the conventions are respected.
[586] *Bosnia v. Serbia* Case, *supra* note 17, para. 430.
[587] *Gambia v. Myanmar* Case, *supra* note 331, para. 79 (ruling that "Myanmar must, in accordance with its obligations under the Convention, in relation to the members of the

violations.[588] Bringing a request for an Advisory Opinion to the ICJ on the questions raised in this chapter are certainly "means reasonably available" and "means at the[] disposal" of states parties to these conventions.

By virtue of use of the veto, and threat of the veto, in situations of ongoing atrocity crimes or their serious risk, the UN Security Council is not acting as designed under the UN Charter. Surely, in the face of agreeing to allow veto use even when a permanent member was directly involved in the situation (as detailed in Chapter 1), the drafters of the Charter did not envisage that this would include situations that transgressed established legal rules – especially when this put the permanent member in a situation of blocking Security Council efforts to prevent or curtail the commission of genocide, crimes against humanity, and/or war crimes. Such veto use is akin to making the vetoing permanent member – who often is involved in the situation in question and/or has close political, military, or economic ties to the regime – akin to an accessory to the crimes. The General Assembly has the ability to question this state of affairs and should do so. Currently there is *no restraint* on veto use in the face of genocide, crimes against humanity, and/or war crimes – at least by the three permanent members that refuse to endorse voluntary veto restraint. This challenge to unrestrained veto use should be brought and/or states should confirm their understanding of the hard law obligations in a General Assembly resolution. Until that time, states should continue to press forward in making arguments calling into question, as a legal matter, unrestrained veto use in the face of genocide, crimes against humanity, and/or war crimes.

    Rohingya group in its territory, take all measures within its power to prevent the commission of all acts within the scope of Article II of the Convention . . . .").

[588] See Dörmann & Serralvo, *supra* note 364, at 735 ("[Common Article] 1 . . . [obligates] States not party to a particular armed conflict [to] use *every means at their disposal* to ensure that the belligerents comply with the Geneva Conventions and [Additional Protocol] 1, and probably the whole body of IHL.") (emphasis added).

5

Case Studies

Veto Use Related to the Situation in Syria and Veto Threats Related to the Situation in Darfur

The conflict in Syria has redefined the meaning of the word horror. The continuation of this nightmare will forever darken the legacy of this generation of world leaders.[1]

INTRODUCTION

This final chapter presents two case studies, one where the veto was utilized while atrocity crimes were being committed, and one where the veto was threatened (expressly or implicitly) while atrocity crimes were being committed. The first case study traces climbing death tolls and growing recognition that mass atrocity crimes were occurring in Syria, while Russia, sometimes joined by China, invoked the veto on fourteen separate occasions. The vetoes blocked recognition of crimes, investigation of crimes, prosecution of crimes, as well as other measures. While sometimes somewhat comparable resolutions later passed, in other situations the veto resulted in permanent blockage. It is not claimed that passage of any single one of the vetoed resolutions would have halted all the crimes. On the other hand, that a significant number of resolutions that would have condemned regime and/or opposition crimes failed to pass or were significantly delayed could not have failed to send a metaphorical "green light" to the perpetrators; thus, the vetoes are partly responsible for the still unfolding human tragedy. The second case study traces climbing death tolls in the early 2000s while the Sudanese military and Janjaweed militia committed mass atrocity crimes against the Fur, Masalit, Zaghawa, and other ethnic groups in the

---

[1] UN Office of the High Commissioner of Human Rights, Human Rights Council, 36th Sess., Opening Statement by Zeid Ra'ad Al Hussein, United Nations High Commissioner for Human Rights, *Darker and More Dangerous: High Commissioner Updates the Human Rights Council on Human Rights Issues in 40 Countries*, at www.ohchr.org/EN/NewsEvents/Pages/DisplayNews.aspx?NewsID=22041.

Darfur region of Sudan. These crimes likely constituted genocide, and, at minimum, war crimes and crimes against humanity. During the key years when the crimes were occurring, China blocked by threat of the veto: initially, any imposition of sanctions on the Government of Sudan, and, permanently, any oil embargo, as well as peacekeeping that was not consensually negotiated with the Government of Sudan. Eventually, a hybrid peacekeeping mission was agreed to and deployed, but only after the height of the killing had occurred and with a weakened mandate. While there were no express vetoes cast related to the situation in Darfur, the Security Council's delays and tepid approach to sanctions and peacekeeping, which significantly increased the death toll, are at least partly attributable to Chinese threats (both express and implied)[2] to use the veto. One might also view the two situations discussed in this chapter through the lens of Russia having strategic and military ties to the regime of Syrian President Bashar al-Assad (and, in fact, militarily involved in the war in Syria), and China having economic and strategic ties to the regime of then-Sudanese President Omar Hassan Ahmad al-Bashir, including as a major importer of Sudanese petroleum. China was also a weapons supplier to the Sudanese military.

While this chapter presents these two case studies, all veto use or threats of veto use in the face of ongoing genocide, crimes against humanity, and/or war crimes (or the serious risk of these crimes occurring)[3] is repugnant, regardless of which permanent member is utilizing the veto or threat of veto. The selection of these two case studies is by no means intended to suggest they are the only problematic situations. Chapter 1 additionally details veto use, or threats or implicit threats of veto use, while atrocity crimes were occurring in South Africa during the apartheid era (by the US, France, and UK), in Rwanda during the 1994 genocide (by the US, France, and, by some accounts, the UK), related to Israel (by the US), related to Sri Lanka (by China), related to Myanmar (by China, sometimes joined

---

[2] For discussion of what constitutes a "threat" and how it could be express or implied, see note 316 *infra* and accompanying text (interviews with Andras Vamos-Goldman).
[3] Chapter 4 discusses the ICJ's *Bosnia v. Serbia* Case, where the ICJ held that Serbia's responsibility to "prevent" genocide was triggered by the "serious risk" of the crime occurring. Case Concerning Application of the Convention on the Prevention and Punishment of the Crime of Genocide (Bosn & Herz. v. Serb. and Montenegro), Judgment of 26 February 2007, para. 431. While the case pertained only to the crime of genocide, there is no reason not to have an analogous approach regarding crimes against humanity and war crimes. For example, as to the obligation to "ensure" respect for the Geneva Conventions in Common Article 1, it makes no sense for a state to have to wait until war crimes fully manifest before the state tries to "ensure" they do not occur.

by Russia), and related to Yemen (by Russia). The author's arguments are relevant to all these situations.[4]

5.1 ANALYSIS OF VETO USE RELATED TO THE SITUATION IN SYRIA

A full narrative of the outbreak of the war in Syria and its conduct, involving multiple outside states and other actors, is beyond the scope of this chapter. This section presents only a brief overview of the war and then a snapshot of what was occurring on the date of each veto at the Security Council related to the situation in Syria. It summarizes the crimes believed to have been occurring on the date of each veto and the total estimated death tolls. The chapter is based almost entirely on publicly available source materials, and therefore does not necessarily capture the true dynamics of negotiations at the Security Council, which would likely be known only to persons present, as much of the Council's work occurs behind closed doors.[5] The chapter does not mean to suggest the vetoes caused all fatalities in Syria, but it probably was a contributing factor to some, while it likely would be impossible to calculate which. There are times that actions by external states have direct and dire consequences on the ground – such as when Belgium withdrew its peacekeeping contingent from Rwanda near the start of the genocide and the 3,000 Tutsi taking shelter near the Belgian's UN compound were immediately taken away to be slaughtered.[6] This section, however, does not make such a direct linkage between any single veto and particular fatalities. Nonetheless, the overall picture of fourteen vetoes of resolutions that would have, inter alia, condemned crimes by the Syrian Government and its

---

[4] The case studies in this chapter were selected because Syria is a recent and still ongoing example of a prolonged situation involving veto use in the face of mass atrocity crimes, while Darfur is an example of a prolonged situation involving veto threats (and a permanent member insisting that resolutions be diluted) in the face of mass atrocity crimes.

[5] Even then, elected members of the Security Council often complain that they are excluded from the drafting and negotiation of resolutions, and only presented with completed drafts to vote on – so true negotiations over the text of resolutions appear to occur primarily among the permanent members.

[6] After ten Belgian peacekeepers who had been part of the United Nations Assistance Mission to Rwanda (UNAMIR) were killed, Belgium withdrew its troop contingent, even though approximately 3,000 Tutsi refugees had fled to the Kicukiro Technical School (ETO) where UNAMIR was based, seeking protection. After the troop withdrawal, these refugees were taken to Nyanza and slaughtered. *Rwanda Remembers Thousands Abandoned by UN Troops at Nyanza*, HOPE MAGAZINE (Apr. 12, 2017), *at* www.hope-mag.com/index.php?com=news&option=read&ca=1&a=2991. The mass graves of the victims are near the former UN compound. Trahan January 2019 visit to mass graves at Nyanza.

military forces,[7] or which blocked other measures, appears to portray a systematic attempt to "protect" one side in the war from Security Council and other external scrutiny, while comparable resolutions condemning crimes by the so-called Islamic State (ISIL) passed.[8]

5.1.1 A Brief Background

The war commenced on March 15, 2011, as part of the wider wave of "Arab Spring" protests, when protesters in the southern city of Deraa demanding release of political prisoners were shot.[9] Despite the protests remaining peaceful for almost nine months, the Syrian Government's use of violence led to violence spreading nationwide.[10] By October 2011, aligned Syrian opposition

---

[7] As discussed further below, when resolutions were vetoed that also, to some extent, "protected" crimes by anti-Government opposition forces from scrutiny, although this "protection" may have been inadvertent. *See* text accompanying note 250 *infra*.

[8] *See, e.g.*, S/RES/2139 (condemning "terrorist attacks" "carried out by organizations and individuals associated with Al-Qaeda, its affiliates, and other terrorist groups, and reiterating its call on all parties to commit to putting an end to terrorist acts perpetrated by such organizations and individuals, while reaffirming that terrorism in all its forms and manifestations constitutes one of the most serious threats to international peace and security, and that any acts of terrorism are criminal and unjustifiable, regardless of their motivation, wherever, whenever and by whomsoever committed"); S/RES/2170 (2014) (condemning gross, widespread abuse of human rights by extremist groups in Iraq and Syria, and expressing the need for accountability for "ISIL, [al Nusra Front] and all other individuals, groups, undertakings, and entities associated with Al-Qaida"); S/RES/2199 (2015) (condemning the abduction, exploitation, trafficking, and abuse of women and children including forced marriages committed by ISIL, the Nusra Front, and other entities associated with Al-Qaida); S/RES/2249 (2015) (reaffirming that "terrorism in all forms and manifestations constitutes one of the most serious threats to international peace and security and that any acts of terrorism are criminal and unjustifiable regardless of their motivations, whenever, wherever and by whomsoever committed"); S/RES/2332 (2016), pmbl. (taking note of the "negative impact of [ISIL's] presence, violent extremist ideology and actions on stability in Syria and the region, including the devastating humanitarian impact on the civilian populations" in areas under their control); S/RES/2347 (2017) (thematic resolution aimed at protecting cultural property that identifies the involvement of non-state actors, including ISIL); S/RES/2393 (Dec. 19, 2017) (condemning a long list of crimes, and, inter alia, expressing "grave concern" "at the movement of foreign terrorist fighters and other terrorists and terrorist groups into and out of Syria"). Beth Van Schaack makes the point that, additionally, individuals associated with terrorist groups were able to be listed for sanctions as part of a preexisting Al-Qaida sanctions program, but there were no sanctions imposed on Syria overall. Beth Van Schaack, *The Security Council and International Crimes in Syria: A Study of Dysfunction*, in IMAGINING JUSTICE FOR SYRIA: WATER ALWAYS FINDS ITS WAY (forthcoming OUP 2020) (unpublished manuscript on file with the author). Van Schaack provides an excellent discussion of the vetoes including analysis of the (often very self-serving) statements made by the permanent members when casting the vetoes.

[9] *Syria Profile – Timeline*, BBC NEWS (Jan. 14, 2019), *at* www.bbc.com/news/world-middle-east -14703995.

[10] *Id.*

groups establish the "Syrian National Council."[11] After a year of faltering performance by the Council, the international community established the "National Coalition for Syrian Revolutionary and Opposition Force," by announcement made in November 2012 in Doha, Qatar.[12] By 2012, the uprising against President Assad had turned into full-scale civil war,[13] with armed opposition forming the "Free Syrian Army."[14] By December 2012, the US, UK, France, Turkey, and Gulf States formally recognize the National Coalition as the "legitimate representative" of the Syrian people.[15]

After having overrun large portions of Iraq, ISIL emerged in 2013 in northern and eastern Syria.[16] By June 2014, ISIL declared a "caliphate," controlling territory from Aleppo to the eastern Iraqi province of Diyala.[17] By September 2014, the US and five Arab countries commenced air strikes against ISIL forces.[18] Since then, many additional countries (particularly NATO members) contributed militarily or financially to combatting ISIL.[19]

Russia has been a close ally of the Syrian regime dating back to the 1970s when President Hafez al-Assad, father of the current Syrian president, allowed "Russia to keep its only naval base outside the former Soviet Union at the Syrian Mediterranean port of Tartus."[20] Russia first intervened militarily in the Syrian conflict, carrying out its first air strikes, in September 2015.[21] Russia claims to have targeted "terrorist groups," but has

---

[11] *Syrian Civil War Fast Facts*, CNN (Dec. 27, 2018), *at* www.cnn.com/2013/08/27/world/meast/syria-civil-war-fast-facts/index.html.
[12] *Id.*
[13] *Id.*
[14] The Free Syrian Army was originally comprised of defectors from the Syrian Armed Forces, but later attracted a variety of groups opposed to the Assad regime, including radical Islamist groups.
[15] BBC News, *supra* note 9. The US, EU, Arab League countries, and Turkey also impose various economic sanctions on Syria. *See* CNN, *supra* note 11.
[16] *Syria's Civil War Explained from the Beginning*, AL JAZEERA (Apr. 14, 2018), *at* www.aljazeera.com/news/2016/05/syria-civil-war-explained-160505084119966.html.
[17] BBC News, *supra* note 9.
[18] *Id.*; CNN, *supra* note 11. While certain European states joined the air strikes (France, the UK, and Belgium), other European states did not join vis-à-vis strikes against ISIL within Syria. JEFFREY L. DUNOFF, STEVEN R. RATNER & DAVID WIPPMAN, INTERNATIONAL LAW NORMS, ACTORS, PROCESS: A PROBLEM-ORIENTED APPROACH 767 (4th ed. 2015).
[19] *US-Led Coalition to Battle IS Group for "as Long as It Takes,"* FRANCE 24, *at* www.france24.com/en/20141203-kerry-coalition-islamic-state-brussels-nato-iraq.
[20] Michael P. Scharf, *How the Syrian Airstrikes Changed International Law*, 19 CHI. J. INT'L L. 586, 590 (2018), *citing* Sam LaGrone, *Russia, Syria Agree on Mediterranean Naval Base Expansion, Refit of Syrian Ships*, USNI NEWS (Jan. 20, 2017), *at* http://perma.cc/68QG-4UDQ.
[21] Patrick J. McDonnell, W. J. Hennigan & Nabih Bulos, *Russia Launches Airstrikes in Syria Amid U.S. Concern About Targets*, L.A. TIMES (Sept. 30, 2015), *at* www.latimes.com/world/europe/la-fg-kremlin-oks-troops-20150930-story.html.

in fact most often targeted opposition forces.[22] Prior to September 2015, Russian involvement consisted mainly of supplying arms and equipment to the Syrian Army.[23] By May 2013, Iranian-backed Lebanese Hezbollah groups had also joined the conflict, assisting the Syrian Army.[24]

Since 2016, Turkish troops intervened both in response to Kurdish forces operating near the Turkish border and in operations against ISIL.[25] Turkey has also provided assistance to Turkish-backed Arabs and Turkmen using the name "Free Syrian Army," which has partly reorganized into the "Syrian National Army."[26] Kurdish forces eventually came to control approximately one-quarter of the territory of Syria.[27] In October 2019, Turkish forces launched an incursion into Kurdish-held northeastern Syria, seizing territory along the Turkish border.[28]

Under the Obama Administration, the US provided military assistance to moderate armed groups that were part of the Free Syrian Army,[29] although that assistance ceased under the Trump Administration.[30] The US has also

---

[22] *Syrian Crisis: Russia Air Strikes "Strengthen IS,"* BBC News (Oct. 2, 2015), *at* www.bbc.com/news/world-middle-east-34431027 ("Moscow insists its air strikes – which began on Wednesday – are targeting IS. But the Syrian opposition and others have suggested non-IS rebels are bearing the brunt of Russian attacks."); *see, e.g.,* Raja Abdulrahim, *Syrian, Russian Airstrikes Target Rebels in Last Stronghold,* Wall St. J. (Apr. 14, 2019), *at* www.wsj.com/articles/syrian-russian-airstrikes-target-rebels-in-last-stronghold-11552572960 ("Syrian government and Russian airstrikes on the last rebel stronghold in Syria have intensified in recent days."). One source attributes 14% of Russian airstrikes as directed at ISIL targets. *Only 14% of Russian Airstrikes in Syria Hit Islamic State Targets, Report Says,* Moscow Times (May 16, 2018), *at* www.themoscowtimes.com/2018/05/16/only-14-percent-russian-airstrikes-syria-hit-islamic-state-targets-report-says-a61470.

[23] Richard Galpin, *Russian Arms Shipments Bolster Syria's Embattled Assad,* BBC News (Jan. 10, 2012), *at* www.bbc.com/news/world-middle-east-16797818.

[24] *Timeline of the Syrian Conflict as It Enters 8th Year,* Assoc. Press (Mar. 15, 2018), *at* www.apnews.com/792a0bd7dd6a4006a78287f170165408.

[25] Al Jazeera, *supra* note 16.

[26] CNN, *supra* note 11. Al Jazeera, *supra* note 16.

[27] Assoc. Press, *supra* note 24.

[28] Zia Weise, *Turkey's Invasion of Syria Explained,* Politico (Oct. 15, 2019), *at* www.politico.eu/article/8-questions-about-turkeys-incursion-into-syria-answered/.

[29] Assistance was said to have included "salaries, training, ammunition and in some cases guided anti-tank missiles." Tom Perry, Suleiman Al-Khalidi & John Walcott, *Exclusive: CIA-Backed Aid for Syrian Rebels Frozen After Islamist Attack – Sources,* Reuters (Feb. 21, 2017), *at* www.reuters.com/article/us-mideast-crisis-syria-rebels/exclusive-cia-backed-aid-for-syrian-rebels-frozen-after-islamist-attack-sources-idUSKBN1601BD. Turkey, the UK, Saudi Arabia, and other Gulf States have also provided assistance to the Free Syrian Army. The "Friends of Syria Group" of states has provided non-military aid.

[30] John Walcott, *Trump Ends CIA Arms Support for Anti-Assad Syria Rebels: U.S. Officials,* Reuters (July 19, 2017), *at* www.reuters.com/article/us-mideast-crisis-usa-syria/trump-ends-cia-arms-support-for-anti-assad-syria-rebels-u-s-officials-idUSKBN1A42KC.

provided weapons and Special Operations forces to assist Kurdish forces.[31] The US also was part of the group of states conducting military strikes against ISIL commencing in 2014.[32] As discussed in Chapter 2, the US additionally launched missile strikes into Syria in April 2017 targeting a Syrian Government air base in response to a chemical weapons attack on the town of Khan Sheikhoun in the opposition-held Idlib Province,[33] and, in April 2018, launched a similar strike, joined by the UK and France, in response to a chemical weapons attack in Eastern Ghouta, also in the Idlib Province.[34] Israel has also carried out air strikes, reportedly against Hezbollah, Iranian forces, and Syrian Government forces.[35]

At the time of writing, the Syrian Army had recaptured most of the areas formerly controlled by anti-regime opposition groups, with the exception of Idlib Province,[36] which is supposed to be a de-escalation zone.[37] As the last remaining rebel stronghold, dire consequences are predicted should Idlib fall to the Syrian Army.[38] Kurdish forces continue to control approximately one-third of Syria's territory,[39] with ISIL thought to have been largely defeated.[40]

The fighting has killed an estimated 465,000, with more than 5.5 million refugees and 6.5 million internally displaced.[41] (The death toll is actually believed to be much higher, but there is no official count as the UN Office of the High Commissioner for Human Rights (OHCHR) stopped updating death tolls in 2014.)[42] Multiple rounds of peace negotiations between the Syrian Government and opposition conducted over the years – in Vienna,

---

[31] CNN, *supra* note 11. The "People's Protection Units" (YPG) are a mostly Kurdish militia that leads the "Syrian Democratic Forces."
[32] See text accompanying note 18 *supra*.
[33] Assoc. Press, *supra* note 24.
[34] CNN, *supra* note 11.
[35] Al Jazeera, *supra* note 16.
[36] The Tahir Institute for Middle East Policy, *TIMEP Brief: Situation in Syria's Idlib Province* (Feb. 21, 2019), at https://timep.org/reports-briefings/timep-brief-situation-in-syrias-idlib-province.
[37] Idlib Province was one of the de-escalation zones Russia, Turkey and Iran agreed to in Astana with the support of the UN Special Envoy Staffan de Mistura. *Russia, Iran, Turkey Set Up Syria De-escalation Zones for at Least Six Months: Memorandum*, Reuters (May 6, 2017), at www.reuters.com/article/us-mideast-crisis-syria-memorandum/russia-iran-turkey-set-up-syria-de-escalation-zones-forat-least-six-months-memorandum-idUSKBN1820C0.
[38] *Id.*
[39] Al Jazeera, *supra* note 16 (map).
[40] Bethan McKernan, *Isis Defeated, US-Backed Syrian Democratic Forces Announce*, Guardian (Mar. 23, 2019), at www.theguardian.com/world/2019/mar/23/isis-defeated-us-backed-syrian-democratic-forces-announce.
[41] Al Jazeera, *supra* note 16.
[42] Trahan e-mail exchange with Mohammad Al Abdallah, Executive Director, Syrian Justice and Accountability Center (SJAC), 6/4/19.

Geneva, and Astana,[43] under the auspices of UN Special Envoys Kofi Annan, Lakhdar Brahimi, and Staffan de Mistura – failed to produce a negotiated settlement.[44]

Given the complexities of the war, no simple solution ever emerged, with hope resting on the rounds of peace negotiations to find an inclusive Syrian-led solution. What the Security Council could, in these circumstances, have done, however, was send an *unequivocal and consistent message* of the *unacceptability of mass atrocity crimes being perpetrated* during the war, such as mass detention, mass torture, indiscriminate aerial bombardment, and use of chemical weapons.[45] The Council could also have sent, and failed to send due to veto use, a clear and consistent message that accountability would follow[46] – as the Allied Powers did during World War II.[47] While it is impossible to prove

---

[43] Astana was the capital of Kazakhstan, but now goes by the name Nur-Sultan.

[44] For a chronology of the peace negotiations, see *Syria Diplomatic Talks: A Timeline*, AL JAZEERA (Sept. 15, 2017), *at* www.aljazeera.com/news/2017/09/syria-diplomatic-talks-timeline-170915083153934.html.

[45] See Report of the Independent International Commission of Inquiry on the Syrian Arab Republic, UN Doc. A/HRC/21/50 (Aug. 16, 2012), *at* www.ohchr.org/Documents/HRBodies/HRCouncil/RegularSession/Session21/A-HRC-21-50_en.pdf [hereinafter, 3rd Report] (covering, inter alia, mass detention and torture); Report of the Independent International Commission of Inquiry on the Syrian Arab Republic, UN Doc. A/HRC/22/59 (Feb. 5, 2013), *at* https://www.ohchr.org/Documents/HRBodies/HRCouncil/CoISyria/A.HRC.22.59_en.pdf [hereinafter, 4th Report] (covering, inter alia, indiscriminate aerial bombardment); *Chemical Weapons Attacks Documented by the Commission (Infographic)*, OHCHR, *at* www.ohchr.org/SiteCollectionImages/Bodies/HRCouncil/IICISyria/COISyria_ChemicalWeapons.jpg (covering chemical weapons attacks). As described below, various resolutions condemning crimes did pass the Council although often years after a resolution that would have originally condemned the crimes was vetoed.

[46] As explored below, the Council sent inconsistent messages, for instance, stressing, at one point, that those "responsible" "must be brought to justice" (S/RES/2139 (2014)), but later that year failing to refer the situation to the International Criminal Court (ICC). S/2014/348 (vetoed by the Russian Federation and China). By now, however, it remains quite unclear whether any kind of comprehensive accountability will be possible (given that the Assad regime remains in power); to date, the General Assembly has only created an investigative mechanism. *See* note 124 *infra* and accompanying text.

[47] During World War II, the Allied Powers sent strong messages to the Nazis, warning that accountability would follow. As recited in the Judgment of the *Alstötter* case: "Notice of intent to punish was repeatedly given by the only means available in international affairs, namely, the solemn warning of the governments of the states at war with Germany. [The defendants were] warned of swift retribution by the express declaration of the Allies at Moscow of 30 October 1943." United States v. Joseph Alstötter, 3 TRIALS OF WAR CRIMINALS BEFORE THE NUREMBERG TRIBUNALS UNDER CONTROL COUNCIL LAW NO. 10, at 954 (1948). Of course, accountability did follow, in the form of the trial before the International Military Tribunal at Nuremberg, as well as many other waves of trials. For background on the Nuremberg trials, see generally MICHAEL R. MARRUS, THE NUREMBERG WAR CRIMES TRIAL 1945–46: A DOCUMENTARY HISTORY (1997). A very significant difference, of course,

that such a message necessarily would have altered the behavior of perpetrators on the ground,[48] clearly the absence of such a message (or mixed messages) meant there was no consistent attempt to deter the commission of Government or opposition crimes, including crimes against humanity and war crimes.[49] (As mentioned, numerous resolutions condemning ISIL and other "terrorist" crimes, by contrast, passed the Security Council.)[50] In this situation, a case can be made that the veto – exercised by a permanent member of the Security Council with political and military ties to the Government in Syria (and actually militarily engaged in the conflict), and sometimes joined by another permanent member (China)[51] – was

> was that the USSR was aligned with the US, UK, and France during World War II, and therefore in agreement on pursuing accountability.

[48] For one study suggesting that deterrence can work, see Jacqueline R. McAllister, *Deterring Wartime Atrocities: Hard Lessons from the Yugoslav Tribunal*, 44 INT'L SEC. 84 (2019–20). This chapter also suggests a correlation between chemical weapons investigation mechanisms being created and declining chemical weapons attacks in Syria. See notes 192–94 *infra* and accompanying text.

[49] See, e.g., Report of the Independent International Commission of Inquiry on the Syrian Arab Republic, UN Doc. A/HRC/21/50 (Aug. 16, 2012), at www.ohchr.org/Documents/HRBodies/HRCouncil/RegularSession/Session21/A-HRC-21-50_en.pdf (concluding war crimes and crimes against humanity were being committed by Government and aligned forces).

[50] See note 8 *supra*. Syria has Al-Qaida affiliated groups. One is Jabhat al-Nusra (or the Nusra Front), which in July 2016 became Hayat Tahrir al-Sham, aligned with forces against the Assad regime. Hayat Tahrir al-Sham claims that it has severed its Al-Qaida affiliation. See Center for Strategic and International Studies, *Transnational Threats Project, Hayat Tahrir al-Sham (HTS), TNT Terrorism Backgrounder*, at www.csis.org/programs/transnational-threats-project/terrorism-backgrounders/hayat-tahrir-al-sham-hts. Another is the Khorasan group (also known as Khorasan), believed to be a group of senior Al-Qaida members operating in Syria. Mariam Karouny, *Insight – U.S.-Led Strikes Pressure Al Qaeda's Syria Group to Join with Islamic State*, REUTERS (Sept. 26, 2014), at https://uk.reuters.com/article/uk-syria-crisis-nusra-insight/insight-u-s-led-strikes-pressure-al-qaedas-syria-group-to-join-with-islamic-state-idUKKCN0HL11520140926.

[51] For one analysis of China's relationship to the Assad regime, see Dan Hemenway, *Chinese Strategic Engagement with Assad's Syria*, ATLANTIC COUNCIL (Dec. 21, 2018), at www.atlanticcouncil.org/blogs/syriasource/chinese-strategic-engagement-with-assad-s-syria. Hemenway writes:

> China has several incentives to cooperate with the Assad regime and support what it hopes will prove a stable and friendly government to China. These interests are linked to Chinese President Xi Jinping's more assertive foreign policy, which envisions China using its formidable economic and political might to counter American influence globally. Beijing aims to incorporate Syria into its Belt and Road Initiative (BRI) as a major transit hub, along with Iran and Iraq. Syria announced in September 2017 that China, together with Russia and Iran, is given priority as a friendly government for all infrastructure and reconstruction projects when the war is over.

Id. He also writes that "China is also concerned about the five thousand Uighur Muslims from the Turkistan Islamic Party (TIP) ... that fight alongside Hay'at Tahrir al-Sham (HTS) in Idlib

a contributing factor in enabling the continued perpetration of at least certain crimes, blocking condemnation, blocking investigations, and blocking prosecutions.[52]

The discussion below roughly groups the vetoes chronologically into those blocking: (1) condemnation of crimes; (2) referral of the situation in Syria to the ICC; (3) measures to alleviate the humanitarian emergency during the siege of Aleppo; and (4) condemnation of chemical weapons use and blocking renewal or creation of a chemical weapons inspections regime that would have attributed responsibility to the side using chemical weapons.

5.1.2 *The First Vetoes Related to the Situation in Syria: Blocking Condemnation of Crimes*

The first three vetoes blocked condemnation of crimes occurring in Syria, including in the early stages of the war, when it could have been most crucial to deliver the message to Government (and, later, opposition) forces that Security Council Member States were vigilant in their monitoring of the situation and prepared to impose at least some measures to try to stem the tide of atrocity crimes.

5.1.2.1 Vetoing a Call to End Violence and Hold Perpetrators Accountable

The first Syria-related veto – a double-veto by Russia and China[53] – occurred on October 4, 2011, when the Security Council had before it a resolution that would have demanded an end to the use of force by the Syrian authorities and called for an end to violence and human rights violations during demonstrations, stressing the need to hold to account those responsible.[54] The resolution would also have called on "all States to exercise vigilance and restraint over the

---

province. China would rather defeat TIP in Syria than have to deal with them upon return to Central Asia or China itself." *Id.* Additionally, "Beijing views cooperation with the Assad regime as a way to strengthen military ties with Russia." *Id.* See also Blessing Nneka Iyase & Sheriff Folami Folarin, *A Critique of Veto Power System in the United Nations Security Council*, Acta Universitatis Danubius, 11 INT'L RELATIONS 104, 111 (2018) ("China has been the second longest non-Arab investor in Syria").

[52] As will be detailed below, ICC investigations and prosecutions were blocked, as well as renewal of a chemical weapons inspection regime that would have attributed responsibility – thus, those investigations were also blocked.

[53] While on this veto, other countries also did not agree on this resolution (with India, South Africa, Brazil, and Lebanon abstaining), as more and more atrocities were committed, Russia ended up alone (sometimes with China) in opposing resolutions. Assoc. Press, *Russia and China Veto UN Resolution against Syrian Regime*, GUARDIAN (Oct. 4, 2011), at www.theguardian.com/world/2011/oct/05/russia-china-veto-syria-resolution.

[54] S/2011/612 (vetoed by the Russian Federation and China).

direct or indirect supply, sale or transfer to Syria of arms and related materiel of all types, as well as technical training, financial resources or services, advice, or other services or assistance related to such arms and related materiel[.]"[55] In addition to protecting its Mediterranean port and demonstrating steadfastness to an ally by not abandoning a then seemingly doomed Assad regime, Russia also had incentive to cast this veto as the resolution would have impacted Russia's sale of arms to Syria, at a time when much of the arms being sold to the Government were coming from Russia.[56]

Only a little over a month after the veto, the Independent Commission of Inquiry on the Syrian Arab Republic (Commission), a body of experts created by the Human Rights Council[57] to establish the facts related to human rights violations and crimes being committed in Syria[58] concluded it had "reasonable suspicion" to believe[59] that "crimes against humanity" were being committed by Syrian military and security forces,[60] and Syrian militia forces, including the (Government-aligned)

[55] *Id.*, para. 9. There was, for example, a Presidential Statement issued in August 2011 condemning the violence, calling on the Syrian regime to respect human rights, urging all parties to act with restraint, and recalling that those responsible for human rights violations should be held to account. S/PRST/2011/16 (Aug. 3, 2011). However, a Presidential Statement is non-binding. "A Presidential Statement is an instrument that follows consultations and is based on unanimity, but is not put to a vote—unlike a formal resolution in both respects. They often serve as precursors to a binding resolution." Marko Milanović, *Can UNSC Presidential Statements Be Legally Binding?*, EJIL: *TALK!* (Apr. 15, 2009), *at* www.ejiltalk.org/can-unsc-presidential-statements-be-legally-binding/.

[56] "President Putin has hailed Russia's military campaign in Syria as a 'priceless' opportunity to test new weaponry, including missile systems." Marc Bennetts, *UK Arms Sales Eclipsed as Moscow Cashes in on Syria*, SUNDAY TIMES (Dec. 10, 2018), *at* www.thetimes.co.uk/article/syria-conflict-spurs-russian-arms-sales-6fjnht87s.

[57] S-17/1, Situation of Human Rights in the Syrian Arab Republic, Resolution adopted by the Human Rights Council at its seventeenth special session, *at* www.ohchr.org/Documents/HRBodies/HRCouncil/CoISyria/ResS17_1.pdf. The Human Rights Council first created a Fact-Finding Mission, but soon after created the Commission of Inquiry. Of course, there is no veto at the Human Rights Council, so it was able to create a Commission of Inquiry, and renew its mandate through the present time, without being hampered by Security Council permanent members.

[58] For details, see Independent International Commission of Inquiry on the Syrian Arab Republic, Mandate, *at* www.ohchr.org/EN/HRBodies/HRC/IICISyria/Pages/CoIMandate.aspx.

[59] The Commission's fact-finding used the standard of "reasonable suspicion." "This standard was met when the commission obtained a reliable body of evidence, consistent with other information, indicating the occurrence of a particular incident or event." Report of the Independent International Commission of Inquiry on the Syrian Arab Republic, UN Doc. A/HRC/S-17/2/Add.1, para. 5 (Nov. 23, 2011), *at* www.ohchr.org/Documents/Countries/SY/A.HRC.S-17.2.Add.1_en.pdf.

[60] "The State security apparatus is reported to be large and effective, with a multitude of security forces and intelligence agencies that have overlapping missions . . . . The internal security apparatus includes police forces under the Ministry of the Interior, Syrian Military

Shabbiha militia.[61] At that time, the crimes were believed to include summary execution, arbitrary arrests, enforced disappearances, torture and other forms of ill-treatment, sexual violence, as well as violations of children's rights.[62] By October 2011, while the killing and hostilities had not yet fully engulfed Syria, already an estimated 3,000 people had been killed, including at least 187 children.[63]

5.1.2.2 Vetoing Condemnation of Arbitrary Detention, Enforced Disappearances, and Other Crimes

The second veto – again cast by Russia and China – occurred on February 4, 2012. By this point, the pace of the killing and the crimes being committed had rapidly accelerated. The Commission, in its second report, continued to find that Government forces were committing "crimes against humanity" as well as "widespread, systematic and gross human rights violations," including arbitrary arrests, torture, abductions, and enforced disappearances.[64] By then, the Commission reported that "[a]nti-Government groups have also committed abuses, although not comparable in scale and organization to those carried out by the State."[65]

Notwithstanding, Russia and China vetoed a resolution "dedicated to encouraging a peaceful resolution of the conflict."[66] Specifically, the resolution would have expressed "grave concern at the deterioration of the situation in Syria" and "the death of thousands," and called "for an immediate end to all violence."[67] It would also have condemned "arbitrary executions, killing and persecution of protesters and members of the media, arbitrary detention, enforced disappearances, interference with access to medical treatment, torture, sexual violence, and ill-treatment, including against

---

Intelligence, Air Force Intelligence, the National Security Bureau, the Political Security Directorate and the General Intelligence Directorate." *Id.*, para. 19.

[61] "The militia includes the *Shabbiha*, which is composed of an estimated 10,000 civilians, who are armed by the Government and are widely used to crush anti-Government demonstrations alongside national security forces; and the People's Army, a Baath party militia with an estimated 100,000 reservists, designed to provide additional security and protection in cities in times of war." *Id.*, para. 20.

[62] *Id.*, at Summary.

[63] *Syria Uprising: UN Says Protest Death Toll Hits 3,000*, BBC NEWS (Oct. 14, 2011), at www.bbc.com/news/world-middle-east-15304741.

[64] Report of the Independent International Commission of Inquiry on the Syrian Arab Republic, UN Doc. A/HRC/19/69 (Feb. 22, 2012), *at* www.ohchr.org/Documents/HRBodies/HRCouncil/RegularSession/Session19/A-HRC-19-69_en.pdf.

[65] *Id.*, at Summary.

[66] Van Schaack, *supra* note 8.

[67] S/2012/77 (vetoed by the Russian Federation and China).

children."[68] The resolution would additionally have demanded that the "Syrian authorities cooperate fully with the Office of the High Commissioner for Human Rights and with the Commission of Inquiry dispatched by the Human Rights Council."[69]

At the time of the veto, 7,500 people had been killed, including at least 2,493 civilians.[70] At this point, the General Assembly stepped in and issued a resolution – supported by 137 states[71] – condemning the violence and stressing the need for accountability,[72] but, of course, such a resolution is non-binding and lacks the force of a Security Council resolution. Yet, the number of affirmative votes the resolution garnered is a clear reflection of both immense frustration by over two-thirds of UN Member States with the crimes being committed, as well as the vetoes being cast.[73]

5.1.2.3 Vetoing Condemnation of Bombing and Shelling of Population Centers, and Detention of Thousands in Government-Run Facilities

The third veto occurred on July 19, 2012, with crimes further spreading in both number and type. By August 3, 2012, in its third report, the Commission concluded that Syria was in a state of non-international armed conflict, and that both crimes against humanity and war crimes were occurring.[74] Specifically, the Commission found Government forces and the *Shabbiha* militia had committed the crimes against humanity of murder and torture, and war crimes including unlawful killing, torture, arbitrary arrest and detention, sexual violence, indiscriminate attack, and pillaging and destruction of property.[75] The Commission also found reasonable ground to believe

---

[68] *Id.*, para. 1.
[69] *Id.*, para. 11.
[70] *Syria Unrest: Death Toll Passes 7,500, UN Says*, BBC NEWS (Feb. 29, 2012), *at* www.bbc.com/news/world-middle-east-17194593.
[71] The resolution was adopted by 137 votes to 12 against, with 17 abstentions.
[72] UN Doc. A/Res/66/253 (Feb. 16, 2012).
[73] The comments of Costa Rica are illustrative of concern about veto use:

> Working with the other countries of the so-called group of five small nations, we have expressed our concern about the use of a veto by two permanent members of the Security Council on 4 February (see S/PV.6711). We have reiterated our call for the veto not to be used in situations relating to genocide, crime against humanity, ethnic cleansing or war crimes.

General Assembly, 97th Plenary Meeting, February 16, 2012, UN Doc. A/66/PV.97, *at* www.un.org/en/ga/search/view_doc.asp?symbol=A/66/PV.97.
[74] 3rd Report, *supra* note 45.
[75] *Id.*, at Summary.

5.1 Analysis of Veto Use Related to Syria

organized anti-Government armed groups were committing the war crimes of murder, extrajudicial execution, and torture, but, still, "[t]he violations and abuses committed by anti-Government armed groups did not reach the gravity, frequency and scale of those committed by Government forces and the *Shabbiha*."[76]

Despite these crimes, on July 19, 2012, Russia and China vetoed a resolution that would have condemned bombing and shelling of population centers, and detention of thousands in Government-run facilities.[77] The resolution would also have demanded an end to troop movements toward population centers and the use of heavy weapons in such centers, renewed the mandate of the UN Supervision Mission in Syria (UNSMIS),[78] and stated that non-compliance would result in the immediate imposition of measures under Article 41 of the UN Charter (non-forceful measures).[79]

While passage of these three resolutions quite likely would not have halted the perpetration of the crimes, it could have been a crucial first step, indicating that the Security Council *was watching the situation* and united in condemning the crimes. The failure of the Security Council to voice condemnation at this point, by contrast, was a troubling preliminary indication that the Security Council would not seriously attempt to rein in the commission of mass atrocity crimes (here, crimes against humanity and war crimes). While some of the crimes were able to be condemned under later resolutions,[80] that was two years, and many crimes, later.[81] None of these resolutions proposed action by the Security Council, yet, their passage nevertheless would have been very significant. Had they passed, and had any of the parties named failed to comply with the terms of the resolutions, it

---

[76] *Id.*
[77] S/2012/538 (vetoed by the Russian Federation and China).
[78] *Id.*, paras. 4, 10. UNSMIS was created in Security Council Resolution 2043 (Apr. 21, 2012) to monitor a cessation of armed violence. Its mandate ended in August 2012. Russia had introduced the text of what became Resolution 2043. Van Schaack, *supra* note 8.
[79] S/2012/538, para. 14 (vetoed by the Russian Federation and China). There is a possible counter-narrative on this veto. Namely, at the time, there was a "six-point" peace plan proposed by Kofi Annan, acting as Joint Special Envoy for the UN and League of Arab States. The draft resolution contained a threat of sanctions; yet, that apparently was not part of the peace plan. Thus, some might claim that the draft resolution went beyond what had been agreed upon.
[80] *See, e.g.*, S/RES/2139 (2014), paras. 3, 11 (condemning indiscriminate shelling and aerial bombardment, and torture in detention facilitates). There were also two weakly worded resolutions condemning "human rights" violations in 2012. S/RES/2042 (2012); S/RES/2043 (2012).
[81] Van Schaack also points out that later condemnation only came when the resolutions condemned crimes on both sides, but, earlier, when only or primarily Government crimes were being committed, there were vetoes. Van Schaack, *supra* note 8.

would have shown a deliberate pattern of non-compliance, potentially warranting the imposition of further measures.[82] But one also cannot underestimate the vital importance of even Security Council resolutions that condemn crimes and call for their commission to be halted, even without repercussions.

5.1.3 Vetoing Referral of the Situation in Syria to the ICC

By 2013, crimes continued to accelerate, including a large-scale sarin gas attack on Al-Ghouta in August 2013, and the use of siege warfare. Notwithstanding the many crimes being committed, as detailed further below in Chapter 5.1.3.4, Russia and China vetoed referral of the situation in Syria to the ICC, a court with jurisdiction to prosecute both crimes against humanity and war crimes.[83] Their vetoes[84] largely blocked the possibility of ICC prosecution of both Government and opposition forces, as well as crimes by ISIL.

5.1.3.1 Acceleration of Crimes

By the time of its fourth report, on February 5, 2013, the Commission summarized the situation in Syria as follows:

> The depth of the Syrian tragedy is poignantly reflected in the accounts of its victims. Their harrowing experiences of survival detail grave human rights violations, war crimes and crimes against humanity. The destructive dynamics of the civil war not only have an impact on the civilian population

---

[82] There are a myriad of measures the Security Council could have imposed, had there been the will (and no veto). *See* Charter of the United Nations (1945), 892 UNTS 119 (1945) [hereinafter, UN Charter], Art. 40 (provisional measures), Art. 41 (non-forceful measures), Art. 42 (forceful measures). While some states justify "humanitarian intervention," that position is not widely endorsed. For a comprehensive discussion of humanitarian intervention (including whether US missile strikes into Syria in 2017, and US, UK, and French missile strikes into Syria in 2018 fell within that doctrine), see Chapter 2.

[83] Rome Statute of the International Criminal Court, Arts. 7–8, UN Doc. A/CONF.183/9*, July 18, 1998 (Rome Statute). In addition, the ICC has jurisdiction over the crime of genocide and the crime of aggression. *See id.*, Art 6 (genocide); Resolution ICC-ASP/16/Res.5, adopted by consensus, December 14, 2017 (activating jurisdiction regarding the crime of aggression).

[84] While Russia and China are hardly proponents of the ICC, they do not always veto referral of situations to the ICC, as neither vetoed the Darfur or Libya referrals. S/RES/1953; S/RES/1970. The United States, particularly under the Trump Administration, is also no proponent of the ICC, but did not veto the Syria referral (perhaps knowing or assuming that Russia and/or China would do so).

but are also tearing apart the country's complex social fabric, jeopardizing future generations and undermining peace and security in the entire region.

The situation of human rights in the Syrian Arab Republic has continued to deteriorate. Since 15 July 2012, there has been an escalation in the armed conflict between Government forces and anti-Government armed groups. The conflict has become increasingly sectarian, with the conduct of the parties becoming significantly more radicalized and militarized.[85]

In its fourth, fifth, and sixth reports during 2013, the Commission found continued evidence of Government forces and affiliated militias committing crimes against humanity including murder, torture, rape, enforced disappearance, other inhumane acts,[86] and forcible displacement.[87] The reports also documented Government forces and affiliated militias committing war crimes including arbitrary arrest and detention, unlawful attack, attacking protected objects, pillaging and destruction of property,[88] summary execution,[89] torture, hostage-taking, murder, execution without due process, and rape.[90] The Commission's findings included documentation of deliberate targeting of medical personnel[91] and hospitals, denial of medical access,[92] destruction of cultural heritage property,[93] as well as laying siege to towns in order to make conditions of life unbearable by preventing incoming supplies of food, water, fuel, and medicine, and shelling water towers and electricity generators.[94]

---

[85] 4th Report, *supra* note 45, at 1.
[86] *Id.*
[87] Report of the Independent International Commission of Inquiry on the Syrian Arab Republic, UN Doc. A/HRC/23/58 (June 18, 2013), *at* https://documents-dds-ny.un.org/doc/UNDOC/GEN/G13/156/20/PDF/G1315620.pdf?OpenElement [hereinafter, 5th Report].
[88] 4th Report, *supra* note 45.
[89] 5th Report, *supra* note 87.
[90] Report of the Independent International Commission of Inquiry on the Syrian Arab Republic, UN Doc. A/HRC/24/46 (Aug. 16, 2013), *at* www.ohchr.org/EN/HRBodies/HRC/RegularSessions/Session24/Documents/A_HRC_24_46_en.DOC [hereinafter, 6th Report].
[91] "Physicians for Human Rights (PHR) has documented at least 757 killings of medical personnel since the popular democratic uprisings began in March 2011. The Syrian government, its ally Hezbollah and Russia are responsible for more than 90% of those deaths." Adham Sahloul, *Obituary: A Hospital in Aleppo (2013–2016)*, TIME (Dec. 14, 2016), *at* http://time.com/4599498/aleppo-hospital-obituary/.
[92] 4th Report, *supra* note 45, para. 138.
[93] *Id.*, paras. 148–49.
[94] 6th Report, *supra* note 90, paras. 172–79.

By this time, the Commission reports also start documenting extensive crimes by anti-Government armed groups, such as war crimes including murder, torture, hostage-taking, attacking protected objects,[95] sentencing and execution without due process, pillage,[96] and besieging and indiscriminately shelling civilian neighbourhoods.[97] The sixth report additionally documented anti-Government and Kurdish armed groups recruiting and using child soldiers.[98]

5.1.3.2 The Sarin Gas Attack on Al-Ghouta

One of the most horrifying single episodes of the war came with a large-scale sarin gas attack on August 21, 2013, in the Al-Ghouta region, a suburb of Damascus, where Syrian forces had been attempting to expel rebel forces.[99] Over 1,000 may have died,[100] including many non-combatants, with an estimated 3,000 left suffering from "neurotoxic symptoms."[101] Those launching the attack had access to the Syrian military chemical weapons stockpile and expertise and equipment to manipulate large amounts of chemical agents,[102] leading to the conclusion that the attack was launched by Government forces.[103] The use of chemical weapons was later confirmed by a UN Investigative

---

[95] 4th Report, *supra* note 45.
[96] 5th Report, *supra* note 87.
[97] 6th Report, *supra* note 90.
[98] *Id.*
[99] *Id.*
[100] Arms Control Association, *Timeline of Syrian Chemical Weapons Activity, 2012–2019*, at www.armscontrol.org/factsheets/Timeline-of-Syrian-Chemical-Weapons-Activity. Death toll estimates vary from 281 to 1,729. *See* France-Diplomatie – Ministry of Foreign Affairs and International Development, Syria/Syrian Chemical Programme – National Executive Summary of Declassified Intelligence, Paris, September 3, 2013 (using the figure 281), *at* www.diplomatie.gouv.fr/IMG/pdf/Syrian_Chemical_Programme.pdf; *Bodies Still Being Found After Alleged Syria Chemical Attack: Opposition*, DAILY STAR (Aug. 22, 2013), *at* www.dailystar.com.lb/News/Middle-East/2013/Aug-22/228268-bodies-still-being-found-after-alleged-syria-chemical-attack-opposition.ashx (using the figure 1,729).
[101] Médecins Sans Frontières, *Syria: Thousands Suffering Neurotoxic Symptoms Treated in Hospitals Supported by MSF* (Aug. 24, 3013), *at* www.msf.org/syria-thousands-suffering-neurotoxic-symptoms-treated-hospitals-supported-msf.
[102] *Chemical Weapons Attacks Documented by the Commission (Infographic)*, *supra* note 45.
[103] "[B]y examining the debris field and impact area where the rockets struck in Muadhamiya and Ein Tarma, the inspectors found 'sufficient evidence' to calculate azimuths, or angular measurements, that allow their trajectories to be determined 'with a sufficient degree of accuracy.' When plotted on a map, the trajectories converge on a site that Human Rights Watch said was a large military base on Mount Qassioun that is home to the Republican Guard 104th Brigade.... The White House said US agencies had assessed 'with high confidence' that the Syrian government was responsible." *Syria Chemical Attack: What We Know*, BBC NEWS (Sept. 24, 2013), *at* www.bbc.com/news/world-middle-east-23927399.

Commission,[104] with the Al-Ghouta attack having been preceded by several smaller chemical weapons attacks.[105] As discussed in Chapter 2, it was after the Al-Ghouta chemical weapons attack that President Obama, who had previously stated that use of chemical weapons would cross a "red line,"[106] expressed his intent to seek Congressional authorization for a limited US military strike into Syria to deter further chemical weapons use.[107] President Obama later postponed Congress' vote while negotiations were pursued to implement a chemical weapons inspection and disarmament regime proposed by Russia.[108]

5.1.3.3 The Dire Consequences of Siege Warfare

Another tragedy of the war in Syria has been the extensive use of siege warfare. The Commission in its seventh report in February 2014 discussed the consequences of siege warfare as well as its concern that "[t]he warring parties do not fear being held accountable for their acts." The Commission wrote:

> More than 250,000 people are besieged in the Syrian Arab Republic and subjected to relentless shelling and bombardment. They are denied humanitarian aid, food and such basic necessities as medical care, and must choose between surrender and starvation. Siege warfare is employed in a context of egregious human rights and international humanitarian law violations. *The warring parties do not fear being held accountable for their acts.*[109]

The Commission concluded that many of the same crimes against humanity were continuing, with additional war crimes by Government forces and

---

[104] United Nations Mission to Investigate Allegations of the Use of Chemical Weapons in the Syrian Arab Republic, Report on the Alleged Use of Chemical Weapons in the Ghouta Area of Damascus on 21 August 2013, September 13, 2013, *at* www.un.org/zh/focus/northafrica/cw investigation.pdf (finding "clear and convincing evidence that surface-to-surface rockets containing the nerve agent Sarin were used").

[105] The Commission document attacks on: Uteibah on March 19, 2013; Khan Al-Asal on March 19, 2013 (using chlorine gas); Sheik Maqsood Neighborhood on April 13, 2013; and Saraqib on April 29, 2013. *Chemical Weapons Attacks Documented by the Commission (Infographic), supra* note 45.

[106] Glenn Kessler, *President Obama and the "Red Line" on Syria's Chemical Weapons*, WASH. POST (Sept. 6, 2013), *at* www.washingtonpost.com/news/fact-checker/wp/2013/09/06/president-obama-and-the-red-line-on-syrias-chemical-weapons/?noredirect=on&utm_term=.fdac9d3acdfa.

[107] Peter Baker & Jonathan Weisman, *Obama Seeks Approval by Congress for Strike in Syria*, N.Y. TIMES (Aug. 31, 2013), *at* www.nytimes.com/2013/09/01/world/middleeast/syria.html.

[108] *See* Arms Control Association Timeline, *supra* note 100.

[109] Report of the Independent International Commission of Inquiry on the Syrian Arab Republic, U.N. Doc. A/HRC/25/65 (Feb. 12, 2014), *at* www.refworld.org/docid/53182eed4.html [hereinafter, 7th Report] (emphasis added).

affiliated militia of targeting civilians in sniper attacks, barrel bombing, and indiscriminate and disproportionate aerial bombardment and shelling.[110] Non-state armed groups also continued to commit extensive war crimes,[111] and now additionally crimes against humanity.[112] As of May 2014, 162,000 people had been killed, including almost 54,000 civilians (over 8,600 of whom were children),[113] and, as of June 2013, there were 4.25 million internally displaced.[114]

5.1.3.4 Vetoing ICC Referral

While the Security Council was able to muster enough agreement to issue a resolution condemning an extensive list of crimes,[115] calling for the lifting of sieges including of Aleppo, and "recalling" that "starvation of civilians as a method of combat is prohibited by international humanitarian law,"[116] what the Security Council more significantly could have done at this point was try to *deter* commission of the crimes, and *deliver a clear message* that accountability would follow – had there actually been the will – by referring the situation in Syria to the ICC. Yet, despite the vast number of crimes being committed, including the large-scale sarin gas attack on Al-Ghouta[117] and the

---

[110] Id.
[111] The war crimes included murder, execution without due process, torture, hostage-taking, enforced disappearances, rape and sexual violence, recruiting and using children in hostilities, attacking protected objects, forcibly displacing civilians, targeting medical and religious personnel and journalists, and besieging and indiscriminately shelling civilian neighborhoods. Id.
[112] The crimes against humanity included widespread detention and torture. Id.
[113] *Syria War Death Toll Tops 160,000*, CBC News (May 19, 2014), at www.cbc.ca/news/world/syria-war-death-toll-tops-160-000-1.2647285.
[114] 5th Report, *supra* note 87.
[115] S/RES/2139, para. 1 (Feb. 22, 2014) (condemning "all forms of sexual and gender-based violence, as well as all grave violations and abuses committed against children in contravention of applicable international law, such as recruitment and use, killing and maiming, rape, attacks on schools and hospitals as well as arbitrary arrest, detention, torture, ill treatment and use as human shields"). One reason this resolution may have passed was that it condemned crimes by both "Syrian authorities, as well as the human rights abuses and violations of international humanitarian law by armed groups." Id., para. 1; *see also* Van Schaack, *supra* note 8.
[116] S/RES/2139, para. 5. *See also* S/RES/2332 (Dec. 21, 2016); S/RES/2393 (2017) (reaffirming that sieges of civilian populations are a violation of international humanitarian law); S/RES/2417 (2018) (condemning starvation of civilians as a method of warfare and prohibited by international humanitarian law); S/RES/2165; S/RES/2139.
[117] Admittedly, the ICC does not have jurisdiction to prosecute use of chemical weapons during non-international armed conflict; however, when such weapons are used during non-international armed conflict, other war crimes covered by the Rome Statute are committed. *Compare* Rome Statute, Art. 8.2(b) (xvii–xviii) (war crimes during international armed conflict, including "[e]mploying poison or poisoned weapons" and "asphyxiating, poisonous

widespread use of siege warfare, as well as the Commission *specifically warning* that "[t]he warring parties do not fear being held accountable for their acts,"[118] and the Security Council elsewhere reaffirming a commitment "for violations and abuses in Syria [to] be brought to justice,"[119] on May 22, 2014, Russia and China vetoed a resolution that would have referred the situation in Syria to the ICC.[120]

The vetoed resolution also would have reaffirmed "strong condemnation of the widespread violations of human rights and international humanitarian law by the Syrian authorities and pro-Government militias, as well as the human rights abuses and violations of international humanitarian law by non-State armed groups . . . ."[121] That resolution was co-sponsored by sixty-five states.[122] The large number of states co-sponsoring was a clear indication of widespread support for the referral among UN Member States, and intended to exert political pressure on Russia and China to refrain from using their vetoes.[123]

---

or other gases"); *with id.* Art. 8(c), (e) (war crimes during non-international armed conflict, not containing the same).

[118] 7th Report, *supra* note 109.

[119] S/RES/2139, para. 13.

[120] S/2014/348 (vetoed by the Russian Federation and China). The veto of referral was also preceded by the publication of the "Caesar photos," documenting horrific and gruesome mass torture in Government-run detention facilities. *See Goal Stories: The Caesar Photos*, at www.goalglobal.org/stories/post/what-are-the-caesar-photographs ("The photographer, a former military policeman now code-named Caesar, defected from Syria and brought with him upwards of 55,000 such images (of 11,000 people) taken by himself and other military photographers between 2011 and 2013.").

[121] S/2014/348, para. 1 (vetoed by the Russian Federation and China). The resolution would also have expressed "commitment to an effective follow-up of the [referral]." *Id.*, para. 5. Such a commitment would have been extremely helpful had referral occurred, given the lack of past Security Council follow up on its referrals to the ICC of the situations in Darfur and Libya. S/RES/1593; S/RES/1970.

[122] They were: Albania, Andorra, Australia, Austria, Belgium, Botswana, Bulgaria, Canada, Central African Republic, Chile, Côte d'Ivoire, Croatia, Cyprus, Czech Republic, Democratic Republic of the Congo, Denmark, Estonia, Finland, France, Georgia, Germany, Greece, Hungary, Iceland, Ireland, Italy, Japan, Jordan, Latvia, Libya, Liechtenstein, Lithuania, Luxembourg, Malta, Marshall Islands, Mexico, Monaco, Montenegro, Netherlands, New Zealand, Norway, Panama, Poland, Portugal, Qatar, Republic of Korea, Republic of Moldova, Romania, Samoa, San Marino, Saudi Arabia, Senegal, Serbia, Seychelles, Slovakia, Slovenia, Spain, Sweden, Switzerland, The former Yugoslav Republic of Macedonia, Turkey, Ukraine, United Arab Emirates, the UK, and the US.

[123] Trahan e-mail exchange with Sina Alavi, Legal Adviser to the Permanent Mission of Liechtenstein to the UN, 4/23/19. The call for referral originated with a January 2013 letter initiated by Switzerland, with 50 signatory states. Letter to H.E. Mr. Mohammad Masood Khan, President of the Security Council for the month of January 2013, from the Permanent Mission of Switzerland to the United Nations (Jan. 14, 2013), *at* www.newsd.admin.ch/newsd/

The absence of referral could mean that the vast bulk of the crimes in Syria escape prosecution. Syria is not a party to the ICC's Rome Statute, so that absent referral, the ICC has only quite limited jurisdiction over a small subset of the crimes in Syria – namely, it has jurisdiction over "foreign fighters" who are nationals of Rome Statute States Parties, but not Syrian or other non-State Party nationals. As noted in Chapter 4, after veto of the ICC referral, the General Assembly created a new type of mechanism (the IIIM),[124] with a mandate "to collect, consolidate, preserve and analyse evidence of violations of international humanitarian law and human rights violations and abuses . . ." in Syria.[125] The IIIM, however, is not an accountability mechanism – it has no capacity to conduct prosecutions.[126] Its evidence collection can, to the extent possible, feed into domestic cases in Europe (or elsewhere) that may be pursued against isolated perpetrators who, for example, travel to such countries or where victims are located.[127] While the prosecution of individual isolated cases is significant, it does not supplant the need for the ICC, or creation of other, legitimate, credible ways to prosecute the crimes in Syria, either of which could evaluate the totality of the crime base and develop a prosecutorial strategy based on inclusion of the key perpetrators and gravest crimes, considering additional factors such as prosecuting all sides and including the key types of crimes perpetrated.[128]

5.1.3.5 ISIL Crimes against the Yazidis

Blocking ICC referral also meant the ICC would be unable to prosecute ISIL crimes. While ISIL perpetrators are implicated in extensive crimes against

---

message/attachments/29293.pdf. The letter also reflected the broad base of support that existed for referral and presumably was also intended to pressure the Security Council to refer.

[124] The full name is the International, Impartial and Independent Mechanism to Assist in the Investigation and Prosecution of Persons Responsible for the Most Serious Crimes Under International Law Committed in the Syrian Arab Republic Since March 2011. The IIIM is mostly engaged in gathering "information" already collected by others; sifting through it; trying to verify and determine what may be useful and usable in any future accountability process; and putting this information into a usable form to hold those responsible accountable. Trahan 5/30/19 interview with Andras Vamos-Goldman.

[125] UN GA Res. 71/248, para. 4 (Dec. 21, 2016).

[126] *Id.*

[127] The presence of victims alone, would not, however, allow prosecutions absent apprehension of the perpetrators unless the country is one where criminal trials *in absentia* are permitted. For a survey of the law on universal jurisdiction, see Amnesty International, *Universal Jurisdiction: A Preliminary Survey of Legislation Around the World – 2012 Update* (2012), at www.amnesty.org/download/Documents/24000/ior530192012en.pdf.

[128] Current political realities, for now, preclude such prosecutions, although the political climate could shift in the future.

humanity and war crimes, their attacks on the Yazidi community brought them particular notoriety. ISIL forces are believed to have committed genocide,[129] as well as crimes against humanity and war crimes, against members of the Yazidi religious group,[130] in addition to targeting other groups.[131] It is believed that as many as 6,800 Yazidi women and girls[132] were forced into sexual slavery with ISIL fighters (sometimes having been sold in slave markets), after men of the communities were executed.[133] The attack on the Yazidis has been characterized as "a brutal campaign to eliminate the Yazidi identity, involving violations committed on a massive scale, forced conversions to Islam, the separation of families and enslavement of surviving women and children, considered as spoils of war."[134] The Commission, in a special report, characterized the crimes committed against the Yazidis as genocide, crimes against humanity, and war crimes based on sexual slavery, enslavement, torture and inhuman and degrading treatment, forcible transfer causing serious bodily and mental harm, the infliction of conditions of life that bring about a slow death, and preventing births.[135]

Absent referral, most ISIL crimes are also beyond the scope of the ICC's jurisdiction. As with the crimes in Syria more generally, the ICC only has jurisdiction over a limited subset of ISIL crimes – namely, those committed by

---

[129] Tom Gjelten, *State Department Declares ISIS Attacks on Christians Constitute Genocide*, NPR (Mar. 17, 2016), *at* www.npr.org/2016/03/17/470861310/state-department-declares-isis-attacks-on-christians-constitute-genocide.

[130] "The Yazidis are one of the world's smallest and oldest monotheistic religious minorities. Their religion is considered a pre-Islamic sect that draws from Christianity, Judaism, and the ancient monotheistic religion of Zoroastrianism." Joshua Berlinger, *Who Are the Religious and Ethnic Groups Under Threat from ISIS?*, CNN (Aug. 8, 2014), *at* www.cnn.com/2014/08/08/world/meast/iraq-ethnic-groups-under-threat-isis/index.html.

[131] ISIL, for example, is also believed to have "tortured, raped, kidnapped and executed Christians in Iraq and Syria." Counter Extremism Project, *ISIS's Persecution of Religions*, *at* www.counterextremism.com/content/isiss-persecution-religions.

[132] *See* Reliefweb, *Sexual Violence against Yazidis: ISIL Foreign Fighters Should Be Prosecuted for Genocide and Crimes against Humanity* (Oct. 25, 2018) (a report published by the Kinyat Organization for Documentation and FIDH estimates as of October 2018 "4300 [who] have allegedly escaped or been bought back [and] 2500 members of the community ... still believed to be 'missing'").

[133] The number killed is estimated at 2,000–5,500. Kinyat Organization for Documentation and FIDH, *Sexual and Gender-Based Crimes against the Yazidi Community: The Role of ISIL Foreign Fighters*, at 5 (Oct. 2018), *at* www.fidh.org/IMG/pdf/irak723angweb.pdf. Of those, "1,400 were executed, and 1,700 died on Mount Sinjar during the August 2014 siege." *Id.*

[134] Reliefweb, *supra* note 132.

[135] Report of the Independent International Commission of Inquiry on the Syrian Arab Republic, "They Came to Destroy": ISIS Crimes against the Yazidis, UN Doc. A/HRC/32/CRP.2 (June 15, 2016), *at* www.ohchr.org/Documents/HRBodies/HRCouncil/CoISyria/A_HRC_32_CRP.2_en.pdf.

"foreign fighters" from Rome Statute States Parties, but not Syrian (or Iraqi) or other non-State Party nationals.[136] While the IIIM's mandate includes evidence-collection regarding ISIL crimes in Syria, and the Security Council also later created a mechanism to investigate ISIL crimes in Iraq – the UN Investigative Team for Accountability of Da'esh (UNITAD)[137] – neither mechanism has any ability to conduct prosecutions. While isolated ISIL fighters could be prosecuted in European (or other) countries if they return, unless some other prosecution mechanism is established, the lack of referral could also mean most ISIL crimes either escape prosecution, or end in summary forms of vengeful justice in Iraq or Syria. There have already been extremely troubling news accounts of mass executions of ISIL perpetrators in Iraq after brief trials.[138]

Thus, veto of the referral both (i) jettisoned any kind of consistent message that perpetrators could face accountability,[139] which could have been sent in an attempt to deter further crimes, and (ii) made attempts to prosecute the crimes significantly more difficult, if not impossible, for the vast bulk of the crimes,[140] at least while the current Syrian Government remains in power.

---

[136] One report documents crimes by foreign ISIL fighters of French, German, American, Saudi, Libyan, Tunisian, Lebanese, Palestinian, Yemeni, and Chinese nationalities; yet, of those, only France, Germany, Tunisia, and Palestine are Rome Statute States Parties, but there would be no need for ICC prosecution of at least French and German nationals, as their national judiciaries are fully capable of such prosecutions. See Kinyat and FIDH Report, *supra* note 133, at 28. The ICC Prosecutor has declared that "the jurisdictional basis ... is too narrow at this stage." See ICC Office of the Prosecutor, *Statement of the Prosecutor of the International Criminal Court, Fatou Bensouda, on the Alleged Crimes Committed by ISIS* (Apr. 8, 2015), at www.icc-cpi.int/Pages/item.aspx?name=otp-stat-08-04-2015-1.

[137] UNITAD was created by Security Council resolution 2379 (Sept. 21, 2017). S/2017/2379. UNITAD is charged with supporting Iraqi domestic efforts to hold ISIL perpetrators accountable for crimes committed in Iraq. *Id.*

[138] See Ben Taub, *Iraq's Post-ISIS Campaign of Revenge*, NEW YORKER (Dec. 17, 2018), *at* www.newyorker.com/magazine/2018/12/24/iraqs-post-isis-campaign-of-revenge ("Thousands of men and boys have been convicted of ISIS affiliation, and hundreds have been hanged."). Given concerns about lack of due process and potential imposition of the death penalty in Iraqi courts, it remains entirely unclear what UNITAD will do with most of the evidence it collects, as a UN mechanism should not turn over evidence to courts lacking due process protections or retaining the death penalty. The creation of an evidence-collecting mechanism that only investigates the crimes of one side in a conflict also sets an extremely problematic precedent. For discussion of concerns with UNITAD's mandate, see Jennifer Trahan, *International Justice and the International Criminal Court at a Critical Juncture*, in THE FUTURE OF GLOBAL AFFAIRS: MANAGING DISCONTINUITIES, DISRUPTIONS, AND DESTRUCTION (C. P. Ankersen & W.P.S. Sidhu eds., forthcoming 2020).

[139] As noted, there were resolutions calling for accountability, *see, e.g.*, S/RES/2139, para. 13, but the ICC referral would have actually been a *step towards* making this possible.

[140] Admittedly, the ICC could not have prosecuted numerically that many perpetrators either (mainly due to budgetary limitations), but it could have tackled prosecutions systematically.

5.1.4 Vetoes Related to the Siege of Aleppo

The next two vetoes of Security Council resolutions relate to the siege of Aleppo, another of the many tragedies of the Syrian civil war.[141] Despite the dire circumstances in which the population trapped in Aleppo found itself, with numerous crimes being committed, including indiscriminate aerial bombardment by Syrian and Russian air forces and destruction of hospitals, the vetoes blocked condemnation of the crimes, and blocked a seven-day ceasefire that would have allowed humanitarian assistance to reach those trapped by the fighting. China declined to join Russia on the first of the two vetoes. While there was an Aleppo-related resolution that was able to pass, it came only once the city had fallen to Government forces, so did nothing to alleviate conditions during the siege.[142] Many other cities in Syria were also subjected to siege warfare; thus, the siege of Aleppo was far from the only instance.[143]

5.1.4.1 The Siege of Aleppo

The fighting in Aleppo began in 2012,[144] and lasted until December 2016, when Government forces regained control of the city.[145] The situation became particularly desperate for those trapped in the city particularly by the fall of 2016. In September 29, 2016, "[a]irstrikes by forces loyal to the Syrian government ... bombed out of service the two largest hospitals in besieged eastern Aleppo," which hospitals had been serving a quarter of

---

Universal jurisdiction prosecutions (or domestic prosecution based on other grounds of jurisdiction) will depend more on the happenstance of where perpetrators travel and can be apprehended, and which victims (with the wherewithal to press the authorities to initiate investigations) reside in the diaspora communities of which countries.

[141] The siege during the current war in Syria was pre-dated by a 1980 siege on Aleppo, also by Government forces, that left an estimated 1,000–2000 dead. Human Rights Watch, Middle East Watch, *Syria Unmasked: The Suppression of Human Rights by the Assad Regime* (1991).

[142] S/RES/2328 (Dec. 19, 2016) (calling for evacuation of civilians from Aleppo and access to ensure humanitarian assistance). There was also a resolution two years prior that called for the lifting of sieges, including in Aleppo. S/RES/2139, para. 5 (2014).

[143] See, e.g., S/RES/2139, para. 5 (calling for the lifting of the sieges "of populated areas, including in the Old City of Homs (Homs), Nubl and Zahra (Aleppo), Madamiyet Elsham (Rural Damascus), Yarmouk (Damascus), Eastern Ghouta (Rural Damascus), Darayya (Rural Damascus), and other locations, and demand[ing] that all parties allow the delivery of humanitarian assistance ....").

[144] Luke Harding & Martin Chulov, *Syrian Rebels Fight Assad Troops in Aleppo*, GUARDIAN (July 22, 2012), *at* www.theguardian.com/world/2012/jul/22/syrian-rebels-fight-aleppo.

[145] For a chronology of the fighting in Aleppo, see David Sim, *The Fall of Aleppo Timeline: How Assad Captured Syria's Biggest City*, IB TIMES (Dec. 16, 2016), *at* www.ibtimes.co.uk/fall-aleppo-timeline-how-assad-captured-syrias-biggest-city-1596504.

a million.[146] Doctors described the situation of "children who are coming to us as body parts. We collect the body parts and wrap them in shrouds and bury them."[147] The airstrikes followed a week of intense military activity by Syrian military forces in the area after a ceasefire agreement had collapsed, with Aleppo "virtually cut off from medical and food supplies."[148] Human Rights Watch called the September and October 2016 bombings conducted by a joint Russian and Syrian aerial campaign war crimes, documenting over 950 impact sites from airstrikes characterized as "recklessly indiscriminate," with use of "cluster munitions and incendiary weapons," and deliberate targeting of at least one of the medical facilities.[149] By November 20, 2016, the Syrian Observatory for Human Rights reported the number of casualties across Aleppo and surrounding areas had reached over 1,000 since September 2016 alone.[150]

In its eighth, ninth, and tenth reports in 2014–15, the Commission continued to find evidence of many of the same crimes as previously reported, such as Government and affiliated forces committing massacres, disregarding the special protection accorded to hospitals and medical and humanitarian personnel, as well as the use of chlorine gas.[151] It also continued to find a host of crimes committed by non-state armed groups, such as targeting medical and religious personnel and journalists.[152] In the tenth report, the Commission, likely in response to the Security Council's failure to refer the situation in

---

[146] Kareem Shaheen & Julian Borger, *Two Aleppo Hospitals Bombed out of Service in "Catastrophic" Airstrikes*, GUARDIAN (Sept. 28, 2016), at www.theguardian.com/world/2016/sep/28/aleppo-two-hospitals-bombed-out-of-service-syria-airstrikes.

[147] *Id.*

[148] Erin Cunningham & Brian Murphy, *Syrian Airstrikes Hammer Aleppo amid Expanding Offensive against Rebels*, WASH. POST (Sept. 23, 2016), at www.washingtonpost.com/world/middle_east/syrian-airstrikes-hammer-aleppo-amid-expanding-offensive-against-rebels/2016/09/23/4d247c50-818a-11e6-b002-307601806392_story.html.

[149] Human Rights Watch, *Russia/Syria: War Crimes in Month of Bombing Aleppo* (Dec. 1, 2016), at www.hrw.org/news/2016/12/01/russia/syria-war-crimes-month-bombing-aleppo.

[150] Laura Smith-Spark, Eyad Kourdi & Kareem Khadder, *Syria Activists: Airstrikes Knock out Hospitals in Rebel-held Aleppo*, CNN (Nov. 20, 2016), at www.cnn.com/2016/11/19/middleeast/syria-aleppo-airstrikes-hospitals/index.html.

[151] Report of the Independent International Commission of Inquiry on the Syrian Arab Republic, UN Doc. A/HRC/27/60 (Aug. 13, 2014), at www.ohchr.org/EN/HRBodies/HRC/RegularSessions/Session27/Documents/A_HRC_27_60_ENG.doc [hereinafter, 8th Report]. *See also* Report of the Independent International Commission of Inquiry on the Syrian Arab Republic, UN Doc. A/HRC/28/69 (Feb. 5, 2015), at https://documents-dds-ny.un.org/doc/UNDOC/GEN/G15/019/37/PDF/G1501937.pdf?OpenElement [hereinafter, 9th Report]; Report of the Independent International Commission of Inquiry on the Syrian Arab Republic, UN Doc. A/HRC/30/48 (Aug. 13, 2015), at www.ohchr.org/EN/HRBodies/HRC/RegularSessions/Session30/Documents/A_HRC_30_48_ENG.doc [hereinafter, 10th report].

[152] 8th Report, *supra* note 151.

Syria to the ICC, wrote: "It is the ... particular obligation of the Security Council, in the context of the war in the Syrian Arab Republic, to open a path to justice."[153] The General Assembly's creation of the IIIM, discussed above, is a start, by having evidence collected and preserved, but it is *not a justice mechanism*; the Security Council has created *no path* to justice.

In its eleventh and twelfth reports in 2016, the Commission continued to find further evidence of crimes against humanity and war crimes,[154] with the twelfth report focusing particular attention on the dire situation in Aleppo:

> Nearly 600,000 people are now under siege, with fears growing for those living in Aleppo city. Humanitarian access, including to provide lifesaving essentials such as surgical kits and medicine, is currently being blocked by some of the belligerents .... Medical workers and facilities have come under sustained and targeted attack. As a consequence, there has been a severe weakening of health-care infrastructure, particularly in areas of the country not under government control, with devastating consequences for civilians .... Away from the battlefield, civilians and *hors de combat* fighters continue to be disappeared, taken hostage, tortured and subjected to sexual violence, often in the context of detention. Unlawful killings, including deaths in detention and summary executions, remain a hallmark of this blood-soaked conflict.[155]

5.1.4.2 Vetoing Expressions of Outrage at the Alarming Number of Civilian Casualties, Including Those Caused by Indiscriminate Aerial Bombing, in Aleppo

Despite the horrific crimes being committed in Aleppo and elsewhere, on October 8, 2016, Russia vetoed a resolution that would have expressed outrage at the alarming number of civilian casualties, including those caused by indiscriminate aerial bombings, in Aleppo.[156] The resolution would also have expressed distress at the 13.5 million Syrians in need of humanitarian

---

[153] 10th Report, *supra* note 151.
[154] Report of the Independent International Commission of Inquiry on the Syrian Arab Republic, UN Doc. A/HRC/31/68 (Feb. 11, 2016), *at* www.ohchr.org/Documents/HRBodies/HRCouncil/CoISyria/A-HRC-31-68.pdf [hereinafter, 11th report]; Report of the Independent International Commission of Inquiry on the Syrian Arab Republic, UN Doc. A/HRC/33/55 (Aug. 11, 2016), *at* https://documents-dds-ny.un.org/doc/UNDOC/GEN/G16/178/60/PDF/G1617860.pdf?OpenElement [hereinafter, 12th report].
[155] 12th Report, *supra* note 154.
[156] S/2016/846 (vetoed by the Russian Federation).

assistance and six million internally displaced, and demanded an end to aerial bombardments.[157] The resolution would additionally have called for attacks to cease

> against civilians and civilian objects, including those involving attacks on schools, medical facilities and the deliberate interruptions of water supply, the indiscriminate use of weapons, including artillery, barrel bombs and air strikes, indiscriminate shelling by mortars, car bombs, suicide attacks and tunnel bombs, as well as the use of starvation of civilians as a method of combat, including by the besiegement of populated areas, and the widespread use of torture, ill-treatment, arbitrary executions, extrajudicial killings, enforced disappearances, sexual and gender-based violence, as well as all grave violations and abuses committed against children[.][158]

At the time Russia invoked its veto, Russian air forces were conducting, with the Syrian military, a joint aerial campaign in Aleppo,[159] so obviously Russia would not join in condemning or allowing condemnation of its own airstrikes.[160] (Russia's purported explanation for the veto raised the Libya

---

[157] Id.
[158] Id. This resolution was also supported by a long list of states: Andorra, Australia, Austria, Belgium, Bulgaria, Canada, Costa Rica, Croatia, Cyprus, Czech Republic, Denmark, Estonia, Finland, France, Georgia, Germany, Greece, Hungary, Iceland, Ireland, Italy, Latvia, Lithuania, Luxembourg, Malta, Mexico, Monaco, Morocco, Netherlands, Norway, Poland, Portugal, Qatar, Romania, San Marino, Saudi Arabia, Senegal, Slovakia, Slovenia, Spain, Sweden, Turkey, Ukraine, United Arab Emirates, the UK, and the US. Id.
[159] Suleiman Al-Khalidi, *Syrian and Russian Aircraft Step Up Bombing of Aleppo City*, REUTERS (June 4, 2016), at www.reuters.com/article/us-mideast-crisis-syria-aleppo/syrian-and-russian-aircraft-step-up-bombing-of-aleppo-city-monitor-idUSKCN0YR0DI; Max Fischer, *Russia's Brutal Bombing of Aleppo May Be Calculated and It May Be Working*, N.Y. TIMES (Sept. 28, 2016), at www.reuters.com/article/us-mideast-crisis-syria-aleppo/syrian-and-russian-aircraft-step-up-bombing-of-aleppo-city-monitor-idUSKCN0YR0DI; *Syria Conflict: Heavy Air Strikes Resume on Aleppo*, BBC NEWS (Oct. 11, 2016), at www.bbc.com/news/world-middle-east-37625785; Emma Graham-Harrison, *Aleppo Airstrikes Restart as Russia Announces Major Syria Offensive*, GUARDIAN (Nov. 15, 2016), at www.theguardian.com/world/2016/nov/15/aleppo-airstrikes-resume-as-russia-announces-major-syria-offensive.
[160] A prior resolution condemning "barrel bombs in Aleppo" did manage to pass, S/RES/2165 (July 14, 2014), but at the time Russia was not yet militarily engaged in any air campaign involving Aleppo. (The resolution condemned "the continuing indiscriminate attacks in populated areas, including an intensified campaign of aerial bombings and the use of barrel bombs in Aleppo and other areas, artillery, shelling and air strikes, and the widespread use of torture, ill-treatment, sexual and gender-based violence as well as all grave violations and abuses committed against children."). See also S/RES/2139, pmbl., paras. 3, 5 (Feb. 22, 2014) (expressing alarm at the "hundreds of thousands of civilians trapped in besieged areas," "indiscriminate ... shelling and aerial bombardment, such as the use of barrel bombs," and calling for lifting of sieges, including of Aleppo).

intervention.)[161] The Russian veto very clearly reveals the harm of the UN Charter having no provision to disqualify from voting a permanent member involved in the situation at issue; as discussed in Chapter 1, during the San Francisco negotiations of the UN Charter, states opposed the absence of such a disqualification provision, but did not prevail in creating one under Chapter VII.[162]

5.1.4.3 Vetoing a Seven-Day Ceasefire in Aleppo That Would Have Allowed Humanitarian Assistance

Despite the dire situation in Aleppo, on December 5, 2016, Russia and China then vetoed a resolution that would have implemented a seven-day ceasefire in Aleppo to allow provision of humanitarian assistance.[163] The resolution would also have expressed distress at the millions in need of humanitarian assistance, the vast number of individuals internally displaced, and the thousands living in besieged areas.[164] It would additionally have condemned threats on medical and humanitarian assistance personnel.[165]

Two days after the veto, Canada, France, Germany, Italy, the UK, and the US issued a poignant statement about the tragedy unfolding in Aleppo:

> A humanitarian disaster is taking place before our very eyes. Some 200,000 civilians, including many children, in eastern Aleppo are cut off from food and medicine supplies. Aleppo is being subjected to daily bombings and artillery attacks by the Syrian regime, supported by Russia and Iran. Hospitals and schools have not been spared. Rather, they appear to be the targets of attack in an attempt to wear people down. The images of dying children are heart breaking. We condemn the actions of the Syrian regime and its foreign backers, especially Russia, for their obstruction of humanitarian aid, and strongly condemn the Syrian regime's attacks that have devastated civilians and medical facilities and use of barrel bombs and chemical weapons.[166]

---

[161] See Statement by the Russian Federation, Security Council, 7785th Meeting, Saturday, October 8, 2016, UN Doc. S/PV.7785, at https://undocs.org/en/S/PV.7785. It is well-known that Russia believes that it was misled as to the Libya intervention, which Russia claims exceeded the force mandate authorized. Even if that argument has validity, one might well ask how long that serves as an excuse for Russia's voting related to Syria.

[162] See Chapter 1. The Charter disqualifies in other circumstances (under Chapter VI and Article 52(3)) a "party to a dispute" from voting. See UN Charter, Art. 27(3).

[163] S/2016/1026 (vetoed by the Russian Federation and China).

[164] Id.

[165] Id., para. 4.

[166] UK Prime Minister's Office Press Release, Joint Statement on Aleppo: 7 December 2016 (Dec. 7, 2016), at www.gov.uk/government/news/joint-statement-on-aleppo-7-december-2016.

The statement noted the urgent need "for an immediate ceasefire to allow the United Nations to get humanitarian assistance to people in eastern Aleppo and to provide humanitarian relief."[167] These states were also explicit that *"Russia is blocking the UN Security Council, which is therefore unable to do its work and put an end to the atrocities."*[168]

As to the two Aleppo-related vetoes, it is difficult to reach any conclusion other than that a permanent member (Russia), militarily assisting the Syrian military at the time, including in the aerial assault on Aleppo, wanted *not to alleviate the siege* in order to advance Syrian military objectives in retaking the city, which was considered a key turning point in the war.[169] The vetoes appear to have come at a clear cost of denying humanitarian aid, while the civilians trapped in Aleppo were under aerial bombardment from Syrian and Russian airstrikes.[170] As mentioned, a resolution related to the siege was passed, but it came only once the siege was over.[171]

5.1.5 *Vetoes Related to Chemical Weapons Use*

The next six Syria-related vetoes all relate to chemical weapons use – blocking condemnation of use of the weapons, blocking requests for documentation such as flight plans and access to air bases from which chemical weapons were believed to have launched, and blocking inspections that would have attributed responsibility to the side using them.[172] The vast bulk of the chemical weapons attacks – with thirty-four attacks documented by the Commission[173] and eighty-five documented by Human Rights Watch[174] – are attributed to Government

---

[167] *Id.*
[168] *Id.* (emphasis added).
[169] Ben Hubbard, *Turning Point in Syria as Assad Regains All of Aleppo*, N.Y. TIMES (Dec. 22, 2016), *at* www.nytimes.com/2016/12/22/world/middleeast/aleppo-syria-evacuation.html. Russia claimed that lifting the siege would have allowed opposition forces time to replenish their ranks and supplies. Van Schaack, *supra* note 8.
[170] *Syrian and Russian Airstrikes Flattening Aleppo*, CBS EVENING NEWS (Oct. 12, 2016), *at* www.youtube.com/watch?v=yS3LFA7dNUQ; U.N. *Photos of Eastern Aleppo, Before and After Syrian and Russian Airstrikes*, WASH. POST, *at* www.washingtonpost.com/apps/g/page/world/un-photos-of-eastern-aleppo-before-and-after-syrian-and-russian-airstrikes/2097/?noredirect=on.
[171] S/RES/2328 (Dec. 19, 2016) (calling for evacuation of civilian from Aleppo and access to ensure humanitarian assistance).
[172] *See* Chapters 5.1.5.3–5.6 *infra*.
[173] Arms Control Association Timeline, *supra* note 100.
[174] Human Rights Watch, *Syria: A Year on, Chemical Weapons Attacks Persist: International Action for Deterrence, Justice Ineffective* (Apr. 4, 2018), *at* www.hrw.org/news/2018/04/04/syria-year-chemical-weapons-attacks-persist.

forces,[175] although not all attacks are attributed and some are attributed to other groups, including ISIL.[176] On five of the six vetoes, China again did not join Russia's veto.[177] While other resolutions condemning use of chemical weapons were able to pass,[178] as to some measures (particularly, as to investigations that would have attributed responsibility to the side using chemical weapons), the veto meant investigations attributing responsibility simply ended.

5.1.5.1 Attempts at Destroying Syria's Chemical Weapons Stockpile

After the large-scale chemical weapons attack on Al-Ghouta in August 2013,[179] as well as several other prior attacks,[180] the international community embarked on extensive efforts to force Syria to destroy its chemical weapons stockpile. These efforts (at least Russia's participation in them) can be explained in part by President Obama's willingness, after the Al-Ghouta attack, to seek Congressional authorization for a limited US military strike into Syria to deter further chemical weapons use.[181] As mentioned above, President Obama later postponed Congress' vote[182] presumably because at the time Russia appeared willing to work toward chemical weapons disarmament.[183]

[175] Sarah Almukhtar, *Most Chemical Attacks in Syria Get Little Attention. Here Are 34 Confirmed Cases*, N.Y. TIMES (Apr. 13, 2018), *at* www.nytimes.com/interactive/2018/04/13/world/middleeast/syria-chemical-attacks-maps-history.html (attributing most attacks discussed in that report to regime forces, and some as "unknown" in source); Human Rights Watch, *Syria: A Year On*, *supra* note 174 ("Of the 85 chemical weapon attacks analyzed from these sources, more than 50 were identified by the various sources as having been committed by Syrian government forces." "The groups found that the Islamic State group (also known as [ISIL]) carried out three chemical weapon attacks using sulfur mustard. One attack was by non-state armed groups using chlorine. Those responsible for the remaining attacks in the data set are unknown or unconfirmed.").
[176] For example, a November 6, 2015, OPCW-FFM press release claimed with "utmost confidence" ISIL's use of sulfur mustard gas on August 21, 2015 in Marea, in northern Syria. Arms Control Association Timeline, *supra* note 100.
[177] China joined only the first chemical-weapons related veto: S/2017/172 (vetoed by the Russian Federation and China).
[178] *See* note 186 *supra* (resolution condemning chemical weapons use).
[179] *See* Chapter 5.1.3.2 *supra*.
[180] The Commission documented previous attacks on: Uteibah on March 19, 2013; Khan Al-Asal on March 19, 2013 (using chlorine gas); Sheik Maqsood neighborhood on April 13, 2013; and Saraqib on April 29, 2013. *Chemical Weapons Attacks Documented by the Commission (Infographic)*, *supra* note 45.
[181] Peter Baker & Jonathan Weisman, *Obama Seeks Approval by Congress for Strike in Syria*, N.Y. TIMES (Aug. 31, 2013), *at* www.nytimes.com/2013/09/01/world/middleeast/syria.html.
[182] Arms Control Association Timeline, *supra* note 100. *See also* Chapter 2.3.1.
[183] *See* Alicia Sanders-Zakre, Arms Control Association, *What You Need to Know About Chemical Weapons Use in Syria*, *at* www.armscontrol.org/blog/2018-09-23/what-you-need-know-about-chemical-weapons-use-syria ("To avoid a military strike in Syria, Russia approached the

Thereafter, on September 14, 2013, the US and Russia concluded a Framework Agreement for Elimination of Syrian Chemical Weapons,[184] and Syria became a party to the Convention on the Prohibition of the Development, Production, Stockpiling and Use of Chemical Weapons and on their Destruction (CWC).[185] Inspections and disarmament obligations were memorialized in Security Council Resolution 2118, which endorsed the Framework Agreement.[186] On September 27, 2013, the Organization for the Prohibition of Chemical Weapons (OPCW) established "special procedures" to supervise inspection and destruction of Syria's chemical weapons.[187]

Notwithstanding these efforts, chemical weapons attacks continued. The Commission documented attacks (after the above developments) on: Kafr Zeita on April 11, 2014 (by Government forces using chlorine gas); Kafr Zeita and Al Tamana on April 12, 2014 (two incidents by Government forces using chlorine gas); Kafr Zeita on April 16, 2014 (by Government forces using chlorine gas); Kafr Zeita and Al Tamana on April 18, 2014 (two incidents by Government forces using chlorine gas); and Tal Minnis on April 21, 2014 (by Government forces).[188]

Because of these continuing chemical weapons attacks, the Director-General of the OPCW on April 29, 2014, announced the creation of an OPCW Fact-Finding Mission (the OPCW-FFM) to investigate the use of chemical weapons in Syria.[189] Thereafter, on August 7, 2015, in Resolution

---

United States proposing an international effort to identify and destroy Syria's chemical stockpile. Obama accepted this alternative . . . .").

[184] Joint National Paper by the Russian Federation and the United States of America, Framework for Elimination of Syrian Chemical Weapons, EC-M-33/NAT.1 (Sept. 17, 2013), at www.opcw.org/fileadmin/OPCW/EC/M-33/ecm33nato1_e_.pdf.

[185] Syria had already on November 22, 1968 acceded to the Protocol for the Prohibition of the Use in War of Asphyxiating, Poisonous or Other Gases and of Bacteriological Methods of Warfare.

[186] See S/RES/2118 (2013) (requiring Syria to dispose of its chemical weapons stockpiles and cooperate with the OPCW). The resolution also condemned use of chemical weapons in Ghouta. Thus, this resolution condemning chemical weapons did manage to pass the Security Council. See id., paras. 1–2 ("[d]etermines that the use of chemical weapons anywhere constitutes a threat to international peace and security"; and "[c]ondemns in the strongest terms any use of chemical weapons in the Syrian Arab Republic, in particular the attack on 21 August 2013, in violation of international law").

[187] Id.

[188] Chemical Weapons Attacks Documented by the Commission (Infographic), supra note 45. There were also earlier attacks documented.

[189] "In response to persistent allegations of chemical weapon attacks in Syria, the OPCW Fact Finding Mission (FFM) was set up in 2014 'to establish facts surrounding allegations of the use of toxic chemicals, reportedly chlorine, for hostile purposes in the Syrian Arab Republic.'" Organisation for the Prohibition of Chemical Weapons ("OPCW"), at www.opcw.org/special-sections/syria/the-fact-finding-mission.

2235, the Security Council created an OPCW-UN Joint Investigative Mechanism (JIM) to identify those responsible for chemical weapons use.[190]

Creation of these two investigative mechanisms appears to have had a positive impact, in that after creation of the OPCW-FFM[191] and through at least the early work of the JIM,[192] there is a nearly two-year gap in chemical weapons attacks documented by the Commission.[193] In fact, a draft Security Council resolution expressly mentioned that "immediately after the JIM's establishment there was a decrease in the number of allegations of use of chemicals as weapons in the Syrian Arab Republic."[194] This gap fairly clearly shows that deterrence can be created by the establishment of investigative mechanisms – that is, the gap in attacks suggests that what happens in the international community *can have deterrent impact* on perpetrators on the ground.

After large amounts of chemical weapons were shipped out of Syria or destroyed, the OPCW stated, as of January 2016, that the chemical weapons stockpile that Syria's Government had declared had been destroyed.[195]

5.1.5.2 Continued Chemical Weapons Use

Unfortunately, notwithstanding these efforts, chemical weapons attacks continued, suggesting either that there had been significant omissions in Syria's reporting of its chemical weapons or that its chemical weapons production capabilities were not fully dismantled.[196] After the OPCW announcement, the Commission documented additional attacks – almost all attributed to Government forces – on: Sheik Maqsood neighborhood on April 5, 2016

---

[190] See S/RES/2235 (2015). The JIM's mandate was extended twice. S/RES/2314 (2016); S/RES/2319 (2016). The OPCW FFM's findings were the basis for the work of the JIM.
[191] On April 29, 2014, the Director-General of the OPCW announced the creation of the OPCW FFM.
[192] The Security Council created the JIM on August 7, 2015, in Resolution 2235. S/2015/2235.
[193] See *Chemical Weapons Attacks Documented by the Commission (Infographic)*, supra note 45 (listing no chemical weapons attacks between April 2014 and April 2016). Human Rights Watch, by contrast, does document some chemical weapons attacks in 2015. Human Rights Watch, *Chemical Weapons Attacks in Syria Since 2013*, at www.hrw.org/news/2018/04/04/syria-year-chemical-weapons-attacks-persist.
[194] See S/RES/172 (2017) (vetoed by the Russian Federation and China).
[195] "The OPCW reported that 581 metric tonnes of the precursor chemical for sarin gas were destroyed. In total, 96% of the chemical weapons stockpile (that the Syrian government had declared) was removed, according to the OPCW. The complete destruction of the stockpile was reported in January 2016." *Syria: Does Russia Always Use a Veto at the UN Security Council?*, BBC NEWS (Apr. 16, 2018), at www.bbc.com/news/world-43781954.
[196] Van Schaack, *supra* note 8.

(using chlorine gas); Saraqeb on August 1, 2016 (by Government forces); Al-Sukkari neighborhood on September 6, 2016 (by Government forces using chlorine gas); M10 Hospital[197] in Aleppo on October 1, 2016 (by Government forces using chlorine gas); Al-Kalasa, Bustan Al-Qasr, and Al-Firdous neighborhoods on December 8, 2016 (three incidents by Government forces using chlorine gas); Al-Kalasa and Bustan Al-Qasr neighborhoods on December 9, 2016 (two incidents by Government forces using chlorine gas); Al-Hayat Hospital on December 10, 2016 (by Government forces); Bseema village on January 8, 2017 (by Government forces using chlorine gas); and Sultan Al-Marj village on January 30, 2017 (by Government forces using chlorine gas).[198]

5.1.5.3 Vetoing Condemnation of Chemical Weapons Use

Despite these continuing chemical weapons attacks, and Russia's having concluded the Framework Agreement and initially voted to create the JIM, Russian willingness (or apparent willingness)[199] to rein in Syria's chemical weapons use, to the extent it existed,[200] apparently ceased by 2017. On

---

[197] "'M10' was the nom de guerre of the Sakhour Hospital, an underground trauma hospital servicing the besieged civilians of eastern Aleppo City. It was destroyed in October 2016." Adham Sahloul, *Obituary: A Hospital in Aleppo (2013–2016)*, TIME (Dec. 14, 2016), at http://time.com/4599498/aleppo-hospital-obituary.

[198] *Chemical Weapons Attacks Documented by the Commission (Infographic)*, *supra* note 45. In its March 2017 report, the Commission additionally wrote about the consequences of Government forces committing war crimes by attacking civilians and civilian objects by prohibited weapons such as cluster munitions, incendiary weapons, and weaponized chlorine canisters. Human Rights Abuses and International Humanitarian Law Violations in the Syrian Arab Republic, 21 July 2016–28 February 2017, Conference Room Paper of the Independent International Commission of Inquiry on the Syrian Arab Republic, UN Doc. A/HRC/34/CRP.3 (Mar. 10, 2017), at www.ohchr.org/EN/HRBodies/HRC/IICISyria/Pages/IndependentInternationalCommission.aspx. A report by the International Center for Transitional Justice (ICTJ) and ten Syrian civil society groups forming the "Save Syrian Schools Project" also chronicles how the destruction of schools and consequences of the war impacted a generation of Syrian children by depriving them of schooling. Badael Foundation, Center for Civil Society and Democracy, Dawlaty, International Center for Transitional Justice, Lawyers and Doctors for Human Rights, Startpoint, Syrian Institute for Justice, Syrian Network for Human Rights, The Day After, Violation Documentation Center, and Women Now for Development, *"We Didn't Think It Would Hit Us": Understanding the Impact of Attacks on Schools in Syria* (Sept. 2018), at www.ictj.org/sites/default/files/Report_Save_Syrian_Schools_English_Web.pdf (chronicling a total of 1,292 schools that were attacked from 2011 to mid-2017).

[199] One theory is that Russia supported creation of the JIM until Russia realized the JIM would start attributing responsibility for chemical weapons attacks to the Syrian military. Trahan e-mail exchange with Mohammad Al Abdallah, 4/19/19.

[200] As noted, there were earlier resolutions condemning chemical weapons use that passed. *See, e.g.*, note 186 *supra*.

February 28, 2017, Russia and China jointly vetoed a resolution that would have condemned "any use of toxic chemicals as a weapon in the Syrian Arab Republic," and recalled the Security Council's "determination to identify those parties in Syria responsible for the use of any chemical weapons," and demanded compliance with the OPCW.[201] The resolution would also have expressed the Security Council's "conviction that those individuals responsible for the use of chemical weapons in the Syrian Arab Republic should be thoroughly investigated, and prosecuted, as appropriate, before a competent tribunal which is both independent and impartial."[202] Again, the resolution received widespread support from a large number of states.[203]

Russia's veto of this resolution, and its next five vetoes related to chemical weapons use (detailed below in Chapters 5.1.5.4–5.6), suggest that Russia perhaps had never been genuine in its commitment to pursuing accountability for Syrian chemical weapons use.[204] One theory is that Russian efforts in creating the Framework Agreement and initially authorizing the JIM only appeared genuine enough to forestall President Obama from pursuing Congressional authorization for a US military strike into Syria.[205] Once President Obama's "red line" moment had passed and he declined to seek Congressional authorization for a military strike, and the JIM started identifying Syrian military involvement in chemical weapons attacks, Russian vetoes related to chemical weapons resumed.[206]

5.1.5.4 Further Vetoing Condemnation of Chemical Weapons Use, and Requests for Documentation Such as Flight Plans and Access to Air Bases from Which Chemical Weapons Were Believed to Have Been Launched

In March 2017, Syrian Government forces launched three more chemical weapons attacks: on Al-Latamneh Hospital on March 25, 2017, using

---

[201] S/2017/172 (vetoed by the Russian Federation and China).
[202] *Id.*, para. 4. The resolution, in its Annex 1, also would have named senior Syrian military and intelligence officials thought to be responsible for Syria's chemical weapons program, who would have been subject to sanctions, including asset freezes and a travel ban. *See id.*, Annex I.
[203] Supporting states were: Albania, Australia, Austria, Belgium, Bulgaria, Canada, Croatia, Cyprus, Czechia, Denmark, Estonia, Finland, France, Germany, Greece, Iceland, Ireland, Israel, Italy, Japan, Latvia, Liechtenstein, Lithuania, Luxembourg, Malta, Montenegro, Netherlands, New Zealand, Norway, Poland, Portugal, Qatar, Romania, Saudi Arabia, Slovakia, Spain, Sweden, Turkey, Ukraine, United Arab Emirates, the UK, and the US. *Id.*
[204] Trahan e-mail exchange with Mohammad Al Abdallah, 4/19/19.
[205] *Id. See also* notes 181–83 *supra*.
[206] Trahan e-mail exchange with Mohammad Al Abdallah, 4/19/19.

improvised chlorine barrel bombs; on Qabun Municipality on March 29, 2017; and on Al-Latamneh village on March 30, 2017.[207] Then, on April 4, 2017, came a large-scale sarin gas attack on the town of Khan Shaykhun in the opposition-held Idlib Province,[208] with estimated fatalities exceeding eighty, attributed to Syrian Government forces.[209] As discussed in Chapter 2.3.2 and noted above in Chapter 5.1.1, it was in response to the April 4 attack, that the US on April 6, 2017 (under the Trump Administration), launched missile strikes targeting the air base from which it is believed the chemical weapons attack was launched.[210] Just the next day, on April 7, 2017, Government forces launched another chemical weapons attack, on Al-Hayat Hospital.[211]

Nonetheless, on April 12, 2017, Russia vetoed a resolution that would have condemned the chemical weapons attack on Khan Shaykhun.[212] The resolution would also have expressed "outrage that individuals continue to be killed and injured by chemical weapons in the Syrian Arab Republic" and expressed "determination that those responsible must be held accountable."[213] Additionally, the resolution would have requested documentation such as flight plans and access to air bases from which chemical weapons were believed to have been launched.[214] China did not join Russia on this veto,[215] starting a trend of not joining Russia on vetoes related to chemical weapons use. At this point in the war, over 465,000 had been killed, of whom over 96,000 were civilians (including over 14,000 killed by torture in prison), and 145,000 were reported missing.[216]

---

[207] *Chemical Weapons Attacks Documented by the Commission (Infographic)*, supra note 45.
[208] Assoc. Press, *supra* note 24.
[209] *UN Panel Blames Syrian Forces for Khan Sheikhoun Attack*, AL JAZEERA (Oct. 27, 2017), at www.aljazeera.com/news/2017/10/panel-blames-syrian-forces-khan-sheikhoun-attack-1710262 12414046.html.
[210] *See* Arms Control Association Timeline, *supra* note 100. *See* Scharf, *supra* note 20, at 591 ("The US fired fifty-nine Tomahawk missiles at the Shayrat Airfield in Syria. President Trump said the airstrike was conducted in response to the Assad regime's use of sarin gas, a chemical weapon, on the town of Khan Sheikhoun .... Shayrat Airfield was targeted because it had been used to store chemical weapons and aircraft employed in the April 4 attack."), *citing* Remarks on United States Military Operations in Syria, 2017 DAILY COMP. PRES. DOC. 238 (Apr. 6, 2017).
[211] *Chemical Weapons Attacks Documented by the Commission (Infographic)*, supra note 45.
[212] S/2017/315 (vetoed by the Russian Federation).
[213] *Id.*, para. 1.
[214] *Id.*, para. 5.
[215] *Id.*
[216] *Syrian War Monitor Says 465,000 Killed in Six Years of Fighting*, REUTERS (Mar. 13, 2017), at www.reuters.com/article/us-mideast-crisis-syria-casualties/syrian-war-monitor-says-465000-killed-in-six-years-of-fighting-idUSKBN16K1Q1.

5.1.5.5 Vetoing Renewal of the Mandate for Investigations That Would Have Attributed Responsibility to the Side Using Chemical Weapons

Four more chemical weapons attacks followed later in 2017, all by Government forces, and all using chlorine gas: on Al-Tamana on April 29, 2017, Ayn Tarma on July 1, 2017, Zamalka on July 2, 2017, and Jowbar on July 8, 2017.[217] Despite these new chemical weapons attacks (and all prior chemical weapons attacks), on October 24, 2017, Russia vetoed a resolution that would have renewed the mandate of the JIM.[218] This resolution again had received widespread support.[219]

As noted above, the JIM had been created as a partnership between the UN and the OPCW, and had the mandate to:

> identify, to the greatest extent feasible, individuals, entities, groups or governments who were perpetrators, organizers, sponsors or otherwise involved in the use of chemicals as weapons, including chlorine or any other toxic chemical, in Syria where the OPCW fact-finding mission determines or has determined that a specific incident in the Syrian Arab Republic involved or likely involved the use of chemicals as weapons.

On this veto, China again did not join Russia.[220] The lapse of the JIM's mandate left in place only the OPCW-FFM, which could identify chemical weapons use, but could not attribute responsibility to the side using chemical weapons.[221]

5.1.5.6 Further Vetoing Condemnation of Chemical Weapons Use, and Furthering Vetoing Renewal of the Mandate for Inspections That Would Have Attributed Responsibility

November brought two additional vetoes related to chemical weapons use. On November 16, 2017, Russia vetoed a resolution that would have condemned

---

[217] *Chemical Weapons Attacks Documented by the Commission (Infographic)*, *supra* note 45.
[218] S/2017/884 (vetoed by the Russian Federation). As explained above, the JIM was originally created by Security Council Resolution 2235 on August 7, 2015, with its mandate twice renewed in 2016.
[219] States supporting the resolution were: Albania, Australia, Austria, Belgium, Bulgaria, Canada, Croatia, Cyprus, [Czech Republic], Denmark, Estonia, Finland, France, Germany, Greece, Hungary, Iceland, Ireland, Israel, Italy, Japan, Latvia, Liechtenstein, Lithuania, Luxembourg, Malta, Montenegro, Netherlands, Norway, Poland, Portugal, Qatar, Republic of Korea, Romania, Slovakia, Slovenia, Spain, Turkey, Ukraine, the UK, and the US. S/2017/884 (vetoed by the Russian Federation).
[220] S/2017/884 (vetoed by the Russian Federation).
[221] "[T]he OPCW Fact Finding Mission (FFM) was set up in 2014 'to establish facts surrounding allegations of the use of toxic chemicals, reportedly chlorine, for hostile purposes in the Syrian Arab Republic.'" Organisation for the Prohibition of Chemical Weapons, *at* www.opcw.org/special-sections/syria/the-fact-finding-mission.

the use of toxic chemicals as weapons, expressed grave concern that civilians continue to be killed and injured by such weapons, renewed the mandate of the JIM, and stated that "no party in Syria shall use, develop, produce, otherwise acquire, stockpile or retain, or transfer chemical weapons."[222] Then, the next day, on November 17, 2017, Russia again vetoed renewal of the mandate of the JIM.[223] China did not join either veto. One day later, on November 18, 2017, a chemical weapons attack occurred on Harasta, attributed to Government forces.[224] By February 2018, over 500,000 Syrians had been killed. In 2017 alone, over 11,000 had been killed, including over 10,000 civilians; 5.5 million Syrians had fled the country, and 6.1 million were internally displaced.[225]

The next spring brought yet another large-scale chemical weapons attack, this time on the Syrian town of Douma, on April 7, 2018, potentially using both chlorine and sarin gas, killing at least several dozen civilians.[226] (Oddly, the attack fell almost on the one-year anniversary of the Khan Sheikhoun chemical weapons attack.) According to news accounts of a US Government briefing, "[e]yewitnesses reported multiple government helicopters over Douma on April 7th, and said barrel bombs were dropped from those helicopters.... They said the only forces with military aircraft such as helicopters in Syria belong to Assad's government."[227]

Notwithstanding the Douma attack (and all prior chemical weapons attacks), on April 10, 2018, Russia cast its twelfth veto related to the situation in Syria, and sixth veto related to chemical weapons use. Russia vetoed a resolution that would have condemned "use of any toxic chemical, including chlorine, as a weapon in the Syrian Arab Republic," expressed outrage

---

[222] S/2017/962, pmbl., paras. 1, 3 (vetoed by the Russian Federation).
[223] S/2017/970 (vetoed by the Russian Federation).
[224] *Chemical Weapons Attacks Documented by the Commission (Infographic)*, supra note 45.
[225] I Am Syria, *Death Tolls*, at www.iamsyria.org/death-tolls.html.
[226] *What Is Known About Suspected Chemical Weapons Attack in Syria*, EYEWITNESS NEWS (Apr. 15, 2018), at http://ewn.co.za/2018/04/16/what-is-known-about-suspected-chemical-weapons-attack-in-syria; *Security Council Fails to Adopt Three Resolutions on Chemical Weapons Use in Syria*, UN NEWS (Apr. 10, 2018), at https://news.un.org/en/story/2018/04/1006991; *UN Secretary-General Should Activate Independent Mechanism to Attribute Responsibility for Chemical Attacks in Syria*, RELIEF WEB (Apr. 13, 2018), at https://reliefweb.int/report/syrian-arab-republic/un-secretary-general-should-activate-independent-mechanism-attribute.
[227] Anne Gearan & Missy Ryan, *U.S. and Allies Warn Syria of More Missile Strikes if Chemical Attacks Used Again*, WASH. POST (Apr. 13, 2018), at www.washingtonpost.com/world/national-security/us-launches-missile-strikes-in-syria/2018/04/13/c68e89d0-3f4a-11e8-974f-aacd97698cef_story.html?utm_term=.226a93dd75a7; Phil Stewart & Tom Perry, *U.S. Says Air Strikes Cripple Syria Chemical Weapons Program*, REUTERS (Apr. 12, 2018), at www.reuters.com/article/us-mideast-crisis-syria/trump-says-ordered-precision-strikes-against-syria-chemical-weapons-capabilities-idUSKBN1HJ0ZS.

"that civilians continue to be killed and injured by chemical weapons and toxic chemicals as weapons in the Syrian Arab republic," and demanded access for the OPCW-FFM and unimpeded passage for medical and humanitarian personnel.[228] The resolution also would have established a UN Independent Mechanism of Investigation (UNIMI) "to identify to the greatest extent feasible, individuals, entities, groups, or governments who were perpetrators, organizers, sponsors or otherwise involved in the use of chemical weapons, including chlorine or any other toxic chemical, in the Syrian Arab Republic...."[229] China again did not join this final chemical weapons-related veto. As discussed in Chapter 2.3.2 and noted above in Chapter 5.1.1, the US, UK, and France, on April 13, 2018, launched missile strikes targeting three chemical weapons facilities in response to the Douma attack.[230]

Total estimates of the number of fatalities in Syria due to chemical weapons use stand around 1,500.[231] As mentioned, various of the vetoed resolutions received significant support from states, including states not serving on the Security Council,[232] which demonstrates widespread support for these resolutions within the UN, and likely was an attempt to exert political pressure against use of the veto.[233] China's declining to join five of the six chemical weapons-related vetoes suggests that China – with incentives for alignment with the Syrian regime[234] – was reticent about being seen as aligned when it came to chemical weapons use; alternatively, perhaps China knew Russia would veto, so saw no pressing need to join and could save itself the

---

[228] S/2018/321, paras. 1, 5, 6 (vetoed by the Russian Federation).

[229] Id., para. 8.

[230] Julian Borger & Peter Beaumont, *Syria: US, UK and France Launch Strikes in Response to Chemical Attack*, GUARDIAN (Apr. 14, 2018), at www.theguardian.com/world/2018/apr/14/syria-air-strikes-us-uk-and-france-launch-attack-on-assad-regime. *See also* Scharf, *supra* note 20, at 592 ("One hundred three missiles were fired from a variety of naval vessels and jets — about double what was launched in April 2017. The chairman of the US Joint Chiefs of Staff, Joseph Dunford, said the targets were 'specifically associated' with Syria's chemical weapons program. They included a scientific research facility in Damascus, a chemical weapons storage facility west of Homs, and a chemical weapons equipment storage site and command post near Homs."), citing *Syria Air Strikes: US and Allies Attack "Chemical Weapons Sites,"* BBC (Apr. 14, 2018), at http://perma.cc/5H3Q-WW7J; *Gen. Dunford Says Targets Linked to Chem Weapons*, ASSOC. PRESS (Apr. 13, 2018), at http://perma.cc/B84U-3DPL. "A Russian-sponsored Security Council resolution that would have condemned the attack was soundly defeated by a vote of [only] three in favor...." Scharf, *supra* note 20, at 593.

[231] Kareem Shaheen, *"Almost 1,500 Killed in Chemical Weapons Attacks" in Syria*, GUARDIAN (Mar. 14, 2016), at www.theguardian.com/world/2016/mar/14/syria-chemical-weapons-attacks-almost-1500-killed-report-united-nations.

[232] See notes 203, 219 *supra*.

[233] See note 123 (e-mail with Sina Alavi).

[234] See note 51 *supra* (suggesting reasons why China might want to align politically with the Syrian Government).

embarrassment. As noted, other prior Security Council resolutions did pass condemning chemical weapons use;[235] thus, the vetoes discussed above did not fully block condemnation, but they did block all condemnation starting in 2017. The vetoes also fully blocked other measures, such as requests for documentation of flight plans and access to air bases from which chemical weapons were believed to have been launched, and renewal of the JIM and creation of the UNIMI, which would have been able to attribute responsibility to the side using chemical weapons.

While extremely horrific, fatalities from chemical weapons use represent just a fraction of the total number killed by indiscriminate aerial bombardment and other crimes.[236] Syrian victims sometimes resent the extensive coverage and condemnation of chemical weapons use to the exclusion of attention to other crimes.[237]

Yet another dispiriting thirteenth veto (a double veto by Russia and China) was cast on September 19, 2019, of a resolution that would have created a ceasefire in Syria's war-torn Idlib province, called for a halt to the aerial bombing campaign there, and demanded humanitarian access and safe passage for medical personnel.[238] A final, dispiriting fourteenth veto was cast on December 20, 2019 (again by Russia and China) of a resolution that would have called for improved humanitarian assistance, reiterated the obligation to comply with international humanitarian law and international human rights law, and called for "safe, unimpeded and sustained access" for humanitarian convoys.[239]

5.1.6 Overall Impact of the Vetoes Related to the Situation in Syria

These fourteen vetoes detailed above were cast during the commission of a massive number of crimes against humanity and war crimes in Syria. The Commission has documented the crimes to include:

- summary execution,
- unlawful killing,

---

[235] See, e.g., note 186 supra.
[236] Trahan conversation with Mohammad Al Abdallah.
[237] Id.
[238] S/2019/756 (vetoed by the Russian Federation and China). "The Syrian Observatory for Human Rights says the offensive [in Idlib] has killed close to 1,000 civilians." French Press Agency – AFP, *Russia's 13 UN Security Council Vetoes on Syria*, DAILY SABAH MIDEAST (Sept. 20, 2019), at www.dailysabah.com/mideast/2019/09/20/russias-13-unsecurity-council-vetoes-on-syria.
[239] S/2019/961 (vetoed by the Russian Federation and China).

- arbitrary arrests and detentions,
- enforced disappearances,
- torture,
- rape and other sexual violence,
- pillage,
- destruction of property,
- attacking protected objects,
- hostage-taking,
- attacking civilians,
- recruiting and using child soldiers in hostilities,
- barrel bombing,
- laying siege,
- forcibly displacing civilians,
- deliberate use of starvation,[240]
- indiscriminate and disproportionate aerial bombardment and shelling,
- disregarding the special protection accorded to hospitals,
- use of chemical weapons including chlorine and sarin gas,
- targeting medical, humanitarian, and religious personnel, and journalists,
- cutting off civilians from food and medical access,
- targeting hospitals and schools,
- destruction of cultural heritage, and
- obstructing humanitarian aid.[241]

As noted, many of the crimes were reported to be committed by Government forces and affiliated militia, while extensive crimes were also attributed to anti-Government opposition groups.[242]

---

[240] Starvation of civilians as a method of warfare during non-international armed conflict has been a crime under both Additional Protocol II as well as customary international law, but was not until recently included in the ICC's Rome Statute. *See, e.g.*, Protocol Additional to the Geneva Conventions of 12 August 1949, and relating to the Protection of Victims of Non-International Armed Conflicts (Protocol II), June 8, 1977, Art. 14. Switzerland spearheaded the recent efforts that succeeded in having this crimes added to the Rome Statute. Res. ICC-ASP/18/Res.5, adopted Dec. 6, 2019, by consensus.

[241] *See* reports of the Independent Commission of Inquiry on the Syrian Arab Republic *at* www.ohchr.org/EN/HRBodies/HRC/IICISyria/Pages/Documentation.aspx. Some of the crimes enumerated above constitute war crimes; some constitute crimes against humanity; some constitute both.

[242] As discussed above, ISIL members are also believed to have committed genocide, as well as war crimes and crimes against humanity. *See* Chapter 5.1.3.5 *supra*.

The vetoes, inter alia: (1) blocked or delayed[243] condemnation of crimes (while numerous resolutions condemning crimes by ISIL and other "terrorist" groups passed);[244] (2) blocked prosecution before the ICC of war crimes and crimes against humanity by Government forces and affiliated militia; blocked prosecution before the ICC of genocide, crimes against humanity, and war crimes by ISIL; and blocked prosecution before the ICC of crimes against humanity and war crimes by any other actors within Syria, including anti-Government armed groups;[245] (3) blocked humanitarian assistance to alleviate the suffering of civilians during the siege of Aleppo;[246] and (4) blocked inspections as to chemical weapons use that would have attributed responsibility to those using the weapons (blocking renewal of the mandate of the JIM three times[247] and blocking creation of the UNIMI).[248]

The above chronology of events suggests an attempt by one permanent member (often joined by another permanent member) to shield Government crimes in Syria from Security Council and other scrutiny, while Syrian Government forces, militarily assisted by the first permanent member, were committing large-scale crimes against humanity and war crimes. The chronology also suggests an attempt by one permanent member to shield Government forces from condemnation, scrutiny, and accountability *even when using chemical weapons*, at least commencing in 2017.[249] Admittedly, many of the vetoes also had the effect of shielding crimes by anti-Government opposition groups, who then also did not receive condemnation under Security Council resolutions or referral to the ICC; this shielding, however, was likely inadvertent, in that it simply followed when resolutions condemning Government crimes were vetoed.[250]

---

[243] As explained, sometimes after a veto, a resolution condemning the crimes did follow a few years later. Thus, not all condemnation of crimes was permanently blocked, but the resolutions that were able to pass often suggested an equivalency between Syrian Government and opposition crimes. Van Schaack, *supra* note 8.

[244] See note 8 *supra* (Security Council resolutions condemning ISIL and other "terrorist" crimes).

[245] S/2014/348 (vetoed by the Russian Federation and China).

[246] S/2016/1026 (vetoed by the Russian Federation and China).

[247] S/2017/884 (vetoed by the Russian Federation); S/2017/962 (vetoed by the Russian Federation); S/2017/970 (vetoed by the Russian Federation).

[248] S/2018/321 (vetoed by the Russian Federation).

[249] As mentioned above, the initial creation of the JIM in 2015 and renewal of its mandate in 2016 both passed the Security Council, and Russia initially appeared willing to work towards chemical weapons containment when it entered into the Framework Agreement for Elimination of Syrian Chemical Weapons. *See* note 190 *supra* and accompanying text (JIM); note 184 *supra* (Framework Agreement).

[250] While some of the earlier vetoed resolutions would have condemned crimes by Government forces, most later resolutions generically condemned crimes, without identifying which side was allegedly responsible.

All in all, the Security Council has clearly failed in its primary responsibility of maintaining international peace and security with respect to the situation in Syria. All the members of the Security Council and the international community more generally have also completely failed to implement any "responsibility to protect," causing one to legitimately wonder what has become of this doctrine if it can be so completely ignored in the context of Syria.[251] While the author acknowledges the extreme complexity of resolving the conflict, and that myriad rounds of peace negotiations were attempted but unable to reach a negotiated settlement, what the Council, at minimum, could have done in these circumstances was vociferously and consistently condemn the commission of mass atrocity crimes *by all sides in the conflict*, refer the situation in Syria to the ICC in an attempt to deter crimes and ensure accountability, alleviate civilian suffering such as during the siege of Aleppo, and continue with chemical weapons inspections that were attributing responsibility to the side using the weapons – *which appeared to be deterring chemical weapons attacks*.[252] While none of the vetoed resolutions, had they passed, would have ended the war, the measures that were blocked could have at least attempted to mitigate some of the war's more horrific aspects.

The way the veto was used arguably helped enable the perpetration of a vast number of crimes in Syria, because it ensured that *no consistent message* attempting to deter the crimes, and no consistent message that accountability would follow, was ever delivered regarding Syrian Government or opposition crimes. The vetoes conveyed exactly the opposite message – that perpetrators of crimes against humanity and war crimes by the Government or its forces would be "protected" or "shielded" from scrutiny, often even when using chemical weapons, because they had a "protector" (sometimes two)[253] on the Security Council. No country – Syria or *any other country*[254] – should receive this message that it is above the rule of law.

Moreover, the way these vetoes were utilized – shielding, inter alia, Government perpetration of atrocity crimes – raises serious legal questions (detailed in Chapter 4). A strong argument can be made that the UN Charter's voting provisions should not be read in a way that essentially allows veto use (a power granted under the Charter) to be used to facilitate the ongoing

---

[251] For discussion of the responsibility to protect, see Chapter 2.2.
[252] *See* text accompanying notes 191–94 *supra* (drop in attacks when inspections commenced).
[253] China did not join five of the six vetoes related to chemical weapons use and did not join one Aleppo-related veto, but joined eight other vetoes.
[254] The author *in no way* limits her arguments to the situation in Syria (or Darfur), but means them to apply equally to any use (or threat of use) of the veto while genocide, crimes against humanity, and/or war crimes are occurring, or are at serious risk of occurring.

commission of atrocity crimes – here, crimes against humanity and war crimes by Syrian Government forces, as well as crimes against humanity, war crimes, and genocide, when ISIL crimes failed to be referred to the ICC.

5.2 ANALYSIS OF VETO THREATS RELATED TO THE SITUATION IN DARFUR

As with the situation in Syria, a full narrative of the years of hostilities and atrocity crimes committed in the Darfur region of Sudan is beyond the scope of this chapter. This section presents only a brief overview of the conflict and then provides a snapshot of some of what the Security Council was able to pass in terms of resolutions, but also focuses on where its work was blocked. There were no express vetoes related to the situation in Darfur, but there were threats to invoke the veto, or insistence by a permanent member on weakening resolution language that amounted to an implied threat.[255] This resulted in delayed imposition of sanctions, complete blockage of an oil embargo, limitations of arms and other sanctions, delayed deployment of UN peacekeeping, and blocking a disarmament mandate for peacekeepers. Follow-up on ICC arrest warrants also appears to have been blocked. Additionally, because of China's well-known political alignment with the regime of then Sudanese President Omar Hassan al-Bashir, further measures that otherwise could have been proposed and voted on at the Security Council never were. While it is admittedly harder here to trace the role that the veto power played, it still appears to have played a role, perhaps just as much as express veto use would have. It is more difficult, however, for the outside world (beyond the UN) to know of this, because China was not pressed to vote on resolutions. Thus, unlike express vetoes, mere inaction, veto threats, or implied threats rarely make newspaper headlines. (Why this apparent difference in treatment exists between Russia – where Russia was pressed to vote on resolutions and forced to publicly use its veto related to Syria, with China sometimes joining – and the situation in Darfur,[256] where China generally was not, is an interesting question.)[257]

---

[255] See note 316 *infra* and accompanying text on what amounts to a "threat" (interview with Andras Vamos-Goldman).
[256] The same is true for Sri Lanka and Myanmar. As to Myanmar, there was one express veto, but only one, and none with respect to Sri Lanka. See Chapter 1.3.2.
[257] The author will surmise that the difference could relate to China's significant economic power and countries being more concerned that they not jeopardize their bilateral relationship by publicly embarrassing China. Additionally, if a permanent member is not forced to use its veto, the permanent member may be more willing to negotiate a Presidential Statement, although that is non-binding. Another explanation is that: "As Russia's intransigence set in [regarding

This section of this chapter traces the developments in Darfur and the extent to which the Security Council was able to act or not. It also chronicles the rising death tolls while the crimes were being committed, with the crimes certainly constituting crimes against humanity and war crimes, but most likely also genocide. Again, material is derived from publicly available sources, and therefore does not necessarily capture the true dynamics of negotiations within the Security Council, which would be known only to persons present. As with the discussion of events in Syria, this section does not intend to suggest that the veto threats caused all fatalities in Darfur, but it appears to have been a contributing factor. The overall picture of weakening sanctions – for example, blocking an oil embargo, initially excluding the Government from an arms embargo, limiting travel sanctions, and an asset freeze – as well as blocking and delaying the deployment of UN peacekeepers and restricting their mandate, clearly suggest that China's veto power hampered the Security Council's ability to function while ongoing atrocity crimes were being committed. In fact, the delays in UN peacekeeping and lack of a true peacekeeping force arguably resulted in many tens, if not hundreds, of thousands of additional deaths, rapes, and displaced persons.[258]

5.2.1 A Brief Background

In 2003, while the international community's attention was focused on negotiating a peace agreement to end the twenty-year civil war between northern and southern Sudan, another major conflict was beginning in Darfur, in western Sudan.[259]

The conflict in Darfur has historical roots in intercommunal conflict between nomadic Arab camel- and cattle-herders, and sedentary farmers (including the Fur, Masalit, and Zaghawa ethnic groups), who have historically competed for land and water resources.[260] Until the 1980s, these

---

Syria], the rest of the Council dispensed with diplomatic decorum and advanced draft resolutions knowing full well that they would fail. The P-3 [the UK, France, and US] highlight these predictable results to underscore Russia's complicity with the Syrian government – a pattern not lost on the Russian delegation." Van Schaack, *supra* note 8. "This willingness to isolate and attempt to shame Russia on Syria is also attributable to the Europeans' and the Americans' aggravation over Russia's actions in Ukraine." *Id.*

[258] Trahan interview with Darfur scholar Eric Reeves, 6/18/19.
[259] World Without Genocide, *Darfur Genocide*, at http://worldwithoutgenocide.org/genocides-and-conflicts/darfur-genocide [hereinafter, *Darfur Genocide*].
[260] Jennifer Trahan, *Why the Killing in Darfur Is Genocide*, 31 FORDHAM J. INT'L L. 990, 995 (2008), at http://ir.lawnet.fordham.edu/cgi/viewcontent.cgi?article=2107&context=ilj

tensions were mostly kept in abeyance by traditional conflict resolution mechanisms.[261] However, in the following years, tensions worsened due to extended periods of drought, competition for scarce resources, lack of good governance, and the availability of weapons.[262] In 1994, the Sudanese Government also reorganized, giving Arab groups new positions of power in Darfur, which the Fur, Masalit, and Zaghawa viewed as an attempt to undermine their leadership roles and power in the region.[263]

The conflict, which has serious racial and ethnic overtones,[264] escalated in February 2003 when two armed rebel groups, the Sudan Liberation Army/Movement (SLA/M) and the Justice and Equality Movement (JEM) – drawn from members of the Fur, Masalit, and Zaghawa ethnic groups[265] – rose up against the Sudanese Government, accusing it of neglecting the region and arming Arab militias against civilians.[266] Early demands included an end to prolonged economic marginalization, an end to tribal militias, and power-sharing with the central Government.[267]

At first, the local authorities in Darfur seemingly looked for a peaceful solution to the insurgency.[268] However, by the end of March 2003, the

---

[hereinafter, *Why the Killing in Darfur Is Genocide*]. For more extensive background on the conflict and discussion of the crimes occurring, see ERIC REEVES, A LONG DAY'S DYING: CRITICAL MOMENTS IN THE DARFUR GENOCIDE (2007); Eric Reeves, *Compromising with Evil: An Archival History of Greater Sudan, 2007–2012*, at www.compromisingwithevil.org.

[261] Trahan, *Why the Killing in Darfur Is Genocide*, supra note 260, at 995, citing Human Rights Watch, *Darfur Destroyed: Ethnic Cleansing By Government and Militia Forces in Western Sudan* 6 (2004), at www.hrw.org/reports/2004/sudan0504/ [hereinafter, *Darfur Destroyed*].

[262] *Id.*

[263] *Id.*; Trahan, *Why the Killing in Darfur Is Genocide*, supra note 260, at 995–96, n. 24 ("The 1994 reorganization created the three Darfur states of North, South and West Darfur. The effect of the reorganization was to negate in particular the political power of the Fur, the largest ethnic group in Darfur."), citing Interview with Eric Reeves, 01/05/08.

[264] Human Rights Watch, *Sudan, Darfur in Flames: Atrocities in Western Sudan*, 8 (2004), at www.hrw.org/reports/2004/sudan0404/sudan0404.pdf [hereinafter, *Darfur in Flames*].

[265] The JEM was supported largely by the Zaghawa people, and the SLA/M drew most of its followers from the Fur people. David H. Shinn, *China and the Conflict in Darfur*, XVI BROWN J. FOR. AFF. 85, 86 (2009). The SLA/M split into two main factions: the SLA Abdul Wahid (SLA-AW) and the SLA Mini Minnawi (SLA-MM), over disagreements related to the May 2006 Darfur Peace Agreement. By 2011, all rebel groups consolidated into the Sudan Revolutionary Front. Security Council Report, Chronology of Events – Sudan (Darfur), rev. 1 May 2019, at www.securitycouncilreport.org/chronology/sudan-darfur.php.

[266] *Darfur Destroyed*, supra note 261, at 1.

[267] *Id.*; *Darfur in Flames*, supra note 264, at 9.

[268] Amnesty International, *Sudan: Darfur – Too Many People Killed for No Reason*, 2 (Feb. 3, 2004), at www.amnesty.org/download/Documents/92000/afr540082004en.pdf [hereinafter, *Darfur – Too Many People Killed for No Reason*].

Sudanese forces and the Arab "Janjaweed"[269] militias it armed and mobilized decided to respond by force.[270]

On April 25, 2003, the rebels attacked the airport in Al-Fasher, the capital city of North Darfur, reportedly killing approximately seventy Government soldiers and destroying planes.[271] The SLA/M declared that the attack was a demonstration against the Government's perceived failure to protect villagers from attacks by nomadic groups and the underdevelopment and marginalization of the region.[272]

The attack on Al-Fasher was a turning point. Soon thereafter, Government forces and the Janjaweed adopted a "scorched earth policy," attacking not only rebel fighters but also launching a full-scale attack against the civilian population of Darfur. While the Fur, Masalit, and Zaghawa[273] were the primary original targets, soon other non-Arab/African tribes became targets: the Berti, Birgid, Tunjur, Tama, and many others.[274]

The Janjaweed, whose tactics were notoriously brutal, moved in on horses and camels, raping and sexually violating women and children, killing and torturing civilians, burning and looting entire villages, and poisoning water wells.[275] While these attacks happened from the ground, Government forces attacked by air, using helicopter gunships.[276]

The fighting continued over the next decade despite occasional lulls,[277] with the crimes committed in 2003–04, discussed at length below, representing the

---

[269] Trahan, *Why the Killing in Darfur Is Genocide*, supra note 260, at 995 (the Janjaweed are primarily "camel-herding nomads who migrated to Darfur from the 1970s, and from Arab camel-herding tribes from North Darfur").

[270] *Darfur – Too Many People Killed for No Reason*, supra note 268, at 2; Shinn, supra note 265, at 86; Trahan, *Why the Killing in Darfur Is Genocide*, supra note 260, at 995 n.17 ("The term 'Janjaweed' ... is reported to be an amalgamation of three Arabic words for ghost, gun, and horse that historically referred to criminals, bandits or outlaws.").

[271] *Darfur – Too Many People Killed for No Reason*, supra note 268, at 2.

[272] *Id.*

[273] Trahan, *Why the Killing in Darfur Is Genocide*, supra note 260, at 995–96; *Darfur Destroyed*, supra note 261, at 7.

[274] Human Rights Watch, *Targeting the Fur: Mass Killings in Darfur A Human Rights Watch Briefing Paper*, at 3 n. 9 (Jan. 24, 2005), *at* www.hrw.org/legacy/backgrounder/africa/darfur0105/darfur0105.pdf.

[275] *Darfur – Too Many People Killed for No Reason*, supra note 268, at 3–4; *Darfur Genocide*, supra note 259; Jewish World Watch, *Darfur Genocide*, *at* www.jww.org/conflict-areas/sudan/darfur; Samuel Totten, *The UN International Commission of Inquiry on Darfur: New and Disturbing Findings*, 4 GENOCIDE STUD. & PREVENTION 354, 362–63, 366 (2009), *at* http://scholarcommons.usf.edu/cgi/viewcontent.cgi?article=1126&context=gsp.

[276] Trahan, *Why the Killing in Darfur Is Genocide*, supra note 260, at 996; *Darfur Destroyed*, supra note 261, at 7.

[277] Geneva Academy, *Sudan: Several Overlapping Non-international Armed Conflicts in Darfur, Kordofan and Blue Nile State* (Jan. 21, 2019), *at* www.rulac.org/news/sudan-several-overlapping-non-international-armed-conflicts-in-darfur-kordo.

height of the killing.[278] On April 2, 2004, the United Nations described Darfur as one of the world's worst humanitarian crises[279] and on September 9, 2004, US Secretary of State Colin Powell declared that genocide had been committed.[280] "Others who have described the situation as genocide include the Parliament of the European Union, the Defense Minister of the Government of Germany, General Roméo Dallaire of Canada (UN peacekeeping force commander in Rwanda), and a great many international genocide scholars."[281]

By July 2004, African Union (AU) forces, as part of an African Union Mission in Sudan (AMIS), began deploying in small numbers to the region.[282] Due to the Government of Sudan's refusal to consent to the deployment of UN peacekeepers to Darfur,[283] it was not until July 2007 that the Security Council authorized a 26,000-strong[284] joint United Nations/African Union Mission in Darfur (UNAMID).[285] UNAMID formally took over from AMIS on December 31, 2007, with its deployment only gradually rolled-out thereafter. UNAMID incorporated and expanded on the relatively small

[278] Trahan, *Why the Killing in Darfur Is Genocide*, *supra* note 260, at 996; Human Rights Watch, *Entrenching Impunity: Government Responsibility for International Crimes in Darfur*, 8 (2005), at www.hrw.org/reports/2005/darfur1205 [hereinafter, *Entrenching Impunity*] ("The pervasive pattern of government-militia coordinated attacks on villages [in Darfur] has declined in 2005 in comparison with previous years, but this is largely because most of the targeted population has already been displaced from the most fertile, desirable rural areas.").

[279] *TIMELINE: Darfur Conflict and Peace Efforts*, REUTERS (Oct. 1, 2007), at www .reuters.com/article/us-sudan-darfur-time/timeline-darfur-conflict-and-peace-efforts-idUSGOR14023720071001.

[280] *Powell Calls Sudan Killings Genocide*, CNN (Sept. 9, 2004), at www.cnn.com/2004/WOR LD/africa/09/09/sudan.powell.

[281] Eric Reeves, *Report of the International Commission of Inquiry on Darfur: A Critical Analysis (Part II)*, IDEA (Oct. 14, 2005), at www.ideajournal.com/articles.php?id=39. Additional groups that have declared the crisis in Darfur to be genocide include: Physicians for Human Rights, US Committee for Refugees, Africa Action, Justice Action (UK), Yad Vashem, Genocide Watch, and The Campaign to Prevent Genocide. Trahan, *Why the Killing in Darfur Is Genocide*, *supra* note 260, at 992 n. 6, citing Interview with Eric Reeves, 01/05/08.

[282] AMIS was charged with monitoring and observing compliance with "ceasefire agreements, in particular the N'djamena Ceasefire Agreement." "AMIS ha[d] the additional mandate of assisting in the process of confidence building; contributing to a secure environment for the delivery of humanitarian relief and, ultimately, the return of IDPs and refugees to their homes; and contributing generally to the improvement of the security situation throughout Darfur." Nsongurua J. Udombana, *When Neutrality Is a Sin: The Darfur Crisis and the Crisis of Humanitarian Intervention in Sudan*, 27(4) HUM. RTS. Q. 1149, 1187 (2005), at https://pa pers.ssrn.com/sol3/papers.cfm?abstract_id=1803678.

[283] As will be detailed below, it was China that insisted on making the deployment of UN peacekeepers to Darfur contingent on Sudan's consent. See Chapters 5.2.4.1–2.

[284] The actual deployment figures were 17,300 military personnel, 3,300 police personnel, and 16 Formed Police Units. Trahan interview with Eric Reeves, 6/18/19.

[285] S/RES/1769 (July 31, 2007); UNAMID, *About*, at https://unamid.unmissions.org/about-unamid-0.

AMIS force, but was burdened by so many limitations and hostility from the Government of Sudan that it was never effective.[286]

Serious crimes against the civilian population have continued, including deliberate and indiscriminate attacks, rapes, killings, mass displacements, torture, destruction of property, and looting of livestock.[287] United Nations and humanitarian personnel have also come under attack.[288]

By 2010, the UN estimated that since the conflict began, more than 2.7 million people had been forced to flee their homes, some living in displaced persons camps.[289] Even in the camps, those fleeing found no safety, with patrolling Janjaweed continuing to kill men and rape women venturing out in search of firewood or water.[290] The majority of the casualties in Darfur have been civilian.[291] Early estimates placed the death toll at 200,000;[292] however, in 2008, the UN revised its estimate to over 300,000.[293] While fatality estimates are often in the 200,000–300,000 range,[294] a more accurate figure is probably 400,000.[295]

---

[286] Trahan interview with Eric Reeves, 6/18/19.
[287] See, e.g., Human Rights Watch, *World Report: Sudan*, at www.hrw.org/world-report/2006/country-chapters/sudan [Events of 2006]; Human Rights Watch, *"Men with No Mercy": Rapid Support Forces Attacks against Civilians in Darfur, Sudan* (Sept. 9, 2015), at www.hrw.org/report/2015/09/09/men-no-mercy/rapid-support-forces-attacks-against-civilians-darfur-sudan [hereinafter, *"Men with No Mercy"*].
[288] See, e.g., HRW, Events of 2006, *supra* note 287.
[289] *Q&A: Sudan's Darfur Conflict*, BBC (Feb. 23, 2010), at http://news.bbc.co.uk/2/hi/africa/3496731.stm. According to Sudan expert Eric Reeves:

> the 2.7 million figure has constantly fluctuated wildly and has been heavily politicized; it also includes people who have been displaced more than once (or twice), and not all those displaced ended up in camps, or have been counted. The UN recently lowered its 2017 figure to 2.1 million. According to the UN High Commissioner for Refugees ("UNHCR") there are still approximately 350,000 Darfuri refugees in Eastern Chad.

Trahan 6/18/19 interview with Eric Reeves, 6/18/19.
[290] See, e.g., Second Periodic Report of the United Nations High Commissioner for Human Rights on the Human Rights Situation in Sudan, 14 (Jan. 27, 2006), at www.ohchr.org/Documents/Countries/sudanjanuary06.pdf.
[291] *Darfur – Too Many People Killed for No Reason*, *supra* note 268, at 2.
[292] Louis Charbonneau, *UN Says Darfur Dead May Be 300,000 as Sudan Denies*, REUTERS (Apr. 22, 2008), at www.reuters.com/article/us-sudan-darfur-un/u-n-says-darfur-dead-may-be-300000-as-sudan-denies-idUSN2230854320080422; Oxfam, *Overview of the Crisis in Darfur* (Sept. 29, 2008), at www.oxfamamerica.org/explore/stories/overview-of-the-crisis-in-darfur ("The Government of Sudan pegs the figure at 10,000, while many activists say the true [number] is up to 400,000.").
[293] Charbonneau, *supra* note 292.
[294] Over ten years later, the UN and news sources still generally cite the death toll as 200,000–300,000. See, e.g., UNICEF, *Darfur Overview*, at www.unicef.org/infobycountry/sudan_darfuroverview.html.
[295] Phillip Manyok, *Oil and Darfur's Blood: China's Thirst for Sudan's Oil*, 4 J. POL. SCI. & PUB. AFF. (2016), at www.omicsonline.org/open-access/oil-and-darfurs-blood-chinas-thirst-

Then, in mid-2013, the Rapid Support Forces (RSF) – a Sudanese Government force with members drawn from paramilitary forces, including the Janjaweed – was created, with the goal of defeating rebel groups in Sudan.[296] In 2014 and 2015, the RSF led two counterinsurgency campaigns in Darfur (Operation Decisive Summer I and II),[297] and, in 2016, led a horrific, brutal assault on Jebel Marra.[298] Forces reportedly committed crimes against humanity, including killings, mass rape and torture of civilians, forced displacement of communities, and destruction of physical infrastructure and infrastructure necessary for sustaining life.[299] According to UN estimates, about 600,000 people were displaced during 2014 and the first half of 2015,[300] and an additional 100,000 during the assault on Jebel Marra in 2016.[301]

After the Security Council referred the situation in Darfur to the ICC,[302] the ICC in 2007 issued arrest warrants against Ahmad Muhammad Harun, then Sudan's Minister of State for the Interior, and Ali Muhammad Ali Abd-Al-Rahman (Ali Kushayb), one of the most senior Janjaweed commanders, charging crimes against humanity and war crimes.[303] In 2009 and 2010, the ICC issued arrest warrants for then Sudanese President Bashir on charges of crimes against humanity, war crimes, and genocide.[304] And, in 2012, the ICC issued an additional arrest warrant also charging crimes against humanity

---

for-sudans-oil-2332-0761-1000189.php?aid=69390 ("The UN Office for the Coordination of Humanitarian Affairs (OCHA) estimated that 396,563 people have died as a result of war in Darfur alone."); *see also* Eric Reeves, *Quantifying Genocide: Darfur Mortality Update*, August 6, 2010 (updated November 2016), SUDAN: RESEARCH, ANALYSIS, AND ADVOCACY (Jan. 5, 2017), at http://sudanreeves.org/2017/01/05/quantifying-genocide-darfur-mortality-update-august-6-2010/.

[296] "Men with No Mercy," *supra* note 287.
[297] *Id.*
[298] Eric Reeves, *Jebel Marra: Accelerating Civilian Destruction and Displacement—Consequences of International Expediency and Indifference*, SOUTH SUDAN NEWS AGENCY (Feb. 26, 2016), at https://southsudannewsagency.org/index.php/2016/02/26/jebel-marra-accelerating-civilian-destruction-and-displacement.
[299] "Men with No Mercy," *supra* note 287.
[300] *Id.*
[301] Reeves, *Jebel Marra*, *supra* note 298.
[302] S/RES/1593 (Mar. 31, 2005).
[303] The Prosecutor v. Ahmad Muhammad Harun ("Ahmad Harun") and Ali Muhammad Ali Abd-Al-Rahman ("Ali Kushayb"), ICC-02/05-01/07, at www.icc-cpi.int/darfur/harunkushayb (twenty counts of crimes against humanity, twenty-two counts of war crimes).
[304] The Prosecutor v. Omar Hassan Ahmad Al Bashir, ICC-02/05-01/09, at www.icc-cpi.int/darfur/albashir. An ICC Pre-Trial Chamber initially only agreed to a warrant charging crimes against humanity and war crimes, but after the Prosecutor's successful appeal, a second warrant charging genocide was also issued. Second Warrant of Arrest for Omar Hassan Ahmad Al Bashir, ICC-02/05-01/09-95, July 12, 2010 (charging genocide).

and war crimes against Abdel Raheem Muhammad Hussein, Sudan's Minister of National Defense, for activities while he was Minister of the Interior.[305] President Bashir remained in power until forced out by a military coup on April 11, 2019,[306] but neither he nor any other Government or Janjaweed charged have been transferred to the ICC.[307] At the time of writing, Bashir faces domestic corruption charges, and Mohamed Hamdan Dagolo ("Hemeti"), a former Janjaweed leader who is heavily implicated in atrocity crimes, is reportedly leading Sudan's "transition."[308]

5.2.2 How Veto Threats Hampered the Security Council's Ability to Pass Resolutions Related to the Situation in Darfur

The discussion below roughly groups the events in Darfur and inaction or delayed action of the Security Council chronologically into: (1) Chinese threats (explicit or implicit)[309] related to the imposition of sanctions; and (2) Chinese threats (explicit or implicit) related to the deployment of UN peacekeepers to Darfur. As will be detailed below, China used the threat of veto to delay, limit, or completely block imposing various sanctions. As to

---

[305] The Prosecutor v. Abdel Raheem Muhammad Hussein, ICC-02/05-01/12, *at* www.icc-cpi.int /darfur/hussein (seven counts of crimes against humanity, six counts of war crimes).

[306] *Sudan's Omar al-Bashir Forced Out in Coup*, CNN (Apr. 11, 2019), *at* www.cnn.com/africa/ live-news/sudan-latest-updates/h_36cb0aae3db11e523b0fc33d21aa5fdb.

[307] As will be explained below, the lack of follow-up is also partly attributable to the veto power, as some on the Council *did* try to follow up regarding the first two warrants, but the Presidential Statement calling for execution of the warrants was blocked by China. *See infra* section 5.2.5. Originally, three rebel leaders were also summoned and appeared voluntarily before the ICC regarding attacks against AU peacekeepers in 2007, killing twelve peacekeepers: Bahr Idriss Abu Garda (Vice-President of JEM at the time of the alleged crimes); Abdallah Banda Abakaer Nourain (Commander-in-Chief of the JEM Collective-Leadership); and Saleh Mohammed Jerbo Jamus (former Chief-of-Staff of the SLA-Unity). Thereafter, charges against Abu Garda were not confirmed, charges against Jerbo were terminated in 2013 after his death, while an arrest warrant against Banda was issued in September 2014 and remains outstanding. *See* Prosecutor v. Bahr Idriss Abu Garda, ICC-02/05-02/09, *at* www.icc-cpi.int/darfur/abugarda (charges not confirmed); Prosecutor v. Abdallah Banda Abakaer Nourain, ICC-02/05-03/09, *at* www.icc-cpi.int/darfur/banda (three counts of war crimes against Banda; proceedings against Jerbo terminated).

[308] Khalid Abdelaziz, *Sudan's Ex-President Bashir Charged with Corruption, Holding Illicit Foreign Currency*, REUTERS (Aug. 31, 2019), *at* www.reuters.com/article/us-sudan-politics-b ashir/sudans-ex-president-bashir-charged-with-corruption-holding-illicit-foreign-currency-id USKCN1VL0AJ; Jérôme Tubiana, *The Man Who Terrorized Darfur Is Leading Sudan's Supposed Transition*, FOR. POL'Y (May 14, 2019), *at* https://foreignpolicy.com/2019/05/14/m an-who-terrorized-darfur-is-leading-sudans-supposed-transition-hemeti-rsf-janjaweed-bashir-khartoum.

[309] *See* note 316 *infra* and accompanying text (express and implied threats).

peacekeeping, China also used the threat of the veto to require that any UN peacekeeping deployment to Darfur be consensually negotiated with the Government of Sudan – consent which was later refused, resulting in significant delays in UN peacekeepers reaching Darfur. China also insisted on weakening the eventual hybrid peacekeeping force's mandate by removing a disarmament obligation. China additionally blocked the issuance of a Presidential Statement[310] that would have called for the execution of the first two arrest warrants issued by the ICC.

While China was "protecting" the Sudanese Government through the use of its veto power, the Sudanese military and Janjaweed militia were jointly committing mass atrocity crimes – acknowledged, as mentioned, to constitute crimes against humanity and war crimes,[311] and most likely also genocide.[312] The above analysis should also be viewed through the lens of China's strong economic ties to the Sudanese Government – purchasing significant amounts of oil from Sudan, making huge capital investments in Sudan, and extending many loans as a way to cultivate Sudan as a client state in Africa.[313] China was also a supplier of weapons to Sudan, including during the period when the crimes were at their height.[314] Accordingly, China and Sudan both benefited

---

[310] As explained below, technically, there is no veto over a Presidential Statement, yet Chinese objections resulted in the Presidential Statement not being issued, as the Security Council President could not speak for all members. See text accompanying notes 507–09 *infra*.

[311] All the ICC's warrants against Government of Sudan and Janjaweed leaders charge crimes against humanity and war crimes. See notes 303–05 *supra*.

[312] See note 304 *supra* (Bashir warrant for genocide).

[313] Human Rights Watch, *Sudan, Oil, and Human Rights*, 456–58 (2003) at www.hrw.org/reports/2003/sudan1103/sudanprint.pdf [hereinafter, *Sudan, Oil, and Human Rights*]; Manyok, *supra* note 295. Eric Reeves explains China's economic ties to Sudan related to oil:

> Over the last decade, with its economy booming and its need for cheap fossil fuels climbing at a fantastic clip, China has been Khartoum's primary partner in oil development projects. Of the 500,000 barrels of oil Sudan produces every day, China imports roughly two-thirds. That would translate into more than $7 billion a year in costs, if the oil were purchased on the open market. But because China dominates the two major oil production consortia in southern Sudan, Beijing's petroleum bill was only slightly more than half that. It's no wonder the Chinese have been so keen on funneling money – some $10 billion – into Sudanese oil infrastructure projects like pipeline construction, all-weather road building, and exploration rigs. Don't expect the relationship to change any time soon either: China's petroleum import bill has risen by more than 10% per year for more than a decade and shows no signs of slowing.

Eric Reeves, *Partners in Genocide: A Comprehensive Guide to China's Role in Darfur* (Dec. 19, 2007), *at* http://sudanreeves.org/2007/12/19/partners-in-genocide-a-comprehensive-guide-to-chinas-role-in-darfur. For additional discussion of China's financial ties to Sudan, see Shinn, *supra* note 265, at 87–88.

[314] According to United Nations Comtrade data:

financially by China blocking the oil embargo and initially limiting the arms embargo.[315]

The discussion below covers veto "threats," both express and implied. When a permanent member of the Security Council states an objection to language in a resolution, it may not sound like a "threat," but it indicates to drafters and supporters of the resolution, that, if put to a vote, the permanent member could invoke the veto. Andras Vamos-Goldman, who served as political coordinator and then legal adviser to the Canadian Mission to the United Nations from 1997 to 2002, explains:

> Any indication (formal or informal) from a permanent member that it disagrees with a proposed action (or language) essentially constitutes a "threat." What makes it a "threat" is not the form or even the strength of such opposition, it is the power of the negative vote behind anything and everything a permanent member says and does. When it is said by a permanent member, all other Security Council members have it in the backs of their minds that it always has the potential to stop the Security Council from acting.[316]

> China has transferred a lot of weapons and small arms valued at $1 million in 2002, $23 million in 2005. This finding is also confirmed by Human Rights First research which stated that China's military sales to Sudan have exponentially increased since 1999, which is exactly when Sudan's oil production increased. The same report showed that Sudan's small arms purchases tripled between 1999 and 2000. It quadrupled during 2001, increased fifteen-fold in 2002. By [the] end of ... 2005, the report stated small arms imports to Sudan have risen to more than 680 times of what Sudan's arms imports were in 1999. This means, Sudan's Arms imports from China have been on the rise and so were military cooperation between Beijing and Khartoum. The top China-Sudan military leaders have had several meetings in 2002, 2003, 2005 and 2007, at the top official levels. In April of 2007, China's Defense Minister Mr. Cao Gangchuan openly made a disclosure that the two countries are further working to develop military cooperation in all areas.

Manyok, *supra* note 295.

[315] As discussed below, even when the arms embargo was expanded to include the Government, a UN Panel of Experts concluded China was violating the embargo. *See* note 447 *infra* and accompanying text.

[316] Trahan 6/3/19 interview with Andras Vamos-Goldman. He further explains:

> For example, if a permanent member were to indicate in negotiations that it would "have concerns" with certain wording in a draft resolution, depending on the importance of that text to the substance of the resolution, it can be a "flag" to the drafters and sponsors of the resolution that the text at issue could trigger a veto. Since negotiations tend to be fluid, involving many considerations, even direct questions such as "will you veto the resolution with this wording" can at time receive an enigmatic response such as "we will have to consider all our options carefully." Until the last stages of negotiations, the drafters and sponsors of the resolution often only have such information on which to make their calculation of whether the permanent member in question will or will not invoke the veto.

5.2.3 How Veto Threats Weakened Sanctions

In the face of large-scale atrocity crimes being committed in Darfur, one sees five known instances where China threatened, expressly or implicitly, to utilize its veto power if certain sanctions were imposed on the Sudanese Government. (There may have been additional veto threats, but it is difficult to know; those discussed below appear in publicly available sources.) Prompt imposition of arms sanctions on the Government as well as an oil embargo – both of which were blocked – could have delivered a crucial message that the states serving on the Security Council were vigilantly monitoring the situation and prepared to impose costly economic measures to try to stem the tide of atrocity crimes. A sufficient number of states on the Security Council appeared to be willing to take such steps to pressure the Government of Sudan to cease its role in the attacks and rein in the Janjaweed militias it was arming, paying, and coordinating.[317] While the Council eventually was able to agree on certain sanctions – an arms embargo (that initially excluded the Government) and limited asset freezes and travel bans[318] – the veto threats delayed imposing sanctions, weakened the sanctions imposed, and entirely blocked sanctions related to Sudan's oil exports. While the Security Council also imposed a ban on offensive military flights, the resolution was completely ignored, with no consequences imposed for violations.

5.2.3.1 The First Implicit Threat to Veto Sanctions

The first known implicit threat occurred on or prior to July 30, 2004, related to what became Resolution 1556. China insisted that language be removed from the resolution that would have threatened sanctions on the Government of Sudan if it did not comply with the resolution. The Security Council eventually passed Resolution 1556, imposing an arms embargo on "non-governmental entities and individuals" in Darfur,[319] but not on the Government.

Trahan 5/29/19–5/30/19 interviews with Andras Vamos-Goldman. By "express" threat, the author means a situation where a permanent member says words to the effect "we will be forced to veto (or cast a negative vote) if that language is not removed"; by "implied" threat, the author means a situation where a permanent member expresses "concerns" with certain resolution language that "would be difficult to accept," but is not expressly threatening to veto.

[317] As noted below, Human Rights Watch found that the Sudanese Government reportedly recruited as many as 20,000 militia members, uniformed and armed them, paid new recruits fee ranging from $100 to 400 and monthly stipends, and condoned their attacks. *Darfur in Flames, supra* note 264, at 22, 24.

[318] S/RES/1591. Only four persons were subject to the travel ban and asset freeze after China refused to endorse seventeen individuals being listed. *See* S/RES/1672 (Apr. 25, 2006) (listing four individuals).

[319] S/RES/1556, para. 7.

By July 2004, however, a huge number of the early warning mechanisms within the UN system, as well as various NGOs, had already reported that a massive number of crimes were being committed by the Sudanese military and Janjaweed militia[320] in Darfur. For example:

- As early as February 2003, Amnesty International called for a commission of inquiry into the crisis in Darfur[321] (a call that was renewed in January 2004).[322]
- By March 2003, the Special Rapporteur on the Situation of Human Rights in Sudan expressed concern that the ongoing conflict in Darfur had a high potential to destabilize the country, and human rights groups accused the Government of arming the Janjaweed against Darfuri groups.[323]
- By September 2003, the UNHCR reported that nearly 70,000 Sudanese refugees had fled to Chad.[324] The newly arrived refugees told a UN interagency mission team that they fled Darfur when Government forces bombed their villages.[325]
- By October 2003, the number of internally displaced persons (IDPs) had risen to over 500,000,[326] including 200,000 of whom fled in October alone.[327] The USAID Administrator also reported that over 7,000 people had died and stated that "the conflict in Darfur was the worst in the region since independence."[328]

---

[320] There were also crimes committed by rebel groups, although far less extensive in scale.
[321] Amnesty International, *Sudan: Urgent Call for Commission of Inquiry in Darfur as Situation Deteriorates* (Feb. 21, 2013), *at* www.amnesty.org.uk/press-releases/sudan-urgent-call-commission-inquiry-darfur-situation-deteriorates.
[322] Amnesty International, *Sudan: Killings, Abductions of Children and Arbitrary Detention in Darfur* (Jan. 7, 2004), *at* https://reliefweb.int/report/sudan/sudan-killings-abductions-children-and-arbitrary-detention-darfur.
[323] UN Commission on Human Rights, Experts Describe Situations in Sudan, South-east Europe and Afghanistan (Mar. 28, 2003), *at* https://reliefweb.int/report/afghanistan/experts-describe-situations-sudan-south-east-europe-and-afghanistan.
[324] UN High Commissioner for Refugees, More Sudanese Refugees Flee to Neighbouring Chad (Sept. 12, 2003), *at* https://reliefweb.int/report/chad/more-sudanese-refugees-flee-neighbouring-chad.
[325] UNHCHR, UNHCR Briefing Notes: Sudan, Uganda, Chad, Afghanistan (Sept. 2, 2003), *at* https://reliefweb.int/report/sudan/unhcr-briefing-notes-sudan-uganda-chad-afghanistan.
[326] IRIN, *Sudan: Rising Numbers of Displaced in Darfur* (Oct. 23, 2003), *at* https://reliefweb.int/report/sudan/sudan-rising-numbers-displaced-darfur.
[327] *Widespread Insecurity in Darfur Despite Ceasefire*, THE NEW HUMANITARIAN (Oct. 3, 2003), *at* www.thenewhumanitarian.org/report/46513/sudan-widespread-insecurity-darfur-despite-ceasefire.
[328] IRIN, *Sudan: Deadlock in Darfur Peace Talks* (Oct. 31, 2003), *at* https://reliefweb.int/report/sudan/sudan-deadlock-darfur-peace-talks.

- According to the UNHCR, thousands of newly arrived Sudanese refugees had fled in late November and early December 2003, after aerial bombardment of homes and villages, ethnic cleansing by Arab militias, and humanitarian relief being blocked.[329]
- By December 2003, the Secretary-General's Special Envoy for Humanitarian Needs in Sudan visited Darfur and observed that the crisis had reached "unprecedented proportions," with one million war-affected.[330] The Under-Secretary-General for Humanitarian Affairs and Emergency Relief Coordinator called the humanitarian situation in Darfur "one of the worst in the world" and was deeply concerned that access to people in need of aid was being blocked by the parties to the conflict.[331] UN Secretary-General Kofi Annan also expressed alarm at "the rapidly deteriorating humanitarian situation in Darfur" and "reports of widespread abuses against civilians, including killings, rape, and the burning and looting of entire villages."[332]
- By January 2004, the High Commissioner for Human Rights also expressed deep concern over the deteriorating human rights and humanitarian situation in Darfur, and called for the establishment of a commission of inquiry.[333]
- On February 3, 2004, Amnesty International released its full-length report *Darfur – Too Many People Killed for No Reason*, outlining the Government's continuous disproportionate and indiscriminate use of helicopter gunships often targeting fleeing civilians, with Government forces at best failing to distinguish between civilian and military persons and objects, and at worst appearing to deliberately target civilians.[334] These aerial attacks were also frequently followed by the Janjaweed's ground attacks, where they would surround villages and surprise civilians who had no time

---

[329] UNHCR, More Sudanese Flee into Chad; UNHCHR Starts Work on Relocation Site (Dec. 8, 2003), at https://reliefweb.int/report/chad/more-sudanese-flee-chad-unhcr-starts-work-relocation-site.

[330] UNOCHA, Humanitarian Envoy Shocked by Worsening Conditions in Darfur, Sudan (Dec. 8, 2003), at https://reliefweb.int/report/sudan/humanitarian-envoy-shocked-worsening-conditions-darfur-sudan.

[331] UNOCHA, Situation in Darfur, Sudan, a Humanitarian Crisis (Dec. 5, 2003), at https://reliefweb.int/report/sudan/situation-darfur-sudan-humanitarian-crisis.

[332] UN Secretary General, UN SC Alarmed by Deteriorating Humanitarian Situation in Darfur Region of Sudan (Dec. 9, 2003), at https://reliefweb.int/report/sudan/un-sg-alarmed-deteriorating-humanitarian-situation-darfur-region-sudan.

[333] UN Office of the High Commissioner for Human Rights, Acting Rights Chief Concerned Over Deteriorating Situation in Darfur Region of Sudan (Jan. 29, 2004), at https://reliefweb.int/report/sudan/acting-rights-chief-concerned-over-deteriorating-situation-darfur-region-sudan.

[334] *Darfur – Too Many People Killed for No Reason*, supra note 268, at 2, 15.

to defend themselves or flee.[335] During the ground attacks, the Janjaweed, sometimes accompanied by Government soldiers, would reportedly destroy entire villages and loot cattle,[336] rape women and girls,[337] abduct civilians,[338] and arrest and torture people from African tribes, most predominantly, those of Fur, Zaghawa, and Masalit ethnicity.[339]

Despite all these early warning signs, the first UN Security Council briefing exclusively devoted to Darfur did not take place until April 2, 2004 – more than a year after the crisis erupted and two months after Amnesty International's report.[340] It is clear the Security Council was slow to respond to the crisis in Darfur because it was focused on concluding the North-South Peace Agreement.[341] However, as will be shown below, China's veto threats continued to "protect" the Government, stymying the Security Council, well after that agreement was concluded.

On the same day that the Security Council met to discuss Darfur, Human Rights Watch released its report *Darfur in Flames: Atrocities in Western Sudan*, characterizing the crimes as crimes against humanity and war crimes.[342] Notably, Human Rights Watch reported that the Sudanese Air Force would drop hundreds – if not thousands – of bombs in northern Darfur, sometimes repeatedly bombing the same villages day after day.[343] The bombings forced people to flee their villages and move into *wadis* (tree-lined riverbeds), where they were also then attacked.[344] Additionally, there was a deliberate campaign to destroy water sources[345] – by poisoning wells, tearing apart irrigation systems, and forcing the

---

[335] Id. at 9–14.
[336] Id. at 19–21.
[337] Id. at 17–19.
[338] Id. at 22.
[339] Id. at 23.
[340] UN, Press Briefing on Humanitarian Crisis in Darfur, Sudan (Apr. 2, 2004), at www.un.org/press/en/2004/egelandbrf.DOC.htm.
[341] Human Rights Watch, *The United Nations and Darfur* (Jan. 2005), at www.hrw.org/legacy/wr2k5/darfur/4.htm [hereinafter, *The United Nations and Darfur*] ("False optimism that th[e] [North-South peace] negotiations would lead to a quick settlement that would change the overall political situation in Sudan may have caused some member states to discount the warning signs of a growing crisis in Darfur"; "the Security Council may have tried to keep Darfur off of its agenda out of fear that a discussion of Darfur would cause the Government in Khartoum to pull out of the [North-South] Naivasha talks."). According to Eric Reeves, the delay in reaching the north-south agreement was deliberate because the Government knew the agreement was so valued by Western nationals that it provided time for the Government to complete its military offensive in Darfur. Trahan interview with Eric Reeves, 6/18/19.
[342] *Darfur in Flames*, supra note 264, at 13.
[343] Id. at 18.
[344] Id. at 19.
[345] Id. at 20.

abandonment of traditional water storage facilities.[346] Human Rights Watch noted far less use of aerial bombardment in South and West Darfur, but reported that Janjaweed ground attacks became increasingly brutal by October 2003, and even more numerous and violent by early 2004.[347] Villages were generally selected on the basis of ethnicity, where African/non-Arab villages were destroyed and emptied, yet other villages in close proximity populated by other ethnicities remained untouched.[348] Human Rights Watch also found that a campaign of forced displacement was taking place and concluded that the character and scale of abuses committed by the Janjaweed would not have been possible without the Government's clear support.[349] In particular, Human Rights Watch found the Sudanese Government recruited as many as 20,000 Janjaweed militia members,[350] uniformed and armed them, paid new recruits fees and monthly stipends,[351] and condoned their attacks.[352] At the same time, the Government disregarded the pleas of the Zaghawa, Masalit, and Fur for protection,[353] and almost entirely obstructed international humanitarian aid to displaced civilians, while providing virtually no assistance of its own.[354]

In May 2004, Human Rights Watch, issued a second report entitled *Darfur Destroyed*,[355] in which it concluded that the Sudanese Government, working with the Janjaweed militia, was committing "ethnic cleansing,"[356] along with crimes against humanity and war crimes.[357] In particular, Human Rights Watch concluded that the Government was responsible for launching aerial bombardments and participating in joint attacks with the Janjaweed on Masalit and Fur villages, which were attacked and burned repeatedly "until the population was finally driven away."[358] Even after the villages were destroyed, the Government-supported Janjaweed continued to attack displaced civilians in camps and settlements, beating and raping women and children who ventured out to find food and firewood, and torturing and killing men who attempted to return to their

---

[346] Trahan interview with Eric Reeves, 6/18/19.
[347] *Darfur in Flames, supra* note 264, at 20.
[348] *Id.* at 22.
[349] *Id.* at 16.
[350] *Id.* at 22.
[351] *Id.* at 24.
[352] *Id.* at 16, 22–24.
[353] *Id.* at 16, 24–26.
[354] *Id.* at 33–34.
[355] *Id.* at 39–42.
[356] "Ethnic cleansing" is an imprecise term that is used to connote killings perpetrated on an ethnic basis, but not yet necessarily constituting genocide.
[357] *Darfur Destroyed, supra* note 261.
[358] *Id.* at 41–42.

villages.[359] On December 31, 2003, then-President Bashir said "the horsemen" (that is, Janjaweed) would be one of the weapons he would use, alongside the army, to defeat the rebellion,[360] although the Government later denied any involvement with the Janjaweed as international criticism grew. Then Foreign Minister Mustafa Osman Ismail also admitted "common cause" with the Janjaweed.[361]

On May 7, 2004, the High Commissioner for Human Rights also reported that a systematic or widespread pattern of human rights and humanitarian law violations was taking place in Darfur by both the Armed Forces of Sudan and the Janjaweed[362] including: indiscriminate attacks against civilians;[363] rape and other serious forms of sexual violence;[364] destruction of property and pillage;[365] forced displacement;[366] disappearances;[367] and persecution and discrimination.[368] The report, which found that rebel forces were to some extent also violating human rights and humanitarian law,[369] characterized the situation as a "reign of terror in Darfur."[370]

After an "Arria-formula" meeting[371] on May 25, 2004, the Council released a Presidential Statement on May 26,[372] mentioning for the first time the crisis in

---

[359] Id.
[360] Id. at 43, citing *Sudanese President Says the War against Outlaws Is a Government Priority*, ASSOC. PRESS (Dec. 31, 2003).
[361] *Darfur Destroyed, supra* note 261, at 43.
[362] Report of the United Nations High Commissioner for Human Rights and Follow-up to the World Conference on Human Rights, Situation of Human rights in the Darfur Region of the Sudan, at 46, E/CN.4/2005/3 (May 7, 2004), at https://undocs.org/E/CN.4/2005/3.
[363] Id., paras. 57–64.
[364] Id., paras. 65–69.
[365] Id., paras. 70–73.
[366] Id., paras. 74–81.
[367] Id., paras. 82–84.
[368] Id., paras. 85–90.
[369] Id. at 3.
[370] Id., para. 92.
[371] A 1993–95 Supplement of the Repertoire of the Practice of the Security Council describes an Arria-formula meeting:

> The practice of the Arria-formula meetings ... was initiated in March 1992 by the then-President of the Security Council, Ambassador Diego Arria (Venezuela) .... Arria-formula meetings are not ... meetings of the Security Council. They are [meetings "of members" of the Security Council [as opposed to meetings "of" the Security Council] convened ... in order to hear the views of individuals, organizations or institutions on matters within the competence of the Security Council.

Security Council Report, UN Security Council Working Methods, Arria-Formula Meetings, *at* www.securitycouncilreport.org/un-security-council-working-methods/arria-formula-meetings.php.
[372] S/PRST/2004/18.

Darfur, and calling on the Government of Sudan to disarm the Janjaweed.[373] The Presidential Statement, inter alia:

> [e]xpresse[d] grave concern over the deteriorating humanitarian and human rights situation in the Darfur region of Sudan. Noting that thousands have been killed and that hundreds of thousands of people are at risk of dying in the coming months, the Council emphasize[d] the need for immediate humanitarian access to the vulnerable population. The Council also expresse[d] its deep concern at the continuing reports of large-scale violations of human rights and of international humanitarian law in Darfur, including indiscriminate attacks on civilians, sexual violence, forced displacement and acts of violence, especially those with an ethnic dimension, and demand[ed] that those responsible be held accountable.[374]

Two months later, China (along with other Council members) reportedly insisted that language of a draft resolution being negotiated, S/2004/611, be changed so that it *not include a threat of sanctions* against the Sudanese Government if the Government failed to comply with the resolution.[375] According to one source, "the US [was required by China and other states to] soften the language of what became Resolution 1556 to substitute a threat of sanctions to instead reference possible 'further actions, including measures as provided for' in Article 41 of the UN Charter in the event of noncompliance."[376] China later abstained from voting on Resolution 1556,[377] which demanded that the Government of Sudan disarm the Janjaweed and bring to justice those leaders who had incited and carried out the

---

[373] Security Council Report, Chronology of Events – Sudan (Darfur), rev. 1, May 2019, at www.securitycouncilreport.org/chronology/sudan-darfur.php.

[374] S/PRST/2004/18.

[375] Udombana, *supra* note 282, at 1183.

[376] Id. S/RES/1556, para. 6. The source describes the demands as made by "seven of the fifteen council members – including Algeria, China, and Pakistan." Udombana, *supra* note 282, at 1183. Admittedly, if seven of fifteen Security Council members were "reluctant" to endorse sanctions, there were not nine (only eight) positive votes lined up; thus, here China's veto power alone was not the sole impediment.

[377] Vamos-Goldman explains why a permanent member might abstain from voting on a resolution:

> While there can be a myriad of reasons why a permanent member abstains on any given resolution, one obvious one is that it wishes to record its disagreement with some or all of the resolution, but does not wish to go as far as to block Security Council action. In this particular case, China may have obtained its most important goal in negotiations (sanctions), but still did not agree with the language in the resolution. While only those involved in the negotiations would be able to verify, it could also be that a deal may have been arrived at among Security Council members, where China agreed not to "veto" the resolution in exchange for the drafters and supporters dropping the imposition of sanctions on the Government.

Trahan interview with Andras Vamos-Goldman, 6/10/19.

abuses.[378] While Resolution 1556 also imposed an arms embargo, it did so only on sales of arms to all "non-governmental entities and individuals" in Darfur.[379] In other words, it covered only the rebels and Janjaweed militias, but not the Government that was arming the Janjaweed.[380]

While the wording change is not described as caused by a "threat" to veto, obviously, if a permanent member, such as China, does not want to endorse the threat of sanctions, that change needs to be accommodated or there will be a risk of veto.[381] Human Rights Watch describes the role of the veto power: "[b]y July 2004, stronger measures directed at the government were justified and necessary, but they weren't adopted because at least one permanent member – China – and possibly another – Russia – presumably would have vetoed any resolution that included sanctions against the government or authorized direct UN intervention."[382]

As demonstrated above, the insistence that the resolution *not* threaten sanctions against the Government of Sudan, and exclude the Government from any arms embargo occurred in the context of China selling significant amounts of military equipment to the Government of Sudan,[383] at the same time as high-level UN officials, including the Secretary-General,[384] were reporting that Government forces were implicated in atrocity crimes, described at that point as crimes against humanity, war crimes, and "ethnic cleansing."[385]

As of July 2004, there were approximately 1,260,421 IDPs in the region, and *Médecins Sans Frontières* was reporting a death toll "three times the internationally accepted threshold indicating an emergency situation," and "severe acute malnutrition."[386]

---

[378] S/RES/1556, para. 6.
[379] S/RES/1556. Specifically, the resolution:

> *Decides* that all states shall take the necessary measures to prevent the sale or supply, to all non-governmental entities and individuals, including the Janjaweed, operating in the states of North Darfur, South Darfur and West Darfur, by their nationals or from their territories ... of arms and related materiel of all types, including weapons and ammunition, military vehicles and equipment, paramilitary equipment, and spare parts for the aforementioned, whether or not originating in their territories.

Id., para. 7.
[380] *The United Nations and Darfur, supra* note 341.
[381] See note 316 *supra* and accompanying text (Andras Vamos-Goldman interview).
[382] *The United Nations and Darfur, supra* note 341.
[383] See note 314 *supra* (arms sales).
[384] See note 332 *supra* (Secretary-General).
[385] See notes 355–57 *supra* and accompanying text (HRW).
[386] Office of the UN Resident and Humanitarian Coordinator for the Sudan, Darfur Humanitarian Profile No. 4, at 2, 13 (July 1, 2004), at https://reliefweb.int/sites/reliefweb.int/files/resources/B02B487627CD5CFB49256EF60004EDEE-unrc-sud-1jul.pdf.

5.2.3.2 A Second Threat to Veto Sanctions

A second threat (this time explicit) to veto sanctions against the Government of Sudan occurred on or prior to September 18, 2004, related to Resolution 1564, when China insisted that *oil trading sanctions not be imposed* on the Government of Sudan.

Yet, by this time, the Secretary-General was describing the situation in Darfur as involving a "scorched-earth policy."[387] Specifically, in an August 30, 2004 report, the Secretary-General concluded that "most of the targeted violence resulted from a scorched-earth policy adopted by armed militias, and resulted in the forced displacement of more than 1.3 million people within Darfur and across the border to Chad."[388] The Secretary-General also concluded that the Government of Sudan had not met its obligation to stop attacks against civilians and ensure their protection, noting that "[a]ttacks against civilians [were] continuing," "the vast majority of armed militias [had] not been disarmed," and the Government had taken no concrete steps to "bring to justice ... any of the perpetrators ...."[389] Further, the Secretary-General concluded that after eighteen months of conflict, the Government had been unable to resolve the crisis in Darfur,[390] and displaced civilians have been "terrorized and traumatized" and have "lost confidence in the authorities."[391] The Secretary-General was of the view that a "substantially increased international presence" was required in Darfur "as quickly as possible."[392]

By August 2004, the Special Rapporteur on Extrajudicial, Summary or Arbitrary Executions, also reported "beyond doubt that the Government of Sudan is responsible for extrajudicial and summary executions of large numbers of people over the last several months in Darfur."[393]

By September 2004, the US Department of State reported that there was "a consistent and widespread pattern of atrocities committed against non-Arab

---

[387] Report of the Secretary-General Pursuant to Paragraphs 6 and 13 to 16 of Security Council Resolution 1556 (2004), S/2004/703 (Aug. 30, 2004), *at* https://undocs.org/S/2004/703. The Secretary-General was acting pursuant to Security Council Resolution 1556 to, inter alia, report on the progress of Sudan's commitments to disarm the Janjaweed militias and bring to justice those who have incited and carried out human rights and international humanitarian law violations and other atrocities.

[388] *Id.*, para. 59.

[389] *Id.*, para. 61.

[390] *Id.*

[391] *Id.*, para. 62.

[392] *Id.*, para. 64.

[393] Report of Asma Jahangir, Special Rapporteur on extrajudicial, summary or arbitrary executions – Mission to the Sudan, at 2, E/CN.4/2005/7/Add.2 (Aug. 6, 2004), *at* http://daccess-ods.un.org/access.nsf/Get?Open&DS=E/CN.4/2005/7/Add.2&Lang=E.

villagers in the Darfur region."[394] The State Department report also described crimes against humanity being committed with "close coordination between [Government of Sudan] forces and Arab militia elements, ... known as the [Janjaweed], with abuses against the non-Arab population form[ing] a consistent pattern including murder, rape, beatings, ethnic humiliation, and destruction of property."[395]

By September 9, 2004, US Secretary of State Colin Powell told the US Senate Foreign Relations Committee that the State Department had concluded that genocide had been committed and that the Sudanese Government and the Janjaweed bore responsibility.[396] Soon after, President Bush announced in a speech to the UN General Assembly that the US Government had concluded the crimes in Darfur amounted to genocide.[397]

Notwithstanding the vast number of crimes being committed, with the US taking the position that the crimes constituted genocide, China on or prior to September 18, 2004, reportedly threatened to veto draft resolution S/2004/744 if it included oil trading sanctions against the Government of Sudan.[398] The resolution was later adopted as Resolution 1564, which declared "grave concerns" over Sudan not meeting its obligations to protect civilians, disarm the Janjaweed, and identify and bring Janjaweed perpetrators to justice.[399] However, the resolution did not impose oil-related sanctions. It merely stated that the Security Council would "consider taking additional measures ... such as actions to affect Sudan's petroleum sector."[400] Not coincidentally, as mentioned above, Sudan had significant oil exports to China[401] and China was the

---

[394] US State Department, Bureau of Democracy, Human Rights, and Labor and Bureau of Intelligence and Research, *Documenting Atrocities in Darfur*, State Publication 11182 (Sept. 2004), *at* https://2001-2009.state.gov/g/drl/rls/36028.htm.

[395] *Id.*

[396] *The Crisis in Darfur*, Secretary Colin L. Powell, Testimony Before the Senate Foreign Relations Committee, Washington, DC, Sept. 9, 2004.

[397] *President Bush's Speech to the UN*, GUARDIAN (Sept. 21, 2004), *at* www.theguardian.com/world/2004/sep/21/iraq.usa3.

[398] *China Threatens to Veto UN Darfur Resolution over Oil Sanctions*, SUDAN TRIBUNE (Sept. 18, 2004), *at* www.sudantribune.com/spip.php?article5500 ("China will veto the US draft resolution threatening to impose United Nations oil trading sanctions on Sudan for failure to end the humanitarian crisis in Darfur unless the warning is dropped, China's UN envoy said."); *see also* Manyok, *supra* note 295 ("In 2004, China threated to veto UN Security Council Resolution 1564 which called for [an] oil embargo on Sudan.").

[399] Resolution S/RES/1564, para. 7. The resolution also called for an expansion of the AU monitoring mission in Darfur (AMIS), and requested the Secretary-General to establish a commission of inquiry to investigate reports of atrocities in Darfur. *Id.*, paras. 2, 12.

[400] *Id.*, para. 14.

[401] *See* note 313 *supra* (oil trade).

322   Case Studies

largest investor in Sudan's oil industry infrastructure,[402] both in the eastern and western concession areas (part of the Muglad Basin geological structure), and China has also invested heavily in Sudan in other ways (dams, bridges, port work, roads, etc.).[403] China abstained from voting on the resolution.[404]

As of September 27, 2004, the Special Representative of the Secretary-General on Internally Displaced Persons, Francis M. Deng, reported that 200,000 Darfuri refugees had fled to Chad, an estimated 30,000 to 50,000 persons had been killed or died due to war-related causes, and, in total, about 2.2 million had been affected by the conflict.[405]

5.2.3.3 The Third Threat to Veto Sanctions

A third known threat to veto sanctions against the Government of Sudan occurred on or prior to November 19, 2004, related to Resolution 1574, passed during a special Security Council session in Nairobi, Kenya. China threatened a veto if the resolution imposed sanctions on the Government of Sudan, resulting in the resolution being issued without sanctions.

Yet, by that date, UN officials were continuing to report on a massive number of crimes occurring and that the Government of Sudan was failing to meet its obligations imposed under prior resolutions. For instance, Francis M. Deng concluded that the Government had failed to disarm the Janjaweed and to prevent ongoing attacks by them on civilians. He further found that contrary to Government assertions, it was not safe for IDPs to return to their villages, given evidence of ongoing killing, rape, and armed robbery, among other abuses.[406]

---

[402] According to a 2004 news article:

> China is the largest investor in a Sudanese pipeline project that moves about 270,000 barrels of Sudan's estimated 345,000 barrels in daily production, mostly exported to China and India, according to the U.S. Energy Department. China National United, or Chinaoil, and China National Chemicals, known as Sinochem, were awarded contracts last month to buy about half the Nile Blend crude oil for sale in the last quarter of this year, according to traders. Chinaoil is a unit of PetroChina Co., a state-run refiner, and Sinochem is China's largest petrochemicals trader.

SUDAN TRIBUNE, *supra* note 398.

[403] Trahan interview with Eric Reeves, 6/18/19.

[404] Manyok, *supra* note 295 ("China abstained from voting on Security Council resolution 1564, even when it has forced [the] Security Council to removed explicit threats of sanctions on Sudan's oil sector if Bashir's regime refuses to comply with the resolution.").

[405] Report of Francis M. Deng, Representative of the Secretary-General on Internally Displaced Persons – Mission to the Sudan – The Darfur Crisis, at 2, E/CN.4/2005/8, *at* http://daccess-ods.un.org/access.nsf/Get?Open&DS=E/CN.4/2005/8&Lang=E.

[406] *Id.*, para. 21.

On October 4, 2004, the Secretary-General issued a second report that found that Government attacks against civilians continued during August and September 2004.[407] Janjaweed attacks also continued in Southern Darfur, killing civilians and causing a new wave of IDPs.[408] The Janjaweed even reportedly launched attacks against persons who had already been displaced.[409] The Secretary-General concluded that the Government had not made any progress in implementing a ceasefire, stopping attacks on the civilian population, disarming the militia, or prosecuting perpetrators of the atrocities.[410] The Secretary-General, in a third report issued November 2, 2004,[411] further concluded that the violence in Darfur continued to increase on an unacceptable scale.[412] He reported that there were "strong indications that war crimes and crimes against humanity [had] been committed in Darfur on a large and systematic scale."[413]

Harvard Program on Humanitarian Crises and Physicians for Human Rights additionally reported in an October 2004 report that "the *Janjaweed* in collaboration with forces of the Government of Sudan ... have inflicted a massive campaign of rape as a deliberate aspect of their military assault."[414] Human Rights Watch also continued to report on the crimes, finding, as of November 14, 2004, that Government forces and militias had systematically targeted civilian communities that shared the same ethnicity as the rebel groups, killing, looting, raping, forcibly displacing and destroying hundreds of villages."[415]

Notwithstanding all these crimes being committed, China then reportedly threatened to veto draft resolution S/2004/904 if it included sanctions against

[407] Report of the Secretary-General on the Sudan Pursuant to Paragraph 15 of Security Council Resolution 1564 (2004) and paragraphs 6, 13 and 16 of Security Council Resolution 1556 (2004), at paras. 10–11, S/2004/787, *at* https://undocs.org/S/2004/787.
[408] *Id.*
[409] *Id.*, para. 11.
[410] *Id.*
[411] Report of the Secretary-General on the Sudan Pursuant to Paragraph 15 of Security Council Resolution 1564 (2004) and Paragraphs 6, 13 and 16 of Security Council Resolution 1556 (2004), S/2004/881, *at* https://undocs.org/S/2004/881.
[412] *Id.*, para. 61.
[413] *Id.*, para. 11.
[414] Tara Gingerich, et al., *The Use of Rape as a Weapon of War in the Conflict in Darfur, Sudan*, Program on Humanitarian Crises and Human Rights, Harvard School of Public Health, & Physicians for Human Rights, at 1 (Oct. 2004), *at* https://reliefweb.int/sites/reliefweb.int/files/resources/B119C9EFB7DCAA2DC1256F5F004FBEA9-hu-sud-31oct.pdf.
[415] Human Rights Watch, *If We Return, We Will Be Killed: Consolidation of Ethnic Cleansing in Darfur, Sudan* (Nov. 14, 2004), *at* www.hrw.org/report/2004/11/14/if-we-return-we-will-be-killed-consolidation-ethnic-cleansing-darfur-sudan.

the Government of Sudan in the event of noncompliance with the resolution.[416] The resolution, which demanded "that Government and rebel forces and all other armed groups immediately cease all violence and attacks," was later adopted unanimously as Resolution 1574, without any mention of sanctions.[417] Moreover, the resolution even weakened language from prior resolutions to a vague warning that it might in the future consider taking "appropriate action against any party failing to fulfill its commitments."[418]

As of November 2004, the number of fatalities was estimated at 70,000, the number of IDPs was estimated at 1.5 million, and the International Committee for the Red Cross (ICRC) was warning of rural communities facing famine.[419]

5.2.3.4 The Fourth Threat to Veto Sanctions

A fourth known threat to veto sanctions occurred on or prior to March 29, 2005, regarding Resolution 1591. China's veto threats again ensured there would be no oil embargo, although the resolution was able to expand the arms embargo to include the Government of Sudan, and did impose a mechanism for travel bans and asset freezes. However, China succeeded in diluting the travel bans and asset freezes by minimizing the number of persons subject to them and was later accused of violating the arms embargo. Resolution 1591 also included a ban on offensive military flights over Darfur, which was thereafter simply violated.

By the date the resolution passed, Security Council members clearly recognized the severity of the situation, including: (i) the failure of all parties to fully comply with their commitments and demands made in previous resolutions;[420] (ii) continuing violations of international law, including Government-led air strikes and rebel attacks on villages;[421] (iii) continuing sexual violence and violence against civilians in the Darfur region;[422] and (iv) a stalled peace process and no improvement in the humanitarian situation.[423]

---

[416] *The United Nations and Darfur, supra* note 341 ("At the council's special November 2004 session in Nairobi, China, and possibly Russia, which is thought to be the main arms supplier to the Sudanese government, used the threat of a veto to pressure other members to water down Resolution 1574.").
[417] Resolution S/RES/1574, para. 11.
[418] *Id.*, para. 12; *The United Nations and Darfur, supra* note 341.
[419] Imogen Foulkes, *Darfur Villagers "Facing Famine,"* BBC NEWS (Oct. 18, 2004), *at* http://news.bbc.co.uk/2/hi/africa/3754766.stm.
[420] Resolution 1591 (2005), last pmbl. clause.
[421] *Id.*, pmbl. clauses and first operative clause.
[422] *Id.*, pmbl. clauses.
[423] *Id. See also* Press Release SC/8346, UN Security Council (Mar. 29, 2005), *at* www.un.org/press/en/2005/sc8346.doc.htm.

Additionally, the tragic situation in Darfur continued to be chronicled in numerous UN reports. By December 3, 2004, the Secretary-General issued a fourth report, concluding that "chaos" in Darfur was "looming as order [was] collapsing."[424] The report noted that the violence reached an apex on November 22, when the SLA/M attacked Tawilla in Northern Darfur.[425] In response, the Sudanese Army launched heavy retaliatory attacks, reportedly using bomber planes.[426] The Secretary-General also expressed concern about reports of continuing rape and sexual violations by tribesmen within IDP camps,[427] arbitrary arrests escalating in Northern Darfur,[428] police continuing to threaten IDPs,[429] and children continuing to be abducted in Southern Darfur.[430]

By January 2005, the International Commission of Inquiry on Darfur, a body of experts that had been established under Resolution 1564,[431] found that:

> [The] Government of the Sudan and the Janjaweed are responsible for serious violations of international human rights and humanitarian law amounting to crimes under international law. In particular, ... Government forces and militias conducted indiscriminate attacks, including killing of civilians, torture, enforced disappearances, destruction of villages, rape and other forms of sexual violence, pillaging and forced displacement,

---

[424] Report of the Secretary-General on the Sudan Pursuant to Paragraphs 6, 13 and 16 of Security Council Resolution 1556 (2004), Paragraph 15 of Security Council Resolution 1564 (2004), and Paragraph 17 of Security Council Resolution 1574 (2004), at para. 55, S/2004/947, at https://undocs.org/S/2004/947.

[425] *Id.*, para. 2.

[426] *Id.*

[427] *Id.*, paras. 37–38. Rape in Darfur has almost entirely consisted of Arab men raping non-Arab girls, women, and sometimes boys. Rape was a central weapon of war for the Janjaweed. See Eric Reeves, *Continuing Mass Rape of Girls in Darfur: The Most Heinous Crime Generates No International Outrage, January 2016*, SUDAN: RESEARCH, ANALYSIS, AND ADVOCACY (Oct. 15, 2017), at http://sudanreeves.org/2017/10/15/continuing-mass-rape-of-girls-in-darfur-the-most-heinous-crime-generates-no-international-outrage-january-2016.

[428] Report of the Secretary-General on the Sudan Pursuant to Paragraphs 6, 13, and 16 of Security Council Resolution 1556 (2004), *supra* note 424, para. 39.

[429] *Id.*, para. 40.

[430] *Id.*, para. 41.

[431] The Security Council, in Resolution 1564, requested that the Secretary-General "rapidly establish an international commission of inquiry in order immediately to investigate reports of violations of international humanitarian law and human rights law in Darfur by all parties, to determine also whether or not acts of genocide have occurred, and to identify the perpetrators of such violations with a view to ensuring that those responsible are held accountable." S/RES/1564.

throughout Darfur. These acts were conducted on a widespread and systematic basis, and therefore may amount to crimes against humanity. The extensive destruction and displacement have resulted in a loss of livelihood and means of survival for countless women, men and children. In addition to the large-scale attacks, many people have been arrested and detained, and many have been held incommunicado for prolonged periods and tortured. The vast majority of the victims of all of these violations have been from the Fur, Zaghawa, Massalit, Jebel, Aranga and other so-called "African" tribes.[432]

The Commission expressed particular alarm that attacks on villages, killing of civilians, rape, pillaging, and forced displacement continued even during the Commission's mandate.[433]

The Commission additionally rejected Sudan's version that the attacks were carried out for counterinsurgency purposes,[434] and instead found that "most attacks were deliberately and indiscriminately directed against civilians."[435] Furthermore, even if rebels were present in some villages – which the Commission considered unlikely except for in a very small number of cases – it found the attackers did not take precautions to shield civilians from attack and the military response was manifestly disproportionate to any threat posed by the rebels.[436] However, at this point in time, the Commission took the view that there was no policy to commit genocide, while finding "that in some instances individuals, including Government officials, may commit acts with genocidal intent."[437]

Despite all the crimes occurring, on or prior to March 29, 2005, China reportedly threatened (implicitly or expressly) to veto Resolution 1591 if it included a threat of an oil embargo on Sudan in the event of non-compliance with the resolution.[438] Ultimately, China abstained from voting on Resolution 1591, and

---

[432] Report of the International Commission of Inquiry on Darfur to the United Nations Secretary-General Pursuant to Security Council Resolution 1564 of 18 September 2004, at 3 (Jan. 25, 2005), at www.un.org/News/dh/sudan/com_inq_darfur.pdf.
[433] Id.
[434] Part of Human Rights Watch's rationale for not calling the crimes in Darfur "genocide," rested on the (ultimately false) conclusion that the crimes were carried out for counter-insurgency purposes.
[435] Report of the International Commission of Inquiry, *supra* note 432, at 3.
[436] Id. The Commission also found credible evidence that the SLA/M and JEM were responsible for serious violations of international human rights and humanitarian law, which may amount to war crimes – particularly cases of murder of civilians and pillage – although it did not find a systematic or widespread patter to these violations. Id. at 4.
[437] Id. Their finding makes little sense as either the *dolus specialis* (special mental state requirement of genocide) is met or not.
[438] Manyok, *supra* note 295 ("China abstained from voting on resolution 1591 even after it made [the] Security Council ... remove the threat [of an] oil embargo in the event of noncompliance.").

5.2 Analysis of Veto Threats Related to Darfur

the resolution, which "deplore[d]" the Government's failure to comply with prior resolutions including "the failure of the Government of Sudan to disarm the Janjaweed militia and apprehend and bring to justice Janjaweed leaders,"[439] was adopted without any mention of an oil embargo. The resolution did, however, manage to expand the arms embargo that had initially omitted the Government of Sudan to include transfers of arms to Sudanese armed forces operating in Darfur.[440] A UN panel of experts, however, later concluded that China was violating the arms embargo.[441]

The resolution also "demanded that the Government of Sudan in accordance with its commitments under [certain ceasefire agreements] immediately cease conducting offensive military flights in and over the Darfur region."[442] However, the Government of Sudan later simply violated the flight ban – which was later rearticulated in Resolution 1769[443] – without any consequences.[444] The resolution also created a Sanctions Committee whereby

---

[439] S/RES/1591, para. 1.
[440] "In March 2005 Security Council Resolution 1591... expanded the arms embargo to include all parties to the N'djamena Ceasefire Agreement (including Sudanese government forces active in the region, the SLA/M and the JEM) and any other belligerents in North Darfur, South Darfur and West Darfur, Sudan." Stockholm International Peace Research Institute, *UN Arms Embargo on Sudan (Darfur Region)*, at www.sipri.org/databases/embargoes/un_arms_embargoes/sudan. Specifically, paragraph 7, of Resolution 1591 "[r]eaffirms the measures imposed by paragraphs 7 and 8 of resolution 1556 (2004), and decides that these measures shall immediately upon adoption of this resolution, also apply to all the parties to the N'djamena Ceasefire Agreement [which would include the Government of Sudan] and any other belligerents in the states of North Darfur, South Darfur and West Darfur." S/RES/1591, para. 7. Paragraphs 7 and 8 of Resolution 1556 imposed the initial arms embargo. S/RES/1566, paras. 7–8.
[441] "In 2006, the United Nations Panel of Experts condemned China's arms sales to Sudan and declared it as a total violation of [the] arms embargo on Sudan. The report stated that China's weapons and military equipment have been found in Darfur and are being used by the Sudan Army Forces against the civilians in [the] Darfur region." Manyok, *supra* note 295, *citing* Save Darfur Briefing Paper, *China in Sudan: Having It Both Ways* (2008). For discussion of China's arms sales to Sudan, see Shinn, *supra* note 265, at 88–89.
[442] S/RES/1591, para. 6.
[443] S/RES/1769 ("*Demanding* that there should be no aerial bombings and the use of United Nations markings on aircraft used in such attacks ....").
[444] Enough Project, *President Obama's Immediate Sudan Challenge*, at n. 2 (Jan. 2009), at https://enoughproject.org/reports/president-obama-immediate-sudan-challenge ("President Obama and other key members of his administration have taken a robust position in the past regarding the need to counter Sudan's aerial attacks on civilians in Darfur, and have voiced support for enforcing a no-fly zone. Continued Sudanese aerial attacks in Darfur – there were over 40 last year and the Sudanese government launched a new aerial campaign last week – have rightly generated considerable attention. The UN Security Council has demanded an end to offensive military flights several times, most recently in Resolution 1769, which authorized UNAMID. UNAMID has not enforced that demand."). *See also* Report of the Panel of Experts Established Pursuant to Paragraph 3 of Resolution 1591

asset freezes and travel bans could be imposed on select individuals who were responsible for offensive military flights or violating the ban on arms sales;[445] however, that became diluted when China insisted on trimming the list of persons who would be covered from seventeen to four individuals.[446] Furthermore, the Sanctions Committee created in Resolution 1591 appears to have repeatedly delayed publishing Panel of Experts reports that found the Government of Sudan to be in breach of the arms embargo and ban on offensive military flights.[447] Even when published, "[t]he Security Council did not act effectively on the findings."[448]

On March 31, 2005, two days after the watered-down Resolution 1591 was adopted, the Security Council did manage to refer the situation in Sudan to the ICC, with China and the US abstaining.[449] As discussed above in

---

(2005) Concerning the Sudan, at 7, 67–71, UN Doc. S/2006/65 (Jan. 30, 2006), at www.undocs.org/pdf?symbol=en/S/2006/65.

[445] S/RES/1591, para. (3)(c)–(e).

[446] Manyok, *supra* note 295 ("China trimmed the sanction's targets on seventeen government and military officials to only [four]."). See also S/RES/1672 (Apr. 25, 2006) (listing four individuals) (China abstaining). Sudan appointed Janjaweed leader Musa Hilal, who was on the Council's targeted sanctions list, as a government adviser. Security Council Report, Chronology of Events – Sudan (Darfur), rev. 1 May 2019, at www.securitycouncilreport.org/chronology/sudan-darfur.php.

[447] Enough Project, *Irresolution: The U.N. Security Council on Darfur* (July 14, 2008), at https://enoughproject.org/reports/irresolution-un-security-council-darfur#ftn.id07 ("The Sanctions Committee has repeatedly delayed – or even prevented – the publication of reports of the independent Panel of Experts. In January 2006, for example, the committee finally released the final version of the panel's first report, having delayed its publication for the previous two months. The report detailed massive violations of the arms embargo, found multiple instances of breaches to the ban on offensive military flights, and, in a confidential annex, identified a list of 17 individuals impeding the peace process.") (footnotes omitted). See also note 443 *supra* (Security Council demanding an end to aerial bombing).

[448] Enough Project, *supra* note 447, at text accompanying note 7.

[449] S/RES/1593. Algeria and Brazil also abstained. As will be discussed below, the Security Council in subsequent years completely failed to provide any follow-up to its referral, resulting in all ICC arrest warrants related to the situation being outstanding.

An interesting question arises, given the various veto threats detailed in this Chapter, why China did not simply veto referral to the ICC. Some sources suggest China gradually started to moderate its stance vis-à-vis the Government of Sudan – pressing it to stop the killing and no longer offering unconditional support. It is suggested China took this posture partly in response to international pressure to acts as a "responsible stakeholder" and to strengthen China's ties with Western powers. See Gaafar Karrar Ahmed, *The Chinese Stance on the Darfur Conflict*, at 6–8 (South African Institute of International Affairs, Occasional Paper No. 67, Sept. 2010) (discussing China moderating its stance vis-à-vis the Government of Sudan and becoming less uncritically supportive, abstaining on Resolution 1556 despite attempts by Sudanese Government officials to get China to veto, and not vetoing Resolution 1564 or ICC referral); Laura Barber, *Chinese Foreign Policy in the "Going Out" Era: Confronting Challenges and "Adaptive Learning" in Cases of China-Sudan and South Sudan Relations*, at 140 (The London

Chapter 5.2.1, the ICC ultimately charged the crimes to include genocide.[450]

As of March 2005, it was reported that 180,000 people had died including from hunger and disease, with an average of 10,000 civilians dying each month.[451]

As to the Commission of Inquiry's finding that there was no policy to commit genocide, first, having a "policy" is not a required element of genocide, and, second, the crimes were clearly targeting members of different ethnic groups (African tribes including the Fur, Masalit, Zaghawa, and other African/non-Arab groups, as opposed to the Arab Janjaweed), with fairly clear intent to destroy at least a significant part of the groups through a "scorched-earth policy" that left nothing behind.[452] The elements of genocide, therefore, prima facie, appear to be met,[453] and, the ICC has charged the crimes as genocide.[454] However, the veto threats appear problematic even if the crimes are characterized as crimes against humanity and war crimes.

5.2.3.5 The Fifth Threat to Veto Sanctions

A fifth threat to veto sanctions occurred on or prior to July 31, 2007, related to Resolution 1769.[455] China reportedly refused to allow Resolution 1769 if it included sanctions against the Sudanese Government in the event of non-compliance with the resolution.[456] Resolution 1769 was then adopted

>School of Economics and Political Science, PhD thesis, June 2014) (China "did not use its veto to block the referral ... ultimately because China did want to apply pressure on Sudan to respond to the Darfur issue .... Sudanese diplomats have since articulated that Beijing's position had not been one of support for the ICC referral, as Beijing later affirmed that it underestimated its eventual impact and believed the US would block the motion regardless. However, China's reluctance to use its veto to protect those accused of atrocities in Darfur from facing international justice also signaled China's concerns that such a stand would leave China out of favour with the wider international community.") (footnotes omitted).

[450] See note 304 supra (Bashir warrant for genocide).
[451] Jeevan Vasagar, et al., 180,000 Die from Hunger in Darfur, GUARDIAN (Mar. 15, 2005), at www.theguardian.com/world/2005/mar/16/sudan.ewenmacaskill.
[452] S/2004/703, supra note 387 (Secretary-General concluding there was a "scorched-earth policy").
[453] For a detailed analysis of why the crimes constitute genocide, see Trahan, Why the Killing in Darfur Is Genocide, supra note 260. See also notes 281, 396–97 supra and accompanying text (additional authorities recognizing the crimes as genocide).
[454] See note 304 supra (Bashir warrant for genocide).
[455] The crimes being committed in Darfur after the fourth and before the fifth veto threats are discussed below, as the first threat related to peacekeeping occurred prior to the fifth threat related to sanctions. See Chapter 5.2.4.1 ("The First Veto Threat Related to Peacekeeping").
[456] Partners in Genocide, supra note 313 ("Resolution 1769 (July 2007) was a weakened substitute for 1706 .... China ... refused to approve any sanctions measure in the inevitable event of Khartoum's non-compliance with the terms of 1769.").

unanimously without any wording on sanctions.[457] A few months later, in November 2007, "President Bashir visited China for China-Africa Cooperation where he thanked China for its support at the Security Council."[458]

All in all, the threats to veto (both express and implied): (i) initially delayed the imposition of sanctions; (ii) completely prevented imposition of an oil embargo; (iii) initially limited the arms embargo only to cover arms sales to all "non-governmental entities and individuals" in Darfur; and (iv) weakened the travel ban and asset freeze by having only four not seventeen individuals listed. Thus, while the veto threats did not fully prevent the Council from imposing sanctions, they *weakened the sanctions regime*: "Beijing's actions at the UN undermined the effectiveness of United Nations sanctions against Bashir and his regime."[459] The veto threats likely also conveyed to the Government of Sudan that it had a "protector" on the Council, and also protected China's oil imports from Sudan,[460] as well as Sudan's arms purchases from China.[461] Meanwhile, the crimes that Government forces and the Janjaweed were believed to be implicated in included war crimes and crimes against humanity,[462] and most likely genocide,[463] with the ICC, as noted above, ultimately charging the crimes as genocide.[464]

5.2.4 *How Veto Threats Weakened Peacekeeping*

An additional source of veto threats relates to the deployment of peacekeeping forces. As mentioned above, in July 2004, AU forces were deployed to the region as part of the AU observer mission AMIS.[465] However, AMIS was reportedly "overstretched to address the security concerns' in Darfur and 'lack[ed] basic elements of a balanced military force."[466] It also lacked any kind of robust mandate.[467] Despite all the crimes being committed and the

---

[457] *Partners in Genocide, supra* note 313.
[458] Manyok, *supra* note 295.
[459] *Id.*
[460] See notes 313, 402 *supra* (oil trade).
[461] See note 314 *supra* (arms trade).
[462] Report of the International Commission of Inquiry on Darfur, *supra* note 432, at 3.
[463] See Trahan, Why the Killing in Darfur Is Genocide, note 260 *supra*. See also notes 281, 396–97 *supra* and accompanying text (additional authorities recognizing the crimes as genocide).
[464] See note 304 *supra* (Bashir warrant for genocide).
[465] Trahan, *Why the Killing in Darfur Is Genocide, supra* note 260, at 997; *Entrenching Impunity, supra* note 278, at 7.
[466] Udombana, *supra* note 282, at 190.
[467] "The major problem [with AMIS] remains with its mandate." *Id.*

5.2 *Analysis of Veto Threats Related to Darfur*   331

recognized need for the deployment of additional peacekeepers, China made at least two known veto threats related to peacekeeping, significantly delaying deployment of UN peacekeepers and weakening their mandate.

5.2.4.1 The First Veto Threat Related to Peacekeeping

The first known threat related to peacekeeping occurred on or prior to August 31, 2006, related to Resolution 1706 and an attempt to deploy UN peacekeepers to Darfur. UNMIS had been initially mandated to support implementation of the Comprehensive Peace Agreement[468] resolving the North-South conflict. Resolution 1706 expanded UNMIS's mandate[469] to additionally support implementation of the Darfur Peace Agreement,[470] which had been entered into in an attempt to conclude a peace agreement for Darfur. As detailed below, China insisted that any UN peacekeeping deployment to Darfur be consensually negotiated with the Government of Sudan. Consequently, when the Government withheld consent, neither UNMIS, nor any new UN peacekeeping force,[471] was able to deploy to Darfur. Only much later was the hybrid force UNAMID able to gradually roll out its deployment on a consensual basis.

The dire consequences of permanently blocking a fully UN peacekeeping force from Darfur and later delaying the deployment of the hybrid peacekeeping force should be seen in light of the significant numbers of crimes still occurring and the pressing need to try to implement the Darfur Peace Agreement:

- As of July 2005, the High Commissioner for Human Rights reported that "rape and gang rape continue to be perpetrated by armed elements in Darfur," including by members of armed forces and law enforcement,

---

[468] Comprehensive Peace Agreement Between The Government of The Republic of The Sudan and The Sudan People's Liberation Movement / Sudan People's Liberation Army (Jan. 9, 2005), *at* www.refworld.org/pdfid/4c0377872.pdf.
[469] S/RES/1706, para. 8.
[470] Darfur Peace Agreement (May 5, 2006), *at* www.un.org/zh/focus/southernsudan/pdf/dpa.pdf. The Darfur Peace Agreement was entered into on May 5, 2006, between the Government of Sudan and the SLA/M (led by Minni Minawi), but not the JEM nor the SLA/M (led by Abdul Wahid).
[471] While Resolution 1706 suggests there were plans to expand UNMIS to Darfur, according to Eric Reeves, the Department of Peacekeeping Operations (UNDPKO) had primarily been working to develop a new robust UN peacekeeping force with about 22,000 personnel – not drawn from UNMIS, which was already overstretched in South Sudan. Trahan 6/18/19 interview with Eric Reeves.

and that the Government was "either unable or unwilling to hold [the perpetrators] accountable."[472]
- The Office of the High Commissioner for Human Rights (OHCHR) reported on a significant numbers of continuing crimes in the second half of 2005 through 2006:
  - The second OHCHR report highlighted that Government forces, at times in cooperation with the Janjaweed, launched "at least eight organized armed attacks ... on over a dozen IDP camps or villages," deliberately targeting civilians and civilian property and displacing thousands.[473] The human rights situation was made worse by the Government, which failed to "prevent and protect the internally displaced and villagers from being killed, assaulted, and raped by armed militias."[474] The report concluded that the Government's "inability or unwillingness to prosecute perpetrators of human rights abuses and violations of international humanitarian law" continued to fuel impunity in Darfur.[475]
  - The third OHCHR report noted that between January and April 2006, "the conflict in Darfur [had] reached a new level of violence, both in intensity and frequency."[476] During the reporting period, the humanitarian crisis deteriorated even further with the Government and militia seriously limiting access to humanitarian aid by creating "real or *de facto* blockades on civilian populations."[477]
  - The fourth OHCHR report emphasized there had been "no improvement in the situation of human rights in Darfur."[478] For instance, armed militias, supported on at least one occasion by Government forces, launched at least twenty attacks on civilian villages, torturing,

---

[472] Report of the United Nations High Commissioner for Human Rights on Access to Justice for Victims of Sexual Violence, at 2, July 29, 2005, *at* www.ohchr.org/Documents/Countries/darfur29july05.pdf.

[473] Second Periodic Report of the United Nations High Commissioner for Human Rights on the Human Rights Situation in Sudan, at para. 11, Jan. 27, 2006, *at* www.ohchr.org/Documents/Countries/sudanjanuary06.pdf.

[474] *Id.*, para. 14.

[475] *Id.*, paras. 5, 17, 28–34.

[476] Third Periodic Report of the United Nations High Commissioner for Human Rights on the Human Rights Situation in Sudan, at para. 27, April 2006, *at* www.ohchr.org/Documents/Countries/3rdOHCHRApril06.pdf.

[477] *Id.*, para. 30.

[478] Fourth Periodic Report of the United Nations High Commissioner for Human Rights on the Human Rights Situation in Sudan ("Deepening Crisis in Darfur Two Months After the Darfur Peace Agreement: An Assessment"), at 2, July 25, 2006, *at* www.ohchr.org/Documents/Countries/4thOHCHRjuly25final.pdf.

killing, raping, and sexually abusing civilians.[479] The attacks further displaced civilian populations, some of whom had already been displaced at least once or twice before.[480]

Notwithstanding these continuing crimes and the agreed need for UN peacekeeping forces to deploy to Darfur, China reportedly threatened to veto Resolution 1706 on or prior to August 31, 2006, if it did not include the consent of the Government of Sudan for the deployment of peacekeepers.[481] Resolution 1706 was then approved, with the caveat of requesting consent from the Sudanese Government for deployment of UN peacekeepers to Darfur.[482] The Government later declined to give its consent, *keeping a fully UN peacekeeping force permanently out of Darfur.*[483] China abstained from voting on the resolution.

5.2.4.2 The Second Veto Threat Related to Peacekeeping

With the failed UN peacekeeping deployment, attention next focused on trying to deploy a joint AU-UN hybrid peacekeeping force, UNAMID, to Darfur. While UNAMID eventually was able to deploy, it was disastrously conceived as an extension of AMIS,[484] with its deployment only rolled out slowly, contingent on Sudan's consent. Furthermore, China insisted that

---

[479] *Id.*
[480] *Id.*
[481] Hannah Yiu, Jus Cogens, *the Veto and the Responsibility to Protect: A New Perspective*, 7 N.Z. Y.B. INT'L L. 207, 226 (2009), *at* www.austlii.edu.au/nz/journals/NZYbkIntLaw/2009/8.pdf ("In 2006, [China] was instrumental in ensuring that the peacekeeping troops authorised by [Security Council] Resolution 1706 could only be deployed in Darfur with the consent of the Khartoum government."). Eric Reeves similarly writes:

> Resolution 1706 (August 2006) authorized more than 20,000 U.N. peacekeepers and civilian police to protect civilians and humanitarian workers in Darfur. China abstained, and would have vetoed the measure had language not been inserted that "invited" the consent of the Khartoum regime. The National Islamic Front declined the "invitation" and refused to accept the U.N. peacekeeping force. China supported Khartoum's defiance by declaring its belief in "non-interference" in the domestic matters of sovereign nations.

Partners in Genocide, supra note 313.
[482] S/RES/1706, para. 1 (inviting "the consent of the Government of National Unity for the deployment").
[483] *See supra* note 481 (Yiu & Reeves). While UNMIS never fully deployed to Darfur, it did provide equipment and staff (including military advisers, police officers, and civilian officials) as part of a three-stage plan negotiated between the UN, AU, and Government of Sudan.
[484] Trahan interview with Eric Reeves, 6/18/19.

UNAMID have no obligation to disarm combatants – specifically, that it *not* be charged in Resolution 1769 with seizing and disposing of weapons found in contravention of the arms embargo in Resolution 1556.

Again, this veto threat – insisting that UNAMID *not* be able to seize and dispose of weapons – should be seen in the context of crimes known to have been continuing in Darfur throughout 2006–07:

- The fifth OHCHR report, issued in October 2006, underscored that hundreds of armed militia launched large-scale attacks on approximately forty-seven villages in South Darfur, consisting mainly of the Zaghawa, Massalit, and Misseriya Jebel tribes, killing several hundred civilians and burning entire villages to the ground.[485] According to several witnesses, "the motive behind the attacks was to change the demography of the region before the arrival of international troops," and seemed to be an attempt to remove the African tribes to make the area entirely Arab.[486] The report concluded that "Government knowledge, if not complicity, in the attacks [was] almost certain."[487]
- A sixth OHCHR report issued in November 2006 noted that the Janjaweed continued to launch brutal attacks against villages and one IDP camp near Jebel Moon, in Western Darfur, killing scores of civilians.[488] At best, the report concluded that the attacks demonstrate the Government's "continued failure to disarm the militia"; at worst, they demonstrate the Government's use of the Janjaweed to "target civilian populations."[489]
- In a February 23, 2007, report, the Secretary-General deplored the "aerial bombings by Sudanese Government forces" and urged the Government of Sudan to "take immediate action to hold accountable the perpetrators of attacks against civilians."[490] The report further noted

---

[485] Fifth Periodic Report of the United Nations High Commissioner for Human Rights on the Situation of Human Rights in the Sudan ("Killings of Civilians by Militia in Buram Locality, South Darfur"), at paras. 1–6 (Oct. 6, 2006), *at* www.ohchr.org/Documents/Countries/5thOHCHRsept06.pdf.

[486] *Id.*, para. 5.

[487] *Id.*, para. 26.

[488] Sixth Periodic Report of the United Nations High Commissioner for Human Rights on the Human Rights Situation in Sudan ("29 October 2006: Attack on Villages Around the Jebel Moon Area"), at 2 (Nov. 3, 2006), *at* www.ohchr.org/Documents/Countries/6thOHCHR5nov06.pdf.

[489] *Id.*

[490] Monthly Report of the Secretary-General on Darfur, S/2007/104, at para. 48 (Feb. 23, 2007), *at* https://undocs.org/pdf?symbol=en/S/2007/104.

that IDPs living in camps continued to be killed, looted, and harassed, and women continued to be assaulted and raped.[491]
- In a July 2007 report, the Secretary-General also expressed extreme concern that "UNMIS and AMIS peacekeepers and United Nations and non-governmental organization aid personnel [had] increasingly become the target of violent attacks."[492]

Notwithstanding all these crimes, China reportedly threatened to veto (expressly or impliedly)[493] Resolution 1769 if it included an obligation to disarm combatants in UNAMID's mandate (and, as discussed above, if it included sanctions against the Sudanese Government).[494] Resolution 1769 was then adopted unanimously *without any disarmament mandate* (or any wording on sanctions).[495] Specifically, the disarmament that had been proposed was for UNAMID to "seize and dispose" of weapons found in Darfur in contravention of the arms embargo (Resolution 1556), and this was "diluted in the final text [in that] the force was permitted merely to 'monitor' the [presence of such arms]."[496]

As of July 2007, 4.3 million people had been affected by the conflict;[497] more than 200,000 had been killed;[498] 2.2 million had been internally displaced, of whom, 190,000 had been displaced in the first seven months of 2007; and even though more than 12,000 humanitarian workers had been deployed to the region, more than half a million people were cut off from humanitarian assistance.[499]

---

[491] *Id.*, paras. 15–16.
[492] Report of the Secretary-General on Darfur, S/2007/462, at para. 60 (July 27, 2007), *at* https://undocs.org/pdf?symbol=en/S/2007/462. See note 483 *supra* (explaining why there were some UN forces in Darfur, but not the full UNMIS deployment).
[493] China's statements were made in negotiations to which the author does not have access, so it is not possible to say how explicit China was about casting a negative vote if certain language were included in the final text of the resolution.
[494] See Chapter 5.2.3.5 *supra*.
[495] *Partners in Genocide*, *supra* note 313 ("Resolution 1769 (July 2007) was a weakened substitute for 1706. The idea was to authorize a 'hybrid' U.N./African Union force of some 26,000 troops and civilian police to protect civilians and humanitarians. China eventually voted for the resolution, but only after stripping it of a mandate to disarm combatants.").
[496] Save Darfur Briefing paper, *supra* note 441; S/RES/1769, para. 9 ("*Decides* that UNAMID shall monitor whether any arms or related material are present in Darfur in violation of the Agreements and the measures imposed by paragraphs 7 and 8 of Resolution 1556 (2004).").
[497] UN Department of Public Information, Peace and Security Section, The United Nations and Darfur, Fact Sheet (Aug. 2007), *at* www.un.org/News/dh/infocus/sudan/fact_sheet.pdf.
[498] *Id.* In April 2008, nine months after July 2007, John Holmes, head of OCHA used a figure of 300,000. See Roxanne Escobales, *Darfur Dead "Could Number 300,000,"* GUARDIAN (Apr. 23, 2008), *at* www.theguardian.com/world/2008/apr/23/sudan.unitednations.
[499] UN Department of Public Information, Peace and Security Section, *supra* note 497.

5.2.4.3 The Lingering Impact of Veto Threats Weakening Peacekeeping

China's insistence that any peacekeeping deployment be consensually negotiated with the Government of Sudan meant that UN peacekeepers[500] would not reach Darfur until UNAMID's deployment, which the Government only permitted to be rolled out very gradually. This both weakened and delayed peacekeeping.

Hannah Yiu explains:

> [R]esolution [1769] authorised an AU/UN hybrid force ("UNAMID") under Chapter VII to implement the Darfur Peace Agreement of 5 May 2006, but *the force did not provide meaningful protection* for Darfur's people because transition to UNAMID peacekeeping was made contingent on the consent of the Sudanese government. As at July 2008, the UNAMID force only comprised some 9,400 troops, consisting mainly of ex-AMIS forces, due in large part to the *obstructionary tactics* of the government in Sudan. Although the total strength of UNAMID had reached 15,444 by 30 November 2008, this was still a far cry from the actual authorised deployment of 26,000 troops.[501]

The delay in deployment and the Government of Sudan's obstructionary tactics, such as withholding consent, occurred during key years when the Sudanese Armed Forces, acting with the Janjaweed, were committing mass atrocity crimes. China eventually did reportedly urge the Government of Sudan to accept UNAMID's deployment[502] – after being encouraged to do so by the US[503] and after Chinese concerns "over the harm to its image resulting from its relationship with Sudan"[504] particularly in advance of the Beijing 2008 Olympics.[505] However, the harm to peacekeeping – and consequent failure to protect Darfuris who were being killed in large numbers – had already been accomplished.

---

[500] See note 483 *supra* (explaining why there were some UN forces in Darfur).
[501] Yiu, *supra* note 481, at 226 (footnotes omitted) (emphasis added).
[502] In February 2007, "China's President Hu visited Sudan and encouraged Sudanese government [officials] to allow [the] hybrid forces." Manyok, *supra* note 295.
[503] In January 2007, "U.S. Presidential Envoy to Sudan Andrew Natsios visited China to ask China to accept the UN's troop[] deployments in Sudan." *Id.* Others suggest also that China was moving away from unconditional support of the Government of Sudan, realizing that such support came at a diplomatic cost. *See, e.g.*, Ahmed, *supra* note 449.
[504] Shinn, *supra* note 265, at 92.
[505] *Id.* at 95 ("China's intense desire to hold successful Olympic Games in Beijing in 2008 was a huge incentive to focus on the Darfur issue and manage the challenge so that it would detract minimally or not at all from the success of the games"). For example, in February 2007, "China announced $10 million in China's aid to Darfur victims and contributed 275 military engineers to be part of the UN peacekeeping." Manyok, *supra* note 295.

5.2.5 Threats Blocking Follow-Up on the ICC Referral

While unrelated to any specific Security Council resolution, there was yet another way in which China's threats "protected" the Government of Sudan (and its officials) – by ensuring there would be no "follow-up" on the Security Council's referral of the Darfur situation to the ICC.

Specifically, in December 2007, China blocked a Presidential Statement that would have called for the arrest of two of those wanted by the ICC on charges of crimes against humanity and war crimes:

> [In early December 2007,] Britain introduced a toughly worded Presidential Statement at the U.N. Security Council, demanding that Khartoum's National Islamic Front regime turn over two genocidaires to the International Criminal Court. The first, Ahmed Haroun, who, in a grotesque bit of irony, [at the time was serving] as Sudan's minister of humanitarian affairs, is accused of having directly orchestrated many of the vicious crimes documented by the U.N. and independent human rights organizations in Darfur. Similarly, Ali Kushayb, a Janjaweed militia leader, is deeply implicated in the most egregious violations of international law– targeted ethnic slaughter and the use of rape as a weapon of war among them.
>
> The Presidential Statement should've easily passed: The evidence against both men is strong, and because of U.N. Security Council Resolution 1593, the ICC has jurisdiction over the matter. What ended up happening, though, was hardly a surprise to anyone who has watched Darfur closely over the last five years. *China threatened to veto the non-binding declaration unless its language was essentially gutted*, and rather than force the issue, Britain, France, and the US – as well as the other Security Council members – quietly decided to drop the matter. As a result, not only will Haroun and Kushayb remain free, but the government in Khartoum will feel as if it can block the extradition of those subsequently accused by the Court . . . .[506]

While, technically, there is no "veto" of a Presidential Statement, the power of a permanent member can work in an analogous fashion, blocking such a statement from issuing. Andras Vamos-Goldman explains:

> Presidential Statements and "Statements to the Press" are made by the current President of the Security Council "on behalf of the Security Council." Thus, any member can threaten "not to join" such a statement, which deprives the President from making it "on behalf of the Security Council." When a permanent member refuses to join, given their power, it sends a qualitatively more significant message. While it is technically not a veto, because it is not a resolution, it nevertheless effectively scuttles the

---

[506] *Partners in Genocide, supra* note 313 (emphasis added).

Presidential Statement or Statement to the Press "by the Security Council." The option that the drafters and supporters have is to issue a statement without that permanent member, which then becomes merely a statement by several Security Council members, but without the Security Council's weight behind it.[507]

Thus, China's position resulted in the Security Council *not even being able to issue a non-binding Presidential Statement* calling for the execution of ICC arrest warrants charging crimes against humanity and war crimes.[508] While technically not a veto, this instance "exemplifies the many ways permanent members influence the work of the Security Council, at every level of activity."[509] Later, in 2008, China did permit a Presidential Statement to be issued calling for the Government of Sudan and other parties to the conflict in Darfur to "cooperate" with the ICC,[510] but that merely restated, in a non-binding document, what was already mandated by Resolution 1593.[511]

The first unsuccessful attempt at ICC follow-up and the experience of only being able to issue a tepidly worded Presidential Statement in 2008, may also have deterred other Council members from pursuing more aggressive measures for following-up on outstanding arrest warrants related to Darfur.[512] Once the ICC issued an arrest warrant for then-President Bashir, any hope of serious follow-up evaporated, due to China's close relationship with him.[513] In fact, China, along with Russia, supported the AU's request to have the Security Council defer the warrants against Bashir under Article 16 of the Rome Statute.[514] It is difficult not to reach the conclusion: "To some extent, Beijing's actions at the UN are premediated with clear intention of protecting

---

[507] Trahan interview with Andras Vamos-Goldman, 6/3/19.
[508] Harun and Kushayb were not charged with genocide.
[509] Trahan interview with Andras Vamos-Goldman, 6/3/19.
[510] S/PRST/2008/21 (June 16, 2008).
[511] See S/RES/1593 (2005) ("*Decides* that the Government of Sudan and all other parties to the conflict in Darfur, shall cooperate fully with and provide any necessary assistance to the Court and the Prosecutor . . . .").
[512] Russia (and possibly also the US) might additionally not have supported aggressive follow-up. While the US, under the Trump Administration, is decidedly hostile to the ICC, the Obama Administration was more supportive, so might have permitted follow-up.
[513] Manyok, *supra* note 295 ("President Hu Jintao and Bashir have become very close friends. They often stand in solidarity with each other or defend each other particularly at the UN and other forums that are hostile to Beijing and Khartoum. In essence, [the] economic relationship between Beijing and Khartoum has metamorphosed into a political one.").
[514] Shinn, *supra* note 265, at 95; Edith Lederer, *African Union Asks UN to Delay al-Bashir Prosecution*, MAIL & GUARDIAN (Sept. 25, 2010), *at* https://mg.co.za/article/2010-09-25-african-union-asks-un-to-delay-albashir-prosecution. *See also* Rome Statute, Art. 16 (providing for Security Council deferrals). The deferral was not granted.

Bashir's regime from being held accountable for the crimes committed in [Darfur]."[515] As of fall 2019, as mentioned above, all ICC arrest warrants charging crimes by Government of Sudan and Janjaweed leaders in Darfur remain outstanding, some for over a decade.[516] Of course, the initial referral resolution, Resolution 1593, issued under Chapter VII, long ago required cooperation from the Government of Sudan,[517] and ICC States Parties have also been under statutory obligations to effectuate arrests[518] when those covered by ICC arrest warrants traveled to their territories.[519] Yet, without consequences following for violation of these obligations, there is simply no enforcement of warrants.[520]

While this chronological discussion of the crimes ends here, as noted above, crimes in Darfur have continued. As mentioned, in 2014, 2015, and 2016, there were brutal counterinsurgency campaigns in Darfur in which forces reportedly committed crimes against humanity, including killing, mass rape and torture of civilians, forced displacement of communities, destruction of physical infrastructure and infrastructure necessary for sustaining life.[521] Amnesty International additionally reported the use of chemical weapons in Darfur in 2016.[522]

---

[515] Manyok, *supra* note 295.
[516] Note that "the Chinese threat to ICC follow-up could also have included an element of Chinese opposition to the ICC – not just the situation with Sudan. The Chinese (many countries, with the US included) never wanted the ICC to have real 'teeth,' like the ability to execute arrest warrants." Trahan interview with Andras Vamos-Goldman, 6/3/19. On this Presidential Statement, however, it appears the US may have been supportive; of course, a Presidential Statement is non-binding.
[517] S/RES/1593 (2005).
[518] See Rome Statute, Art. 88 *et seq.* (obligations to cooperate).
[519] There have been numerous ICC findings of non-cooperation against Rome Statute States Parties based on their failure to arrest President Bashir when he traveled to their territories.
[520] The ICC's Assembly of States Parties and the ICC itself also share responsibility when States Parties fail to adhere to their Rome Statute obligations. However, where a situation has been referred by the Security Council (as was the Darfur situation) the Council should shoulder its share of responsibility to ensure that its referral can be effective.
[521] Human Rights Watch, "Men with No Mercy," *supra* note 287. See also Bassam Hatoum & Samy Magdy, *Amnesty Warns War Crimes Continuing in Sudan's Darfur*, AP NEWS (June 11, 2019), *at* https://apnews.com/99b4d76a0a434e9d94476347377c00b7.
[522] For example, in September 2016, Amnesty International, in its report *Scorched Earth, Poisoned Air* found that: "a large number of serious violations of international humanitarian and international human rights law [had been] committed by Sudanese government forces, including scores of instances where government forces deliberately targeted civilians and civilian property." Amnesty International, *Scorched Earth, Poisoned Air: Sudanese Government Forces Ravage Jebel Marra, Darfur*, at 4 (Sept. 26, 2016), *at* www.amnestyusa.org/wp-content/uploads/2017/04/jebel_marra_report_c2.pdf. Amnesty found that attacks against civilians in the Jebel Marra were clear violations of international

5.2.6 Overall Impact of the Veto Threats Regarding the Situation in Darfur

The seven (explicit or implicit) veto threats discussed above thus: (1) delayed the imposition of sanctions; (2) prevented imposition of an oil embargo; (3) initially limited the imposition of arms sanctions to exclude the Government; (4) limited travel bans and asset freezes from seventeen to four listed individuals; (5) blocked a fully UN peacekeeping deployment; (6) delayed the hybrid UNAMID deployment by requiring consent from the Government of Sudan; and (7) weakened the eventual hybrid UNAMID deployment by eliminating a disarmament mandate. The threats thus benefitted the Government of Sudan (and, to some extent, also the Janjaweed), while both were heavily implicated in atrocity crimes – crimes against humanity and war crimes, and, most likely, genocide. Blocking the imposition of an oil embargo also directly benefited both China and Sudan, given Sudan's oil exports to China.[523] Initially excluding the Government of Sudan from the arms embargo also benefited both in light of China's arms sales to Sudan, including during the period when the crimes were at their height,[524] with Chinese weapons casings found in Darfur.[525] While China, according to some sources, eventually modified its stance, becoming less uncritically supportive of the Government of Sudan,[526] this change appears to have come only after "western" pressure on China[527] and after much of the killing had occurred.

> humanitarian law and amounted to war crimes, and, particularly with respect to forced displacement and unlawful killings, may also amount to crimes against humanity. *Id.* at 6. Amnesty also extensively documented the use of chemical weapons against civilians, including very young children, finding evidence that "strongly suggest[ed] that Sudanese government forces repeatedly used chemical weapons during attacks in Jebel Marra." *Id.* at 5. In particular, its investigation, which was conducted through the use of satellite imagery and more than 200 in-depth interviews with survivors and experts, indicated that at least 30 chemical attacks took place in the Jebel Marra area between January and September 2016, and reported that "between 200 and 250 people may have died from exposure to chemical weapons agents." *Id.* at 5, 17, 69–94.

[523] *Sudan, Oil, and Human Rights, supra* note 313, at 456–58; Manyok, *supra* note 295.
[524] *Id.*
[525] *Chinese Bullet Casings Found in Darfur*, RADIO FRANCE INTERNATIONALE, at http://en.rfi.fr/africa/20101021-chinese-bullet-casings-found-darfur ("China has dismissed a United Nations report on Sudan that says a dozen brands of Chinese-made bullet casings were found at attack sites in Darfur."). Apparently, there was also a veto threat made by China not to renew the mandate of a panel of experts [on sanctions] if it included a reference in its report to Chinese-made bullets being found in Darfur. *China Seeks to Block U.N. Report on Darfur, Diplomats Say*, REUTERS (Oct. 19, 2010), *at* www.nytimes.com/2010/10/20/world/asia/20sudan.html.
[526] *See, e.g.,* Ahmed, *supra* note 449.
[527] *See* note 503 *supra* (Natsios visit to China); *see also* note 505 *supra* (concerns to reputation in advance of the Beijing Olympic games).

While the above chronology discusses veto threats, what it does not discuss are resolutions that *might have been tabled*, and might have been voted on, had other members of the Security Council not in effect preemptively silenced themselves, knowing that China would have vetoed other, more proactive, measures. "[A]s a Permanent Member of the United Nations Security Council, China's ... position on Sudan doesn't allow other Permanent Members to act ... ."[528] One can only imagine the kinds of resolutions that might have been passed (had there been the will), including, for example, a "no-fly" zone over Darfur so that Sudanese Armed Forces could no longer indiscriminately target Darfuri villagers through their campaign of indiscriminate bombing; creation of humanitarian aid corridors to reach IDPs in camps who were in dire need of humanitarian assistance; or a far earlier deployment of a fully UN peacekeeping force, with a disarmament mandate and a mandate to protect IDPs in camps. One can also imagine, had China been willing early on to exert true leverage over the Government of Sudan (as it was well-positioned to have done) that events might have played out far differently. China, at the outbreak of hostilities, could have pressed the Government of Sudan not to use its armed forces to commit atrocity crimes, not to arm, equip, and pay the Janjaweed, but to disarm them and bring perpetrators to justice, and work towards concluding a truly sustainable peace agreement for Darfur.

Veto threats and the existence of China's veto power did not completely paralyze the Council regarding Darfur as the Council was able to pass numerous resolutions and did ultimately refer the situation to the ICC (while providing no follow-up that might have resulted in arrest warrants being executed). Yet, clearly, *the Council could have done far more* to rein in the commission of atrocity crimes had it not been hampered by veto threats, and simply self-censorship by other Council members who did not draft resolutions they knew could not pass. While in such a situation it is harder to fully detect how the veto power operated – which was admittedly clearer in the situation of Syria where it was overtly used fourteen times – the threat of the veto, and China's simply having the veto power, appear to have directly affected what the Security Council was able to accomplish, hampering it from fulfilling its primary responsibility of maintaining international peace and security, while there were ongoing mass atrocity crimes being committed in Darfur, including by the Sudanese military. "[I]n only three years, more than 396,563 people have lost their lives in the hands of Khartoum's regime of

---

[528] Manyok, *supra* note 295.

which China has played a role in aiding ... in committing these grave[] atrocities."[529]

5.3 CONCLUSION

The chronological analysis above related to crimes in Syria and veto use, and crimes in Darfur and veto threats, amply demonstrates the problem at hand. Namely, certain permanent members of the Security Council have no compunction regarding using, or threatening to use, their veto, regardless of the severity of the crimes being committed and regardless of whether the crimes are characterized as crimes against humanity, war crimes, or genocide. These chronologies thus serve as one more plea to states to challenge the current state of affairs. The veto power, granted by UN Member States in the UN Charter, should not be used in a way that countenances or facilitates the ongoing commission of atrocity crimes, as it has done in both Syria and Darfur, as well as other situations.

---

[529] Manyok, *supra* note 295.

Index

Abd-Al-Rahman, Ali Muhammad (a/k/a Ali Kushayb), 308
Accountability, Coherence and Transparency Group. *See* ACT Code of Conduct
Acheson, Dean, 22, 25
Acheson Plan. *See* Uniting for Peace Resolution
ACT (Accountability, Coherence and Transparency Group) Code of Conduct
  purpose of, 115–116
  as soft law, 102–103
  voluntary veto restraint for atrocity crimes, 114–116, 140
    application of, 115
    criteria of atrocity crimes under, 123–124
    formation of, 114–115
    French/Mexican initiative compared to, 116
    validity of veto under, 135–136
Adams, Simon, 105–106
African Mission in Sudan (AMIS), 306–307
Akande, Dapo, 160, 164
  on judicial review by ICJ, 252, 254
  on UN Security Council, 182–183, 184, 186, 190–191, 248
Albright, Madeline, 118
Aleppo, Syria. *See* siege of Aleppo
Alvarez, José, 245, 251
Amin, Idi, 54, 55
AMIS. *See* African Mission in Sudan
Annan, Kofi, 49, 64, 65–66, 266–267
apartheid regime, South Africa; 188
  UN Security Council veto use, 38
arbitrary detention, 271–274
Arbour, Louise, 76–77

Arria, Diego, 317
Articles on the Responsibility of International Organizations for Internationally Wrongful Acts, 172
Articles on the Responsibility of States for Internationally Wrongful Acts, 172–174
al-Assad, Bashar, 72–73, 129
atrocity crimes. *See also* chemical weapons use; crimes against humanity; genocide; veto power; veto use; war crimes
  definition of, 30
  in FRY, 58–59
  legal limits to veto for, 5–6
  UN Security Council on. *See* UN Security Council
  voluntary veto restraint and. *See* voluntary veto restraint
Australia, response to chemical weapons use by Syria, 204
Austria, response to chemical weapons use by Syria, 204–205

Ban Ki-moon, 106
al-Bashir, Omar Hassan Ahmad, 38–39, 261, 302
Bassiouni, M. Cherif, 154–155, 157–158
Belgium, response to chemical weapons use by Syria, 204–205
Bihozagara, Jacque, 35
Bokassa, Jean-Bedel, 55
Bolton, John, 105–106
Bosnia, 245
  Srebrenica massacre, 58

Brahimi, Lakhdar, 266–267
Butler, Richard, 32

Carswell, David, 195, 196–197
chemical weapons use by Syria, 1
　under Article 27(3), 1
　under al-Assad, 90–95
　Australia response to, 204
　Belgium response to, 204–205
　continuation of, 291–292
　Cyprus response to, 204–205
　destruction of weapons stockpiles, 289–291
　　under Framework Agreement for Elimination of Syrian Chemical Weapons, 290
　　Organization for the Prohibition of Chemical Weapons, 290–291
　Egypt response to, 203
　France response to, 202, 204–205
　Georgia response to, 204
　as grave breach of law, 237–238
　humanitarian intervention in response to, 86–95
　investigative mechanisms for, 90
　Italy response to, 204–205
　Kuwait response to, 202–203, 204–205
　Liechtenstein response to, 204–205, 214
　Lithuania response to, 204–205
　Mexico response to, 203
　military strikes in response to, 86–95
　　proportionality criterion for, 92–93
　　U.K. response, 88–89, 91–92, 93–94
　　U.S. response, 87–88
　Netherlands' response to, 202–203, 204
　Norway response to, 203
　Peru response to, 202–203
　Poland response to, 202–203
　Portugal response to, 204–205
　proportionality criterion for, 92–93
　Slovenia response to, 204–205
　Sweden response to, 204
　Turkey response to, 203
　U.K. response to, 201, 202
　Ukraine response to, 202–203, 204, 205
　UN Security Council resolutions
　　condemnation of chemical weapons use, 292–293
　　for condemnation of chemical weapons use, 292–293
　　documentation requests, 293–294
　　objections to veto use for atrocity crimes, 201–206
　　Purposes and Principles of UN, as influence on, 198–209
　　R2P and, 73–74
　　renewal of inspection mandates, 295–298
　　renewal of investigation mandates, 295
　　vetoes of, 199–201, 206–209, 288–302
　Uruguay response to, 202–203
　U.S. response to, 201
Chesterman, Simon, 161
Chiang Kai-shek, 10–11
China
　in Darfur, to UN Security Council veto threats on, 310–311, 312–319, 337–339. See also specific resolutions
　Myanmar and, 39–42
　Syrian conflict, 268–269
　UN Security Council veto use, 38–42
　veto power of under Article 27(3), 1
　veto power of under UN Charter, 10–11
　veto threats regarding Darfur, 6–7, 302–42
Christenson, Gordon, 152
Churchill, Winston, 11
Cohen, William, 118
Connally, Tom, 18–19
Constantinides, Aristotle, 160, 184, 188
Corell, Hans, 117–118, 126
Court of First Instance (Europe), 162, 166–167, 248
Crawford, James, 161
crime of aggression, ICC, 97–99, 145
crimes against humanity. See also treaty obligations; veto use
　definition and scope of, 155–156, 229
　R2P for, 82–84
　under Rome Statute, 156
　voluntary veto restraint for, criteria for, 131–134
Cyprus, response to chemical weapons use by Syria, 204–205

Darfur, UN Security Council veto use, 302–342. See also al-Bashir, Omar Hassan Ahmad
　African Mission in Sudan, 306–307
　African Union, 306–307
　background of, 303–309
　ethnic conflict in, 304
　genocide in, 306
　Justice Equality Movement, 304

Index

Rapid Support Forces, 308
Sudan Liberation Army/Movement, 304
veto threats, 6–7, 302–42. *See also* veto threats
de Mistura, Staffan, 266–267
Deng, Francis M., 322
destruction of chemical weapons in Syria, 289–291
  under Framework Agreement for Elimination of Syrian Chemical Weapons, 290
  Organization for the Prohibition of Chemical Weapons, 290–291
disappearances. *See* enforced disappearances
documentation requests, chemical weapons use, Syria, 293–294
Doehring, Karl, 161
due diligence standards
  for R2P, legal authority of, 77
  treaty obligations for veto use, 229–230
    drafting resolutions, 228
    under Genocide Convention, 213–214, 218
    negotiations of resolutions, 228
    voting on resolutions, 228
Dugard, John, 153
Dulles, John Foster, 24–25
Dumbarton Oaks Conference, UN Charter at, 10–11, 180
Dunford, Joseph, 297
Dörmann, Knut, 80–81, 217–218

Economic Community of West African States (ECOWAS), 56
Egypt, response to chemical weapons use by Syria, 203
"The Elders," 4–5
  members of, 117
  voluntary veto restraint proposal by, 117–118
  criteria for atrocity crimes in, 123–124
enforced disappearances, 271–272
ethnic cleansing
  definition of, 144
  voluntary veto restraint for, 124–125
European Convention for the Protection of Human Rights and Fundamental Freedoms, 175–177
  treaty obligations and veto use, 223
European Court of Human Rights, 175–177, 222
European Court of Justice, 175–177, 222
Evans, Gareth, 64–65, 70, 133

extradite, obligations to
  ILC and, for genocide, 224–225, 241

Fabius, Laurent, 111, 112
Falk, Richard, 60
Farrall, Jeremy, 183–184, 247–248
Federal Republic of Yugoslavia (FRY). *See also* Kosovo
  atrocity crimes in, 58–59
Fitzmaurice, Sir Gerald, 152
Framework Agreement for Elimination of Syrian Chemical Weapons, 290
France
  "not to veto" initiative with Mexico, 4–5
    as soft law, 102–103
  response to chemical weapons use by Syria, 202, 204–205
  Uniting for Peace Resolution and support for, 25
  veto power of under Article 27(3), 1
  voluntary veto restraint and, 138. *See also* French/Mexican initiative
Frass, Michael, 246
Free Syrian Army, 264
  U.S. assistance to, 265–266
French/Mexican initiative, 4–5, 110–113, 140
  ACT Code of Conduct compared to, 116
  criteria for atrocity crimes under, 123–124
  Hollande, François, 111, 112–113
  origins of, 110–111
  purpose of, 113
  scope of, 110
  as soft law, 102–103
FRY. *See* Federal Republic of Yugoslavia

Gaza territory, U.S. veto use, 37–38
Geneva Conventions (1949), 5–6
  Article 1, 216–220
  Article 3, 216
  grave breaches of, 215–216, 227, 237–238, 241–242
  ICJ judicial review of, 244
  jus cogens norms under, 157
  Myanmar and, 232–234
  R2P under, 79–82
  ratification of, 158
  starvation of citizens under, 299
  treaty obligations for veto use under, 215–220, 221–222
    ICJ and, 219–220
    ICRC and, 217–218

Geneva Conventions (1949) (cont.)
    international humanitarian law, 217
    voting obligations, 225–226
    veto use, 149–150
genocide. *See also* treaty obligations; veto power; veto use
    definition of, 155, 229
    ICJ recognition of, 190
    in Myanmar, 230–232
    obligation to investigate, 224
    under Rome Statute, 156
    voluntary veto restraint for, 123–126, 130–134
Genocide Convention, 5–6
    Bosnia and, 245
    ICJ judicial review of, 244
    jus cogens norms under, 154
    Myanmar and, 234–235
    R2P under, 76–77, 85
    treaty obligations relevant to veto use, 221–222, 272
        due diligence standards, 213–214, 218
        extradition and prosecution of genocide, 224–225
        ICJ decisions on, 210–213
        investigation of genocide, 224
        voting obligations, 224
    veto power under UN Charter, 145–146
    veto use, 149–150
Georgia, response to chemical weapons use by Syria, 204
Goldstone, Richard, 60
grave breaches
    chemical weapons use as, 237–238
    under Geneva Conventions, 215–216, 227, 237–238, 241–242
    as *jus cogens* norms, 169, 170–171, 172–174
Gromyko, Andrei (Soviet Ambassador), 12
Gulf War, "humanitarian intervention" after, 56–57

Hague Convention, 157
hard law
    R2P and, 84–85
    veto use under UN Charter, 144–148
    voluntary veto restraint and, 120–121
Harun, Ahmad Muhammad, 308
Hathaway, Oona, 218
Heieck, John, 213–214
Hollande, François, 89, 111, 112–113
Hull, Cordell, 12

human rights abuses. *See also* crimes against humanity; ethnic cleansing; genocide; war crimes
    Office of the High Commissioner for Human Rights, 266–267
    UN Security Council veto use, 37–38
Human Rights Council, 72
    Myanmar, 230–235
    Syria, 270–271
Human Rights Watch, 312–319, 323
humanitarian intervention
    abuse of invocation of, 63
    for chemical weapons attacks, 86–95
        investigative mechanisms for, 90
        military strikes in response to, 86–95
        proportionality criterion for, 92–93
        in Syria, 90–95
        U.K. response to, 88–89, 91–92, 93–94
        U.S. response to, 87–88
    criteria for, 67
    definition of, 54
    development of, 4
    doctrine of, 54–65, 86, 99–101
        contestation of, 95–97
        development of, 4
        interpretation of, 62–63
        origins of, 55
    by ECOWAS, 56
    after Gulf War, 56–57
    ICC jurisdiction, 99
        under crime of aggression, 97–99
        definition of, 97–98
    ICISS and, 64–65
    international endorsement of, 99
    under international law, 62, 96
    Khmer Rouge and, 55
    legal status of, 86–99
    legalization of, 64–65
    in Liberia, 56
    limitations of application of, 63–64
    limited historical precedent for, 54–57
    by NATO in Kosovo, 4, 53
        at ICJ, 59–60
        Kosovo Commission Report, 62
        UN Security Council endorsement of, 59–60
    R2P and, 94
    rejection of, 64–65
    selective application of, 95–97
    in Sierra Leone, 56
    triggers for, 66

under UN Charter articles, 58, 61–62, 96
wariness about, 63–65
Hussein, Abdel Raheem Muhammad, 308–309
Al-Hussein, Zeid Ra'ad, 41–42, 191, 260

ICC. *See* International Criminal Court
ICISS Commission. *See* International Commission on Intervention and State Sovereignty
ICJ. *See* International Court of Justice
ICRC. *See* International Committee of the Red Cross
ICTR. *See* International Criminal Tribunal for Rwanda
ICTY. *See* International Criminal Tribunal for the former Yugoslavia
Ignatieff, Michael, 74
IHL. *See* international humanitarian law
IIIM. *See* International, Impartial and Independent Mechanism
ILC. *See* International Law Commission
inspection mandates, for chemical weapons use, Syria, 295–298
International, Impartial and Independent Mechanism (IIIM), 28, 29–30
International Commission on Intervention and State Sovereignty (ICISS), 27–28
humanitarian intervention and, 64–65
veto use, 144
International Committee of the Red Cross (ICRC), 80–82
Geneva Conventions, 217–218
International Court of Justice (ICJ)
Geneva Conventions and treaty obligations, 219–220
Genocide Convention and treaty obligations, 210–213
humanitarian intervention in Kosovo, 59–60
judicial review by. *See* judicial review by ICJ
jus cogens norms and, 154, 158–159, 166
recognition of genocide, 190
veto use under UN Charter, judicial review by, 143
International Covenant on Civil and Political Rights, 189–190
International Criminal Court (ICC)
Darfur, UN Security Council veto threats, 337–339
humanitarian interventions and, 99
under crime of aggression, 97–99
under Rome Statute, 98–99
Syria and, 274–283
acceleration of crimes in, 274–276
gender-based violence in, 278
jurisdiction issues, 278–279
sarin gas attacks, in Al-Ghouta, 276–277
siege warfare in, 277–280
vetoing of referral, 278–282
International Criminal Tribunal for Rwanda (ICTR), 155–156
judicial review of creation of, 250
International Criminal Tribunal for the former Yugoslavia (ICTY), 155–156, 160, 182
judicial review of creation of, 249–250, 253
international humanitarian law (IHL)
amnesty under, 235
international law
hierarchy of norms, 150–152
humanitarian intervention under, 62
ICJ judicial review of, 243–251
jus cogens norms under, 150, 167–168
Purposes and Principles of UN Charter under, 186–187
R2P under, 75–77, 83
UN Security Council veto use under, 34
veto power under UN Charter, 146–147
International Law Commission (ILC)
Articles on the Responsibility of International Organizations for Internationally Wrongful Acts, 172
Articles on the Responsibility of States for Internationally Wrongful Acts, 172–174
jus cogens norms and, 150–152, 157, 170, 179
obligations to extradite and prosecute, for genocide, 224–225, 241
obligations to investigate genocide, 224
investigation mandates, for chemical weapons use, by Syria, 295
Islamic State of Iraq and the Levant (ISIL), crimes by, 262–263, 264, 280–282
Israel, 119
Italy, response to chemical weapons use by Syria, 204–205

JEM. *See* Justice Equality Movement
judicial review by ICJ, 6, 242–257
advisability of, 256–257
Akande on, 252, 254
alternatives to, 256–257
discretion in, 254–256

judicial review by ICJ (cont.)
  of Geneva Conventions, 244
  of Genocide Convention, 244
  of international law, compliance with, 243–251
  of UN Charter application
    through advisory opinions, 254–256
    for legal compliance with Charter, 243–251
    legal standards for, 252
    of non-justiciable political questions, 251–254
  veto use under UN Charter, 6
jus cogens norms, 5, 142–143, 146, 148, 150–179
  breaches of, 169, 170–171, 172–174
  criteria for, 169–172
  definition of, 150
  European Court of First Instance, 162, 166–167
  Geneva Conventions, 157
  Genocide Convention, 154
  Hague Convention, 157
  hierarchical superiority of, 153
  ICJ and, 154, 158–159, 166
  ILC and, 150–152, 157, 170, 179
  under international law, 150, 167–168
  hierarchy of norms, 150–152
  as legal concept, 152
  legal consequences of, 165–168
  peremptory norms and, 150–153
    content of, 155–158
    prohibitions under, 153–155
  UN obligations for, 158–164
    through UN Security Council, 158–164
  UN Security Council and
    binding obligations for, 161–164, 165–168
    legal limitations of, 158–161
    legal obligations for, 158–164
    Permanent Members' requirements, 177–179
    violation of norms by, 164, 165–168
  use of, relationship between
    consistency with, 175–177
    limitations on, 172–174
  under Vienna Convention on the Law of Treaties, 150, 153
Justice Equality Movement (JEM), 304

Khmer Rouge, humanitarian intervention because of, 55

Koh, Harold, 87–88
Korean War, Uniting for Peace Resolution and, 24
Kosovo, humanitarian intervention in, by NATO, 4, 53
  at ICJ, 59–60
  Kosovo Commission Report, 62
  UN Security Council endorsement of, 59–60
  voluntary veto restraint and, 104
Kuwait, response to chemical weapons use by Syria, 202–203, 204–205

Lauterpacht, Eli, 165, 166
law. *See specific topics*
League of Nations, 19
legal limits to veto use
  for atrocity crimes, 5–6
  jus cogens norms. *See jus cogens* norms
  recognition of, 5–6
Lemkin, Raphael, 145–146
Levin, Daniel, 35
Liberia, humanitarian intervention in, 56
Libya, R2P in, 4, 53, 70–72
  NATO and, 71–72
  regime change as result of, 71
  UN Security Council authorization of, 70–71
Liechtenstein, response to chemical weapons use by Syria, 204–205, 214
Lithuania, response to chemical weapons use by Syria, 204–205
Litvinov, Maxim, 19
Luck, Edward, 19, 33

Manfredi, Zachary, 218
Meeker, Leonard, 29
Mexico. *See also* French/Mexican initiative
  response to chemical weapons use by Syria, 203
  on veto power of UN Security Council, 198
MH17, Malaysia Airlines Flight, 43
Milanović, Marko, 214, 215
Milošević, Slobodan, 36–37
Myanmar
  under Geneva Conventions, 232–234
  under Genocide Convention, 234–235
  genocide in, 230–232
  Human Rights Council in, 230–235
  treaty obligations regarding veto use and, 230–235
  UN Security Council veto use regarding, 39–42

NAM. *See* Non-Aligned Movement
NATO. *See* North Atlantic Treaty Organization
Netherlands, response to chemical weapons use by Syria, 202–203, 204–205
Non-Aligned Movement (NAM), 48–49
North Atlantic Treaty Organization (NATO)
  humanitarian intervention by, in Kosovo, 4, 53
  at ICJ, 59–60
  Kosovo Commission Report, 62
  UN Security Council endorsement of, 59–60
  voluntary veto restraint and, 104
  R2P in Libya and, 71–72
  UN Security Council veto use and, 36–37
Norway, response to chemical weapons use by Syria, 203
"not to veto" initiative, in French/Mexican initiative. *See* French/Mexican initiative

Obama, Barack, 87–88
  Free Syrian Army assistance under, 265–266
  voluntary veto restraint approach under, 118–119, 138–139
obligations to extradite. *See* extradite
obligations to prosecute. *See* prosecute
obligatory abstention rule, 180
Office of the High Commissioner for Human Rights (OHCHR), 266–267
oil trading sanctions, in Darfur, 320–322
OPCW. *See* Organization for the Prohibition of Chemical Weapons
Operation Provide Comfort, 57
Orakhelashvili, Alexander, 161, 167–168, 223
Organization for the Prohibition of Chemical Weapons (OPCW), 290–291

Pasvolsky, Leo, 15
Paust, Jordan, 184
peremptory norms, 150–153
  content of, 155–158
  prohibitions under, 153–155
Permanent Five members, of UN Security Council, 30, 31. *See also* China; France; Russia; treaty obligations; Union of Soviet Socialist Republics; United Kingdom; United States

jus cogens norms and, requirements as to, 177–179
reform proposals and veto power, 47–48
voluntary veto restraint and threat of veto in, 134–135
Peru, response to chemical weapons use by Syria, 202–203
Peters, Anne, 160–161, 195–196, 197–198, 214
Poland, response to chemical weapons use by Syria, 202–203
Portugal, response to chemical weapons use by Syria, 204–205
Powell, Colin, 306, 321
principle of unanimity. *See* unanimity
prosecute, obligation to
  ILC and, for genocide, 224–225, 241

al-Qaddafi, Muammar, 70

R2P. *See* responsibility to protect
Rapid Support Forces (RSF), 308
Reinisch, August, 223
Report of the Secretary-General, "Implementing the Responsibility to Protect" (2009), 68–69
Report of the Secretary-General's High-Level Panel on "Threats, Challenges and Change, A More Secure World: Our Shared Responsibility" (2004), 67
residual power arguments, 24
"responsibility not to veto,", 4–5, 102–103
  voluntary veto restraint and
  French response to, 122
  legal weight of, 120–122
  R2P and, 104–107
  as soft law, 120, 122
  U.K. response to, 122
responsibility to protect (R2P), 4
  for crimes against humanity, 82–84
  development of, 65–85
  criteria in, 67
  formulation of, 53–54
  first, 66–67
  Geneva Conventions and, 79–82
  Genocide Convention and, 76–77
  humanitarian intervention and, 94
  ICRC and, 80–82
  under international law, 75–77, 83
  legal authority of, 75–77
  due diligence standards, 77

responsibility to protect (R2P) (cont.)
    through hard law, 84–85
    in ICJ rulings, 77–79
    in Libya, 4, 53, 70–72
        NATO and, 71–72
        regime change as result of, 71
        UN Security Council authorization of, 70–71
    pillars of, 68–69
    prosecution obligations, 83–84
    protection duties of, 69
    in *Report of the Secretary-General "Implementing the Responsibility to Protect"* (2009), 68–69
    in *Report of the Secretary-General's High-Level Panel on "Threats, Challenges and Change, A More Secure World: Our Shared Responsibility"* (2004), 67
    "responsibility not to veto" and, 102–103
    voluntary veto restraint and, 104–107
    revitalization of, 75–85
    S5 initiative and, 102–103
    as soft law, 75–76
    Syria, 53, 72–75
        Human Rights Council and, 72
        international community response to, 74
        UN Security Council resolutions for, 73–74
        Torture Convention and, 82–84
        UN Security Council and, 69–71, 73–74, 85
        voluntary veto restraint and, 104–107, 121
            "responsibility not to veto" within, 104–107
    in World Summit Outcome Document, 68
Reummler, Kathryn, 87
Rhodesia, 188
Rodley, Nigel, 154–155
Rome Statute
    crimes defined under, 156
    ICC, 98–99
    starvation of citizens under, Rome Statute amendment, 299
Roosevelt, Franklin Delano, 10, 11
RSF. *See* Rapid Support Forces
Russia, 11. *See also* Union of Soviet Socialist Republics
    in Syria, 264–265
    UN Security Council veto use by, 42–44
    veto power of under Article 27(3), 1
    voluntary veto restraint and, 109
Rwanda, 34–36

S5 initiative, 4–5
    criteria for atrocity crimes under, 123–124
    defeat of, 109
        Russian involvement in, 109
    origins of, 107
    R2P and, 102–103
    UN Security Council and, 107–108
    voluntary veto restraint and, 107–109
San Francisco Conference, UN Charter, 10–21
sarin gas attacks, in Al-Ghouta, Syria, 276–277
Saudi Arabia, UN Security Council veto use, 46–47
Seger, Paul, 109, 127
Serralvo, Jose, 80–81, 217–218
siege of Aleppo, in Syria, UN Security Council vetoes related to, 283–288
    civilian casualties, 285–287
    seven-day ceasefire for humanitarian assistance, 287–288
siege warfare, in Syria, 277–280
Simma, Bruno, 195
SLA/M. *See* Sudan Liberation Army/Movement
Slovenia, response to chemical weapons use by Syria, 204–205
soft law
    Code of Conduct as, 102–103
    French/Mexican initiative as, 102–103
    R2P as, 75–76
Soong, T. V., 19
South Africa, apartheid regime in, 188
    UN Security Council veto use, 38
Srebrenica massacre, 58
Sri Lanka, 39–40
Stalin, Joseph, 11
    on USSR exceptionalism, 15–16
starvation of citizens, as war crime, 299
Stettinius, Edward R., 12
Sudan. *See* Darfur
Sudan Liberation Army/Movement (SLA/M), 304
Syria (Syrian Arab Republic)
    chemical weapons use. *See* chemical weapons use by Syria
    Chinese involvement, 268–269
    Free Syrian Army, 264
        U.S. assistance to, 265–266
    Human Rights Council, 270–271
    prosecution, 274–283

acceleration of crimes, 274–276
gender-based violence, 278
jurisdiction, 278–279
sarin gas attacks, in Al-Ghouta, 276–277
siege warfare, 277–280
vetoing of referral, 278–282
R2P, 53, 72–75
international community response to, 74
Russia in, 264–265
siege of Aleppo, vetoes related to, 283–288
civilian casualties, 285–287
seven-day ceasefire, for humanitarian assistance, 287–288
treaty obligations relevant to veto use and, 237–242
Turkey in, 265
UN Security Council resolutions
objections to veto use for atrocity crimes, 201–206
Purposes and Principles of UN, as influence on, 198–209
R2P and, 73–74
sponsors of, by country, 279
vetoes of, 199–201, 206–209
UN Security Council veto use regarding, 44–45, 262–302
accountability, 269–271
arbitrary detention, 271–274
blocking condemnation of crimes, 269–274
calls to end violence, 269–271
condemnation of bombing, 272–274
enforced disappearances, 271–272
ISIL, crimes by, 262–263, 264, 280–282
for siege of Aleppo, 283–288
U.S. involvement in, through assistance to Free Syrian Army, 265–266
vetoes related to, 6–7, 262–302
Yazidis in, ISIL crimes against, 280–282
Syrian National Council, 263–264

Tladi, Dire, 157
Torture Convention, 82–84
treaty obligations, as to veto use, 209–242, 257–259
applicability of, for UN Security Council members, 220–223
inconsistency, 220–221
voting obligations, 224
application of foundational obligations, 230–242

Myanmar, 230–235
Syria, 237–242
due diligence standards, 229–230
for drafting resolutions, 228
under Genocide Convention, 213–214, 218
for negotiation of resolutions, 228
for voting on resolutions, 228
under European Convention for the Protection of Human Rights and Fundamental Freedoms, 223
European Court of Human Rights, 222
European Court of Justice, 222
Geneva Conventions, 215–220, 221–222
Common Article 1, 217
ICJ and, 219–220
ICRC and, 217–218
voting obligations under, 225–226
Genocide Convention, 221–222, 272
due diligence standard, 213–214, 218
extradition and prosecution of genocide, 224–225
ICJ decisions on, 210–213
investigation of genocide, 224
voting obligations, 224
in ICJ decisions
under Geneva Conventions, 219–220
under Genocide Convention, 210–213
negotiations of resolutions, 228–230
due diligence standards, 228
relevance of, 224–228
voting on resolutions, 228–230
due diligence standards for, 228
Turkey
response to chemical weapons use by Syria, 203
in Syria, 265

U.K. *See* United Kingdom
Ukraine
response to chemical weapons use by, 202–203, 204, 205
on veto power of UN Security Council, 198
UN Assistance Mission for Rwanda (UNAMIR), 34–35, 36
UN Charter. *See* United Nations Charter
UN Security Council. *See also* veto power
Akande on, 182–183, 184, 186, 190–191, 248
on chemical weapons use. *See* chemical weapons use
creation of, 10
Darfur and. *See* Darfur; veto threats

UN Security Council (cont.)
  jus cogens norms and
    binding obligations for, 161–164, 165–168
    legal limitations of, 158–161
    legal obligations for, 158–164
    Permanent Members' requirements, 177–179
    violation of, 164, 165–168
  legal limitations of, 189
  Myanmar and lack of response in, 1
  NAM and, 48–49
  obligatory abstention rule, 180
  Permanent Five members, 30, 31. See also China; France; Russia; Union of Soviet Socialist Republics; United Kingdom; United States
    jus cogens norms and, requirements of, 177–179
    reform proposals and, veto power over, 47–48
    voluntary veto restraint and threat of veto in, 134–135
  Purposes and Principles of the United Nations, 179–209. See also Syria; United Nations Charter
    "good faith" obligation, 194–198
    under international law, 186–187, 194–198
    legal obligations to act in accordance with, 179–184, 185–194
    limitations of powers under, 183–184
    scope of in UN Charter Articles, 185–191
    veto use and, 191–194
  R2P and, 69–71, 73–74, 85
  reform proposals, 47–51
    composition of Security Council, 48–50
    expansion of Security Council, 50
    Permanent Five veto power, 47–48
    veto use, 48, 50–51
  Roosevelt on purpose and scope of, 10
  S5 initiative and, 107–108
  in Syria. See chemical weapons use; Syria
  treaty obligations of, for UN Security Council members, 220–223
    inconsistency with, 220–221
    voting obligations, 224
  UNAMIR, 34–35, 36
  Uniting for Peace Resolution and, 9
  veto use, for atrocity crimes. See treaty obligations; veto use
  voluntary veto restraint resolutions, 137–138
UNAMIR. See UN Assistance Mission for Rwanda
unanimity, principle of, 11, 13
UNGA. See United Nations, General Assembly
Union of Soviet Socialist Republics (USSR)
  Uniting for Peace Resolution and opposition to, 25
  veto power of, under UN Charter, 10–16
    exceptionalism of by Stalin, 15–16
    principle of unanimity and, 11, 13
    Russian Federation and, 11
United Kingdom (U.K.)
  humanitarian intervention for chemical weapons attacks, 88–89, 91–92, 93–94
  response to chemical weapons use by Syria, 201, 202
  Uniting for Peace Resolution and support for, 25
  veto power of on UN Security Council, 198
    under Article 27(3), 1
  voluntary veto restraint and, 113, 138, 140
  "responsibility not to veto" and response to, 122
United Nations (UN). See also UN Security Council
  General Assembly
    emergency special sessions, 28
    IIIM and, 28, 29–30
    membership expansion of, 26
    Uniting for Peace Resolution and, 22–30
    voluntary veto restraint resolutions, 21–30, 103–104, 133
  international humanitarian law and, 221
  jus cogens norms and obligations regarding, 158–164
  through UN Security Council, 158–164
  military alliance, 19
United Nations (UN) Charter, 3–4. See also veto power
  Article 1, 185
  Article 1(1), 164, 185–186, 188, 190
  Article 1(3), 187, 188, 190
  Article 2(4), 61–62, 64
  Article, 12, 247
  Article 18(2), 108–109
  Article 24, 23, 183–184
  Article 24(1), 178–179
  Article 24(2), 180–181, 182, 190, 192, 193–194
  Article 25, 183–184

Index

Article 27(3), 180, 192, 193–194, 197–198
  veto power in, scope of, 1
Article 39, 251–252
Article 41, 190
Article 52, 180
Article 53(1), 58
Article 56, 187
Article 96, 242
Article 103, 5–6, 220, 221–222, 241
Dumbarton Oaks Conference, 10–11, 180
humanitarian intervention under, 58, 61–62, 96
ICJ judicial review of
  through advisory opinions, 254–256
  for legal compliance with Charter, 243–251
  legal standards for, 252
  of non-justiciable political questions, 251–254
non-use of force in, 64
purpose of, 164
San Francisco Conference, 10–21
UN Security Council under. *See* UN Security Council
veto use under. *See* veto use
Vienna Convention on the Law of Treaties, 163
voting procedures under, 21
Yalta Conference, 11, 15–16
United States (U.S.)
  Genocide Prevention Task Force, 118
  "humanitarian interventions" for chemical weapons attacks, 87–88
  Israel and, 119
  "Operation Provide Comfort," 57
  response to chemical weapons use by Syria, 201
  in Syria, 265–266
  veto power of under Article 27(3), 1
  voluntary veto restraint and, under Obama administration, 118–119, 138–139
  Israel and, 119
Uniting for Peace Resolution (1950), 3
  application of, 26–30
  under Article, 24, 23
  Dulles and, 24–25
  French support for, 25
  Korean War and, 24
  reconciling with Charter, 26
  residual power arguments, 24
  U.K. support for, 25

UN General Assembly and, 22–30
use of, 27
USSR opposition to, 25
veto power of UN Security Council and, 9
Uruguay, response to chemical weapons use by Syria, 202–203
U.S. *See* United States
USSR. *See* Union of Soviet Socialist Republics

Vamos-Goldman, Andras, 311–312, 337–338
Van Schaack, Beth, 73
VCLT. *See* Vienna Convention on the Law of Treaties
Védrine, Hubert, 110–111
Verdross, Alfred, 152
veto. *See specific topics*
veto power, under UN Charter
  for atrocity crimes. *See* UN Security Council
  China and, 10–11
  creation of, 145–146
  Genocide Convention and, 145–146
  Mexico on, 198
  negotiations for, historical development of, 10–21
    at San Francisco Conference, international arguments in, 16–21
    before San Francisco Conference, 10–16
    for voting procedures, 11–12, 13–15
  U.K. on, 10–16, 198
  Ukraine on, 198
  UN General Assembly and, 21–30
  veto restraint resolutions, 21–22
  Uniting for Peace Resolution and, 9
  U.S. and, 10–16
  USSR and, 10–16
    exceptionalism of by Stalin, 15–16
    principle of unanimity and, 11, 13, 19–20
    Russian Federation and, 11
veto threats
  in Darfur, to UN Security Council resolutions, 6–7, 309–342
    Chinese involvement in, 310–311, 312–319, 337–339. *See also specific resolutions*
    Human Rights Watch and, 312–319, 323
    ICC referral, 337–339
    oil trading sanctions, 320–322
    peacekeeping weakened by, 330–336
    Resolution 1556, 312–319
    Resolution 1564, 320–322, 325
    Resolution 1574, 322–324
    Resolution 1591, 324–329

veto threats (cont.)
　Resolution 1593, 328–329
　Resolution 1706, 331–333
　Resolution 1769, 329–330, 333–335, 336
　weakening of sanctions as result of, 312–330
　Rwanda, 34–36
　Sri Lanka, 39–40
　UN Security Council veto use and, 33–47
veto use, under UN Charter. *See also jus cogens* norms; Syria
　for atrocity crimes, 30–47
　　under apartheid regime, South Africa, 38
　　by China, 38–42
　　by France, 32, 34–36
　　Gaza, 37–38
　　history of, 32
　　human rights abuses, 37–38
　　under international law, 34
　　Israel, 37–38
　　Myanmar, 39–42
　　overview of, 30–33
　　by Permanent Five members, 30, 31
　　reform proposals for, 48, 50–52
　　by Russia, 42–44
　　Saudi Arabia, 46–47
　　Srebrenica, 42–43
　　Syria. *See* Syria
　　by U.K., 32, 34–36
　　by U.S., 32, 34–36, 37–38
　　veto threats and, 33–47
　　Yemen, 45–46
　　Zimbabwe, 37–38
　Geneva Conventions, 149–150
　Genocide Convention, 149–150
　hard law, 144–148
　ICISS, 144
　ICJ and judicial review by, 143
　ILC and, 146–147
　international law, 148
　jus cogens norms. *See jus cogens* norms
　legal arguments against summary of, 148–150
　scope of UN Charter, 148–149
　treaty obligation considerations for. *See* treaty obligations
Vienna Convention on the Law of Treaties (VCLT), 163, 236
　jus cogens norms, 150, 153
voluntary veto restraint, for atrocity crimes, 1, 4–5, 103–119
　ACT Code of Conduct and, 114–116, 140

application of, 115
criteria for atrocity crimes under, 123–124
formation of, 114–115
French/Mexican initiative compared to, 116
purpose of, 115–116
U.K. support of, 113
validity of veto under, 135–136
criteria for atrocity crimes, assessment of, 123–126
　by approach, 123–124
　for crimes against humanity, 131–134
　for ethnic cleansing, 124–125
　for genocide, 123–126, 130–134
　for war crimes, 131–134
"The Elders," proposal by, 117–118
　criteria for atrocity crimes in, 123–124
　members of, 117
evaluation of approaches to, 119–138
　variations in, 122–138
France and, 138
French/Mexican initiative and, 110–113, 140
　ACT Code of Conduct compared to, 116
　criteria for atrocity crimes under, 123–124
　Hollande, François, 111, 112–113
　origins of, 110–111
　purpose of, 113
　scope of, 110
hard law and, 120–121
implementation of, obstacles to, 139–140
origins of, 103–104
R2P and, 104–107, 121
　"responsibility not to veto" within, 104–107
requirement of explanation for, 126–127
resolutions for, passage criteria for, 136
"responsibility not to veto" and
　French response to, 122
　legal weight of, 120–122
　R2P and, 104–107
　as soft law, 120, 122
　U.K. response to, 122
S5 initiative, 107–109
　criteria for atrocity crimes under, 123–124
　defeat of, 109
　Russian involvement in, 109
threat of veto by permanent members, 134–135
U.K. and, 113, 138, 140
　"responsibility not to veto" and response to, 122

UN Security Council resolutions on, 137–138
UNGA resolutions on, 21–22, 103–104, 133
U.S. approach to under Obama administration, 118–119, 138–139
  Israel and, 119
validity of vetoes, 135–138
vital national interests, 127–130
vital state interests, 127–130

war crimes. *See also* treaty obligations; veto power; veto use
  definition and scope of, 155–156, 229
  under Rome Statute, 156
  starvation of citizens, 299
  voluntary veto restraint for, 131–134
Wolfrum, Rüdiger, 185–186
World Summit Outcome Document, 68

Yalta Conference, UN Charter at, 11, 15–16
Yazidis, in Syria, 280–282
Yemen, UN Security Council veto use in, 45–46
Yiu, Hannah, 162, 336

Zimbabwe, UN Security Council veto use, 37–38

CPSIA information can be obtained
at www.ICGtesting.com
Printed in the USA
LVHW080336290721
693964LV00002B/35